EUCOTAX Series on European Taxation

UCITS and Taxation

EUCOTAX Series on European Taxation

VOLUME 25

Series Editors

Prof. Dr Peter H.J. Essers
Prof. Dr Eric Kemmeren

Fiscal Institute Tilburg/Center for Company Law, Tilburg University

Prof. Dr Michael Lang

Vienna University of Economics and Business

The titles in this series are listed at the back of this volume.

KLUWER LAW INTERNATIONAL

EUCOTAX Series on European Taxation

UCITS and Taxation

Towards Harmonization of the Taxation of UCITS

Raymond Adema

Wolters Kluwer
Law & Business

AUSTIN BOSTON CHICAGO NEW YORK THE NETHERLANDS

Published by:
Kluwer Law International
PO Box 316
2400 AH Alphen aan den Rijn
The Netherlands
Website: www.kluwerlaw.com

Sold and distributed in North, Central and South America by:
Aspen Publishers, Inc.
7201 McKinney Circle
Frederick, MD 21704
United States of America
Email: customer.service@aspenpublishers.com

Sold and distributed in all other countries by:
Turpin Distribution Services Ltd.
Stratton Business Park
Pegasus Drive, Biggleswade
Bedfordshire SG18 8TQ
United Kingdom
Email: kluwerlaw@turpin-distribution.com

Printed on acid-free paper.

ISBN 978-90-411-2839-3

Printed in Great Britain.

Table of Contents

Preface

By the time I graduated in law from the University of Groningen, I had decided to do research for a dissertation. I had not made up my mind, however, about the topic and started working as a tax lawyer. After a few years, I became fascinated with the fragmentation of the market for units in UCITS and other collective investment funds by the national borders of the Member States. The consequences of taxation by cross-border investments in and by UCITS puzzled me and has resulted in the (revised version of the) dissertation in front of you.

Almost twenty-five years after the agreement on the UCITS Directive, the circulation of units in UCITS is for the most part still fragmented by the national borders of the Member States. Taxation has been identified and ranked as one of the major obstacles to cross-border trade in units of UCITS.

Little literature is available on the taxation of cross-border investments in and by UCITS. This study makes an effort to fill that gap. It provides for a comprehensive overview of the tax consequences of the cross-border trade in units of UCITS in Austria, Germany, the Netherlands, and the United Kingdom. It demonstrates that the tax laws of the countries studied hinder cross-border investments in and by UCITS. The results are considered to be of importance for cross-border trade in units of UCITS in other Member States, too. The study ends with recommendations on removing tax obstacles to the cross-border trade in units of UCITS in the European Union by way of harmonization or coordination.

The book is intended for academics, lawmakers, and lawyers working in the field of cross-border trade in units of UCITS.

Raymond Adema
R.P.C.Adema@rug.nl

List of Statutes

The United Kingdom

Introduction

This book studies the taxation of investments in and by undertakings for collective investment in transferable securities (hereafter, UCITS) in Austria, Germany, the Netherlands, and the United Kingdom.

In 1985, the agreement of the European Council on the UCITS Directive improved the conditions of competition among UCITS. The UCITS Directive replaced the diverging laws, regulations, and administrative provisions of the Member States regarding the obligations and control of UCITS with standardized rules. This allows a UCITS to market its units in another Member State without that Member State being able to subject this undertaking or its units to any additional provisions on these subjects. In the case that a UCITS is authorized as such by the financial market authorities of the resident state, that authorization is valid in all other Member States of the European Economic Area. A UCITS that intends to offer its units in another Member State has to notify the financial market authorities of the other Member State of its intention and to demonstrate to the financial market authorities of the other Member State that it has taken the necessary measures to ensure that any participants residing in that Member State can easily exercise their financial rights in their Member State of residence and are provided with the necessary information.

The aim of the UCITS Directive, to wit 'the removal of the restrictions on the free circulation of the units of collective investment undertakings in the Community, and [. . .] to bring about a European capital market', has so far not been fully achieved. The trade of units of UCITS is fragmentized by the national borders of the Member States. As a result, the size of the average UCITS is still five times smaller than its counterpart in the United States of America.[1] Research has shown that the average costs decrease above a certain size of a UCITS, which helps its

1. Green Paper of the European Commission on the enhancement of the EU framework for investment funds, SEC 947 (2005): 3.

performance.[2] The burden of the fragmentation is thus carried by the unitholders. According to academic and industry research,[3] because of the scale effect the unitholders annually pay an estimated EUR 2 billion to EUR 6 billion more in fees than what they would have if the fund market were unified.

A European capital market would improve the conditions of competition among UCITS in the European Union. The latter is in the interest of unitholders. Investors would benefit from this through a bigger supply of better performing UCITS to choose from. In addition, increased competition may force fund managers to decrease the management fee for their UCITS to remain competitive. To improve the conditions of competition between UCITS, the European Union and its Member States should remove the obstacles that continue to hinder cross-border trading in the units of UCITS.

Taxation is identified by asset managers as one of the most important obstacles to cross-border trade in units of UCITS.[4] Taxation of investments in UCITS has not been harmonized or coordinated by the UCITS Directive; nor has the taxation investments by UCITS.

Studies have examined the taxation of investments in and by UCITS and other collective investment funds. Taxation at source of income from the investments by collective investment funds was the topic of the Congresses of the International Fiscal Association in 1962, 1971, and 1997. Taxation of income from investments by and in collective investment funds has been a subject of study by the Organization for Economic Cooperation and Development in 1977[5] and 1999.[6] International coordination is, nevertheless, still absent. Currently, the subject is being studied by the Organization for Economic Cooperation and Development once again.

The aim of this book is to examine whether the differences between the tax laws of Austria, Germany, the Netherlands, and the United Kingdom hinder or facilitate cross-border trading in the units of UCITS. Recent European studies have concentrated on tax discrimination, such as the denial of more special tax treatment or the application of such treatment only after harsh tax administrative conditions are fulfilled.[7] Taking away tax discriminatory barriers for investments in non-resident UCITS is, as this book shows in Parts II to IV, not enough to establish a single market for the trading in units of UCITS where investors will be able to

2. F. Heinemann, et al., 'Towards a Single European Market in Asset Management'. *ZEW* (2003): 24 and 25.
3. F. Heinemann, et al., 'Towards a Single European Market in Asset Management'. *ZEW* (2003): 24; and 'Building of an Integrated European Fund Management – Cross Border Mergers of Funds – A Quick Win?' Invesco (2005): 4.
4. F. Heineman, et al., 'Towards a Single European Market in Asset Management', *ZEW* (2003), 49.
5. OECD (1977), *Taxation of Collective Investment Institutions.*
6. OECD (1999), *Taxation of Cross Border Portfolio Investment: Mutual Funds and Possible Tax Distortions.*
7. See for example, PricewaterhouseCoopers/FEFSI (2001) *Discriminatory tax barriers in the Single European Investment Funds market: A Discussion Paper*; PricewaterhouseCoopers/ FEFSI (2003) *Discriminatory tax barriers in the Single European Investment Funds market: A Progress Report*; and T. Viitala, *Taxation of Investment Funds in the European Union* (Amsterdam: IBFD, 2005).

make their selection on true economic factors only. The cross-border trade in units of UCITS may be hindered or facilitated by taxation if the differences between the national tax legislation of the Member States are substantial (disparities). These differences are the subject of study of this book.

This study therefore examines the taxation of investments in and by UCITS residing in Austria, Germany, the Netherlands, and the United Kingdom. The tax laws of these countries have been chosen for study because they cover all five methods used in the European Union to avoid economic double taxation for investments by way of UCITS, such as:

(1) Transparency (Austria and the Netherlands).
(2) Subjective exemption (Germany and the Netherlands).
(3) Reduced tax base (United Kingdom).
(4) Reduced tax rate (Netherlands and the United Kingdom).
(5) Compensation for the unitholders (United Kingdom).

So far, most of the other studies on collective investment funds were limited to the treatment of individuals. In this study, not only the taxation of individuals other than entrepreneurs (hereafter, individuals) but also that of institutional investors, such as banks and pension funds, will be taken into consideration. Institutional investors hold a fair share of the units in UCITS. Hence, it is quite important to take the tax treatment of institutional investors into consideration as well. The taxation of institutional investors differs from that of individuals, because institutional investors are subject to corporate income tax, subjectively exempt from tax or subject to special tax treatment. Because of the character of UCITS, the substantial interest measures, participation exemption, and group relief measures fall outside the scope of the study. So do the tax treatment of investments by and in fund of funds.

The study consists of the following five parts.

Part I includes two chapters. Chapter 1 introduces the concept of the UCITS. It comments on the cross-border trade in units. Chapter 2 gives an overview of the taxation of UCITS and their unitholders with the aim of analysing whether the differences between the Member States may be too substantial to invest in non-resident UCITS without risking or experiencing a higher tax burden. The following factors are examined:

(1) The tax liability of the UCITS and the unitholders.
(2) The nature and source of the income.
(3) The recognition of income.
(4) The deduction and crediting of withholding tax.

From Chapter 2 it follows that there are substantial differences between the Member States' taxation of UCITS and their investors and that these differences may lead to a higher or lesser tax burden for investments in and by non-resident UCITS compared to investments in and by resident UCITS. Parts II–IV will therefore examine the differences and their origins.

Part II comprises three chapters. It examines the taxation of investments by UCITS in the source state. The source state is the state where the investments are situated and where the issuer of the investments resides or governs, respectively. Chapter 3 will analyse the factors that decide the tax burden at source of income derived by way of UCITS. In Chapter 4 follows an evaluation and comparison of the source taxation for income derived by way of UCITS that are established in the countries studied. The origins of any differences will be established. The conclusions of this analysis for the cross-border trading in the units of UCITS that can be drawn from the comparisons are discussed in Chapter 5.

In Part III, which consists of Chapters 6–8, the taxation of investments in and by UCITS in the state of residence of the UCITS (UCITS country) is studied. It concerns the subjective tax liability of UCITS and the taxation on distributions by UCITS to the unitholders. Chapter 6 considers the factors that make up the tax burden of the income from the investments at the level of UCITS residing in Austria, Germany, the Netherlands, and the United Kingdom. Chapter 7 assesses and compares the tax burden of UCITS in the countries studied. A discussion of the conclusions for the cross-border trading in the units of UCITS follows in Chapter 8.

Part IV is made up of the Chapters 9–14. It examines the taxation of investments in UCITS in the state of residence of the unitholders (unitholder country). Because of the size of the topic, the taxation of unitholders in the countries studied is discussed in separate chapters. In Chapter 9, the tax burden of an investment in UCITS in Austria is analysed. Chapters 10–12 provide the same information for Germany, the Netherlands, and the United Kingdom, respectively. Chapter 13 compares the tax burden for an investment in a resident UCITS with that of an investment in a non-resident UCITS. The conclusions from this comparison for the cross-border trade in units of UCITS are discussed in Chapter 14.

Part V contains Chapter 15, which provides a comprehensive overview of the tax advantages and disadvantages that occur in the cross-border trading. From this overview can be concluded that the cross-border trade in units of UCITS in Austria, Germany, the Netherlands, and the United Kingdom is hindered or facilitated by the differences between the tax laws of these countries, and measures are required to counter this, by way of either harmonization or coordination. Chapter 15 formulates recommendations for the taxation of investments in and by UCITS in the European Union to improve the competition among UCITS. Part V ends with a summary of the book.

The law referred to is that in force on 31 March 2009.

Part I

Introduction of the Concept and the Taxation of Undertakings for Collective Investment in Transferable Securities

In 1985, the agreement of the European Council on a Directive for Undertakings for Collective Investment in Transferable Securities (UCITS) had to remove the restrictions on the cross-border trade in the units of undertakings in collective investments in transferable securities and to establish a European capital market. The UCITS Directive therefore standardized the Member States' diverging laws and regulations regarding the obligations and control of UCITS. The application of standardized rules had to level the conditions of competition between UCITS.

More than twenty years after the adoption of the UCITS Directive, the market in units of UCITS is still fragmentized by the national borders of the Member States. Taxation has been ranked as one of the most important obstacles to cross-border trade in the units of UCITS.

The UCITS Directive does not, however, cover taxation of UCITS, nor is it addressed elsewhere in secondary European Community (EC) law. Most of the Member States therefore simply referred to the existing tax regulations for collective investment funds. A higher tax burden for investments in the units of UCITS or other collective investment funds is in most Member States prevented by the adoption of the principle of transparency. According to this principle, the tax burden for investments by way of UCITS or other collective investment funds should be similar to that of a direct investment.

Chapter 1 introduces the concept of UCITS. Chapter 2 discusses that the measures used by the Member States to establish transparency vary to a large extent because these measures are based on the diverging tax laws of the Member States. As a result, an investment in the units of a non-resident UCITS may at all times result in a higher tax burden for investors compared to an investment in the units of resident UCITS.

Chapter 1

Introduction of the Concept of Undertakings for Collective Investment in Transferable Securities

As early as 1976, the European Commission made a proposal for the coordination of the Member States' diverging laws, regulations, and administrative provisions relating to undertakings for collective investment in transferable securities (UCITS). It was submitted because of the lack of a level field for these undertakings. It was not until 1985 that the Council of the European Communities (European Council) agreed on a Directive on the coordination of the Member States' diverging laws, regulations, and administrative provisions relating to UCITS (UCITS Directive).

The UCITS Directive provides a system under which UCITS are authorized as such by the competent authorities of the Member State in which it is established. This authorization is valid in all other Member States. Another Member State thus is not able to subject non-resident UCITS to any provision whatsoever falling within the field of the UCITS Directive. The only additional conditions for UCITS that intend to market units in another Member State are that they inform the competent authorities of that Member State two months in advance and take all necessary measures to ensure that participants in that Member State can exercise their financial rights in their Member State of residence with ease and are provided with the necessary information. As from 1994, the UCITS Directive is also operative in the European Economic Area (EEA).

In spite of the introduction of the UCITS Directive, the market for units in UCITS is still fragmented along the national borders. No substantial cross-border investments in UCITS take place in the European Union (EU). This is different only for Irish and Luxembourg-resident UCITS. The internal market for capital thus does not as yet function optimally. Taxation has been identified and ranked as one of the major obstacles to the cross-border investments in units of UCITS.

1.1. INTRODUCTION

Savings, pension contributions, and insurance premiums, among other things, often are invested through collective investment funds. Thus, investors, independent of their deposit, are able to spread risk and to use the knowledge of professional asset managers. As a result, collective investment funds on the European market manage more than EUR 5 trillion of assets. They are one of the key actors on the European capital market.[1] Because of the importance of capital for the achievement of the objectives of the European Community (EC),[2] collective investment funds should be able to attract capital by issuing units in all Member States. An investor should be able to select the best-performing collective investment funds within the investor's preferred risk profile, regardless of whether that investment fund is established in the investor's state of residence.

The free movement of capital in the EC is ensured by the founding fathers of the Community in the Treaty establishing the European Community (hereafter, EC Treaty) through the creation of an internal market, which is defined therein as an area without internal frontiers in which the free movement of goods, persons, services, and capital is ensured in accordance with the provisions of that treaty.[3] Capital, among other production factors, should flow between Member States without restrictions. The Articles 56 and 58 of the EC Treaty therefore guarantee the free movement of capital in the internal market by prohibiting all restrictions on these movements between Member States and between Member States and third countries. An obstacle to the free movement of capital caused by a Member State can be removed by the European Court of Justice, unless it can be justified[4] (negative integration). In addition, the free movement of capital can be improved by voluntary mutual recognition or harmonization of national regulations (positive integration).[5] Sometimes, harmonizing rules is necessary to fully establish an internal market, such as removing barriers in the national regulations of a Member State that infringe on the free movement of capital with other Member States or third states, and sometimes it fixes operative problems,[6] for example, by removing disparities between national regulations that distort the free movement of capital within the EC.

1. Green Paper of the European Commission on the enhancement of the EU framework for investment funds, SEC (12 Jul. 2005) 947: 2.
2. The European Community has the following objectives: a harmonious, balanced, and sustainable development of economic activities throughout the Community, a high level of employment and of social protection, equality between men and women, sustainable and non-inflationary growth, a high degree of competitiveness and convergence of economic performance, a high level of protection and improvement of the quality of the environment, the raising of the standard of living and quality of life, and economic and social cohesion and solidarity among Member States.
3. Article 14(2) EC Treaty.
4. Article 58 EC Treaty.
5. P.J.G. Kapteijn & P. Verloren van Themaat, *Inleiding tot het recht van de Europese Gemeenschappen* (Deventer: Kluwer, 1995), 347.
6. G.T. Davies, *European Union – Internal Market Law* (London: Cavendish, 2003), 137.

The free movement of capital is also guaranteed in the Agreement on the European Economic Area (hereafter, EEA Treaty), which includes the EC Member States, Iceland, Liechtenstein, and Norway.[7] The EEA Treaty does not, however, guarantee the free movement of capital between Member States and third states.

1.2. UCITS DIRECTIVE

1.2.1. THE AIM OF THE UCITS DIRECTIVE

The Commission for the European Communities (hereafter: European Commission) submitted a proposal for the coordination of laws, regulations and administrative provisions relating to UCITS in 1976. The Member States' diverging laws and regulations, especially regarding the obligations and control of these collective investments funds, which distorted the competition among them and did not offer unitholders the same protection, were the reason for this proposal.[8] It would not be until 1985 that the Council of the European Communities (hereafter, European Council) agreed on a Directive on the coordination of the laws, regulations, and administrative provisions relating to UCITS to bring about a European capital market.[9] The coordination of these regulations was meant to improve the conditions of competition between UCITS in the EC by standardizing the Member States' regulations regarding the obligations and control of these investment funds.[10] The application of standardized rules guarantees that UCITS can market units in another Member State without that Member State being able to subject this investment fund or its units to any provision whatsoever falling within the field covered by the UCITS Directive. Among other things, a Member State's tax or advertisement regulations may not contain any requirements that are inconsistent with the provisions of the UCITS Directive. Otherwise, Member States could still obstruct the free circulation of units in non-resident UCITS.

The UCITS Directive provides a system under which UCITS are authorized as such by the competent authorities of the Member State in which they are established. This authorization is valid in all other Member States. The only additional conditions for UCITS that intend to market their units in another Member State are that it informs the competent authorities of that Member State two months in advance and it takes all necessary measures to ensure that participants in that Member State can exercise their financial rights in their Member State of residence with ease and are provided with the necessary information.[11] Although the scope of the UCITS Directive is limited to UCITS, the coordination of laws, regulations, and administrative provisions relating to other collective investments funds should

7. Article 40, EEA Treaty.
8. Preamble of the Proposal by the European Commission, 29 Apr. 1976 (OJ C 171/1, 26 Jul. 1976).
9. Directive 85/611/EEC of 20 Dec. 1985 (OJ L 375/3, 31 Dec. 1985).
10. Preamble of the UCITS Directive.
11. Articles 45–47, UCITS Directive.

follow in a later stage to facilitate the free circulation of units in all undertakings for collective investment in the EC.[12]

As of 1 January 1994, the UCITS Directive is operative not only in the EC but also in the other Member States of the EEA: Iceland, Liechtenstein, and Norway. The Member States of the EEA have so far adopted all of the amendments to the UCITS Directive.

1.2.2. Concept of a UCITS

The UCITS Directive defines UCITS as undertakings (i) the sole object of which is the collective investment in transferable securities or in liquid financial assets of capital raised from the public and that operates on the principle of risk-spreading, and (ii) the units of which are, at the request of holders, repurchased or redeemed, directly or indirectly, out of the undertaking's assets (open-end fund).[13]

UCITS must invite investors publicly to invest their capital in their units for collective investment. Investors are, in practice, invited by the sponsoring parent company, being the company that has established the UCITS or its parent, or third parties. UCITS must enable invited investors to make an informed judgment about participation in their units and the risks attached thereto.[14] Therefore, the prospectus of UCITS must contain information about their *investment policy* and risk profile. In addition, their articles of association or fund rules must be attached so that the investor is also informed about the *legal structure and organization* of the UCITS.[15] The UCITS should operate in accordance with its prospectus and articles of association or fund rules. Any violation may be subject to actions by the competent authorities of the Member State in which the UCITS is established.[16]

An advantage of UCITS is that they concern open-end funds. Investors are therefore able to buy or sell units of UCITS on a regular basis against a price that does not differ substantially from the net asset value. The net asset value reflects the market value of the underlying investments and other liquid assets of the UCITS minus its liabilities. Any change in the value of the underlying investments or any income generated from them thus affects the net asset value.

12. Preamble of the UCITS Directive.
13. Article 1(2) UCITS Directive. The actions taken by UCITS to ensure that the stock exchange value of their units does not significantly vary from their net asset value are regarded as equivalent to re-purchase or redemption.
14. Article 28(1) UCITS Directive.
15. Article 29(1) UCITS Directive. Instead, UCITS may also opt to inform the investor that the articles of association or the fund rules are sent on request or they can be consulted at the place where the units are placed on the market.
16. Article 52(1) UCITS Directive.

1.2.3. Investment Policy of UCITS

1.2.3.1. Qualitative and Quantitative Investment Restrictions

The capital attracted from the unitholders is invested by the UCITS in accordance with the investment policy stated in its prospectus, articles of association, or fund rules. The investment policy of UCITS is, as mentioned above, restricted to investments in transferable securities or other liquid financial assets,[17] in accordance with the principle of risk-spreading. The UCITS Directive contains an exhaustive list of potential investment products:[18]

(1) Transferable securities[19] and money market instruments[20] admitted to or traded on an official stock exchange in a Member State or another regulated market in a Member State that operates regularly and is recognized and open to the public.
(2) Deposits with credit institutions that are repayable on demand or have the right to be withdrawn and mature in no more than twelve months.[21]
(3) Financial derivative instruments, including equivalent cash-settled instruments, traded on a regulated market referred to above or financial derivative instruments traded 'over the counter'.[22]
(4) Money market instruments other than those traded on a regulated market.[23]

---

17. Referred to in Art. 19 UCITS Directive.
18. Article 19(1) UCITS Directive.
19. Including recently issued transferable securities, provided that the terms of issue include an undertaking that application is made for admission to official listing and such admission is secured within 1 year of issue.
20. Instruments normally traded on the money market are liquid and have a value that can be accurately determined at any time.
21. Provided that the credit institution has its registered office in a Member State or, if the registered office of the credit institution is situated in a non Member State, provided that it is subject to prudential rules considered by the UCITS' competent authorities as equivalent to those laid down in Community law.
22. Provided that the underlying investment consists of instruments covered by this paragraph, financial indices, interest rates, or foreign exchange rates or currencies in which the UCITS may invest according to its investment objectives as stated in the UCITS' fund rules or instruments of incorporation; the counterparties to 'over-the-counter' derivative transactions are institutions subject to prudential supervision and belonging to the categories approved by the UCITS' competent authorities; and the 'over-the-counter' derivatives are subject to reliable and verifiable valuation on a daily basis and can be sold, liquidated, or closed by an offsetting transaction at any time at their fair value at the UCITS' initiative.
23. If the issue or issuer of such instruments is itself regulated for the purpose of protecting investors and savings, and provided that they are (i) issued or guaranteed by a central, regional, or local authority or central bank of a Member State, the European Central Bank, the EU or the European Investment Bank, a non-Member State or, in the case of a Federal State, one of the members making up the federation, or a public international body to which one or more Member States belong; (ii) issued by an undertaking any securities that are traded on regulated markets; (iii) issued or guaranteed by an establishment subject to prudential supervision, in accordance with criteria defined by Community law or by an establishment that is subject to and complies with prudential rules considered by the competent authorities to be at least as stringent as those

Investments in transferable securities that are admitted to the official listing on a stock exchange or another regulated market outside the EU are subject to further conditions.[24]

The investment policy of UCITS is restricted not only by the endorsed type of investment products but also by limitations to an interest in or the risk exposure of these products. Therefore, UCITS may not invest more than 5% of their assets in transferable securities or money market instruments issued by the same body. Deposits may not be made for more than 20% with the same credit institution, and the risk exposure of a counterparty of UCITS in an 'over-the-counter' derivative transaction may not exceed 10% of their assets when the counterparty is a credit institution or 5% of its assets in other cases. In spite of these individual limits, the combined investment in a single body may not exceed 20% of the UCITS's assets. For some of these limitations, Member States may opt to implement a higher percentage instead.

1.2.3.2. Classes of UCITS

Based on its investment policy, the UCITS can be categorized as an equity fund, bond fund, money market fund, or balanced fund (Figure 1.1).

Figure 1.1 Classes of UCITS Available for Investors

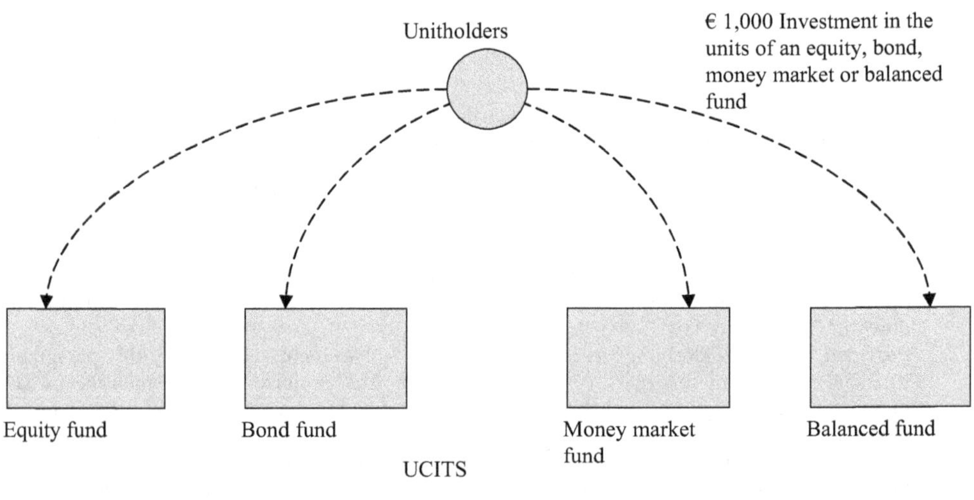

laid down by Community law; or (iv) issued by other bodies belonging to the categories approved by the UCITS' competent authorities, provided that investments in such instruments are subject to investor protection equivalent to that laid down in (i) to (iii) and provided that the issuer is a company whose capital and reserves amount to at least EUR 10 million and that presents and publishes its annual accounts in accordance with Directive 78/660/EEC, is an entity that, within a group of companies that includes one or several listed companies, is dedicated to the financing of the group or is an entity that is dedicated to the financing of securitization vehicles that benefit from a banking liquidity line.

24. Article 19(3) UCITS Directive.

Equity Funds

An equity fund is an investment fund that for the most part invests in *common shares* to participate fully in the growth of an economy or a specific segment of an economy (Figure 1.2).[25] A common share represents a share in the ownership of a company. It usually carries the right to vote on key decisions and to receive dividends. An equity fund aims to realize capital growth and dividends.

In addition, equity funds make use of *financial derivative instruments* to generate extra income or to hedge price or currency risks. A financial derivative instrument generally is a contract under which the contracting parties agree to buy or sell 'a specific quantity of the underlying, at a specific price on a specific future date (or over a specific future period)' or one of the parties has a right to do so.[26] The contracting parties may also agree to set off their obligations in cash on the specific future date. The underlying investment can cover a wide range of products, for instance, securities, interest rates, or foreign exchange rates.

Figure 1.2 Equity Fund

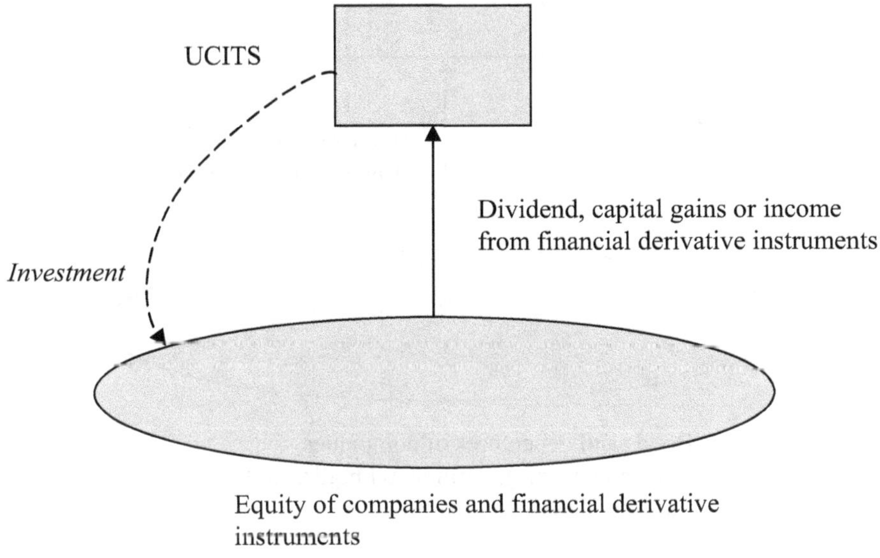

25. Certain equity funds limit their investments to companies that are involved in a certain industry, such as natural resources, pharmacy, or technology. By investing in a specific segment of the economy, these UCITS expect to generate more capital growth and dividends than those of the whole economy on average.
26. C.T. Plambeck, H.D. Rosenbloom, & D.M. Ring, *General Report of the IFA Congress of 1995 on the Tax Aspects of Derivative Financial Instruments* (London: International Fiscal Association, 1995), 663.

Bond Funds

A bond fund is an investment fund mainly made up of bonds and debentures (Figure 1.3). The objective of a bond fund is to generate a steady flow of interest. A bond or debenture is a debt instrument issued for more than twelve months by companies, governments, or governmental bodies to raise capital by borrowing. In return of the providing of capital, the holder of a bond or debenture is paid interest, which is either fixed,[27] floating,[28] or payable at the maturity date.[29] Fixed interest and floating interest are paid annually or semi-annually, usually by way of redemption of the interest coupons that are attached to the bonds, whereas interest payable at maturity date is paid at once on that date.

Like equity funds, bond funds may also use financial derivatives to earn additional income or to hedge price, interest or currency risks.

Figure 1.3 Bond Fund

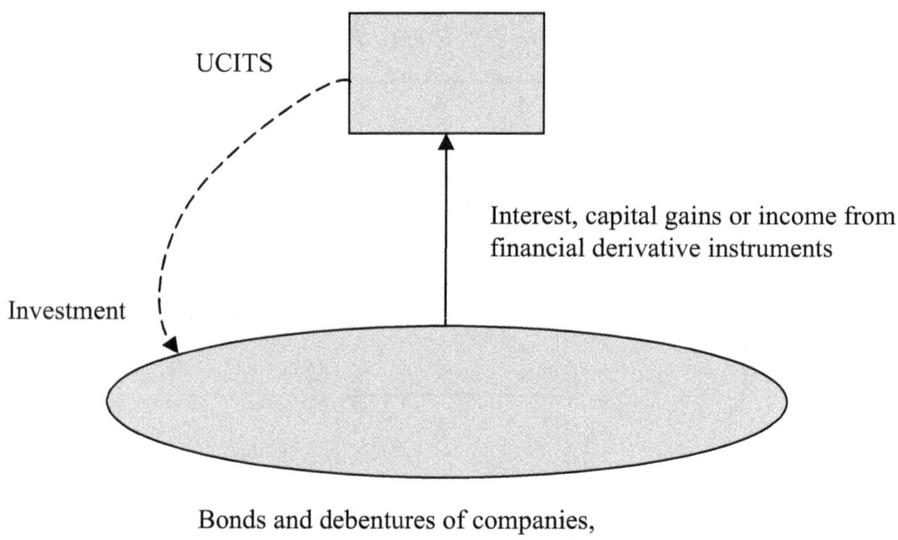

27. A fixed interest rate is a predetermined rate that remains until the maturity date. It is determined on the basis of the interest rate on the capital market at the time of issuing, together with the credit rating of the issuer at that time. The credit rating indicates the ability of the issuer to repay the par value of the bond on the maturity date. The lower the credit rating, the higher the fixed interest rate to compensate the investor for the higher risk.
28. Instead of a fixed interest rate, some bonds have a floating interest rate. By a floating rate, the interest rate is reset from time to time against the interest rate of a specific index or other interest base.
29. A third group of bonds do not generate interest (non-interest – generating bonds). Instead, these bonds are issued at a price deeply below their par value. The difference between the par value and the issue price represents the interest paid during the entire term of the bond. The interest is, however, not paid by the issuer until the maturity date.

Money Market Funds

A money market fund is an investment fund that holds large denominations of money market instruments to provide high income with no loss of capital (Figure 1.4). Contrary to bonds and debentures, money market instruments are debt instruments issued by (large) companies, governments, or governmental bodies for a period of twelve months or less, for example, to raise cash needed for current transactions.[30] For that reason, these instruments are also known as short-term papers. They generate interest.

Extra income might, like equity and bond funds, be generated by the use of financial derivatives, although the latter may also be used to hedge interest or currency risks.

Figure 1.4 Money Market Fund

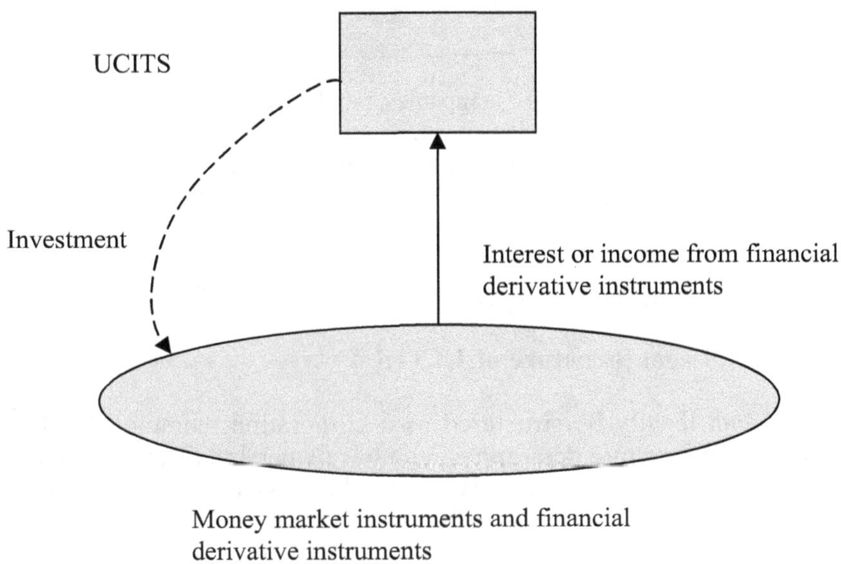

Balanced Funds

A balanced fund is an investment fund that spreads its investments over equities, bonds, and, sometimes, money market instruments to maintain greater stability of capital and income (Figure 1.5). Its aim is to derive a combination of dividends, interest, or capital growth.

A balanced fund may, for the same reasons as given earlier for equity, bond, and money market funds, make use of financial derivatives to generate extra income or to hedge currency, interest, or price risks.

30. 'The Short Term Paper Market in Europe – Recommendations for the Development of a Pan-European Market', a consultation report of 2 Sep. 2002 by the Euribor-ACI Short-Term European Paper Task Force, 9.

Figure 1.5 Balanced Fund

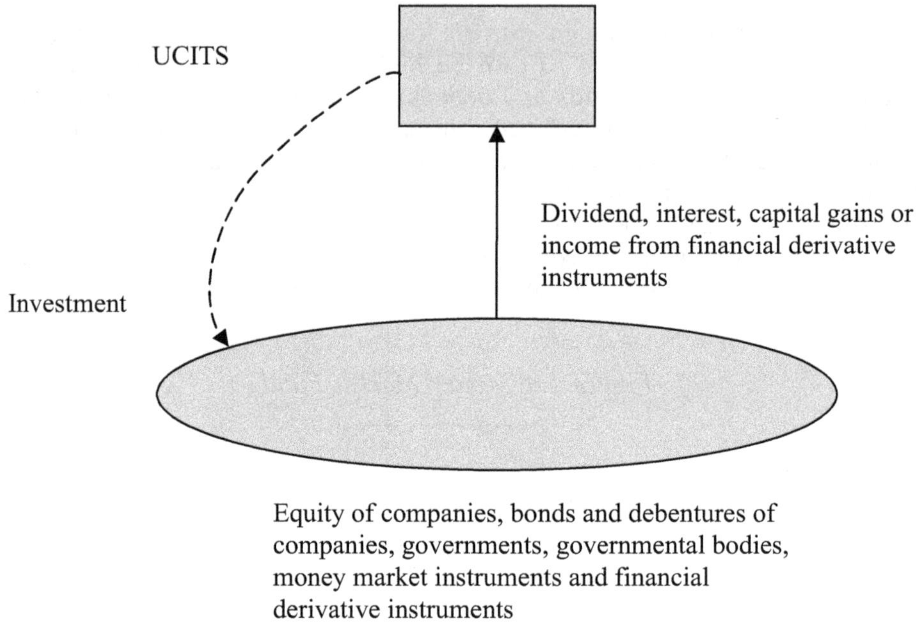

1.2.4. LEGAL STRUCTURE AND ORGANIZATION OF UCITS

1.2.4.1. Legal Structure of UCITS

The UCITS can legally be structured as a corporation, common fund, or unit trust.[31] The legal structure determines who has ownership of the UCITS's assets and who is entitled to the income derived from these assets – the UCITS or the joint unitholders. As a legal entity the investments of an incorporated UCITS are part of the corporation's own assets, which are separated from its unitholders' assets. Consequently, it is also the UCITS that is entitled to the yield of its investments. In contrast to incorporated funds, common funds and unit trusts have no legal personality. A common fund is established by contract. The assets of a common fund are managed and kept in accordance with the fund rules for the benefit of the joint unitholders. Each of the unitholders owns a proportion of the investments. Any earnings from the fund's investments are received by the fund for the account of its investors. A unit trust is vested by a deed. The assets of a unit trust are, contrary to common funds, owned by the trustee, although not for the trustee's own benefit, unless otherwise authorized by the terms of the trust. The property is held

31. Article 1(32) UCITS Directive.

as independent property available only for the beneficiaries.[32] As a result of the trustee's title to the investments, any income deriving from these investments is the trustee's but for the benefit of the beneficiaries.

The UCITS Directive leaves it to the Member States whether they provide for one or more than one legal form for UCITS. The same applies for whether a UCITS is structured with one class or multiple classes of units (umbrella fund). In the case of an umbrella fund, each class of units, also known as a sub-fund, corresponds to a separately administered investment portfolio with its own investment objective, for example, European equity, US bonds, and high yield money market instruments. A unitholder can switch between these investment portfolios because each unit can be converted, or switched, to a unit of another class at its net asset value. This provides unitholders with more flexibility to switch between investment objectives. An umbrella fund is also attractive for its host parent because the costs of the fund are less as a result of being spread over several sub-funds. Furthermore, classes of units with new investment objectives can be introduced easily.[33]

1.2.4.2. Organization of UCITS

The management of UCITS is generally handled by a management company that is authorized by one of the Member States, although an incorporated UCITS does not have to appoint a management company (Figure 1.6). The management activities include, among other things, investment management, administration, and marketing.[34] Investment decisions are made and carried out by the management company. The administration includes legal and fund management accounting services, the distribution of income, and unit issues and redemptions. The UCITS Directive does not cover the marketing of UCITS so UCITS are subject to marketing regulations of the Member State in which they would like to market or market their units. The management company receives a fee from the UCITS for management activities. This fee is sometimes subdivided into a management fee, an administration fee, and a performance fee. Whereas the management and administration fees are determined as a percentage of the UCITS's total assets, the performance fee depends on the difference in total return of the benchmark and the UCITS's return.

The assets of the UCITS must be placed in the custody of an authorized depositary so that the assets of the UCITS and the management company are separated. The depositary, in addition, makes sure that, in accordance with the law and the fund rules, the sale, issue, re-purchase, redemption, and cancellation of units effected on behalf of a corporation, common fund, unit trust, or management company are carried out; the net asset value of units is calculated correctly;

32. D.J. Hayton, *The Law of Trusts* (London: Sweet & Maxwell, 2003), 4.
33. N.V. Ponsen & P. Klemann, 'Beleggingsinstellingen nader belicht', *Preadviezen voor de Vereniging voor Effectenrecht 2000* (Kluwer, 2000): 76.
34. Article 5(2) UCITS Directive in combination with Annex II.

Figure 1.6 Organization of a UCITS

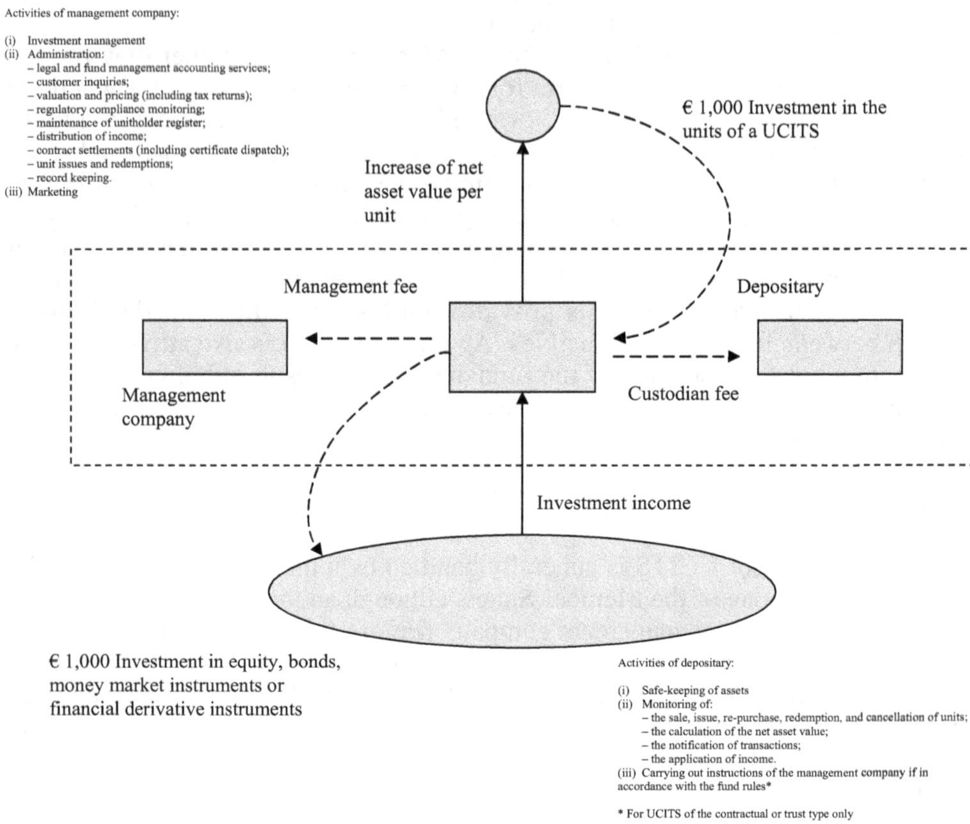

consideration is paid in regard to the usual time limit for the transfer of transactions by the management company; and the income of a corporation, common fund, or unit trust is applied correctly. It also carries out instructions of the management company, unless these instructions violate the law or the fund regulations.[35] The depositary receives a fee from the UCITS for its activities.

1.3. CROSS-BORDER TRADING IN THE UNITS OF UCITS

Despite the aim of the UCITS Directive, in 2004 only 16.1% of the undertakings that are authorized as UCITS sold their shares or units on a cross-border basis.[36]

35. Articles 7(3) and 14(3), UCITS Directive.
36. 'Green Paper of the European Commission on the Enhancement of the EU Framework for Investment Funds', (Washington, DC, SEC (12 Jul 2005) 947: 3.

With the exception of the trading in units of Irish and Luxembourg funds, no substantial cross-border trading in the units of UCITS takes place in the EU. The market for units in UCITS is, despite the UCITS Directive, fragmentized by national borders (Figure 1.7). Austrian investors invest in Austrian, Irish, or Luxembourg-resident UCITS; German investors in German, Irish, or Luxembourg-resident UCITS; and so on. Despite much case law and harmonization efforts, the internal market for capital does not function optimally as yet.

Although there is no simple answer to the fragmentation as a result of the Member States' national borders, obstacles have been identified by academics and in industry research in the past years. These obstacles have been ranked by UK asset managers of UCITS on the request of the Centre for European Economic Research in Mannheim. Because of the ranking of these obstacles, this research is quite unique. It provides a framework for a debate on policy priorities to remove the existing obstacles. In addition, it stimulates further research on the identified obstacles and possible solutions. Taxation has been ranked by the asset managers as one of the most important obstacles to cross-border trade in the units of UCITS.

It is hard for a non-resident UCITS to trade its units in Member States that have imposed tax regulations that discriminate against investment in the units of non-resident UCITS. A discriminatory measure provides for either a tax benefit that is not available for investments in the units of non-resident UCITS or a tax disadvantage that applies only to non-resident UCITS and not to domestic ones, as a result of which investors may be inclined to invest in the units of a domestic UCITS.[37] The problem of tax discrimination is also mentioned by INVESCO.[38] The problem with tax discrimination that is inconsistent with the EC Treaty or the EEA Treaty is that it often requires a procedure before the European Court of Justice to get the discrimination removed. This is costly and time consuming. Tax discriminatory obstacles also can be brought before the European Court of Justice by the European Commission (infringement proceedings).[39] Before it does this, the European Commission will give a Member State the possibility to explain its regulations or to remove such regulations voluntarily. No infringement proceedings by the European Commission regarding tax discrimination by investments in and by non-resident collective investment funds were found.

---

37. PricewaterhouseCoopers/EFAMA, 'Tax discrimination against foreign funds: Light at the end of the tunnel', (2005): 5.
38. 'Building of an integrated European Fund Management: Cross border mergers of funds, a quick win?', INVESCO (2005): 16.
39. Article 226 EC Treaty and Art. 109(1) of the EEA Treaty. The European Commission is not only entrusted with several duties under the EC Treaty but it is also obliged to ensure that the European Community and its Member States fulfil the obligations under the EEA Treaty. On the other hand, the EFTA Surveillance Authority needs to make sure that the EEA Treaty is properly applied in Iceland, Liechtenstein, and Norway. Any tax discriminatory obstacles found by the EFTA Surveillance Authority are, however, brought before the EFTA Court of Justice.

Figure 1.7 The Fragmentation of (Cross-Border) Distribution of Units in UCITS (2001)

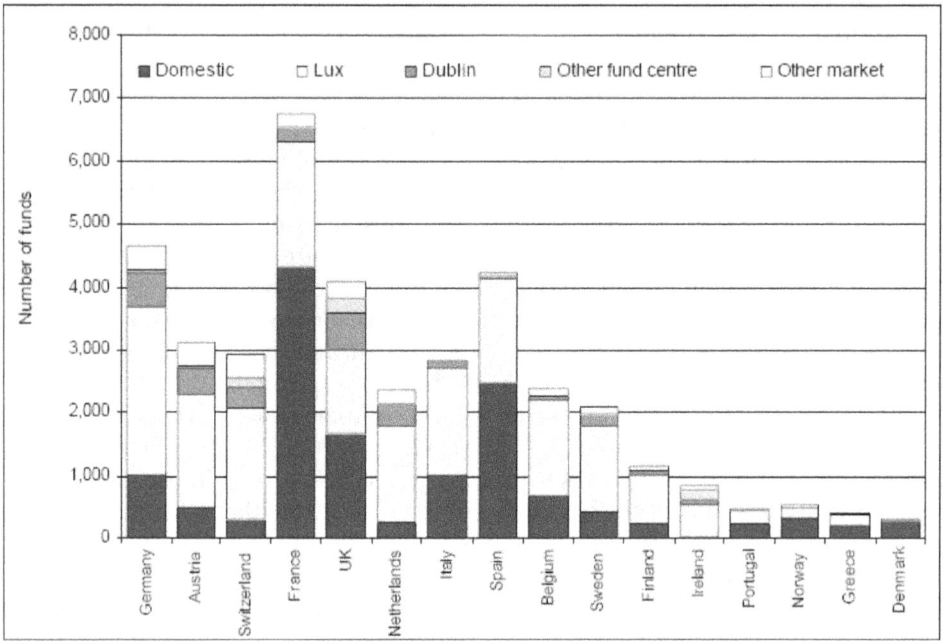

Source: Lipper.

The trading in units of UCITS in another Member State also may be hindered by differences between the tax laws of the Member States under which an investment in the units of a non-resident UCITS results in a higher tax burden compared to an investment in the units of a resident UCITS. UCITS would in that case have difficulties in trading units in the other Member State because investors would be declined to invest in its units. An appeal to the principle of non-discrimination does not give comfort because the EC Treaty and the EEA Treaty do not prohibit disparities. Nor can the European Commission bring disparities to the European Court of Justice. The differences in the tax laws of Member States can be removed only through harmonization or coordination.[40] If an investment in the units of non-resident UCITS, or certain non-resident UCITS, carries a higher tax burden, additional measures are necessary to improve the conditions of competition between UCITS.

This chapter explains the framework for UCITS as laid down in the UCITS Directive. It also deals with the investment policy, legal form, and organization of UCITS. It ends with a discussion on the consequences of taxation on cross-border investments in UCITS.

40. Court of Justice of the European Communities, *Gilly* case (C – 336/96).

Chapter 2

Introduction of the Taxation of Undertakings for Collective Investment in Transferable Securities

The Directive on Undertakings for Collective Investment in Transferable Securities (UCITS) does not harmonize or coordinate the taxation of investments in and by UCITS. Nor is the taxation harmonized or coordinated by other secondary European Community (EC) law. The Member States of the EU are sovereign in the field of direct taxation. The authority to impose personal or corporate income tax on investments in and by UCITS is divided over several jurisdictions.

The concept of transparency helps compare the taxation of investments in and by UCITS among the Member States. In accordance with the concept of transparency, the taxation of investments by way of UCITS should not be more or less than a direct investment. A more favourable tax treatment is undesirable. In that case, investors would be inclined to invest collectively instead of directly, which would distort the financial market and result in a loss of revenue for the Member State. The opposite is also undesirable for socioeconomic reasons.

The tax burden of a direct investment in securities and other financial instruments is determined by the investor's personal or corporate income tax liability, the nature and source of income, the recognition of income, and the deduction and crediting of withholding taxes. Not surprisingly, the taxation of direct investments is not the same in Member States. After all, they are free to determine who is liable to tax, adjust the tax base, set the tax rates and provide relief from tax for certain persons or activities.

The majority of Member States have chosen to follow the concept of transparency for investments in and by UCITS, albeit to a certain degree. On the basis of the specifics of the domestic tax laws, Member States have imposed their own set of tax rules so that income that is derived by way of UCITS is not subject to more taxation or less taxation than a direct investment (transparency). These tax regulations often achieve transparency for only domestic investments, domestic unitholders or investments in resident UCITS.

The Member States' tax laws on investments in and by UCITS are not optimally designed for foreign investments, non-resident unitholders or investments in and by non-resident UCITS. After all, they frequently originate from a time that cross-border investments in and by undertakings for collective investments were not common. The Member States have failed to modernize the taxation of these investments, not to mention to harmonize or coordinate the taxation. Cross-border investments in and by UCITS have therefore the potential to result in numerous tax disadvantages and tax advantages, which would weaken the conditions of competition between UCITS.

2.1. INTRODUCTION

The UCITS Directive covers only Member States' regulations concerning the obligations and control of UCITS. It does not contain regulations regarding the taxation of investments in and by UCITS. Neither will such rules be found elsewhere in secondary EC law. In contrast to federal states such as Canada, the Swiss Confederation, or the United States, the power to tax income, including capital gains and capital, is not shared between the EU and its Member States. Nor is it, as is the case in Australia's system, the exclusive competence of the federative level. The Member States of the EU are sovereign in designing direct tax laws; they are free to define who is liable to tax, adjust their tax base, set the applicable tax rates, and impose special tax regimes for certain persons or activities. The authority to impose (corporate) income tax legislation for UCITS and their investors in the European Union (EU) is thus divided over several jurisdictions.

The Member States' sovereignty is, nevertheless, not unrestricted. It is limited in three ways. The Member States' power to tax is, first, limited by the fundamental freedoms and non-discrimination clauses of the EC Treaty and the EEA Treaty, which cover both discriminatory and restrictive rules. For the taxation of UCITS and investors in UCITS, the freedoms of establishment, services and capital are the most relevant. UCITS must, for example, be able to relocate their residence to another Member State without being hindered by the tax regulations of the former Member State of residence (restriction) or the new one (discrimination). Neither may the trade in units of UCITS be hindered by the tax regulations of their state of residence or another Member State.

Second, it is prohibited for Member States to distort the trade between Member States by way of tax regulations that favour the activities of a particular branch of industry or that of some specific taxpayers (forbidden state aid).[1] However, in

1. Article 87 EC Treaty.

Italian Republic v. Commission[2] the European Commission did not characterize the Italian normal scheme for UCITS and other collective investment funds, as forbidden state aid. Instead, an additional tax scheme for UCITS and other collective investment funds that invest at least two-thirds of the value of their assets in small or medium-sized quoted capitalization companies was considered to be prohibited state aid. Compared to the aforementioned normal tax scheme, the additional tax scheme provided for a tax rate of 5% instead of 12.5%. Without proper consultation of the European Commission it provided a tax incentive for specific groups of investors and particular investments.[3,4]

Third, a few areas of direct tax law have been harmonized to improve the establishment or functioning of the internal market. Based on Article 94 of the EC Treaty, tax matters require unanimity among the Member States. For this reason, in the past many proposals by the European Commission on direct taxation were not adopted. So far, only four directives on direct taxation have been agreed on: the Parent-Subsidiary Directive, the Merger Directive, the Interest and Royalty Directive, and the Savings Taxation Directive. The Savings Taxation Directive is the only one of these directives that involves the taxation of income, that is, interest, derived through a UCITS. Although it regulates among other things the exchange of information about the amount of interest that is distributed to individual unitholders of UCITS,[5] it also allows Austria, Belgium, and Luxembourg to charge a withholding tax on distributed interest of currently 20% in case an individual unitholder has not opted for information exchange. A discussion of the Savings Taxation Directive falls outside the scope of this study, because individual unitholders can avoid Austrian, Belgium, and Luxembourg withholding tax on distributed interest by opting for information exchange, and the Directive does otherwise not concern the taxation of income derived from investments of UCITS.

2.1.1. Historical Developments

At the time of introduction of the UCITS Directive in 1985, the majority of Member States already had separate tax regulations in force for the taxation of undertakings for collective investment. For the taxation of UCITS, most of the Member States simply referred to these existing, non-harmonized, tax regulations. The tax regulations of the Western Member States often date from the 1960s. Because of

---

2. Action brought on 16 Nov. 2005 to the Court of First Instance, *Italian Republic v. Commission* (OJ C 22/23, 28 Jan. 2006). The case is pending before the Court.
3. European Commission Decision, 6 Sep. 2005 (OJ L 268/1, 27 Sep. 2006).
4. See for an extensive discussion, R.H.C. Luja, 'Investment Funds, Tax Planning and State Aid', *European Taxation* 12 (2006): 565–569.
5. See for a more comprehensive discussion, R.P.C. Adema, 'Collective Investment Vehicles and the Savings Taxation Directive from a Dutch Perspective', in *The Taxation of Interest Savings Income in the European Capital Market*, ed. D. Aigner, L. Gläser & M. Tumpel (Vienna: Linde Verlag, 2006), 135–150.

the (socio)-economic developments in Western Europe after World War II (WWII), an increasing number of people were able to invest in securities. Undertakings for collective investment provided these investors with the spread of risk and professional asset management, among other advantages. In addition, the issuing of a unit in an undertaking for collective investment usually requires no more than a small deposit. On the other hand, undertakings for collective investment also made the necessary capital available for the growing economy.[6] Despite the advantages of collective investment, investors would probably favour direct investments in the securities otherwise held collectively if an investment in the units of an undertaking for collective investment would bear a significant higher tax burden than a direct investment. A higher tax burden means that more tax leaks out and the investor will, after taxation, end up with less income. For socioeconomic reasons, a higher tax burden for investments in undertakings for collective investment was prevented or reduced in most Member States by the adoption of the concept of transparency. The transparency concept implies that investors who invest through the use of an undertaking for collective investment are taxed no better or worse than if they had invested directly. By 1961, most Western European states had imposed separate tax regulations for undertakings for collective investment. Some eliminated or reduced double taxation on the income of undertakings for collective investment (tax opaque entity), whereas others prevented taxation at the level of undertakings for collective investment by the use of non-taxable persons (tax transparent entity). It was not until the 1980s that the two most northern Member States, Finland and Sweden, introduced special tax regulations for undertakings for collective investments. In the 1990s, after the collapse of the 'Iron Curtain', the Eastern Member States followed.

2.2. CONCEPT OF TRANSPARENCY

The concept of transparency may be helpful to compare the taxation of investment in the units of UCITS among the Member States. According to the concept of transparency, the tax burden for an investment in a UCITS should be similar to that of a direct investment. If the tax burden of an investment in UCITS is treated more favourably, more investors will be inclined to invest collectively instead of directly, which may distort the financial market and result in a loss of revenue for the Member State. The opposite is attained by a less favourable tax treatment. Investors will be inclined to prefer direct investments rather than collective ones, which is not desirable for socioeconomic reasons. Hence, the tax burden of an investment in a UCITS should ideally match with that of a direct investment. For this reason, it is important to know the composition of the tax

6. E.G. Renk, *Fiscal Problems Arising in Connection with Investment Trusts of International Character: General Report* (The Hague: Cahiers de Droit Fiscal International, 1962), XLV.

burden of a direct investment. The tax burden of a direct investment is determined by the following factors:

(1) The investor's liability to personal or corporate income tax (tax status)
(2) The nature and source of income
(3) The recognition of income
(4) The deduction and crediting of withholding taxes

Together, these factors affect the amount of tax that leaks out and thus determine the amount of income remaining after taxation. A brief explanation of these factors follows. Each factor will be given more consideration in the subsequent sections.

2.2.1. Investing Directly in Securities and Other Financial Instruments

2.2.1.1. Tax Status

The amount of tax due by an investor depends, first, on whether the investor is liable to personal or corporate income tax.

2.2.1.2. Nature and Source of Income

The Member States are, in the absence of any unification or harmonization, free to define who is liable to tax, to describe what types of income are included in a taxable person's tax base, and to set tax rates. Particular types of income may be subject to special treatment. Some Member States provide for more than one tax rate or set of progressive tax rates for dividends, interest, or capital gains. Other Member States exclude capital gains realized by disposal of investment from the tax base of individuals.

2.2.1.3. Recognition of Income

The recognition of income is determined by the accounting principles of a national tax system. These principles are especially of importance for the recognition of capital gains, capital losses, and income from financial derivatives. Generally, these items of income are either recognized (1) at the time of sale, refund or redemption of shares or bonds, the time of maturity of a contract, or at the time of maturity of a contract to deliver or when the contract is eliminated through an offsetting transaction (realization principle); (2) at the end of the year for the profits or losses shown in the accounts based on the market price in the financial markets (mark-to-market principle); or (3) at the end of the year or at one of the times mentioned under (1) (hybrid forms).[7] Another question that occurs with regard to

7. O.H. Jacobs & J. Haun, 'Financial Derivatives in International Tax Law – A Treatment of Certain Key Considerations', *Intertax* (1995): 407.

income from financial derivatives is in regard to categorizing the type of income. Income derived from the selling of options can, for example, be regarded as capital gains or as ordinary income. Again, different positions have been taken in the Member States' accounting principles.

2.2.1.4. Deduction and Crediting of Withholding Tax

In some Member States, certain items of income are not subject to (corporate) income tax because the withholding tax levied at source is a final taxation. In other Member States, the withholding tax may be credited against the investor's (corporate) income tax liability, although the crediting may be subject to further conditions. The crediting of foreign withholding tax is generally limited to the part of the (corporate) income tax liability related to the foreign income. The part of the foreign withholding tax that is not creditable will be an additional tax burden for the investor. The overall tax burden is in that case the sum of the (corporate) income tax due and the difference between the amount of foreign withholding tax levied and the amount of foreign withholding tax credited against the tax liability. In a few Member States, the non-creditable part of the foreign withholding tax may be carried forward to the following year or deducted from the income as an expense.

If an investor is not liable to (corporate) income tax, the charging of withholding tax, if any, will be the only tax suffered on the income derived from an investment. In the case of foreign investments, investors who are not liable to (corporate) income tax are generally not entitled to a reduction of withholding tax under the applicable tax treaty. A reduction of withholding tax is generally available only to persons who are liable to (corporate) income tax in the state of residence. As a result, the amount of tax withheld on foreign income paid to investors who are not liable (corporate) income tax is often more than the tax withheld on foreign income paid to investors who are liable to (corporate) income tax. This is different only in the absence of a tax treaty or in the case in which the domestic tax rate of the source state is less than the reduced tax rate agreed on in the applicable tax treaty.

In Figure 2.1 it is assumed that an investor keeps shares issued by a foreign company. The shares generate a dividend of EUR 100,000. The dividend, in this example, is subject to a withholding tax of 25% in the source state, unless the investor is entitled to a reduction of withholding tax under the tax treaty between the source state and the investor's residence state. In that case, the withholding tax rate is reduced to, in this example, 15%.

The dividend is assumed to be subject to (corporate) income tax at a rate of 40% in the investor's residence state, unless the investor is exempt from (corporate) income tax. Otherwise, the tax withheld by the source state generally may be credited against the (corporate) income tax treaty under the applicable tax treaty. Hence, the investor owes EUR 25,000 (corporate) income tax to the tax authorities of the residence state. In this example, there is no additional tax burden, because the foreign withholding tax can be credited completely against the investor's tax liability.

Figure 2.1 Tax Burden on a Direct Investment

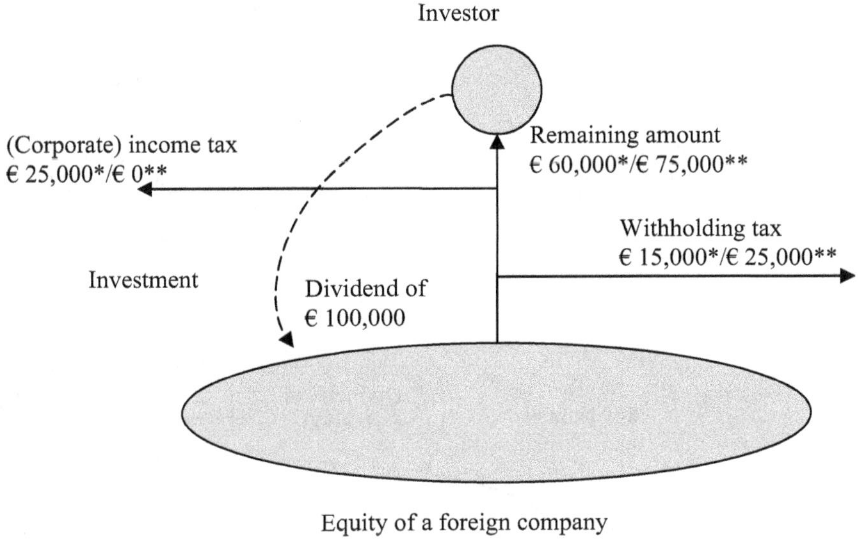

* In the case that the investor is liable to (corporate) income tax.
** In the case that the investor is not liable to (corporate) income tax.

The investor's overall tax burden is thus 40%, which is equal to the amount of (corporate) income tax on the dividend. Consequently, the investor maintains 60% of the dividend. In the case that an investor is not liable to (corporate) income tax, the tax burden is solely formed by the withholding tax levied by the source state, which is 25%. In that case, the investor is left with 75% of the dividend.

2.2.2. Investing by Way of UCITS

The deduction and crediting of withholding taxes, the recognition of the income, and the nature and source of the income should, in accordance with the concept of transparency, be left intact when investors invest collectively instead of directly. Otherwise, the tax burden on a collective investment may be more or less favourable than a direct investment. Thus, it is not sufficient for a Member State to do no more than just neutralize taxation at the level of UCITS. The Member States' tax regulations for an investment in UCITS should be designed to take an investor's tax status into consideration, because the tax burden of a direct investment is primarily determined by the investor's tax status. In addition, the nature and the source of income should not get lost because of the use of a UCITS. Nor should the recognition of the income be different from a direct investment.

Figure 2.2 Tax Burden on an Indirect Investment

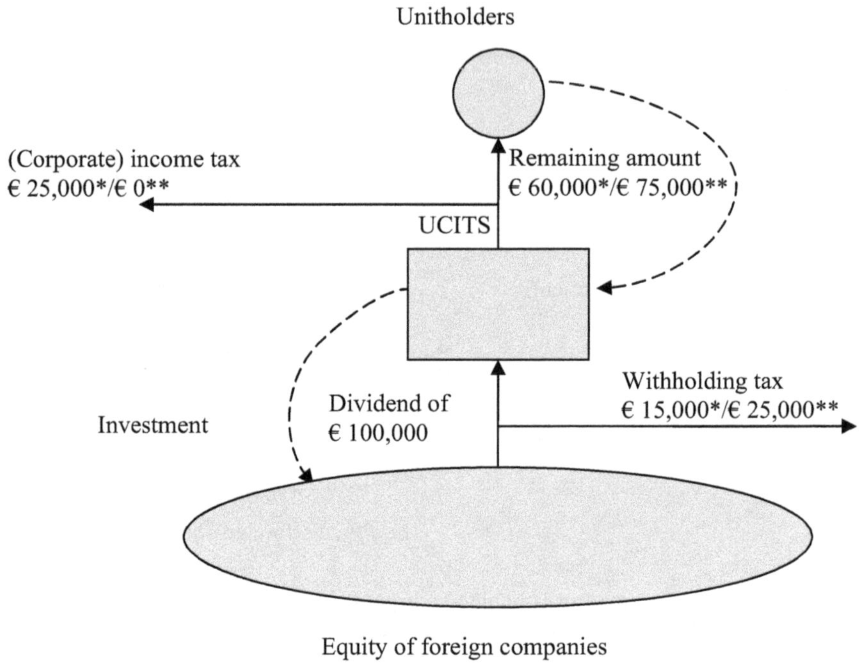

* In the case that the investor is liable to (corporate) income tax.
** In the case that the investor is not liable to (corporate) income tax.

In the example in Figure 2.1, the overall tax burden of income derived from a direct investment is EUR 40,000 for an investor who is liable to (corporate) income tax and EUR 25,000 for an investor who is not liable to such tax. The tax burden of an investment in a UCITS should, in accordance with the concept of transparency, not be more or less than a direct investment. The tax burden of an indirect investment should thus be determined by the same factors as for a direct investment, as illustrated in Figure 2.2. To achieve a similar tax burden, the outcome of these factors may not differ from a that of direct investment. In addition, the income derived from the investment should not be subject to taxation at the level of the UCITS or the level of its investors. The taxation at both levels should be tailored so that the tax status of the investor is taken into account. Hence, the amount of tax due by an investor must still depend on whether the investor is liable to personal or corporate income tax.

2.2.2.1. Exempt Corporate Unitholder

The tax burden of an investor who is not liable to (corporate) income tax is generally determined by the withholding tax levied at the source of the income, if any. The amount of withholding tax levied at source should not be different because of the use of a UCITS. The objective and subjective tax liability (tax status) of UCITS should not be taken into account by the deduction of withholding tax. The amount of withholding tax should still depend on the tax status of the investor. Otherwise, the investor may, for example, benefit from a UCITS's entitlement to a reduction of withholding tax or an exemption from withholding tax under the domestic laws of the source state or the applicable tax treaty. The investor would not have had such a benefit in the case of a direct investment. The opposite may also be true. To meet the conditions of the concept of transparency, the tax status of the investor should thus be taken into consideration by the deduction of withholding tax.

2.2.2.2. Individual and Corporate Unitholders

The tax burden for an investor who is liable to (corporate) income tax is determined by the (corporate) income tax due on the income derived from the investment. To achieve the same tax burden, the amount of income may not be subject to more or less (corporate) income tax than a direct investment. Consequently, the nature and source of income together with the recognition of the income should not change because of the use of a UCITS. Thus, a capital gain realized by the UCITS should also be taxed as a capital gain in the hands of the investor after distribution by the UCITS, unless the capital gain has been finally taxed at the level of the UCITS. Otherwise, the capital gain may be taxed, for example, in the hands of the investors as a dividend or other distribution from shares in a company. The recognition of the income in the hands of the investor should also remain the same. An investment in UCITS would, otherwise, enable investors to defer the (corporate) income tax due on the income received from the underlying investments. The income should thus be considered for (corporate) income tax purposes to be received by the unitholders in the same year as in the case of a direct investment.

In addition, the deduction and crediting of withholding tax at the source of the income should take place as if the investor had invested directly. The objective and subjective tax liability (tax status) of the UCITS should not play a role as discussed above for exempt corporate unitholders.

2.2.2.3. Concept of Transparency by Cross-Border Trading

Despite the IFA Congresses of 1962, 1971, and 1997, all of which concerned the taxation of undertakings for collective investment, any international coordination on the taxation of investments in and by non-resident undertakings for collective investment is lacking, even within the EU. The Member States may have taken different approaches to tailoring the taxation at the level of the investments and that of the UCITS with the taxation at the level of the investors. Where these differences are considerable, Member States may only be able to tailor taxation of an investment in UCITS in accordance with the concept of transparency for investments in domestic securities and other financial instruments, resident investors, or investments in resident UCITS. Member States cannot exercise power over taxation at the level of foreign investments or a non-resident UCITS unless it has a source of income within its jurisdiction. The differences between the national tax systems may result in a tax advantage or a tax disadvantage for an investment in a non-resident UCITS. A tax advantage may facilitate cross-border trading in units of UCITS; whereas cross-border trading may be hindered by a tax disadvantage. A tax advantage or tax disadvantage for investments in units of non-resident UCITS could be the result of considerable differences between measures taken by Member States to establish transparency at the source of income, at the level of the UCITS, and at the level of the investors. If taxation at source of income derived from the investments of a non-resident UCITS differs from that of a resident UCITS, this may result in a higher or lesser tax burden. The same applies for differences between the measures taken at the level of a non-resident UCITS and those taken at the level of the investor.

The subsequent sections will therefore examine the Member States' regulations for the taxation of income derived by way of UCITS. The Member States' tax regulations will be viewed from the perspective of the concept of transparency. The concept of transparency makes it possible to compare the tax burden of an investment in the units of a UCITS, and, thus, of the amount of income that remains after taxation. After that, a conclusion will be drawn whether or not the Member States' tax regulations for investments in UCITS differ so much that this may result in tax advantages and disadvantages for an investment in the units of a non-resident UCITS that may stop investors from investing in the units of non-resident UCITS or certain non-resident UCITS.

2.3. THE TAXATION OF UCITS

2.3.1. THE TAX STATUS OF A CORPORATE UCITS

The design of tax regulations for investments in and by UCITS depends to a great extent on the tax status of UCITS. Whether a UCITS is a taxable person depends on the tax regulations of its Member State of residence. The tax laws of Member States do not necessarily have to correspond with the legal status of UCITS under civil law.[8] In practice, the determination of the tax status of a corporate UCITS does not cause many difficulties. In Member States that provide for this type of UCITS, only fourteen Member States,[9] UCITS are considered taxable persons (tax opaque entity). Consequently, the income and capital gains of these UCITS are, under the general tax provisions for companies, subject to (corporate) income tax at the level of the UCITS. Consequently, income and capital gains are taxed twice – first, at the

8. A.J. Easson & V. Thuronyi, 'Fiscal Transparency', in *Tax Law Design and Drafting*, ed. V. Thuronyi (Washington, D.C.: International Monetary Fund, 1998) Ch. 21, 2.
9. Belgium, Cyprus, France, Hungary, Ireland, Italy, Lithuania, Luxembourg, Malta, the Netherlands, Poland, Romania, Spain, and the United Kingdom.

level of the UCITS and, second, by distribution or on sale, refund, or redemption of the units in the UCITS, at the level of the investor. The double taxation of the income and capital gains is, in most Member States, eliminated or reduced by a subjective exemption, a reduced tax base, or a reduced tax rate.

Instead of eliminating or reducing double taxation at the level of the UCITS, two Member States, Portugal and the United Kingdom, take another approach, that is, eliminating or reducing double taxation at the level of the investor by way of a tax credit or an exemption. Double taxation is sometimes eliminated or reduced by combining two ore more of these measures.

2.3.1.1. Subjectively Exempt

Although a corporation is liable to tax, a corporate UCITS may be subjectively exempt. Sometimes, certain conditions must be fulfilled by the UCITS to be exempt. As a result of the exemption, the income and capital gains of the UCITS will thus not be taxed. Therefore, at the level of the UCITS, no tax is levied. This method of eliminating double taxation on the income and capital gains of UCITS is used in France, Hungary, Ireland, the Netherlands, Lithuania, Luxembourg, and Poland.

Example 2.1

A corporate UCITS receives from its investments in the shares of companies a dividend of EUR 1,000,000. In addition, it has realized a net capital gain on the disposal of shares for an amount of EUR 4,000,000. Because of its subjective exemption, no tax is imposed on the total income of EUR 5,000,000. Consequently, no tax leaks away at the level of the UCITS.

2.3.1.2. Reduced Tax Base

Unlike UCITS that are exempt, UCITS whose tax base is reduced to eliminate or reduce double taxation is still liable to tax. A reduced tax base simply keeps investment income, capital gains, or both, outside the tax base of the UCITS. Consequently, no tax is paid by the UCITS on its income and capital gains. Belgium, Cyprus, Malta, and the United Kingdom use a reduced tax base. In the Netherlands, a reduced tax base is optional for UCITS.

Example 2.2

When the corporate UCITS in Example 2.1 is subject to a reduced tax base instead of a subjective exemption, the income will be kept outside its tax base, as a result of which no tax is imposed on the income of EUR 5,000,000. The reduced tax base prevents the leakage of tax at the UCITS's level.

2.3.1.3. Reduced Tax Rate

In the case of a reduced tax rate, the income and capital gains of a UCITS are still part of its tax base but are taxed at a special tax rate. The tax rate is either reduced or nil. Consequently, the UCITS is liable to tax. A reduced tax rate applies in Italy, the Netherlands, Spain, and the United Kingdom.

Example 2.3

In the case of a reduced tax rate, the income of the corporate UCITS in Example 2.1 is part of its tax base and subject to tax. No tax will, however, be imposed by a tax rate of nil. Again, no tax leaks away.

2.3.1.4. Fully Liable to Tax

Only Portugal and the United Kingdom eliminate or reduce double taxation on the income and capital gains of a UCITS at the level of the investor. Double taxation is prevented in Portugal by a combination of an exemption for proceedings from UCITS and a tax credit. The United Kingdom offers a tax credit that can be set off against the investor's tax liability or applies an exemption for distributed income. Consequently, the UCITS is fully liable to tax in these Member States, although the tax base as well as the tax rate of an UK-resident UCITS is reduced.

Example 2.4

The income of the corporate UCITS in Example 2.1 is now fully taxed. Although (corporate) income tax is levied at the level of the UCITS, the income is not taxed twice because of an exemption or a tax credit at the level of the unitholder.

2.3.2. The Tax Status of a Contractual UCITS

The determination of the tax status of a contractual UCITS is more complicated than that of a corporate UCITS. A contractual UCITS is an arrangement between the unitholders, the management company, and the depositary and lacks legal personality. Although in many Member States the tax status of an entity is established by tax law and does not always correspond with its status under civil law,[10] a contractual UCITS is, in several Member States, to wit Austria, Belgium, France, Ireland, Latvia, and Luxembourg, still transparent for (corporate) income tax purposes (tax transparent entity). The transparency of UCITS prevents the income and capital gains from

---

10. A.J. Easson & V. Thuronyi, 'Fiscal Transparency', in *Tax Law Design and Drafting*, ed. V. Thuronyi (Washington, DC: International Monetary Fund, 1998), Ch. 21, 2.

being taxed twice: first, at the level of a UCITS and second at the level of its investors. The income and capital gains of the UCITS are split up proportionately among its unitholders, although it must sometimes be distributed to be considered to be the investor's.

Example 2.5

A contractual UCITS receives from its investments in the shares of a number of companies a dividend of EUR 1,000,000. In addition, it has realized a net capital gain on the disposal of shares for an amount of EUR 4,000,000. The dividend and capital gains are considered to be those of the unitholders. Unitholder A has an interest of 0.1% in the UCITS. Consequently, A is deemed to have earned a dividend of EUR 1,000 and to have realized a capital gain of EUR 4,000. As the UCITS is disregarded, the income is taxed at the unitholder's level only.

In the remaining Member States, that is, Cyprus, Czech Republic, Denmark, Finland, Germany, Greece, Italy, Lithuania, Malta, the Netherlands, Poland, Portugal, Romania, Slovak Republic, Slovenia, Spain, and Sweden, a contractual UCITS is, like UCITS of the corporate type, treated as a taxable person (tax opaque entity). Consequently, it is considered to be the recipient of the income and capital gains. In principle, it is taxable on these receipts in accordance with the general tax provisions for companies. The Member States have taken the same measures to avoid double taxation on the income and capital gains as described for corporate UCITS in the previous subsection.

2.3.3. The Tax Status of a Unit Trust UCITS

In three Member States, Ireland, Malta, and the United Kingdom, UCITS also can be constituted as a unit trust. In these states, UCITS of the unit trust type are subject to tax (tax opaque entity). In Ireland and Malta, a UCITS of the unit trust type is, however, not charged with (corporate) income tax because it is subjectively exempt from tax. In the United Kingdom, it has, on the other hand, a reduced corporate tax base and, moreover, it is subject to a reduced corporate tax rate. The United Kingdom compensates the unitholders for the tax liability of the UCITS by way of a tax credit or an exemption for distributed income.

Example 2.6

A UCITS of the trust type receives from its investments in the shares of a number of companies a total amount of EUR 1,000,000. In addition, it has realized a net capital gain on the disposal of shares for an amount of EUR 4,000,000. The income and capital gains are considered to be those of the UCITS. In Ireland the UCITS would be subjectively exempt whereas in the United Kingdom the capital gains of the EUR 4,000,000 would be exempt and the other income of EUR 1,000,000 would be subject to a reduced corporate tax rate for which the unitholders will receive a tax credit.

Figure 2.3 The Possible Tax Rules for UCITS

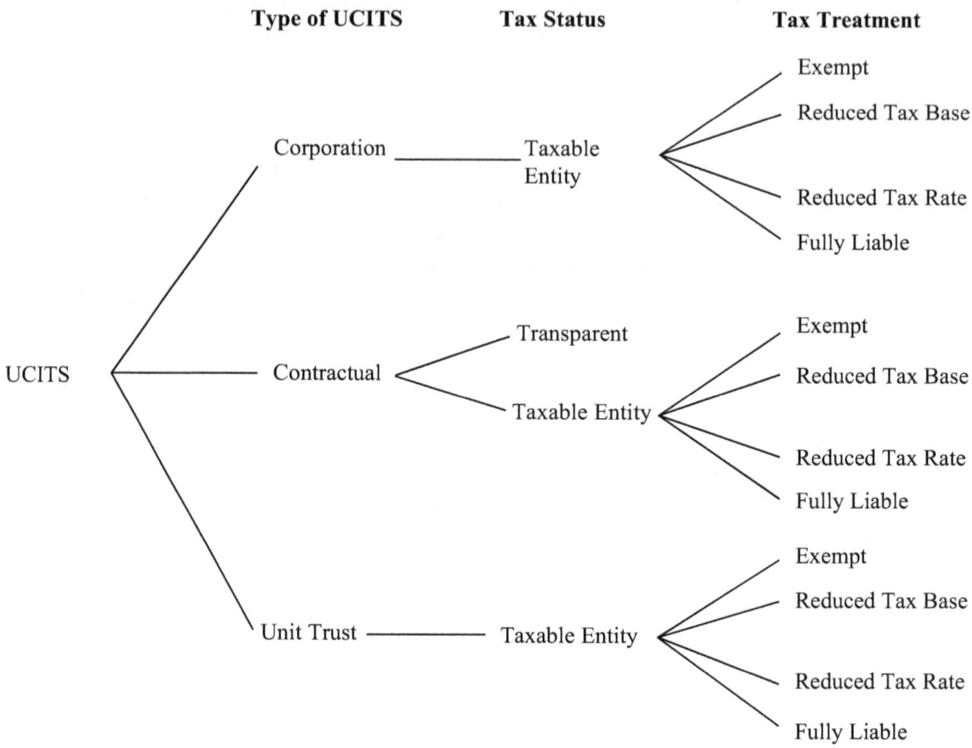

2.4. TAXATION AND CREDITING OF WITHHOLDING TAX

Income from investments of capital is often taxed at source with a withholding tax for the account of the recipient.[11] The amount of income derived from the investments is thus reduced by the withholding tax. For income derived from domestic investments, the withholding tax is an advance tax payment for the recipient.[12] The withholding tax may be credited against the recipient's (corporate) income tax liability. Nevertheless, some states have introduced a final withholding tax on certain types of income for resident recipients. Such types of income are not subject to further taxation with (corporate) income tax.

11. Some Member States also levy a withholding tax on foreign income from capital that has no source in that Member State other than that it is paid on an account of the beneficiary present in that Member State or by the use of a resident paying agent.
12. L. Burns & R. Krever, 'Taxation of Income from Business and Investment', in *Tax Law Design and Drafting*, ed. V. Thuronyi (Washington, D.C.: International Monetary Fund, 1998), Ch. 16, 70.

The type of income earned by a UCITS depends on its investment policy. The investments made by the UCITS may, based on its investment policy, generate dividends, interest, or capital gains. Whereas some UCITS specialize in domestic investments, others spread the risks of their investments geographically. Such UCITS do not, or do not only, invest domestically but rather pan-European or in regions outside the EU. Global funds, for instance, spread their investments worldwide and over all segments of the economy. Another reason to invest outside the residence state of the UCITS may be due to expected economic developments in certain regions, like Eastern Europe, Asia or Latin America, or even states, like Turkey, China, or Brazil. The income derived from these foreign investments may, for the account of the recipient, have been subject to withholding taxes at source, too. For non-resident recipients, such withholding taxes are a final taxation in the source state, although in a few states these investors are explicitly exempt from withholding tax.

The types of income from capital that are subject to withholding tax differ among the source states. Hence, source states may not levy a withholding tax on all types of income from capital. Some states, such as the Netherlands, levy a withholding tax on dividends only, whereas in, for instance, Austria and Germany, dividend as well as interest is subject to a withholding tax. Capital gains realized on portfolio investments are in the majority of Member States not subject to withholding tax. Neither is income from financial derivative instruments.[13] UCITS that limit their investments to their state of residence or other Member States (hereafter, EU funds) are usually thus confronted with the deduction of domestic or foreign withholding taxes on dividends or interest only. Any capital gains realized on the sale, refund, or redemption of investments or income from financial derivatives is generally not subject to withholding tax. Outside the EU, these types of income may be more often subject to withholding tax. Consequently, UCITS that also or especially invest outside the EU (hereafter, global funds) may be confronted with withholding taxes on dividends, interest, capital gains, or income from financial derivatives.

Moreover, withholding taxes may be levied at different times because the accounting principles of the source states differ. This may occur especially with respect to income from financial derivatives because of their more complex functioning.

Furthermore, the rate of the withholding tax also varies among the source states. Dividends may in one state be subject to a withholding tax of 28% while in another state they are taxed at a rate of only 15%. In the EU, the withholding tax rate for portfolio dividends varies between 0% and 30%. The withholding tax rate for interest varies from 0% to 30%.

The deduction and crediting of withholding taxes is affected by the liability to tax of UCITS and the measures taken to prevent the income derived from the investments made by the UCITS from being taxed twice. Therefore, the crediting of domestic withholding taxes and the deduction and crediting of foreign

13. OECD (1994), Taxation of New Financial Instruments.

withholding taxes are discussed hereafter to determine whether or not there are some substantial differences between the Member States.

2.4.1. Domestic Withholding Tax

2.4.1.1. Crediting of Domestic Withholding Tax

Unless the withholding tax is meant as a final tax, any domestic withholding tax may usually be credited by the recipient against the recipient's (corporate) income tax liability. The recipient is either the unitholder or the UCITS. The unitholder is considered to be the recipient of the income by a contractual UCITS that is considered to be transparent (hereafter, *tax transparent* UCITS). Similar to a direct investment, it therefore depends on the tax liability of the unitholder whether or the unitholder can credit the domestic withholding tax. The crediting of domestic withholding taxes thus does not cause a higher or lesser tax credit for an investment in the units of a tax transparent UCITS than a direct investment. In the case of a non-resident unitholder, the crediting of the withholding taxes by the residence state of the UCITS depends on the laws of the residence state of the investor and the tax treaty between the two states. The crediting of foreign withholding taxes will be discussed in Section 2.4.2.

Unlike a tax transparent UCITS, a UCITS that is considered a taxable person (hereafter, *tax opaque* UCITS) is considered to be the recipient of the income instead of its unitholders. The liability to tax of the UCITS is thus taken into account instead of that of its unitholders because the domestic withholding tax can be credited against the tax liability of the UCITS. If a UCITS does not actually pay any (corporate) income tax as a result of a reduced tax base or a reduced tax rate, the domestic withholding tax will be refunded. Subjectively exempt UCITS are, on the other hand, not liable to (corporate) income tax and thus do not have the possibility to credit the domestic withholding taxes. Nor are they entitled to a refund of those taxes. An investment in the units of a UCITS that is subjectively exempt leads to a *higher* tax burden for investors who are liable to (corporate) income tax. For that reason, some Member States have introduced the possibility for unitholders, or certain unitholders, to credit domestic withholding taxes levied on income of the UCITS against their tax liability as if they had invested directly. In these Member States, an investment in the units of a subjectively exempt UCITS does not cause a higher tax burden than a direct investment.

For other UCITS, it depends on the amount of the (corporate) income tax due regardless of whether all withholding taxes can be fully credited. The amount of domestic withholding tax that is not creditable will be refunded. For practical reasons, a few Member States have introduced an exemption for domestic withholding tax for dividend and interest derived by UCITS. In either situation, the tax burden of an investment in the units of tax opaque UCITS is for unitholders who are not liable to (corporate) income tax *lower* than that of a direct investment, because the UCITS may credit the domestic withholding taxes and will get a refund for the amount of domestic withholding taxes that is not creditable, whereas in the case of a direct investment, these unitholders would not have a refund.

In conclusion, the crediting of withholding taxes levied on income from domestic investments made by UCITS varies among Member States. On the one hand, it depends on the tax liability of the unitholder for tax transparent UCITS. For tax opaque UCITS, it instead depends on the tax liability of the UCITS. UCITS that are not subjectively exempt are entitled to a tax credit or a refund, whereas those that are subjectively exempt are not so entitled. In a few Member States, the unitholders of subjectively exempt UCITS are entitled to credit domestic withholding taxes instead.

2.4.2. Foreign Withholding Tax

2.4.2.1. Levying of Foreign Withholding Tax

In the case of cross-border payments there is generally the risk that such payments are taxed twice – first by the source state and then by the residence state. Any (potential) double taxation on the income of a UCITS may be eliminated or reduced by a bilateral agreement for the avoidance of double taxation on income and capital between the source state and the residence state (hereafter, tax treaty). The right to tax capital gains on, and income other than dividends and interest derived from, the portfolio investments (hereafter, other portfolio income) is allocated by tax treaties that are based on the Organization for Economic Cooperation and Development (OECD) Model Tax Convention to the residence state of the UCITS.[14] The right to tax dividends and interest income is, on the other hand, shared between both states.[15] The right of the source state[16] is, however, limited. It has been agreed in tax treaties that the withholding tax on dividends or interest may not exceed a certain percentage of the gross amount.[17] The OECD Model Tax Convention suggests 15% for portfolio dividends[18] and 10% for

14. Instead of the residence state, the source state is allowed to tax any capital gains or capital losses, or other portfolio income that is connected with a permanent establishment in the source state (Art. 7 OECD Model Tax Convention). Otherwise, the provisions on capital gains and other income apply, and the right to tax lies with the residence state.
15. Instead of the source state's right to tax, the residence state's right to tax will be limited when the dividends or interest income is connected with a permanent establishment in the source state (Arts 10(4) and 11(4) OECD Model Tax Convention). Otherwise, the provisions on dividends and interest income take priority over the provision on business profits.
16. The necessary tie with the source state is expressed by requiring that it is allowed to levy a withholding tax only in the case that the dividend is paid by a company resident in the source state or the interest arose in the source state.
17. Articles 10 and 11 OECD Model Tax Convention.
18. Dividends other than inter-company dividends. According to Art. 10(3) the term 'dividend' within the meaning of Art. 10 is income from shares, 'jouissance' shares or 'jouissance' rights, mining shares, founders' shares or other rights, not being debt claims, participating in profits, as well as income from other corporate rights, which is subjected to the same taxation treatment as income from shares by the law of the State of which the company making the distribution is a resident.

interest.[19] Often lower rates are applied. Unless the ordinary withholding tax on dividends or interest is less than the percentage agreed on under the applicable tax treaty, either the payer of the income may be authorized to apply the percentage agreed on in the applicable tax treaty (maximum withholding tax rate) or the beneficiary may, afterward, request a refund of the amount that is withheld by the source state in excess of the maximum withholding tax rate agreed on in the applicable tax treaty. Both situations require a certificate or official document of the residence state in which the provisions of the applicable tax treaty apply to the beneficiary.[20]

The source state's right to tax dividends, interest, capital gains, and other portfolio income will, however, be limited only if the applicable tax treaty applies to the beneficiary. A tax treaty that is based on the OECD Model Tax Convention applies only to persons that are resident in one or both[21] of the Contracting States,

---

19. Interest is defined by Art. 10(3) OECD Model Tax Convention as income from debt claims of every kind, whether or not secured by mortgage and whether or not carrying a right to participate in the debtor's profits, particularly, income from government securities, bonds, or debentures, including premiums and prizes attaching to such securities, bonds, or debentures. Penalty charges for late payments are not regarded as interest for the purposes of Art. 11.
20. K. Vogel, 'Klaus Vogel on Double Taxation Conventions: a Commentary to the OECD', *UN and US Model Conventions for the Avoidance of Double Taxation of Income and Capital. With Particular Reference to German Treaty Practice* (Amsterdam: Kluwer Law International, 1997), Preface to Arts 10–12, 32.
21. In contrast to the OECD Model Tax Convention, some tax treaties do not apply to persons that are dual resident. The (corporate) income tax regulations of the Member States apply to persons other than an individual that are resident in a Member State or have a source of income in a Member State. Unless a Member State adheres to the principle of territoriality, residents are generally liable to tax on their worldwide income in the Member State of residence, whereas non-residents are liable to only certain income with a source in that Member State. For the purposes of the UCITS Directive, a corporate UCITS is deemed to have its residence in the Member State where its registered office is located. The residence of a UCITS of the contractual type or the unit trust type is considered to be that of its management company's registered office. A registered office means its statutory seat. For tax purposes, however, the criteria used for the determination of the residence of persons other than an individual differ among the Member States. In some Member States a person other than an individual is resident when it is incorporated under or receives its legal status from the law of a Member States, whereas in others it is decided, on criteria such as the basis of its seat, its management, or its central management and control. The criteria may be used on their own or may be combined.

    The diverging rules of the Member States together with differences in the interpretation of the same criterion, or differences resulting from the complicated nature of a criterion may cause dual residence. Dual residence may occur when some activities of the UCITS, such as its management or its board of directors' meetings, are performed outside the Member State of authorization. As a result, the UCITS may be considered to be resident in Member State A and incorporated under the law of A, as well as in Member B, with its management is located in B. Consequently, the income and capital gains of the UCITS may be taxed twice, or not at all. A typical example where dual residence may come up is the authorization of a UCITS in a Member State by order of a promoter that is resident in another Member State with the aim of distributing the units in the UCITS in the last Member State. In exchange for the selling of units in the UCITS, the promoter receives a fee for the units sold. Typically, for this example, the promoter would likely keep some sort of control on the UCITS to guarantee its performance.

being the states that entered into the agreement. Being a person resident in one of the Contracting States is not only of importance for the application of a tax treaty but in most tax treaties it is also a condition for the application of the rules for dividends, interest, capital gains and other portfolio income. The term 'person' includes an individual, a company or any other body of persons. To qualify as a

---

It is the performance of a UCITS that determines the demand for its units by investors and thus the amount of the promoter's fee for the units sold. Control of the UCITS can be secured by a majority in the board of directors of the UCITS or its management company. Depending on the criteria for the determination of a resident in the promoter's Member State of residence, this may cause dual residence.

Any double taxation on the income and capital gains of a UCITS resulting from the dual residence may be eliminated or reduced by a bilateral agreement for the avoidance of double taxation on income and capital between the Member States concerned (hereafter, tax treaty). A tax treaty that is based on the OECD Model Tax Convention applies only to persons that are resident in one or both of the Contracting States, being the states that entered into the agreement. The OECD Model Convention defines a resident as any person who, under the domestic laws of a Contracting State, is liable to tax in that Contracting State by reason of his domicile, residence, place of management, or any other criterion of a similar nature. It is not enough to be liable only to tax on income with a source in that state or capital located in that state. What is meant is a comprehensive liability to tax. Member States have, however, different views on the meaning of the term 'liable to tax'. In the case that a UCITS is liable to tax in both Contracting States, a tax treaty that is based on the OECD Model Tax Convention deems the Contracting State in which the place of effective management of the UCITS is located as its residence, the 'tie-breaker rule'. In absence of a definition of the place of effective management in the OECD Model Convention, the Member States tend to interpret this term in accordance with concepts used under their domestic law. This will undermine the effectiveness of the tie-breaker rule if it results in a different outcome. The OECD Commentary, therefore, defines, since 2003, the place of effective management as 'the place where the key management and commercial decisions that are necessary for the conduct of the [UCITS's] business are in substance made. [This] will ordinarily be the place where the most senior person or group of persons (e.g., a board of directors) makes its decisions, the place where the actions to be taken by the entity as a whole are determined'. This is a matter of fact. The key management and commercial decisions are generally made for a UCITS by its board of directors or by its management company. Thus, the location of the board of directors' meeting or the residence of its management company will be decisive, unless the crucial decisions are made by other officials. The term 'substance' means that other persons may have to be taken into account when they have the power to make the essential decisions. Hence, if the board of directors only approves decisions that are performed by the promoter, the place of effective management is localized in the promoter's Member State of residence.

The tie-breaker rule does not, however, solve all cases of dual residence. It is not effective when one of the Contracting States disagrees about whether a UCITS is liable to tax in both Contracting States. As mentioned, the Member States have different views on the meaning of the term 'liable to tax'. According to some Member States, it includes persons that are in principle subject to tax but on whom no tax is levied. The UCITS is, for example, exempt from (corporate) income tax when certain criteria are met. Other Member States disagree with this view. Consequently, only one of the Contracting States applies the tie-breaker rule, because it considers the UCITS to be liable to tax in both States. The other deems it to be a resident, because according to its interpretation, it is not liable to tax in the other State. The effectiveness of the tie-breaker rule in these cases depends on the location of the place of effective management of the UCITS.

company, it is not necessary that the body is corporate. It is enough that it is treated as a body corporate for tax purposes. Thus, it includes not only UCITS of the corporate type, but also UCITS of the contractual and unit trust type that are considered taxable persons under domestic law. The phrase 'any other body of persons' includes structures that have no legal personality and are not considered a taxable entity.[22] Consequently, a contractual UCITS that is, in the absence of legal personality, considered to be transparent, may constitute as any other body of persons and thus qualify as a person for the OECD Model Tax Convention.

In addition, a person must be resident in one or both Contracting States. The OECD Model Tax Convention defines a resident as any person who, under the domestic laws of a Contracting State, is liable to tax in that Contracting State by reason of his domicile, residence, place of management, or any other criterion of a similar nature.[23] It is not sufficient to be liable to tax on income with a source in that state or capital located in that state. What is meant is a comprehensive liability to tax according to domestic rules. Unless a Contracting State adheres to the principle of territoriality, residents are generally liable to tax on their worldwide income in the Contracting State of residence, whereas non-residents are liable to only certain income with a source in that Contracting State. Although the actual levy of tax is an indication that a person is liable to tax, it is not necessary that tax be imposed. Taking the function of the definition of a resident person into account, the distributive rules, like rules similar to the Articles 10 and 11 of the OECD Model Tax Convention, do not require that the resident actually be taxed as a resident by the residence state, for example, on the dividend and interest income.[24] 'A tax treaty is still applicable if one state does not exercise its right to tax provided for in the applicable tax treaty. The tax exemption of income in one State does not prevent the taxpayer from claiming tax treaty benefits in the other Contracting State.'[25] Hence, not only UCITS that are fully liable to tax, but also those that have a reduced tax base or tax rate, or are subjectively exempt, might be considered to be liable to tax as well, and thus qualify as a treaty subject.

However, in practice, Member States have different views on the meaning of the term 'liable to tax'.[26] Consequently, some source states deny the application of a tax treaty for certain types of taxation of *tax opaque* UCITS. Generally, a reduced tax base does not block the application of a tax treaty by the source state.

22. K. Vogel, Klaus Vogel on Double Taxation Conventions: a Commentary to the OECD, UN, and US Model Conventions for the Avoidance of Double Taxation of Income and Capital. With Particular Reference to German Treaty Practice (Amsterdam: Kluwer Law International, 1997), Arts 3, 17.
23. See Art. 4(1) OECD Model Tax Convention.
24. K. Vogel, Klaus Vogel on Double Taxation Conventions: a Commentary to the OECD, UN and US Model Conventions for the Avoidance of Double Taxation of Income and Capital. With Particular Reference to German Treaty Practice (Amsterdam: Kluwer Law International, 1997), Arts 4, 24a.
25. M. Lang, *The Application of the OECD Model Tax Convention to Partnerships* (Vienna: Linde Verlag/The Hague: Kluwer Law International, 2000), 38.
26. P.J.M. Bongaarts & L.J. Ed, *General Report of the IFA Congress of 1997 on the Taxation of Investment Funds* (International Fiscal Association, 1997), 44.

Neither does a reduced tax rate. Netherlands and UK-resident UCITS, for example, which are subject to a reduced tax base as well as a reduced tax rate, are considered liable to tax by source states and thus may apply the provisions of the tax treaties between those source states and the Netherlands or the United Kingdom. A subjective exemption, on the other hand, is generally not considered a liability to tax by source states. Because of a subjective exemption under domestic law, the application of tax treaties by Luxembourg-resident UCITS of the corporate type is, according to the Luxembourg Tax Administration, denied by nine EU Member States and discussed by five others. Other states that refuse the use of tax treaties by Luxembourg-resident UCITS of the corporate type are, among other countries, Brazil, Japan, and the United States. The other twelve EU Member States apply the tax treaty to Luxembourg-resident UCITS of the corporate type.[27] Some of these latter Member States, however, deny the application of tax treaties by German-resident UCITS even while these UCITS are likewise subjectively exempt from tax. The German tax treaties are often not applied by the source states to German-resident UCITS. It is odd that the very same tax measure, a subjective exemption, results in different applications of tax treaties by source states. A possible explanation could be that some source states take the position that German-resident UCITS are transparent and thus not a treaty subject.[28] According to Articles 3 and 4 OECD Model Tax Convention, it depends, however, on the domestic law whether a tax treaty applies. Thus, it is not within the power of a source state to consider German-resident UCITS to be transparent for tax treaty purposes while they are, under domestic law, considered to be a taxable person.

If a tax opaque UCITS fails to be classified as a treaty subject, the source state's right to tax is not limited. Hence, the source state may impose withholding taxes on capital gains and other portfolio income and, for dividends and interest income, it may do so at a higher tax rate. Consequently, more tax leaks out than would have in the case of a direct investment, unless the unitholder is not liable to (corporate) income tax and, thus, would not have been classified as a treaty subject by a direct investment either. This may result in economic double taxation of the UCITS's income. Even though the residence state of the UCITS may not impose tax because of the measures discussed in Section 2.2, the foreign portfolio income may be taxed again in the hands of its unitholders on distribution or the disposal of the units in the UCITS.

27. See the website of the Luxembourg Tax Administration or <www.impotsdirects.public.lu/dossiers/conventions/opc/sicav/index.html>.
28. In the case of German contractual UCITS, it is noted in the German literature that some source states may take the position that they are transparent and thus not a treaty subject (U. Sorgenfrei, Steuerlichter Transparenzgrundsatz und DBA-Berechtigung deutscher offener Investmentfonds, *IStR* 10 (1994): 468–469). According to the Arts 3 and 4 OECD Model Tax Convention, it depends on the domestic law whether a tax treaty applies. Hence, it is not within the power of a source state to consider German UCITS of the contractual type to be transparent, because they are under domestic law considered a taxable person.

Example 2.7

A corporate UCITS resident in State A receives from an investment in the shares of a company resident in State B a total amount of EUR 100,000. State B levies a withholding tax of EUR 25,000. The tax treaty concluded between State A and State B limits the source state's right to tax dividend income to 15%. The corporate UCITS does, according to State B, not qualify as a treaty subject because of a subjective exemption. Consequently, State B is not limited by the tax treaty to levy a withholding tax of 25% and an amount of EUR 25,000 for withholding tax leaks out. If individual C, who resides in State A, had invested directly instead of through the UCITS, he would qualify as a treaty subject and the source state would have taxed the dividend with 15% instead of 25%. Consequently, 10% less tax leaks out.

A contractual UCITS that is, for tax purposes, considered to be *transparent* in its residence state is not liable to tax. The tax treaties concluded by its residence state do not therefore apply to such a UCITS. Because of the transparency, the income and capital gains of such UCITS are, based on the proportional share in the UCITS, attributable to each of the unitholders, although domestic laws, sometimes, require the distribution of the income and capital gains. Hence, the unitholders are, for tax treaty purposes, considered to be the beneficiaries of the income and capital gains. A source state's right to tax the beneficiary's share in any dividend, interest income, capital gains, or other income earned by the UCITS from a source in that state will be limited only if a unitholder is liable to (corporate) income tax and, thus, qualifies as a treaty subject. Hence, the tax status of the unitholder is taken into account so that the tax burden is similar to a direct investment. In the case of a non-resident unitholder where a tax treaty between the source state and the unitholder's residence state is absent, the source state's right to tax will not be limited. This result, however, is no different than for a direct investment.

Because of the use of a UCITS, the unitholders are not aware of any withholding taxes until further notice by the UCITS. Regularly, this takes place at the end of the year, which is after the withholding of tax by the source state. Each of the unitholders who qualifies as a treaty subject thus has to make a request to the source state to limit its right to tax and ask for a refund of the tax that is withheld in breach of or in excess of the provisions of the applicable tax treaty.[29] It is time consuming for the source state to process returns for each unitholder. Moreover, this practice may lead to an interest disadvantage for the unitholders. Only a few tax treaties provide for a practical solution. The tax treaty between Belgium and the Netherlands,[30] for example, applies to tax transparent UCITS[31] instead of to their

29. J. Täske, National Report on Germany of the IFA Congress of 1997 on the Taxation of Investment Funds (International Fiscal Association 1997), 463.
30. Article 25 of the tax treaty between Belgium and the Netherlands.
31. Although the tax treaty uses the same abbreviation as used in the Netherlands for UCITS, it also applies to other undertakings for collective investment. According to the joint explanatory notes

unitholders. The application is limited to tax transparent UCITS resident in Belgium or the Netherlands that receive dividends or interest income from the other Contracting State. Such UCITS may apply the tax treaty instead of their unitholders, but only for those unitholders that are resident in the same Contracting State as the UCITS. Thus, it cannot apply the tax treaty instead of unitholders that reside outside the undertaking's residence state. Nevertheless, it may request the source state to limit its withholding tax on dividend or interest income to, respectively, 15%,[32] and 10%,[33] if at least 75% of its unitholders are resident in the same state as the undertaking.[34] Instead of individual requests by all unitholders, the undertaking for collective investment in securities makes one collective request. UCITS that are listed on a stock exchange may, however, have difficulty in verifying the residence of their unitholders.

2.4.2.2. Crediting of Foreign Withholding Tax

To avoid double taxation of dividends and interest, the residence state has to provide for a tax credit for the limited withholding tax levied by the source state under a tax treaty that is based on the OECD Model Tax Convention. The amount of withholding tax levied by the source state thus may be credited against the beneficiary's tax liability. In contrast to the crediting of domestic withholding taxes, a foreign tax credit is limited to the amount of tax levied by the residence state on the beneficiary's total amount of taxable income related to the dividend or interest.[35] In the absence of a tax treaty, any dividends, interest, capital gains and other portfolio income, such as income from financial derivatives, from a foreign source runs the risk of double taxation. Therefore, in some Member States, a beneficiary may, in the absence of a tax treaty with the source state, credit those foreign withholding taxes against his tax liability, too. The crediting may, however, be subject to certain limitations regarding the amount of the tax credit or the source states that have levied the withholding tax.

The unitholder of a *tax transparent* UCITS is, for the unitholder's share, considered to be the beneficiary of the foreign income. Consequently, the foreign withholding taxes may be credited against the unitholder's (corporate) income tax liability. Similar to the crediting of domestic withholding taxes, the unitholder's tax liability is taken into account. The tax burden thus *does not differ*

to the tax treaty, the term 'undertaking for collective investment in securities' refers to undertakings for collective investment that are, for tax purposes, transparent. In Belgium these are a *gemeenschappelijke beleggingsfondsen* and in the Netherlands a *besloten fonds voor gemene rekening* (Memorie van Toelichting, Tweede Kamer, vergaderjaar 2001–2002, 28 259, nr. 3, 58). The term 'undertaking for collective investment in securities' is thus broader than transparent UCITS. It also covers other Belgian and Dutch transparent undertakings for collective investment that invest in securities.

32. Article 10(2)(b) Tax Treaty between Belgium and the Netherlands.
33. Article 11(2) Tax Treaty between Belgium and the Netherlands.
34. Article 25(1) Tax Treaty between Belgium and the Netherlands.
35. Articles 23A(2) and 23B(1) OECD Model Tax Convention.

from that of a direct investment. For non-resident unitholders, the crediting of foreign withholding taxes depends on the tax regulations of, and applicable tax treaties concluded by, the state of residence.

In contrast to a tax transparent UCITS, a *tax opaque* UCITS is considered the recipient of the income rather than its unitholders. The liability to tax of the UCITS is thus taken into account instead of that of its unitholders, as the foreign withholding tax can be credited against the tax liability of the UCITS but not for more than that part of the (corporate) income tax levied on the worldwide income of the UCITS related to the foreign income. Some UCITS, however, do not actually pay any (corporate) income tax as a result of a reduced tax base or tax rate, or are subjectively exempt from such tax. Hence, they cannot credit any foreign withholding tax, because the foreign tax credit is reduced to nil. Consequently, the tax burden of an investment in the units of such UCITS is for unitholders who are liable to (corporate) income tax *higher* than a direct investment, because the UCITS cannot set off foreign withholding taxes and these unitholders could have done so in the case of a direct investment. Other UCITS may pay (corporate) income tax on the income derived from their investments, because not all income is exempt or the tax rate is not nil. For these UCITS, it depends on the amount of the (corporate) income tax due whether foreign withholding taxes can be fully or only partly credited. Otherwise, the tax burden is formed by the amount of withholding tax that cannot be credited. A few Member States have introduced the availability of a refund of such tax to ensure that the levy of foreign withholding taxes does not cause a tax burden for investment in the units of tax opaque UCITS. Consequently, no tax burden is borne by an investment in the units of such UCITS, which results in a *lower* tax burden for investors who are not liable (corporate) income tax. Other Member States have imposed regulations that allow the unitholders to credit foreign withholding taxes against their (corporate) income tax liability as if they had invested directly. As a result of this, the tax burden of an investment in the units of UCITS resident of one of these Member States is similar to that of a direct investment.

In conclusion, the crediting of withholding taxes levied on the income derived from foreign investments made by UCITS differs widely among the Member States. This leads to differences in the tax burden of investments in the units of UCITS. For tax transparent UCITS, the crediting of foreign withholding taxes depends on the tax liability of the unitholder, because the unitholder is considered the beneficiary of the income. For tax opaque UCITS, foreign withholding taxes are credited against the tax liability of the UCITS. Nevertheless, tax opaque UCITS often do not pay any (corporate) income tax or pay (corporate) income tax at a reduced rate so that the foreign tax credit is limited to nil or cannot be completely credited, respectively. Other UCITS are not entitled to a foreign tax credit, because they are subjectively exempt from (corporate) income tax. Some Member States have therefore introduced a refund of the foreign withholding tax at the level of the UCITS or a credit of the foreign withholding tax at the level of the unitholders.

2.5. RECOGNITION OF INCOME

If an investor is liable to (corporate) income tax, the income derived from and the capital gains realized on investments would, in the case of a direct investment, be taxable in the year of receipt. If an investor is not liable to (corporate) income tax, the withholding tax, if any, levied at source, is a final tax for that investor. The recognition of income is determined by the accounting principles of a national tax system. The national tax systems differ, as mentioned in Section 2.2.1, so that the same income, for example, income from a financial derivative, may be considered to be received by investors of different Member States in different tax years.

Based on the concept of transparency, the income should not be recognized as being received in the hands of the investors at a different moment in the case of the use of a UCITS than in the case of a direct investment. Otherwise, it would enable investors to defer the levy of (corporate) income tax on the income. A *tax opaque* UCITS is, however, a separate taxable person. Its property is, for tax purposes, divided from that of its unitholders. It requires a distribution before the income is considered to be received by its unitholders. In the case of a UCITS of the *transparent* type, its unitholders are considered to be the recipients of the income. Nevertheless, in most Member States a distribution of the income is required before the income is taxable in the hands of its investors. Hence, the income needs to be distributed before it can be taxed.

Surprisingly, not all UCITS are obliged to distribute their income and capital gains. Approximately ten Member States[36] have imposed regulations to ensure that the income can be taxed in the hands of the unitholders of UCITS. These Member States make use of different methods. Some simply prohibit accumulation of income, in other words the income must be distributed, whereas others deem any accumulated income to be distributed or tax the unitholders on the increase in value of the units in the UCITS together with any distributed income. In the case of a distribution or deemed distribution, it is important to note that the income must be distributed or is deemed to be distributed before the end of the financial or calendar year in most Member States. In the Netherlands, the income must, however, be distributed within eight months after the end of the financial year of certain UCITS. Consequently, the income may be taxable in the hands of the unitholders of these UCITS one year later than when it was received by the UCITS. Capital gains from the disposal of the underlying investments do not have to be distributed to the unitholders if the UCITS has opted for a reinvestment account. In the other Member States, UCITS may accumulate income and capital gains, which may offer an opportunity to defer the levy of (corporate) income tax on the income at the level of the unitholder. The accumulated income is not received by the unitholders until a later distribution or the disposal of the units in the UCITS.

36. Among other states, Austria, Czech Republic, Germany, the Netherlands and the United Kingdom.

2.6. NATURE AND SOURCE OF INCOME

Not only the tax year in which the income is received but also the nature and source of the income should remain intact to ensure that the income is taxed as if the investor had invested directly. This is, again, of importance only for investors who are liable to (corporate) income tax, because the withholding tax levied at the source of the income was already a final tax for other investors. Some types of income are subject to favourable tax treatment under the tax laws of some Member States. The income might be wholly or partially exempt, although thresholds may apply, for example, an exemption of dividend or interest payments up to EUR 6,000 a year. Such favourable treatment should be available not only for direct investments but also if the investor made use of a UCITS. Otherwise, more tax would be due than for a direct investment. The nature of the income will, however, not be an issue if a special tax treatment for certain types of income is lacking.

The source of the income should remain the same as well, because some national tax systems attach different tax credits to domestic and foreign income. In addition, the crediting of foreign withholding taxes, in some Member States, takes place on a country-by-country basis. However, in the absence of such measures, the source of the income does not play a role in the taxation of the income.

A *tax opaque* UCITS is considered a taxable person. A distribution of income earned by the UCITS is considered a dividend or other income from a domestic source. Without further measures, the original nature and source of the income and capital gains of the UCITS would disappear. Special measures are therefore necessary to maintain the nature and source of the income so that the unitholders are taxed as if they had invested directly. In addition, the unitholders must be informed of the nature and source of their share of the annual income so that they can file their tax returns correctly. As a result of differences among the national tax systems, the Member States apply different regulations. Because of the special tax treatment of dividends and interest for corporate income tax purposes in Germany, for example, the income of German-resident UCITS is considered to keep its nature and source after distribution. German-resident UCITS are therefore required to inform the unitholders of the composition of the annual income. Others, such as Luxembourg-resident UCITS, are not obliged to exchange such information. The income from these UCITS is considered a dividend from a domestic source.

Tax transparent UCITS have the advantage that their income is considered to be earned by the unitholders. Consequently, the source and nature of the income is maintained and any withholding taxes attached to the income and capital gains can, in accordance with the applicable regulations, be credited by the investor against the investor's tax liability. Such UCITS only have to inform the unitholders of the nature and the source of their share in the annual income of the UCITS.

Different tax regulations are applicable in the Member States regarding the nature and source of the income distributed by a UCITS or realized on disposal of the units in a UCITS. Like the levy and crediting of withholding taxes, the nature and the source of the income are affected by the tax status of a UCITS. The nature and source of the income earned by tax transparent UCITS remains intact as a result of its transparency, whereas that of tax opaque UCITS disappears because these UCITS are considered to be separate taxable persons. Some Member States have imposed special measures to ensure that the nature and source of the income of tax opaque UCITS remain intact. Because not all Member States have imposed similar measures, the nature and source of the income earned by tax opaque UCITS remains intact in some Member States and disappears entirely in others.

2.7. CONCLUSION

From this chapter it follows that there are some substantial differences between the Member States' tax regulations for income derived from the investments of UCITS. In the absence of any harmonization or coordination, each of the Member States has imposed its own set of tax regulations to prevent the income earned by the use of UCITS from being subject to more severe taxation or lesser taxation than a direct investment. The majority of these measures are, however, designed in accordance with the national tax legislation and, thus, for domestic investments, resident unitholders or investments in resident UCITS.

The differences between the tax regulations of the Member States may therefore result in a tax disadvantage or a tax advantage for investments in the units of a UCITS by non-resident investors. This may either facilitate or hinder the trading in the units of UCITS. Either way, it affects the competition between UCITS. Moreover, the differences make it hard for investors to compare the performances of UCITS, because some measures, such as tax credits, take place in some Member States at the level of the UCITS and in others at the level of the unitholders. In other Member States, such measures are missing. Hence, the performance of some UCITS include, for instance, a tax credit for foreign withholding taxes, whereas others do not because the tax credit is granted at the level of the unitholder and thus is not included in the performance of the UCITS.

In addition, there may be higher costs for UCITS to attract capital from non-resident investors than from resident ones. To prevent non-resident unitholders from being subject to more severe taxation in their residence state, the UCITS or the non-resident unitholder sometimes has to submit information on the unitholder's share in the income from the underlying investments and its composition. This information must be compiled in accordance with the tax regulations and accounting principles of the unitholder's residence state, which may, because of the differences between the Member States, be costly. Moreover, non-professional investors generally lack the knowledge to compile the required information, especially when the accounting principles of the Member States at stake differ. This may give domestic promoters of UCITS an advantage over foreign promoters. Therefore, UCITS may be inclined to limit the issue of units to residents of Member States, whose tax regulations are, more or less, in line with those of the UCITS in order that additional costs are avoided. This may decrease the competition between UCITS.

Further research is required to examine whether, and to what extent, these differences actually cause a higher or lesser taxation and to what extent the information that must be submitted by non-resident UCITS to prevent more severe taxation is a barrier. Therefore, in the next chapters, the tax laws of Austria, Germany, the Netherlands and the United Kingdom are compared. The origins of any additional tax burden for investments in the units of UCITS will be analysed, commented on, and compared. The conclusions of this comparison may also be helpful in formulating guidelines, should additional measures be necessary.

This chapter explains the necessity of measures to establish that dividend, interest, capital gains, and other portfolio income derived by way of UCITS are not subject to more severe taxation (or a lesser taxation) than a direct investment (transparency). From this chapter follows that the Member States have taken different measures to establish transparency.

Part II
Taxation of the Income at Source

Income from investments of undertakings for collective investment in transferable securities (UCITS) is often taxable in the state of source. Usually, a withholding tax will be charged on the gross amount of the income. To ensure that the income is subject to the same amount of withholding tax as for a direct investment (transparency), the same tax base, tax rates, and exemptions should be used. Neither should the application of tax treaties differ from a direct investment in the case of income from investments situated *outside* the jurisdiction of the UCITS state.

The research in the Chapters 3–5 shows that taxation at source of the income derived from investments situated *within* and *outside* the UCITS state varies substantially among UCITS residing in Austria, Germany, the Netherlands, and the United Kingdom. As a result of differences in taxation at source of income, it will make a difference for investors as to the country in which the UCITS is a resident or the country in which the UCITS will invest. Many differences can be found. Most important are the following:

(1) uniform rules for the taxation at source of income from the investments situated *within* the UCITS country are lacking; and
(2) a uniform application of the tax treaties to income derived by way of UCITS from investments situated *outside* the UCITS countries is also missing.

Because of the differences in taxation at source of income, the cross-border trade in units of UCITS results in distortions for Austrian, Dutch, German, and UK unitholders, even though measures have been taken by the UCITS Directive to remove restrictions on the free circulation of units in UCITS. The cross-border trade in units of UCITS is still restricted by differences in the national tax legislation of the countries studied. This distorts the conditions of competition between UCITS.

Figure II.1 Taxation of Income at Source

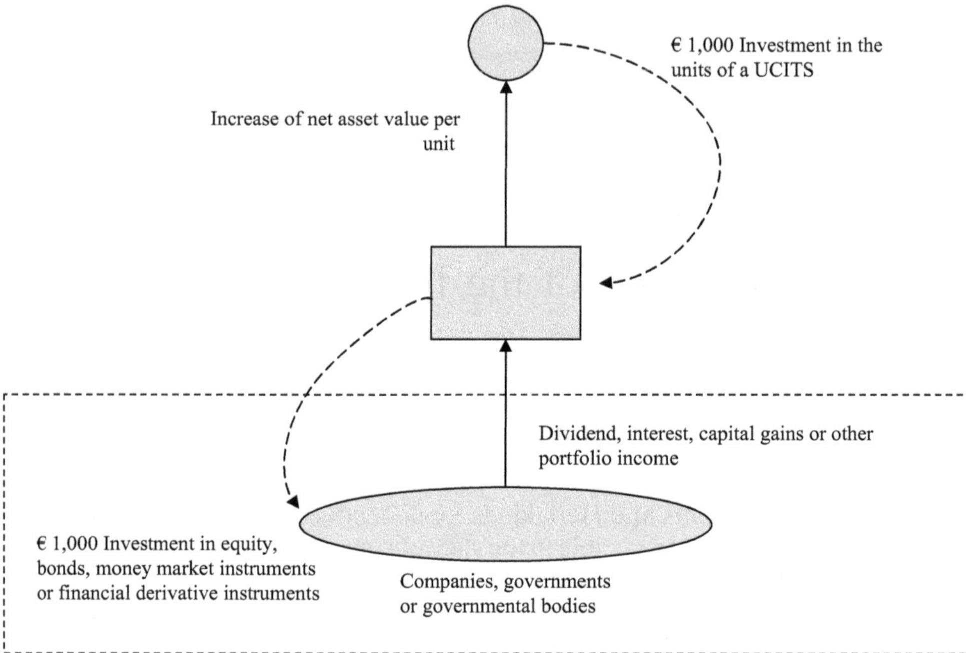

It should be noted that the distortions not only hinder cross-border trade among the countries studied. In some cases, it supports cross-border trade. Although the latter results in a tax advantage for the unitholders, it frustrates the higher aim of the UCITS Directive.

Part II examines the situation in which income is derived by an UCITS from investments in equity, bonds, and money market instruments in combination with financial derivatives other than for the hedging of risks.

Chapter 3
Taxation of Income from the Underlying Investments in the Source State

In the countries studied, income from securities and other financial instruments is frequently subject to withholding tax at source. The withholding tax needs to be deducted by the paying company or the paying agent from the gross amount of the income before paying out to the recipient and must be remitted to the tax authorities. In the absence of any harmonization or coordination by the European Union or Organization for Economic Cooperation and Development, the tax base, tax rate, and available exemptions from withholding tax are not the same in the countries studied.

Although income from securities and other financial instruments paid to UCITS should not be subject to more withholding tax (or less withholding tax) than a direct investment (transparency), income paid to resident UCITS is for the most part exempt from withholding tax in the countries studied or the tax withheld is refundable. The available exemption from withholding tax or refund of the tax withheld is generally restricted to resident UCITS, which seems to infringe on the free movement of capital as laid down in Articles 56 and 58 of the European Community (EC) Treaty and Article 40 of the European Economic Area (EEA) Treaty. As a result, income paid to non-resident UCITS is frequently subject to more taxation than income paid to resident UCITS.

In only a few cases, income paid to non-resident UCITS results in lesser taxation compared to income paid to resident UCITS, because of the application of a reduced tax rate under a tax treaty. The applicable tax rates do not differ only between resident and non-resident UCITS; they also differ between non-resident UCITS because the application of tax treaties is not the same for UCITS.

Overall, the source taxation on income paid to resident and non-resident UCITS in the countries studied is complex, unclear, and (seems) discriminatory.

Not only the countries studied but also other countries make use of withholding taxes to impose tax on income from securities and other financial instruments. The other state's right to tax may, however, be limited in the presence of a tax treaty, but only if the beneficiary of the income is a person residing in one of the Contracting States (a person for the purposes of the tax treaty). The size of the tax treaty network of the countries studied varies, especially outside the European Economic Area. For portfolio investments, the tax treaty network of the United Kingdom is the most comprehensive compared to the other countries studied. In some regions, the United Kingdom has concluded twice the number of tax treaties than the other countries studied. Nevertheless, the tax treaty network of the United Kingdom does not fully overlap with that of the other countries studied and shows some significant gaps too.

The beneficiary of the income is generally considered to be a person for the purposes of a tax treaty if it is liable to tax in a state, which is a party to the tax treaty, by reason of his domicile, residence, place of management, or any other criterion of a similar nature under the domestic laws of that Contracting State. Usually, individuals and corporate bodies, like banks and insurance companies, are fully liable to personal and corporate income tax on their worldwide taxable income. Pension funds and charities are generally not fully liable to tax on their worldwide taxable income. Instead, they are often subjectively exempt from corporate income tax. As a result, some source states do not consider pension funds and charities to be a person for the purposes of a tax treaty. Most recent Netherlands tax treaties, therefore, explicitly state that pension funds and charities are considered to be a person for the purposes of these tax treaties. The tax treaties of the other countries do not provide for such. This is different only for the Austrian and UK tax treaties with Saudi Arabia and the UK tax treaty with Moldova.

A source state's right to tax may be limited if a tax treaty provides for a reduction of withholding tax or an exemption from withholding tax. The right to tax dividends and interest is usually allocated to both states. The source state's right to tax is often limited to a percentage agreed on in the tax treaty. From the Tables 3.1 to 3.16, it follows that the countries studied have not agreed on the same percentages in their tax treaties. In addition, the tax treaties concluded by the countries studied often contain a special rule for interest paid by the Government or a governmental body of the Contracting State, or interest paid to banks, financial institutions, or pension funds.

The majority of tax treaties concluded by the countries studied eliminate the source state's right to tax capital gains and other portfolio income. In these tax treaties the right to tax is exclusively allocated to the residence state of the alienator and recipient of the income, respectively. Nevertheless, the source state's right to tax capital gains or other portfolio income is not eliminated by some UK tax treaties. Moreover, a third of the German tax treaties do not eliminate the source state's right to tax capital gains from the disposal of shares in a company that is a resident of the source state.

The application of tax treaties for income derived by way of UCITS should not differ from that of a direct investment. The source state should take into account the tax liability of the unitholder and not that of the UCITS. However, the objective and subjective tax liability of UCITS, which differs for UCITS residing in the countries studied, affects the application of tax treaties. As a result, the application of tax treaties is not the same for income derived by way of UCITS residing in the countries studied. In some cases, tax treaties are applied to the UCITS, whereas in other cases they are applied to the unitholders. In other cases, the application of tax treaties is denied to both the UCITS and the unitholders.

Differences in the number, provisions, and application of tax treaties will make a difference as to the country in which the UCITS is a resident or in which the UCITS will invest.

3.1. INTRODUCTION

To ensure that the income derived from investments of UCITS is not subject to more withholding tax (or less withholding tax, as the case may be) than a direct investment, the country of source should ignore the tax status of the UCITS. Instead, it should, just as for a direct investment, take into account the tax status of the unitholder. This also applies for the application of tax treaties. In this chapter the degree of transparency of the taxation at source of income derived from the investments of UCITS will be analysed.

3.2. TAX LIABILITY AT SOURCE OF INCOME FROM THE INVESTMENTS SITUATED IN THE UCITS COUNTRY

Member States of the EU and the EEA frequently impose taxes on income from securities and other financial instruments by way of withholding at source. The paying company or the paying agent is obliged to deduct tax from the gross amount and to pay it to the tax authorities on behalf of the beneficiary. In the absence of a claim for reduced withholding tax being made under an appropriate tax treaty, the personal and family circumstances of the beneficiary are not taken into account. Nor is any notice taken of his obligation to file a tax return. Relief from withholding tax, that is, a reduced rate or an exemption, for certain persons or activities may be mentioned explicitly in the domestic tax legislation of the Member State. Relief could be granted either (1) at the source or (2) by way of a refund afterward.

The Member States have sovereign right to impose withholding tax on income from securities and other financial instruments. After all, the taxation of dividends, interest, capital gains, and other portfolio income is not harmonized by the EC Treaty, the EEA Treaty, or any secondary EC law. Nor is it coordinated by the European Union or the Organization for Economic Cooperation and Development. Hence, the items of income from securities and other financial instruments on which tax has to be withheld at the source, the withholding tax rate and the availability of any relief from withholding tax for certain persons or activities, such as UCITS, differ substantially among the Member States.

Articles 56 and 58 of the EC Treaty and Article 40 of the EEA Treaty, however, prohibit a different treatment of portfolio investments by resident and non-resident taxpayers in the same Member State. The treaties establish that the withholding tax on dividends, interest, capital gains, and other portfolio income paid to non-residents may not be higher than the combination of withholding tax and income tax in a domestic situation.[1] Accordingly, a Member State should not apply a higher withholding tax rate to non-resident taxpayers. Nor may an exemption from withholding tax or a refund of the tax withheld be restricted to resident taxpayers.[2] Such discriminatory taxation may be brought before the European Court of Justice by the non-resident taxpayer[3] or the European Commission (infringement procedure). The European Commission has recently started infringement procedures to remove discriminatory taxation on dividend and interest payments to non-resident pension funds[4] and charities. In the Member States in question, dividends or interest payments paid to non-resident pension funds or charities were subject to higher taxation than if these payments were paid to resident pension funds or charities.

Section 3.2 discusses the level, operation, and transparency of source taxation in the countries studied. The following issues will be dealt with: source taxation in the countries studied with regard to a direct investment and an investment by way of an UCITS. In addition, it examines whether income paid to non-resident UCITS is subject to higher taxation in Austria, Germany, the Netherlands, and the United Kingdom compared to resident UCITS. Section 3.2.5 contains the conclusions that could be drawn from this research.

1. See Communication from the European Commission on Dividend taxation of individuals in the Internal Market, 19 Dec. 2003, COM (2003) 810 final, 17.
2. The same applies for the availability of taxation of the income from securities and other financial instruments under the general tax rules so that the personal and family circumstances are taken into account. On the basis of *Schumacker* C-279/93 of 14 Feb. 1995, a Member State should not restrict the taxation under general tax rules to resident taxpayers if the situation of non-resident taxpayers is similar to that of resident taxpayers. A similar situation occurs where a non-resident receives a major part of his income and almost all his family income in a Member State other than his residence state. However, it remains unclear whether this situation frequently occurs in the case of portfolio investments. See for a more in-depth discussion of the *Schumacker* case G. Kofler, *Doppelbesteuerungsabkommen und Europäisches Gemeinschaftsrecht* (Vienna: Linde Verlag, 2007), 64; and P.J. Wattel, in B. Terra & P.J. Wattel, *European Tax Law* (Deventer: Kluwer, 2005), 3.2.8.3(ii).
3. Examples of such are *Maninnen* C-319/02 of 7 Sep. 2004, *Verkooijen* C-35/98 of 6 Jun. 2006 and *Denkavit* C-170/05 of 14 Dec. 2006.
4. See also the press releases by the European Commission 26 Jun. 2008 (IP/08/1022), 6 May 2008 (IP/08/712), 28 Feb. 2008 (IP/08/334), 31 Jan. 2008 (IP/08/143), 23 Jul. 2007 (IP/07/1152), 7 May 2007 (IP/07/616), 22 Jan. 2007 (IP/07/66) and 25 Jun. 2006 (IP/06/1060).

3.2.1. Austrian Source Taxation

3.2.1.1. Investing Directly in Securities and Other Financial Instruments

Tax Base and Tax Rate

Austria imposes a 25% withholding tax at source on distributions (dividends), interest, and other earnings from shares or other equity participations.[5] The withholding tax has to be deducted by the paying company from the gross amount of the distribution (dividend), interest, or other earnings from shares or other equity participations.[6] No withholding tax is charged if the paying company resides outside Austria, unless the distribution or other earnings are paid out by the use of an Austrian paying agent. In that case, the latter has to deduct the withholding tax from the gross amount.[7] A paying agent is the credit institution that pays the foreign distribution, interest, or earning to the shareholder or participant.[8]

In spite of the above, the withholding tax on (portfolio) dividends paid to non-resident companies is higher than the combination of withholding tax and corporate income tax in a domestic situation. (Portfolio) dividends are exempt from corporate income tax in the hands of resident companies as a result of which the tax withheld at source is refunded.[9] The higher taxation of (portfolio) dividends paid to non-resident companies seems to infringe the free movement of capital as laid down in Articles 56 and 58 of the EC Treaty and Article 40 of the EEA Treaty. An in-depth study of such infringement, however, falls outside the scope of this study.[10]

A withholding tax of 25% is further charged on the following:[11]

(1) *Interest* from deposits or other debts with domestic credit institutions or a domestic branch of a foreign credit institution.
(2) *Interest* from bonds and other debt securities.

A paying agent is in the case of interest other than interest from shares either the clearinghouse that pays the interest to the holder of a coupon, the credit institution or bank that pays to that person the interest at the pay date, or the part of the

5. Section 93(2) and (3) Income Tax Act (Einkommensteuergesetz 1988), BGBl. 1988/400, 7 Jul. 1988.
6. Section 93(2)(a) Income Tax Act.
7. Section 93(2)(e) Income Tax Act.
8. Section 95(3)(4) Income Tax Act.
9. Section 10(1) of the Corporate Tax Act (Körperschafsteuergesetz), BGBl. Nr 401/1988, 7 Jul. 1988.
10. See also the press release by the European Commission of 26 Jun. 2008 (IP/08/1022). A more in-depth discussion on the free movement of capital may be found in B.J.M. Terra & P.J. Wattel, *European Tax Law* (Deventer: Kluwer, 2008); T. Viitala, *Taxation of Investment Funds in the European Union* (Amsterdam: IBFD, 2005); and S. Norberg et al., *EEA Law – A Commentary on the EEA Agreement* (Stockholm: Fritzes, 1993).
11. Section 93(2) and (3) Income Tax Act.

proceeds from the disposal of bonds or other debt securities that is related to interest.[12]

Exemption from Withholding Tax

A resident pension fund or charity may, however, appeal to an exemption from withholding tax on dividends or a share in the profits other than by liquidation that is paid out on shares or other equity participation held in a resident corporate body (domestic dividends).[13,14] The exemption is, however, restricted to resident pension funds and charities. As a result, domestic dividends paid to non-resident pension funds and charities are taxed more heavily than those paid to resident pension funds and charities, which might infringe on Articles 56 and 58 of the EC Treaty and Article 40 of the EEA Treaty.[15]

No withholding tax has to be deducted on interest other than from shares that is paid to a resident pension fund.[16,17] Nor does tax have to be withheld on interest paid to non-resident pension funds. Like other non-residents, the latter are entitled to a general exemption from withholding tax on interest other than from shares or a loan other than a debt security that is secured by a mortgage on immovable property in Austria.[18,19] The general exemption for non-residents also applies to foreign dividends, interest from shares, or other equity participations.

Reduction of Withholding Tax

A paying agent may be authorized to apply a reduced tax rate in the presence of a tax treaty but only if the beneficiary of the income is a resident for the purposes of the tax treaty;[20] see Section 3.3 for a more in-depth discussion. The Austrian tax treaties with Germany, the Netherlands, and the United Kingdom provide for a reduced tax rate of 15%

12. Section 95(3)(2) Income Tax Act.
13. Section 94(6)(a) Income Tax Act.
14. A resident pension fund or charity needs to claim the exemption. Any regulations on the format of a claim could not be traced. It is free format. The pension fund or charity has to inform the paying agent about the entitlement to the exemption. It could not be traced whether or not it is necessary to inform the paying agent for every receipt of dividend.
15. See also the press release by the European Commission of 26 Jun. 2008 (IP/08/1022) in which the Commission mentioned that it has already sent a letter of formal notice to Austria on 23 Nov. 2007 regarding the higher taxation of dividends paid to foreign pension funds.
16. Section 94(6)(c) Income Tax Act.
17. A claim on the application of the exemption is free format. The paying agent needs to be informed by the pension fund about the entitlement to the exemption. It could not be traced whether or not the paying agent needs to be informed for every interest payment.
18. See for more information C. Ludwig, *Einkommensteuergesetz* Kommentar (WUV-Universitätsverlag, looseleaf), EStG, § 98, at 80 and 81.
19. Section 98(1)(5)(a)Income Tax Act.
20. E. Lechner, *Kapitalertragsteuer und Doppelbesteuerungsabkommen*, in Lechner, Staringer & Tumpel, *Kapitalertragsteuer* (2003), 252.

3.2.1.2. Investing by Way of Austrian-Resident UCITS

Dividend, Interest, or Other Earnings from Shares

Domestic dividends from shares or other equity participations paid to resident UCITS are subject to withholding tax under the same conditions as for a direct investment. Austria does not provide for relief from withholding tax at source of domestic dividends. Instead, Austria provides for an exemption at the time of distribution by the UCITS. The same applies for interest and other earnings from such shares or other equity participations.

Interest from Bonds, Debentures, and Other Debt

The taxation of interest from bonds or debentures paid to resident UCITS differs from a direct investment. Instead, it is exempt from withholding tax.[21] The same applies to foreign distributions (dividends), interest, and other earnings from shares or other equity participations. The exemption is, however, not available to non-resident UCITS, such as German, Netherlands, and UK-resident UCITS. The restriction to resident UCITS seems to infringe Articles 56 and 58 of the EC Treaty and Article 40 of the EEA Treaty.

Interest from bonds or debentures paid to non-resident UCITS may be subject to more taxation than that paid to domestic UCITS because non-resident UCITS are considered to be transparent under the domestic laws of Austria.[22] For that reason, the application of the general exemption for interest paid to non-residents, which has been discussed previously for a direct investment, depends on the place of residence of the unitholders. The more unitholders that reside in Austria, the lesser is the amount of the exemption, whereas resident UCITS are entitled to a full exemption.

Reduction of Withholding Tax

The withholding tax on domestic dividends, interest, and other earnings from shares or other equity participations is considered to be charged for the account of the unitholders, because resident UCITS are considered to be transparent.[23] Hence, non-resident unitholders are entitled to a reduced tax rate under the same conditions as a direct investment.[24]

---

21. Section 94(10) Income Tax Act.
22. Section 98(1)(5)(a) Income Tax Act in combination with s. 42 of the Law on Investment Funds. See also BMF 22 Oct. 2008, SWI 2009, 1.
23. S. Kirchmayr, National Report of Austria for the IFA Congress of 1997 on the Taxation of Investment Funds (International Fiscal Association, 1997), 266.
24. In practice, Austrian-resident UCITS have introduced a special class of units for non-resident unitholders. The paying agent does not have to withhold tax on any distributions or deemed distributions to the holders of units from this class if the management company and the depositary bank have confirmed that none of the units of the special class are held by persons subject to withholding tax; see also s. 13(3) of the Law on Investments Funds.

3.2.2. German Source Taxation

3.2.2.1. Investing Directly in Securities and Other Financial Instruments

Tax Base and Tax Rate

Germany charges a 26.375% withholding tax at source of dividends or other distributions from shares or other equity participations.[25] The withholding tax has to be deducted by the paying company. No withholding tax is charged if the securities are held outside Germany.

Notwithstanding, these (portfolio) dividends paid to non-resident companies seems to be subject to more taxation than those paid to resident companies. Under the Corporate Tax Act (portfolio) dividends are for 95% of the gross amount exempt from corporate income tax in the hands of resident companies.[26] Hence, most of the tax withheld at source is refunded to resident companies. For the reasons discussed in Section 3.2, the higher taxation of (portfolio) dividends seems to infringe Articles 56 and 58 of the EC Treaty and Article 40 of the EEA Treaty.[27]

A withholding tax of 26.375% is also charged at source of interest from convertible and profit-sharing bonds or other debt securities.[28] The withholding tax has to be deducted by the paying company. As for dividends, no withholding tax is charged if the securities are kept outside Germany.

In addition, it imposes a withholding tax of 26.375% at source of interest from bonds or other debt securities other than convertible or profit-sharing ones.[29] The withholding tax has to be deducted by the German paying agent from the gross amount. A paying agent is the credit institution, bank, or other financial institution that pays or credits the interest to the person that produces the interest coupon or holds the bond or debt security. If a paying agent is missing, the debtor is considered to be the paying agent.[30]

Finally, tax is withheld at a rate of 26.375% at source of capital gains from the disposal of shares and other financial instruments.[31,32] The withholding tax

25. Sections 43(1)(1) and 43a(1)(1) Income Tax Act (Einkommensteuergesetz).
26. Section 8b(1), (2) and (5) of the Corporate Tax Act (Körperschafsteuergesetz), BGBl. I 1976/2597 and 2599, 31 Aug. 1976.
27. See also the press release by the European Commission of 26 Jun. 2008 (IP/08/1022).
28. Sections 43(1)(2) and 43a(1)(1) Income Tax Act.
29. Sections 43(1)(7) and 43a(1)(1) Income Tax Act.
30. Section 44(1) Income Tax Act.
31. Sections 43(1)(7) and 43A(1)(1) Income Tax Act.
32. A capital gain is considered to be the difference between the proceeds from the disposal after deduction of any connected costs and the cost price. A transitional arrangement applies to capital gains on shares or other financial instruments that were acquired before 1 Jan. 2008. These capital gains remain tax exempt, but only if the financial instruments were held for at least 1 year.

needs to be deducted by the credit institution or financial service provider, which is charged by the alienator to execute the disposal.[33]

The withholding tax is in each of these cases charged on the gross amount.[34]

Exemption from Withholding Tax

No tax is withheld on interest paid to and capital gains realized by exempt corporate bodies, such as pension funds and charities.[35,36] The exemption does not, however, apply to interest from convertible and profit-sharing bonds or other debt securities. The latter follows the taxation of dividends.

The exemption does not apply to non-resident pension funds and charities. Like with other non-residents, these pension funds and charities are exempt from withholding tax on interest from bonds or other debt securities and on capital gains.[37,38]

Reduction of Withholding Tax

A non-resident beneficiary of domestic dividends may be entitled to a reduction of withholding tax in the presence of a tax treaty; see Section 3.3 for the conditions. Germany has agreed on a reduced tax rate of 15% in the tax treaties with Austria, the Netherlands, and the United Kingdom.

3.2.2.2. Investing by Way of German-Resident UCITS

Dividend and Interest from Convertible and Profits-Sharing Bonds and Debentures

A refund of the tax withheld at the source avoids that dividends and interest from convertible and profit-sharing bonds or other debt securities are subject to withholding tax twice – at source and at the time of distribution. No refund, however, is available for UCITS residing outside Germany. The restriction of the refund to UCITS residing in Germany seems to infringe the free movement of capital as laid down in Articles 56 and 58 of the EC Treaty or Article 40 of the EEA Treaty. Non-resident UCITS appear to be treated less favourably than resident UCITS.[39]

33. Section 44(1) Income Tax Act.
34. Section 43a(2) Income Tax Act.
35. Section 44a(4) Income Tax Act.
36. A resident pension funds needs to claim the exemption. It needs to submit a copy of the declaration from the tax authorities that it is subjectively exempt from corporate income tax as a pension fund. Whether it is necessary to submit a copy of the declaration for every interest payment could not be traced.
37. Section 49(5) Income Tax Act.
38. To obtain the exemption, a non-resident pension fund needs to submit proof that it is entitled to such. No regulations on the format of a claim could be traced. It seems free format. Whether it is necessary to submit proof for every interest payment could not be traced.
39. See also the press release by the European Commission of 31 Jan. 2008 (IP/08/143) in which the Commission states that it has sent a letter of formal notice to Germany regarding the higher taxation of dividends paid to foreign pension funds.

Interest from Bonds and Debentures Other Than Convertible and Profit-Sharing Ones and Capital Gains

An exemption at source avoids double withholding tax on interest from bonds and other debt securities other than from convertible and profit-sharing bonds or other debt securities (interest), as well as capital gains derived by way of a resident UCITS.[40] Instead, interest and capital gains are subject to withholding tax at the time of distribution. The exemption at source of interest and capital gains is restricted to resident UCITS. Nevertheless, it does not necessarily infringe on the free movement of capital as laid down in Articles 56 and 58 of the EC Treaty and Article 40 of the EEA Treaty, because of the availability of a general exemption for interest and capital gains paid to non-resident taxpayers. The latter seem to include non-resident UCITS.[41]

3.2.3. NETHERLANDS SOURCE TAXATION

3.2.3.1. Investing Directly in Securities and Other Financial Instruments

Tax Base and Tax Rate

The Netherlands charges a 15% withholding tax at source of dividends paid by Netherlands-resident companies. The withholding tax has to be deducted by the paying company from the gross amount of the dividend.[42] The tax is withheld for the account of the beneficiary.

Refund of Withholding Tax

Exempt corporate bodies, like *pension funds* and *charities*, may request for a refund of the withholding tax charged on dividend paid out by a Netherlands-resident company.[43,44] The refund is also available for non-resident pension funds and charities but only where they would also be exempt from tax if they

40. Section 44a(4) Income Tax Act in combination with s. 11(1) of the Investment Taxation Act (Investmentsteuergesetz), BGBl. I 2003/2724, 15 Dec. 2003.
41. Section 2(1) Corporate Tax Act. See also J. Täske, *National Report on Germany of the IFA Congress of 1997 on the Taxation of Investment Funds* (International Fiscal Association, 1997), at 461.
42. Section 7(1) and (2) Dividend Tax Act (Wet op de dividendbelasting), *Stb.* 1965, 621, 23 Dec. 1965.
43. Article 10(1) Dividend Tax Act.
44. A request for a refund can be made by way of a special form issued by the Dutch tax authorities. The form can be used for more than one receipt of dividend. The original dividend invoices should be attached.

had resided in the Netherlands.[45,46] The restriction of the refund to exempt corporate bodies residing in the Netherlands or a Member State of the European Union seems to infringe the free movement of capital between the Member States of the European Economic Area as laid down in Article 40 of the EEA Treaty. Exempt corporate bodies residing in Iceland, Liechtenstein or Norway are, unlike their EU counterparts, not entitled to a refund. They are therefore treated less favourable than their EU counterparts.

Reduction of Withholding Tax

In the presence of a tax treaty, the paying company may be authorized to apply a reduction of the withholding tax on dividend; see Section 3.3 for an in-depth discussion about which shareholders may appeal to a reduction of withholding tax. A number of the Netherlands tax treaties provide in a lower percentage than the domestic tax rate of 15%. The Netherlands tax treaties with Austria, Germany and the United Kingdom, however, provide for 15%, which equals the domestic tax rate.

3.2.3.2. Investing by Way of Netherlands-Resident UCITS

Netherlands-Resident (EII) UCITS

The Netherlands does not provide for an exemption at source or a refund of the tax withheld if the dividends are derived by way of a resident UCITS if they are considered as exempt investment institution (hereafter, resident (EII) UCITS).[47] Resident (EII) UCITS are subjectively exempt from corporate income tax.[48] Instead of an exemption or refund, double withholding tax is avoided in the form of an exemption at the time of distribution by these UCITS to the unitholders.

Netherlands-Resident (FII) UCITS

Any domestic dividends paid to resident UCITS that are regarded as fiscal investment institution (hereafter, resident (FII) UCITS) are subject to withholding tax as described above for a direct investment. The tax is considered to be withheld for the account of the UCITS and not that of the unitholders. These UCITS are subject to corporate income tax but at a rate of only nil percent.[49] In order to avoid

45. Article 10(1) and (3) Dividend Tax Act.
46. The Dutch tax authorities have issued a special form for such request.
47. Section 1(4) Dividend Tax Act in combination with s. 6(a) of the Corporate Tax Act.
48. The objective and subjective tax liability of these UCITS is further discussed in Section 6.2.3.
49. See for more details Section 6.2.3.

double withholding tax, a refund of the tax withheld[50] at source is available at the time of distribution.[51] The refund of withholding tax is under no circumstances available for non-resident UCITS, that is Austrian, German or UK-resident UCITS. The restriction of the refund to certain UCITS residing in the Netherlands seems to infringe the free movement of capital as laid down in Articles 56 and 58 of the EC Treaty and Article 40 of the EEA Treaty. Non-resident UCITS seem to be treated less favourably than resident (FII) UCITS.[52]

Netherlands-Resident (TII) UCITS

Any Netherlands source dividend derived by way of resident UCITS which are known as transparent investment institution (hereafter, resident (TII) UCITS) is considered to be that of the unitholders. Resident (TII) UCITS[53] are considered to be transparent for the purposes of taxation in the Netherlands. Hence, the amount of source taxation does not differ from a direct investment as any refund or reduction of withholding tax is available under the same conditions.

3.2.4. UK Source Taxation

3.2.4.1. Investing Directly in Securities and Other Financial Instruments

Tax Base and Tax Rate

The United Kingdom does not withhold any tax on dividend payments. Under certain tax treaties, the beneficial owner of any dividends is entitled to a tax credit. Following the abolition of Advanced Corporation Tax (ACT) in April 1999, and a corresponding reduction in input tax credits, the entitlement to the tax credit gives no benefit except in a very limited number of circumstances under treaties

50. It concerns a refund in the form of a payment reduction for the tax that has to be withheld by Netherlands-resident (FII) UCITS at the time of the annual distribution to the unitholders. The tax withheld at source may be set off by Netherlands-resident (FII) UCITS against the 15% tax that needs to be withhold for the account of the unitholders at the time of distribution. A Netherlands-resident (FII) UCITS does, thus, not have to pay the full amount of tax withheld at the time of distribution to the tax authorities. The payment reduction is, however, not a credit for the tax withheld at source to the unitholders but a *refund of the tax withheld at source* to Netherlands-resident (FII) UCITS. The tax withheld at the time of distribution is namely fully creditable by the unitholders. Hence, the difference between the tax withheld on the distribution and the tax paid by the UCITS to the tax authorities results in an increase of the intrinsic value of the UCITS. The amount of the difference equals that of the tax withheld at source; see for a more in-depth discussion subs. 6.3.2.
51. Section 11a Dividend Tax Act in combination with section 28 of the Corporate Tax Act.
52. See also *BNB* 2008/290c annotated by I.J.J. Burgers.
53. See Section 6.3.2 for a discussion of the objective and subjective tax liability of these UCITS.

with Belgium, Italy, Luxembourg, Netherlands, Sweden, Switzerland and the United States.

The United Kingdom withholds an amount that reflects the savings rate, which is currently 20% from interest paid on debts that are capable of exceeding one year. The withholding tax is applied at the source of interest paid by deposit-takers.[54] Withholding tax on interest has to be deducted by the deposit-taker from the gross amount of the interest paid in respect to a deposit to individuals. A deposit-taker includes the Bank of England, a bank or other person that has permission to accept deposits or a local authority.[55]

A deposit is defined as a sum of money paid on terms, which means that it will be repaid with or without interest.[56] It explicitly excludes deposits for which qualifying certificates of deposit have been issued,[57] debts on securities listed on a recognized stock exchange, and loans made by the deposit-taker in the ordinary course of his business.[58]

Tax is also withheld at a rate of 20% in the case of a payment of yearly interest. The withholding tax has to be deducted by the person that pays the yearly interest or the person through whom the payment of yearly interest is made (paying agent).[59]

Yearly interest, which is also known as annual interest, concerns interest that arises in the United Kingdom and is paid by a company, a local authority, by or on behalf of a partnership of which a company is a member, or by any person to another person whose usual place of residence is outside the United Kingdom.[60] It explicitly excludes listed bonds and other (debt) securities that are issued by a company and that carry a right to interest, which are known as quoted Eurobonds.[61] Nor does it include interest paid by deposit-takers, UK public revenue dividends or interest paid in the ordinary course of business being wholly or mainly dealing in financial instruments by a person authorized under the Financial Services and Market Act 2000.[62,63]

A 20% withholding tax is further charged by the United Kingdom on UK public revenue dividends. The person that pays the UK public revenue dividends or the person through whom the payment of UK public revenue dividends is made (paying agent) is obliged to deduct the withholding tax.[64]

---

54. Section 851(1) and (2) Income Tax Act 2007, c.3.
55. Section 853(2) Income Tax Act.
56. Section 938 Income Tax Act.
57. Qualifying certificates of deposit are certificates of deposit under which the amount payable is at least GBP 50,000, exclusive of interest, and that amount is payable to whoever holds the certificate at a specified time within five years (s. 985(1) Income Tax Act).
58. Sections 865 and 870(1) Income Tax Act.
59. Section 874(2) Income Tax Act.
60. Section 874(1) Income Tax Act.
61. Sections 882 and 987 Income Tax Act.
62. Chapter 8.
63. Sections 876, 877, 878 and 885 Income Tax Act.
64. Section 892(2) Income Tax Act.

UK public revenue dividends concern income from bonds and debt securities other than those issued by local authorities that is paid out of the public revenue of the United Kingdom or Northern Ireland.[65] The income from these securities is subject to withholding tax, unless the securities are considered to be gross-paying securities. In that case the charging of withholding tax is omitted. Gross-paying securities are gilt-edged securities[66] or other securities that are the subject of a Treasury direction.[67]

The withholding tax is charged on the gross amount.

Exemption from Withholding Tax

No withholding tax needs to be deducted by a deposit-taker on interest paid to (exempt) companies.[68] The same applies for non-resident (exempt) companies.

Reduction of Withholding Tax

A non-resident may be entitled to a reduced tax rate or an exemption in the presence of a tax treaty but only if the beneficiary of the income is a resident for the purposes of the tax treaty;[69] an in-depth discussion on the latter follows in Section 3.3. The source state's right to tax interest is eliminated in the UK tax treaties with Austria, Germany and the Netherlands.

3.2.4.2. Investing by Way of UK-Resident UCITS

Interest Paid by Deposit-Takers

As a company, interest paid by a deposit-taker to resident UCITS is not subject to withholding tax. By contrast, full exemption is not necessarily available for interest paid by a deposit-taker to non-resident UCITS. It should be noted that the absence of such exemption may be considered to be an infringement of the free movement of capital as laid down in Articles 56 and 58 of the EC Treaty and Article 40 of the EEA Treaty.

Interest paid to a non-resident UCITS is not necessarily exempt from tax in the case in which the UCITS is considered transparent under the domestic laws of the United Kingdom.[70] The application of one of the exemptions for interest paid by a deposit-taker, which have been discussed previously for a direct investment, does

65. Section 891 Income Tax Act.
66. As listed in Sch. 9 of the Taxation of Chargeable Gains Act 1992, c.12.
67. Section 893(2)(b) Income Tax Act.
68. Section 856(3) Income Tax Act.
69. E. Lechner, *Kapitalertragsteuer und Doppelbesteuerungsabkommen*, in Lechner, Staringer and Tumpel, *Kapitalertragsteuer* (2003), 252.
70. C. Hurley, National Report on the United Kingdom of the IFA Congress of 1997 on the Taxation of Investment Funds (International Fiscal Association, 1997), 840.

in that case depend on the place of residence of the unitholders and the category of unitholders.

Yearly Interest and UK Public Revenue Dividends

The United Kingdom does not provide for relief at source of yearly interest and UK public revenue dividends that are derived by way of resident UCITS. The withholding tax deducted on these items of income may, however, be set off by resident UCITS against the corporate income tax liability, whereas the part of the withholding tax that cannot be set off is refundable.[71]

3.2.5. Conclusion

The measures taken by the countries studied, except with respect to Netherlands-resident (EII/TII) UCITS, prevent the income from the underlying investments situated within the UCITS country from being subject to withholding tax at source. In this way, the expenses made at the level of the UCITS can be set off against the income. The income is, therefore, either exempt from withholding tax at source or the withholding tax charged at source is refunded to the UCITS. Instead, the countries studied charge withholding tax at the time of distribution to the unitholders, which ensures that the tax status of the unitholders is, like a direct investment, taken into account by the charging of withholding tax.

Austria, however, does not apply an exemption for the withholding tax charged at source of dividends paid by Austrian companies. Nor does it refund the withholding tax to resident UCITS. The withholding tax is, however, considered to be charged on the account of the unitholders, as these UCITS are considered to be transparent. The withholding tax is therefore not charged differently from a direct investment. Any expenses made at the level of the UCITS can, however, be set off against the dividends; see Section 6.4.1 for a more detailed discussion.

The taxation at source of domestic income from the investments of Netherlands-resident (EII) UCITS is not removed by the Netherlands. Instead, it does not charge withholding tax at the time of distribution by these UCITS. Although double withholding tax is avoided, this measure does not establish transparency because the tax status of the unitholders is not taken into account by the charging of withholding tax.

The taxation at source of domestic income derived by way of Netherlands-resident (TII) UCITS applies as if the unitholders had invested directly.

Finally, the United Kingdom does not avoid withholding tax at source of yearly interest and UK public revenue dividends. The withholding tax can, however, be credited at the level of the UCITS.

71. D. Smailes & A. Flint, *Tolley's Income Tax 2006–07* (London: LexisNexis Tolley, 2006), 23.1.

3.3. TAX LIABILITY AT SOURCE OF THE INCOME FROM THE INVESTMENTS SITUATED OUTSIDE THE UCITS COUNTRY

The taxation at source on income from securities and other financial instruments situated outside the jurisdiction of the UCITS country is determined by the domestic laws of the state in which jurisdiction the investments are situated (local tax legislation). The source state's right to tax dividends, interest, capital gains, and other portfolio income may, however, be limited in the presence of a tax treaty. It is usually the case that only beneficial owners of income can claim the limitations of a source state's right to tax under a tax treaty.

This paragraph contains an overview of the number, provisions, and application of tax treaties. Like in the previous section, the situation of a direct investment will be compared with that of an investment by way of an UCITS. However, hereafter the application of tax treaties will be described first to discuss the conditions under which a source state's right to tax is limited by a tax treaty. The conclusion is drawn in Section 3.3.6.

3.3.1. The Application of Tax Treaties

The tax treaties of the countries studied generally apply if the beneficial owner of the income is a person (or any body of persons) residing in one of the Contracting States (hereafter, a person for tax treaty purposes). As a general rule a person for tax treaty purposes is one of the following:

(1) an individual;
(2) a body corporate; or
(3) a partnership or other association; that is fully liable to tax in the state of residence.

3.3.1.1. Individuals and Corporate Entities

A person is usually regarded as being a resident for the purposes of a tax treaty if it is liable to tax in a state, which is a party to the tax treaty, by reason of domicile, residence, place of management, or any other criterion of a similar nature under the domestic laws of that Contracting State.[72] In EU and EEA residents, for example, individuals and corporate bodies, such as banks or insurance companies, are generally fully liable to personal and corporate income tax on their worldwide taxable income.

Charities will usually take the form of a body corporate and hence fall within the definition of 'person' for treaties that follow the OECD Model Tax Convention.

72. See Art. 4(1) OECD Model Tax Convention.

Similarly, tax authorities will often regard authority approved pension schemes as falling within the 'any body of persons' in the OECD definitions articles.

3.3.1.2. Pension Funds and Charities

However, an issue arises for pension funds and organizations that are operated exclusively for religious, charitable, scientific, cultural, education, or public purposes (hereafter, charities) because they are usually not fully liable to tax in the state of residence. Instead, they are often subjectively exempt from corporate income tax. For that reason, some source states do not consider pension funds and charities to be a person for the purposes of a tax treaty,[73] even while the OECD Model Tax Convention does not require that a resident is actually taxed in the state of residence.[74] Most of the recent Netherlands tax treaties therefore explicitly consider pension funds[75] and charities[76] to be a person for purposes of these tax treaties. This approach could not be found in the tax treaties of the other countries studied. An exception to this is the Austrian and UK tax treaties with Saudi Arabia and UK tax treaty with Moldova. These tax treaties explicitly consider pension funds to be a person for purposes of these tax treaties.

The Netherlands[77] and UK[78] tax authorities generally regard pension funds and charities to be tax treaty eligible even while such is not explicitly stated in a tax treaty. This is due to the fact that these entities are usually considered to be liable to tax, even if they are not specifically subject to tax. Under most UK tax treaties, if pension funds and charities are resident in the UK, they will be treated as residents for treaty purposes. However, the access to tax benefits may be restricted if there is a 'subject to tax' condition. It should be noted that as a result of the ambiguity surrounding pension schemes, some tax treaties now contain specific wording in

73. See F. Wassermayer, in G.H. Debatin & F. Wassermeyer, *Doppelbesteuerung* (Munich: Verlag C.H. Beck, looseleaf), Arts 4, 8.3.
74. K. Vogel, Klaus Vogel on Double Taxation Conventions: a Commentary to the OECD, UN and US Model Conventions for the Avoidance of Double Taxation of Income and Capital. With Particular Reference to German Treaty Practice (Amsterdam: Kluwer Law International, 1997), Arts 4, 24a.
75. These are the tax treaties with Albania, Armenia, Argentina, Belgium, Canada, Estonia, Finland, Georgia, Ghana, Iceland, Jordan, Latvia, Lithuania, Macedonia, Mexico, Moldavia, Mongolia, Poland, Portugal, Romania, Russia, Slovenia, South Africa, Taiwan, Uganda, Ukraine, the United States, Uzbekistan, and Vietnam.
76. These are the tax treaties with Belgium, Canada, Estonia, Georgia, Latvia, Lithuania, Russia, Ukraine, and the United States.
77. According to the Netherlands, its tax treaties should, nonetheless, be applied to these entities. It therefore issues certificates of residence to Netherlands-resident pension funds and charities. In accordance with that view, the Netherlands also applies its tax treaties to pension funds and charities residing in the jurisdiction of a tax treaty partner but only on a reciprocal basis; see the letter by the state secretary for Finance of the 14 Aug. 1997, *VN 1997/3140*). An overview of the tax treaty partners that apply the applicable tax treaty with the Netherlands to Netherlands-resident pension funds and charities could, however, not be traced.
78. E. Dungworth & O. Farnworth, 'Foreign Taxes', in *Tolley's Taxation of Collective Investment*, ed. S. Newcombe et al. (London: LexisNexis Tolley, 2003), 293.

respect to how they should be treated. Furthermore, as a result of this position, the Netherlands tax authorities also apply a tax treaty to pension funds or charities that reside in the jurisdiction of the tax treaty partner but only on a reciprocal basis. An overview of the tax treaty partners that have agreed to do so or in practice do so is, however, missing.

Unfortunately, the Austrian and German view in this matter could not be determined.

3.3.1.3. Beneficial Owner

A reduction of withholding tax or an exemption from withholding tax on dividend, interest, and, sometimes, other portfolio income applies only if the beneficial owner of these payments is a resident of the state, which is a party to the treaty.[79] Otherwise, a source state's right to tax is not limited by the tax treaty. The condition of beneficial ownership is introduced to avoid treaty shopping. The concept of tax treaty rates of withholding tax being available to the ultimate beneficial owners of any income is designed to prevent tax avoidance where a person channels income by way of an entity residing in another state that has a tax treaty with more attractive provisions and to which that person would not have been entitled in the case of a direct receipt.[80]

A definition of beneficial owner is missing in the OECD Model Tax Convention. From the Commentary to Article 10 of the OECD Model Tax Convention follows that it does not include agents, nominees, or conduit companies acting as a fiduciary.[81] A beneficial owner is thus not somebody who merely acts on behalf of and for the benefit of another person. Instead, it is '(...) he who is free to decide (i) whether or not the capital or other assets should be used or made available for use by others or (ii) on how the yields therefrom should be used or (iii) both'.[82]

A bank, which collects dividend or interest for the account of its customers, does usually not own these payments formally. Nor is it entitled to them. Hence, it is not considered to be the beneficial owner of the dividend or interest. This is not different for a person who keeps equity or bonds on the basis of a management agreement for a principal.[83]

79. P. Baker, 'Beneficial Ownership: After Indofood', GITC VI, no. 1 (2007): 15.
80. Although the condition was introduced in the OECD Model Convention of 1977, it is considered to have already been embedded in the older tax treaties.
81. See Commentary to Art. 10 of the OECD Model Tax Convention, 12.
82. K. Vogel, Klaus Vogel on Double Taxation Conventions: a Commentary to the OECD, UN and US Model Conventions for the Avoidance of Double Taxation of Income and Capital. With Particular Reference to German Treaty Practice (Amsterdam: Kluwer Law International, 1997), Preface to Arts 10–12, 9.
83. See F. Wassermayer, in G.H. Debatin & F. Wassermeyer, *Doppelbesteuerung* (Munich: Verlag C.H. Beck, looseleaf), Arts 10–11, 57 and 62.

3.3.1.4. Procedure to Claim the Benefits of a Tax Treaty

Taxes on dividends, interest, and, sometimes, capital gains are usually charged by withholding at the source of these payments. The debtor of the payments needs to withhold the tax and to pay it to the tax authorities. In the case that a tax treaty provides in a reduction of withholding tax or an exemption either (1) the debtor needs to apply the domestic tax rate and the part of the tax withheld above the percentage agreed on in the applicable tax treaty is refunded afterward (refund procedure) or (2) the debtor may be authorized to apply the reduced withholding tax (at source relief procedure).

3.3.1.5. Refund Procedure

Under the refund procedure, the payer is obliged by law to withhold tax at the domestic rate. The part of the withholding tax that exceeds the percentage agreed on in the tax treaty is not refunded until the beneficial owner has submitted a claim for such. The documentation required for such claim differs among the tax treaty partners as the procedures for claiming tax treaty benefits has not been harmonized or coordinated by the EU or the Organization for Economic Cooperation and Development yet. Nor does the period that such documents remain valid or the period within such claim needs to be submitted.

Some tax treaty partners have not regulated the format of a claim. It is free format. Other tax treaty partners make use of the existing know-your-customer regulations. A third group of tax treaty partners have developed official forms, which often need to be signed or stamped by the tax authorities of the beneficial owner's residence state. In addition, the period that the required documents are valid varies from tax treaty partner to tax treaty partner. Sometimes, each claim requires separate documents, whereas other times they are valid for a certain period or until revoked.[84]

Generally, a claim needs to be submitted within a certain period of time (claiming period). The claiming period is sometimes explicitly stated in a tax treaty or its implementation order, whereas at other times it depends on domestic law of the tax treaty partner. It varies from two to eight years. The claiming period usually starts after the end of the year in which the tax is withheld.

3.3.1.6. At Source Relief Procedure

Contrary to the refund procedure, a reduced tax rate or an exemption under the source relief procedure is already applied at the time the tax is withheld. The debtor is authorized to apply the benefits of a tax treaty, that is, a reduced tax rate or exemption. As mentioned above, the details of the procedure differs from tax treaty

84. The fact finding study on fiscal compliance procedures related to clearing and settlement within the EU by the European Commission's Clearing and Settlement Fiscal Compliance expert group, 13.

partner to tax treaty partner. Generally, the payer is held responsible for the withholding of the correct amount of tax. Hence, the payer may be declined to apply a reduction of withholding tax or an exemption if there is doubt about the eligibility to a tax treaty. In that case, the excess is, on request, refunded afterward.

The Sections 3.3.2–3.3.5 examine the allocation of the right to tax under the tax treaties concluded by the countries studied. A source state's right to tax dividends, interest, capital gains, and other portfolio income is frequently limited by a tax treaty. In addition, these sections consider whether the application of tax treaties to UCITS results in more taxation in the source state than for a direct investment.

3.3.2. Austrian Tax Treaty Network

3.3.2.1. Investing Directly in Securities and Other Financial Instruments

Austria has concluded seventy-seven tax treaties with respect to taxes on income and capital (Table 3.1). It has tax treaties with all EU Member States, although the tax treaty with Latvia did not enter into force until 1 January 2008. Moreover, Austria has also concluded tax treaties with Liechtenstein and Norway, which are EEA Member States.

Table 3.1 Austrian Tax Treaties in Respect to Dividends

DTC	*State of Source*	*Maximum Tax Rate (%) Allowed in State of Source on Portfolio Investment Dividends*	*Special Features*	*Article*
Albania	C	15	-	10(1) and (2)
Algeria	C	15	-	10(1) and (2)
Armenia	C	15	-	10(1) and (2)
Australia	C	15	-	10(1) and (2)
Azerbaijan	C	15	-	10(1) and (2)
Barbados	C	15	-	10(1) and (2)
Belarus	C	15	-	10(1) and (2)
Belgium	C	15	-	10(1) and (2)
Belize	C	15	-	10(1) and (2)
Brazil	C	15	-	10(1) and (2)

Table 3.1 (cont'd)

DTC	*State of Source*	*Maximum Tax Rate (%) Allowed in State of Source on Portfolio Investment Dividends*	*Special Features*	*Article*
Bulgaria	C	Eliminated	-	8(1)
Canada	C	15	-	10(1) and (2)
China	C	10	-	10(1) and (2)
Croatia	C	15	-	10(1) and (2)
Cuba	C	15	-	10(1) an (2)
Cyprus	C	Eliminated	-	10(1), (2), and (4)
Czechoslovakia	C	10	-	10(1) and (2)
Czech Republic	C	10	-	10(1) and (2)
Denmark	C	15	-	10(1) and (2)
Egypt	C	15	-	VIII(2)
Estonia	C	15	-	10(1) and (2)
Finland	C	10	-	10(1) and (2)
France	C	15	Avoir fiscal	10(1), (2), and (3)
Georgia	C	10	-	10(1) and (2)
Germany	C	15	-	10(1) and (2)
Greece	C	Unrestricted	-	10(1)
Greece (2010)	C	15	-	10(1) and (2)
Hungary	C	10	-	10(1) and (2)
India	C	10	-	10(1) and (2)
Indonesia	C	15	-	10(1) and (2)
Iran	C	10	-	10(1) and (2)
Ireland	C	15	Exemption for inter-corporate dividends if such is available for domestic sourcc dividends	8(1) and (4)

Table 3.1 (cont'd)

DTC	*State of Source*	*Maximum Tax Rate (%) Allowed in State of Source on Portfolio Investment Dividends*	*Special Features*	*Article*
Israel	C	25	-	10(1) and (2)
Italy	C	15	-	10(1) and (2)
Japan	C	20	-	IX(1)
Kazakhstan	C	15	-	10(1) and (2)
Korea	C	15	-	10(1) and (2)
Kyrgyzstan	C	15	-	10(1) and (2)
Kuwait	C	Eliminated	-	10(1)
Latvia	C	10	-	10(1) and (2)
Liechtenstein	C	15	-	10(1) and (2)
Lithuania	C	15	-	10(1) and (2)
Luxembourg	C	15	-	10(1) and (2)
Macedonia	C	15	-	10(1) and (2)
Malaysia	C	Eliminated	-	10(1) and (3)
Malta	C	Eliminated	-	10(1) and (2)
Mexico	C	10	-	10(1) and (2)
Moldova	C	15	-	10(1) and (2)
Mongolia	C	10	-	10(1) and (2)
Morocco	C	10	-	10(1) and (2)
Nepal	C	15	-	10(1) and (2)
Netherlands	C	15	-	10(1) and (2)
New Zealand	C	15	-	10(1) and (2)
Norway	C	15	-	10(1) and (2)
Pakistan	C	15	-	10(1) and (2)
Philippines	C	25	-	10(1) and (2)
Poland	C	15	-	10(1) and (2)
Portugal	C	15	-	10(1) and (2)
Romania	C	5	-	10(1) and (2)

Table 3.1 (cont'd)

DTC	*State of Source*	*Maximum Tax Rate (%) Allowed in State of Source on Portfolio Investment Dividends*	*Special Features*	*Article*
Russia	C	15	-	10(1) and (2)
San Marino	C	15	-	10(1) and (2)
Saudi Arabia	C	5	-	10(1) and (2)
Singapore	C	10	-	10(1) and (2)
Slovak Republic[a]	C	10	-	10(1) and (2)
Slovenia	C	15	-	10(1) and (2)
South Africa	C	15	-	10(1) and (2)
Spain	C	15	-	10(1) and (2)
Sweden	C	10	-	10(1) and (2)
Switzerland	C	15	-	10(1) and (2)
Tajikistan[b]	C	Eliminated	-	8(1)
Thailand	C	20	-	10(1) and (2)
Tunisia	C	20	-	10(1) and (2)
Turkey	C	35	-	10(1) and (2)
Turkmenistan[b]	C	Eliminated	-	8(1)
Ukraine	C	10	-	10(1) and (2)
United Arab Emirates	C	Eliminated	-	10(1)
United Kingdom	C	15	Tax credit	10(2) and (4)
United States	C	15	-	10(1) and (2)
USSR	C	Eliminated	-	8(1)
Uzbekistan	C	15	-	10(1) and (2)
Venezuela	C	15	-	10(1) and (2)

C, The Contracting State with whom Austria has concluded the tax treaty.

[a] The tax treaty concluded with the former Czechoslovakia still applies to the Slovak Republic.

[b] The tax treaty concluded with the former Union of Soviet Socialist Republics applies to Tajikistan and Turkmenistan.

Rate of Tax at Source on Dividends

From Table 3.1 it follows that the Austrian tax treaties allocate the right to tax dividends to the state of residence of the beneficiary. The dividends also may be taxed by the source state. Except for the tax treaty with *Greece*, the source state's right to tax dividends is limited to the percentage agreed on. In the majority of its tax treaties, Austria has agreed on a percentage of either 10% or 15%.

There are only a few exceptions to the rule. The tax treaties with Israel, Japan, the Philippines, Thailand, Tunisia, and Turkey provide for higher percentages while a limitation, as mentioned above, is missing in the tax treaty with Greece.

Diverging rules are also found in the tax treaties with Bulgaria, Cyprus, Kuwait, Malaysia, Malta, Tajikistan, Turkmenistan, and the United Arab Emirates. The source state's right to tax is completely eliminated in those tax treaties. Instead, the right to tax is allocated exclusively to the residence state. The tax treaties with Romania and Saudi Arabia limit the source state's right to tax to 5%.

The tax treaty with Ireland eliminates Austria's right to tax dividend paid by an Irish-resident company to an Austrian-resident company where an exemption is available for inter-corporate dividends paid between Austrian-resident companies.

Special Rules

Because of the partial imputation system of the United Kingdom, the tax treaty with that country provides for a partial refund to individuals and corporate entities for the corporate income tax that is levied at the level of the distributing UK-resident company. The amount of the refund is one-ninth of the dividend payment. The refund is, however, limited to dividends paid by UK companies for which a UK individual would have been entitled to a dividend tax credit. The United Kingdom as the source state has, nevertheless, the right to tax the amount of the dividend together with that of the dividend tax credit but at a rate of 15% of the overall amount.[85]

A similar kind of refund is found in the tax treaty with *France*.

Rates of Tax at Source on Interest

Table 3.2 shows that the right to tax interest is allocated to the state of residence of the beneficiary. Like dividends, the interest also may be taxed by the source state. Most Austrian tax treaties limit a source state's right to tax interest to 10%.

The source state's right to tax, however, is eliminated by a quarter of the Austrian tax treaties, which are mostly tax treaties with industrial countries. These are the tax treaties with Barbados, Belize, Bulgaria, Cyprus, Czech Republic, Denmark, Finland, France, Georgia, Germany, Greece (except for interest on bonds or other debt securities issued by the government or a governmental body of

---

85. Article 10(3) Tax Treaty between Austria and the United Kingdom.

Table 3.2 Austrian Tax Treaties in Respect to Interest

DTC	*State of Source*	*Maximum Tax Rate (%) Allowed in State of Source on Portfolio Investment Interest*	*Special Features*	*Article*
Albania	C	5	-	11(1) and (2)
Algeria	C	10	Special rule regarding interest paid on a loan from a bank Special rule regarding interest derived from the government or a governmental body of the Contracting State Special rule regarding interest derived by a credit institution that is fully owned by the government or a governmental body of the other Contracting State	11(1), (2), (3) and (4)
Armenia	C	10	Special rule regarding interest paid on a loan from a bank	11(1), (2), and (3)
Australia	C	10	-	11(1) and (2)
Azerbaijan	C	10	-	11(1) and (2)
Barbados	C	Eliminated	-	11(1)
Belarus	C	5	-	11(1) and (2)

Table 3.2 (cont'd)

DTC	State of Source	Maximum Tax Rate (%) Allowed in State of Source on Portfolio Investment Interest	Special Features	Article
Belgium	C	15	-	11(1) and (2)
Belize	C	Eliminated	-	11(1)
Brazil	C	15	Special rule regarding interest derived from the government or a governmental body of the Contracting State Special rule regarding interest derived by a financial institution that is fully owned by the government or a governmental body of the other Contracting State	11(1), (2) and (3)
Bulgaria	C	Eliminated	-	9(1)
Canada	C	10	Special rule regarding interest derived from the government or a governmental body of the Contracting State	11(1), (2), and (7)

Table 3.2 (cont'd)

DTC	*State of Source*	*Maximum Tax Rate (%) Allowed in State of Source on Portfolio Investment Interest*	*Special Features*	*Article*
			Special rule regarding interest paid to a pension fund residing in the other Contracting State	
China	C	10	Special rule for bank loans	11(1) and (2) Protocol paragraph 3
Croatia	C	5	-	11(1) and (2)
Cuba	C	10	Special rule regarding interest paid on a loan from a bank	11(1), (2), and (3)
Cyprus	C	Eliminated	-	11(1)
Czechoslovakia	C	Eliminated	-	11(1)
Czech Republic	C	Eliminated	-	11(1)
Denmark	C	Eliminated	-	11(1)
Egypt	C	15	-	X(1) and (2)
Estonia	C	10	Special rule regarding interest derived by a financial institution that is fully owned by the government or a governmental body of the other Contracting State	11(1), (2), and (3)

Table 3.2 (cont'd)

DTC	*State of Source*	*Maximum Tax Rate (%) Allowed in State of Source on Portfolio Investment Interest*	*Special Features*	*Article*
Finland	C	Eliminated	-	11(1)
France	C	Eliminated	-	11(1)
Georgia	C	Eliminated	-	11(1)
Germany	C	Eliminated	-	11(1)
Greece	C	Eliminated	Special rule regarding interest derived from the government or a governmental body of the Contracting State	11(1) and (2)
Greece (2010)	C	8	-	11(1) and (2)
Hungary	C	Eliminated	-	11(1)
India	C	10	-	11(1) and (2)
Indonesia	C	10	Special rule regarding interest derived by a financial institution that is fully controlled by the government or a governmental body of the other Contracting State	11(1) and (2)
Iran	C	5	Special rule regarding interest derived by a bank that is fully owned by the government or a	11(1), (2) and (3)

Table 3.2 (cont'd)

DTC	*State of Source*	*Maximum Tax Rate (%) Allowed in State of Source on Portfolio Investment Interest*	*Special Features*	*Article*
			governmental body of the other Contracting State Special rule regarding interest paid on a loan from a bank residing in the other Contracting State	
Ireland	C	Eliminated	-	9(1)
Israel	C	15	-	11(1) and (2)
Italy	C	10	Special rule regarding interest derived from the government or a governmental body of the Contracting State Special rule regarding interest derived by a financial institution that is fully owned by the government or a governmental body of the other Contracting State	11(1), (2) and (3)

Table 3.2 (cont'd)

DTC	*State of Source*	*Maximum Tax Rate (%) Allowed in State of Source on Portfolio Investment Interest*	*Special Features*	*Article*
Japan	C	10	-	X(1)
Kazakhstan	C	10	Special rule regarding interest derived by a financial institution that is fully owned by the government or a governmental body of the other Contracting State	11(1), (2), and (3)
Korea	C	10	-	11(1) and (2)
Kuwait	C	Eliminated	-	11(1)
Kyrgyzstan	C	10	-	11(1) and (2)
Latvia	C	10	-	11(1) and (2)
Liechtenstein	C	10	-	11(1) and (2)
Lithuania	C	10	Special rule regarding interest derived by a financial institution that is fully owned by the government or a governmental body of the other Contracting State	11(1), (2), and (3)

Table 3.2 (cont'd)

DTC	*State of Source*	*Maximum Tax Rate (%) Allowed in State of Source on Portfolio Investment Interest*	*Special Features*	*Article*
Luxembourg	C	Eliminated	-	11(1)
Macedonia	C	Eliminated	-	11(1)
Malaysia	C	15	A special rule applies if interest is derived from a loan as meant in section 2(1) of the Malaysian Income Tax Act 1967	11(1), (2), and (3)
Malta	C	5	-	11(1) and (2)
Mexico	C	10	Special rule regarding interest derived from the government or a governmental body of the Contracting State Special rule regarding interest paid to a pension fund residing in the other Contracting State	11(1), (2), and (3)
Moldova	C	5	-	11(1) and (2)
Mongolia	C	10	-	11(1) and (2)
Morocco	C	10	-	11(1) and (2)

Table 3.2 (cont'd)

DTC	*State of Source*	*Maximum Tax Rate (%) Allowed in State of Source on Portfolio Investment Interest*	*Special Features*	*Article*
Nepal	C	15	Special rule regarding interest derived by a financial institution that is fully controlled by the government or a governmental body of the other Contracting State Special rule regarding interest from the Contracting State to a bank residing in the other Contracting State	11(1), (2) and (3)
Netherlands	C	Eliminated	-	11(1)
New Zealand	C	10	-	11(1) and (2)
Norway	C	Eliminated	-	11(1)
Pakistan	C	15	Special rule regarding interest derived from the government or a governmental body of the Contracting State	11(1), (2), and (3)

Table 3.2 (cont'd)

DTC	*State of Source*	*Maximum Tax Rate (%) Allowed in State of Source on Portfolio Investment Interest*	*Special Features*	*Article*
Philippines	C	15	Special rule regarding interest paid by a company residing in the Contracting State, which is registered under the Philippines Investment Stimulating Acts	11(1), (2), and (3)
Poland	C	5	Special rule regarding interest paid on a loan from a bank residing in the other Contracting State	11(1), (2), and (3)
Portugal	C	10	-	11(1) and (2)
Romania	C	3 (Eliminated)	Special rule regarding interest as long as Austria applies an exemption to interest paid to residents of the Contracting State	11(1) and (2) Protocol paragraph 2
Russia	C	Eliminated	-	11(1)

Table 3.2 (cont'd)

DTC	*State of Source*	*Maximum Tax Rate (%) Allowed in State of Source on Portfolio Investment Interest*	*Special Features*	*Article*
San Marino	C	Eliminated	Special rule regarding interest derived from the government or a governmental body of the Contracting State Special rule regarding interest derived by a financial institution that is fully owned by the government or a governmental body of the other Contracting State	11(1) and (2)
Saudi Arabia	C	5	Special rule regarding interest derived from the government or a governmental body of the Contracting State Special rule regarding interest derived by a financial institution that is	11(1), (2), and (3)

Table 3.2 (cont'd)

DTC	*State of Source*	*Maximum Tax Rate (%) Allowed in State of Source on Portfolio Investment Interest*	*Special Features*	*Article*
			fully owned by the government or a governmental body of the other Contracting State	
Singapore	C	5	Special rule regarding interest paid by a bank residing in the Contracting State to a bank, which is a resident of the other Contracting State	11(1), (2), and (3)
Slovak Republic[a]	C	Eliminated	-	11(1)
Slovenia	C	5	-	11(1) and (2)
South Africa	C	Eliminated	-	11(1)
Spain	C	5	-	11(1) and (2)
Sweden	C	Eliminated	-	10A(1)
Switzerland	C	Eliminated	-	11(1)
Tajikistan[b]	C	Eliminated	-	9(1)
Thailand	C	25	Special rule regarding interest derived by a credit institution that is fully owned by the government	11(1), (2) and (3)

Table 3.2 (cont'd)

DTC	*State of Source*	*Maximum Tax Rate (%) Allowed in State of Source on Portfolio Investment Interest*	*Special Features*	*Article*
			or a governmental body of the other Contracting State	
Tunisia	C	10	-	11(1) and (2)
Turkey	C	15	-	11(1) and (2)
Turkmenistan[b]	C	Eliminated	-	9(1)
Ukraine	C	5	-	11(1) and (2)
United Arab Emirates	C	Eliminated	-	11(1)
United Kingdom	C	Eliminated	Special rule for interest derived from listed bonds or other debt securities if the interest is not subject to tax in the residence state of beneficiary and the securities are disposed within 3 months after their purchase	11(1) and (5)
United States	C	Eliminated	-	11(1)
USSR	C	Eliminated	-	9(1)
Uzbekistan	C	10	-	11(1)
Venezuela	C	10	4.95% for bank loans Special rule for interest paid by the Government	11(1), (2) and (3)

Table 3.2 (cont'd)

DTC	*State of Source*	*Maximum Tax Rate (%) Allowed in State of Source on Portfolio Investment Interest*	*Special Features*	*Article*
			Special rule for interest derived by instrumentality of government	

C, The Contracting State with whom Austria has concluded the tax treaty.

[a] The tax treaty concluded with the former Czechoslovakia still applies to the Slovak Republic.

[b] The tax treaty concluded with the former Union of Soviet Socialist Republics applies to Tajikistan, and Turkmenistan.

Greece), Hungary, Ireland, Kuwait, Luxembourg, Macedonia, The Netherlands, Norway, Russia, San Marino, Slovak Republic, South Africa, Sweden, Switzerland, Tajikistan, Turkmenistan, the United Arab Emirates, the United Kingdom, and the United States. Instead, the right to tax is allocated exclusively to the residence state. The source state's right to tax interest from listed bonds or other debt securities is, however, not eliminated under the tax treaty with the United Kingdom if the interest is not subject to tax in the residence state of the beneficiary and the securities are disposed within three months after their purchase. The Protocol to the tax treaty with Romania also allocates the right to tax interest exclusively to the residence state as long as Austria does not withhold tax at source on interest paid to Romanian residents.

Furthermore, Austria has agreed on lower percentages in the tax treaties with Albania, Belarus, Croatia, Greece (2010), Iran, Malta, Moldova, Poland, Saudi Arabia, Singapore, Slovenia, Spain, and Ukraine.

The percentages agreed on in the tax treaties with Argentina, Belgium, Brazil, Egypt, Israel, Malaysia, Nepal, Pakistan, the Philippines, Thailand, and Turkey exceed 10%. These are mostly tax treaties with developing countries.

Exclusive Rates

The tax treaties with Algeria, Armenia, Cuba, Iran, Poland, and Singapore provide for an exemption at source of interest that is paid to banks. However, this is sometimes subject to conditions. The exemption under the tax treaty with Singapore is limited to interest paid by a bank residing in the Contracting State to a bank that is a resident of the other Contracting State. The source state's right to tax is limited to 10% and 4.95% by the tax treaty with Nepal and Venezuela, respectively, in the case of interest paid to a bank. For bank loans the tax treaty with China reduces the source state's right to tax to 70% of the gross amount.

The tax treaties with Canada and Mexico apply an exemption at source on interest paid to a pension fund residing in the other Contracting State so far as the interest also remains exempt from tax in the residence state of the pension fund.

If interest is paid by the Government or a governmental part of a Contracting State, the tax treaties with Algeria, Canada, Italy, Mexico, Pakistan, Saudi Arabia, and Venezuela apply an exemption at source on the interest. The opposite is, however, found in the tax treaties with Brazil and Greece. These tax treaties provide an exemption in the state of residence of the beneficiary.

In addition to a general exemption for interest in the source state, the tax treaty with San Marino also eliminates the residence state's right to tax for interest paid by the Government or a governmental part of a Contracting State or interest paid to a bank, financial institution or credit institution that is fully owned by the Government or a governmental part of one of the other Contracting States. As a result, such interest remains exempt in the source state as well as the residence state.

Moreover, the source state's right is eliminated in the tax treaties with Algeria, Brazil, Estonia, Indonesia, Iran, Italy, Kazakhstan, Lithuania, Nepal, Saudi Arabia, and Thailand, where interest is paid to a bank, financial institution, or credit institution that is fully owned or controlled by the Government or a governmental part of one of the Contracting States. In that case the interest may be taxed exclusively by the state of residence of the bank, financial institution, or credit institution.

Malaysia and the Philippines have agreed in the tax treaty with Austria to exempt interest that is derived from a loan within the meaning of section 2(1) of the Malaysian Income Tax Act 1967 or paid by a company residing in the Contracting State that is registered under the Philippines Investment Stimulating Acts.

Rates of Tax at Source on Capital Gains

From Table 3.3 it can be concluded that the right to tax gains from the disposal of portfolio investments is, with the exception of Brazil, and China, allocated exclusively by the Austrian tax treaties to the state of residence of the alienator. These tax treaties fully eliminate the source state's right to tax. Although a provision on capital gains is missing, the right to tax capital gains is under the tax treaties with Luxembourg, Sweden, and the former Union of Soviet Socialist Republics, which as mentioned earlier still applies to Tajikistan and Turkmenistan, allocated to residence state by the provision on other portfolio income.

The tax treaties with India, Israel, Luxembourg, Mexico, Sweden, and Thailand do not, however, allocate the right to tax gains from the disposal of shares in a resident company exclusively to the residence state of the alienator. Under these tax treaties, these gains also may be taxed by the company's residence state, although the tax treaty with Israel limits the taxation in the source state to capital

Table 3.3 Austrian Tax Treaties in Respect to Capital Gains from Portfolio Investments

DTC	*State of Source*	*Catch-All Clause for the Gains from the Alienation of Portfolio Investments*	*Special Features*	*Article*
Albania	C	Residence state	-	13(4)
Algeria	C	Residence state	-	13(4)
Armenia	C	Residence state	-	13(6)
Australia	C	No rule	The right to tax is allocated exclusively to the residence state of the alienator by the other portfolio income clause	-
Azerbaijan	C	Residence state	-	13(5)
Barbados	C	Residence state	-	13(4)
Belarus	C	Residence state	-	13(4)
Belgium	C	Residence state	-	13(3)
Belize	C	Residence state	-	13(4)
Brazil	C	Both states	-	13(3)
Bulgaria	C	Residence state	-	15(4)
Canada	C	Residence state	-	13(5)
China	C	Both states	-	13(6), and 22(2)
Croatia	C	Residence state	-	13(4)
Cuba	C	Residence state	-	13(4)
Cyprus	C	Residence state	-	13(4)
Czechoslovakia	C	Residence state	-	13(4)
Czech Republic	C	Residence state	-	13(4)
Denmark	C	Residence state	-	13(4)
Egypt	C	Residence state	-	XII(1)
Estonia	C	Residence state	-	13(4)
Finland	C	Residence state	-	13(5)

Table 3.3 (cont'd)

DTC	*State of Source*	*Catch-All Clause for the Gains from the Alienation of Portfolio Investments*	*Special Features*	*Article*
France	C	Residence state	-	13(6)
Georgia	C	Residence state	-	13(4)
Germany	C	Residence state	-	13(5)
Greece	C	Residence state	-	13(3)
Greece (2010)	C	Residence state	-	13(4)
Hungary	C	Residence state	-	13(3)
India	C	Residence state	Special rule regarding gains from the alienation of shares in a resident company	13(5) and (6), and 23(2)
Indonesia	C	Residence state	-	13(4)
Iran	C	Residence state	-	13(4)
Ireland	C	Residence state	-	11(5)
Israel	C	Residence state	Special rule for capital gain from the disposal of shares in an unquoted company	13(3), and 24(2)
Italy	C	Residence state	-	13(3)
Japan	C	Residence state	-	XVIII(1)
Kazakhstan	C	Residence state	-	13(4)
Korea	C	Residence state	-	13(5)
Kuwait	C	Residence state	-	13(4)
Kyrgyzstan	C	Residence state	-	13(5)
Latvia	C	Residence state	-	13(4)
Liechtenstein	C	Residence state	-	13(3)
Lithuania	C	Residence state	-	13(4)

Table 3.3 (cont'd)

DTC	*State of Source*	*Catch-All Clause for the Gains from the Alienation of Portfolio Investments*	*Special Features*	*Article*
Luxembourg	C	Residence state	The application of the clause on capital gains is limited to gains from the disposal of shares in a company residing in the Contracting State The clause on other portfolio income applies to gains from the disposal of other portfolio investments	8
Macedonia	C	Residence state	-	13(4)
Malaysia	C	Residence state	-	13(3)
Malta	C	Residence state	-	13(3)
Mexico	C	Residence state	Special rule regarding gains from the alienation of shares in a resident company	13(3) and (6)
Moldova	C	Residence state	-	13(4)
Mongolia	C	Residence state	-	13(4)
Morocco	C	Residence state	-	13(5)
Nepal	C	Residence state	-	13(4)
Netherlands	C	Residence state	-	14(4)

Table 3.3 (cont'd)

DTC	*State of Source*	*Catch-All Clause for the Gains from the Alienation of Portfolio Investments*	*Special Features*	*Article*
New Zealand	C	Residence state	-	13(5)
Norway	C	Residence state	-	13(5)
Pakistan	C	Residence state	-	14(6)
Philippines	C	Residence state	-	13(5)
Poland	C	Residence state	-	13(5)
Portugal	C	Residence state	-	13(3)
Romania	C	Residence state	-	13(5)
Russia	C	Residence state	-	13(4)
San Marino	C	Residence state	-	13(5)
Saudi Arabia	C	Residence state	-	13(5)
Singapore	C	Residence state	-	13(5)
Slovak Republic[a]	C	Residence state	-	13(4)
Slovenia	C	Residence state	-	13(4)
South Africa	C	Residence state	-	13(4)
Spain	C	Residence state	-	13(3)
Sweden	C	No rule	The application of the clause on capital gains is limited to gains from the disposal of shares in a company residing in the Contracting State The clause on other portfolio income applies to gains from the disposal of other portfolio investments	8

Table 3.3 (cont'd)

DTC	*State of Source*	*Catch-All Clause for the Gains from the Alienation of Portfolio Investments*	*Special Features*	*Article*
Switzerland	C	Residence state	-	13(3)
Tajikistan[b]	C	No rule	The right to tax is allocated exclusively to the residence state of the alienator by the other portfolio income clause	-
Thailand	C	Residence state	Special rule regarding gains from the alienation of shares in a resident company. The same applies for the gains from the disposal of bonds or other debt securities	13(4) and (5)
Tunisia	C	Residence state	-	13(3)
Turkey	C	Residence state	Special rule regarding gains from the alienation of portfolio investments that are disposed of within 6 months after the purchase	13(3)
Turkmenistan[b]	C	No rule	The right to tax is allocated exclusively to	-

Table 3.3 (cont'd)

DTC	*State of Source*	*Catch-All Clause for the Gains from the Alienation of Portfolio Investments*	*Special Features*	*Article*
			the residence state of the alienator by the other portfolio income clause	
Ukraine	C	Residence state	-	13(5)
United Arab Emirates	C	Residence state	-	13(4)
United Kingdom	C	Residence state	-	13(4)
United States	C	Residence state	-	13(6)
USSR	C	No rule	The right to tax is allocated exclusively to the residence state of the alienator by the other portfolio income clause	-
Uzbekistan	C	Residence state	-	13(4)
Venezuela	C	Residence state	-	13(6)

C, The Contracting State with whom Austria has concluded the tax treaty.

[a] The tax treaty concluded with the former Czechoslovakia still applies to the Slovak Republic.

[b] The tax treaty concluded with the former Union of Soviet Socialist Republics applies to Tajikistan, and Turkmenistan.

gains realized on the disposal of shares in an unquoted company resident of one of the Contracting States and to the part of these gains that is related to property situated in the company's residence state. The tax treaties with Israel and Mexico, however, limit the right to tax of the company's residence state to 15% and 20%, respectively. The tax treaty with Thailand does not allocate the right to tax gains from the disposal of bonds and other debt securities exclusively to the residence state of the alienator, either. Under that tax treaty, these gains may also be taxed by the residence state of the debtor who issued the securities.

The right to tax gains from the disposal of portfolio investments is, under the tax treaty with Turkey, allocated to both states if an investment is disposed of within six months after the purchase. Otherwise, these gains are allocated exclusively to the residence state of the alienator.

The tax treaties with Brazil and China do not allocate the right to tax capital gains exclusively to the source state or the residence state of the alienator. Instead, these tax treaties allocate the right to tax to both states. The source state's right to tax is, thus, not limited.

Rates of Tax at Source on Other Portfolio Income

Table 3.4 shows that the Austrian tax treaties generally allocate the right to tax other portfolio income exclusively to the state of residence of the beneficiary. The right to tax, however, is not allocated exclusively to the residence state of the beneficiary in the tax treaties with Armenia, Australia, Azerbaijan, Canada, China, Cuba, India, Malaysia, Mexico, Nepal, New Zealand, Pakistan, Saudi Arabia, and Singapore. In these tax treaties it is allocated to both states.

The tax treaties with Thailand and Turkey allocate the right to tax other portfolio income exclusively to the source state. An allocation of the right to tax other portfolio income is, finally, missing in the tax treaty with Japan. Hence, the source state's right to tax other portfolio income is not limited by this tax treaty.

3.3.2.2. Investing by Way of Austrian-Resident UCITS

Application of Tax Treaties

Austrian-resident UCITS do not qualify as a resident for purposes of the Austrian tax treaties. The income from the underlying investments of these UCITS is considered to be that of the unitholders under the domestic laws of Austria.[86] The Austrian tax treaties therefore apply as if the unitholders had invested directly in the underlying investments.

Individual Requests by the Unitholders

Except for the tax treaties with France and Switzerland, an Austrian-resident UCITS cannot claim a reduced tax rate or an exemption available under one of the Austrian tax treaties on behalf of the unitholders. Instead, each unitholder has to submit a separate request for a refund of the part of the withholding tax that exceeds the percentage agreed on in the applicable tax treaty afterward. The unitholders,

86. S. Kirchmayr, National Report on Austria of the IFA Congress of 1997 on the Taxation of Investment Funds (International Fiscal Association, 1997), 275.

Table 3.4 Austrian Tax Treaties in Respect to Other Portfolio Income

DTC	*State of Source*	*Catch-All Clause for Portfolio Income Not Expressly Mentioned*	*Special Features*	*Article*
Albania	C	Residence state	-	21(1)
Algeria	C	Residence state	-	21(1)
Armenia	C	Both states	-	21(1) and (3)
Australia	C	Both states	-	21(1) and (2)
Azerbaijan	C	Both states		21(1) and (3)
Barbados	C	Residence state	-	22(1)
Belarus	C	Residence state	-	21(1)
Belgium	C	Residence state	-	21
Belize	C	Residence state	-	20(1)
Brazil	C	Residence state	-	21
Bulgaria	C	Residence state	-	16
Canada	C	Both states	-	21(1) and (2)
China	C	Both states	-	2(1) and (3)
Croatia	C	Residence state	-	21(1)
Cuba	C	Both states	-	22(1) and (3)
Cyprus	C	Residence state	-	21(1)
Czechoslovakia	C	Residence state	-	21(1)
Czech Republic	C	Residence state	-	20(1)
Denmark	C	Residence state	-	22(1)
Egypt	C	Residence state	-	XIX
Estonia	C	Residence state	-	21(1)
Finland	C	Residence state	-	21(1)
France	C	Residence state	-	21(1)
Georgia	C	Residence state	-	21(1)
Germany	C	Residence state	-	21(1)
Greece	C	Residence state	-	21
Greece (2010)	C	Residence state	-	21(1)
Hungary	C	Residence state	-	20
India	C	Both states	-	22(1) and (3)

Table 3.4 (cont'd)

DTC	*State of Source*	*Catch-All Clause for Portfolio Income Not Expressly Mentioned*	*Special Features*	*Article*
Indonesia	C	Both states	-	22(1) and (3)
Iran	C	Residence state	-	21(1)
Ireland	C	Residence state	-	20
Israel	C	Residence state	-	22
Italy	C	Residence state	-	21(1)
Japan	C	No rule	In the absence of clause on other portfolio income, the source state's right to tax is not limited	-
Kazakhstan	C	Residence state	-	21(1)
Korea	C	Residence state	-	21(1)
Kuwait	C	Residence state	-	21(1)
Kyrgyzstan	C	Residence state	-	21(1)
Latvia	C	Residence state	-	22(1)
Liechtenstein	C	Residence state	-	21
Lithuania	C	Residence state		22(1)
Luxembourg	C	Residence state	-	2
Macedonia		Residence state	-	20(1)
Malaysia	C	Both states	-	21
Malta	C	Residence state	-	21(1)
Mexico	C	Both states	-	20(1) and (3)
Moldova	C	Residence state	-	20(1)
Mongolia	C	Residence state	-	22(1) and (3)
Morocco	C	Residence state	-	22(1)
Nepal	C	Both states	-	21(1) and (3)
Netherlands	C	Residence state	-	22
New Zealand	C	Both states	-	20(1)
Norway	C	Residence state	-	22(1)

Table 3.4 (cont'd)

DTC	State of Source	Catch-All Clause for Portfolio Income Not Expressly Mentioned	Special Features	Article
Pakistan	C	Both states	-	23(1) and (3)
Philippines	C	Residence state	-	22(1)
Poland	C	Residence state	-	22(1)
Portugal	C	Residence state	-	21
Romania	C	Residence state	-	22(1)
Russia	C	Residence state	-	21(1)
San Marino	C	Residence state	-	21(1)
Saudi Arabia	C	Both states	-	22(3)
Singapore	C	Both states	-	21(1) and (3)
Slovak Republic[a]	C	Residence state	-	21(1)
Slovenia	C	Residence state	-	22(1)
South Africa	C	Residence state	-	21(1)
Spain	C	Residence state	-	22
Sweden	C	Residence state	-	2
Switzerland	C	Residence state	-	21
Tajikistan[b]	C	Residence state	-	12
Thailand	C	Source state	-	22, and 24(3)
Tunisia	C	Residence state	-	21
Turkey	C	Source state	-	21(1), and 23(1)
Turkmenistan[b]	C	Residence state	-	12
Ukraine	C	Residence state	-	21(1)
United Kingdom	C	Residence state	-	22
United States	C	Residence state	-	21(1)
USSR	C	Residence state	-	12
Uzbekistan	C	Residence state	-	21(1)
Venezuela	C	Both states	-	22(1) and (3)

C, The Contracting State with whom Austria has concluded the tax treaty.

[a] The tax treaty concluded with the former Czechoslovakia still applies to the Slovak Republic.

[b] The tax treaty concluded with the former Union of Soviet Socialist Republics applies to Tajikistan, and Turkmenistan.

however, may have difficulties to submit proof that they are the beneficial owners of the dividends, interest, or capital gains because these items of income are claimed by the custodian in the name of the UCITS.

A non-resident unitholder of an Austrian-resident UCITS needs to appeal to the tax treaty concluded between the source state and the residence state of that unitholder, if any. As a non-resident, he cannot claim the benefits of the applicable Austrian tax treaty.

A Collective Request by the UCITS

The tax treaty with France[87] and a bilateral ministerial arrangement with Switzerland[88] provide for a collective request by Austrian-resident UCITS on behalf of resident unitholders. It concerns those unitholders who would have been entitled to a reduced tax rate or an exemption under one of the Austrian tax treaties if they had invested directly.

Austrian-resident UCITS thus cannot claim a reduced tax rate or an exemption under the tax treaty with France or Switzerland on behalf of non-resident unitholders. These unitholders have to claim the benefits of the applicable tax treaty themselves. The applicable tax treaty concerns the tax treaty between the source state and their residence state.

3.3.3. German Tax Treaty Network

3.3.3.1. Investing Directly in Securities and Other Financial Instruments

Germany has concluded eighty-three tax treaties with respect to taxes on income and capital. It has treaties with all Member States of the European Union. Germany has, furthermore, concluded tax treaties with two of the three other Member States of the European Economic Area: Iceland and Norway.

Rates of Tax at Source on Dividends

Table 3.5 shows dividends are taxable in the state of residence of the beneficiary. However, they may also be taxed in the source state. Most German tax treaties limit the source state's right to 15%.

A higher percentage of tax may, nonetheless, be charged by the source state under the tax treaties with Greece, Iran, Israel, Ivory Coast, Trinidad and Tobago, Turkey, and Zimbabwe. The source state's right to tax dividends is, in the tax treaties with Ireland, Mauritius, and Thailand, not restricted at all. The tax treaty

87. Protocol to the tax treaty between Austria and France, para. V, BGBl Nr 1994/613.
88. The bilateral ministerial arrangement between Austria and Switzerland of 19 Aug. 1960, Zl 53.467-8/1960.

Table 3.5 German Tax Treaties in Respect to Dividends

DTC	State of Source	Maximum Tax Rate (%) Allowed in the State of Source on Portfolio Investment Dividends	Special Features	Article
Algeria	C	15	-	10(1) and (2)
Argentina	C	15	-	10(1) and (2)
Armenia[a]	C	15	-	7(1) and (2)
Australia	C	15	-	10(1)
Austria	C	15	-	10(1) and (2)
Azerbaijan	C	15	-	10(1) and (2)
Bangladesh	C	15	-	10(1) and (2)
Belarus	C	15	-	10(1) and (2)
Belgium	C	15	-	10(1) and (2)
Bolivia	C	15	-	10(1)
Bosnia-Herzegovina[b]	C	15	-	11(1)
Bulgaria	C	15	-	9(1) and (2)
Canada	C	15	-	10(1) and (2)
China	C	10	-	10(1) and (2)
Croatia	C	15	-	10(1) and (2)
Cyprus	C	Eliminated	Subject to tax clause	10(1), (2) and (4) Protocal paragraph 2
Czechoslovakia	C	15	-	10(1) and (2)
Czech Republic[c]	C	15	-	10(1) and (2)
Denmark	C	15	-	10(1) and (2)
Ecuador	C	15	-	10(1)
Egypt	C	15	-	10(1) and (2)
Estonia	C	15	-	10(1) and (2)
Finland	C	15	-	10(1) and (2)
France	C	15	-	9(1) and (2)

Table 3.5 (cont'd)

DTC	*State of Source*	*Maximum Tax Rate (%) Allowed in the State of Source on Portfolio Investment Dividends*	*Special Features*	*Article*
Georgia	C	10	-	10(1) and (2)
Ghana	C	15	-	10(1) and (2)
Greece	C	25	-	VI(1) and (2)
Hungary	C	15	-	10(1) and (2)
Iceland	C	15	-	10(1) and (2)
India	C	10	-	10(1) and (2)
Indonesia	C	15	-	10(1)
Iran	C	20	-	10(1) and (2)
Ireland	C	Unrestricted	Exemption for surtax in Ireland	VI (1)
Israel	C	25	-	12(1)
Italy	C	15	Refund of *maggiorazione di conguaglio* paid by the distributing enterprise	10(1), (2), and (5)
Ivory Coast	C	15 or 18	-	10(1) and (2) Protocol paragraph 1
Jamaica	C	15	-	10(1) and (2)
Japan	C	15	-	10(1) and (2)
Kazakhstan	C	15	-	10(1) and (2)
Kenya	C	15	-	10(1) and (2)
Korea	C	15	-	10(1) and (2)
Kosovo[b]	C	15	-	11(1)
Kuwait	C	15	-	10(1) and (2)
Kyrgyzstan	C	15	-	10(1) and (2)

Table 3.5 (cont'd)

DTC	*State of Source*	*Maximum Tax Rate (%) Allowed in the State of Source on Portfolio Investment Dividends*	*Special Features*	*Article*
Latvia	C	15	-	10(1) and (2)
Liberia	C	15	-	10(1) and (2)
Lithuania	C	15	-	10(1) and (2)
Luxembourg	C	15	-	13(1), (2), and (3)
Macedonia[b]	C	15	-	11(1)
Malaysia	C	Eliminated	-	10(1) and (2)
Malta	C	Eliminated	-	10(1) and (3)
Mauritius	C	Unrestricted	-	10(1) and (3)
Mexico	C	15	-	10(1) and (2)
Moldova[a]	C	15	-	7(1) and (2)
Mongolia	C	10	-	10(1)
Montenegro[b]	C	15	-	11(1)
Morocco	C	15	-	10(1) and (2)
Namibia	C	15	-	10(1)
Netherlands	C	15	-	13(1) and (2)
New Zealand	C	15	-	10(1) and (2)
Norway	C	15	-	10(1) and (2)
Pakistan	C	15	-	10(1) and (2)
Philippines	C	15	-	10(1) and (2)
Poland	C	15	-	10(1) and (2)
Portugal	C	15	-	10(1) and (2)
Romania	C	15	-	10(1) and (2)
Russia	C	15	-	10(1)
Serbia[b]	C	15	-	11(1)
Singapore	C	Eliminated	-	10(1), (2), and (4)
Slovak Republic[c]	C	15	-	10(1) and (2)

Table 3.5 (cont'd)

DTC	*State of Source*	*Maximum Tax Rate (%) Allowed in the State of Source on Portfolio Investment Dividends*	*Special Features*	*Article*
Slovenia	C	15	-	10(1) and (2)
South Africa	C	15	-	7(1) and (2)
Spain	C	15	-	10(1) and (2)
Sri Lanka	C	15	-	10(1) and (2)
Sweden	C	15	-	10(1) and (2)
Switzerland	C	15	-	10(1) and (2)
Tajikistan	C	15	-	10(1) and (2)
Thailand	C	Unrestricted	20% if paid by industrial enterprises	10(1) and (2)
Trinidad and Tobago	C	20	-	10(1) and (2)
Tunisia	C	15	-	10(1) and (2)
Turkey	C	20	-	10(1) and (2)
Turkmenistan[a]	C	15	-	7(1) and (2)
Ukraine	C	10	-	10(1) and (2)
United Arab Emirates	C	15	-	10(1) and (2)
United Kingdom	C	15	Subject to tax	VI(1)
United States	C	15	Special rule for pension funds and charities	10(1), (2), and (3), 27(1)
Uruguay	C	15	-	10(1)
USSR	C	15	-	7(1) and (2)
Uzbekistan	C	15	-	10(1) and (2)
Venezuela	C	15	-	10(1)
Vietnam	C	15	-	10(1) and (2)
Yugoslavia	C	15	-	11(1)

Table 3.5 (cont'd)

DTC	*State of Source*	*Maximum Tax Rate (%) Allowed in the State of Source on Portfolio Investment Dividends*	*Special Features*	*Article*
Zambia	C	15	Subject to tax clause	10(1) and (2) Protocal paragraph 2
Zimbabwe	C	20	-	10(1) and (2)

C, The Contracting State with whom Germany has concluded the tax treaty.

[a] The tax treaty concluded with the former Union of Soviet Socialist Republics applies to Armenia, Moldova, and Turkmenistan.

[b] The tax treaty concluded with the former Republic of Yugoslavia still applies to Bosnia-Herzegovina, Macedonia, and Serbia. The official positions of Kosovo and Montenegro are not clear.

[c] The tax treaty concluded with the former Czechoslovakia still applies to the Czech Republic and the Slovak Republic.

with Thailand, however, applies a tax rate of 20% at source of dividend if it is paid by an industrial enterprise.

Instead of a limitation of the source state's right to tax, the tax treaties with Cyprus, Malaysia, Malta, and Singapore eliminate the source state's right to tax dividends by allocating the right to tax completely to the beneficiary's state of residence. The tax treaties with Armenia, China, India, Mongolia, and Ukraine reduce the source state's right to tax to either 5% or 10%.

Special Rules

No tax is withheld at source on interest paid to pension funds and charities under the tax treaty with the United States. The source state's right to tax is completely eliminated.

The tax treaty with Italy provides conditionally for a (partial) refund of the corporate income tax charged at the level of a distributing Italian resident company.

Rates of Tax at Source on Interest

Table 3.6 shows that the beneficiary's state of residence is allocated the right to tax interest. In most tax treaties, the interest may also be taxed in the source

Table 3.6 German Tax Treaties in Respect to Interest

DTC	*State of Source*	*Maximum Tax Rate (%) Allowed in the State of Source on Portfolio Investment Interest*	*Special Features*	*Article*
Algeria	C	10	-	11(1), (2), and (3)
Argentina	C	15	10% for bank loans	11(1) and (2)
Armenia[a]	C	5 (Eliminated)	Special rule as long as Germany applies an exemption for interest paid to residents of the Contracting State	8(1) and (2)
Australia	C	10	-	11(1)
Austria	C	Eliminated	-	11(1)
Azerbaijan	C	10	-	11(1) and (2)
Bangladesh	C	10	-	11(1) and (2)
Belarus	C	5	-	11(1) and (2)
Belgium	C	15	Special rule for interest paid to enterprises regarding loans other than bonds and other debt securities	11(1), (2), and (3)
Bolivia	C	15	-	11(1)
Bosnia-Herzegovina[b]	C	Eliminated	-	12(1)
Bulgaria	C	Eliminated	-	10(1)
Canada	C	10	Special rule regarding interest derived from the government or a	11(1), (2) and (3)

Table 3.6 (cont'd)

DTC	*State of Source*	*Maximum Tax Rate (%) Allowed in the State of Source on Portfolio Investment Interest*	*Special Features*	*Article*
			governmental body of the Contracting State Special rule for pension funds	
China	C	10	-	11(1) and (2)
Croatia	C	Eliminated	-	11(1)
Cyprus	C	10	Subject to tax clause	11(1) and (2) Protocal paragraph 2
Czechoslovakia	C	Eliminated	-	11(1)
Czech Republic[c]	C	Eliminated	-	11(1)
Denmark	C	Eliminated	-	11(1)
Ecuador	C	15	10% for bank loans	11(1)
Egypt	C	15	Special rule regarding interest derived from the government or a governmental body of the Contracting State	11(1), (2) and (3)
Estonia	C	10	-	11(1) and (2)
Finland	C	Eliminated	-	11(1)
France	C	Eliminated	-	10(1)
Georgia	C	Eliminated	-	11(1)
Ghana	C	10	0% for bank loans	11(1), (2), and (4)

Table 3.6 (cont'd)

DTC	*State of Source*	*Maximum Tax Rate (%) Allowed in the State of Source on Portfolio Investment Interest*	*Special Features*	*Article*
Greece	C	10	-	VII(1) and (2)
Hungary	C	Eliminated	-	11(1)
Iceland	C	Eliminated	-	11(1)
India	C	10	-	11(1) and (2)
Indonesia	C	10	Interest paid to financial institutions fully owned by government	11(1) and (3)
Iran	C	15		11(1) and (2)
Ireland	C	Eliminated	-	VII(1)
Israel	C	15	-	13(1)
Italy	C	10	Special rule regarding interest derived from the government or a governmental body of the Contracting State Special rule for bank-to-bank loans	11(1), (2) and (3) Protocol paragraph 11
Ivory Coast	C	15	-	11(1) and (2)
Jamaica	C	12.5	10% for bank loans	11(1) and (2)
Japan	C	10	Special rule regarding interest derived from the government	11(1), (2), and (3)

Table 3.6 (cont'd)

DTC	*State of Source*	*Maximum Tax Rate (%) Allowed in the State of Source on Portfolio Investment Interest*	*Special Features*	*Article*
Kazakhstan	C	10	-	11(1) and (2)
Kenya	C	15	-	11(1) and (2)
Korea	C	10	-	11(1) and (2)
Kosovo[b]	C	Eliminated	-	12(1)
Kuwait	C	Eliminated	-	11(1)
Kyrgyzstan	C	5	-	11(1) and (2)
Latvia	C	10	-	11(1) and (2)
Liberia	C	20	10% for bank loans	11(1) and (2)
Lithuania	C	10	-	11(1) and (2)
Luxembourg	C	Eliminated	-	14(1)
Macedonia[b]	C	Eliminated	-	12(1)
Malaysia	C	15	-	11(1)
Malta	C	Eliminated	-	11(1)
Mauritius	C	Unrestricted	0% for bank loans	11(1), (2) and (3)
Mexico	C	15		11(1), (2), and (3)
Moldova[a]	C	5 (Eliminated)	Special rule as long as Germany applies an exemption for interest paid to residents of the Contracting State	8(1) and (2)
Mongolia	C	10	-	11(1)
Montenegro[b]	C	Eliminated	-	12(1)
Morocco	C	10	-	11(1) and (2)
Namibia	C	Eliminated	-	11(1)

Table 3.6 (cont'd)

DTC	*State of Source*	*Maximum Tax Rate (%) Allowed in the State of Source on Portfolio Investment Interest*	*Special Features*	*Article*
Netherlands	C	Eliminated	-	14(1)
New Zealand	C	10	-	11(1) and (2)
Norway	C	Eliminated	-	11(1)
Pakistan	C	20	10% for bank loans	11(1) and (2)
Philippines	C	10	10% for bank loans Special rule for public issued bonds or other debt securities	11(1) and (2)
Poland	C	5	Special rule for bank loans	11(1), (2), and (3)
Portugal	C	15	10% if a bank loan is given for operation with economic or social interest for Contracting State	11(1) and (2)
Romania	C	3	-	11(1) and (2)
Russia	C	Eliminated	-	11(1)
Serbia[b]	C	Eliminated	-	12(1)
Singapore	C	8	-	11(1) and (2)
Slovak Republic	C	Eliminated	-	11(1)
Slovenia[c]	C	5	-	11(1) and (2)
South Africa	C	10	-	8(1) and (2)
Spain	C	10	-	11(1) and (2)
Sri Lanka	C	10	Special rule for bank loans	11(1), (2), and (4)
Sweden	C	Eliminated	-	11(1)

Table 3.6 (cont'd)

DTC	*State of Source*	*Maximum Tax Rate (%) Allowed in the State of Source on Portfolio Investment Interest*	*Special Features*	*Article*
Switzerland	C	Eliminated	-	11(1)
Tajikistan	C	Eliminated	-	11(1)
Thailand	C	25	10% if bank loan is given to industrial enterprise Special rule regarding interest derived from the government Special rule for interest derived by financial institutions fully owned by government	11(1), (2), (3), and (4)
Trinidad and Tobago	C	15	10% for bank loans	11(1) and (2)
Tunisia	C	10	-	11(1) and (2)
Turkey	C	15	-	11(1) and (2)
Turkmenistan[a]	C	5 (Eliminated)	Special rule as long as Germany applies an exemption for interest paid to residents of the Contracting State	8(1) and (2)
Ukraine	C	5	2% for bank loans	11(1) and (2)
United Arab Emirates	C	Eliminated	-	11(1)

Table 3.6 (cont'd)

DTC	*State of Source*	*Maximum Tax Rate (%) Allowed in the State of Source on Portfolio Investment Interest*	*Special Features*	*Article*
United Kingdom	C	Eliminated	Subject to tax clause	VII(1)
United States	C	Eliminated	-	11(1)
USSR	C	5 (Eliminated)	Special rule as long as Germany applies an exemption for interest paid to residents of the Contracting State	8(1) and (2)
Uruguay	C	15	-	11(1)
Uzbekistan	C	5	-	11(1) and (2)
Venezuela	C	5	-	11(1)
Vietnam	C	10 (5)	-	11(1) and (2) Protocol paragraph 5
Yugoslavia	C	Eliminated	-	12(1)
Zambia	C	10	Subject to tax clause	11(1) and (2) Protocal paragraph 2
Zimbabwe	C	10	-	11(1) and (2)

C, The Contracting State with whom Germany has concluded the tax treaty.

[a] The tax treaty concluded with the former Union of Soviet Socialist Republics applies to Armenia, Moldova, and Turkmenistan.

[b] The tax treaty concluded with the former Republic of Yugoslavia still applies to Bosnia-Herzegovina, Macedonia, and Serbia. The official positions of Kosovo and Montenegro are not clear.

[c] The tax treaty concluded with the former Czechoslovakia still applies to the Czech Republic, and the Slovak Republic.

state, although that right is, except for the tax treaty with Mauritius, limited to the percentage agreed on. In most of these tax treaties Germany has agreed on 10%.

In the tax treaties with industrialized countries, the source state's right to tax interest is frequently eliminated by allocating the right to tax exclusively to the beneficiary's state of residence. This is the case in the tax treaties with Austria, Belarus, Bulgaria, Czech Republic, Denmark, Finland, France, Hungary, Iceland, Ireland, Kuwait, Luxembourg, Malta, Namibia, the Netherlands, Norway, Russia, Serbia and Montenegro, Slovakia, Sweden, Switzerland, Tajikistan, the United Arab Emirates, the United Kingdom, and the United States of America. This covers a third of the German tax treaties. The tax treaties with Armenia, Moldova, and Turkmenistan also allocate the right to tax exclusively to the beneficiary's state of residence, provided that state does not charge tax at source on interest paid to residents of the source state.

The German tax treaties with Kyrgyzstan, Poland, Romania, Singapore, Slovenia, Ukraine, Uzbekistan, and Venezuela provide for a percentage that is less than 10%. The tax treaty with Vietnam provides for 5% as long as Germany does not withheld tax on interest paid to residents of Vietnam.

By contrast, in its tax treaties with mostly developing countries Germany has often agreed on a percentage that exceeds 10%. These are the tax treaties with Argentina, Belgium, Bolivia, Ecuador, Egypt, Iran, Israel, Ivory Coast, Jamaica, Kenya, Liberia, Malaysia, Mexico, Pakistan, Portugal, Thailand, Turkey, and Uzbekistan. A restriction of the source state's right to tax interest is missing in the tax treaty with Mauritius.

Exclusive Rates

The tax treaties with Ghana, Italy, Mauritius, Poland and Sri Lanka, sometimes subject to further conditions, provide for an exemption for tax in the source state if interest is paid to a bank residing in the other Contracting States. Under the tax treaty with Italy, however, the exemption is limited to bank-to-bank loans. The tax treaties with Argentina, Ecuador, Jamaica, Liberia, Pakistan, the Philippines, Portugal, Thailand, Trinidad and Tobago, and Ukraine provide for a reduction of the tax rate at source on interest that is paid to a bank residing in the other Contracting State. The exemption under the tax treaty with Thailand is limited to interest paid to a bank by an industrial enterprise.

Under the tax treaties with Belgium and the Philippines interest paid in respect to public issued bonds and other debt securities is exempt from tax in the source state. The exemption is limited under the tax treaty with Belgium to situations in which the beneficiary of the interest is an enterprise.

No tax is further withheld at source on interest paid to pension funds under the tax treaty with Canada. The source state's right to tax is completely eliminated.

Interest paid by the Government or a governmental body of the Contacting State to a resident of the other Contracting State is exempt from tax in the source state under the tax treaties with Canada, Egypt, Italy, Japan, and Thailand. These tax treaties allocate the right to tax exclusively to the residence state of the beneficiary.

Finally, the tax treaties with Indonesia and Thailand provide for an exemption at source for interest paid *to* a bank or credit institution that is wholly owned by the Government or a governmental body of the other Contracting State. The application of the exemption however is decided from situation to situation under the tax treaty with Indonesia.

Rates of Tax at Source on Capital Gains

From Table 3.7 it can be concluded that the right to tax gains from the disposal of portfolio investments is, with the exception of the tax treaties with Australia, China, Egypt, and Trinidad and Tobago, allocated exclusively to the state of the residence of the alienator. Under the tax treaties with Argentina, Bolivia, Bulgaria, Cyprus, Czech Republic, Ecuador, India, Jamaica, Kenya, Liberia, Luxembourg, Mauritius, Mexico, the Philippines, Slovak Republic, Sri Lanka, Tunisia, and Uruguay, the capital gains from the disposal of shares in a resident company may also be taxed in the company's residence state.

The right to tax gains realized by the disposal of shares in a resident company is even allocated exclusively to the company's residence state in the tax treaties with Armenia, Bangladesh, Moldova, Turkmenistan, Uruguay, and Zimbabwe. Almost a third of the German tax treaties thus contain a special rule for gains from the disposal of a resident company. These tax treaties, however, allocate the right to tax gains from the disposal of other portfolio investments exclusively to the alienator's residence state.

If a portfolio investment is disposed of within a year after purchase, the gain from the disposal, under the tax treaty with Turkey, may also be taxed by the Contracting State in which jurisdiction the investment is situated. Otherwise, the gain is taxed exclusively in the residence state of the alienator.

The tax treaties with China and Egypt allocate the right to tax any capital gains from the disposal of portfolio investments to the Contracting State in which jurisdiction the investment is situated as well as the residence state of the alienator. These tax treaties do not provide for a limitation of the source state's right to tax. The tax treaties with Australia and Trinidad and Tobago, for lack of a provision on capital gains and other portfolio income, do not provide for a limitation of the source state's right to tax either.

Table 3.7 German Tax Treaties in Respect to Capital Gains from Portfolio Investments

DTC	*State of Source*	*Catch-All Clause for the Gains from the Alienation of Portfolio Investments*	*Special Features*	*Article*
Algeria	C	Residence state	-	13(5)
Argentina	C	Residence state	Special rule regarding gains from the alienation of shares in a resident company. In that case the gains may also be taxed in the company's residence state	13(3) and (5), and 23(1)
Armenia[a]	C	Residence state	Special rule regarding gains from the alienation of shares in a resident company. In that case the gains may be taxed *exclusively* in the company's residence state	11(3) and (4)
Australia	C	No rule	Since a clause on other portfolio income is also missing, the source state's right to tax is not limited	-
Austria	C	Residence state	-	13(5)
Azerbaijan	C	Residence state	-	13(5)

Table 3.7 (cont'd)

DTC	*State of Source*	*Catch-All Clause for the Gains from the Alienation of Portfolio Investments*	*Special Features*	*Article*
Bangladesh	C	Residence state	Special rule regarding gains from the alienation of shares in a resident company. In that case the gains may be taxed *exclusively* in the company's residence state	13(4) and (5)
Belarus	C	Residence state	-	13(4)
Belgium	C	Residence state	-	13(3)
Bolivia	C	Residence state	Special rule regarding gains from the alienation of shares in a resident company. In that case the gains may also be taxed in the company's residence state	13(3) and (4), and 23(1)
Bosnia-Herzegovina[b]	C	Residence state	-	14(5)
Bulgaria	C	Residence state	Special rule regarding gains from the alienation of shares in a resident company. In that	12(4) and (5), and 22(1)

Table 3.7 (cont'd)

DTC	*State of Source*	*Catch-All Clause for the Gains from the Alienation of Portfolio Investments*	*Special Features*	*Article*
			case the gains may also be taxed in the company's residence state	
Canada	C	Residence state	-	13(6)
China	C	Both states	-	13(4), and 24(2)
Croatia	C	Residence state	-	13(5)
Cyprus	C	Residence state	Subject to tax clause Special rule regarding gains from the alienation of shares in a resident company. In that case the gains may also be taxed in the company's residence state	13(3) and (4), and 23(1) Protocol paragraph 2
Czechoslovakia	C	Residence state	Special rule regarding gains from the alienation of shares in a resident company. In that case the gains may also be taxed in the company's residence state	13(3) and (4), and 23(1)

Table 3.7 (cont'd)

DTC	*State of Source*	*Catch-All Clause for the Gains from the Alienation of Portfolio Investments*	*Special Features*	*Article*
Czech Republic[c]	C	Residence state	Special rule regarding gains from the alienation of shares in a resident company. In that case the gains may also be taxed in the company's residence state	13(3) and (4), and 23(1)
Denmark	C	Residence state	-	13(4)
Ecuador	C	Residence state	Special rule regarding gains from the alienation of shares in a resident company. In that case the gains may also be taxed in the company's residence state	13(3) and (4), and 23(1)
Egypt	C	Both states	-	13(4), and 24(1)
Estonia	C	Residence state	-	13(4)
Finland	C	Residence state	-	13(4)
France	C	Residence state	The application of the clause on capital gains is limited to gains from the	7(1)

Table 3.7 (cont'd)

DTC	*State of Source*	*Catch-All Clause for the Gains from the Alienation of Portfolio Investments*	*Special Features*	*Article*
			disposal of shares in a company residing in the Contracting State The clause on other portfolio income applies to gains from the disposal of other portfolio investments	
Georgia	C	Residence state	-	13(5)
Ghana	C	Residence state	-	13(5)
Greece	C	Residence state	-	IX(1)
Hungary	C	Residence state	-	13(3)
Iceland	C	Residence state	-	13(3)
India	C	Residence state	Special rule regarding gains from the alienation of shares in a resident company. In that case the gains may also be taxed in the company's residence state	13(4) and (5), and 23(1)
Indonesia	C	Residence state	-	13(4)
Iran	C	Residence state	-	13(3)
Ireland	C	Residence state	-	X(1)

Table 3.7 (cont'd)

DTC	*State of Source*	*Catch-All Clause for the Gains from the Alienation of Portfolio Investments*	*Special Features*	*Article*
Israel	C	Residence state	-	7(1)
Italy	C	Residence state	-	13(4)
Ivory Coast	C	Residence state	-	13(4)
Jamaica	C	Residence state	Special rule regarding gains from the alienation of shares in a resident company. In that case the gains may also be taxed in the company's residence state	13(3) and (4), and 23(1)
Japan	C	Residence state	-	13(3)
Kazakhstan	C	Residence state	-	13(5)
Kenya	C	Residence state	Special rule regarding gains from the alienation of shares in a resident company. In that case the gains may also be taxed in the company's residence state	13(4) and (5), and 23(1)
Korea	C	Residence state	-	13(5)
Kosovo[b]	C	Residence state	-	14(5)
Kuwait	C	Residence state	-	13(4)
Kyrgyzstan	C	Residence state	-	13(5)

Table 3.7 (cont'd)

DTC	*State of Source*	*Catch-All Clause for the Gains from the Alienation of Portfolio Investments*	*Special Features*	*Article*
Latvia	C	Residence state	-	13(4)
Liberia	C	Residence state	Special rule regarding gains from the alienation of shares in a resident company. In that case the gains may also be taxed in the company's residence	13(3) and (4), and 23(1)
Lithuania	C	Residence state	-	13(4)
Luxembourg	C	Residence state	The application of the clause on capital gains is limited to gains from the disposal of shares in a company residing in the Contracting State. The clause on other portfolio income applies to gains from the disposal of other portfolio investments	8(1)
Macedonia[b]	C	Residence state	-	14(5)
Malaysia	C	Residence state	-	13(3)

Table 3.7 (cont'd)

DTC	*State of Source*	*Catch-All Clause for the Gains from the Alienation of Portfolio Investments*	*Special Features*	*Article*
Malta	C	Residence state	-	13(5)
Mauritius	C	Residence state	Special rule regarding gains from the alienation of shares in a resident company. In that case the gains may also be taxed in the company's residence state	13(3) and (4), and 24(1)
Mexico	C	Residence state	Special rule regarding gains from the alienation of shares in a resident company. In that case the gains may also be taxed in the company's residence state	13(4) and (5), and 23(2)
Moldova[a]	C	Residence state	Special rule regarding gains from the alienation of shares in a resident company. In that case the gains may be taxed *exclusively* in the company's residence state	11(3) and (4)

Table 3.7 (cont'd)

DTC	*State of Source*	*Catch-All Clause for the Gains from the Alienation of Portfolio Investments*	*Special Features*	*Article*
Mongolia	C	Residence state	-	13(4)
Montenegro[b]	C	Residence state	-	14(5)
Morocco	C	Residence state	-	13(3)
Namibia	C	Residence state	-	13(4)
Netherlands	C	Residence state	The application of the clause on capital gains is limited to gains from the disposal of shares in a company residing in the Contracting State The clause on other portfolio income applies to gains from the disposal of other portfolio investments	8(1)
New Zealand	C	Residence state	-	13(4)
Norway	C	Residence state	-	13(6)
Pakistan	C	Residence state	-	13(6)
Philippines	C	Residence state	Special rule regarding gains from the alienation of shares in a resident company. In that case the gains may also be	13(3) and (4), and 24(1)

Table 3.7 (cont'd)

DTC	*State of Source*	*Catch-All Clause for the Gains from the Alienation of Portfolio Investments*	*Special Features*	*Article*
			taxed in the company's residence state	
Poland	C	Residence state	-	13(5)
Portugal	C	Residence state	-	13(4)
Romania	C	Residence state	-	13(5)
Russia	C	Residence state	-	13(4)
Serbia[b]	C	Residence state	-	14(5)
Singapore	C	Residence state	-	13(5)
Slovak Republic[c]	C	Residence state	Special rule regarding gains from the alienation of shares in a resident company. In that case the gains may also be taxed in the company's residence state	13(3) and (4), and 23(1)
Slovenia	C	Residence state	-	13(4)
South Africa	C	Residence state	-	11(2)
Spain	C	Residence state	-	13(3)
Sri Lanka	C	Residence state	Special rule regarding gains from the alienation of shares in a resident company. In that case the gains may also be	13(3) and (4), and 23(1)

Table 3.7 (cont'd)

DTC	*State of Source*	*Catch-All Clause for the Gains from the Alienation of Portfolio Investments*	*Special Features*	*Article*
			taxed in the company's residence state	
Sweden	C	Residence state	-	13(4)
Switzerland	C	Residence state	-	13(3)
Tajikistan	C	Residence state	-	13(5)
Thailand	C	Residence state	-	13(3)
Trinidad and Tobago	C	No rule	Because a clause on other portfolio income is also lacking, the source state's right to tax is not limited	-
Tunisia	C	Residence state	Special rule regarding gains from the alienation of shares in a resident company. In that case the gains may also be taxed in the company's residence state	13(3) and (4), and 23(1)
Turkey	C	Residence state	Special rule regarding gains from the alienation of portfolio investments that are disposed	13(3), and 23(1)

Table 3.7 (cont'd)

DTC	*State of Source*	*Catch-All Clause for the Gains from the Alienation of Portfolio Investments*	*Special Features*	*Article*
			within 1 year after the purchase. In that case the gains may also be taxed in the source state	
Turkmenistan[a]	C	Residence state	Special rule regarding gains from the alienation of shares in a resident company. In that case the gains may be taxed *exclusively* in the company's residence state	11(3) and (4)
Ukraine	C	Residence state	-	13(5)
Uruguay	C	Residence state	Special rule regarding gains from the alienation of shares in a resident company. In that case the gains may also be taxed in the company's residence state	13(3) and (4), and 23(1)
United Arab Emirates	C	Residence state	-	13(4)

Table 3.7 (cont'd)

DTC	*State of Source*	*Catch-All Clause for the Gains from the Alienation of Portfolio Investments*	*Special Features*	*Article*
United Kingdom	C	Residence state	-	VIII(3)
United States	C	Residence state	-	13(5)
USSR	C	Residence state	-	11(3) and (4)
Uzbekistan	C	Residence state	-	13(5)
Venezuela	C	Residence state	-	13(4)
Vietnam	C	Residence state	-	13(5)
Yugoslavia	C	Residence state	-	14(5)
Zambia	C	Residence state	Subject to tax clause	13(3) Protocol paragraph 2
Zimbabwe	C	Residence state	Special rule regarding gains from the alienation of shares in a resident company. In that case the gains may be taxed *exclusively* in the company's residence state	13(4) and (5), and 23(1)

C, The Contracting State with whom Germany has concluded the tax treaty.

[a] The tax treaty concluded with the former Union of Soviet Socialist Republics applies to Armenia, Moldova, and Turkmenistan.

[b] The tax treaty concluded with the former Republic of Yugoslavia still applies to Bosnia-Herzegovina, Macedonia, and Serbia. The official positions of Kosovo and Montenegro are not clear.

[c] The tax treaty concluded with the former Czechoslovakia still applies to the Czech Republic and the Slovak Republic.

Rates of Tax at Source on Other Portfolio Income

Table 3.8 demonstrates that the residence state of the beneficiary is, with a few exceptions, exclusively granted the right to tax other portfolio income arising in one of the Contracting States. In the case of Cyprus, Kenya, Morocco, Portugal, South Africa, the United Kingdom, and Zambia, this depends, however, on whether the other portfolio income is subject to tax in the residence state.

Table 3.8 German Tax Treaties in Respect to Other Portfolio Income

DTC	*State of Source*	*Catch-All Clause for Portfolio Income Not Expressly Mentioned*	*Special Features*	*Article*
Algeria	C	Residence state	-	21(1)
Argentina	C	Residence state	-	21(1)
Armenia[a]	C	Residence state	-	17
Australia	C	No rule	In the absence of a clause on other portfolio income, the source state's right to tax is not limited	-
Austria	C	Residence state	-	21(1)
Azerbaijan	C	Residence state	-	21(1)
Bangladesh	C	Both states	-	21(1) and (2)
Belarus	C	Residence state	-	21
Belgium	C	Residence state	-	21
Bolivia	C	Residence state	-	21
Bosnia-Herzegovina[b]	C	Residence state	-	22(1)
Bulgaria	C	Residence state	-	20
Canada	C	Both states	-	21(1) and (3)
China	C	Both states	-	22(1) and (3)
Croatia	C	Residence state	-	21(1)
Cyprus	C	Residence state	Subject to tax clause	21 Protocol paragraph 2

Table 3.8 (cont'd)

DTC	*State of Source*	*Catch-All Clause for Portfolio Income Not Expressly Mentioned*	*Special Features*	*Article*
Czechoslovakia	C	Residence state	-	21
Czech Republic[c]	C	Residence state	-	21
Denmark	C	Residence state	-	21(1)
Ecuador	C	Residence state	-	21
Egypt	C	Both states	-	22(1) and (2)
Estonia	C	Residence state	-	21(1)
Finland	C	Residence state	-	21
France	C	Residence state	-	18
Georgia	C	Residence state	-	21(1)
Ghana	C	Residence state	-	21(1)
Greece	C	No rule	In the absence of clause on other portfolio income, the source state's right to tax is not limited	-
Hungary	C	Residence state	-	21
Iceland	C	Residence state	-	21
India	C	Residence state	-	21(1)
Indonesia	C	Residence state	-	21(1)
Iran	C	Residence state		22
Ireland	C	No rule	In the absence of clause on other portfolio income, the source state's right to tax is not limited	-
Israel	C	Residence state	-	17
Italy	C	Residence state	-	22(1)

Table 3.8 (cont'd)

DTC	*State of Source*	*Catch-All Clause for Portfolio Income Not Expressly Mentioned*	*Special Features*	*Article*
Ivory Coast	C	Residence state	-	21
Jamaica	C	Residence state	-	21
Japan	C	Residence state	-	22
Kazakhstan	C	Residence state	-	21(1)
Kenya	C	Residence state	Subject to tax	21
Korea	C	Residence state	-	21(1)
Kosovo[b]	C	Residence state	-	22(1)
Kuwait	C	Residence state	-	21(1)
Kyrgyzstan	C	Residence state	-	21(1)
Latvia	C	Residence state	-	21(1)
Liberia	C	No rule	In the absence of clause on other portfolio income, the source state's right to tax is not limited	-
Lithuania	C	Residence state	-	21(1)
Luxembourg	C	Residence state	-	16
Macedonia[b]	C	Residence state	-	22(1)
Malaysia	C	Residence state	-	21(1)
Malta	C	Residence state	-	21(1)
Mauritius	C	Residence state	-	22(1)
Mexico	C	Both states	-	21(1) and (2)
Moldova[a]	C	Residence state	-	17
Mongolia	C	Residence state	-	21(1)
Montenegro[b]	C	Residence state	-	22(1)
Morocco	C	Residence state	-	21
Namibia	C	Residence state	-	21(1)
Netherlands	C	Residence state	-	16
New Zealand	C	Both states	-	21(1)

Table 3.8 (cont'd)

DTC	*State of Source*	*Catch-All Clause for Portfolio Income Not Expressly Mentioned*	*Special Features*	*Article*
Norway	C	Residence state	-	21(1)
Pakistan	C	Residence state	-	21(1)
Philippines	C	Both states	-	22
Poland	C	Residence state	-	22(1)
Portugal	C	Residence state	Subject to tax clause	22(1)
Romania	C	Residence state	-	21(1)
Russia	C	Residence state	-	21
Serbia[b]	C	Residence state	-	22(1)
Singapore	C	Residence state	-	21(1)
Slovak Republic[c]	C	Residence state	-	21
Slovenia	C	Residence state	-	21(1)
South Africa	C	Residence state	Subject to tax clause	19
Spain	C	Residence state	-	21
Sri Lanka	C	No rule	In the absence of clause on other portfolio income, the source state's right to tax is not limited	-
Sweden	C	Residence state	-	21(1)
Switzerland	C	Residence state	-	21
Tajikistan	C	Residence state	-	20(1)
Thailand	C	No rule	In the absence of clause on other portfolio income, the source state's right to tax is not limited	-

Table 3.8 (cont'd)

DTC	*State of Source*	*Catch-All Clause for Portfolio Income Not Expressly Mentioned*	*Special Features*	*Article*
Trinidad and Tobago	C	No rule	In the absence of clause on other portfolio income, the source state's right to tax is not limited	-
Tunisia	C	Residence state	-	21
Turkey	C	Both states	-	21(1)
Turkmenistan[a]	C	Residence state	-	17
Ukraine	C	Residence state	-	21(1)
Uruguay	C	Residence state	-	21
United Arab Emirates	C	Residence state	-	21(1)
United Kingdom	C	Residence state	Subject to tax clause	XV
United States	C	Residence state	-	21(1)
USSR	C	Residence state	-	17
Uzbekistan	C	Residence state	-	21(1)
Venezuela	C	Residence state	-	21(1)
Vietnam	C	Residence state	-	21(1)
Yugoslavia	C	Residence state	-	22(1)
Zambia	C	Residence state	Subject to tax clause	21 Protocol paragraph 2b
Zimbabwe	C	Residence state	-	21

C, The Contracting State with whom Germany has concluded the tax treaty.

[a] The tax treaty concluded with the former Union of Soviet Socialist Republics applies to Armenia, Moldova, and Turkmenistan.

[b] The tax treaty concluded with the former Republic of Yugoslavia still applies to Bosnia-Herzegovina, Macedonia, and Serbia. The official positions of Kosovo and Montenegro are not clear.

[c] The tax treaty concluded with the former Czechoslovakia still applies to the Czech Republic and the Slovak Republic.

The tax treaties with Bangladesh, Canada, China, Egypt Mexico, New Zealand, the Philippines, and Turkey allocate the right to tax to both states. None of these tax treaties, however, provide for a limitation of the source state's right to tax. An allocation of the right to tax other portfolio income is, finally, missing in the tax treaties with Australia, Greece, Ireland, Liberia, Sri Lanka, Thailand, and Trinidad and Tobago. Hence, the source state is not limited in the taxation of capital gains under that tax treaty.

3.3.3.2. Investing by Way of German-Resident UCITS

Application of Tax Treaties

German-resident UCITS are in the view of Germany tax treaty eligible because they are initially subject to tax on their worldwide taxable income.[89] From an enquiry of the German investment and asset management association in 1995, it follows that this view is shared only by Belgium, Denmark, Portugal, and Spain. Furthermore, Austria,[90] Italy, and the Netherlands do not consistently consider German-resident UCITS as tax treaty eligible.[91] Thus, most German tax treaty partners do not share the view that German-resident UCITS are tax treaty eligible.

Transparent

Some tax treaty partners assume that German-resident UCITS are transparent. In the view of these states the income from the investments of German-resident UCITS is not that of the UCITS. Instead, it is considered to be that of the unitholders. These tax treaty partners apply their tax treaty with Germany as if the unitholders had invested directly.

Individual Requests by the Unitholders

Except for the tax treaties with France, Switzerland, and the United States, German-resident UCITS cannot automatically claim the benefits of a tax treaty on behalf of the unitholders. Instead of a collective request by the UCITS, the unitholders have to submit individual requests for the application of a reduction of withholding tax on or an exemption from withholding tax on dividend or interest afterward.

A non-resident unitholder, such as an Austrian, a Dutch, or a UK unitholder, cannot claim the benefits of the German tax treaties. Instead, the unitholder has to

89. U. Sorgenfrei, Steuerlicher Transparenzgrundsatz und DBA-Berechtigung deutscher offener Investmentsfonds, *IStR 1994/10*, 468.
90. See on the contrary BMF 5 Dec. 1994, *EAS* 535. According to this publication German-resident UCITS are in the view of the Austrian tax authorities treaty eligible.
91. D. Lübbehüsen, in J. Brinkhaus & P. Scherer, *KAGG and AuslInvestment-Gesetz – Kommentar* (Munich: Verlag C.H. Beck, 2003), KAGG § 38, 50.

apply the applicable tax treaty between the source state and the unitholder's state of residence, for example, Austria, the Netherlands, or the United Kingdom.

Collective Request by the UCITS

The tax treaty with France,[92] an agreement with the competent tax authorities of Switzerland,[93] provides for a collective request by the UCITS on behalf of resident unitholders. A resident unitholder is a unitholder who would have been entitled to the benefits of the applicable tax treaty if the unitholder had invested directly. A German-resident UCITS can thus not claim a reduction of withholding tax or an exemption from withholding tax collectively for non-resident unitholders. These unitholders have to file separate requests to the France or Swiss tax authorities afterward.

The tax treaty with the United States also provides for a collective request by the UCITS on behalf of the unitholder but under conditions that are generally not feasible for a German-resident UCITS.[94]

3.3.4. NETHERLANDS TAX TREATY NETWORK

3.3.4.1. Investing Directly in Securities and Other Financial Instruments

The Netherlands has concluded eighty tax treaties with respect to taxes on income and on capital. With the exception of Cyprus, it has tax treaties with all Member States of the European Union. The Netherlands has, furthermore, concluded tax treaties with Iceland and Norway. These countries have also signed the EEA Treaty.

The tax relations between Aruba, the Netherlands, and the Netherlands Antilles are not regulated by a tax treaty. Instead, they are laid down in a statute law: the Tax Charter for the Kingdom of the Netherlands.[95] However, the functioning of the Tax Charter does not differ from that of a tax treaty.

Rates of Tax at Source on Dividends

From Table 3.9 it follows that the right to tax dividends is allocated to the residence state under all of the Netherlands tax treaties as well as under the Tax Charter for the Kingdom of the Netherlands. Dividends may also be taxed in the source state, although the source state's right to tax is, in the majority of the Netherlands tax

92. Article 25B Tax Treaty between France and Germany.
93. Finmin NRW 14 Dec. 1964, S. 1303-27-V B 1, DB 1965, 53.
94. Sorgenfrei, Steuerlichter Transparenzgrundsatz und DBA-Berechtigung deutscher offener Investmentfonds, IStR 1994, 471.
95. Belastingregeling voor het Koninkrijk, *Trb.* 1964, 528, 28 Oct. 1965.

Table 3.9 Netherlands Tax Treaties and Tax Charter for the Kingdom in Respect to Dividends

DTC	*State of Source*	*Maximum Tax Rate (%) Allowed in the State of Source on Portfolio Investment Dividends*	*Special Features*	*Article*
Albania	C	15	Special rule for pension funds	10(1) and (2) Protocol paragraph XII
Argentina	C	15	Special rule for pension funds	10(1) and (2) 31
Armenia	C	15		10(1) and (2)
Aruba[a]	C	15	-	11(1) and (2)
Australia	C	15	-	10(1) and (2)
Austria	C	15	-	10(1) and (2)
Azerbaijan[b]	C	15	-	7(1) and (2)
Bangladesh	C	15	-	10(1) and (2)
Barbados	C	15	-	10(1) and (2)
Belarus	C	15	-	10(1) and (2)
Belgium	C	15	-	10(1) and (2)
Bosnia-Herzegovina[c]	C	15	-	10(1) and (2)
Brazil	C	15	-	10(1) and (2)
Bulgaria	C	15	-	10(1) and (2)
Canada	C	15	-	10(1) and (2)
China	C	10	-	10(1) and (2)
Croatia	C	15	-	10(1) and (2)
Czechoslovakia	C	10	-	10(1) and (2)
Czech Republic[d]	C	10	-	10(1) and (2)
Denmark	C	15	-	10(1) and (2)
Egypt	C	15	-	10(1) and (2)
Estonia	C	15	-	10(1) and (2)

Table 3.9 (cont'd)

DTC	*State of Source*	*Maximum Tax Rate (%) Allowed in the State of Source on Portfolio Investment Dividends*	*Special Features*	*Article*
Finland	C	15	Special rule for pension funds	10(1), (2), and (3)
France	C	15	Avoir fiscal	10(1), (2), and (3)
Georgia	C	15	-	10(1) and (2)
Germany	C	15	-	13(1) and (3)
Ghana	C	10	Special rule for pension funds	10(1) and (2) Protocol paragraph IX
Greece	C	35	-	10(1) and (2)
Hungary	C	15	-	10(1) and (2)
Iceland	C	15	-	10(1) and (2)
India	C	10	-	10(1) and (2) Protocol paragraph IV
Indonesia	C	10	-	10(1) and (2)
Ireland	C	15	Exemption from surtax in Ireland	8(1), (2), and (6)
Israel	C	15	-	11(1) and (2)
Italy	C	15	Refund of *maggirazione di conguaglio* paid by distributing company	10(1), (2), and (5)
Japan	C	15	-	11(1) and (2)
Jordan	C	15	Special rule for pension funds	10(1) and (2) Protocol paragraph VIII
Kazakhstan	C	15	-	10(1) and (2)

Table 3.9 (cont'd)

DTC	*State of Source*	*Maximum Tax Rate (%) Allowed in the State of Source on Portfolio Investment Dividends*	*Special Features*	*Article*
Korea	C	15	-	10(1) and (2)
Kuwait	C	10	-	10(1) and (2)
Kyrgyzstan[b]	C	15	-	7(1) and (2)
Latvia	C	15	-	10(1) and (2)
Lithuania	C	15	-	10(1) and (2)
Luxembourg	C	15	-	10(1) and (2)
Macedonia	C	15	-	10(1) and (2)
Malawi	C	Eliminated	Subject to tax clause	VI(1)
Malaysia	C	Eliminated	-	11(1) and (3)
Malta	C	Eliminated	Incentive for industrial companies resident in the Contracting State	10(1) and (3)
Mexico	C	15	-	10(1) and (2)
Moldova	C	15	-	10(1) and (2)
Mongolia	C	15	-	10(1) and (2)
Morocco	C	25	-	10(1) and (2)
Netherlands Antilles[a]	C	15	-	11(1) and (2)
New Zealand	C	15	-	10(1) and (2)
Nigeria	C	15	-	10(1) and (2)
Norway	C	15	-	10(1) and (2)
Pakistan	C	20	-	10(1) and (2)
Philippines	C	15	-	10(1) and (2)
Poland	C	15	-	10(1) and (2)
Portugal	C	10	-	10(1) and (2)
Romania	C	15	-	10(1) and (2)

Table 3.9 (cont'd)

DTC	*State of Source*	*Maximum Tax Rate (%) Allowed in the State of Source on Portfolio Investment Dividends*	*Special Features*	*Article*
Russia	C	15	-	10(1) and (2)
Serbia and Montenegro[c]	C	15	-	10(1) and (2)
Singapore	C	Eliminated	-	10(1) and (3)
Slovak Republic[d]	C	10	-	10(1) and (2)
Slovenia	C	15	-	10(1) and (2)
South Africa	C	10	-	10(1) and (2)
Spain	C	15	-	10(1) and (2)
Sri Lanka	C	15	-	10(1) and (2)
Surinam	C	20	15% if the beneficiary is not subject to tax	10(1) and (2)
Sweden	C	15	-	10(1) and (2)
Switzerland	C	15	-	9(1) and (2)
Taiwan	C	10	-	10(1) and (2)
Tajikistan[b]	C	15	-	7(1) and (2)
Tax Charter for the Kingdom	C	15	-	11(1) and (2)
Thailand	C	25	Special rule for distribution of industrial enterprises	10(1) and (2)
Tunisia	C	20	-	10(1) and (2)
Turkey	C	20	-	10(1) and (2)
Uganda	C	15	-	10(1) and (2)
Ukraine	C	15	-	10(1) and (2)
United Kingdom	C	15	Tax credit	10(1), (2), and (3)

Table 3.9 (cont'd)

DTC	State of Source	Maximum Tax Rate (%) Allowed in the State of Source on Portfolio Investment Dividends	Special Features	Article
United States	C	15	Special rule for pension funds and charities	10(1) and (2) 35(1)
USSR	C	15	-	7(1) and (2)
Uzbekistan	C	15	-	10(1) and (2)
Venezuela	C	10	-	10(1) and (2)
Vietnam	C	15	-	10(1) and (2)
Yugoslavia	C	15	-	10(1) and (2)
Zambia	C	15	-	10(1) and (2)
Zimbabwe	C	20	-	10(1) and (2)

C, The Contracting State with whom the Netherlands has concluded the tax treaty.

[a] The Tax Charter of the Kingdom applies between Aruba, the Netherlands, and the Netherlands Antilles.

[b] The tax treaty concluded with the former Union of Soviet Socialist Republics applies to Azerbaijan, Kyrgyzstan, and Tajikistan.

[c] The tax treaty concluded with the former Republic of Yugoslavia still applies to Serbia and Montenegro. The official position of Bosnia-Herzegovina is not clear.

[d] The tax treaty concluded with the former Czechoslovakia still applies to the Czech Republic and the Slovak Republic.

treaties, limited to either 10% or 15%. The tax treaties with Greece, Morocco, Surinam, Thailand, Tunisia, Turkey, and Zimbabwe, however, provide for higher percentages.

The tax treaties with Malawi, Malaysia, Malta, and Singapore are the exceptions to the rule that dividends also may be taxed in the source state. The right to tax is in these tax treaties allocated exclusively to the residence state.

Special Rules

The Netherlands tax treaty with the United Kingdom, like the Austrian tax treaty with that country, provides for a partial refund to individuals and corporate entities for the corporate income tax that is charged at the level of the distributing

UK company.[96] At the same time, the United Kingdom as the source state has, likewise, the right to tax the amount of the dividends and the dividend tax credit together at a rate of 15%. Similar kinds of refunds can be found in the tax treaties with France and Italy.

Furthermore, the tax treaties with Albania, Argentina, Finland, Ghana, Jordan, and the United States provide for an exemption in the source state in the case of a dividend paid to a pension fund.

The source state's right to tax is also eliminated under the tax treaty with the United States if dividend is paid to a charity.

Rates of Tax at Source on Interest

Table 3.10 shows that the Netherlands tax treaties and the Tax Charter for the Kingdom of the Netherlands allocate the right to tax interest to the residence state of the beneficiary. The source state may, however, tax the interest at the percentage agreed on, which, under the majority of the Netherlands tax treaties, is 10%.

The tax treaties with Austria, Azerbaijan, Bulgaria, Croatia, Czech Republic, Denmark, Germany, Finland, Georgia, Germany, Hungary, Iceland, Ireland, Kuwait, Kyrgyzstan, Luxembourg, Macedonia, Malawi, Norway, Russia, Serbia and Montenegro, Slovak Republic, South Africa, Sweden, Tajikistan, the United Kingdom, and the United States, however, eliminate the source state's right to tax. These tax treaties, which represent more than a quarter of the tax treaties concluded by the Netherlands, allocate the right to tax interest exclusively to the residence state of the beneficiary. The Protocol to the tax treaties with Romania and Uzbekistan also eliminate the source state right to tax interest for as long as the Netherlands does not withhold tax at source on interest paid by a Netherlands-resident debtor to residents of these states.

Lower percentages are provided for in the tax treaties with Armenia, Barbados, Belarus, Ghana, Jordan, Moldova, Poland, Slovenia, Switzerland, and Venezuela. The Protocol to the tax treaties with Tunisia and Vietnam provides for a lower percentage for withholding tax on interest than the provision in the tax treaty, provided that the Netherlands does not charge tax at source on interest paid by a Netherlands-resident debtor to residents of one of these states.

The Netherlands has agreed on higher percentages in the tax treaties with Argentina, Brazil, Egypt, Israel, Korea, Mexico, Morocco, Nigeria, Pakistan, the Philippines, Thailand, and Turkey. These are mostly tax treaties with developing countries.

Exclusive Rates

In the tax treaties with Armenia, Belgium, Estonia, France, Ghana, Lithuania, Mongolia, Poland, Slovenia, Taiwan, and Uganda, interest paid to a bank residing

96. Article 10(3) Tax Treaty between the Netherlands and the United Kingdom.

Table 3.10 Netherlands Tax Treaties in Respect to Interest

DTC	*State of Source*	*Maximum Tax Rate (%) Allowed in the State of Source on Portfolio Investment Interest*	*Special Features*	*Article*
Albania	C	10	Special rule regarding interest derived from the government. Special rule regarding interest derived by financial institution owned or controlled by the government	11(1), (2) and (3)
Argentina	C	12	Special rule regarding interest derived from the government Special rule regarding interest derived by financial institution owned or controlled by the government Special rule interest paid to pension fund	12(1), (2) and (3), and 31
Armenia	C	5	Special rule regarding interest derived from the government Special rule for bank loans	11(1), (2), and (3)

Table 3.10 (cont'd)

DTC	*State of Source*	*Maximum Tax Rate (%) Allowed in the State of Source on Portfolio Investment Interest*	*Special Features*	*Article*
Aruba[a]	C	10	-	13(1) and (2)
Australia	C	10	-	11(1) and (2)
Austria	C	Eliminated	-	11(1)
Azerbaijan[b]	C	Eliminated	-	8(1)
Bangladesh	C	10	Special rule regarding interest derived from the government Special rule regarding interest derived by financial institution owned or controlled by the government 7.5% for bank loans as long as the Netherlands applies an exemption at source of interest	11(1), (2), and (3) Protocol paragraph 2
Barbados	C	5	-	11(1) and (2)
Belarus	C	5	Special rule regarding interest derived from the government	11(1), (2) and (3)

Table 3.10 (cont'd)

DTC	*State of Source*	*Maximum Tax Rate (%) Allowed in the State of Source on Portfolio Investment Interest*	*Special Features*	*Article*
			Special rule regarding interest derived by financial institution owned or controlled by the government	
Belgium	C	10	Special rule for interest paid in respect to a loan other than a debt security payable to bearer given to an enterprise Special rule for interest paid to a bank or insurance company regarding bonds or debt securities to bearer, which are held for more than 3 months	11(1), (2), and (3)
Bosnia-Herzegovina[c]	C	10	-	11(1)
Brazil	C	15	Special rule regarding interest derived by financial institution owned or controlled by the government	11(1), (2), and (3)
Bulgaria	C	Eliminated	-	11(1)

Table 3.10 (cont'd)

DTC	*State of Source*	*Maximum Tax Rate (%) Allowed in the State of Source on Portfolio Investment Interest*	*Special Features*	*Article*
Canada	C	10	Special rule regarding interest derived from the government Special rule regarding interest derived by financial institution controlled by the government Special rule interest paid to pension fund	11(1), (2), and (3)
China	C	10	-	11(1) and (2)
Croatia	C	Eliminated	-	11(1)
Czechoslovakia	C	Eliminated	-	11(1)
Czech Republic[d]	C	Eliminated	-	11(1)
Denmark	C	Eliminated	-	11(1)
Egypt	C	12	Special rule regarding interest derived from the government Special rule regarding interest derived by financial institution owned or controlled by the government	11(1), (2), and (3)

Table 3.10 (cont'd)

DTC	*State of Source*	*Maximum Tax Rate (%) Allowed in the State of Source on Portfolio Investment Interest*	*Special Features*	*Article*
Estonia	C	10	Special rule regarding interest derived by financial institution owned or controlled by the government Special rule for bank loans	11(1), (2), and (3)
Finland	C	Eliminated	-	11(1)
France	C	10	Special rule for bank loans	11(1), (2), and (3)
Georgia	C	Eliminated	-	11(1)
Germany	C	Eliminated	-	14(1)
Ghana	C	8	Special rule regarding interest derived from the government Special rule regarding interest derived by an instrumentality (including a financial institution) owned or controlled by the government	11(1), (2), (3), and (4)

Table 3.10 (cont'd)

DTC	*State of Source*	*Maximum Tax Rate (%) Allowed in the State of Source on Portfolio Investment Interest*	*Special Features*	*Article*
			Special rule for bank loans Special rule for pension funds	
Greece	C	10	8% for bank loans	11(1) and (2)
Hungary	C	Eliminated	-	11(1)
Iceland	C	Eliminated	-	11(1)
India	C	10	Special rule regarding interest derived by financial institution fully owned by the government	11(1), (2), and (4)
Indonesia	C	10	Special rule regarding interest derived by financial institution owned or controlled by the government	11(1), (2), and (3) Protocol paragraph IV
Ireland	C	Eliminated	-	9(1)
Israel	C	15	10% for bank loans	12(1) and (2)
Italy	C	10	Special rule regarding interest derived from the government Special rule regarding	11(1), (2), and (3)

Table 3.10 (cont'd)

DTC	State of Source	Maximum Tax Rate (%) Allowed in the State of Source on Portfolio Investment Interest	Special Features	Article
			interest derived by financial institution fully owned by the government	
Japan	C	10	Special rule regarding interest derived by a financial institution fully owned by the government	12(1), (2), and (3)
Jordan	C	5	Special rule regarding interest derived from the government	11(1), (2), and (3)
Kazakhstan	C	10	Special rule regarding interest derived from the government	11(1), (2), and (8)
Korea	C	15	10% in case of loans with a period of more than 7 years Special rule regarding interest derived by financial institution fully owned by the government	11(1), (2), and (3)
Kuwait	C	Eliminated	-	11(1)
Kyrgyzstan[b]	C	Eliminated	-	8(1)

Table 3.10 (cont'd)

DTC	*State of Source*	*Maximum Tax Rate (%) Allowed in the State of Source on Portfolio Investment Interest*	*Special Features*	*Article*
Latvia	C	10	Special rule regarding interest derived by financial institution owned or controlled by the government	11(1), (2), and (3)
Lithuania	C	10	Special rule regarding interest derived by financial institution owned or controlled by the government Special rule for bank loan	11(1), (2), and (3)
Luxembourg	C	Eliminated	-	11(1)
Macedonia	C	Eliminated	-	11(1)
Malawi	C	Eliminated	-	VII(1)
Malaysia	C	10	Special rule regarding interest derived by financial institution fully owned by the government	12(1), (2), and (9)
Malta	C	10	-	11(1) and (2)
Mexico	C	10	Special rule regarding interest derived from the government	11(1), (2), and (3)

Table 3.10 (cont'd)

DTC	*State of Source*	*Maximum Tax Rate (%) Allowed in the State of Source on Portfolio Investment Interest*	*Special Features*	*Article*
			Special rule for pension funds 5% for bank loans and listed bonds and other debt securities	
Moldova	C	5	Special rule regarding interest derived from the government	11(1), (2), and (3)
Mongolia	C	10	Special rule regarding interest derived from the government Special rule regarding interest derived by financial institution fully owned or controlled by the government Special rule for bank loans	11(1), (2), and (3)
Morocco	C	25	-	11(1) and (2)
Netherlands Antilles[a]	C	10	-	13(1) and (2)
New Zealand	C	10	Special rule regarding interest derived by a financial	11(1), (2), and (3)

Table 3.10 (cont'd)

DTC	*State of Source*	*Maximum Tax Rate (%) Allowed in the State of Source on Portfolio Investment Interest*	*Special Features*	*Article*
			institution fully owned by the government	
Nigeria	C	12.5	Special rule regarding interest derived by financial institution owned or controlled by the government	11(1), (2), and (3)
Norway	C	Eliminated	-	11(1)
Pakistan	C	20	10% for bank loans Special rule regarding interest derived by financial institution owned or controlled by the government	11(1), (2), and (3)
Philippines	C	15	Special rule regarding interest derived from the government Special rule regarding interest derived by financial institution owned or controlled by the government	11(1), (2), and (3)

Table 3.10 (cont'd)

DTC	*State of Source*	*Maximum Tax Rate (%) Allowed in the State of Source on Portfolio Investment Interest*	*Special Features*	*Article*
Poland	C	5	Special rule regarding interest derived from the government Special rule regarding interest derived by financial institution owned or controlled by the government Special rule for bank loans	11(1), (2) and (3)
Portugal	C	10	Special rule regarding interest derived from the government Special rule regarding interest derived by financial institution owned or controlled by the government	11(1), (2) and (3)
Romania	C	3 (Eliminated)	-	11(1), (2), and (3) Protocol paragraph IX
Russia	C	Eliminated	-	11(1)

Table 3.10 (cont'd)

DTC	*State of Source*	*Maximum Tax Rate (%) Allowed in the State of Source on Portfolio Investment Interest*	*Special Features*	*Article*
Serbia and Montenegro[c]	C	Eliminated	-	11(1)
Singapore	C	10	-	11(1) and (2)
Slovak Republic[a]	C	Eliminated	-	11(1)
Slovenia	C	5	Special rule regarding interest derived from the government Special rule regarding interest derived by financial institution owned or controlled by the government Special rule for bank loans	11(1), (2), and (3)
South Africa	C	Eliminated	-	11(1)
Spain	C	10	-	11(1) and (2)
Sri Lanka	C	10	5% bank loans Special rule regarding interest derived by a governmental owned/controlled financial institution	11(1), (2), and (3) Protocol paragraph III

Table 3.10 (cont'd)

DTC	*State of Source*	*Maximum Tax Rate (%) Allowed in the State of Source on Portfolio Investment Interest*	*Special Features*	*Article*
Surinam	C	10	5% for bank loans Special rule regarding interest derived by financial institution owned or controlled by the government	11(1), (2), and (3)
Sweden	C	Eliminated	-	11(1)
Switzerland	C	5	-	9(1) and (2)
Taiwan	C	10	Special rule regarding interest derived from the government Special rule regarding interest derived by a governmental controlled financial institution Special rule for bank-to-bank loan	11(1), (2), and (3)
Tajikistan[b]	C	Eliminated	-	8(1)
Tax Charter for the Kingdom	C	10	-	13(1) and (2)
Thailand	C	25	10% for bank loans	11(1) and (2)
Tunisia	C	10 (7.5)	Special rule regarding	11(1), (2), and (3)

Table 3.10 (cont'd)

DTC	*State of Source*	*Maximum Tax Rate (%) Allowed in the State of Source on Portfolio Investment Interest*	*Special Features*	*Article*
			interest derived from the government Special rule regarding interest derived by financial institution owned or controlled by the government	Protocol paragraph Ad 11
Turkey	C	15	10% if the period of a loan is more than 2 years	11(1) and (2)
Uganda	C	10	Special rule for bank loans Special rule regarding a loan with a period of more than 3 years if the interest is derived by a financial institution owned or controlled by the government	11(1), (2), and (3)
Ukraine	C	10	2% for bank loans Special rule regarding interest derived from the government	11(1), (2), and (3)

Table 3.10 (cont'd)

DTC	*State of Source*	*Maximum Tax Rate (%) Allowed in the State of Source on Portfolio Investment Interest*	*Special Features*	*Article*
United Kingdom	C	Eliminated	-	11(1)
United States	C	Eliminated	-	12(1)
USSR	C	Eliminated	-	8(1)
Uzbekistan	C	10 (Eliminated)	-	11(1), (2) Protocol paragraph X
Venezuela	C	5	Special rule regarding interest derived from the government Special rule regarding interest derived by financial institution owned or controlled by the government	11(1), (2), and (3)
Vietnam	C	10 (7)	Special rule regarding interest derived from the government Special rule regarding interest derived by financial institution owned or controlled by the government	11(1), (2), and (3) Protocol paragraph VIII

Table 3.10 (cont'd)

DTC	*State of Source*	*Maximum Tax Rate (%) Allowed in the State of Source on Portfolio Investment Interest*	*Special Features*	*Article*
Yugoslavia	C	Eliminated	-	11(1)
Zambia	C	10	Special rule regarding interest derived by financial institution owned or controlled by the government	11(1), (2), and (3)
Zimbabwe	C	10	-	11(1) and (2)

C, The Contracting State with whom the Netherlands has concluded the tax treaty.

[a] The Tax Charter of the Kingdom applies between Aruba, the Netherlands, and the Netherlands Antilles.

[b] The tax treaty concluded with the former Union of Soviet Socialist Republics applies to Azerbaijan, Kyrgyzstan, and Tajikistan.

[c] The tax treaty concluded with the former Republic of Yugoslavia still applies to Serbia and Montenegro. The official position of Bosnia-Herzegovina is not clear.

[d] The tax treaty concluded with the former Czechoslovakia still applies to the Czech Republic and the Slovak Republic.

in the other Contracting State is sometimes subject to further conditions, exempt from tax at source. In the case of the tax treaty with Taiwan, the exemption is limited to bank-to-bank loans. Occasionally, the exemption also applies to financial institutions[97] other than a bank or an insurance company. The tax treaties with Bangladesh, Greece, Israel, Mexico, Pakistan, the Philippines, Sri Lanka, Thailand, and Ukraine provide for a reduction of the tax rate charged at source on interest for bank loans. The reduction under the tax treaty with Bangladesh applies subject to the condition that the Netherlands does not withhold tax at source of interest paid to Bangladeshi residents.

97. According to the Protocol of the tax treaty with Israel, a financial institution includes a company, which in the normal course of its business receives money on deposit or makes loans.

If the period of a loan exceeds a certain number of years, the tax treaties with Belgium, Kazakhstan, and Turkey provide for an exemption at source for the interest paid to a resident of the other Contracting State. Under the tax treaty with Belgium the exemption is limited to interest paid to an enterprise of the other Contracting State and paid in respect to a loan other than a debt security or deposit payable to bearer.

The tax treaty with Mexico applies a reduction to 5% for interest paid in respect to listed bonds and other debt securities. The tax treaty does not provide for any requirements in respect to the period of these securities.

An exemption applies under the tax treaties with Argentina, Canada, Ghana, and Mexico if the interest is paid to a pension fund residing in the other Contracting State. To qualify for the exemption, the pension fund has to be exempt from tax in the other Contracting State.

Interest paid by the Government, a political subdivision or local authority thereof, or the Central Bank remains exempt from tax in the source state under the tax treaties with Albania, Argentina, Armenia, Bangladesh, Belarus, Belgium, Canada, Egypt, Ghana, Italy, Jordan, Kazakhstan, Mexico, Moldova, Mongolia, the Philippines, Poland, Portugal, Slovenia, Taiwan, Tunisia, Ukraine, Venezuela, and Vietnam.

Under the tax treaties with Albania, Argentina, Bangladesh, Belarus, Brazil, Canada, Egypt, Estonia, Ghana, India, Indonesia, Italy, Japan, Korea, Latvia, Lithuania, Malaysia, Mongolia, New Zealand, Nigeria, Pakistan, Poland, the Philippines, Portugal, Slovenia, Sri Lanka, Taiwan, Tunisia, Uganda, Venezuela, Vietnam, and Zambia, the Netherlands agreed on an exemption at source of interest paid to a financial institution that is owned or controlled by the Government or a governmental body of the other Contracting State. Under the Protocol of the tax treaty with Taiwan a financial institution is considered to be controlled by the government if the latter has an interest of at least 50%.

Rates of Tax at Source on Capital Gains

With the exception of the tax treaties with Argentina, Australia, Brazil, China, Germany, and Malawi, the right to tax gains realized by the disposal of portfolio investments is allocated exclusively to the state of residence of the alienator, as can be concluded from Table 3.11. Under the tax treaty with Germany and the Tax Charter for the Kingdom the allocation of the right to tax is limited to gains from the disposal of shares in a resident company. The right to tax other gains is, however, also allocated exclusively by these tax treaties to the residence state of the alienator although on the basis of the provision on other portfolio income.

The tax treaty with Nigeria does not, however, allocate the right to tax gains from the disposal of shares in a resident company exclusively to the residence state of the alienator. These gains may also be taxed in the company's residence state.

Under the tax treaty with Turkey, in case non-listed shares or bonds issued by a resident company are disposed of to a resident of that state within six months after

Table 3.11 Netherlands Tax Treaties in Respect to Capital Gains from Portfolio Investments

DTC	*State of Source*	*Catch-All Clause for the Gains from the Alienation of Portfolio Investments*	*Special Features*	*Article*
Albania	C	Residence state	-	13(5)
Argentina	C	Both states	Special rule gain derived by a pension funds	14(5), (6), and (7), 25(4), and 31
Armenia	C	Residence state	-	13(4)
Aruba[a]	C	No rule	-	12(1)
Australia	C	No rule	Because a clause on other portfolio income is also lacking, the source state's right to tax is not limited	-
Austria	C	Residence state	-	14(4)
Azerbaijan[b]	C	Residence state	-	11(4)
Bangladesh	C	Residence state	-	13(4)
Barbados	C	Residence state	-	13(4)
Belarus	C	Residence state	-	13(4)
Belgium	C	Residence state	-	13(4)
Bosnia-Herzegovina[c]	C	Residence state	-	13(4)
Brazil	C	Both states	-	13(3)
Bulgaria	C	Residence state	-	13(4)
Canada	C	Residence state	-	13(7)
China	C	Source state	-	13(4)
Croatia	C	Residence state	-	13(4)
Czechoslovakia	C	Residence state	-	14(4)
Czech Republic[d]	C	Residence state	-	14(4)
Denmark	C	Residence state	-	13(4)

Table 3.11 (cont'd)

DTC	*State of Source*	*Catch-All Clause for the Gains from the Alienation of Portfolio Investments*	*Special Features*	*Article*
Egypt	C	Residence state	-	13(4)
Estonia	C	Residence state	-	13(4)
Finland	C	Residence state	-	13(4)
France	C	Residence state	-	13(4)
Georgia	C	Residence state	-	13(4)
Germany	C	No rule	Special rule for gains from the disposal of shares in a company resident in the Contracting State	8(1)
Ghana	C	Residence state	-	13(5)
Greece	C	Residence state	-	14(4)
Hungary	C	Residence state	-	13(4)
Iceland	C	Residence state	-	13(4)
India	C	Residence state	-	13(5)
Indonesia	C	Residence state	-	14(4)
Ireland	C	Residence state	-	12(4)
Israel	C	Residence state	-	15(4)
Italy	C	Residence state	-	13(4)
Japan	C	Residence state	-	14(4)
Jordan	C	Residence state	-	13(4)
Kazakhstan	C	Residence state	-	13(5)
Korea	C	Residence state	-	14(4)
Kuwait	C	Residence state	-	13(4)
Kyrgyzstan[b]	C	Residence state	-	11(4)
Latvia	C	Residence state	-	13(4)
Lithuania	C	Residence state	-	13(4)
Luxembourg	C	Residence state	-	14(4)

Table 3.11 (cont'd)

DTC	*State of Source*	*Catch-All Clause for the Gains from the Alienation of Portfolio Investments*	*Special Features*	*Article*
Macedonia	C	Residence state	-	13(4)
Malawi	C	No rule	Because a clause on other portfolio income is also lacking, the source state's right to tax is not limited	-
Malaysia	C	Residence state	-	14(4)
Malta	C	Residence state	-	14(4)
Mexico	C	Residence state	-	13(5)
Moldova	C	Residence state	-	13(4)
Mongolia	C	Residence state	-	13(4)
Morocco	C	Residence state	-	14(4)
Netherlands Antilles[a]	C	No rule	-	12(1)
New Zealand	C	Residence state	-	13(4)
Nigeria	C	Residence state	Special rule regarding gains from the disposal of shares in a company residing in the Contracting State	13(4) and (5), and 23(3)
Norway	C	Residence state	-	13(4)
Pakistan	C	Residence state	-	13(4)
Philippines	C	Residence state	-	13(4)
Poland	C	Residence state	-	13(4)
Portugal	C	Residence state	-	13(4)
Romania	C	Residence state	-	13(4)
Russia	C	Residence state	-	13(4)

Table 3.11 (cont'd)

DTC	*State of Source*	*Catch-All Clause for the Gains from the Alienation of Portfolio Investments*	*Special Features*	*Article*
Serbia and Montenegro[c]	C	Residence state	-	13(4)
Singapore	C	Residence state	-	14(4)
Slovak Republic[d]	C	Residence state	-	14(4)
Slovenia	C	Residence state	-	13(5)
South Africa	C	Residence state	-	13(4)
Spain	C	Residence state	-	14(4)
Sri Lanka	C	Residence state	-	13(4)
Surinam	C	Residence state	-	14(4)
Sweden	C	Residence state	-	13(4)
Switzerland	C	No rule	The source state's right to tax is eliminated by the clause on other portfolio income	-
Taiwan	C	Residence state	-	13(5)
Tajikistan[b]	C	Residence state	-	11(4)
Tax Charter for the Kingdom	C	No rule	-	12(1)
Thailand	C	Residence state	-	14(4)
Tunisia	C	Residence state	-	13(4)
Turkey	C	Residence state	Special rule regarding gains from the alienation of non-listed shares or bonds issued by a resident company that are disposed within 1 year	13(4) and (5)

Table 3.11 (cont'd)

DTC	*State of Source*	*Catch-All Clause for the Gains from the Alienation of Portfolio Investments*	*Special Features*	*Article*
			after the purchase. In that case the gains may also be taxed in the source state	
Uganda	C	Residence state	-	13(4)
Ukraine	C	Residence state	-	13(5)
United Kingdom	C	Residence state	-	13(4)
United States	C	Residence state	-	14(7)
USSR	C	Residence state	-	11(4)
Uzbekistan	C	Residence state	-	13(4)
Venezuela	C	Residence state	-	13(4)
Vietnam	C	Residence state	-	13(5)
Yugoslavia	C	Residence state	-	13(4)
Zambia	C	Residence state	-	13(4)
Zimbabwe	C	Residence state	-	13(4)

C, The Contracting State with whom the Netherlands has concluded the tax treaty.

[a] The Tax Charter of the Kingdom applies between Aruba, the Netherlands, and the Netherlands Antilles.

[b] The tax treaty concluded with the former Union of Soviet Socialist Republics applies to Azerbaijan, Kyrgyzstan, and Tajikistan.

[c] The tax treaty concluded with the former Republic of Yugoslavia still applies to Serbia and Montenegro. The official position of Bosnia-Herzegovina is not clear.

[d] The tax treaty concluded with the former Czechoslovakia still applies to the Czech Republic and the Slovak Republic.

the purchase, the right to tax the gains from that disposal is allocated to both states. If not, the right to tax is exclusively allocated to the residence state of the alienator.

The tax treaty with China does not allocate the right to tax exclusively to the state of residence of the alienator. Instead, it allocates the right to tax capital gains exclusively to the Contracting State in which jurisdiction the disposed investments are situated.

In the case of the tax treaties with Argentina and Brazil, the right to tax is allocated to both states. The tax treaty with Brazil does not provide for any limitation of the source state's right to tax. Because of the lack of a provision on capital gains and other portfolio income, the same holds true under the tax treaties with Australia and Malawi.

Special Rules

The tax treaty with Argentina provides for an exemption in the source state where a capital gain is derived by a pension fund.

Rates of Tax at Source on Other Portfolio Income

Table 3.12 demonstrates that the residence state of the beneficiary is exclusively granted the right to tax other portfolio income in the majority of the Netherlands tax treaties. In the case of the tax treaties with Barbados and Belgium, it depends on whether or not the other portfolio income is subject to tax in the residence state.

The right to tax other portfolio income is not exclusively allocated to the residence state in the tax treaties with Argentina, Brazil, Canada, China, Malaysia, Mexico, and New Zealand. These tax treaties allocate the right to tax to both states. The source state's right is limited, however, to a percentage agreed on under the tax treaty with Canada, Malaysia, Mexico, and New Zealand. The tax treaty with China does not provide for such a limitation.

An allocation of the right to tax other portfolio income is, finally, missing in the tax treaties with Australia, India, Korea, Malawi, Pakistan, the Philippines, Sri Lanka, and Thailand. Hence, the source state is not limited in the taxation of capital gains under those tax treaties.

Special Rules

The tax treaty with Argentina provides for an exemption in the source state where the other portfolio income is derived by a pension fund.

3.3.4.2. Investing by Way of Netherlands-Resident UCITS

Application of Tax Treaties

Netherlands-Resident (EII) UCITS

A Netherlands-resident (EII) UCITS is initially subject to corporate income tax on its worldwide taxable income as a public corporation or an open-fund for joint account. Nevertheless, it does in the view of the Netherlands not qualify as a person for tax treaty purposes because it has opted for a subjective exemption from

Table 3.12 Netherlands Tax Treaties in Respect to Other Portfolio Income

DTC	*State of Source*	*Catch-All Clause for Portfolio Income Not Expressly Mentioned*	*Special Features*	*Article*
Albania	C	Residence state	-	21
Argentina	C	Both states	Special rule other portfolio income paid to a pension fund	23(1) and (3) 31
Armenia	C	Residence state	-	22(1)
Aruba[a]	C	Residence state	-	20
Australia	C	No rule	In the absence of a clause on other portfolio income, the source state's right to tax is not limited	-
Austria	C	Residence state	-	22
Azerbaijan[b]	C	Residence state	-	16
Bangladesh	C	Residence state	-	22(1)
Barbados	C	Residence state	Subject to tax clause	23(1)
Belarus	C	Residence state	-	21(1)
Belgium	C	Residence state	Subject to tax clause	21(1)
Bosnia-Herzegovina[c]	C	Residence state	-	21(1)
Brazil	C	Both states	-	22 and 23(3)
Bulgaria	C	Residence state	-	22(1)
Canada	C	Both states	Source state's right to tax restricted to 25%	21A(1) and (2)
China	C	Both states	-	22(1) and (3)
Croatia	C	Residence state	-	21(1)
Czechoslovakia	C	Residence state	-	23
Czech Republic[d]	C	Residence state	-	23

Table 3.12 (cont'd)

DTC	*State of Source*	*Catch-All Clause for Portfolio Income Not Expressly Mentioned*	*Special Features*	*Article*
Denmark	C	Residence state	-	21(1)
Egypt	C	Residence state	-	21(1)
Estonia	C	Residence state	-	22(1)
Finland	C	Residence state	-	21(1)
France	C	Residence state	-	22
Georgia	C	Residence state	-	22(1)
Germany	C	Residence state	-	16
Ghana	C	Residence state	-	22(1)
Greece	C	Residence state	-	23(1)
Hungary	C	Residence state	-	22(1)
Iceland	C	Residence state	-	22(1)
India	C	No rule	In the absence of a clause on other portfolio income, the source state's right to tax is not limited	-
Indonesia	C	Residence state	-	23(1)
Ireland	C	Residence state	-	20
Israel	C	Residence state	-	24
Italy	C	Residence state	-	22(1)
Japan	C	Residence state	-	23
Jordan	C	Residence state	-	21(1)
Kazakhstan	C	Residence state	-	22
Korea	C	No rule	In the absence of a clause on other portfolio income, the source state's right to tax is not limited	-
Kuwait	C	Residence state	-	22(1)
Kyrgyzstan[b]	C	Residence state	-	16

Table 3.12 (cont'd)

DTC	*State of Source*	*Catch-All Clause for Portfolio Income Not Expressly Mentioned*	*Special Features*	*Article*
Latvia	C	Residence state	-	22(1)
Lithuania	C	Residence state	-	22(1)
Luxembourg	C	Residence state	-	21
Macedonia	C	Residence state	-	22(1)
Malawi	C	No rule	In the absence of a clause on other portfolio income, the source state's right to tax is not limited	-
Malaysia	C	Both states	Source state's right to tax restricted to 10%	22(1)
Malta	C	Residence state	-	23(1)
Mexico	C	Both states	Source state's right to tax restricted to 17.5%	21(1) and (3), and 22(3)
Moldova	C	Residence state	-	21(1)
Mongolia	C	Residence state	-	22(1)
Morocco	C	Residence state	-	22
Netherlands Antilles[a]	C	Residence state	-	20
New Zealand	C	Both states	Special rule regarding other portfolio income. The income may also be taxed in the source state but not for more than 15% of the income	21A(1) and (3)
Nigeria	C	Residence state	-	22(1)
Norway	C	Residence state	-	21(1)
Pakistan	C	No rule	In the absence of a clause on other	-

Table 3.12 (cont'd)

DTC	State of Source	Catch-All Clause for Portfolio Income Not Expressly Mentioned	Special Features	Article
			portfolio income, the source state's right to tax is not limited	
Philippines	C	No rule	In the absence of a clause on other portfolio income, the source state's right to tax is not limited	-
Poland	C	Residence state	-	22(1)
Portugal	C	Residence state	-	22(1)
Romania	C	Residence state	-	22(1)
Russia	C	Residence state	-	21(1)
Serbia and Montenegro[c]	C	Residence state	-	21(1)
Singapore	C	Residence state	-	21
Slovak Republic[d]	C	Residence state	-	23
Slovenia	C	Residence state	-	21(1)
South Africa	C	Residence state	-	21(1)
Spain	C	Residence state	-	23
Sri Lanka	C	No rule	In the absence of a clause on other portfolio income, the source state's right to tax is not limited	-
Surinam	C	Residence state	-	22
Sweden	C	Residence state	-	22(1)
Switzerland	C	Residence state	-	2(1)
Taiwan	C	Residence state	-	22(1)
Tajikistan[b]	C	Residence state	-	16

Table 3.12 (cont'd)

DTC	*State of Source*	*Catch-All Clause for Portfolio Income Not Expressly Mentioned*	*Special Features*	*Article*
Tax Charter for the Kingdom	C	Residence state	-	20
Thailand	C	No rule	In the absence of a clause on other portfolio income, the source state's right to tax is not limited	-
Tunisia	C	Residence state	-	21(1)
Turkey	C	Residence state	-	22(1)
Uganda	C	Residence state	-	21(1)
Ukraine	C	Residence state	-	22(1)
United Kingdom	C	Residence state	-	21(1)
United States of America	C	Residence state	-	23(1)
USSR	C	Residence state	-	16
Uzbekistan	C	Residence state	-	22(1)
Venezuela	C	Residence state	-	22(1)
Vietnam	C	Residence state	-	22(1)
Yugoslavia	C	Residence state	-	21(1)
Zambia	C	Residence state	-	21
Zimbabwe	C	Residence state	-	22(1)

C, The Contracting State with whom the Netherlands has concluded the tax treaty.

[a] The Tax Charter of the Kingdom applies between Aruba, the Netherlands, and the Netherlands Antilles.

[b] The tax treaty concluded with the former Union of Soviet Socialist Republics applies to Azerbaijan, Kyrgyzstan, and Tajikistan.

[c] The tax treaty concluded with the former Republic of Yugoslavia still applies to Serbia and Montenegro. The official position of Bosnia-Herzegovina is not clear.

[d] The tax treaty concluded with the former Czechoslovakia still applies to the Czech Republic and the Slovak Republic.

corporate income tax. According to the Netherlands, this subjective exemption prevents Netherlands-resident (EII) UCITS from claiming tax treaty benefits in a source state.[98] Consequently, the Netherlands does not issue certificates of residence to Netherlands-resident (EII) UCITS, which are generally required for the application of a reduced tax rate or an exemption under a tax treaty.[99] A Netherlands-resident (EII) UCITS may, therefore, have difficulties by claiming tax treaty benefits even in the case that the source state has a different view on the meaning of the term 'liable to tax' than the Netherlands; see Section 2.4.2 for a more in-depth discussion on the latter.

The taxation at source of income from the underlying investments is, thus, generally not limited by one of the Netherlands tax treaties or the Tax Charter for the Kingdom.

Netherlands-Resident (FII) UCITS

A Netherlands-resident (FII) UCITS is, in practice, considered to be a person for the purposes of a tax treaty.[100] It is liable to corporate income tax on its worldwide taxable income although at a tax rate of nil percent. The latter should, according to the Netherlands, be viewed in combination with the requirement for Netherlands-resident (FII) UCITS to distribute the income available for distribution to the unitholders annually, which guarantees the taxation of that income at the level of the unitholders. The application of tax treaties to Netherlands-resident (FII) UCITS is, therefore, justified in the view of the Netherlands.[101] This view is generally followed by the tax treaty partners.

In the presence of a tax treaty with the Netherlands, a source state's right to tax income from the underlying investments of Netherlands-resident (FII) UCITS is therefore limited by that tax treaty.

Netherlands-Resident (TII) UCITS

Netherlands-resident (TII) UCITS are not considered to be a person for tax treaty purposes because any income from the underlying investments is considered to be that of the unitholders under the domestic laws of the Netherlands (transparency). The Netherlands tax treaties should therefore be applied as if the unitholders had invested directly. This view seems to be confirmed by the first results from a consultation by the Netherlands on the qualification of transparent investment institutions, like Netherlands-resident (TII) UCITS, for tax treaty purposes.

---

98. See the announcement of 9 Jun. 2008 by the Netherlands department of Finance at <www.minfin.nl/dsresource?objectid=2103&type=pdf>.
99. *Ibid.*
100. L.F. Kosters & H. Mooij, National Report on the Netherlands of the IFA Congress of 1997 on the Taxation of Investment Funds (International Fiscal Association, 1997), 649.
101. Explanatory Notes, IIK, 2005–2006, 30.533, nr 3, at 4.

As part of a study on cross-border asset pooling by pension funds and other investors, the Netherlands is currently consulting some of its tax treaty partners about the qualification of transparent investment institutions under the Netherlands tax treaties. Belgium, Denmark, Norway, and Taiwan have already indicated that they indeed consider transparent investment institutions as transparent for tax treaty purposes while Finland will evaluate each request separately.[102] More replies from other tax treaty partners are expected.

Individual Requests by the Unitholders

As the income is considered to be that of the unitholders, it depends on the tax liability of the unitholders whether or not a source state's right to tax is limited by a tax treaty. Except for the tax treaty with Belgium, the Netherlands tax treaties do not provide a collective request for the application of a reduced tax rate or an exemption by Netherlands-resident (TII) UCITS on behalf of the unitholders. Instead, afterward each unitholder has to file an individual request for a refund of the part of the foreign withholding tax that exceeds the percentage agreed on in the applicable tax treaty.

In the case of a non-resident unitholder, the applicable tax treaty concerns the tax treaty concluded between the source state and the residence state of the unitholder, if any.

Collective Request by the UCITS

The recent Netherlands tax treaty with Belgium provides a collective request for the application of a reduced tax rate or an exemption by Netherlands-resident (TII) UCITS on behalf of the unitholders.[103] A Netherlands-resident (TII) UCITS may submit a collective request to either apply a reduced tax rate or an exemption in advance of a dividend or interest payment or for a refund of withholding tax afterward. Instead of a request by each of the unitholders, a collective request by the Netherlands-resident (TII) UCITS is sufficient, which is quite practical for both the source state and the unitholder. It is therefore remarkable that the Netherlands has not asked for a clause on a collective request by Netherlands-resident (TII) UCITS on behalf of the unitholders in other recent tax treaties.

The collective request by a Netherlands-resident (TII) UCITS can be made on behalf of those unitholders who would have been entitled to a reduced tax rate or exemption under the Netherlands tax treaty with Belgium if they had invested directly.[104] A Netherlands-resident (TII) UCITS can thus not request for a reduced tax rate or an exemption on behalf of non-resident unitholders. These unitholders have to submit their request on an individual basis afterward.

102. See the announcement of 9 Jun. 2008 by the Netherlands department of Finance at <www.minfin.nl/dsresource?objectid=2103&type=pdf>.

103. Article 25 of the Netherlands tax treaty with Belgium.

104. C. van Raad, Nederlandse regelingen ter voorkoming van dubbele belasting (Deventer: Kluwer, looseleaf), II.B. (Belgium 2001), 269 and 270.

Table 3.13 UK Tax Treaties in Respect to Dividends

DTC	*State of Source*	*Maximum Tax Rate (%) Allowed in the State of Source on Portfolio Investment Dividends*	*Special Features*	*Article*
Antigua and Barbuda	C	Eliminated	Subject to tax clause	6(1)
Argentina	C	15	-	10(1) and (2)
Australia	C	15	-	10(1) and (2)
Austria	C	15	-	10(1)
Azerbaijan	C	15	Subject to tax clause	10(1) and (2)
Bangladesh	C	15	-	10(1) and (2)
Barbados	C	Eliminated	Subject to tax clause	9(4)
Belarus[a]	C	Eliminated	Subject to tax clause	8(1)
Belgium	C	10	-	10(1) and (2)
Belize	C	Eliminated	Subject to tax clause	6(4)
Bolivia	C	15	-	10(1) and (2)
Bosnia-Herzegovina[b]	C	15	-	10(1) and (2)
Botswana	C	12	-	10(1) and (2)
Brunei	C	Eliminated	Subject to tax clause	6(4)
Bulgaria	C	10	-	9(1) and (2)
Canada	C	15	-	10(1) and (2)
Chile	C	15		10(1) and (2)
China	C	10	-	10(1) and (2)
Croatia[b]	C	15	-	10(1) and (2)
Cyprus	C	Eliminated	-	11(4)
Czechoslovakia	C	15	-	10(1) and (2)
Czech Republic[c]	C	15	-	10(1) and (2)

Table 3.13 (cont'd)

DTC	*State of Source*	*Maximum Tax Rate (%) Allowed in the State of Source on Portfolio Investment Dividends*	*Special Features*	*Article*
Denmark	C	15	-	10(1) and (2)
Egypt	C	20	-	10(2)
Estonia	C	15	-	10(1) and (2)
Falkland Islands		10	-	10(1) and (2)
Fiji		15	-	11(1)
Finland	C	Eliminated	-	11(1)
France	C	15	Avoir fiscal if subject to tax *except for pension funds*	9(6) and (7) Protocol 15 October 1987 paragraph 2
Gambia	C	Eliminated	Subject to tax clause	11(4)
Georgia	C	10	-	10(1) and (2)
Germany	C	15	Subject to tax clause	VI(1)
Ghana	C	15	Subject to tax clause	10(1) and (2)
Greece	C	No rule	Because a clause on other portfolio income is also lacking, the source state's right to tax is not limited	-
Grenada	C	Eliminated	Subject to tax clause	6(1)
Guernsey	C	No rule	Because a clause on other portfolio income is also lacking, the source	-

Table 3.13 (cont'd)

DTC	State of Source	Maximum Tax Rate (%) Allowed in the State of Source on Portfolio Investment Dividends	Special Features	Article
			state's right to tax is not limited	
Guyana	C	15	-	11(1) and (2)
Hungary	C	15	-	10(1) and (2)
Iceland	C	15	-	10(2)
India	C	15	-	11(3)
Indonesia	C	15	-	10(1)
Ireland	C	15	Special rule for pension funds and charities	11(1) and (2)
Island of Man	C	No rule	Because a clause on other portfolio income is also lacking, the source state's right to tax is not limited	-
Israel	C	15	Subject to tax clause	VI(1) and (2)
Italy	C	15	Tax credit	10(1), (2), and (4)
Ivory Coast	C	15 or 18	-	10(1) and (2)
Jamaica	C	15	-	8(4)
Japan	C	10	Special rule for pension funds	10(1), (2), and (3)
Jersey	C	No rule	Because a clause on other portfolio income is also lacking, the source state's right to tax is not limited	-

Table 3.13 (cont'd)

DTC	*State of Source*	*Maximum Tax Rate (%) Allowed in the State of Source on Portfolio Investment Dividends*	*Special Features*	*Article*
Jordan	C	10	-	10(1) and (2)
Kazakhstan	C	15	Subject to tax clause	10(1) and (2)
Kenya	C	15	Subject to tax clause	11(4)
Kiribati and Tuvalu	C	Eliminated	Subject to tax clause	6(4)
Korea	C	15	-	10(1) and (2)
Kuwait	C	15	Subject to tax clause	10(1) and (2)
Latvia	C	15	-	10(1) and (2)
Lesotho	C	10	Subject to tax clause	10(1) and (2)
Lithuania	C	15	-	10(1) and (2)
Luxembourg	C	15	-	X(1) and (2)
Macedonia	C	15	-	10(1) and (2)
Malawi	C	Eliminated	Subject to tax clause	VI(4)
Malaysia	C	10	Subject to tax clause	10(1) and (2)
Malta	C	Unrestricted	-	10(3)
Mauritius	C	15	-	10(4)
Mexico	C	Eliminated	-	10(1)
Moldova	C	10	Special rule for pension funds	10(1) and (2)
Mongolia	C	15	-	10(1) and (2)
Montserrat	C	Eliminated	Subject to tax clause	6(1)
Morocco	C	25	-	10(2)
Myanmar	C	Eliminated	Subject to tax clause	VI(1)

Table 3.13 (cont'd)

DTC	*State of Source*	*Maximum Tax Rate (%) Allowed in the State of Source on Portfolio Investment Dividends*	*Special Features*	*Article*
Netherlands	C	15	-	10(1) and (2)
New Zealand	C	15	-	11(1) and (2)
Nigeria	C	15	Subject to tax clause	10(1) and (2)
Norway	C	15	-	10(1) and (2)
Oman	C	10	Subject to tax clause	10(1) and (2)
Pakistan	C	20	15% if the beneficiary is a company	10(1) and (2)
Papua New Guinea	C	17	-	11(1) and (2)
Philippines	C	25	-	9(1)
Poland	C	10	-	10(1) and (2)
Portugal	C	15	Subject to tax clause	10(1) and (2)
Romania	C	15	-	10(1)
Russia	C	10	Subject to tax clause	10(1) and (2)
St. Christopher (St. Kitts) and Nevis	C	Eliminated	Subject to tax clause	6(1)
Saudi Arabia (2010)	C	15	-	10(1) and (2)
Serbia and Montenegro[b]	C	15	-	10(1) and (2)
Sierra Leone	C	Eliminated	Subject to tax clause	6(1)
Singapore	C	Eliminated	-	10(1), (2), and (3)
Slovak Republic[c]	C	15	-	10(1) and (2)

Table 3.13 (cont'd)

DTC	*State of Source*	*Maximum Tax Rate (%) Allowed in the State of Source on Portfolio Investment Dividends*	*Special Features*	*Article*
Slovenia	C	15	Special rule for pension funds	10(1) and (2) Protocol paragraph 2
Solomon Islands	C	Eliminated	Subject to tax clause	6(4)
South Africa	C	15	-	10(1) and (2)
Spain	C	15	-	10(1)
Sri Lanka	C	15	-	10(1) and (4)
Sudan	C	Eliminated	-	10(1), (2), and (3)
Swaziland	C	15	-	10(1) and (2)
Sweden	C	5	-	10(1)
Switzerland	C	15	-	10(1)
Taiwan	C	10	-	10(1) and (2)
Tajikistan[a]		Eliminated	Subject to tax clause	8(1)
Thailand	C	Unrestricted	20% if paid by industrial undertaking and beneficiary is subject to UK tax	11(3)
Trinidad and Tobago	C	20	-	10(2)
Tunisia	C	20	-	10(1) and (2)
Turkey	C	20	-	10(1) and (2)
Turkmenistan[a]	C	Eliminated	Subject to tax clause	8(1)
Uganda	C	15	-	10(1) and (2)
Ukraine	C	10	Subject to tax clause	10(1) and (2)

Table 3.13 (cont'd)

DTC	*State of Source*	*Maximum Tax Rate (%) Allowed in the State of Source on Portfolio Investment Dividends*	*Special Features*	*Article*
United States	C	15	Special rule for pension schemes	10(1), (2), and (3)
USSR	C	Eliminated	Subject to tax clause	8(1)
Uzbekistan	C	10	Subject to tax clause	10(1) and (2)
Yugoslavia	C	15	-	10(1) and (2)
Venezuela	C	10	-	10(1) and (2)
Vietnam	C	15	Subject to tax clause	10(1) and (2)
Yugoslavia	C	15	-	10(1) and (2)
Zambia	C	15	Subject to tax clause	11(1)
Zimbabwe	C	20	Subject to tax clause	11(4)

C, The Contracting State with whom the United Kingdom has concluded at tax treaty.

[a] The tax treaty concluded with the former Union of Soviet Socialist Republics applies to Belarus, Tajikistan, and Turkmenistan.

[b] The tax treaty concluded with the former Republic of Yugoslavia still applies to Bosnia-Herzegovina, Croatia, and Serbia and Montenegro.

[c] The tax treaty concluded with the former Czechoslovakia still applies to the Czech Republic and the Slovak Republic.

To process a collective request by a Netherlands-resident (TII) UCITS, the tax treaty with *Belgium* requires that more than 75% of the unitholders reside in the Netherlands.[105] Otherwise, the collective request will not be processed and the unitholders have to file individual requests. A Netherlands-resident (TII) UCITS that attracts capital outside the Netherlands is thus subject to a higher

105. Article 25(2) of the Netherlands tax treaty with Belgium.

administrative burden under the tax treaty with *Belgium* than one that attracts little or no capital outside the Netherlands. Nevertheless, this does not necessarily infringe on Articles 56 and 58 of the EC Treaty and Article 40 of the EEA Treaty.

3.3.5. UK Tax Treaty Network

3.3.5.1. Investing Directly in Securities and Other Financial Instruments

The United Kingdom has concluded one-hundred and seven tax treaties with respect to taxes on income and capital. It has tax treaties with all Members of the EU. In addition, the United Kingdom has also concluded tax treaties with Iceland and Norway, which have signed the EEA Treaty.

Rate of Tax at Source of Dividends

From Table 3.13 it follows that the right to tax dividends is allocated to the residence state. Under most tax treaties dividends may also be taxed in the source state. In the majority of these tax treaties, the source state's right to tax is limited to 10%, 12%, or 15%.

The source state's right to tax is often eliminated in the tax treaties with overseas territories or former overseas territories. These are the tax treaties with Antigua and Barbuda, Barbados, Belize, Brunei, Cyprus, Finland, Gambia, Grenada, Kiribati and Tuvalu, Malawi, Mexico, Montserrat, Myanmar, St. Christopher (St. Kitts) and Nevis, Sierra Leone, Singapore, the Solomon Islands, Sudan. and the countries of the former Union of Soviet Socialist Republics. Under some of these tax treaties the application of the exemption depends on whether or not the dividend is subject to tax in the beneficiary's residence state. Otherwise, the source state's right to tax is not limited by the tax treaty.

The tax treaty with Sweden limits the source state's right to tax to 5%.

The United Kingdom has agreed on higher percentages in the tax treaties with Egypt, Ivory Coast, Morocco, Pakistan, Papua New Guinea, the Philippines, Trinidad and Tobago, Tunisia, Turkey, and Zimbabwe. A limitation of the source state's right to tax dividends is, with the exception of dividends paid by an industrial undertaking, missing in the tax treaty with Thailand. The same is true of the tax treaties with Greece, Guernsey, Isle of Man, and Jersey because these tax treaties lack provisions on dividends and other portfolio income.

Special Rules

The tax treaties with Ireland, Japan, Moldova, and the United States, however, provide for an exemption from tax in the source state if dividends are paid to a pension funds residing in the other Contracting State.

Furthermore, a (partial) refund of the corporate income tax charged at the level of distributing France- and Italy-resident companies is, subject to conditions, provided for in the tax treaties with France and Italy, respectively.

Rate of Tax at Source on Interest

In Table 3.14 it is shown that the right to tax interest is allocated to the state of residence of the beneficiary. In most tax treaties, interest may also be taxed in the source state, although the source state's right to tax is limited to an agreed-on percentage. In the majority of these tax treaties, the source state's right to tax is limited to a percentage of 10%.

The United Kingdom has agreed in the tax treaties with most industrial countries to eliminate the source state's right to tax interest. Nevertheless, this sometimes depends on taxation in the beneficiary's residence state. This is the case in the tax treaties with Austria, Bulgaria, Czech Republic, Denmark, the Falkland Islands, Finland, France, Georgia, Germany, Greece, Hungary, Iceland, Ireland, Kuwait, Luxembourg, Malawi, Mauritius, the Netherlands, Norway, Oman, Russian Federation, Saudi Arabia, Slovakia, South Africa, Sweden, Switzerland, Ukraine, the United States, and the *countries* in the former Union of Soviet Socialist Republics. Thus, the right to tax interest is allocated exclusively to the residence state of the beneficiary under more than one-quarter of the UK tax treaties.

The tax treaties with Moldova, Poland, Slovenia, Uzbekistan, and Venezuela limit a source state's right to tax to 5%.

The restriction of the source state's right to tax does not apply under some of these tax treaties if the income is not subject to tax in the hands of the beneficiary and the interest is paid on a holding disposed of by the beneficiary within three months after purchase.

Under the UK tax treaties with developing countries the source state is frequently allowed to apply a tax rate of more than 10%. This is the case in the tax treaties with Argentina, Barbados, Belgium, Bolivia, Chile, Egypt, Gambia, Ghana, Guyana, India, Israel, Ivory Coast, Jamaica, Kenya, Mexico, Nigeria, Pakistan, the Philippines, Spain, Sudan, Thailand, Tunisia, Turkey, and Uganda.

The source state's right to tax is not restricted even in the tax treaties with Antigua and Tobago, Belize, Brunei, Grenada, Guernsey, Isle of Man, Jersey, Kiribati and Tuvalu, Montserrat, Myanmar, St. Christopher and Nevis, Sierra Leone, the Solomon Islands, and Swaziland. These tax treaties lack a provision on interest, and the source state's right to tax interest is not covered by a provision on other portfolio income.

Exclusive Rates

The tax treaties with Argentina, Australia, Moldova, and Japan provide conditionally for an exemption from tax in the source state if interest is paid to a bank resident in the other Contracting State. Under the tax treaty with Japan, the exemption, subject to certain conditions, also applies to insurance companies and dealers

Table 3.14 UK Tax Treaties in Respect to Interest

DTC	*State of Source*	*Maximum Tax Rate (%) Allowed in the State of Source on Portfolio Investment Interest*	*Special Features*	*Article*
Antigua and Barbuda	C	No rule	Because a clause on other portfolio income is also lacking, the source state's right to tax is not limited	-
Argentina	C	12	Special rule regarding interest derived from the government or a governmental body of the Contracting State Special rule for bank loan with a period of five years or more The source state's right to tax is not limited if interest is paid to a beneficiary which is exempt from tax and the loan is disposed within 3 months after the purchase	11(1), (2), (3), and (8)
Australia	C	10	Special rule for bank loan	11(1) and (2)
Austria	C	Eliminated	-	11(1)

Table 3.14 (cont'd)

DTC	State of Source	Maximum Tax Rate (%) Allowed in the State of Source on Portfolio Investment Interest	Special Features	Article
Azerbaijan	C	10	Subject to tax clause The source state's right to tax is not limited if interest is paid to a beneficiary that is exempt from tax on such income and the loan is disposed within 3 months after the purchase Special rule for interest derived by instrumentality of government	11(1), (2), (7), and (9)
Bangladesh	C	10	7.5% for bank loan Special rule for interest derived by instrumentality wholly owned by government	11(1), (2), and (7)
Barbados	C	15	Subject to tax clause	11(1)
Belarus[a]	C	Eliminated	-	9(1)
Belgium	C	15	-	9(1)
Belize	C	No rule	Because a clause on other portfolio income is also lacking,	-

Table 3.14 (cont'd)

DTC	*State of Source*	*Maximum Tax Rate (%) Allowed in the State of Source on Portfolio Investment Interest*	*Special Features*	*Article*
			the source state's right to tax is not limited	
Bolivia	C	15	The source state's right to tax is not limited if interest is paid to a beneficiary which is exempt from tax and the loan is disposed within 3 months after the purchase Special rule for interest derived by instrumentality of government	11(1), (2), (7), and (9)
Bosnia-Herzegovina[b]	C	10	-	11(1) and (2)
Botswana	C	10	-	11(1) and (2)
Brunei	C	No rule	Because a clause on other portfolio income is also lacking, the source state's right to tax is not limited	-
Bulgaria	C	Eliminated	-	10(1)
Canada	C	10	Special rule regarding interest derived from the government	11(1), (2), and (4)

Table 3.14 (cont'd)

DTC	*State of Source*	*Maximum Tax Rate (%) Allowed in the State of Source on Portfolio Investment Interest*	*Special Features*	*Article*
Chile	C	15	5% for bank loans and listed bonds or debt securities	11(1) and (2)
China	C	10	-	11(1) and (2)
Croatia[b]	C	10	-	11(1) and (2)
Cyprus	C	10	-	12(1)
Czechoslovakia	C	Eliminated	-	11(1)
Czech Republic[c]	C	Eliminated	-	11(1)
Denmark	C	Eliminated	-	11(1)
Egypt	C	15	Special rule for interest derived by instrumentality of government	11(1), (2), and (5)
Estonia	C	10	Special rule regarding interest derived from the government	11(1), (2), and (3)
Falkland Islands	C	Eliminated	-	11(1)
Fiji	C	10	The source state's right to tax is not limited if interest is paid to a beneficiary that is exempt from tax and the loan is disposed within 3 months after the purchase	12(1), (2), and (7)

Table 3.14 (cont'd)

DTC	*State of Source*	*Maximum Tax Rate (%) Allowed in the State of Source on Portfolio Investment Interest*	*Special Features*	*Article*
Finland	C	Eliminated	The source state's right to tax is not limited if interest is paid to a beneficiary that is exempt from tax and the loan is disposed within 3 months after the purchase	12(1) and (4)
France	C	Eliminated	-	11(1)
Gambia	C	15	-	12(1) and (2)
Georgia	C	Eliminated	-	11(1)
Germany	C	Eliminated	Subject to tax clause	VII(1)
Ghana	C	12.5	Subject to tax clause The source state's right to tax is *except for charities* not limited if interest is paid to a beneficiary that is exempt from tax and the loan is disposed within 3 months after the purchase income Special rule for interest derived by instrumentality of government	11(1), (2), (8), (10), and (11)

Table 3.14 (cont'd)

DTC	*State of Source*	*Maximum Tax Rate (%) Allowed in the State of Source on Portfolio Investment Interest*	*Special Features*	*Article*
Greece	C	Eliminated	Subject to tax clause	VI(1)
Grenada	C	No rule	Because a clause on other portfolio income is also lacking, the source state's right to tax is not limited	-
Guernsey	C	No rule	Since a clause on other portfolio income is also lacking, the source state's right to tax is not limited	-
Guyana	C	15	Special rule regarding interest derived from the government Special rule for interest derived by instrumentality of government The source state's right to tax is not limited if interest is paid to a beneficiary that is exempt from tax and the loan is disposed within 3 months after the purchase	12(1), (2), (5), (8), and (10)

Table 3.14 (cont'd)

DTC	*State of Source*	*Maximum Tax Rate (%) Allowed in the State of Source on Portfolio Investment Interest*	*Special Features*	*Article*
Hungary	C	Eliminated	-	11(1)
Iceland	C	Eliminated	-	11(1)
India	C	15	10% for bank loans The source state's right to tax is not limited if interest is paid to a beneficiary that is exempt from tax and the loan is disposed within 3 months after the purchase	11(1), (2), (3) and (10)
Indonesia	C	10	-	11(1) and (2)
Ireland	C	Eliminated	-	12(1)
Isle of Man	C	No rule	Because a clause on other portfolio income is also lacking, the source state's right to tax is not limited	-
Israel	C	15	Subject to tax clausc	VII(1)
Italy	C	10	Special rule regarding interest derived from the government The source state's right to tax is not limited if interest is paid to	11(1), (2), (3), and (10)

Table 3.14 (cont'd)

DTC	State of Source	Maximum Tax Rate (%) Allowed in the State of Source on Portfolio Investment Interest	Special Features	Article
			a beneficiary that is exempt from tax and the loan is disposed within 3 months after the purchase	
Ivory Coast	C	15	Special rule for interest derived by instrumentality wholly owned by government	11(1), (2), and (3)
Jamaica	C	12.5	Special rule for interest derived by instrumentality wholly owned by government and not subject to tax The source state's right to tax is not limited if interest is paid to a beneficiary which is exempt from tax and the loan is disposed within 3 months after the purchase	11(1), (2), (4), and (8)
Japan	C	10	Special rule for bank loans	11(1), (2), and (3)

Table 3.14 (cont'd)

DTC	*State of Source*	*Maximum Tax Rate (%) Allowed in the State of Source on Portfolio Investment Interest*	*Special Features*	*Article*
			Special rule for pension funds	
Jersey	C	No rule	Because a clause on other portfolio income is also lacking, the source state's right to tax is not limited	-
Jordan	C	10	-	11(1) and (2)
Kazakhstan	C	10	The source state's right to tax is not limited if interest is paid to a beneficiary that is exempt from tax and the loan is disposed within 3 months after the purchase Special rule for interest derived by instrumentality of government	11(1), (2), (8), and (10)
Kenya	C	15	Subject to tax clause	12(1) and (2)
Kiribati and Tuvalu	C	No rule	Because a clause on other portfolio income is also lacking, the source state's right to tax is not limited	-

Table 3.14 (cont'd)

DTC	*State of Source*	*Maximum Tax Rate (%) Allowed in the State of Source on Portfolio Investment Interest*	*Special Features*	*Article*
Korea	C	10	Special rule for interest derived by financial institution owned by government The source state's right to tax is not limited if interest is paid to a beneficiary than is exempt from tax and the loan is disposed within 3 months after the purchase	11(1), (2), (4), and (9)
Kuwait	C	Eliminated	-	11(1)
Latvia	C	10	Special rule regarding interest derived from the government	11(1), (2), and (3)
Lesotho	C	10	Subject to tax clause Special rule for interest derived by instrumentality of government The source state's right to tax is not limited if interest is paid to a beneficiary	11(1), (2), (8), and (10)

Table 3.14 (cont'd)

DTC	*State of Source*	*Maximum Tax Rate (%) Allowed in the State of Source on Portfolio Investment Interest*	*Special Features*	*Article*
			that is exempt from tax and the loan is disposed within 3 months after the purchase	
Lithuania	C	10	Special rule regarding interest derived from the government	11(1), (2), and (3)
Luxembourg	C	Eliminated	-	XI(1)
Macedonia	C	10	-	11(1) and (2)
Malawi	C	Eliminated	Subject to tax clause	VII(1)
Malaysia	C	10	Subject to tax clause	11(1) and (2)
Malta	C	10	Special rule for interest derived by instrumentality of government	11(1), (2), and (8)
Mauritius	C	Eliminated	Special rule for bank loans	11(1), (2), and (3)
Mexico	C	15	10% for bank-to-bank loan Special rule regarding interest derived from the government Special rule for pension funds	11(1), (2), (3), (4), and (10)

Table 3.14 (cont'd)

DTC	*State of Source*	*Maximum Tax Rate (%) Allowed in the State of Source on Portfolio Investment Interest*	*Special Features*	*Article*
			The source state's right to tax is not limited if interest is paid to a beneficiary that is exempt from tax and the loan is disposed within 3 months after the purchase	
Moldova	C	5	Special rule regarding interest derived from the government or a governmental body of the Contracting State Special rule for interest paid to a financial institution	11(1), (2), and (3)
Mongolia	C	10	7% for bank loans The source state's right to tax is not limited if interest is paid to a beneficiary that is exempt from tax and the loan is disposed within 3 months after the purchase	11(1), (2), (3), and (9)

Table 3.14 (cont'd)

DTC	*State of Source*	*Maximum Tax Rate (%) Allowed in the State of Source on Portfolio Investment Interest*	*Special Features*	*Article*
Montserrat	C	No rule	Because a clause on other portfolio income is also lacking, the source state's right to tax is not limited	-
Morocco	C	10	-	11(1) and (2)
Myanmar	C	No rule	Because a clause on other portfolio income is also lacking, the source state's right to tax is not limited	-
Netherlands	C	Eliminated	-	11(1)
New Zealand	C	10	-	12(1) and (2)
Nigeria	C	12.5	Subject to tax clause Special rule for interest derived by instrumentality of government	11(1), (2), and (3)
Norway	C	Eliminated	-	11(1)
Oman	C	Eliminated	Subject to tax clause	11(1)
Pakistan	C	15	-	11(1) and (2)
Papua New Guinea	C	10	Special rule for interest derived by instrumentality of government	12(1), (2), and (3)

Table 3.14 (cont'd)

DTC	*State of Source*	*Maximum Tax Rate (%) Allowed in the State of Source on Portfolio Investment Interest*	*Special Features*	*Article*
Philippines	C	15	10% public issued bonds and other debt securities of a company	10(1), (2), and (3)
Poland	C	5	Special rule for interest to government and loans insured by government institutions	11(1)
Portugal	C	10	Subject to tax clause	11(1) and (2)
Romania	C	10	-	11(1) and (2)
Russia	C	Eliminated	-	11(1)
St. Christopher (St. Kitts) and Nevis	C	No rule	Because a clause on other portfolio income is also lacking, the source state's right to tax is not limited	-
Saudi Arabia (2010)	C	Eliminated	-	11(1)
Serbia and Montenegro[b]	C	10	-	11(1) and (2)
Sierra Leone		No rule	Because a clause on other portfolio income is also lacking, the source state's right to tax is not limited	-
Singapore	C	10	-	11(1) and (2)

Table 3.14 (cont'd)

DTC	*State of Source*	*Maximum Tax Rate (%) Allowed in the State of Source on Portfolio Investment Interest*	*Special Features*	*Article*
Slovak Republic[c]	C	Eliminated	-	11(1)
Slovenia	C	5	Special rule regarding interest derived from government	11(1), (2), and (3)
Solomon Islands		No rule	Because a clause on other portfolio income is also lacking, the source state's right to tax is not limited	-
South Africa	C	Eliminated	-	11(1)
Spain	C	12	The source state's right to tax is not limited if interest is paid to a beneficiary that is exempt from tax and the loan is disposed within 3 months after the purchase	11(1), (2), and (7)
Sri Lanka	C	10	Special rule regarding interest derived by an UK-resident company from the government or a	11(1), (2), (5), and (6)

Table 3.14 (cont'd)

DTC	*State of Source*	*Maximum Tax Rate (%) Allowed in the State of Source on Portfolio Investment Interest*	*Special Features*	*Article*
			governmental body of the Contracting State Special rule for bank loans	
Sudan	C	15	-	11(1) and (2)
Swaziland	C	No rule	The source state's right to tax is not limited, because the clause on other portfolio income does not apply to interest	20
Sweden	C	Eliminated	-	11(1)
Switzerland	C	Eliminated	-	11(1)
Taiwan	C	10	Special rule for interest derived by instrumentality of government	11(1), (2), and (8)
Tajikistan[a]	C	Eliminated	-	9(1)
Thailand	C	25	Subject to tax clause	12(1) and (2)
Trinidad and Tobago	C	10	Special rule for interest derived by instrumentality of government	11(1), (2), and (3)
Tunisia	C	12	10% for bank loans	11(1) and (2)
Turkey	C	15	-	11(1) and (2)
Turkmenistan[a]	C	Eliminated	-	9(1)

Table 3.14 (cont'd)

DTC	*State of Source*	*Maximum Tax Rate (%) Allowed in the State of Source on Portfolio Investment Interest*	*Special Features*	*Article*
Uganda	C	15	-	11(1) and (2)
Ukraine	C	Eliminated	Subject to tax clause	11(1)
United States	C	Eliminated	-	11(1)
USSR	C	Eliminated	-	9(1)
Uzbekistan	C	5	The source state's right to tax is not limited if interest is paid to a beneficiary that is exempt from tax and the loan is disposed within 3 months after the purchase Special rule for interest derived by instrumentality of government	11(1), (2), (8), and (10)
Venezuela	C	5	Subject to tax clause Special rule regarding interest derived from government	11(1), (2), (3), and (10)
Vietnam	C	10	Subject to tax clause Special rule for interest derived by instrumentality of government	11(1), (2), and (8)

Table 3.14 (cont'd)

DTC	*State of Source*	*Maximum Tax Rate (%) Allowed in the State of Source on Portfolio Investment Interest*	*Special Features*	*Article*
Yugoslavia	C	10	-	11(1) and (2)
Zambia	C	10	Subject to tax clause	12(1) and (2)
Zimbabwe	C	10	Subject to tax clause	11(1), (2), and (3)

C, The Contracting State with whom the United Kingdom has concluded the tax treaty.

[a] The tax treaty concluded with the former Union of Soviet Socialist Republics applies to Belarus, Tajikistan, and Turkmenistan.

[b] The tax treaty concluded with the former Republic of Yugoslavia still applies to Bosnia-Herzegovina, Croatia, and Serbia and Montenegro.

[c] The tax treaty concluded with the former Czechoslovakia still applies to the Czech Republic and the Slovak Republic.

in securities. Instead of an exemption, the tax treaties with Bangladesh, Chile, India, Mexico, Mongolia, and Tunisia reduce the tax rate in the source state to interest paid in respect to a bank loan. Some of these tax treaties also apply the exemption to other credit or financial institutions.[106]

The tax treaty with Chile also reduces the tax rate in the source state for interest paid in respect to bonds and debt securities. The same is provided for in the tax treaty with the Philippines for public issued bonds and other debt securities.

An exemption applies in the tax treaty with Japan and Mexico to interest paid to a pension fund that resides in the other Contracting State.

Interest remains exempt from tax in the source state under the UK tax treaties with Argentina, Canada, Estonia, Italy, Latvia, Lithuania, Mexico, Moldova, and Venezuela if it is paid by the Government or a governmental body of the Contracting State.

106. In the tax treaty with Australia a financial institution is defined as a bank or other enterprises substantially deriving profits by raising debt finance in the financial markets or by taking deposits at interest and using those funds in carrying on a business of providing finance.

Some tax treaties[107] provide for an exemption from tax in the source state where interest is derived by an instrumentality of the Government or a governmental body of the other Contracting State that is wholly owned by the Government or a governmental body of the other Contracting State. An 'instrumentality' does not seem to include a financial institution, because according to the tax treaties with Egypt and Jamaica it means any agency or entity created or organized by the Government of either of the Contracting States to carry out Government functions. A financial institution other than a Central Bank does not necessarily have to carry out such functions.

Rate of Tax at Source on Capital Gains

From Table 3.15 it can be concluded that the right to tax gains realized by the disposal of portfolio investments in most tax treaties is allocated exclusively to the state of residence of the alienator. Under the tax treaties with Argentina and Chile the gains from the disposal of shares in a resident company may also be taxed in the company's residence state but not for more than 15% and 16% of the gain, respectively.

Under the tax treaty with Turkey the right to tax gains from the disposal of portfolio investments is allocated to both states if the investments are disposed of within one year after the purchase. If not, the right to tax is allocated exclusively to the residence state of the alienator.

The tax treaties with Cyprus, Papua New Guinea, and Sudan lack a specific provision for capital gains. The allocation of the right to tax these gains is, however, covered by the provision on other portfolio income, which allocates the right to tax exclusively to the residence state of the beneficiary.

The tax treaties with Australia, China, Guyana, India, Lesotho, Nigeria, and Pakistan allocate the right to tax gains from the disposal of portfolio investments in all cases to both states. The same result is derived under the tax treaty with Trinidad and Tobago, although by way of the provision on other portfolio income.

The right to tax capital gains is not allocated in the tax treaties with Antigua and Barbuda, Belize, Brunei, Gambia, Grenada, Guernsey, Isle of Man, Jersey, Kiribati and Tuvalu, Malawi, Montserrat, Myanmar, St. Christopher and Nevis, and Sierra Leone. The tax treaties with these states thus do not limit the source state's right to tax capital gains.

Rate of Tax at Source on Other Portfolio Income

Table 3.16 above shows that the majority of the UK tax treaties allocate the right to tax other portfolio income exclusively to the state of residence of the beneficiary. Under the tax treaties with Argentina, Australia, Botswana, Canada, Chile, India,

107. These are the tax treaties with Azerbaijan, Bangladesh, Bolivia, Egypt, Ghana, Guyana, Ivory Coast, Jamaica, Kazakhstan, Korea, Lesotho, Malta, Mexico, Nigeria, Papua New Guinea, Taiwan, Trinidad and Tobago, Venezuela, and Vietnam.

Table 3.15 UK Tax Treaties in Respect to Capital Gains from Portfolio Investments

DTC	*State of Source*	*Catch-all Clause for the Gains from the Alienation of Portfolio Investments*	*Special Features*	*Article*
Antigua and Barbuda	C	No rule	Because a clause on other portfolio income is also lacking, the source state's right to tax is not limited	-
Argentina	C	Residence state	Special rule regarding gains from the alienation of shares in a resident company. In that case the gains may also be taxed in the company's residence, but not for more than 15% of the gain	13(6) and (7), and 23(1)
Australia	C	Both states	-	13(6), and 22(2)
Austria	C	Residence state	-	13(4)
Azerbaijan	C	Residence state	Subject to tax clause	13(5)
Bangladesh	C	Residence state	-	13(4)
Barbados	C	Residence state	Subject to tax clause	13(4)
Belarus[a]	C	Residence state	-	12(4)
Belgium	C	Residence state	-	13(4)

Table 3.15 (cont'd)

DTC	*State of Source*	*Catch-all Clause for the Gains from the Alienation of Portfolio Investments*	*Special Features*	*Article*
Belize	C	No rule	Because a clause on other portfolio income is also lacking, the source state's right to tax is not limited	-
Bolivia	C	Residence state	-	13(5)
Bosnia-Herzegovina[b]	C	Residence state	-	13(4)
Botswana	C	Residence state	-	14(5)
Brunei	C	No rule	Because a clause on other portfolio income is also lacking, the source state's right to tax is not limited	-
Bulgaria	C	Residence state	-	12(4)
Canada	C	Residence state	-	13(8)
Chile	C	Residence state	Special rule regarding gains from the alienation of shares in a resident company. In that case the gains may, *except for pension funds*, also be taxed in the company's residence but not for more than 16% of the gain	13(4) and (5)

Table 3.15 (cont'd)

DTC	*State of Source*	*Catch-all Clause for the Gains from the Alienation of Portfolio Investments*	*Special Features*	*Article*
China	C	Both states	-	14(1), and 23(2)
Croatia[b]	C	Residence state	-	13(4)
Cyprus	C	No rule	The right to tax is allocated *exclusively* to the residence state of the alienator by the other portfolio income clause	-
Czechoslovakia	C	Residence state	-	13(4)
Czech Republic[c]	C	Residence state	-	13(4)
Denmark	C	Residence state	-	13(6)
Egypt	C	Residence state	-	13(4)
Estonia	C	Residence state	-	13(5)
Falkland Islands	C	Residence state	-	13(5)
Fiji	C	Residence state	-	14(4)
Finland	C	Residence state	-	14(6)
France	C	Residence state	-	13(3)
Gambia	C	No rule	Because a clause on other portfolio income is also lacking, the source state's right to tax is not limited	-
Georgia	C	Residence state	-	13(5)
Germany	C	Residence state	-	VIII(3)
Ghana	C	Residence state	-	13(5)
Greece	C	Residence state	-	VII

Table 3.15 (cont'd)

DTC	*State of Source*	*Catch-all Clause for the Gains from the Alienation of Portfolio Investments*	*Special Features*	*Article*
Grenada	C	No rule	Because a clause on other portfolio income is also lacking, the source state's right to tax is not limited	-
Guernsey	C	No rule	Because a clause on other portfolio income is also lacking, the source state's right to tax is not limited	-
Guyana	C	Both states	-	15(1), and 24(1)
Hungary	C	Residence state	-	13(4)
Iceland	C	Residence state	-	13(5)
India	C	Both states	-	14
Indonesia	C	Residence state	-	13(4)
Ireland	C	Residence state	Subject to tax clause for individuals	13(5)
Isle of Man	C	No rule	Because a clause on other portfolio income is also lacking, the source state's right to tax is not limited	-
Israel	C	Residence state	Subject to tax clause	VIIIA(4)
Italy	C	Residence state	-	13(4)
Ivory Coast	C	Residence state	-	14(4)

Table 3.15 (cont'd)

DTC	*State of Source*	*Catch-all Clause for the Gains from the Alienation of Portfolio Investments*	*Special Features*	*Article*
Jamaica	C	Residence state	Subject to tax clause	20(3)
Japan	C	Residence state	-	13(6)
Jersey	C	No rule	Because a clause on other portfolio income is also lacking, the source state's right to tax is not limited	-
Jordon	C	Residence state	Subject to tax clause	13(5)
Kazakhstan	C	Residence state	-	13(5)
Kenya	C	Residence state	-	15(4)
Kiribati and Tuvalu		No rule	Because a clause on other portfolio income is also lacking, the source state's right to tax is not limited	-
Korea	C	Residence state	-	13(5)
Kuwait	C	Residence state	-	13(4)
Latvia	C	Residence state	-	13(5)
Lesotho	C	Both states	-	14
Lithuania	C	Residence state	-	13(5)
Luxembourg	C	Residence state	-	XIII(3)
Macedonia	C	Residence state	-	13(5)
Malawi	C	No rule	Because a clause on other portfolio income is also lacking, the source state's right to tax is not limited	-

Table 3.15 (cont'd)

DTC	*State of Source*	*Catch-all Clause for the Gains from the Alienation of Portfolio Investments*	*Special Features*	*Article*
Malaysia	C	Residence state	Subject to tax clause	14(5)
Malta	C	Residence state	Subject to tax clause	13(5)
Mauritius	C	Residence state	-	13(4)
Mexico	C	Residence state	-	13(7)
Moldova	C	Residence state	-	13(5)
Mongolia	C	Residence state	Subject to tax clause	13(5)
Montserrat	C	No rule	Because a clause on other portfolio income is also lacking, the source state's right to tax is not limited	-
Morocco	C	Residence state	-	13(3)
Myanmar	C	No rule	Because a clause on other portfolio income is also lacking, the source state's right to tax is not limited	-
Netherlands	C	Residence state	-	13(4)
New Zealand	C	Residence state	-	14(4)
Nigeria	C	Both states	-	13
Norway	C	Residence state	-	13(6)
Oman	C	Residence state	Subject to tax clause	13(6)
Pakistan	C	Both states	-	14(1)

Table 3.15 (cont'd)

DTC	*State of Source*	*Catch-all Clause for the Gains from the Alienation of Portfolio Investments*	*Special Features*	*Article*
Papua New Guinea	C	No rule	The right to tax is allocated exclusively to the residence state by the other portfolio income clause	-
Philippines	C	Residence state	-	12(4)
Poland	C	Residence state	-	13(4)
Portugal	C	Residence state	-	13(4)
Romania	C	Residence state	-	14(4)
Russia	C	Residence state	Subject to tax clause	13(5)
St. Christopher (St. Kitts) and Nevis	C	No rule	Because a clause on other portfolio income is also lacking, the source state's right to tax is not limited	-
Saudi Arabia (2010)	C	Residence state	-	13(6)
Serbia and Montenegro[b]	C	Residence state	-	13(4)
Sierra Leone	C	No rule	Because a clause on other portfolio income is also lacking, the source state's right to tax is not limited	-
Singapore	C	Residence state	-	13(5)
Slovak Republic[c]	C	Residence state	-	13(4)

Table 3.15 (cont'd)

DTC	*State of Source*	*Catch-all Clause for the Gains from the Alienation of Portfolio Investments*	*Special Features*	*Article*
Slovenia	C	Residence state	-	13(5)
Solomon Islands	C	No rule	Since a clause on other portfolio income is also lacking, the source state's right to tax is not limited	-
South Africa	C	Residence state	-	13(5)
Spain	C	Residence state	-	13(4)
Sri Lanka	C	Residence state	-	13(4)
Sudan	C	Residence state	-	13(4)
Swaziland	C	No rule	The right to tax is allocated exclusively to the residence state by the other portfolio income clause	-
Sweden	C	Residence state	-	13(7)
Switzerland	C	Residence state	-	13(5)
Taiwan	C	Residence state	-	13(5)
Tajikistan[a]	C	Residence state	-	12(4)
Thailand	C	Residence state	-	14(4)
Trinidad and Tobago	C	No rule	The right to tax is allocated exclusively to the *both states* by the other portfolio income clause	-
Tunisia	C	Residence state	-	13(4)
Turkey	C	Residence state	Special rule regarding gains from portfolio	13(4), and 23(1)

Table 3.15 (cont'd)

DTC	*State of Source*	*Catch-all Clause for the Gains from the Alienation of Portfolio Investments*	*Special Features*	*Article*
			investments that are disposed within 1 year after the purchase. In that case the gains may also be taxed in the state in which the gains arise	
Turkmenistan[a]	C	Residence state	-	12(4)
Uganda	C	Residence state	-	14(4)
Ukraine	C	Residence state	Subject to tax clause	13(5)
United States	C	Residence state	-	13(5)
USSR	C	Residence state	-	12(4)
Uzbekistan	C	Residence state	Subject to tax clause	13(5)
Venezuela	C	Residence state	Subject to tax clause	13(5)
Vietnam	C	Residence state	Subject to tax clause	13(5)
Yugoslavia	C	Residence state	-	13(4)
Zambia	C	Residence state	-	14(3)
Zimbabwe	C	Residence state	-	14(4)

C, The Contracting State with whom the United Kingdom has concluded the tax treaty.

[a] The tax treaty concluded with the former Union of Soviet Socialist Republics applies to Belarus, Tajikistan, and Turkmenistan.

[b] The tax treaty concluded with the former Republic of Yugoslavia still applies to Bosnia-Herzegovina, Croatia, and Serbia and Montenegro.

[c] The tax treaty concluded with the former Czechoslovakia still applies to the Czech Republic and the Slovak Republic.

Table 3.16 UK Tax Treaties in Respect to Other Portfolio Income

DTC	*State of Source*	*Catch-all Clause for Portfolio Income Not Expressly Mentioned*	*Special Features*	*Article*
Antigua and Tobago	C	No rule	In the absence of clause on other portfolio income, the source state's right to tax is not limited	-
Argentina	C	Both states	-	21(1) and (5)
Australia	C	Both states	-	20(1) and (3), and 22(2)
Austria	C	Residence state	-	22
Azerbaijan	C	Residence state	-	21(1)
Bangladesh	C	No rule	In the absence of a clause on other portfolio income, the source state's right to tax is not limited	-
Barbados	C	Residence state	Subject to tax clause	21
Belarus[a]	C	Residence state	-	19
Belgium	C	Residence state	-	22(1)
Belize	C	No rule	In the absence of a clause on other portfolio income, the source state's right to tax is not limited	-
Bolivia	C	Residence state	-	21(1)
Bosnia-Herzegovina[b]	C	Residence state	-	21(1)

Table 3.16 (cont'd)

DTC	*State of Source*	*Catch-all Clause for Portfolio Income Not Expressly Mentioned*	*Special Features*	*Article*
Botswana	C	Both states	-	22(1) and (3)
Brunei	C	No rule	In the absence of a clause on other portfolio income, the source state's right to tax is not limited	-
Bulgaria	C	Residence state	-	21
Canada	C	Both states	-	20A(1) and (3)
Chile	C	Both states	-	20(1) and (3)
China	C	No rule	In the absence of a clause on other portfolio income, the source state's right to tax is not limited	-
Croatia[b]	C	Residence state	-	21(1)
Cyprus	C	Residence state	-	23
Czechoslovakia	C	Residence state	-	21
Czech Republic[c]	C	Residence state	-	21
Denmark	C	Residence state	-	21(1)
Egypt	C	No rule	In the absence of a clause on other portfolio income, the source state's right to tax is not limited	-
Estonia	C	Residence state	-	22(1)

Table 3.16 (cont'd)

DTC	*State of Source*	*Catch-all Clause for Portfolio Income Not Expressly Mentioned*	*Special Features*	*Article*
Falkland Islands	C	Residence state	-	22(1)
Fiji	C	No rule	In the absence of a clause on other portfolio income, the source state's right to tax is not limited	-
Finland	C	Residence state	-	23(1)
France	C	Residence state	-	22(1)
Gambia	C	No rule	In the absence of a clause on other portfolio income, the source state's right to tax is not limited	-
Georgia	C	Residence state	-	21(1)
Germany	C	Residence state	Subject to tax clause	XV
Ghana	C	Residence state	Subject to tax clause	23
Greece	C	No rule	In the absence of a clause on other portfolio income, the source state's right to tax is not limited	-
Grenada	C	No rule	In the absence of a clause on other portfolio income, the source state's right to tax is not limited	-

Table 3.16 (cont'd)

DTC	*State of Source*	*Catch-all Clause for Portfolio Income Not Expressly Mentioned*	*Special Features*	*Article*
Guernsey	C	No rule	In the absence of a clause on other portfolio income, the source state's right to tax is not limited	-
Guyana	C	Residence state	-	23
Hungary	C	Residence state	-	22
Iceland	C	Residence state	-	21(1)
India	C	Both states	-	23(1) and (3)
Indonesia	C	No rule	In the absence of a clause on other portfolio income, the source state's right to tax is not limited	-
Ireland	C	Residence state	-	20(1)
Isle of Man		No rule	In the absence of a clause on other portfolio income, the source state's right to tax is not limited	-
Israel	C	Residence state	Subject to tax clause	XVII
Italy	C	Residence state	-	22(1)
Ivory Coast	C	Residence state		22
Jamaica	C	Residence state	Subject to tax clause	21
Japan	C	Residence state	-	21(1)

Table 3.16 (cont'd)

DTC	*State of Source*	*Catch-all Clause for Portfolio Income Not Expressly Mentioned*	*Special Features*	*Article*
Jersey	C	No rule	In the absence of a clause on other portfolio income, the source state's right to tax is not limited	-
Jordan	C	Both states	-	22(1)
Kazakhstan	C	Residence state	-	21(1)
Kenya	C	Residence state	Subject to tax clause	24
Kiribati and Tuvalu	C	No rule	In the absence of a clause on other portfolio income, the source state's right to tax is not limited	-
Korea	C	Residence state	-	22(1)
Kuwait	C	Residence state	-	22(1)
Latvia	C	Residence state	-	22(1)
Lesotho	C	Residence state	-	22(1)
Lithuania	C	Residence state	-	22(1)
Luxembourg	C	Residence state	-	XXII(1)
Macedonia	C	Residence state	-	20(1)
Malawi	C	No rule	In the absence of a clause on other portfolio income, the source state's right to tax is not limited	-
Malaysia	C	Both states	-	23(1)

Table 3.16 (cont'd)

DTC	*State of Source*	*Catch-all Clause for Portfolio Income Not Expressly Mentioned*	*Special Features*	*Article*
Malta	C	Residence state	-	21(1)
Mauritius	C	Residence state	-	22(1)
Mexico	C	Both states	-	21(1) and (3)
Moldova	C	Residence state	-	20(1)
Mongolia	C	Residence state	-	22(1)
Montserrat	C	No rule	In the absence of a clause on other portfolio income, the source state's right to tax is not limited	-
Morocco	C	Residence state	-	21
Myanmar	C	No rule	In the absence of a clause on other portfolio income, the source state's right to tax is not limited	-
Netherlands		Residence state	-	21(1)
New Zealand	C	Both States	-	21A(1) and (3)
Nigeria	C	No rule	In the absence of a clause on other portfolio income, the source state's right to tax is not limited	-
Norway	C	Residence state	-	21(1)
Oman	C	Residence state	-	21(1)

Table 3.16 (cont'd)

DTC	*State of Source*	*Catch-all Clause for Portfolio Income Not Expressly Mentioned*	*Special Features*	*Article*
Pakistan	C	No rule	In the absence of a clause on other portfolio income, the source state's right to tax is not limited	-
Papua New Guinea	C	Residence state	-	22(1)
Philippines	C	No rule	In the absence of a clause on other portfolio income, the source state's right to tax is not limited	-
Poland	C	Residence state	-	21(1)
Portugal	C	Residence state	Subject to tax clause	20
Romania	C	Residence state	-	23
Russia	C	Residence state	-	21(1)
St. Christopher (St. Kitts) and Nevis	C	No rule	In the absence of a clause on other portfolio income, the source state's right to tax is not limited	-
Saudi Arabia (2010)	C	Both states	-	21(1) and (3)
Serbia and Montenegro[b]	C	Residence state	-	21(1)
Sierra Leone	C	No rule	In the absence of a clause on other portfolio	-

Table 3.16 (cont'd)

DTC	*State of Source*	*Catch-all Clause for Portfolio Income Not Expressly Mentioned*	*Special Features*	*Article*
			income, the source state's right to tax is not limited	
Singapore	C	Both states	-	22(1) and (3)
Slovak Republic[c]	C	Residence state	-	21
Slovenia	C	Residence state	-	21(1)
Solomon Islands	C	No rule	In the absence of a clause on other portfolio income, the source state's right to tax is not limited	-
South Africa	C	Both states	-	20(1) and (3)
Spain	C	Residence state	-	22(1)
Sri Lanka	C	No rule	In the absence of a clause on other portfolio income, the source state's right to tax is not limited	-
Sudan	C	Residence state	-	21
Swaziland	C	Residence state	-	20
Sweden	C	Residence state	-	21(1)
Switzerland	C	Residence state	-	21(1)
Taiwan	C	Both states	-	21(1) and (2)
Tajikistan[a]	C	Residence state	-	19

Table 3.16 (cont'd)

DTC	*State of Source*	*Catch-all Clause for Portfolio Income Not Expressly Mentioned*	*Special Features*	*Article*
Thailand	C	No rule	In the absence of a clause on other portfolio income, the source state's right to tax is not limited	-
Trinidad and Tobago	C	Both states	-	22
Tunisia	C	Residence state	-	21
Turkey	C	Residence state	-	22
Turkmenistan[a]	C	Residence state	-	19
Uganda	C	Residence state	-	22
Ukraine	C	Residence state	-	21(1)
United States	C	Residence state	-	22(1)
USSR	C	Residence state	-	19
Uzbekistan	C	Residence state	-	21(1)
Venezuela	C	Both states	-	21(1) and (3)
Vietnam	C	Residence state		21(1)
Yugoslavia	C	Residence state	-	21(1)
Zambia	C	Residence state	Subject to tax clause	22
Zimbabwe	C	Residence state	-	22

C, The Contracting State with whom the United Kingdom has concluded the tax treaty.

[a] The tax treaty concluded with the former Union of Soviet Socialist Republics applies to Belarus, Tajikistan, and Turkmenistan.

[b] The tax treaty concluded with the former Republic of Yugoslavia still applies to Bosnia-Herzegovina, Croatia, Serbia and Montenegro, and Slovenia.

[c] The tax treaty concluded with the former Czechoslovakia still applies to the Czech Republic, and the Slovak Republic.

Jordan, Malaysia, Mexico, New Zealand, Saudi Arabia, Singapore, South Africa, Taiwan, Trinidad and Tobago, and Venezuela, the other portfolio income may also be taxed in the Contracting State in which jurisdiction the investments are situated. These tax treaties do not provide in a limitation of the source state's right to tax.

The right to tax other portfolio income is not allocated in the tax treaties with Antigua and Barbuda, Bangladesh, Belize, Brunei, China, Egypt, Fiji, Gambia, Greece, Grenada, Guernsey, Indonesia, Isle of Man, Jersey, Kiribati and Tuvalu, Malawi, Montserrat, Myanmar, Nigeria, Pakistan, the Philippines, St. Christopher and Nevis, Sierra Leone, Sri Lanka, and Thailand. The source state's right to tax other portfolio income is, thus, not limited in these tax treaties.

3.3.5.2. Investing by Way of UK-Resident UCITS

Application of Tax Treaties

UK-resident UCITS are considered to be a person for the purposes of a tax treaty. They are liable to corporate income tax in the United Kingdom at a rate of 20%.[108] A source state's right to tax is therefore limited by the tax treaty concluded with the United Kingdom.[109] The tax treaties with Japan and Slovenia explicitly state that UK-resident UCITS among other authorized investment funds are considered to be a resident for the purposes of these tax treaties.[110]

Transparent

UK-resident UCITS of the trust type are assumed by a few tax treaty partners to be transparent. The income from the investments is considered by those tax treaty partners to be that of the unitholders.[111] Hence, they apply the tax treaty with the United Kingdom under the same conditions as a direct investment.

108. It should be noted that at the time of writing, the UK tax authorities are considering the redrafting of legislation for the taxation of foreign profits. Under the proposed new regime it is possible that a UK-resident UCITS may become exempt from UK corporate income tax on foreign dividends. If UK UCITS do become generally exempt from foreign dividend income, this could have an impact on UK-resident UCITS access to tax treaty rates of withholding tax. This is because many of the UK's tax treaties require that a person should be liable not only to corporate income tax but also in practice subject to tax, that is they should pay some tax as a matter of practice and not merely be liable.

109. C. Hurley, National Report on the United Kingdom of the IFA Congress of 1997 on the Taxation of Investment Funds (International Fiscal Association, 1997), 833 and 834.

110. See the Exchange of Notes on the Arts 10, 11, and 13 to the tax treaty with Japan and para. 1 of the Protocol to the tax treaty with Slovenia.

111. C. Hurley, National Report on the United Kingdom of the IFA Congress of 1997 on the Taxation of Investment Funds (International Fiscal Association, 1997), 834.

Individual Request by the Unitholders

Apart from the tax treaties with Switzerland, UK-resident UCITS cannot submit a collective request on behalf of the unitholders, if a tax treaty partner assumes that a UK-resident UCITS is transparent. Each unitholder, afterward, has to submit a separate request for a refund of the tax withheld above the percentage agreed on in the applicable tax treaty.

A non-resident unitholder cannot benefit from the UK tax treaties. He should claim the benefits of the tax treaty between the source state and his state of residence.

Collective Request by the UCITS

A UK-resident UCITS may submit a collective claim relating to the benefits of the tax treaty with Switzerland. The claim is made on behalf of those unitholders that are beneficially owned by UK residents, which does not differ from a direct investment.[112] A UK-resident UCITS cannot submit a collective request on behalf of non-resident unitholders. The latter have to file an individual request afterward.

A UK-resident UCITS may claim a full refund of the part of the Swiss withholding tax that exceeds the percentage agreed on if more than 95% of the unitholders are considered to be UK residents for the purposes of the tax treaty with Switzerland. The percentage of units of a UK-resident UCITS that are held by UK-resident unitholders needs to be indicated annually. Switzerland and the United Kingdom are free to bring the necessary controls into place.[113]

3.3.6. Conclusion

The taxation at source on the income from securities and other financial instruments that are situated or issued outside the jurisdiction of the UCITS country does not, with the exception of Austrian-resident UCITS, Netherlands-resident (TII) UCITS and a number of cases in which German and UK-resident UCITS are wrongfully assumed to be transparent, take place as if the unitholders had invested directly. The application of the tax treaties for income derived through German-resident UCITS, Netherlands-resident (EII/FII) UCITS, and UK-resident UCITS differs from a direct investment by the unitholders, because the source states take into account the tax liability of the UCITS instead of that of the unitholders.

The application of the tax treaties to income derived by way of these UCITS is affected by the measures taken in the UCITS country to prevent the income from the investments being subject to (corporate) income tax twice – at the level of the

112. Article 24 of the UK tax treaty with Switzerland in combination with the Memorandum of Understanding regarding investment vehicles of 12 Feb. 2008.

113. Paragraph 3 of the Memorandum of Understanding regarding investment vehicles of 12 Feb. 2008.

UCITS and at the level of the unitholders. As is the case for Austrian-resident UCITS and Netherlands-resident (TII) UCITS, this could have been avoided by considering UCITS to be transparent.

An in-depth discussion of the origins and consequences of the differences in source taxation of income is found in Chapters 4 and 5.

Chapter 4

Comparison of the Source Taxation of Income Derived by Way of Austrian, German, Netherlands, and United Kingdom – Resident Undertakings for Collective Investment in Transferable Securities

For domestic investments, only a few of the countries studied use transparency, and then only for some items of income to make sure that income from securities and other financial instruments paid to undertakings for collective investment in transferable securities (UCITS) is not subject to more taxation (or less taxation as the case may be) than a direct investment. This is surprising because it establishes that the income from securities and other financial instruments, like a direct investment, is considered to be that of the unitholders.

The countries studied favour an exemption from withholding tax or a refund of the tax withheld at source. Instead, these items of income are subject to withholding tax at the time of distribution. This approach is an alternative for transparency. Overall, it has more or less the same result as transparency. Like a direct investment, the tax base, tax rate, and available exemptions are applied on the basis of the tax liability of the unitholders, although at the time of distribution.

A difference with transparency is, however, that the income is subject to withholding tax after deduction of any expenses made at the level of the UCITS, for example, the management fee, administration fee, and collecting fees. The deduction of these expenses results in an inequality compared to a direct investment, as withholding taxes in the countries studied are otherwise deducted from the gross amount of the income. If the restriction of the exemption from withholding tax or refund of the tax withheld to resident UCITS somehow does not infringe on the free movement of capital as laid down in Articles 56 and 58 of the European Community (EC) Treaty or Article 40 of the European Economic Area (EEA) Treaty, the fact that income paid to non-resident UCITS is taxed at the gross amount, whereas income paid to resident UCITS in the end is taxed after the deduction of any expenses seems to do so.

In the case of foreign investments, some of the countries studied make use of transparency to establish that the application of tax treaties for income derived by way of UCITS does not differ from a direct investment. Transparency establishes that the income from securities and other financial instruments is considered to be that of the unitholders. Like a direct investment, the tax liability of the unitholders is therefore taken into account by the application of the tax treaty and not that of the UCITS.

A disadvantage of transparency is that an UCITS under the majority of the tax treaties concluded by the countries studied cannot make a request for the application of a reduction of withholding tax or an exemption from withholding tax on behalf of the unitholders. The unitholders have to make separate requests for such afterward.

Not all of the countries studied have introduced measures to establish that the application of tax treaties for income derived by way of UCITS does not differ from a direct investment. In the absence of any measures, the application of the tax treaties depends on the objective and subjective tax liability of the UCITS. The objective and subjective tax liability of UCITS in the countries studied varies. Some UCITS are entitled to a reduced tax base, a reduced tax rate, or both, whereas other UCITS are subjectively exempt from corporate income tax; see Section 6.2 for a more in-depth discussion of the objective and subjective tax liability of UCITS.

The application of tax treaties to UCITS is convenient and practical for individual and corporate unitholders. They do not have to make any separate requests for the application of a reduction of withholding tax or an exemption from withholding tax.

The application of tax treaties to UCITS, however, may not lead to a result similar to that of the application of tax treaties to the unitholders. It is not neutral. It may result in a tax advantage compared to a direct investment in the case that the UCITS country has more tax treaties with countries in a specific region or a particular state than the residence state of the unitholder or the tax treaties of the UCITS country contain more attractive provisions (tax treaty shopping).

4.1. INTRODUCTION

This chapter evaluates and compares the instruments used by the countries studied to establish that the taxation in the source state does not differ from a direct investment. Not only the taxation of income from investments within Austria, Germany, the Netherlands, and the United Kingdom is evaluated and compared (Section 4.2) but also that of income from investments situated outside these countries (Section 4.3).

4.2. COMPARISON OF THE SOURCE TAXATION OF INCOME FROM INVESTMENTS SITUATED WITHIN THE JURISDICTION OF AUSTRIA, GERMANY, THE NETHERLANDS, AND THE UNITED KINGDOM

Table 4.1. illustrates that the measures taken by Austria, Germany, the Netherlands, and the United Kingdom to establish transparency for income derived from investments situated *within* its jurisdiction produce different results for resident and non-resident UCITS. Furthermore, the source taxation is affected by the application of reduced tax rates under the tax treaties between the countries studied. As a result, the source taxation in the countries studied is not the same for resident and non-resident UCITS.

Table 4.1. Application of Tax Base, Tax Rates and Available Exemptions from Withholding Tax under the Domestic Laws of the Countries Studied

Source state	*Resident UCITS*	*Non-resident UCITS*	*Consequences for Source Taxation*
Austria	Transparency but only for domestic dividends. Application of exemption at source of other items of income	Transparency for domestic dividends and interest. These items of income may, however, be taxed at a reduced tax rate if they are derived through a non-resident UCITS, which is tax treaty eligible, that is, Netherlands-resident (FII) UCITS and UK-resident UCITS	No uniform source taxation of income derived through resident and non-resident UCITS and between non-resident UCITS. By the selection of UCITS, the investment policy and residence state of UCITS matters
Germany	Application of refund of the tax withheld[a] respectively exemption at source[b]	Denial of refund of tax withheld at source of income[a]/ application of exemption at source[b]	No uniform source taxation of income derived through resident and non-resident UCITS and between non-resident UCITS. By the selection of UCITS, the investment policy

Table 4.1. (cont'd)

Source state	*Resident UCITS*	*Non-resident UCITS*	*Consequences for Source Taxation*
			and residence state of UCITS matters
Netherlands	Refund of the tax withheld, although it is not available for resident (EII/TII) UCITS. Instead, an exemption applies at the time of distribution of income by resident (EII) UCITS. Transparency applies to domestic dividends derived through resident (TII) UCITS	Denial of refund of the tax withheld at source. Transparency applies to dividend derived by way of transparent non-resident UCITS	No uniform source taxation of income derived through resident and non-resident UCITS and between non-resident UCITS. By the selection of UCITS, the investment policy and residence state of UCITS matters Exempt corporate unitholders are subject to more severe taxation if they derive income through Netherlands-resident (EII) UCITS or non-resident UCITS
United Kingdom	Application of exemption at source except for yearly interest and UK public revenue dividends	Application of exemption at source. Transparency applies to income derived by way of transparent non-resident UCITS	No uniform source taxation of income derived through resident and non-resident UCITS and between non-resident UCITS. By the selection of UCITS, the investment policy and residence state of UCITS matters

[a] For dividend and interest from convertible or profit-sharing bonds or debentures.

[b] In the case of interest from bonds and debentures other than from convertible or profit-sharing ones, or capital gains from the disposal of securities or other financial instruments.

4.2.1. Availability of Instruments to Establish Taxation as If Invested Directly for Resident UCITS

Transparency

In Austria, dividends derived by way of resident UCITS are considered to be that of the unitholders (transparency). As a result, the tax base, tax rate, and the availability of exemptions does not differ from a direct investment in shares of Austrian companies. Transparency does not only establish that dividends paid to resident UCITS are subject to more taxation (or less taxation) than a direct investment, it also avoids double taxation. Nevertheless, the application of transparency is limited to dividends. It does not apply to interest payments.

The Netherlands also makes use of transparency to establish that dividends derived by way of UCITS are not subject to more withholding tax (or less withholding tax) than a direct investment in the shares of Netherlands companies but only for resident (TII) UCITS.

Exemption at Source or Refund of the Tax Withheld

Germany applies an exemption at source of interest and capital gains derived by way of these UCITS and provides for a refund of the tax withheld on dividend. Instead, these items of income are subject to withholding tax at the time of distribution by the UCITS. Taxation at the time of distribution by the UCITS establishes that the tax status of the unitholder is, like a direct investment, taken into account by the application of exemptions, refunds, and, in the case of non-resident unitholders, reduced tax rates under the tax treaties between the countries studied. It should, however, be noted that the avoidance of double withholding tax and measures to apply exemptions, refunds, and special tax rates as if the unitholders had invested directly are necessary only where the income under the domestic laws of the UCITS country is considered to be that of the UCITS (tax opaque UCITS). This is the case for German-resident UCITS.

Example 4.1

X, a pension fund residing in the Netherlands, keeps units in Y, which is a Netherlands-resident (FII) UCITS. Z, a company residing in the Netherlands, pays a dividend of EUR 100,000 to Y. An amount of EUR 15,000 is withheld on the dividend by Z as tax. The withholding tax of EUR 15,000 is, on request, refunded to Y. When a dividend of EUR 100,000 is distributed by Y at the end of the year, the dividend is subject to 15% withholding EUR 15,000. As a pension fund, X is, like in the case of a direct investment, entitled to a refund of the withholding tax of EUR 15,000.

Taxation in the form of a withholding tax at the time of distribution instead of a withholding tax at source also prevents that income derived by way of tax opaque UCITS is subject to withholding tax twice; at source of the income and at the time of distribution by the UCITS (double withholding tax). In addition, the management fee, administration fee, custodian fee, and other expenses made at the level of the UCITS may be deducted from the income from the investments of the UCITS. Austria therefore applies an exemption at source of interest paid to Austrian-resident UCITS, even while these UCITS are transparent.

Example 4.2

Y, a UCITS residing in Austria, is paid an amount of EUR 100,000 as interest from bonds issued by Z, an Austrian-resident company. After deduction of an amount of EUR 10,000 as expenses, the remaining amount of the interest, EUR 90,000, is distributed by Y. The interest is not subject to withholding tax at the time of receipt by Y. Instead, Austria charges withholding tax at the time of distribution by Y.

The United Kingdom also exempts interest paid by a deposit-taker if it is paid to a resident UCITS, whereas a refund of the tax withheld at source of domestic dividends derived through UCITS is available in the Netherlands. The latter is, however, limited to resident (FII) UCITS and does not apply to resident (EII/TII) UCITS.

Exemption at the Time of Distribution by the UCITS Instead of at Source

Instead of an exemption at source or a refund of the tax withheld, the Netherlands avoids double withholding tax for domestic dividends derived through resident (EII) UCITS by means of an exemption at the time that the domestic dividends are distributed by these UCITS. The management fee, administration fee, custodian fee, and other expenses made at the level of the UCITS are thus not set off against the income from the investments. The withholding tax is thus charged on the gross amount of dividend.

Example 4.3

Y, a Netherlands-resident (EII) UCITS, derives a dividend of EUR 100,000 from Z, a Netherlands-resident company. An amount of EUR 15,000 is withheld on the dividend by the Netherlands as tax. No exemption or refund is available. The dividend is, however, exempt from withholding tax when it is distributed by Y at the end of the year.

An additional measure is necessary, however, to establish that the tax status of the unitholders is taken into account by the application of exemptions and reduced tax rates. Otherwise, Netherlands source dividend derived through resident (EII) UCITS would for some unitholders be subject to more withholding tax than if they had derived such dividends directly. However, the Netherlands has failed to do so even while such transparency could have been introduced simply by means of a refund of the part of the withholding tax that would not have been charged in case of a direct investment.

4.2.2. Application of Instruments to Establish Taxation as If Invested Directly to Non-resident UCITS

Separate from the availability of measures to establish transparency for resident UCITS, the source taxation in the countries studied is affected by the way these measures are applied to income derived by way of non-resident UCITS. The application of an exemption at source or refund of the tax withheld depends on the residence state of the UCITS, because the application is restricted to resident UCITS. As a result, the source taxation differs for income derived by way of resident and non-resident UCITS from investments situated *within* the jurisdiction of the countries studied.

Example 4.4

X, a company residing in the Netherlands, pays a dividend of EUR 100,000 to Y, an Austrian-resident UCITS, and Z, a Netherlands-resident (FII) UCITS. X is required to withhold a tax of EUR 15,000 on each of the dividend. The withholding tax of EUR 15,000 is refunded to Z in the form of a payment reduction. No refund is available for Y.

This is different only for income types in which case an exemption applies at the source. The application of these exemptions, however, has nothing to do with transparency. It originates from a general exemption from withholding tax available under the domestic laws for non-resident taxpayers. The application of the general exemption depends on either the place of residence of the UCITS or its unitholders. The effect of these exemptions, however, is not the same because they are limited to certain types of income, for example, interest from bonds and debentures other than convertible or profit-sharing ones. Therefore, the source taxation of other types of income, for example, dividend, still differs if it is derived through resident and non-resident UCITS.

Example 4.5

X, a UCITS residing in Germany, and Y, a UCITS residing in the United Kingdom, both keep shares and bonds issued by Z, a company residing in Germany. Z pays both X and Y a dividend of EUR 100,000 and interest of EUR 100,000. Z has to withhold EUR 15,000 as tax on the dividend paid to X, whereas it is not required to withhold tax on the interest payments to X as a result of an exemption for interest paid to German-resident UCITS. However, it needs to withhold a tax of EUR 15,000 on the dividend paid to Y, whereas no tax has to be withheld on the interest payment because of an exemption for interest payments to non-residents. Furthermore, the withholding tax of EUR 26,375 charged on the dividend paid to X is, unlike that charged on the dividend paid to Y, refunded to X.

The source taxation of income derived by way of UCITS from investments situated within the countries studied is further affected by the application of a reduced tax rate under the tax treaties between the countries studied. As a result the applicable tax rates do not only differ for resident and non-resident UCITS, but they also differ between non-resident UCITS. Contrary to resident UCITS, non-resident UCITS might be entitled to a reduced tax rate under a tax treaty. The application of a tax treaty for income derived by way of non-resident UCITS is neither uniform. It depends on the tax liability of either the unitholder or the UCITS.

Example 4.6

X, a German-resident company, pays a dividend of EUR 100,000 to both Y, a UCITS residing in Germany, and Z, a UCITS residing in the United Kingdom. X is required to withheld a tax of EUR 25,000 on the dividend paid to Y, whereas the withholding tax on the dividend paid to Z is, in accordance with the German tax treaty with the United Kingdom, only EUR 15,000.

A more in-depth discussion of the application of tax treaties for income derived by way of UCITS follows in the next section.

4.2.3. Conclusion

Isolated the instruments used by Austria, Germany, the Netherlands, and the United Kingdom establish that income derived by UCITS is not subject to more severe taxation (or lesser taxation). This is different only for Netherlands source dividends derived by way of Netherlands-resident (EII) UCITS, because the Netherlands does not provide for an additional measure to establish that the tax status of the unitholders is taken into account for the application of exemptions and reduced tax rates available under the tax treaties between the countries studied.

Nevertheless, the source taxation of income derived by resident and non-resident UCITS in Austria, Germany, the Netherlands, and the United Kingdom shows substantial differences. It is affected by the restriction of an exemption at source or a refund of the tax withheld to resident UCITS only. These differences in the source taxation are further increased because of the application of a reduced tax rate on income derived by some non-resident UCITS. As the reduced tax rates are not applied to every non-resident UCITS, the source taxation also differs between non-resident UCITS.

4.3. COMPARISON OF THE TAXATION OF INCOME FROM INVESTMENTS SITUATED OUTSIDE THE JURISDICTION OF AUSTRIA, GERMANY, THE NETHERLANDS, AND THE UNITED KINGDOM

As is shown in Table 4.2, some countries studied failed to provide for measures to establish that the tax treaties are applied to income derived by way of UCITS as if the unitholders had invested directly. The application of the tax treaties to Austrian, German, Netherlands, and UK-resident UCITS therefore varies.

Table 4.2. Application of Tax Treaties

UCITS Country	*Method*	*Advantage for Unitholders*	*Disadvantage for Unitholders*
Austria	Application of tax treaties to unitholders	As if invested directly	Individual and corporate unitholders have to file individual requests to each source state for a refund
Germany	Denial of tax treaties to UCITS, although in some cases the tax treaties are applied to the unitholders	–	More severe taxation for individual and corporate unitholders
Netherlands			
– Exempt Investment Institution (EII)	Denial of tax treaties to UCITS and unitholders	–	More severe taxation for individual and corporate unitholders
– Fiscal Investment Institution (FII)	Application of tax treaties to UCITS	Individual and corporate unitholders do not have to file requests to each	–

Table 4.2. (cont'd)

UCITS Country	*Method*	*Advantage for Unitholders*	*Disadvantage for Unitholders*
		source state for a refund Enables non-resident unitholders to tax treaty shopping Tax advantage for exempt corporate unitholders	
– Transparent Investment Institution (TII)	Application of tax treaties to unitholders	As if invested directly	Individual and corporate unitholders have to file individual requests to each source state for a refund
United Kingdom	Application of tax treaties to UCITS, although in some cases the tax treaties are applied to the unitholders	Individual and corporate unitholders do not have to file requests to each source state for a refund Enables non-resident unitholders to tax treaty shopping Tax advantage for exempt corporate unitholders	-

4.3.1. Availability of Instruments to Establish Taxation as If Invested Directly for Resident UCITS

4.3.1.1. Transparency

Austrian-resident UCITS and Netherlands-resident (TII) UCITS are transparent under the domestic laws of Austria and the Netherlands, respectively. Any income derived by way of these UCITS is considered to be that of the unitholders.

The application of a tax treaty is, therefore, limited to those unitholders that are liable to tax in the state of residence. The application of tax treaties for income derived through Austrian-resident UCITS and Netherlands-resident (TII) UCITS does, thus, not differ from a direct investment.

Example 4.7

Y, a corporate unitholder residing in Austria, derives interest from bonds issued by the Government of Italy for an amount of EUR 100,000 by way of Z, an Austrian-resident UCITS. Assume that the interest would have been subject to withholding tax at rate of 12.5% under the domestic laws of Italy. For this kind of interest, the Italian tax treaty with Austria provides for an exemption in the source state. Because Y is liable to tax in Austria, the part of the interest that is attributable to Y is in accordance with the tax treaty exempt from withholding tax in Italy. This would have been different if Y was subjectively exempt from corporate income tax. In that case, the exemption in the tax treaty with Italy does not apply to the unitholder because the unitholder is not liable to tax in its residence state.

The tax treaty in question is the tax treaty between the source state and the residence state of the unitholder. Non-resident unitholders thus apply the tax treaty concluded by the source state with the residence state of this unitholder. Thus, this does not differ from a direct investment.

Example 4.8

Where a non-resident corporate unitholder holds units in Y of the example above, the interest paid by the Italian Government remains exempt in the source state only in the presence of an exemption in the Italian tax treaty with the residence state of the unitholder, if any.

4.3.1.2. Absence of Any Measure to Establish Transparency

Germany, the Netherlands, and the United Kingdom have failed to establish that tax treaties are applied for income derived by way of German-resident UCITS, Netherlands-resident (EII/FII) UCITS, and UK-resident UCITS as if the unitholders had invested directly. Any income derived by these UCITS is considered to be that of the UCITS. As a result, the tax status of the UCITS is taken into account by the application of the tax treaty instead of that of the unitholder. The tax treaties are therefore applied only for income derived by way of these UCITS if the latter are (fully) liable to tax in the UCITS country. Otherwise, the application of the tax treaties to the UCITS is denied by source states.

A UCITS is often not considered to be (fully) liable to tax if it does not qualify as a corporate entity that is subject to (corporate) income tax or it is subjectively exempt from (corporate) income tax. This is generally the case for German-resident UCITS and Netherlands-resident (EII) UCITS. As a result of the denial of the tax treaties to these UCITS, the taxation at source of income is more severe for individual and corporate unitholders than a direct investment to the extent that the taxation at source of the income under the local tax legislation without the application of the tax treaty exceeds the taxation with the application of the tax treaties. It does not, however, differ from a direct investment for exempt corporate unitholders except for the application of Netherlands tax treaties that explicitly consider specific exempt corporate unitholders, pension funds, or charities, to be a person for tax treaty purposes.

Example 4.9

Some of the units of Y, a Netherlands-resident (EII) UCITS that is subjectively exempt from corporate income tax, are held by Z, an individual unitholder who also resides in the Netherlands. Y is paid an amount of EUR 100,000 as interest in respect to bonds issued by the Italian Government. An amount of EUR 12,500 as tax is withheld on the interest. The exemption in the Italian tax treaty with the Netherlands is denied by Italy because Y is subjectively exempt from tax in the Netherlands.

Apart from taxation under the general rules, a UCITS seems to be considered (fully) liable to tax in the UCITS country in case it is subject to a reduced tax base or a reduced tax rate. This is the case for Netherlands-resident (FII) UCITS and UK-resident UCITS. The application of tax treaties for income derived by way of these UCITS does not for individual and corporate unitholders differ from a direct investment. Nevertheless, an investment through these UCITS may be considered more convenient and practical than a direct investment because individual and corporate unitholders do not have to file individual requests to each source state for a refund of the part of the withholding tax that is not charged in accordance with the applicable tax treaty.

Example 4.10

Y, a corporate unitholder, derives by way of Z, a UK-resident UCITS, interest from bonds issued by the Government of Italy. Italy charges a withholding tax on interest of, for example, 12.5%. The Italian tax treaty with the United Kingdom provides for an exemption at source for interest derived from the government of the other Contracting State. The interest is, as is the case for a direct investment, exempt from tax in the source state, because the Italian tax treaty with the United Kingdom applies to the UCITS.

The application of the tax treaties to Netherlands-resident (FII) UCITS and UK-resident UCITS results in an advantage for exempt corporate unitholders compared to a direct investment. In that case, the tax treaties would generally not have been applied by the source state, because these unitholders are exempt from tax. An investment by way of these UCITS is therefore more attractive for exempt corporate unitholders than a direct investment.

Example 4.11

Y, an exempt corporate unitholder, holds units in Z, a Netherlands-resident (FII) UCITS. Z derives interest from bonds issued by the Government of Italy. Italy charges a withholding tax on interest of, for example, 12.5%. The Italian tax treaty with the Netherlands provides for an exemption at source for interest paid by the government of the other Contracting State. The interest, unlike a direct investment by Y, remains exempt from tax in the source state, because the Italian tax treaty with the Netherlands applies to Z.

Because the tax treaties of the Netherlands and the United Kingdom are applied to these UCITS, it is possible for non-resident unitholders to take advantage of the tax treaty network of the Netherlands and the United Kingdom if one of these countries has concluded more tax treaties with countries in a certain region or with a specific country that has not concluded a tax treaty with the unitholder's residence state. The same applies in case a clause in one of the tax treaties of the Netherlands or the United Kingdom is more attractive than those of the tax treaties of the unitholder's residence state.

Example 4.12

X, a corporate unitholder residing in Germany, participates in Y, a Netherlands-resident (FII) UCITS. Y is paid interest by a Brazilian-resident company, Z. The interest is subject to Brazilian withholding tax at a rate of, for example, 20%. The Brazilian tax treaty with the Netherlands reduces the tax rate to 15%. In the case of a direct investment, the source state's right to tax would not be reduced, because Germany, the residence state of X, has not concluded a tax treaty with Brazil. An investment by way of Y results in a tax advantage for X.

4.4. CONCLUSION

The application of tax treaties for income derived by way of Austrian-, German-, Netherlands-, and UK-resident UCITS, and thus the source taxation on such income, shows some considerable differences. Transparency, the instrument used by Austria and for (TII) UCITS by the Netherlands, achieves that tax treaties are applied to income derived by way of UCITS as if resident and non-resident unitholders had invested directly. In the absence of any instrument to establish such transparency, the application of tax treaties for income derived by way of German-resident UCITS, Netherlands-resident (EII/FII) UCITS, and UK-resident UCITS depends on the subjective and objective tax liability of these UCITS instead of that of the unitholders. The subjective and objective tax liability of German, Netherlands, and UK-resident UCITS differs, and thus so does the application of tax treaties to income derived by way of these UCITS.

Furthermore, an investment in the units of Netherlands-resident (FII) UCITS or UK-resident UCITS may enable non-resident individual and corporate investors to take advantage of the tax treaty network of the Netherlands and the United Kingdom, respectively. An investment in the units of these UCITS may result in a tax advantage compared to a direct investment if the Netherlands or the United Kingdom has more tax treaties with countries in a certain region or a tax treaty with a particular country that has not concluded a tax treaty with the residence state of an individual or corporate portfolio investor. The same applies in case a source state's right to tax is more restricted in one of the tax treaties of these two countries than in the tax treaty of the residence state of a portfolio investor.

Chapter 5 discusses the consequences of the differences in the source taxation of the income derived by way of UCITS for the cross-border trade in units of UCITS between Austria, Germany, the Netherlands, and the United Kingdom.

Chapter 5

Distortions to the Cross-Border Trade in Units of Undertakings for Collective Investment in Transferable Securities Caused by Differences in the Source Taxation

The countries studied have failed to establish that the trade in units of undertakings for collective investment in transferable securities (UCITS) takes place under the same conditions for investments in securities and other financial instruments that are situated within their jurisdiction (domestic investments). The denial of available exemption of withholding tax under the domestic laws of the countries studied hinders non-resident UCITS by attracting capital in the countries studied. The denial discourages investors to make use of non-resident UCITS, because income paid to non-resident UCITS is taxed more heavily in the countries studied than that paid to resident UCITS.

A level playing field for UCITS is also lacking in the case of investments in securities and other financial instruments that are situated outside the countries studied (foreign investments). Differences in the number, provisions, and application of tax treaties distort the trade in units of non-resident UCITS in the countries studied.

5.1. INTRODUCTION

In the absence of any uniform rules, the taxation at source of income as shown in Chapters 3 and 4 differs substantially for UCITS residing in Austria, Germany, the Netherlands, and the United Kingdom. These differences distort the cross-border trade in units of UCITS because income derived by way of non-resident UCITS

Table 5.1 Taxation at Source of Income from Investments

	Taxation at Source of Income from Investments Situated Within the Unitholder Country	Taxation at Source of Income from Investments Situated Outside Austria, Germany, the Netherlands, and the United Kingdom		
		Application of Tax Treaties	Exceptional Provisions in Tax Treaties	Number of Tax Treaties
Austrian unitholders UCITS				
German-resident UCITS	–[a]/0	–[c]/0[d,e]	0[d]	0[d]
Netherlands-resident (EII) UCITS	–[a]/0	–[f]/0[e]	N/A	N/A
Netherlands-resident (FII) UCITS	+/0[b]	+[e]/0[f]	–[h]/+[i]/0	–[j]/+[k]/0
Netherlands-resident (TII) UCITS	–[a]/0	0	0	0
UK-resident UCITS	+/0[b]	+[e]/0[f,g]	–[h/]+[i]/0	–/+[k]/0
German unitholders UCITS				
Austrian-resident UCITS	–/0[l]	+[c]/0[d,e]	0	0
Netherlands-resident (EII) UCITS	–0[l]	–[d]/0[c,e]	N/A	N/A
Netherlands-resident (FII) UCITS	–/0[l]	+[c,e]/0[d]	–[h]/+[i]/0	–[j]/+[k]/0
Netherlands-resident (TII) UCITS	–/0[l]	+[c]/0[d,e]	0	0
UK-resident UCITS	–/0[l]	+[c,e]/0[d,g]	–[h]/+[i]/0	–[j]/+[k]/0
Netherlands unitholders UCITS*				
Austrian-resident UCITS	–/0[m]	–[e]/0[f]	0	0
German-resident UCITS	–/0[m]	–[c,e]/0[d]	0[d]	0[d]
UK-resident UCITS	–/0[n]	–[g]/0[e,f]	–[h]/+[i]/0	–[j]/+[k]/0

UK unitholders UCITS				
Austrian-resident UCITS	$-^{o}/0$	$-^{e}/0^{f,g}$	0	0
German-resident UCITS	$-^{o}/0$	$-^{c,e}/0^{d,g}$	0^{d}	0^{d}
Netherlands-resident (EII) UCITS	$-^{p}/0$	$-^{e,f}/0^{g}$	N/A	N/A
Netherlands-resident (FII) UCITS	$+^{q}/0$	$+^{g}/0^{e,f}$	$-^{h}/+^{i}/0$	$-^{j}/+^{k}/0$
Netherlands-resident (TII) UCITS	$-^{o}/0$	$-^{e}/0^{f,g}$	0	0

+ Means that the cross-border trading is facilitated as a result of a tax advantage.

0 Signifies that the cross-border trading is not affected in the absence of a tax advantage or tax disadvantage.

– Stands for a tax disadvantage that hinders the cross-border trading.

N/A, Not available or not relevant.

[a] Individual and corporate unitholders for interest from bonds and debentures.

[b] Exempt corporate unitholders in the case of interest from bonds and debentures.

[c] Individual and corporate unitholders for investments in states that do not assume German-resident UCITS to be transparent.

[d] For individual and corporate unitholders if the source state assumes that German-resident UCITS are transparent.

[e] Exempt corporate unitholders.

[f] Individual and corporate unitholders.

[g] Exempt corporate unitholders for investments in states that assume UK-resident UCITS of the trust type to be transparent.

[h] In case the tax treaty of unitholder country restricts the source state's right further than the one of the UCITS country.

[i] Where the source state's right to tax is further reduced by a tax treaty of the UCITS country than that of the unitholder country.

[j] Where the unitholder country has concluded a tax treaty with a state in which the UCITS invests and the UCITS country has not.

[k] If the UCITS invests in a state that has concluded a tax treaty with the UCITS country while there is no tax treaty with unitholder country.

[l] In the case of interest from bonds and other debt securities other than from convertible or profit-sharing ones.

[m] For pension funds and charities if the units of the UCITS are not considered freely transferable.

[n] For pension funds and charities if the units of the UCITS of the trust type are not considered freely transferable.

[o] In the case of individual unitholders for interest paid by a deposit-taker.

[p] For individual unitholders in the case of interest paid by a deposit-taker to a UCITS of the contractual type.

[q] For yearly interest and UK public revenue dividends.

* In comparison with a Netherlands-resident (FII) UCITS. After all, most Netherlands-resident UCITS have opted to be treated as a fiscal investment institution (FII) for tax purposes.

from portfolio investments is, compared to that derived by way of resident UCITS, in a significant number of cases subject to either more severe taxation at source of income (tax disadvantage) or a lesser taxation (tax advantage). The conditions of competition between UCITS in the countries studied are therefore not alike.

5.1.1. Tabular Overview

An overview of the distortions is provided in Table 5.1. The table shows, with respect to Austrian, German, Netherlands, and UK unitholders, which tax disadvantages or tax advantages arise from the differences in source taxation. From the table follows that the occurrence of a tax disadvantage or tax advantage is connected with the investment policy of a non-resident UCITS, its residence state, or the tax liability of the unitholder.

Sections 5.2 and 5.3 present a more detailed explanation of the origins of the tax disadvantages and tax advantages shown in Table 5.1.

5.2. TAXATION AT SOURCE OF INCOME DERIVED FROM INVESTMENTS SITUATED WITHIN THE UNITHOLDER COUNTRY

5.2.1. Introduction

The amount of withholding tax that is charged on income derived by way of resident and non-resident UCITS from investments situated within the jurisdiction of the countries studied (domestic investments) is not the same. In some cases, the source taxation is affected by the restriction of exemption from withholding tax at source or a refund of the tax withheld to resident UCITS only. In other cases, it is affected by the application of a reduced tax rate to some non-resident UCITS. The competition among UCITS does not therefore take place under the same conditions for investments situated within the jurisdiction of the countries studied, which may affect the trade in units of UCITS.

For these reasons, non-resident UCITS, as illustrated in Figure 5.1, may have difficulty in marketing units to individuals and institutional investors in the countries studied. As a result of more severe source taxation, investors may be discouraged to use non-resident UCITS for domestic investments.

5.2.2. Cross-Border Trading of Units in Austria

5.2.2.1. Austrian Unitholder and German-Resident UCITS

The taxation at source of dividends does not hinder or support the trading in units of German-resident UCITS to Austrian investors for domestic investments in equity.

Figure 5.1 A Restriction of an Exemption at Source to Resident UCITS Discourages Individuals and Institutional Investors to Make Use of Non-resident UCITS for Investments within *the Countries Studied*

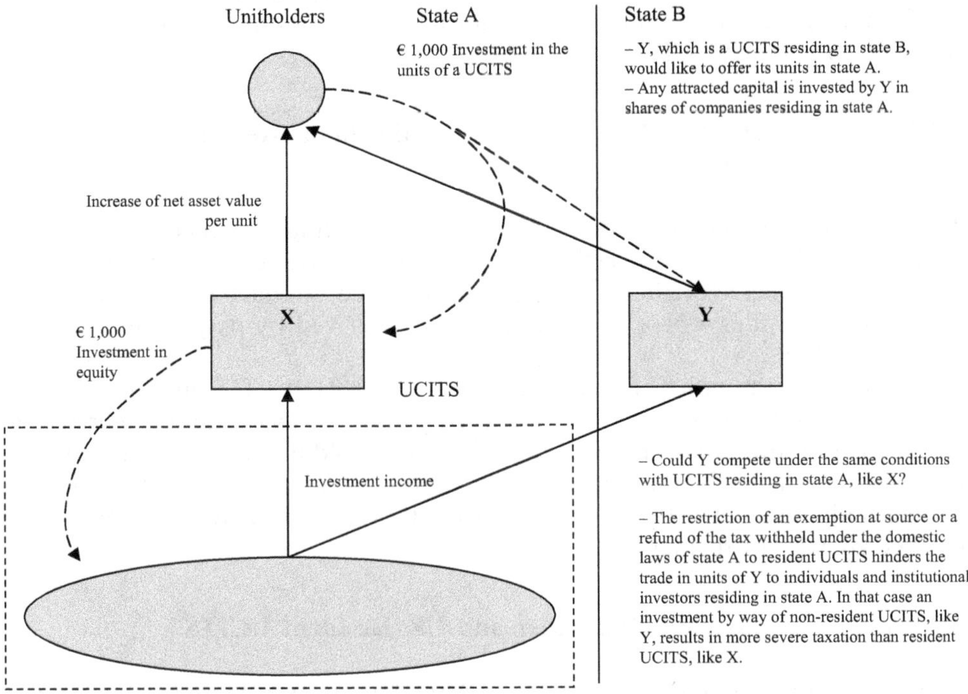

The taxation at source of income derived by these UCITS does not differ from that of resident UCITS. Investments by way of German-resident UCITS are therefore as attractive to Austrian investors as those made by way of resident UCITS.

The trade in units of German-resident UCITS to Austrian individual and corporate investors for domestic investments in bonds and debentures is, however, hindered by the absence of an exemption from withholding tax on interest paid to non-resident UCITS. The taxation at source of interest paid to these UCITS does for that reason exceed that of interest paid to resident UCITS. Austrian investors are therefore discouraged to invest in the units of German-resident UCITS for domestic investments in bonds and debentures.

The taxation at source of interest does not, however, affect the trade in units of German-resident UCITS to Austrian exempt corporate bodies for domestic investments in bonds and debentures. As with a direct investment, exempt corporate bodies are entitled to an exemption from withholding tax so that the taxation of interest derived by way of German-resident UCITS does not differ for these unitholders from that of interest derived by way of resident UCITS.

5.2.2.2. Austrian Unitholder and Netherlands-Resident (EII/TII) UCITS

The taxation at source affects the trade in units of Netherlands-resident (EII/TII) UCITS under the same conditions, and for the same reasons, as discussed earlier for German-resident UCITS.

5.2.2.3. Austrian Unitholder and Netherlands-Resident (FII) UCITS

The taxation at source of dividends facilitates the trading in units of Netherlands-resident (FII) UCITS in Austria for investments in Austrian equity. Under Austrian tax treaty with the Netherlands, the tax rate at source is reduced to 15% and a tax rate of 25% applies where such dividends are derived by way of an Austrian-resident UCITS.

Trading in the units of Netherlands-resident (FII) UCITS in Austria is not affected by the taxation at source of interest paid by an Austrian-resident debtor. Interest paid to these UCITS is exempt from withholding tax under the Austrian tax treaty with the Netherlands. The taxation of interest derived by way of Netherlands-resident (FII) UCITS therefore does not differ from that of interest derived by way of resident UCITS.

5.2.2.4. Austrian Unitholder and UK-Resident UCITS

Trading in units of UK-resident UCITS in Austria is affected as subject to the same conditions as those discussed earlier for Netherlands-resident (FII) UCITS.

5.2.3. Cross-Border Trading of Units in Germany

5.2.3.1. German Unitholder and Austrian-Resident UCITS

The absence of an exemption or a refund from withholding tax on dividends paid to non-resident UCITS hinders Austrian-resident UCITS in attracting capital from German investors for domestic investments. Dividends paid to non-resident UCITS are therefore subject to more taxation than are resident UCITS. German investors are therefore discouraged from investing in the units of Austrian-resident UCITS.

The trade in units of Austrian-resident UCITS to German investors for domestic investments in bonds and debentures is, nevertheless, not affected by the taxation at source of interest. The application of the exemption at source of interest does not differ from that of German-resident UCITS.

5.2.3.2. German Unitholder and Netherlands-Resident (EII/TII) UCITS

The taxation at source of income from investments situated within Germany affects the trade in units of Netherlands-resident (EII/TII) UCITS under the same conditions and for the same reasons as discussed previously for Austrian-resident UCITS.

5.2.3.3. German Unitholder and Netherlands-Resident (FII) UCITS or UK-Resident UCITS

Trading in the units of Netherlands-resident (FII) and UK-resident UCITS in Germany is hindered by the taxation at source of dividends under the same conditions and for the same reasons as discussed earlier for Austrian-resident UCITS.

The taxation at source of interest derived from bonds or other debt securities issued by German-resident companies does not affect Netherlands- and UK-resident UCITS to attract capital in Germany. Interest paid to these UCITS remains exempt from tax under the German tax treaty with the Netherlands and the United Kingdom. The attractiveness of Netherlands- and UK-resident UCITS for domestic investments in bonds and debt securities thus does not differ from that of German-resident UCITS.

5.2.4. Cross-Border Trading of Units in the Netherlands

5.2.4.1. Dutch Unitholder and Austrian-Resident UCITS

The absence of a refund of the tax withheld at source of dividends paid by a Netherlands-resident company hinders trading in the units of Austrian-resident UCITS to individual and corporate investors in the Netherlands. The tax withheld at source on such dividends is not refundable, unlike for Netherlands-resident (FII) UCITS. Austrian-resident UCITS are therefore less attractive to Netherlands investors than Netherlands-resident (FII) UCITS.

Trading in units of Austrian-resident UCITS to exempt corporate investors in the Netherlands is not affected by taxation at source of dividends paid by Netherlands-resident companies. The tax withheld at source is, because of the transparency of Austrian-resident UCITS, refundable for Netherlands exempt corporate unitholders. This result does not differ from that of Netherlands-resident (FII) UCITS.

5.2.4.2. Dutch Unitholder and German-Resident UCITS or UK-Resident UCITS

Taxation at source of dividends paid by a Netherlands-resident company hinders trading in units of German- and UK-resident UCITS in the Netherlands. The tax withheld at source of such dividends is, unlike for Netherlands-resident (FII) UCITS, not refundable to non-resident UCITS. This results in a tax disadvantage for German- and UK-resident UCITS compared to Netherlands-resident (FII) UCITS.

5.2.5. Cross-Border Trading of Units in the United Kingdom

5.2.5.1. UK Unitholder and Austrian-Resident UCITS

Trading in units of Austrian-resident UCITS in the United Kingdom is not affected by taxation at source of yearly interest and UK public revenue dividends. Yearly interest and UK public revenue dividends are subject to a 20% withholding tax at the time of receipt. This does not, however, differ from an investment in the units of UK-resident UCITS. The attractiveness of the units of Austrian-resident UCITS does not therefore differ for UK investors from that of units in UK-resident UCITS.

Taxation at source of interest paid by UK deposit-takers, on the other hand, hinders trading in units of Austrian-resident UCITS to individual investors in the United Kingdom. As a result of the transparency of Austrian-resident UCITS, any interest paid by deposit-takers to Austrian-resident UCITS is considered to be that of the unitholders. Therefore, the part of the interest considered to be derived by individual unitholders is, unlike in the case of such interest is paid to UK-resident UCITS, not exempt from withholding tax. UK investors will therefore find Austrian-resident UCITS less attractive than UK-resident UCITS.

Trading in nits of Austrian-resident UCITS to (exempt) corporate investors is not affected by the withholding tax for interest paid by deposit-takers. Austrian-resident UCITS are considered transparent under the domestic laws of the United Kingdom, so these unitholders are entitled to an exemption. The taxation of interest paid by deposit-takers does not therefore differ from UK-resident UCITS.

5.2.5.2. UK Unitholder and German-Resident UCITS or Netherlands-Resident (EII/TII) UCITS of the Contractual Type

The trade in the units of German-resident UCITS and Netherlands-resident (EII/TII) UCITS of the contractual type in the United Kingdom is affected under the same conditions, and for the same reasons, as discussed earlier for Austrian-resident UCITS.

5.2.5.3. UK Unitholder and Netherlands-Resident (EII/FII) UCITS of the Corporate Type

Taxation at source of yearly interest and UK public revenue dividends does not affect trading in units of UCITS Netherlands-resident (EII/FII) UCITS of the corporate type. The taxation does not differ from that with UK-resident UCITS. An investment in the units of these UCITS does not therefore differ from that of UK-resident UCITS.

Trading in units of Netherlands-resident (EII/FII) UCITS of the corporate type in the United Kingdom is not affected by the exemption at source of interest derived from UK deposit-takers. Just as for UK-resident UCITS, interest derived by Netherlands-resident (EII/FII) UCITS of the corporate type remains exempt from withholding tax. The attractiveness of these UCITS thus does not differ from UK-resident UCITS.

5.3. TAXATION AT SOURCE OF INCOME DERIVED FROM INVESTMENTS SITUATED OUTSIDE AUSTRIA, GERMANY, THE NETHERLANDS, AND THE UNITED KINGDOM

5.3.1. INTRODUCTION

Not only does the withholding tax charged on income derived through UCITS from investments situated within the jurisdiction of the countries studied (domestic investments) differ among UCITS, but also that of income derived from investments situated outside the jurisdiction of these countries (foreign investments). The source taxation is affected by differences in the number, contents, and application of tax treaties. The conditions of competition between UCITS are thus not the same for investments outside the countries studied.

The trade in units of non-resident UCITS in the countries studied may be hindered (or supported, as the case may be), as illustrated in Figure 5.2. Resident individuals and (exempt) corporate investors may be discouraged (or encouraged) to make use of non-resident UCITS for foreign investments because of differences in the application, contents, and number of tax treaties.

5.3.2. CROSS-BORDER TRADING OF UNITS IN AUSTRIA

5.3.2.1. Austrian Unitholder and German-Resident UCITS

Trading in units of German-resident UCITS to individual and corporate investors in Austria is hindered by the denial of tax treaties to UCITS and unitholders. In contrast to Austria, Germany does not provide for any measures to apply tax treaties to German-resident UCITS as if the unitholders had invested directly. Hence, the tax treaties are denied because these UCITS are not liable to tax. German-resident UCITS are therefore less attractive to Austrian individual and corporate investors than Austrian-resident UCITS.

The denial of tax treaties to UCITS and unitholders does not affect the trading in units of German-resident UCITS to exempt corporate investors in Austria.

Figure 5.2 Individuals and Institutional Investors May Be Discourage to Invest in the Units of Non-resident UCITS Due to Differences in the Application, the Contents and the Number of Tax Treaties

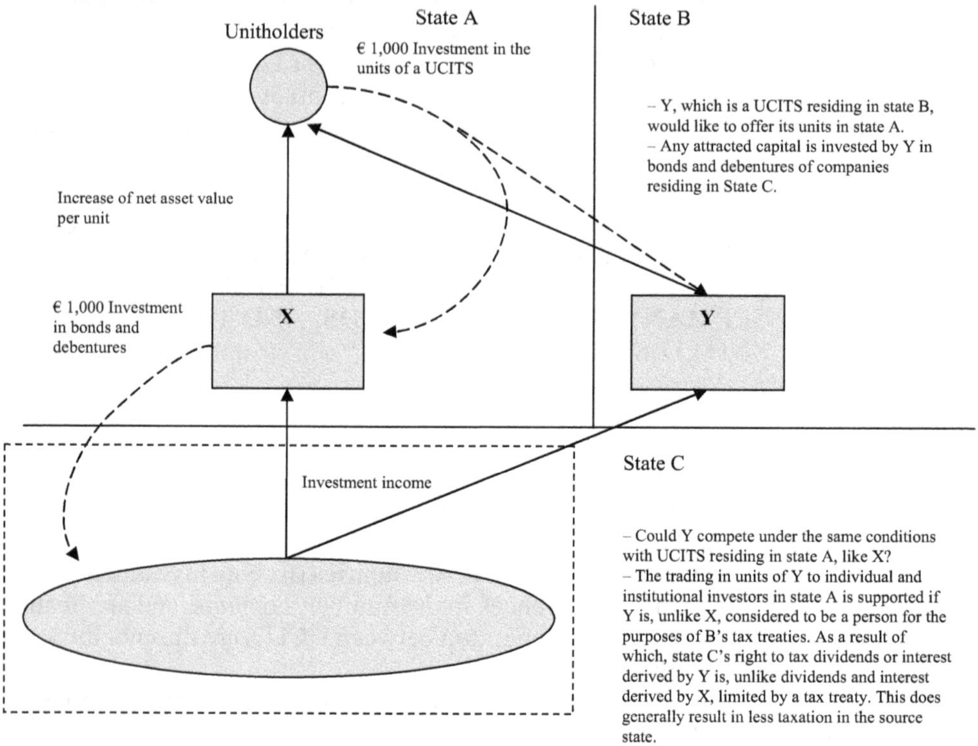

After all, it does not differ from an investment in the units of an Austrian-resident UCITS.

If a source state, however, assumes wrongly that German-resident UCITS are transparent, the application of the tax treaties as if the unitholders had invested directly does not affect the trading in the units of these UCITS by individual and corporate investors in Austria. In such a case, the tax treaties are applied to individual and corporate unitholders of German-resident UCITS. This does not differ from an investment in the units of Austrian-resident UCITS. An overview of the source states that assume German-resident UCITS to be transparent could not be found.

Trading in units of German-resident UCITS by individual and corporate investors in Austria is not affected by the number of tax treaties concluded by Germany. The latter is of no importance where a source state assumes that German-resident UCITS are transparent. In this case, the Austrian tax treaties are applied to individual and corporate investors residing in Austria. This does not differ from an investment in the units of Austrian-resident UCITS.

The incorrect assumption by some source states that German-resident UCITS are transparent does not affect trading in the units of these UCITS by exempt corporate unitholders in Austria. In this case the unitholders are, as is the case for Austrian-resident UCITS, considered to be the beneficiaries of the income. The attractiveness of units in a German-resident UCITS therefore does not differ from that of units in an Austrian-resident UCITS.

5.3.2.2. Austrian Unitholder and Netherlands-Resident (EII) UCITS

The conditions under which the trading in units of Netherlands-resident (EII) UCITS is affected by the denial of tax treaties to these UCITS, and the unitholders do not differ from those discussed earlier for German-resident UCITS.

5.3.2.3. Austrian Unitholder and Netherlands-Resident (FII) UCITS

Trading in units of Netherlands-resident (FII) UCITS to individual and corporate unitholders in Austria is not affected by the application of tax treaties to these UCITS. Netherlands-resident UCITS are considered to be a person for tax treaty purposes. The tax treaties are therefore applied by source states to these UCITS. For individual and corporate unitholders, this does not differ from an investment in the units of Austrian-resident UCITS.

The application of tax treaties supports Netherlands-resident (FII) UCITS to attract capital from exempt corporate investors in Austria. The tax treaties are still applied to Netherlands-resident UCITS if its units are held by exempt corporate investors residing in Austria. An investment in the units of Netherlands-resident UCITS therefore results in a tax advantage compared to an investment in the units of Austrian-resident UCITS.

Trading in units of Netherlands-resident (FII) UCITS to individual and corporate unitholders in Austria is affected by differences in the contents of the Austrian and Netherlands tax treaties. In such a case the taxation at source of the income from the underlying investments of Netherlands-resident UCITS may be more (or less) than that of the income from the underlying investments of Austrian-resident UCITS.

Trading in units of Netherlands-resident (FII) UCITS in Austria is supported where the Netherlands has concluded more tax treaties with countries in a specific region than Austria or in the presence of a Netherlands tax treaty with a particular country that has concluded a tax treaty with Austria. In this case the income derived from the investments of Netherlands-resident (FII) UCITS situated in these countries or in the particular country may be subject to less tax at source. The tax treaty network of the Netherlands includes tax treaties with countries that have not concluded a tax treaty with Austria. These are Aruba, Bangladesh, Ghana, Iceland, Jordan, Malawi, Netherlands Antilles, Nigeria, Serbia and Montenegro, Sri Lanka, Surinam, Taiwan, Uganda, Vietnam, Zambia, and Zimbabwe.

An investment in the units of Netherlands-resident UCITS results in a tax advantage for investments in these countries compared to Austrian-resident UCITS.

In case that the Netherlands has concluded fewer tax treaties with countries in a specific region than Austria, or in the absence of a Netherlands tax treaty with a particular country that has a tax treaty with Austria, the trading in units of Netherlands-resident (FII) UCITS to Austrian individual and corporate investors is hindered. The taxation at source of income from the investments of Netherlands-resident (FII) UCITS may then be more than in case of an investment in the units of Austrian-resident UCITS. Austria has concluded tax treaties with Algeria, Belize, Cuba, Cyprus, Iran, Liechtenstein, Nepal, San Marino, Saudi Arabia, and the United Arab Emirates, whereas the Netherlands has not. An investment in the units of Netherlands-resident UCITS therefore results in a tax disadvantage for investments in these countries compared to Austrian-resident UCITS.

5.3.2.4. Austrian Unitholder and Netherlands-Resident (TII) UCITS

The application of tax treaties does not hinder or support the trade in units of Netherlands-resident (TII) UCITS in Austria. It does not differ from an investment in Austrian-resident UCITS. The conditions of competition among Austrian-resident and Netherlands-resident (TII) UCITS therefore do not differ for foreign investments.

5.3.2.5. Austrian Unitholder and UK-Resident UCITS

Trading in UK-resident UCITS in Austria is affected by the application of tax treaties to these UCITS under the same conditions as discussed above for Netherlands-resident (FII) UCITS.

Differences in the contents of the Austrian and UK tax treaties affect trading in units of UK-resident UCITS to individual and corporate unitholders in Austria. In that case the taxation at source of the income from the underlying investments of UK-resident UCITS may differ from that of the income from the same underlying investments of Austrian-resident UCITS.

The number of tax treaties concluded by the United Kingdom supports the trading in units of UK-resident UCITS in Austria, because the United Kingdom has concluded substantially more tax treaties in respect to income and capital than Austria. The United Kingdom has, unlike Austria, concluded tax treaties with Antigua and Barbuda, Bangladesh, Bolivia, Bosnia-Herzegovina, Botswana, Brunei, Chile, Falkland Islands, Fiji, Gambia, Ghana, Grenada, Guernsey, Guyana, Iceland, Isle of Man, Ivory Coast, Jamaica, Jersey, Jordan, Kenya, Kiribati and Tuvalu, Lesotho, Malawi, Mauritius, Montserrat, Myanmar, Namibia, Nigeria, Oman, Papua New Guinea, St. Christopher and Nevis, Serbia and Montenegro, Sierra Leone, the Solomon Islands, Sri Lanka, Sudan, Swaziland, Taiwan, Uganda, Vietnam, Zambia, and Zimbabwe. An investment in the units of UK-resident

UCITS results in a tax advantage for investments in these countries compared to Austrian-resident UCITS.

Trading in units of UK-resident UCITS is, subject to the same conditions as discussed above for Netherlands-resident (FII) UCITS, hindered by the number of tax treaties concluded by the United Kingdom. Austria has concluded substantially fewer tax treaties than the United Kingdom. Nonetheless, it has concluded tax treaties with Algeria, Brazil, Cuba, Iran, Liechtenstein, Nepal, San Marino, Saudi Arabia, and the United Arab Emirates, whereas the United Kingdom has not. An investment in the units of UK-resident UCITS therefore results in a tax disadvantage for investments in these countries compared to Austrian-resident UCITS.

In case a source state wrongly assumes that UK-resident UCITS of the trust type are transparent, the trading in units of these UCITS to individual and corporate unitholders in Austria is affected by the application of tax treaties, as those discussed for German-resident UCITS earlier. An overview of the source states that assume UK-resident UCITS of the trust type to be transparent could, just as for German-resident UCITS, not be found.

5.3.3. CROSS-BORDER TRADING OF UNITS IN GERMANY

5.3.3.1. German Unitholder and Austrian-Resident UCITS

Trading in units of Austrian-resident UCITS to individual and corporate investors in Germany is facilitated by the application of tax treaties. Austrian-resident UCITS are considered to be transparent so that the application of the tax treaties depends on the tax liability of the unitholders. The tax treaties are therefore applied to individual and corporate unitholders of Austrian-resident UCITS as if they had invested directly. An investment in the units of Austrian-resident UCITS results in a tax advantage, because the tax treaties are not always applied by source states in the case of an investment in the units of German-resident UCITS. This is different only where German-resident UCITS are wrongly assumed to be transparent.

The application of tax treaties does not affect the trading in units of Austrian-resident UCITS to exempt corporate investors in Germany. The application of tax treaties is denied for exempt corporate unitholders of Austrian-resident UCITS. The application of tax treaties therefore does not differ from an investment in the units of German-resident UCITS.

5.3.3.2. German Unitholder and Netherlands-Resident (EII) UCITS

Trading of units of Netherlands-resident (EII) UCITS in Germany is not affected by the denial of tax treaties to these UCITS and the unitholders. This does not differ from German-resident UCITS.

The denial of tax treaties, however, hinders the trading of units in Netherlands-resident (EII) UCITS to individual and corporate unitholders in Germany for investments in states that wrongly assume German-resident UCITS to be transparent. These source states, unlike in the case of Netherlands-resident (EII) UCITS, apply their tax treaties to investors in German-resident UCITS. The units of Netherlands-resident (EII) UCITS are therefore less attractive than those of German-resident UCITS.

5.3.3.3. German Unitholder and Netherlands-Resident (FII) UCITS

The application of tax treaties to Netherlands-resident (FII) UCITS supports the trading of these UCITS in Germany. The tax treaties apply to Netherlands-resident (FII) UCITS, whereas they are often not applied by source states in the case of German-resident UCITS. For this reason, an investment in the units of Netherlands-resident UCITS results in a tax advantage compared to an investment in the units of German-resident UCITS.

Trading in units of Netherlands-resident (FII) UCITS to individual and corporate unitholders is not affected by the application of tax treaties to these UCITS for investments in states that assume German-resident UCITS to be transparent. In this case the tax treaties are also applied to income derived by way of German-resident UCITS, although the unitholders are, unlike investors in Netherlands-resident (FII) UCITS, considered the beneficiary. The latter, however, does not affect the result of the application of the applicable tax treaty.

Differences in the contents of the Netherlands and German tax treaties affect the trading in units of Netherlands-resident (FII) UCITS to individual and corporate unitholders in Germany. In such a case, taxation at the source of the income from the underlying investments of Netherlands-resident UCITS may be more (or less) than that of the income from the underlying investments of German-resident UCITS.

Trading in units of Netherlands-resident UCITS in Germany is supported where the Netherlands has concluded more tax treaties with countries in a specific region than Germany or in the presence of a Netherlands tax treaty with a particular country that has not concluded a tax treaty with Germany. The Netherlands has concluded tax treaties with Albania, Aruba, Brazil, Malawi, Netherlands Antilles, Nigeria, Surinam, Taiwan, and Uganda, whereas these countries do not have a tax treaty with Germany. For investments in these countries, Netherlands-resident (FII) UCITS are more attractive to German individual and corporate investors than German-resident UCITS.

If the Netherlands has concluded fewer tax treaties with the countries in a specific region than Germany, or in the absence of a Netherlands tax treaty with a particular country that has a tax treaty with Germany, the trading in units of Netherlands-resident (FII) UCITS to German individual and corporate investors is hindered. In that case, the units of Netherlands-resident (FII) UCITS are less attractive than the units of German-resident UCITS. Germany has, unlike the

Netherlands, concluded tax treaties with Bolivia, Cyprus, Ecuador, Iran, Ivory Coast, Jamaica, Kenya, Liberia, Mauritius, Namibia, Trinidad and Tobago, United Arab Emirates, and Uruguay. This is, however, the case only where these countries apply the tax treaties to individual and corporate unitholders of German-resident UCITS.

5.3.3.4. German Unitholder and Netherlands-Resident (TII) UCITS

The conditions under which the trade in units of Netherlands-resident (TII) UCITS is affected by the application of tax treaties to these UCITS and the unitholders do not differ from those discussed above for Austrian-resident UCITS.

5.3.3.5. German Unitholder and UK-Resident UCITS

The application of tax treaties to UK-resident UCITS supports the trading in the units of these UCITS in Germany for the same reasons as discussed above for Netherlands-resident (FII) UCITS.

If, however, a UK-resident UCITS invests in a country that wrongly assumes that German-resident UCITS are transparent, the application of the tax treaty to these UCITS does not facilitate the trading in the units of these UCITS to individual and corporate investors in Germany. In that case the tax treaty is applied to the individual and corporate unitholders of German-resident UCITS as they are liable to tax. The attractiveness of UK-resident UCITS in such a case does not differ from German-resident UCITS.

Where the contents of the German and UK tax treaties differ, the trading in units of UK-resident UCITS to individual and corporate unitholders in Germany is affected. In this case the taxation at the source of the income from the underlying investments of UK-resident UCITS may be more (or less) than that of the income from the underlying investments of German-resident UCITS.

Trading in units of UK-resident UCITS is supported where the United Kingdom has concluded more tax treaties with countries in a specific region than Germany or in the presence of an UK tax treaty with a particular country that has not concluded a tax treaty with Germany. The United Kingdom has, in contrast to Germany, concluded tax treaties with Antigua and Barbuda, Barbados, Belize, Botswana, Brunei, Chile, Falkland Islands, Fiji, Gambia, Grenada, Guernsey, Guyana, Isle of Man, Jersey, Jordan, Kiribati and Tuvalu, Lesotho, Malawi, Montserrat, Myanmar, Nigeria, Oman, Papua New Guinea, St. Christopher and Nevis, Sierra Leone, the Solomon Islands, Sudan, Swaziland, Taiwan, and Uganda. An investment in the units of UK-resident UCITS results in a tax advantage for investments in these countries compared to German-resident UCITS.

Where the United Kingdom has concluded fewer tax treaties with the countries in a specific region than Germany, or in the absence of a tax treaty with a particular country that has one with Germany, the trading in units of UK-resident UCITS to individual and corporate investors in Germany is hindered.

Germany has concluded tax treaties with Armenia, Ecuador, Iran, Kyrgyzstan, Liberia, United Arab Emirates, and Uruguay, whereas the United Kingdom has not. An investment in the units of German-resident UCITS is, for investments in these countries, more attractive to individual and corporate unitholders than that of UK-resident UCITS.

A few source states wrongly assume UK-resident UCITS of the trust type to be transparent. Trading in the units of these UCITS to individual and corporate unitholders in Germany is nevertheless facilitated for investments in these countries. In the case of German-resident UCITS, the tax treaties are often not applied. UK-resident UCITS of the trust type that are wrongfully assumed to be transparent are therefore more attractive to individual and corporate unitholders than German-resident UCITS.

The assumption of a source state for purpose of the application of the tax treaty that an UK-resident UCITS of the trust type is transparent does not affect the trading in the units of these UCITS to exempt corporate unitholders in Germany. In such a case these investors are not entitled to the benefits of the tax treaty because they are not liable to tax. However, this does not differ from an investment in the units of German-resident UCITS.

5.3.4. Cross-Border Trading of Units in the Netherlands

5.3.4.1. Dutch Unitholder and Austrian-Resident UCITS

Trading in the units of Austrian-resident UCITS to individual and corporate investors in the Netherlands is not affected by the application of tax treaties to the unitholders of these UCITS. The source state applies the Netherlands tax treaties to Netherlands individual and corporate unitholders of Austrian-resident UCITS. This does not differ from an investment in the units of Netherlands-resident (FII) UCITS.

The application of tax treaties to the unitholders hinders the trading in units of Austrian-resident UCITS to exempt corporate unitholders in the Netherlands. The application of tax treaties is denied to Netherlands exempt corporate unitholders who invest by way of an Austrian-resident UCITS, unless the tax treaty explicitly states that pension funds or charities are considered to be a person for the purposes of the treaty. Otherwise, an investment in the units of Austrian-resident UCITS results in a tax disadvantage compared to investing in a Netherlands-resident (FII) UCITS.

5.3.4.2. Dutch Unitholder and German-Resident UCITS

The denial of the application of tax treaties hinders the trading of units in German-resident UCITS to individual and corporate investors in the Netherlands. An investment in the units of German-resident UCITS therefore results in a tax disadvantage compared to Netherlands-resident (FII) UCITS.

The trading in units of German-resident UCITS to exempt corporate unitholders in the Netherlands is, under the same conditions and for the same reasons as discussed earlier for Austrian-resident UCITS, hindered by the application of tax treaties.

The trading in the units of German-resident UCITS to individual and corporate unitholders in the Netherlands is not affected in case a source state wrongly assumes that these UCITS are transparent. In such a case the tax treaty is applied by the source state to individual and corporate unitholders of these UCITS. This does not differ from Netherlands-resident (FII) UCITS.

5.3.4.3. Dutch Unitholder and UK-Resident UCITS

Trading in units of UK-resident UCITS in the Netherlands is not affected by the application of tax treaties to these UCITS. This does not differ from an investment in the units of Netherlands-resident (FII) UCITS.

Differences in the contents of the Netherlands and UK tax treaties affect trading in units of UK-resident UCITS to individual and corporate unitholders in the Netherlands. In this case the taxation at source of income from the underlying investments of UK-resident UCITS may be more (or less) than that of the income from the underlying investments of Netherlands-resident (FII) UCITS.

Trading in units of UK-resident UCITS in the Netherlands is supported where the Netherlands has concluded fewer tax treaties with the countries in a specific region or in the absence of a Netherlands tax treaty with a particular country. The taxation at source of income from the investments of UK-resident UCITS may in such a case be less than in the case of an investment in the units of Austrian-resident UCITS. The tax treaty network of the United Kingdom, in contrast to that of the Netherlands, includes tax treaties with Antigua and Barbuda, Belize, Bolivia, Botswana, Brunei, Chile, Cyprus, Falkland Islands, Fiji, Gambia, Grenada, Guernsey, Guyana, Isle of Man, Ivory Coast, Jamaica, Jersey, Kenya, Kiribati and Tuvalu, Lesotho, Mauritius, Montserrat, Myanmar, Namibia, Oman, Papua New Guinea, St. Christopher and Nevis, Sierra Leone, the Solomon Islands, Sudan, and Swaziland. An investment in the units of UK-resident UCITS results in a tax advantage for investments in these countries compared to the units of Netherlands-resident UCITS.

If the Netherlands has concluded more tax treaties with the countries in a specific region, or in the presence of a tax treaty with a particular country that has not concluded one with the United Kingdom, the trading in units of UK-resident UCITS in the Netherlands is hindered. The tax treaty network of the Netherlands includes countries that have not concluded a tax treaty with the United Kingdom. These are Albania, Armenia, Aruba, Brazil, Netherlands Antilles, and Surinam. Netherlands-resident UCITS are more attractive for investments in these countries than UK-resident UCITS.

Trading in units of UK-resident UCITS of the trust type to exempt corporate unitholders in the Netherlands is hindered if it is assumed by a source state to be transparent. In such a case, the source state, unlike for Netherlands-resident (FII)

UCITS, does not apply the tax treaty to exempt corporate unitholders of UK-resident UCITS of the trust type. This results in a tax disadvantage compared to UK-resident (FII) UCITS.

5.3.5. Cross-Border Trading of Units in the United Kingdom

5.3.5.1. UK Unitholder and Austrian-Resident UCITS

The trading in units of Austrian-resident UCITS to individual and corporate unitholders in the United Kingdom is not affected by the application of tax treaties. The tax treaties are applied by source states to individual and corporate unitholders of Austrian-resident UCITS. An investment in the units of Austrian-resident UCITS therefore does not differ from that of the units of UK-resident UCITS.

The application of tax treaties hinders the trading in units of Austrian-resident UCITS to exempt corporate unitholders in the United Kingdom. Source states deny the application of tax treaties to exempt corporate unitholders of Austrian-resident UCITS. This differs from an investment in the units of UK-resident UCITS.

5.3.5.2. UK Unitholder and Netherlands-Resident (EII) UCITS

Trading in the units of Netherlands-resident (EII) UCITS in the United Kingdom is hindered by the denial of tax treaties to the UCITS and the unitholders. Netherlands-resident (EII) UCITS are therefore less attractive than UK-resident UCITS.

5.3.5.3. UK Unitholder and Netherlands-Resident (FII) UCITS

The application of tax treaties does not affect the trading in the units of Netherlands-resident (FII) UCITS in the United Kingdom. This is no different from an investment in the units of UK-resident UCITS.

The trading in the units of Netherlands-resident (FII) UCITS is supported where the Netherlands has concluded more tax treaties with countries in a specific region or in the presence of a Netherlands tax treaty with a particular country that has not concluded a tax treaty with the United Kingdom. In such a case an investment in the units of Netherlands-resident UCITS is more attractive than an investment in the units of UK-resident UCITS. A comparison of the tax treaty networks of the Netherlands and the United Kingdom is found in Section 5.3.4.

If fewer tax treaties have been concluded by the Netherlands with countries in a specific region than the United Kingdom or in the absence of a Netherlands tax treaty with a particular country that has concluded a tax treaty with the United Kingdom, the trading in units of Netherlands-resident (FII) UCITS in the United Kingdom is hindered. The United Kingdom has concluded substantially more tax treaties than the Netherlands. An overview of the countries than have concluded a tax treaty with the United Kingdom but have not concluded one with the Netherlands is given in Section 5.3.4.

5.3.5.4. UK Unitholder and German-Resident UCITS

The application of tax treaties affects the trading in units of German-resident UCITS in the United Kingdom subject to the same conditions as those discussed in Section 5.3.4 for the trading in the units of these UCITS in the Netherlands.

5.3.5.5. UK Unitholder and Netherlands-Resident (TII) UCITS

The conditions under which the trade in units of Netherlands-resident (TII) UCITS is affected by the application of tax treaties to these UCITS and the unitholders do not differ from those discussed above for Austrian-resident UCITS.

5.4. CONCLUSION

Circulation of units in UCITS is restricted by the differences in the taxation at source of income from the investments of UCITS. Sometimes, the investor is better served by investing through a resident UCITS. In other cases, this is not of benefit to the investor. The main reason for the differences is the absence of any uniform rules to establish transparency. The conditions of competition in the countries studied therefore diverge for resident and non-resident UCITS and between non-resident UCITS. The measures taken by the UCITS Directive to remove the restrictions in the national legislation of the Member States on the free circulation of units in UCITS are thus not far-reaching enough because none of the differences in taxation at source of income from the investments of UCITS have been removed.

From the previous two chapters it follows that the source taxation of domestic and foreign investments by UCITS is not the same. The differences in the source taxation may hinder UCITS by attracting capital in other Member States. This chapter provides for an overview of such distortions to the trade in units of UCITS.

Part III

Tax Liability of Undertakings for Collective Investment in Transferable Securities

To prevent an investment by way of undertakings for collective investment in transferable securities (UCITS) resulting in more tax than that of a direct investment, the income from the investments should not be subject to tax at the level of the UCITS (avoidance of economic double taxation). For the same reasons, the UCITS state should not charge any withholding tax at the time of distribution. It is, further, not advisable to provide for relief at the level of the UCITS because the relief is shared among all unitholders instead of only those that would have been entitled to relief in the case of a direct investment.

Taxation at the level of UCITS in Austria, Germany, the Netherlands, and the United Kingdom varies to a great extent, as the analysis in the Chapters 6–8 illustrates. For this reason, it is inevitable that unitholders take notice of the state of residence of UCITS by the selection of UCITS, to avoid any tax disadvantages. The following differences are considered the most relevant:

(1) The avoidance of double (corporate) income tax.
(2) The availability of relief for the withholding tax that is charged by the source states at the level of the UCITS.
(3) The charging of withholding tax from UCITS at the time of distribution.

The units of UCITS cannot circulate freely in the countries studied despite the attempt of the UCITS Directive to remove any restrictions for such circulation. The differences between the national tax legislation of the countries studied restrict the cross-border trade in units of UCITS. The competition among UCITS therefore does not take place under the same conditions.

In a couple of cases, an investment in a non-resident UCITS results in a tax advantage for the unitholders compared to an investment in a resident UCITS. Nevertheless, such distortion undermines the aim of the UCITS Directive in establishing a European capital market.

Part III examines taxation of investments in and by UCITS in the UCITS country.

Figure III.1 Tax Liability of UCITS

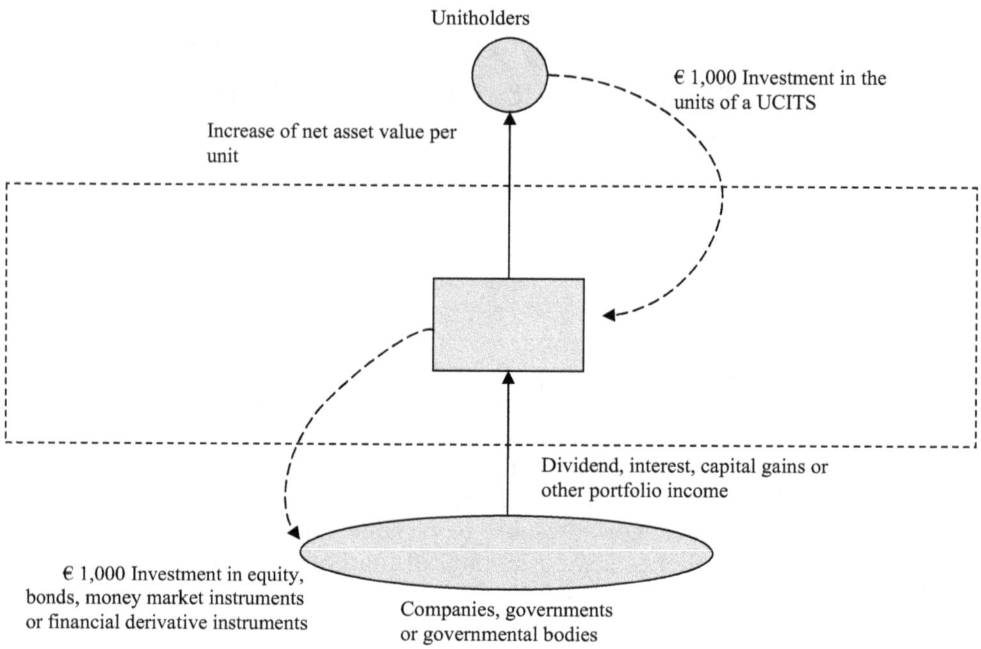

Chapter 6

Taxation of Income from the Investments in the Undertakings for Collective Investment in Transferable Securities Country

In the absence of any harmonization or coordination by the European Union (EU) or the European Economic Area (EEA), the objective and subjective tax liability of undertakings for collective investment in transferable securities (UCITS) in the countries studied is not the same. The tax liability of UCITS does not always correspond with the legal status under civil law. Some of the countries studied consider the income from securities and other financial instruments to be that of the unitholders (transparent), whereas the income in the other countries is considered to be that of the UCITS (intransparent). The latter group of countries do not allow that income to be subject to tax twice – at the level of both the UCITS and the unitholders. They avoid taxation at the level of the UCITS or compensate the unitholders entirely or partly for taxation at the level of the UCITS. Thus, income from securities and other financial instruments derived by way of UCITS is not taxed more heavily than a direct investment.

The avoidance of taxation at the level of the UCITS for domestic dividends seems to infringe on the free movement of capital as laid down in Articles 56 and 58 of the EC Treaty and Article 40 of the EEA Treaty in one of the countries studied, the United Kingdom. For domestic dividends the United Kingdom avoids taxation at the level of the UCITS by way of an objective exemption. This exemption is not, however, available for foreign dividends. As a result, foreign dividends are subject to more taxation at the level of UK-resident UCITS than domestic dividends.

For other items of income such as foreign dividends, the United Kingdom does not avoid taxation at the level of UK-resident UCITS. Instead, it partly compensates the unitholders for taxation at the level of these UCITS. The compensation reduces double taxation only for taxpayers who are liable to personal or corporate income tax in the United Kingdom. Non-resident unitholders are generally not liable to tax in the United Kingdom. They are therefore not compensated by the United Kingdom. Nor are they compensated by the residence state, because most states avoid double taxation at the level of the UCITS and not at that of the unitholders (disparity). UK-resident UCITS may therefore have difficulties in attracting capital in other Member States.

Like a direct investment, the tax withheld should be credited as if the unitholders had invested directly. Nevertheless, the crediting of withholding tax is affected by the objective and subjective tax liability of UCITS. The tax withheld in some of the other countries may be credited by the unitholders as if they had invested directly, whereas the other countries grant relief at the level of the UCITS. The availability and the amount of relief at the level of UCITS differs among the countries studied.

The relief granted to Netherlands-resident (FII) UCITS for foreign withholding tax may, however, be reduced if some of the non-resident unitholders other than EU pension funds, charities, and other exempt corporate bodies are entitled to a reduction of withholding tax or an exemption from withholding tax under a tax treaty. The reduction of the relief discourages Netherlands-resident (FII) UCITS to attract capital in a Member State that has concluded a tax treaty with the Netherlands that provides for a reduction of withholding tax or an exemption from withholding tax, for example, the Czech Republic, Portugal, and Slovakia. The reduction, therefore, seems to infringe on the free movement of capital as laid down in Articles 56 and 58 of the EC Treaty and Article 40 of the EEA Treaty.

The objective and subjective tax liability of UCITS and the availability and amount of relief for foreign withholding taxes for UCITS show some substantial differences in the countries studied.

Finally, taxation on distributions is not the same in the countries studied. This is not only caused by differences in the tax base, tax rate, and available exemptions from withholding tax, but it is also the result of differences in taxation at source of income. Some items of income are subject to withholding tax at source. Other items of income are exempt from withholding tax at source or the tax withheld is refundable by the UCITS. Instead, these items of income are taxed at the time of distribution. The items of income for which an exemption or refund is available at source vary among the countries studied, as does taxation at the time of distribution.

6.1. INTRODUCTION

Investors in UCITS ideally should be placed into the same tax position as if they had made any underlying investments themselves directly. Otherwise, investments in a UCITS could be less efficient than a direct investment. Therefore, it is the case that several methods are available to prevent income from UCITS investments from being subject to corporate income tax at the level of the UCITS. For example, a UCITS may be tax transparent or have access to a subjective exemption, a reduced tax base, or a reduced tax rate. It is also possible to compensate the unitholders for taxation at the level of the UCITS. In case a UCITS is subject to tax, a fiction may be necessary to prevent relief for the tax withheld at source at the level of the UCITS so that instead relief should, as is the case for a direct investment, be available at the level of the unitholders. Finally, an exemption for distributions of UCITS would simply avoid the charging of withholding tax from UCITS at the time of distribution.

6.2. TAX LIABILITY OF THE UCITS FOR THE INCOME FROM THE INVESTMENTS

6.2.1. Austrian-Resident UCITS

Corporate entities resident in Austria are subject to corporate income tax on their worldwide taxable income. Corporate entities include the following:[1]

(1) Legal persons incorporated under civil law.[2]
(2) Commercial enterprises operated by public entities.
(3) Associations, institutions, foundations without legal personality, and other pools of assets set up for a specific purpose (a special-purpose vehicle).

An Austrian-resident UCITS is a special-purpose vehicle that consists of securities, money market instruments, or other marketable financial instruments that are held in joint ownership by the unitholders.[3] As a special-purpose vehicle, it is initially subject to corporate income tax.

A special-purpose vehicle is, however, not subject to corporate income tax where its income is taxable in the hands of another taxpayer on the basis of the Income Tax Act or another federal act.[4] The Law on Investment Funds, which is a federal act, determines that the income from the underlying investments of Austrian-resident UCITS is taxable in the hands of the unitholders. Austrian-resident UCITS are, therefore, not subject to corporate income tax. Instead, they are considered to be transparent under the domestic laws of Austria.

Transparency ensures that the income from the underlying investments of an Austrian-resident UCITS is not taxed twice – at the level of both the UCITS and the unitholders. The transparency results from the characteristics of an

1. Section 1(2) Corporate Tax Act (*Körperschafsteuergesetz*), BGBl. No. 401/1988, 7 Jul. 1988.
2. Examples of such legal persons are public corporations, private corporations with limited liability, and mutual insurance companies.
3. Section 1(1) Law on Investment Funds (*Investmentfondsgesetz* 1993), BGBl. No. 532/1993, 30 Jul. 1993.
4. Section 3 Corporate Tax Act.

Austrian-resident UCITS under the Austrian civil law and the Law on Investment Funds.[5]

6.2.2. German-Resident UCITS

Corporate entities resident in Germany are subject to corporate income tax on their worldwide taxable income. Corporate entities includes the following:[6]

(1) Corporations with a capital that is divided in shares.[7]
(2) Trading or agricultural cooperatives.
(3) Mutual insurance or pension companies.
(4) Other legal persons incorporated under civil law.
(5) Associations, institutions, foundations without legal personality, and other pools of assets set up for a specific purpose (a special-purpose 'Zweckvermögen').
(6) Commercial enterprises operated by public entities.

A German-resident UCITS is a fund that invests in accordance with the principle of risk-spreading in securities, money market instruments, financial derivative instruments and other listed investments for the joint account of its unitholders.[8] The underlying investments are owned either by the unitholders as co-owners or by a management company on behalf of the unitholders. Consequently, any income from the investments has to be split up proportionally among the unitholders.[9] This is not very practical because of the number of unitholders, the varying composition of the unitholders, and, in the case of a listed UCITS, the namelessness of the unitholders.[10] A German-resident UCITS is therefore considered to be a special-purpose 'Zweckvermögen'.[11]

As a special-purpose vehicle, a German-resident UCITS is initially subject to corporate income tax. This makes the splitting up of the income among unitholders unnecessary.[12] The Investment Taxation Act, however, determines that a German-resident UCITS is exempt from corporate income tax and trade tax.[13]

---

5. VwGH 21 Nov. 1995, No. 95/12/0035. See also H. Macher, 'Die Besteuerung inländischer Dachfonds', *ÖStZ* 15, No. 6, March 1999, at 106.
6. Section 1(1) Corporate Tax Act (*Körperschafsteuergesetz*), BGBl. I 1976/2597 and 2599, 31 Aug. 1976.
7. Examples of such corporations are public corporations and private corporations with limited liability.
8. Sections 1 and 2(1) and (2) Investment Act (*Investmentgesetz*), BGBl. I 2003/2676, 15 Dec. 2003.
9. Sections 180(1) or 39(2) Federal Taxation Act (*Abgabenordenung*).
10. D. Lübbehüsen, in *KAGG and AuslInvestment-Gesetz – Kommentar*, ed. J. Brinkhaus & P. Scherer (Munich: Verlag C.H. Beck, 2003), KAGG § 38, 15.
11. Sections 11(1) of the Investment Taxation Act (*Investmentsteuergesetz*), BGBl. I 2003/2724, 15 Dec. 2003.
12. A. Ramackers, in *Das Einkommensteuerrecht*, ed. E. Littmann, H. Bitz, & H. Pust (Stuttgart: Schäffer Poeschel, loose leaf), InvStG § 1 at 50.
13. Section 11(1) Investment Taxation Act.

The subjective exemption prevents the income from the underlying investments of a German-resident UCITS from being taxed twice – at the level of the UCITS and at that of the unitholders. A German-resident UCITS is considered to be semi-transparent under the German tax legislation. The degree of transparency depends on the Investment Taxation Act.

6.2.3. Netherlands-Resident UCITS

Corporate entities resident in the Netherlands are subject to corporate income tax on their worldwide taxable income. Corporate entities include the following:[14]

(1) Public corporations, private corporations with limited liability, open limited partnerships, and other corporations with a capital that is divided in shares.
(2) Cooperatives and foundations on a cooperative basis.
(3) Mutual insurance companies and foundations that act as an insurance company or credit institution.
(4) Foundations authorized under the Housing Act as an organization that operates in the interest of public housing.
(5) Other foundations and other (non-public) legal entities that carry on a business.
(6) Open funds for joint account (a specific subcategory of a special-purpose vehicle).
(7) Those enterprises of public legal entities that are listed in Article 2(3) of the Corporate Tax Act.

A Netherlands-resident UCITS is either incorporated or established by contract. A Netherlands-resident UCITS of the corporate type is a legal person requesting or acquiring funds or other goods for collective investment in order to have the unitholders share in the proceeds of the investments.[15] It may be incorporated either as a public corporation, private corporation with limited liability, cooperative, mutual insurance company, foundation or association.[16]

A Netherlands-resident UCITS of the contractual type is a fund that consists of attracted capital, or other property, with the purpose of making collective investments to let the unitholders share the proceedings from these investments.[17] Because it is a fund established with the purpose of obtaining income for its participants by collective investment or otherwise of the obtained capital, it may be characterized as an open fund for joint account, but only if its certificates

14. Section 2 Corporate Tax Act (*Wet op de Vennootschapsbelasting* 1969), *Stb.* 1969, 445, 8 Oct. 1969.
15. Article 1:1 Act on Financial Supervision.
16. C.M. Grundmann-Van der Krol, *Koersen door de Wet op het financieel toezicht* (Deventer: Kluwer, 2007), 66.
17. Article 1:1 Act on Financial Supervision.

of participation are freely transferable.[18] Otherwise, it is considered a closed fund for joint account, which is transparent for tax purposes.

The units of a Netherlands-resident UCITS of the contractual type are considered freely transferable if the disposal of the units does not need to be approved by all unitholders[19] or such is not limited to close relatives and in-laws only. The Act on Financial Supervision does not require the units of UCITS to be freely transferable. Instead, it merely requires that the units are, at the request of the holders, repurchased or redeemed by the UCITS. Depending on the fund rules, the units of a Netherlands-resident UCITS of the contractual type may be either freely transferable (open fund for joint account) or not (closed fund for joint account).

6.2.3.1. Netherlands-Resident (EII/FII) UCITS

As a public corporation, private corporation with limited liability, other legal person, or open fund for joint account, a Netherlands-resident UCITS is initially subject to corporate income tax (tax opaque UCITS). The Corporate Tax Act, however, provides for special tax regulations. A Netherlands-resident UCITS may opt either for a subjective exemption[20] (exempt investment institution) or a corporate income tax rate of nil percent[21] (fiscal investment institution).

Subjective Exemption

For obtaining a subjective exemption from corporate income tax (hereafter, Netherlands-resident (EII) UCITS), a UCITS, or other investment fund needs to qualify as a public corporation, open fund for joint account, or as entity that is established under the laws of Aruba, the Netherlands Antilles, another Member State of the European Union, or a third country that has concluded a tax treaty with the Netherlands that includes a provision on non-discrimination. An entity that is established under the law of one of the countries mentioned has to be comparable to a public corporation or open fund for joint account.[22]

Tax Rate of Nil Percent

The corporate income tax rate of nil percent (hereafter, Netherlands-resident (FII) UCITS) is open only for UCITS and other investment funds that qualify as a public corporation, private corporation with limited liability, open fund for joint account, or entity that is established under the laws of Aruba, the Netherlands Antilles,

18. Article 2(2) Corporate Tax Act.
19. Decree of 11 of January 2007, CPP2006/1870M.
20. Article 6a Corporate Tax Act.
21. Article 28 Corporate Tax Act in conjunction with Art. 9 of the Decree on Investment Schemes (*Besluit Beleggingsinstellingen* 1970), Stb. 1970, 190, 29 Apr. 1970.
22. Article 6a(2) Corporate Tax Act.

another Member State of the European Union, or a third state that has concluded a tax treaty with the Netherlands that includes a provision on non-discrimination. The entity that is established under the laws of one of the countries mentioned has to be comparable with a public corporation, private corporation with limited liability, or open fund for joint account.[23]

The subjective exemption and the tax rate of nil percent both prevent the income from the underlying investments of a Netherlands-resident UCITS from being taxed twice – at the level of both the UCITS and the unitholders. To fulfil the requirements for obtaining the tax rate of nil percent, a UCITS must distribute the income available for distribution within eight months after the end of each financial year.[24] No distribution is required for obtaining the subjective exemption.[25]

6.2.3.2. Netherlands-Resident (TII) UCITS

As a closed fund for joint account, a Netherlands-resident UCITS of the contractual type whose units cannot be transferred freely is considered transparent. It is known as a transparent investment institution (hereafter, Netherlands-resident (TII) UCITS). The income of a Netherlands-resident (TII) UCITS is that of the unitholders, which avoids (economic) double taxation (transparent UCITS).

6.2.4. UK-Resident UCITS

Companies resident in the United Kingdom are subject to corporate income tax on their worldwide taxable income. A company includes the following:[26]

(1) Any body corporate.
(2) Unincorporated associations other than a partnership, local authority, or a local authority association.

A UK-resident UCITS is either incorporated or established by trust deed. A UK-resident UCITS of the corporate type is an authorized open-end investment company with variable share capital that invests according to its articles of incorporation with the aim of spreading risk and giving its shareholders or unitholders (hereafter, unitholders) the benefit of the results of the management of the investments.[27] As a body corporate, a UK-resident UCITS of the corporate type is subject

23. Article 28(2) Corporate Tax Act.
24. Separate from the obligation to distribute the taxable profits to the unitholders, the Corporate Tax Act sets requirements with respect to the statutory goal and actual activities, debts, unitholders, and board of directors of UCITS or other investment funds.
25. The Corporate Tax Act, however, contains requirements with respect to the statutory goal and actual activities, the kind of investments, and the spreading of risk.
26. Section 832 Income and Corporation Taxes Act 1988, c.1.
27. Section 236(2) Financial Services and Markets Act 2000, c.8.

to corporate income tax. It is, however, exempt under the Taxation of Chargeable Gains Act.[28]

A UK-resident UCITS of the trust type is an authorized unit trust that invests in accordance with the aim of spreading risk and that holds these investments on trust for the unitholders.[29] It does not qualify as a company and, thus, is not subject to corporate income tax. Instead, the trustees of a UK-resident UCITS of the trust type are initially subject to income tax for income from the investments and to capital gains tax for the proceeds from the disposal of investments, as they receive the income[30] or the gains accrue to them.[31] The Income and Corporation Taxes Act, however, determines that the trustees of a UK-resident UCITS of the trust type are considered a company in respect to income arising to them and for the purposes of the provisions of the act relating to relief for capital expenditure[32] while an exemption applies under the Taxation of Chargeable Gains Act.[33]

As a company, a UK-resident UCITS is initially subject to corporate income tax. The Income and Corporation Taxes Act, like for other companies, provides for an exemption for UK-source dividends derived by UK-resident UCITS. The Income and Corporation Taxes Act, further, provides for special tax regulations with a basic income tax rate of 20% (2009).[34] The unitholders of a UK-resident UCITS are compensated for the corporate income tax liability of the UCITS by way of a tax credit, an exemption, or a combination of both. The tax credit, exemption, or combination of both prevents the income from the underlying investments of a UK-resident UCITS from being taxed twice – at the level of the UCITS and at that of the unitholders.

Example 6.1

A UK-resident UCITS derives dividends of EUR 1,000,000. Half of the dividend is paid by a Chinese-resident company. The other half is paid by a UK-resident company. An exemption applies to the UK dividend of EUR 500,000. The Chinese dividend is subject to corporate income tax at the level of the UCITS. The corporate income tax is charged at a tax rate of 20%. The corporate income tax liability of the UCITS for the foreign dividend is EUR 100,000, ignoring the double tax relief potential. After deduction of corporate income tax, an amount of EUR 900,000 of the dividend remains, which has to be distributed or is considered to have been distributed, at the distribution date. The UCITS, for example, distributes the remaining amount of the dividend

28. Section 100 Taxation of Chargeable Gains Act.
29. Section 237(1) Financial Services and Markets Act 2000.
30. Williams v. Singer [1921] 1 AC 65, 71, 7 TC 387, 411.
31. Section 65(1) and (2) Taxation of Chargeable Gains Act 1992, c.12.
32. Section 468(1) Income and Corporation Taxes Act in conjunction with The Authorised Investment Funds (Tax) Regulations 2006, S.I. 2006/964, 29 Mar. 2006.
33. Section 100 Taxation of Chargeable Gains Act.
34. Sections 468(1A) and 468A(1) Income and Corporation Taxes Act.

over 10,000 units so that an amount of EUR 90 is distributed per unit. Individual unitholders are compensated for taxation at the level of the UCITS by way of a tax credit. The tax credit is one-ninth of the dividend of EUR 90: EUR 10. Compensation also is provided to corporate unitholders, which are entitled to a tax credit for the part of the distribution that is not related to UK dividends while an exemption applies to the part that is related to such dividend.

A tax credit is, however, not refundable, so that taxation at the level of the UCITS is not, or is not entirely, removed if the tax credit cannot or cannot entirely be set off by the unitholder.

Example 6.2

A company resident in China pays a dividend of EUR 1,000,000 to a UK-resident UCITS. The corporate income tax liability of the UCITS for the Chinese dividend is EUR 200,000, ignoring any double tax relief potential. After taxation, the dividend is distributed by the UCITS, for example, for over 10,000 units so that the amount per unit is EUR 80. In the absence of a corporate income tax liability, an exempt corporate unitholder cannot benefit from the tax credit to which it is entitled. Exempt corporate unitholders are thus not compensated for taxation at the level of the UCITS.

In the absence of a tax liability in the United Kingdom, non-resident unitholders are generally not able to set off the tax credit or to benefit from an exemption. The UK tax treaties with Austria, Belgium, Cyprus, France, Italy, Luxembourg, Malta, the Netherlands, Poland, Romania, Slovenia, and Sweden therefore provide relief for the corporate income tax charged at the level of UCITS and other companies in the form of a payment by the United Kingdom. The availability of the relief provided under the UK tax treaty with Malta is, however, limited to individual unitholders. The payment under these tax treaties is determined as the amount of a tax credit that exceeds a tax at 15%, or in the case of the UK tax treaty with Belgium, 20%, of the amount of the dividend and the tax credit together.[35] The tax credit is one-ninth of the dividend payment to the unitholder. If the amount of the tax exceeds that of the tax credit, the remaining amount of the tax is considered reduced to nil.[36]

Example 6.3

A non-resident unitholder of a UK-resident UCITS is paid a dividend of United Kingdom Pound (GBP) 900. UK individual unitholders would have been entitled to a tax credit of GBP 100, being one-ninth of the dividend. In the absence of a tax liability in the United Kingdom, the tax credit cannot be set

35. *Simon's Direct Tax Service* (Butterworths, loose leaf), at F1.215.
36. Section 33(10)(c) F(No2)A 1997.

off by the non-resident unitholder. Nonetheless, the non-resident unitholder is, under the UK tax treaty with unitholder's residence state, entitled to a payment of the amount of the tax credit that remains after the charge of a 15% tax on the sum of the dividend and the tax credit. The amount of the payment remaining after the deduction of tax is, however, considered nil: the amount of the tax credit of GBP 100 reduced by that of the tax of GBP 150.

From the example, it follows that a payment under the UK tax treaties with Austria, Belgium, Cyprus, France, Italy, Luxembourg, Malta, the Netherlands, Poland, Romania, Slovenia, and Sweden is not made in the case of non-resident unitholders of UK-resident UCITS. As from 6 April 1999, the amount of the tax credit is one-ninth of a dividend payment and thus never exceeds the tax charged at 15% or 20%. In practice, non-resident unitholders therefore generally do not request a payment.[37]

Qualifying Investment Test

The corporate income tax liability of a UK-resident UCITS is nullified where the UCITS satisfies the qualifying investment test at all times in a distribution period.[38] In that case, each distribution in that period may be considered loan relationship debits, which can be set off against any profits of the UCITS for the distribution period.[39] The part of the interest distribution that cannot be set off against the profits may be carried forward to the following distribution period as a loan relationship deficit.[40] An excess interest distribution cannot be carried back to a previous distribution period.[41] The deduction of distributions as loan relationship debits avoids double taxation of the income from the underlying investments of the UCITS.

Example 6.4

A UK-resident UCITS receives interest for an amount of GBP 100,000. The interest is at the distribution date paid out to its unitholders. If the UK-resident UCITS satisfied the qualifying investment test at all times during the distribution period, the amount of the distribution is deductible from its profits as loan relationship debits. The amount of the profits therefore is nil: the amount of interest of GBP 100,000 reduced by that of the loan relationship debits of GBP 100,000.

---

37. L. Shirley, Authorised Unit Trusts and OEICs, in *Tolley's Taxation of Collective Investment*, ed. S. Newcombe and other contributors (London: NexisLexis Tolley, 2003), 318.
38. Section 17 The Authorised Investment Funds (Tax) Regulations 2006.
39. Section 13 The Authorised Investment Funds (Tax) Regulations 2006.
40. Section 83 FA 1996.
41. Section 14 The Authorised Investment Funds (Tax) Regulations 2006.

The qualifying investment test is satisfied where more than 60% of the market value of the investments of the UCITS consists of money placed at interest, securities other than shares in a company, shares in a building company, derivative contracts whose underlying subject matter consists wholly of money placed at interest, securities other than shares in a company, shares in a building company or currency, contracts for differences whose underlying subject matter consists wholly of interest rates, creditworthiness and currency, other derivative contracts where there is a hedging relationship between that contract and any money placed at interest, securities other than shares in a company or shares in a building society, and alternative finance arrangements.[42] The interest distributions are considered in the hands of the unitholders to be yearly interest.[43] The unitholders are therefore not granted a tax credit, an exemption, or a combination of both.

6.2.5. Conclusion

Although the measures taken by Austria, Germany, and the Netherlands differ, each of the methods avoids taxation at the level of the UCITS. The income from the investments of UCITS is therefore subject to tax once – at the level of the unitholders. In the United Kingdom, taxation of income at the level of the UCITS is not avoided. The unitholders are, however, compensated for taxation at the level of the UCITS in the form of a tax credit, an exemption, or a combination of both. As the tax credit is not refundable, exempt companies like pension funds and charities are not compensated for taxation at the level of the UCITS. The same applies to non-resident unitholders.

Taxation at the level of UK-resident UCITS is avoided only if the UCITS derives solely domestic dividends or satisfies the qualifying investment test at all times during a financial year. The tax liability of the UCITS is in those cases nullified because domestic dividends are exempt from tax, and interest distributions are deductible from the profits of the UCITS.

6.3. CREDITING OF FOREIGN WITHHOLDING TAX

6.3.1. Austrian-Resident UCITS

The Austrian tax treaties and unilateral rules, as discussed in Section 3.3.2.2, do not apply to Austrian-resident UCITS. The latter do not qualify as a person liable to tax, because they are transparent. The withholding tax levied by a source state on income derived from an underlying investment is considered to be levied for the account of the unitholders. It is therefore creditable by the unitholders where one of the Austrian tax treaties or the unilateral rules provides for such (foreign tax credit).

42. Section 20 The Authorised Investment Funds (Tax) Regulations 2006.
43. Section 18(1) The Authorised Investment Funds (Tax) Regulations 2006.

6.3.2. German-Resident UCITS

The German tax treaties and unilateral rules are considered by Germany to apply to German-resident UCITS.[44] The latter qualify as a person liable to tax, because they are initially subject to corporate income tax. The withholding tax levied by a source state on income that is derived from an underlying investment is therefore creditable by the UCITS where one of these regulations provides for such (a foreign tax credit). The foreign tax credit, however, may not be credited by a German-resident UCITS because it is subjectively exempt.

Under the Investment Taxation Act a German-resident UCITS may, however, elect to show foreign withholding tax as either deductible from the taxable income of the unitholders or creditable against the tax liability of the unitholders. In case of the latter, German unitholders may apply the German tax treaties and unilateral rules as if they had invested directly in the underlying investments.[45] In that case, German unitholders are allowed to credit the foreign withholding tax where one of these regulations provides for such a credit.

6.3.3. Netherlands-Resident UCITS

6.3.3.1. Netherlands-Resident (EII) UCITS

Netherlands-resident (EII) UCITS, as mentioned in Section 3.3.4.2, cannot rely on the Tax Charter for the Kingdom of the Netherlands, the Netherlands tax treaties, and unilateral rules. The Corporate Tax Act does not provide for any other relief for the withholding tax levied by a source state on income that is derived from an underlying investment. Nor are the unitholders of these UCITS under the Netherlands Income Tax Act or Corporate Tax Act allowed to credit the foreign withholding tax as if they had invested directly.

6.3.3.2. Netherlands-Resident (FII) UCITS

From Section 3.3.4.2 follows that Netherlands-resident (FII) UCITS are generally considered to be entitled to the benefits of the Tax Charter for the Kingdom of the Netherlands, the Netherlands tax treaties, and unilateral rules. The tax withheld by a source state on income from the underlying investment is creditable by these UCITS where one of these regulations provides for such a credit.

---

44. U. Sorgenfrei, Steuerlicher Transparenzgrundsatz und DBA-Berechtigung deutscher offener Investmentsfonds, *IstR* 1994/10, 468; and J. Täske, *National report on Germany of the IFA congress on the taxation of investment funds* (International Fiscal Association, 1997), 463.
45. Section 4(4) Investment Taxation Act.

Ordinary Tax Credit

The Netherlands does not, under any circumstances, grant a foreign tax credit for more than the part of the corporate income tax liability that is related to the foreign income (ordinary tax credit). The corporate income tax liability of Netherlands-resident (FII) UCITS is, however, always nil, because of the corporate income tax rate of nil percent.

Example 6.5

A Netherlands-resident (FII) UCITS receives an interest payment of EUR 100,000 from a Brazilian-resident corporation. In accordance with Brazil's tax treaty with the Netherlands, Brazil levies a withholding tax of 15% on the interest payment. The foreign tax credit is the lower of the foreign withholding tax levied in accordance with the tax treaty and the ordinary tax credit. The corporate income tax levied on the interest is nil. Therefore, the foreign tax credit is nil as well.

Relief for Withholding Tax on Dividend and Interest

For that reason, the Dividend Tax Act provides relief for the tax withheld at source of dividend and interest. The relief takes place in the form of a payment reduction for the tax that has to be withheld by the UCITS at the time of distribution to the unitholders. Any foreign withholding tax on dividend and interest may be set off by a Netherlands-resident (FII) UCITS against the 15% tax that needs to be withheld for the account of the unitholders at the time of distribution.[46] A Netherlands-resident (FII) UCITS thus does not have to pay the full amount of the withholding tax to the tax authorities while the tax withheld is fully creditable by the unitholders. The difference between the tax withheld on the distribution and the tax paid to the tax authorities increases the intrinsic value of the units in the UCITS.

Example 6.6

X, a Netherlands-resident (FII) UCITS, distributes an amount of EUR 100,000 to its unitholders. It has to deduct EUR 15,000 withholding tax on the distribution. No withholding tax is paid by X to the Netherlands tax authorities because it may credit EUR 15,000 Austrian withholding tax against the tax withheld.

The payment reduction is restricted to foreign withholding tax on dividends and interest. Not only dividend and interest are, however, subject to withholding tax.

46. Article 11a(1) Dividend Tax Act.

Gains realized by the disposal of investments and other portfolio income may also be subject to withholding tax. In some tax treaties, the Netherlands has agreed that the source state has the right to tax these income types. Nevertheless, in these cases, the Dividend Tax Act does not provide relief for such withholding tax even while it would have been creditable if an individual unitholder had invested directly.

Example 6.7

A Netherlands-resident (FII) UCITS derives a capital gain from the disposal of an investment in Brazil. The capital gain, in the absence of any limitation in the tax treaty of the source state's right to tax capital gains, has been subject to withholding tax at a rate of, for example, 25%. The withholding tax on the capital gain would be creditable in the case of a direct investment. No relief is granted to the UCITS for the Brazilian withholding tax, because the relief is limited to withholding tax on dividends and interest and therefore does not apply to withholding tax on capital gains.

The relief for foreign withholding tax is limited to 15% of the gross amount of the dividend or interest. The Netherlands does thus does not provide for more relief than the amount of tax withheld at the time of distribution and against which the foreign withholding tax is credited. The limit is applied on a per-item basis. Some Netherlands tax treaties, however, provide for a withholding tax on dividend or interest of more than 15%. In that case, the Netherlands does not provide relief for the part of the withholding tax that exceeds 15% of the gross amount.

Example 6.8

A Netherlands-resident (FII) UCITS receives a dividend of EUR 100,000, which is paid by a Paraguayan resident corporation. Paraguay, in the absence of a tax treaty with the Netherlands, levies a withholding tax of 25% on the dividend. The foreign withholding tax on the dividend would have been fully creditable in the case of direct investment by an individual unitholder on the basis of the Netherlands' unilateral rules. The relief for the Paraguayan withholding tax available for UCITS is, however, limited to 15% of the gross amount of the dividend.

Full Relief

Finally, the amount of the relief for foreign withholding tax depends under the Dividend Tax Act on the composition of the unitholders of the UCITS. A full relief for foreign withholding tax is granted where none of the non-resident unitholders is entitled under the Tax Charter for the Kingdom or one of the Netherlands tax treaties to a reduction or an exemption from withholding tax at the time of distribution by the UCITS to the unitholder.[47] It concerns the composition of the unitholders at the time the foreign dividend or interest is derived by the UCITS. Because this is impractical for UCITS, the tax authorities may agree to make use of the composition of the unitholders at the beginning of the financial year instead.[48] If the UCITS, for example, because of its listing on a stock exchange, does not have the disposal over the composition of its unitholders, it may estimate this.

Example 6.9

A Netherlands-resident (FII) UCITS receives an interest payment of EUR 100,000, which is paid out by a Brazilian-resident corporation. In accordance with the Brazilian tax treaty with the Netherlands, Brazil levies a withholding tax of 15% on the interest. The withholding tax on the interest qualifies for relief. Half of the unitholders are resident in the Netherlands. The other half of the unitholders are Argentinean and US pension funds. The UCITS is therefore not granted a full relief.

Partial Relief

A Netherlands-resident (FII) UCITS receives only a partial relief for foreign withholding tax if some of the non-resident unitholders other than pension funds or charities residing in the European Union are under the Tax Charter for the Kingdom of the Netherlands or a tax treaty entitled to a reduction of or an exemption from withholding tax at the time of distribution (disqualifying unitholders).[49] Some Netherlands tax treaties provide a withholding tax rate of less than 15%[50] or an exemption from withholding tax.[51] Furthermore, most Netherlands tax treaties apply a reduced tax rate if a unitholder keeps a substantial interest in a company including a Netherlands-resident (FII) UCITS; as mentioned before taxation of substantial interests falls outside the scope of this study.

The partial relief for foreign withholding tax can be expressed by means of the following formula:

$$PR = FWT -/- R$$

FWT is the amount of foreign withholding tax that qualifies for relief.

47. Article 11a(2) Dividend Tax Act.
48. A decree or other publication on such is, however, lacking. On the basis of legal certainty and transparency, it is desirable that this practice would be published instead of agreed on with each individual UCITS or other collective investment fund separately.
49. Article 11a(2) Dividend Tax Act.
50. It concerns the tax treaties with China, the Czech Republic, India, Indonesia, Kuwait, Portugal, the Slovak Republic, Taiwan, or Venezuela.
51. The tax treaties with Albania, Argentina, and the United Kingdom provides for an exemption from withholding tax if dividend is paid to a pension fund.

R is the amount for which the unitholders are under the Tax Charter for the Kingdom, a tax treaty entitled to a reduction, or an exemption at the time of distribution under a tax credit if the dividend or interest would be distributed upon receipt.

From the formula, it follows that the amount of a reduction or an exemption available to the unitholders under the Tax Charter for the Kingdom of the Netherlands or a tax treaty reduces the amount of relief granted to Netherlands-resident (FII) UCITS. The amount of a reduction or an exemption available to the unitholders needs to be determined on receipt of each item of dividend or interest by the UCITS. Hence, the data put in the formula is that of the composition of the unitholders at the time that the foreign dividend or interest is derived by the UCITS. As mentioned earlier, the tax authorities may, in practice, agree to apply the payment reduction on the basis of the composition of the unitholders at the beginning of the financial year.[52]

The formula for partial relief has the result that the more disqualifying unitholders invest in the units of a Netherlands-resident (FII) UCITS the less (partial) relief for foreign withholding taxes is given. A Netherlands-resident (FII) UCITS that attracts capital from Member States or third states that have concluded a tax treaty with the Netherlands that provides a reduced tax rate or an exemption for dividend is therefore treated less favourably than a Netherlands-resident (FII) UCITS that attracts little or no capital outside the Netherlands or from other Member States or third states. This seems to infringe on the free movement of capital as laid down in Articles 56 and 58 of the EC Treaty and Article 40 of the EEA Treaty.[53]

Example 6.10

A Netherlands-resident (FII) UCITS receives an interest payment of EUR 100,000, which is paid out by a Brazilian-resident corporation. In accordance with the Brazilian tax treaty with the Netherlands, Brazil levies a withholding tax of 15% on the interest. The withholding tax on the interest qualifies for relief. Half of the unitholders are resident in the Netherlands. The other half of the unitholders consists of Argentinean and US pension funds. At the time of distribution, these unitholders are entitled to a reduction of EUR 7,500. The UCITS is granted a partial relief of EUR 7,500 (PR = EUR 15,000 –/– EUR 7,500).

In the case of *Orange European Smallcap Fund N.V.*, the European Court of Justice has decided that a restriction of relief for foreign withholding tax to fiscal investment institutions, like Netherlands-resident (FII) UCITS, to the extent to

52. A decree or other publication on such is, however, lacking. For the transparency of the functioning of the payment reduction, it would be desirable that this practise would be published publicly instead of dealing with each individual UCITS or other collective investment fund separately.
53. See also *BNB* 2008/290c annotated by I.J.J. Burgers.

which unitholders are established in other Member States or in third countries infringes on the free movement of capital as laid down in Articles 56 and 58 of the EC Treaty 'since such a reduction adversely affects all the shareholders (...) without distinction'.[54] Although the restriction of relief is now limited to non-resident unitholders who are entitled to a reduction of withholding tax at the time of distribution, it still affects all unitholders without distinction. This is a consequence of the fact that the relief in the form of a payment reduction is granted at the level of the UCITS and not in the form of a tax credit or otherwise at that of the unitholders.

Carry Forward

In the case that the amount of the foreign withholding tax for which the UCITS is entitled to relief exceeds the amount of withholding tax charged at the time of distribution, the excess may be carried forward to the following year.

6.3.3.3. Netherlands-Resident (TII) UCITS

Netherlands-resident (TII) UCITS are, like Austrian-resident UCITS, considered to be transparent and do not qualify as a person for tax treaty purposes. Any foreign withholding tax charged by the source state is considered to be that of the unitholders. If the Tax Charter for the Kingdom, the Netherlands tax treaties, and unilateral rules provide for a foreign tax credit, the withholding tax charged by the source state may be set off against the unitholder's (corporate) income tax liability.

6.3.4. UK-Resident UCITS

The UK tax treaties and unilateral rules, as discussed in Section 3.3.5.2, apply to UK-resident UCITS. These qualify as a person liable to tax for tax treaty purposes because they are subject to corporate income tax in the United Kingdom. The withholding tax levied by a source state on income that is derived from an underlying investment is, therefore, creditable by the UCITS where one of these regulations provides for such credit.

In the presence of a tax treaty, any available foreign tax credit will be limited to the foreign withholding tax that could have been levied in accordance with that treaty. In the absence of a tax treaty or in the event that a tax treaty is present but does not cover taxation of the type of income involved,[55] a credit still may be

54. Judgment of the European Court of Justice of 20 May 2008 in respect of C-194/06 at 97 (*Staatssecretaris van Financiën vs. Orange European Smallcap Fund N.V.*).

55. Any provisions on the taxation of interest, capital gains, and other portfolio income are absent in the tax treaties with Antigua and Barbuda, Belize, Brunei, Grenada, Kiribati, Montserrat, Myanmar, St. Christopher (St. Kitts) and Nevis, Sierra Leone, the Solomon Islands, and Tuvalu. In the agreements with Botswana and Malawi, provisions are missing only for the taxation of capital gains and other portfolio income. Of special interest are the agreements with Guernsey, Island of Man, and Jersey that cover none of income types from portfolio investments.

available in the United Kingdom. Under the unilateral rules if, among other things, the foreign tax levied corresponds to UK (corporate) income tax or capital gains tax.

The UK tax treaties and unilateral rules, however, do not provide for a foreign tax credit where the income or chargeable gain is exempt from UK tax.[56] No foreign tax credit is granted to a UK UCITS for the foreign withholding tax that is levied on capital gains, because UK-resident UCITS are exempt from corporate income tax on chargeable gains.[57,58]

Ordinary Tax Credit

Under no circumstances does the United Kingdom grant a foreign tax credit for more than the part of UK corporate income tax that is related to the foreign income (ordinary tax credit). The ordinary tax credit is determined on a per-item basis.[59] Whether the amount of the foreign withholding tax exceeds the part of UK corporate income tax that is related to the foreign income thus needs to be determined for each item of foreign income separately.

In the case of a UK-resident UCITS, the corporate income tax is charged at a reduced tax rate of 20%. The foreign tax credit is therefore at the most 20% of the foreign income. The part of the corporate income tax that is related to the foreign income will, however, be less than 20% if costs are deducted from the taxable profits of the UCITS or losses from former years can be set off against the taxable profits.

Example 6.11

A UK-resident UCITS that qualifies as a balanced fund receives an interest payment of EUR 100,000, which is paid by a Brazilian-resident corporation. The United Kingdom has not concluded a tax treaty with Brazil, which therefore levies a withholding tax of 25% on the interest. The foreign tax credit is the lower of the foreign withholding tax levied and the ordinary tax credit. The corporate income tax levied on the interest is in the case of a UK UCITS at most 20%. The foreign tax credit is therefore limited to a maximum of EUR 20,000.

---

56. Section 790(4) Income and Corporation Taxes Act.
57. Section 100 Taxation of Chargeable Gains Act in conjunction with s. 97 of The Authorised Investment Funds (Tax) Regulations 2006.
58. See E. Dungworth & O. Farnworth, Authorised Unit Trusts and OEICs, in *Tolley's Taxation of Collective Investment*, ed. S. Newcombe and other contributors (London: LexisNexis Tolley, 2003), 286.
59. Section 797 Income and Corporation Taxes Act.

If a UK-resident UCITS satisfies the qualifying investment test, its corporate income tax liability may be nullified because any interest distributions can be credited against the taxable profits as loan relationship debits. The foreign tax credit is also nullified as it is the lower of the foreign withholding tax levied and the corporate income tax levied on the foreign income.

Example 6.12

A UK-resident UCITS receives an interest payment of EUR 100,000, which is paid by a Brazilian-resident corporation. The United Kingdom has not concluded a tax treaty with Brazil, which for that reason levies a withholding tax of 25% on the interest. The foreign tax credit is the lower of the foreign withholding tax levied and the ordinary tax credit. The corporate income tax levied on the interest is in most cases nil if the UK UCITS satisfied the qualifying investment test at all times during the financial year. The foreign tax credit is therefore limited to nil.

6.3.5. Conclusion

Each of the countries studied provides measures that give relief for the withholding tax charged by a source state, although the Netherlands does not provide relief for Netherlands-resident (EII) UCITS. Austria, Germany, and in the case of Netherlands-resident (TII) UCITS, the Netherlands, provide relief in the form of a foreign tax credit at the level of the unitholders as if they had invested directly. The Netherlands and the United Kingdom also provide relief in the form of a payment reduction and a foreign tax credit, respectively. However, the availability and amount of the relief differs in the Netherlands and the United Kingdom from the amount available in the case of a direct investment. The relief is granted at the level of the UCITS. It is therefore granted indirectly to all unitholders regardless of whether they would have enjoyed relief in the form of a foreign tax credit if they had invested directly or not.

6.4. DISTRIBUTION OF INCOME

6.4.1. Austrian-Resident UCITS

The income from the underlying investments of Austrian-resident UCITS is distributed, accumulated, or both distributed and accumulated. In the case of the latter, the income is partly distributed to certain series of units while the other part is accumulated for other series of units.[60]

---

60. Section 13 Law on Investment Funds.

6.4.1.1. Annual Return

For the application of the Income Tax Act and the Corporate Tax Act, the annual return is considered to be distributed at the earlier of an actual distribution, the disposal of units in the UCITS, and four months after the end of the financial year.[61] The annual return covers the annual income from the underlying investments after provision for expenses.[62]

6.4.1.2. Accounting of Portfolio Investments

The annual return of an Austrian-resident UCITS is determined in accordance with the accountancy principles laid down in commercial law. These accountancy principles therefore determine when income from the investments is added to the annual return.

Marketable and non-marketable securities such as shares, bonds and other debt securities; financial options; or financial futures are valued at cost.

The annual return of an Austrian-resident UCITS does not include any change in value of marketable and non-marketable securities until that change is realized at the time that the securities are disposed of or in the case of options or futures, the expiry date.[63]

A dividend from marketable shares is accounted for when the shares are quoted ex-dividend. If a dividend is paid out on non-marketable shares, the dividend is accounted for at the time that the dividend is declared.[64]

Interest is included in the annual return of an Austrian-resident UCITS at the time that it accrues.[65] If an Austrian-resident UCITS is given compensation in the form of a discount on the par value of the bond or other debt security,[66] the amount of the discount has to be spread linearly over the life of the security as interest. If compensation is paid by an Austrian-resident UCITS at the time of purchase in the form of a premium above the par value,[67] the amount of the premium is spread similarly as costs. Some bonds do not bear interest periodically. Instead, they pay the interest together with the repayment at the date of repayment. In accordance with the principles of commercial law, the growth of interest annually has to be added to the book value of those non-interest-bearing bonds.[68]

---

61. Section 40(1) and (2) Law on Investment Funds.
62. Section 13 Law on Investment Funds.
63. W. Hallas, *Die Prüfung von Investmentfonds* (Verlag Orac, 1997), 200 and 201. See the Guidelines for the Law on Investment Funds (*Investmentfondsrichtlinien* 2008), 17 Oct. 2008, 89–97.
64. W. Hallas, *Die Prüfung von Investmentfonds* (Verlag Orac, 1997), 200.
65. *Ibid.*, at 201–203.
66. A discount on the par value of a bond is given where the interest rate of the bond is less than the interest rate of the capital market.
67. A premium above the par value of a bond is paid where the interest rate of the bond is more than the interest rate of the capital market.
68. See also the Guidelines for the Law on Investment Funds, 83, and W. Doralt & S. Kirchmayr, *Einkommensteuergesetz Kommentar* (WUV-Universitätsverlag, loose leaf), EStG, Anhang I § 93, 14.

6.4.1.3. Deduction of Tax

The tax withheld at source on the income by Austria or other states is creditable by the unitholders of Austrian-resident UCITS. It is therefore not deductible from the income available for distribution.

6.4.1.4. Expenses

All expenses including the management costs have to be deducted from the annual income from the underlying investments.[69] This is different only for expenses directly connected with the purchase or disposal of investments or otherwise connected with capital.[70]

For the application of the Income Tax Act and the Corporate Tax Act, the expenses are considered to be deducted from the income that is not related to the proceeds from the disposal of the investments. If the expenses cannot, or cannot completely, be set off against the other part of the annual return, they are considered to be deducted from the proceeds from the disposal of investments. Any remaining amount is credited against the capital.[71]

6.4.1.5. Loss from the Disposal of Investments

If the amount of the capital losses from the disposal of investments exceeds that of the capital gains, for the application of the Income Tax Act and the Corporate Tax Act, the excess is carried forward to the following financial year. It is thus not set off against the other part of the annual return.

6.4.2. German-Resident UCITS

The income from the underlying investments is distributed, accumulated, or both distributed and accumulated by German-resident UCITS. In the case of the latter, the part of the income from the underlying investments that is related to proceeds from the disposal of investments is accumulated whereas the other part of the income is distributed to the unitholders.[72]

Distribution Account

The income shown in the distribution account as available for distribution is, for the application of the Income Tax Act and Corporate Tax Act, considered to be distributed on distribution or the end of the financial year, whichever is earlier.

---

69. See also the Guidelines for the Law on Investment Funds, 119 and 120.
70. W. Hallas, *Die Prüfung von Investmentfonds* (Verlag Orac, 1997), 221.
71. See also the Guidelines for the Law on Investment Funds, 121.
72. Article 43(4)(6) Investment Act.

The income shown in the distribution account as available for distribution is the annual income from the underlying investments after provision for expenses.

Accounting of Portfolio Investments

The annual return of a German-resident UCITS is determined in accordance with the principle of supply. The Investment Taxation Act, however, provides for a few modifications. The principle of supply and the modifications of the Investment Taxation Act determine when income from the investments is added to the annual return.

Marketable and non-marketable securities such as shares, bonds and other debt securities, financial options, or financial futures are valued at cost.[73]

The annual return of a German-resident UCITS does not include any change in value of marketable and non-marketable securities until that change is realized at the time that the securities are disposed of or in the case of options or futures, the expiry date.

A dividend from marketable shares is accounted for when the shares are quoted ex-dividend. If a dividend is paid out on non-marketable shares, the dividend is accounted for at the time the dividend is declared.[74]

Interest is included in the annual return of a German-resident UCITS at the time that it accrues. If a German-resident UCITS is given compensation in the form of a discount on the par value of the bond or other debt security,[75] the amount of the discount has to be spread linearly over the life of the security as interest. If compensation is paid by a German-resident UCITS at the time of purchase in the form of a premium above the par value,[76] the amount of the premium is spread similarly, although as costs. Some bonds do not bear interest periodically. Instead, they pay the interest together with the repayment at the date of repayment. In accordance with the principles of commercial law, the growth of interest has to be added annually to the book value of those non-interest-bearing bonds.[77]

---

73. K. Beckmann, in *Investment: Handbuch für das gesamte Investmentwesen*, ed. K. Beckmann, R. Scholtz, & L. Vollmer (Berlin: Erich Schmidt Verlag, loose leaf), InvStG § 44, 35.
74. T. Elser, in *Investment: Handbuch für das gesamte Investmentwesen*, ed. K. Beckmann, R. Scholtz, & L. Vollmer (Berlin: Erich Schmidt Verlag, loose leaf), InvStG § 3, 7; and *Investmentsteuergesetz Zweifels-und Auslegungsfragen,* BMF 2 Jun. 2005 – IV C1 – S 1980 – 1 – 87/05, InvStG § 3, 48.
75. A discount on the par value of a bond is given where the interest rate of the bond is less than the interest rate of the capital market.
76. A premium above the par value of a bond is paid where the interest rate of the bond is more than the interest rate of the capital market.
77. K. Beckmann, in *Investment: Handbuch für das gesamte Investmentwesen*, ed. K Beckmann, R. Scholtz, & L. Vollmer (Berlin: Erich Schmidt Verlag, loose leaf), InvStG § 44, 32; and M. Schödermeier & C. Baltzer, in *KAGG and AuslInvestment-Gesetz – Kommentar*, ed. J. Brinkhaus & P. Scherer (Munich:Verlag C.H. Beck, 2003), KAGG § 24a, 31.

Deduction of Tax

As mentioned in Section 6.3.3, the foreign withholding tax charged at source on the income is either deductible from the taxable income of the unitholders or creditable against the tax liability of the unitholders. In the case of the latter, the foreign withholding tax is shown as fully deductible from the income of German-resident UCITS that is available for distribution.

Expenses

All expenses, including management costs, must be deducted from the annual income from the underlying investments. This is different only for expenses directly connected with the purchase or disposal of investments or otherwise connected with capital.

For the application of the Income Tax Act and the Corporate Tax Act, the expenses are considered to be spread proportionally over the different types of income from the underlying investments. The part of the expenses related to income that is exempt from German tax is not deductible. Furthermore, the part of the expenses not related to foreign withholding tax is deductible for only 90%.[78]

Losses

For the application of the Income Tax Act and Corporate Tax Act, a loss may be set off against any income of the same type. A loss of one income type may be set off only against another income type when that other income type is taxed similarly in the hands of all unitholders. Income types are not taxed similarly where one income type is partially exempt in the hands of a unitholder and the other is fully exempt or fully taxable. The entitlement to a foreign tax credit, however, does not constitute a different taxation.[79] If a loss cannot, or cannot entirely, be set off, the non-credible amount is carried forward to the following financial year to be credited against income of the same type.

6.4.3. Netherlands-Resident UCITS

6.4.3.1. Netherlands-Resident (EII) UCITS

The Law on Financial Supervision does not lay down whether the income from the underlying investments of Netherlands-resident (EII) UCITS is distributed or not. The latter is therefore determined by the instrument of incorporation or fund rules.

78. Section 3(1) and (2) Investment Taxation Act.
79. T. Elser, in *Investment: Handbuch für das gesamte Investmentwesen*, ed. K. Beckmann, R. Scholtz, & L. Vollmer (Berlin: Erich Schmidt Verlag, loose leaf), InvStG § 3, 63.

Annual Return

To prevent the income by accumulation not being taxable until the disposal of the units in these UCITS, the Corporate Tax Act requires corporate unitholders to value the units of these UCITS at market value.[80] The market value of the units in UCITS does not significantly vary from the net asset value, which is the difference between the assets and liabilities of a UCITS on a per unit basis. The change in value of the net asset value at the end of the year and that at the beginning of the year equals the annual return from the investments of the UCITS in that period. The annual return includes realized yields from investments, changes in value of the investments and other income.[81]

Accounting of Portfolio Investments

The annual return of a Netherlands-resident (EII) UCITS is determined in accordance with the Netherlands guidelines for annual reporting. The accountancy principles laid down in these guidelines thus determine at what time, and for what amount, income from the investments of the UCITS is included in the annual income.

Marketable and non-marketable securities such as shares, financial options, financial futures, or bonds and other debt securities have to be valued at market value.[82] Any change in value is, therefore, included in the net asset value of the UCITS at the time that it arises.

A dividend from marketable and non-marketable shares is accounted for at the time that the UCITS derives a right to the payment of the dividend.[83] This is generally the time that the dividend is declared by the paying company.

Interest is included in the net asset value of a Netherlands-resident (EII) UCITS at the time that it accrues.[84] If a Netherlands-resident (EII) UCITS is given compensation at the time of purchase in the form of a discount on the par value of a bond or other debt security,[85] the amount of the discount needs to be spread linearly over the life of the security as interest. If compensation is paid by a Netherlands-resident (EII) UCITS at the time of purchase in the form of a premium above the par value of a bond or other debt security,[86] the amount of the premium, like a discount, must be spread linearly over the life of the security as negative interest. Some bonds or other debt securities do not generate interest on a periodical

---

80. Section 8(1) Corporate Tax Act in conjunction with s. 3.29a(1) of the Income Tax Act (Wet Inkomstenbelasting 2001), *Stb.* 2000, 215, 11 May 2000.
81. Netherlands Guidelines for Annual Reporting 615, 303.
82. Netherlands Guidelines for Annual Reporting 615, 201.
83. Netherlands Guidelines for Annual Reporting 615, 303, in conjunction with 270, 125.
84. Netherlands Guidelines for Annual Reporting 615, 101, in conjunction with 270, 125.
85. A discount on the par value of a bond is given where the interest rate of the bond is less than the interest rate of the capital market.
86. A premium above the par value of a bond is paid where the interest rate of the bond is more than the interest rate of the capital market.

basis. The interest on these securities is, instead, paid at once at the redemption date.[87]

Deduction of Tax

The annual return is reduced by the withholding tax charged by the Netherlands and other states at source on income from the investments. The withholding tax is deductible from the annual income because no relief is available in the Netherlands.

Expenses

All expenses, including the management fee, must be deducted from the annual return. If expenses are connected with the purchase of investments, these expenses are included in the cost price of the investments instead of being deducted from the annual return.[88]

Losses

The Corporate Tax Act does not contain any special rules if the amount of the capital losses from the disposal of investments in a financial year exceeds that of the capital gains.

6.4.3.2. Netherlands-Resident (FII) UCITS

A Netherlands-resident (FII) UCITS has to distribute the income available for distribution within eight months after the end of each financial year. The income available for distribution is determined as (1) the business income of a Netherlands-resident (FII) UCITS reduced by (2) any changes in the value of the underlying investments where the UCITS has opted for a reinvestment account; (3) the non-deductible expenses listed in Article 2 of the Decree on Investment Schemes; and (4) creditable deficits from former years.[89]

Business Income

Income is considered to be business income if it is derived from the business assets of a corporate entity. The portfolio investments of Netherlands-resident (FII) UCITS of the corporate type are always considered business income. As public corporations or private corporations with limited liability, these UCITS are

87. Netherlands Guidelines for Annual Reporting 615 at 101 in conjunction with 270, 126.
88. Netherlands Guidelines for Annual Reporting 615, 101, in conjunction with 214, 205.
89. Article 28(2)(b) Corporate Tax Act in conjunction with Arts 1A and 2 of the Decree on Investment Schemes.

considered to carry on their business with their entire capital.[90] The same applies to the portfolio investments of Netherlands-resident (FII) UCITS of the contractual type, because funds for joint account are also considered to carry on their business with their entire capital.[91]

Tax Accounting Principles

The business income of a Netherlands-resident (FII) UCITS is determined by the principles of sound business practice.[92] The principle of sound business practice, which has been developed in the case law because it is not further defined in the Corporate Tax Act or the Income Tax Act, has the aim of having only those benefits and expenses included in the profits of a financial year that are related to that year only. In principle, a Netherlands-resident (FII) UCITS must use the principles of business economics by determining annual profits, unless these principles are not in accordance with the Corporate Tax Act or the Income Tax Act, or the aim or a principle of one of these acts (principle of sound business practice).[93]

Tax Accounting of Portfolio Investments

The business income in the financial year of a Netherlands-resident (FII) UCITS is generally determined by a comparison of the value of the business assets by the end of that year with that in the beginning. Any change in value is thus taxable as business income. When a change in value of investments in equity, bonds and debt securities, options, and futures is included in the business income, it is determined by sound business practice. Sound business practice also determines when other income from the investments such as dividends or interest is entered into the books.

Marketable securities such as shares,[94] financial options,[95] or financial futures[96] can be valued either at the lower of cost and market value or at market value. If marketable securities are valued at the lower of cost and market value, the business income of a corporate entity does not include any increase in value of the securities until that increase is realized by the disposal of the securities or in the case of options or futures, at the expiry date. A decrease in value, on the other hand, is taken into account at the time that it arises. An increase in value is taken into account the following year but not for more than the original cost of the securities Any change in value is included in the business income of a corporate entity at the time that it arises if marketable securities are valued at market value.

90. Article 2(5) Corporate Tax Act.
91. Article 2(2) Corporate Tax Act.
92. Article 8(1) Corporate Tax Act in conjunction with Art. 3.25 Income Tax Act.
93. Supreme Court of the Netherlands, 8 May 1957, *BNB* 1957/208.
94. L.W. Sillevis et al., *Cursus Belastingrecht (Inkomstenbelasting)* (Deventer: Kluwer, loose leaf), 3.2.18.G.b.
95. P.M. Verhagen, *Financiële derivaten in de fiscale winst* (Lelystad: Vermande, 1997), 169.
96. *Ibid.*, 79 and 80.

Non-marketable securities such as shares,[97] financial options,[98] or financial forwards,[99] on the other hand, are valued at cost. The business income of a corporate entity does not include any change in value of non-marketable securities until that change is realized at the time that the shares are disposed of or in the case of options or futures, the expiry date.

A dividend from shares is included in the business income of a corporate entity at the time that the decision to do so is taken by the corporation that makes the payment of dividend.

Bonds and other debt instruments are valued at market value or at par value. If bonds are purchased with the intention of keeping them only for a short period, they have to be valued at market value. In that case, any change in value is included in the business income of the corporate entity at the time that the change arises.

Bonds and debt instruments have to be valued at par value if a corporate entity has the intention of keeping them until the repayment date. If the corporate entity is given compensation in the form of a discount on the par value of the bond,[100] the amount of the discount is either credited at once against other business income or is entered into the books as a temporary item that is marked down for depreciation linearly during the financial years until the repayment date. If compensation is paid by the corporate entity at the time of purchase in the form of a premium above the par value,[101] the amount of the premium is entered into the books as a temporary item, which is marked down for depreciation linearly during the financial years until the repayment date.[102] Hence, the premium is deducted during these financial years as a loss.

Interest is included in the business income of a corporate entity at the time that it accrues. Some bonds do not bear interest periodically, but instead they pay the interest together with the repayment at the date of repayment. In accordance with the principle of sound business practice, the accrued interest must be added annually to the book value of those non-interest-bearing bonds. As a result of this, because of the increase in value of the bond, the accrued interest is included in the income of the financial year concerned.[103] The Secretary of State for Finance is of the opinion that this practice is also applicable to zero-bonds, deep-discount bonds, and savings certificates.[104]

97. L.W. Sillevis et al., *Cursus Belastingrecht (Inkomstenbelasting)* (Kluwer, loose leaf) at 3.2.18.G.b.
98. P.M. Verhagen, *Financiële derivaten in de fiscale winst* (Lelystad: Vermande, 1997), at 169.
99. *Ibid.*, at 79 and 80.
100. A discount on the par value of a bond is given where the interest rate of the bond is less than the interest rate of the capital market.
101. A premium above the par value of a bond is paid where the interest rate of the bond is more than the interest rate of the capital market.
102. HR 13 Nov. 1991, No. 27.563, *BNB* 1992/109.
103. HR 28 Feb. 1968, No. 15.847, *BNB* 1968/93.
104. Decision of the Secretary of State for Finance of 11 Mar. 1996, DB96/805M, 1186, *BNB* 1996/157.

Changes in Value of the Investments and Reinvestment Account

Despite the above, a change in value of the underlying portfolio investments is excluded from the business income if the UCITS has opted for a reinvestment account. In that case the changes in value of the underlying portfolio investments do not have to be distributed. By accumulation, the changes in value are not realized by the unitholders until the disposal of the units in the UCITS. The choice for a reinvestment account needs to be made before the tax assessment of the first financial year becomes final.[105]

If a Netherlands-resident (FII) UCITS has opted for a reinvestment account, the management costs are not fully deductible from the business income of the UCITS. In that case, only a proportional part of the management costs[106] is deductible from the business income, whereas the other part reduces the reinvestment account.[107] The management costs thus have to be spread among the income available for distribution and the reinvestment account.

Deduction of Tax

The part of the foreign withholding tax that exceeds the relief granted by the Netherlands for the withholding tax is not available for distribution to the unitholders. Therefore, this part is deductible from the business income. The same applies for withholding tax on capital gains and other portfolio income for which no relief is available.

Non-deductible Expenses

Non-deductible expenses are taken into account in determining income available for distribution because they have reduced the income available for distribution. These expenses are, with respect to UCITS, the non-deductible amount of the remuneration of a member of the supervisory board, the non-deductible part of donations, and the non-deductible part of the general costs of the UCITS that also contain a personal element.[108]

Non-deductible expenses cannot be fully credited against the income available for distribution if a Netherlands-resident (FII) UCITS has opted for a reinvestment account. A proportional part of the non-deductible expenses[109] may be credited

105. Article 4(1) Decree on Investment Schemes.
106. A proportional part of the management costs is the part of the amount of the economic value of the assets reduced by the amount of the reinvestment account in the beginning of the financial year in relation to the amount of the economic value of the assets, or in the case of UCITS of the contractual type of the UCITS itself (Art. 2(6) Decree on Investment Schemes).
107. Sections 2(2) and 4(1) Decree on Investment Schemes.
108. Article 2(1) Decree on Investment Schemes.
109. A proportional part of the non-deductible costs is the part of the amount of the economic value of the assets reduced with the amount of the reinvestment account in the beginning of the

against income available for distribution while the other part reduces the reinvestment account.[110] The non-deductible expenses thus have to be spread among the income available for distribution and the reinvestment account.

Creditable Deficits

A creditable deficit may be set off against the income available for distribution in the following eight years. A creditable deficit is one made during the period that a UCITS had opted for the special tax regulations for UCITS and other investment funds.[111]

6.4.3.3. Netherlands-Resident (TII) UCITS

The fund rules of Netherlands-resident (TII) UCITS determine whether or not the income from the underlying investments is distributed since the Law on Financial Supervision does not stipulate such.

Annual Return

The annual return from the underlying investments of Netherlands-resident (TII) UCITS is for tax purposes considered to be received by the unitholders at the time of arising. Any expenses made at the level of these UCITS other than for collecting income from the underlying investments are therefore not deductible by the unitholders.

Accounting of Portfolio Investments

The annual return of Netherlands-resident (TII) UCITS is, in practice, determined in accordance with the principles of sound business practice only, as the income of individual unitholders is determined as a fixed percentage on the average value of the units in the UCITS; see Section 11.2.1.1 for more information on the latter. The annual return is thus determined in accordance with the same principles as discussed in Section 6.4.3.2 for Netherlands-resident (FII) UCITS.

A point of particular interest is the allocation of capital gains and losses realized by the disposal of the underlying investments among the unitholders. These investments are considered to be disposed not only by their sale or redemption but also each time that a Netherlands-resident (TII) UCITS issues units. After the issuing of units, the underlying investments are held by more unitholders than before. The existing unitholders have, thus, disposed a part of their share in the investments to the new unitholders. Netherlands-resident (TII) UCITS therefore

---

financial year in relation to amount of the economic value of the assets, or in the case of UCITS of the contractual type of the UCITS itself (Art. 2(6) Decree on Investment Schemes).

110. Articles 2(2) and 4(3) Decree on Investment Schemes.
111. Article 2(3) Decree on Investment Schemes.

need to administer the amount of the capital gain or loss realized by the unitholder at each issue date. Unlike Austria and Germany, the Netherlands has neglected to provide for a practical solution for such disposals.

Deduction of Tax

The tax withheld by a source state is considered to be that of the unitholders. It may therefore be set off against the (corporate) income tax liability of the unitholders. It is not deducted from the amount of the annual return.

Expenses

As mentioned earlier, the costs made at the level of the UCITS are not deductible. This is different only for the expenses made for collecting income from the underlying investments. These expenses are deductible.

Losses

Any loss realized by the disposal of the *underlying investments* is considered to be that of the unitholders. It is thus deductible at the time of arising. In the case that a loss cannot or cannot fully be set off against the other income of the unitholder, the non-creditable part of the loss is carried back to the previous year or carried forward to the following year.

6.4.4. UK-Resident UCITS

Under the instrument of incorporation or the trust deed of a UK-resident UCITS, the income from the underlying investments is distributed, accumulated, or both distributed and accumulated. Where the income is both distributed and accumulated, it is partially distributed to certain series of units while the other part is accumulated for other series of units. The proceeds from the disposal of investments, except in the case of liquidation, may not be distributed to the unitholders.[112]

Distribution Account

The income shown in the distribution account as available for distribution is, for the application of the Tax Acts, considered to be distributed as dividends or yearly interest at the distribution date.[113] The distribution date is the end of a distribution

112. *Simon's Direct Tax Service* (London: Butterworths, loose leaf), D4.1311.
113. Sections 15(1), 17(1), 18(1), and 22(1) the Authorized Investment Funds (Tax) Regulations 2006). The articles of incorporation or, as the case may be, the trust deed of some UK UCITS

period, unless by or in accordance with the instrument of incorporation or trust deed, another date is specified. A distribution period is defined the length of time between payments of distributions. It is at the most a year, but the articles of incorporation or trust deed may stipulate a shorter distribution period, such as a month, quarter, or half of a year.[114]

Income Available for Distribution

The income shown in the distribution account as available for distribution means 'the available income after provision for tax and expenses'.[115] The income shown in the distribution account does not include any proceeds from the disposal of investments. These proceeds are not realized by the unitholders until the disposal of the units in the UCITS.

Accounting of Income from Underlying Investments

The distribution account of a UK-resident UCITS is determined in accordance with the accountancy principles laid down in the Investment Management Association's Statement of Recommended Practice (SORP) relating to Authorized Funds and agreed by the UK's Audit Standard Board (ASB).[116] This statement is compulsory for UK-resident UCITS under the Financial Services Authority (FSA) sourcebook for collective investment schemes. The accountancy principles laid down in the statement of recommended practice determine when income from the investments, such as dividends and interest, is added to the distribution account.

A dividend from marketable shares is accounted for when the shares are quoted ex-dividend, that is, at the date at which a purchaser of the stock would not have a right to dividends or the date when the quoted price fell to reflect the value of a dividend concerned. If a dividend is paid out on non-marketable shares, the dividend is accounted for at the time that the dividend is declared. In the case of UK dividends, a dividend tax credit is not taken into account.[117]

---

states that no distribution takes place if the distribution account is less than an agreed amount (*de minimis* limit). In that case, the amount of the distribution account is, under certain conditions, not considered to be distributed to the unitholders. The UCITS may in that case waive the amount of the distribution account that is less than the *de minimis* limit (*de minimis* amount) and carry that amount forward as available for distribution to the annual income of the following year. It should be noted that none of the units in the UCITS may be in bearer form (s. 23 The Authorized Investment Funds [Tax] Regulations 2006).

114. L. Shirley, Authorised Unit Trusts and OEICs, in S. Newcombe et al., *Tolley's Taxation of Collective Investment* (London: LexisNexis Tolley, 2003), 27.

115. A. Macfarlanes, *Collective Investment Schemes: the Law and Practice* (London: Sweet and Maxwell, loose leaf), B1.006.

116. As reissued in 21 Nov. 2008 by the Investment Management Association.

117. Statement of Recommended Practice relating to Authorised Funds, para. 2.28.

Interest or other income from non-equity securities such as bonds and other debt securities is included in the distribution account of a UK-resident UCITS at the time it is earned. The part of the proceeds from the disposal of bonds or other interest-bearing securities related to accrued interest therefore needs to be added to the distribution account.

Interest from debt securities should be recognized as revenue using the effective interest method of accounting. This is a method of calculating the amortized cost of a financial asset or financial liability and allocating the interest income or interest expense over a relevant investment period. For example, if a UK-resident UCITS is given compensation in the form of a discount on the par value of the bond or other debt security,[118] the amount of the discount has to be spread linearly over the life of the security as interest. If compensation is paid by a UCITS at the time of purchase in the form of a premium above the par value,[119] the amount of the premium is spread similarly as costs.

The size of any discount or premium should be reviewed on a regular basis when an expected maturity date changes or a premium or discount changes, it may be appropriate to revise cash flow estimates.[120]

Gains and losses from financial options and financial futures are included in the distribution account where they are undertaken to generate income or protect income. Gains and losses generated from positions to protect or enhance capital are not.

Deduction of Tax

Taxation is taken into account because it reduces the income available for distribution either in the financial year in which it arises or a following year. Such taxation is the corporate income tax liability of the UCITS after relief for double taxation and the withholding tax levied at source on income. If the corporate income tax liability on certain income is deferred because of a difference in the time that income is recognized for accountancy and for tax purposes, the income available for distribution is, nevertheless, reduced by the deferred tax. The amount of the deferred tax has to be paid to the revenue in the future and is thus not available for distribution. The deferred tax balances may, however, change over time as a result of legislative changes. The income available for distribution is also affected by adjustments in respect of previous periods. The adjustments reduce the income available for distribution in the financial year in which they occur.

118. A discount on the par value of a bond is given where the interest rate of the bond is less than the interest rate of the capital market.
119. A premium above the par value of a bond is paid where the interest rate of the bond is more than the interest rate of the capital market.
120. Statement of Recommended Practice relating to Authorised Funds, paras 1.25, 1.26, 2.36–2.50.

Expenses

All expenses must be deducted from any income, but only if they are allowable for tax purposes. This is different only for expenses directly connected with the purchase or disposal of investments or otherwise connected with capital.[121]

6.4.5. Conclusion

To tax the income from the underlying investments of UCITS as if the unitholders had invested directly, the countries studied provide measures to distribute the income to the unitholders or measures with a similar effect. The Netherlands requires Netherlands-resident (FII) UCITS to actually distribute the income that is available for distribution. The other countries do not require an actual distribution. Nor does the Netherlands for Netherlands-resident (EII/TII) UCITS. The part of the income available for distribution that is not actually distributed is nevertheless considered by these countries to be distributed to the unitholders. Although the measures taken are mostly similar, the countries studied apply different principles to determine the amount of income available for distribution.

The income from the investments of Netherlands-resident (EII) UCITS does not have to be distributed or is considered to be distributed. Instead, the units of these UCITS have to be valued at market value by corporate unitholders so that any income derived from the investments during the financial year of the unitholders is taxable.

6.5. WITHHOLDING TAX LEVIED BY THE UCITS COUNTRY

6.5.1. Austrian-Resident UCITS

Tax Base and Tax Rate

Austria charges a 25% withholding tax from Austrian-resident UCITS at the time of distribution or the disposal of the units in the UCITS. The withholding tax is charged on the part of a distribution or the proceeds from a disposal that is related to the following:[122]

(1) Interest from deposits or other debts with domestic credit institutions or a domestic branch of a foreign credit institution
(2) Interest from bonds or other debt securities
(3) Income from speculative transactions

121. Statement of Recommended Practice relating to Authorised Funds, para. 2.35.
122. Article 93(3)(4) Income Tax Act.

(4) Dividends, interest or other distributions from shares in non-resident companies.

The withholding tax needs to be deducted by the clearinghouse, bank, or credit institution that pays the distribution or the proceeds from the disposal to the unitholder (paying agent) from the gross amount of the tax object. The tax withheld is remitted to the Austrian tax authorities on behalf of the unitholders.

Any of the above-mentioned items of income that are not distributed within four months after the end of the year in which they arose is considered to be distributed at the end of that period (deemed distribution). In that case the UCITS is required to make a distribution to the unitholders for the amount of the withholding tax due on the deemed distribution.[123]

Exemption from Withholding Tax

Distributions paid to resident pension funds are not subject to withholding tax.[124] The same applies for distributions paid to non-resident pension funds and other non-resident unitholders.[125] Distributions paid to non-resident pension funds are thus not subject to more taxation than that paid to resident pension funds.

Reduction of Withholding Tax

An appeal to a reduction of withholding tax under one of the Austrian tax treaties is not necessary because distributions paid to non-residents are exempt from tax on the basis of the Austrian unilateral rules as discussed earlier.

6.5.2. German-Resident UCITS

Tax Base and Tax Rate

Germany charges a withholding tax from German-resident UCITS at the time of distribution. A 26.375% (2009) withholding tax is charged on the part of a distribution that is related to the following:[126]

(1) Dividends or other distributions from shares or other equity participations.
(2) Interest from bonds or other debt securities.
(3) Capital gains from the disposal of shares and other financial instruments.[127]

123. Section 13 Law on Investment Funds.
124. Article 94(6) Income Tax Act.
125. Article 98(1)(5) Income Tax Act.
126. Section 32d Income Tax Act in combination with s. 7(1), (2) and (4) Investment Taxation Act.
127. A capital gain is considered to be the difference between the proceeds from the disposal after deduction of any connected costs and the cost price. A transitional arrangement applies to

A resident UCITS that makes the distribution is obliged to withhold tax on the gross amount of that part and pay the tax to the German tax authorities on behalf of the unitholders within ten days after the end of the month.

Any of these items of income that are not distributed at the end of the year are considered to be so for the purposes of withholding tax. Exceptions to the rule are accumulated capital gains from the disposal of shares and other financial instruments. These capital gains are subject to withholding tax only in the case that they are actually distributed to the unitholders or realized at the time of disposal of the units in the UCITS.[128]

A withholding tax of 26.375% is further charged by Germany on capital gains realized by the disposal of *units* in a German-resident UCITS.[129] The credit institution or financial service provider that is charged by the alienator to execute the disposal, is obliged to withhold tax on the proceeds from the disposal. The tax needs to be remitted to the German tax authorities on behalf of the alienator within ten days after the end of the month.

Exemption from Withholding Tax

An exemption applies to interest from bonds and debentures other than from convertible and profit-sharing ones distributed to resident pension funds, charities, and other exempt corporate unitholders. These distributions are not subject to withholding tax. The same is true for interest from bonds and debentures other than from convertible and profit-sharing ones paid to non-resident pension funds, charities and other non-resident taxpayers.

Reduction of Withholding Tax

In the presence of a tax treaty, the withholding tax on the part of a distribution to non-resident individual or corporate unitholders that is related to dividends or other distributions from shares or other equity participations or the proceeds from the disposal of dividend coupons is charged at the most at the percentage agreed on for dividends. The majority of the German tax treaties provide for a lower percentage for dividends than the domestic percentage of 26.375%. In the German tax treaties with the other countries studied, the source state's right to tax dividends is limited to a maximum of 15%.

---

capital gains on shares or other financial instruments that were acquired before 1 Jan. 2008. These capital gains remain tax exempt but only if the financial instruments were held for at least one year.

128. See s. 1(3) Investment Tax Act.

129. Section 32d Income Tax Act in combination with s. 8(5) and (6) Investment Taxation Act.

6.5.3. Netherlands-Resident UCITS

6.5.3.1. Netherlands-Resident (EII) UCITS

Exemption from Withholding Tax

The Netherlands does not charge a withholding tax from Netherlands-resident (EII) UCITS at the time of distribution. The distributions of these UCITS are exempt from withholding tax.[130]

6.5.3.2. Netherlands-Resident (FII) UCITS

Tax Base and Tax Rate

The Netherlands imposes a withholding tax of 15% from Netherlands-resident (FII) UCITS at the time of distribution or redemption of the units in the UCITS. The tax is withheld by the UCITS on the gross amount of the distribution or the part of the redemption price that exceeds the paid-up capital.[131] The withholding tax must be remitted to the Netherlands tax authorities on behalf of the unitholder within one month.

An exemption applies to a distribution at the expense of the reinvestment account, but only if it is shown in the books likewise and the unitholders are informed about the nature of the distribution.[132] The exemption also applies to the part of the redemption price that is related to the reinvestment account. In both cases, the exemption realizes that capital gains and losses from the underlying investments, which are included in the reinvestment account as discussed in Section 6.4.3.2, are not subject to more taxation than in the case of a direct investment.

Refund of Withholding Tax

A refund of withholding tax is available for distributions paid to pension funds and charities residing in the Netherlands because they are exempt from corporate income tax.[133] The same applies to pension funds and charities residing in another Member State of the European Union.[134] The refund is, however, limited to pension funds and charities that would also be exempt from tax if they had resided in the Netherlands. Either way, no refund is available for the part of the withholding tax charged at the time of distribution for which a Netherlands-resident (FII)

130. Article 1(4) Dividend Tax Act.
131. Article 1(1), 1(2) and 3 Dividend Tax Act.
132. Article 3b Dividend Tax Act in combination with the Decree of 12 Dec. 2008, CPP2008/708M, *NTFR* 2009/33, 7.2.
133. Article 10(1) Dividend Tax Act.
134. Article 10(1) and (3) Dividend Tax Act.

UCITS is granted relief for foreign withholding tax.[135] Otherwise, the Netherlands would not only refund domestic withholding tax but indirectly also foreign withholding tax. This is not considered desirable.

The restriction of the refund to pension funds and charities residing in the Netherlands or a Member State of the EU seems to infringe the free movement of capital between the Member States of the EEA as laid down in the Article 40 of the EEA Treaty. Exempt corporate unitholders residing in Iceland, Liechtenstein, or Norway are, unlike their resident or EU counterparts, not entitled to a refund. These non-resident unitholders are therefore treated less favourably than their resident counterparts.

Reduction of Withholding Tax

In the presence of a tax treaty, the withholding tax on a distribution to non-resident individuals and corporate unitholders is charged at the most at the percentage agreed on by the Contracting States for dividends. Some Netherlands tax treaties provide in a lower percentage for dividends than the domestic tax rate of 15%. The Netherlands tax treaties with the other countries studied, however, provide for 15%, which is equal to the domestic tax rate.

6.5.3.3. Netherlands-Resident (TII) UCITS

The distributions of Netherlands-resident (TII) UCITS are not subject to withholding tax in the Netherlands because these UCITS are not considered to be a company. The Netherlands does not charge a withholding tax on distributions by entities other than a company.

6.5.4. UK-Resident UCITS

Tax Base and Tax Rate

The United Kingdom charges a withholding tax from UK-resident UCITS at the time of distribution. The 20% withholding tax is, however, charged only in the case of distributions of yearly interest (interest distribution).[136] The resident UCITS, which pays the interest distribution, or the person through whom the interest distribution is made, needs to deduct the withholding tax from the gross amount of that payment.

Any income shown in the distribution account as available for an interest distribution is considered to be distributed as yearly interest at the distribution date; see also Section 6.4.4. In such a case, the UCITS must deduct the withholding

135. Article 10(1) Dividend Tax Act.
136. Section 349(2) Income and Corporation Tax Act in conjunction with s. 26(1) The Authorized Investment Funds (Tax) Regulations 2006.

tax from the amount of the distribution account and to remit it to the UK tax authorities on behalf of the unitholders.[137]

Exemption from Withholding Tax

No withholding tax is, however, charged on distributions paid to companies, including exempt companies like pension funds or charities.[138] Nor is it charged on distributions paid to non-resident companies and other non-resident unitholders.[139] These distributions are explicitly exempt from withholding tax. Apparently, the United Kingdom would like to restrict the deduction of withholding tax to distributions paid to resident individual taxpayers.

Reduction of Withholding Tax

An appeal to a reduction of withholding tax under one of the UK tax treaties is not necessary because distributions paid to non-residents are not subject to withholding tax under the UK unilateral rules as discussed earlier.

6.5.5. Conclusion

To ensure that the income is subject to the same amount of withholding tax as a direct investment, Austria, Germany, and the Netherlands provide measures to charge withholding tax on the part of the distribution by resident UCITS that has, as discussed in Section 3.2, been exempt from tax at source, on receipt by the UCITS, or for which the tax withheld at source has been refunded to the UCITS. The Netherlands also charges a withholding tax on the part of the distribution for which relief for the tax withheld by other states has been granted.

Austria, the Netherlands and in the case of interest distributions, the United Kingdom further charge a withholding tax on certain other parts of the distribution to ensure the (corporate) income tax liability for the unitholders.

Chapter 7 will provide a more comprehensive discussion of the differences in taxation at the level of the UCITS.

137. Section 26(6) The Authorized Investment Funds (Tax) Regulations 2006.
138. Section 47(2) The Authorized Investment Funds (Tax) Regulations 2006.
139. Section 26(4) The Authorized Investment Funds (Tax) Regulations 2006.

Chapter 7

Comparison of Taxation of Income from the Investments in the UCITS Country Undertakings for Collective Investment in Transferable Securities

One of the countries studied, Austria, makes use of transparency to avoid double taxation. Transparency establishes that the income from securities and other financial instruments is in the undertaking for collective investment in transferable securities (UCITS) country considered to belong to the unitholders and, thus, is subject to tax once. Otherwise, the income is considered to be that of the UCITS. This is the case in Germany and the United Kingdom. These countries avoid double taxation by way of a subjective exemption, reduced tax rate, reduced tax base, or compensation to the unitholder for taxation at the level of the UCITS.

One of the countries studied, the Netherlands, provides for a dual approach. On the basis of the legal status of the UCITS under civil law, UCITS are for tax purposes considered to be transparent or opaque. In the case of the latter, they may opt for a subjective exemption or a reduced tax rate of nil percent. This enables a Netherlands-resident UCITS to optimize its taxation on the basis of the investments and the tax status of the unitholders.

The United Kingdom makes use of more than one instrument to avoid double taxation. The type of income determines what instrument is used to avoid double taxation. An objective exemption avoids double taxation in the case of domestic dividends, a reduced tax base avoids double taxation of interest and other income where the qualifying investment test is satisfied, and in other cases compensation to the unitholders should take away double taxation. Compensation at the level of the unitholders is, however, not an effective instrument to avoid double taxation. It does not take away double taxation if the unitholder is not liable to tax in the United Kingdom, that is, exempt corporate unitholders or non-resident unitholders.

The objective and subjective tax liability of UCITS does not only affect the application of tax treaties for income derived by way of UCITS, but it also affects the crediting of the tax withheld at source. Additional measures are necessary to establish that the crediting of these withholding taxes does not differ from the crediting applied in the case of a direct investment. Nevertheless, the majority of the countries studied that consider resident UCITS to be opaque have failed to take such measures. Instead, they provide relief at the level of the UCITS. The availability and the amount of the relief is not the same as for a direct investment.

As an alternative to transparency, certain items of income in the countries studied are exempt from withholding tax or the tax withheld is refunded to the UCITS. Instead, these items of income are subject to withholding tax at the time of distribution. The tax base, tax rate, and available exemptions should be applied as if the unitholders had invested directly. This is, however, not entirely the case in the countries studied, so taxation at the time of distribution is not necessarily the same as taxation at source in the case of a direct investment.

7.1. INTRODUCTION

This chapter provides a more in-depth discussion of the instruments used by the countries studied to establish that taxation in the UCITS country does not differ from a direct investment. Section 7.2 analyses and compares the objective and subjective tax liability of UCITS in the countries studied. In Section 7.3 follows an examination of the crediting of withholding tax at the level of the UCITS. Section 7.4 ends with an evaluation and comparison of taxation on distributions.

7.2. MEASURES TAKEN TO AVOID ECONOMIC DOUBLE TAXATION OF THE INCOME DERIVED BY WAY OF UCITS

Table 7.1 demonstrates that Austria, Germany, the Netherlands, and the United Kingdom do not apply the same instruments to establish that the use of UCITS does not result in more taxation (or less taxation) than a direct investment. Taxation in the UCITS country therefore differs in Austria, Germany, the Netherlands, and the United Kingdom.

Table 7.1 Comparison of the Subjective and Objective Tax Liability of UCITS in the Countries Studied

UCITS Country	*Resident Unitholders*	*Non-resident Unitholders*	*Consequences of Taxation in the UCITS Country*
Austria	Avoidance of double taxation by way of transparency.	Avoidance of double taxation by way of transparency.	Fully avoids double taxation.
Germany	Avoidance of double taxation by way of a subjective exemption from corporate income tax.	Avoidance of double taxation by way of a subjective exemption from corporate income tax.	Fully avoids double taxation.
Netherlands	Avoidance of double taxation by way of transparency, a subjective exemption or a reduced tax rate.	Avoidance of double taxation by way of transparency, a subjective exemption or a reduced tax rate.	Fully avoids double taxation.
United Kingdom	Avoidance of double taxation through a reduced tax base, but only if the UCITS solely derives UK dividends or satisfies the qualifying investments test. Otherwise, double taxation is reduced only by way of a reduced tax rate in combination with compensation in	Avoidance of double taxation through a reduced tax base, but only if the UCITS solely derives UK dividends or satisfies the qualifying investments test. Otherwise, the double taxation is reduced only by way of a reduced tax rate. Non-resident unitholders are	Double taxation is only avoided if the UCITS solely derives UK dividends or satisfies the qualifying investment test. Otherwise, exempt corporate unitholders and non-resident unitholders are not compensated for taxation at the level of the UCITS, whereas the other

Table 7.1 (cont'd)

UCITS Country	*Resident Unitholders*	*Non-resident Unitholders*	*Consequences of Taxation in the UCITS Country*
	the form of a tax credit or an exemption at the level of the unitholder. Exempt corporate unitholders are, not compensated for taxation at the level of the UCITS.	not compensated for taxation at the level of the UCITS.	unitholders are only partly compensated for such.

7.2.1. Available Instruments to Avoid Double Taxation at the Level of Resident UCITS

7.2.1.1. Transparency

Austria considers income derived by way of Austrian-resident UCITS to be that of the unitholders because these UCITS are transparent for tax purposes. The income is therefore not subject to tax at the level of the UCITS. An advantage of transparency is that the avoidance of double taxation is not limited to Austrian-resident unitholders. It also avoids double (corporate) income tax for non-resident unitholders. The same applies for Netherlands-resident (TII) UCITS.

Example 7.1

Y, a UCITS residing in Austria, derives a dividend of EUR 100,000 from Z, an Austrian-resident company. The dividend is considered to be that of the unitholders of Y. No (corporate) income tax is due at the level of Y.

7.2.1.2. Subjective Exemption

Any income derived by way of German-resident UCITS and Netherlands-resident (EII/FII) UCITS is in Germany and the Netherlands considered to be that of the UCITS. A tax liability for these income types at the level of the UCITS is, however, prevented by way of a subjective exemption. The subjective exemption is optional in the Netherlands. Instead, an opaque Netherlands-resident UCITS may also opt for a reduced tax rate, which will be discussed later. Like transparency, a subjective exemption also prevents corporate income tax at the level of the UCITS for non-resident unitholders.

Example 7.2

Y, a German-resident company, pays a dividend of EUR 100,000 to Z, a UCITS residing in Germany. The dividend remains exempt at the level of the UCITS so that no corporate income tax is due by Z on the income.

7.2.1.3. Reduced Tax Rate

The Netherlands and the United Kingdom consider income derived by way of respectively Netherlands-resident (FII) UCITS and UK-resident UCITS to be that of the UCITS. Both countries apply for a reduced tax rate, which does not affect the UCITS's subjective liability to tax. The income from the investments forms part of its tax base. It is subject to corporate income tax at a rate of nil percent in the Netherlands and 20% in the United Kingdom. The tax liability of a Netherlands-resident (FII) UCITS is reduced to nil. The tax liability of an UK-resident UCITS is not nullified. Instead, it is determined in combination with a tax credit/exemption, a reduced tax rate, or both, as discussed later. The application of a reduced tax rate does not differ because of the participation of any non-resident unitholders.

Example 7.3

Y, a Netherlands-resident (FII) UCITS, is paid a dividend of EUR 100,000 by Z, a Netherlands-resident company. At the level of Y the dividend is subject to corporate income tax at a rate of nil percent. Y does not have to pay any corporate income tax on the income.

7.2.1.4. Compensation for the Unitholders

Income derived by way of UK-resident UCITS is considered to be that of the UCITS. Under the compensation method, the income derived by UK-resident UCITS is, under the general tax rules, subject to corporate income tax at the level of the UCITS, although at a reduced tax rate of 20%. The unitholders are then partly compensated for the tax liability of the UCITS. The compensation takes place in the form of a tax credit, an exemption, or a combination of both.

Example 7.4

X, an individual residing in the United Kingdom, keeps units in Y, a UK-resident UCITS. Y derives a dividend of EUR 100,000 from Z, a company residing in the Netherlands. The dividend is subject to UK corporate income tax at the level of Y. The corporate income tax due is EUR 20,000. After deduction of corporate income tax, the remaining amount of EUR 80,000 is distributed by Y to the unitholders. X derives an amount of EUR 800. He is entitled to a tax credit of EUR 89, while the corporate income tax liability at the level of Y that is related to the part of the dividend derived by X is EUR 200.

In the case in which the tax credit cannot, or cannot entirely, be set off by a unitholder, to the extent the non-creditable part is not refundable, it does not fully compensate the unitholder for taxation at the level of the UCITS. The same applies for an exemption in case the unitholder is subjectively exempt from tax. Among other persons, this is the case for pension funds or charities. For these investors, a direct investment is more attractive than an investment through an UK-resident UCITS.

Example 7.5

Some of the units in X, a UK-resident UCITS, are held by Y, a pension fund residing in the United Kingdom. Z, a Netherlands-resident UCITS, pays X a dividend of EUR 100,000. The dividend is subject to UK corporate income tax at the level of X. The corporate income tax due is EUR 20,000. After deduction of corporate income tax, the remaining amount of EUR 80,000 is distributed by X. Y derives an amount of EUR 800 instead of its share in the dividend, EUR 1,000.

Non-resident unitholders are generally not liable to (corporate) income tax in the United Kingdom. They are therefore not able to set off the tax credit or cannot benefit from an exemption for the distributed income or the income considered to be distributed.

7.2.1.5. Reduced Tax Base

The United Kingdom applies a reduced tax base to keep certain income from investments outside the tax base of UK-resident UCITS by way of either an exemption or a deduction. In either case, these income types are therefore not subject to tax at the level of the UCITS. An exemption applies to dividend paid by UK-resident companies and capital gains, whereas any distributed income may be deducted by a UK-resident UCITS from its taxable income as loan relationship debits if it satisfies the qualifying investment test. The application of a reduced tax base does not differ in case of non-resident unitholders.

Example 7.6

Y, a UK-resident UCITS, is paid a dividend of EUR 100,000 by Z, a UK-resident company. The dividend remains exempt from UK corporate income tax at the level of Y.

7.2.2. Conclusion

Although Austria, Germany, and the Netherlands make use of different instruments, each of these instruments ensures that income derived by way of UCITS results in the avoidance (corporate) income tax at the level of the UCITS and that of the unitholders (avoidance of double taxation). The instruments used by the United Kingdom prevent double taxation only for dividends paid by UK companies, for capital gains, or if a UCITS satisfies the qualifying investment test. Otherwise, the double taxation is for UK unitholders only partially taken way by the tax credit insofar as the tax credit can be fully set off against the income tax liability of these unitholders, whereas double taxation is not avoided for UK exempt corporate unitholders and non-resident unitholders.

7.3. MEASURES TO PROVIDE RELIEF FOR THE WITHHOLDING TAX CHARGED BY THE SOURCE STATE

Table 7.2 shows that not all of the countries studied have taken measures to establish that the crediting of the tax withheld at source of income derived by way of resident UCITS takes place for unitholders as if they had invested directly. Instead, the Netherlands and the United Kingdom provide relief for such withholding tax at the level of Netherlands-resident (EII/FII) UCITS and UK-resident UCITS. As a result, the overall taxation of UCITS is not the same in Austria, Germany, the Netherlands, and the United Kingdom.

Table 7.2 Comparison of the Availability of Relief at the Level of UCITS in the Countries Studied

UCITS Country	*Resident Unitholders*	*Non-resident Unitholders*	*Consequences of Taxation in the UCITS Country*
Austria	–	–	–
Germany	–	–	–

Table 7.2 (cont'd)

UCITS Country	*Resident Unitholders*	*Non-resident Unitholders*	*Consequences of Taxation in the UCITS Country*
Netherlands	Full payment to the UCITS for the withholding charged on dividend and interest that would have been available under a tax treaty for Dutch individual unitholders (FII), deduction from the annual return (EII), or no payment to the UCITS (TII).	No or a partial payment to the UCITS for the withholding charged on dividend and interest that is related to unitholders who are entitled to a reduction or an exemption from withholding tax if these items of income are distributed (FII), deduction from the annual return (EII), or no payment to the UCITS (TII).	Discourages Netherlands-resident (FII) UCITS to attract capital from states Member States or third states that have concluded a tax treaty with the Netherlands that provides in a reduced tax rate or an exemption for dividend.
United Kingdom	Foreign tax credit to the UCITS.	Foreign tax credit to the UCITS.	–

7.3.1. Availability of Instruments for Relief at the Level of Resident UCITS

7.3.1.1. Payment Relief at the Level of the UCITS

With the exception of (TII) UCITS, the Netherlands considers income derived by way of UCITS to be that of the UCITS. The tax withheld at source on such income is, for that reason, considered to be charged for the account of the UCITS. Unlike a direct investment, the amount of the foreign tax withholding tax that can be credited depends on the tax liability of the UCITS. Because of the nullified corporate income tax liability, Netherlands-resident (FII) UCITS are not able to set off any of the foreign withholding tax. The Netherlands therefore provides for relief in the form of a payment reduction for the tax that has to be withheld at the time of distribution. The relief, however, is limited to the tax withheld at source of dividends and interest.

Example 7.7

Y, a Netherlands-resident (FII) UCITS, is paid a dividend of EUR 100,000 by Z, a company residing in China. Z is required to withhold a tax of EUR 10,000 on the dividend. Assuming that the unitholders of Y are residing in the Netherlands, Y is granted by the Netherlands a payment reduction of EUR 10,000 for the Chinese tax withheld on the dividend.

Contrary to a direct investment, no relief is available for the withholding tax charged on capital gains and other portfolio income for which a tax treaty would in the case of a direct investment have provided for a foreign tax credit. The relief available for withholding tax on capital gains and other portfolio income derived by way of a Netherlands-resident (FII) UCITS from investments situated in a state that is under a tax treaty entitled to charge withholding tax on such income is for individual and corporate investors less than the relief available for a direct investment.

Example 7.8

Y, a Netherlands-resident (FII) UCITS, disposes shares in Z, a company residing in Panama. Assuming that Panama charges withholding tax on capital gains realized by the disposal of shares in resident companies, Y is not entitled to relief for the Panamanian withholding tax because such is limited to withholding tax on dividend and interest.

Unlike a direct investment, the amount of relief available for withholding tax charged on dividends and interest derived by way of Netherlands-resident (FII) UCITS is affected by the participation of non-residents (other than EU pension funds, charities, and other exempt corporate bodies) who are entitled to a reduction or an exemption from withholding tax under a tax treaty (disqualifying unitholders). The amount of the reduction or exemption granted to the unitholders on the gross amount of the dividend or interest under a tax treaty reduces the amount of relief granted to Netherlands-resident (FII) UCITS. The more disqualifying unitholders participate in a Netherlands-resident (FII) UCITS the less relief the UCITS derives. The Netherlands justifies the restriction by arguing that it reflects the financing of the relief by way of the final taxation on distributions for non-resident unitholders. The financing argument does not, however, seem to be valid, because more appropriate measures are available. Instead, the

Netherlands could, like Austria and Germany, provide relief at the level of the unitholders without restricting the circulation of units in Netherlands-resident (FII) UCITS.

Example 7.9

Y, a Netherlands-resident (FII) UCITS, is paid a dividend of EUR 100,000 by Z, a company residing in China. Z is required to withhold a tax of EUR 10,000 on the dividend. Assuming that half of the unitholders of Y are individuals residing in the Czech Republic, Portugal, or Slovakia, which are entitled to a reduced tax rate of 10% under the tax treaties with these states, Y is granted by the Netherlands a payment of EUR 5,000 for the Chinese tax withhold of EUR 10,000 on the dividend, whereas a Netherlands-resident (FII) UCITS with resident unitholders would have been granted a payment of only EUR 10,000.

A direct investment is, therefore, more attractive for individual and corporate unitholders than an investment by the use of a Netherlands-resident (FII) UCITS whose units are partly held by unitholders who are entitled to a reduction or exemption under a tax treaty.

Example 7.10

Y, a Netherlands-resident (FII) UCITS, is paid a dividend of EUR 100,000 by Z, a company residing in China. Z is required to withhold a tax of EUR 10,000 on the dividend. Assuming that half of the unitholders of Y are US pension funds, Y is granted by the Netherlands a payment of EUR 0 for the Chinese withholding tax of EUR 10,000.

The availability of relief at the level of the UCITS in the form of a payment reduction results in an advantage for exempt corporate unitholders compared to a direct investment. In that case, they would not have been entitled to relief in the form of a foreign tax credit under most of the Netherlands tax treaties or if they were they would not have been able to benefit from it in the absence of a tax liability.

7.3.1.2. Deduction from the Annual Return

As mentioned earlier, income derived by way of UCITS is considered by the Netherlands to be that of the UCITS. Netherlands-resident (EII) UCITS, however, are subjectively exempt from corporate income tax so that none of the foreign withholding tax can be set off. Instead, the tax withheld at source on income is deductible as expenses from the amount of income available for distribution by a

Netherlands-resident (EII) UCITS. The deduction of foreign withholding tax does not provide that the amount of the relief equals that of a direct investment because it is credited against the taxable income derived by the unitholder instead of the tax liability of the unitholder. An investment by way of a Netherlands-resident (EII) UCITS may therefore be less attractive for individual and corporate unitholders than a direct investment.

Example 7.11

Y, a Netherlands-resident (EII) UCITS, derives a dividend of EUR 100,000 from Z, a company residing in China. The latter is required to withhold a tax of EUR 10,000 on the dividend. The Chinese withholding tax of EUR 10,000 is deductible from the annual return of Y.

In the absence of a tax liability the deduction of the withholding tax from the amount of income does not help exempt corporate unitholders, unless they are only partly exempt from tax. In that case, the comments made earlier for individual and corporate unitholders also apply to them.

7.3.1.3. Foreign Tax Credit

Like the Netherlands, the United Kingdom considers income derived by way of UK-resident UCITS to be that of the UCITS. On the basis of the UK tax treaties and unilateral rules, the withholding tax charged by the source state on dividend, interest, and other portfolio income is creditable against the corporate income tax liability of the UCITS. It is not possible for UK-resident UCITS to credit the withholding tax charged on capital gains because these UCITS are not subject to corporate income tax at the level of UK-resident UCITS. The availability of relief for individual and corporate unitholders, except for the withholding tax charged on capital gains, does not differ from a direct investment.

Example 7.12

Y, a UK-resident UCITS, is paid a dividend of EUR 100,000 by Z, a company residing in China. Z needs to withhold a tax of EUR 10,000 on the dividend. The Chinese withholding tax of EUR 10,000 can be set off against the corporate income tax liability of Y.

The United Kingdom does not grant a foreign tax credit under any circumstances for more than the part of the corporate income tax liability of the beneficiary that is related to the foreign income (ordinary tax credit). In contrast to a direct investment, the tax liability of the UCITS is taken into account and not that of the unitholders. This gives another result, if the UCITS satisfies the qualifying investment test at all times during the financial year. In that case, none of the withholding tax is creditable because the corporate income tax liability is nullified as a result of the deduction of the distributed income or income that is considered to be distributed.

Example 7.13

Y, a company residing in China, pays Z, a UK-resident UCITS, interest for an amount of EUR 100,000. Y is required to withhold a tax of EUR 10,000 on the interest payment. The Chinese withholding tax of EUR 10,000 cannot be set off by Z as the qualifying investment test was satisfied at all times during the financial year of Z.

An investment through a UK-resident UCITS, for the same reasons as mentioned for Netherlands-resident (FII) UCITS, may result in an advantage for exempt corporate unitholders compared to a direct investment.

7.3.2. Conclusion

The availability of instruments to establish that the crediting of withholding tax charged by source states on income derived by way of UCITS does not differ from a direct investment varies in Austria, Germany, the Netherlands, and the United Kingdom. As a result, the availability and the amount of relief for such withholding tax at the level of the UCITS varies among Austrian-, German-, Netherlands-, and UK-resident UCITS, whereas in the Netherlands it varies even between Netherlands-resident (FII) UCITS and Netherlands-resident (EII) UCITS.

7.4. TAXATION ON DISTRIBUTIONS BY UCITS TO THE UNITHOLDERS

As discussed in Section 4.3, all of the countries studied provide for an exemption at source of certain items of income derived by way of UCITS from investments within the UCITS country or a refund of the tax withheld on such items to establish that the source taxation of these income types does not differ from a direct investment. Instead, the countries studied charge withholding tax at the time of distribution by the UCITS to the unitholders. The availability of measures to establish that taxation at the time of distribution takes place as if these items of income were derived directly varies. As a result, taxation on distributions by UCITS to the unitholders in Austria, Germany, the Netherlands, and the United Kingdom also vary.

Table 7.3 Comparison of Taxation on Distributions by UCITS to Unitholder

UCITS Country	*Resident Unitholders*	*Non-resident Unitholders*	*Consequences of Taxation in the UCITS Country*
Austria	Transparency except for income from speculative transactions	Transparency	–
Germany	Transparency	Transparency	–
Netherlands	Absence of any measures to establish transparency	Absence of any measures to establish transparency	Results frequently in more severe taxation in the case of bond funds and money market funds.
United Kingdom	Absence of any measures to establish transparency	Absence of any measures to establish transparency	Results in more severe taxation for UK individual unitholders but only if the UCITS satisfies the qualifying investment test

7.4.1. Availability of Instruments to Establish that Taxation on Distributions in the UCITS Country Does Not Result in More Severe Taxation than a Direct Investment

7.4.1.1. Transparency

Austria and Germany limit taxation on distributions by UCITS to the part of a distribution that is related to items of income for which an exemption at source applied or the tax withheld was refunded. This is different in Austria only for income from speculative transactions that is distributed to resident unitholders, which would not have been subject to withholding tax if it were derived directly by these unitholders. Furthermore, any exemptions, refunds, or in case of non-resident unitholders reduced tax rates under the one of the tax treaties between the countries studied are applied as if the unitholders had invested directly.

Example 7.14

Y, a company residing in Austria, pays Z, an Austrian-resident UCITS an amount of EUR 100,000 as interest. Y is not required to withhold tax on the interest. Instead, X is required to withhold tax on the distribution of the interest to the unitholders.

7.4.1.2. Absence of Any Measures to Establish Transparency

Unlike Austria and Germany, the Netherlands fails to provide any measures to establish that taxation on distributions by Netherlands-resident (FII) UCITS does not result in more withholding tax than if the unitholders had invested directly. Instead, the full amount of the distribution is subject to withholding tax even if related to interest or foreign dividend. An exception applies for capital gains, but only if the UCITS has opted for a reinvestment account.

Example 7.15

X, a Netherlands-resident (FII), derives interest from Y, a Netherlands-resident company, and dividend from Z, a Canadian-resident company, for an amount of EUR 100,000 each. Y is not required to withhold tax on the interest payment, whereas EUR 15,000 has to be withheld by Z. X needs to withhold EUR 30,000 as tax at the time that the Netherlands source interest and Canadian source dividend is distributed to the unitholders.

The refund of the tax withheld is applied to exempt corporate unitholders, like pension funds and charities, are applied similar to a direct investment. The same applies for the application of a reduced tax rate under a tax treaty between the countries studied.

Similar to the Netherlands, the United Kingdom has not provided for any measures to establish that taxation on distributions by UK-resident UCITS does not result in more withholding tax (or less withholding tax) than a direct investment. Instead, the full amount of the distribution is subject to withholding tax if it satisfies the qualifying investment test at all times during the financial year. Otherwise, the distributed income is fully exempt from withholding tax even when it contains interest, which would have been subject to withholding tax if it was derived directly by some unitholders.

7.4.2. Conclusion

Taxation on distributions by UCITS in Austria, Germany, the Netherlands, and the United Kingdom does not take place uniformly. Separate from differences in tax bases and tax rates, the availability of instruments is not the same to establish that taxation on distributions by the UCITS to the unitholders does not differ from a direct investment in case an exemption applied at source or the tax withheld was refunded. Transparency, the instrument used by Austria and Germany, provides that taxation on distributions does not differ from that on a direct investment. In the absence of any measures to establish transparency, the distributions by Netherlands-resident (FII) UCITS may be subject to more taxation than if the income would have been derived directly by the unitholders. For the same reasons, the distributions by UK-resident UCITS produce either more severe taxation or a lesser taxation compared to a direct investment.

Chapter 8 deals with the consequences of the differences in taxation at the level of the UCITS for the cross-border trading in units of UCITS in Austria, Germany, the Netherlands, and the United Kingdom.

Chapter 8

Distortions to the Cross-Border Trade in Units of UCITS Caused by Differences in Taxation in the UCITS Country

The countries studied have not been successful in establishing a level playing field for UCITS. Investments in non-resident UCITS result in more taxation than investments in resident UCITS where the UCITS country of the non-resident UCITS has failed to avoid taxation at the level of the UCITS or to compensate non-resident unitholders for taxation at the level of the UCITS. In that case UCITS may have difficulties in attracting capital from investors in other Member States.

The conditions of competition between UCITS are further hampered by the availability of relief for the tax withheld at source at the level of the UCITS instead of at the level of the unitholders. The availability of relief at the level of the UCITS improves the UCITS's performance, which may encourage non-resident unitholders to invest in its units.

Finally, the playing field for UCITS in the countries studied is undermined by the differences in taxation on distributions. It concerns differences in the tax base, tax rates, and the availability of exemptions from withholding tax.

8.1. INTRODUCTION

From Chapters 6 and 7 it follows that taxation in the UCITS country shows differences for the countries studied that distort the cross-border trade in units of UCITS. The differences in taxation in the UCITS country result in distortions because income derived by way of a non-resident UCITS is in some cases subject to more severe taxation (tax disadvantage) in the UCITS country than income derived by way of a resident UCITS, whereas in other cases it results in a lesser taxation (tax advantage). UCITS therefore do not compete under the same conditions.

8.1.1. Tabular Overview

An overview of the distortions is given in Table 8.1. Tax disadvantages or tax advantages that arise from the differences in taxation in the UCITS country for income derived through non-resident UCITS in comparison with income derived through resident UCITS are indicated for Austrian, German, Netherlands, and UK unitholders. Table 8.1 demonstrates that the existence of the tax advantages and disadvantages is related to the investment policy and the residence state of the UCITS together with the tax status of the unitholders.

Table 8.1 Taxation of the Income from the Underlying Investments at the Level of the UCITS

	Tax Liability of the UCITS	*Relief for the Withholding Tax Charged by the Source State*	*The Withholding Tax Charged by the UCITS Country at the Time of Distribution*
Austrian unitholders UCITS			
German-resident UCITS	0	0	–[c]/+
Netherlands-resident (EII) UCITS	0	0	+/0[d]
Netherlands-resident (FII) UCITS	0	+	+/–[c]/0[e]
Netherlands-resident (TII) UCITS	0	0	+/0[d]
UK-resident UCITS	–/0[a]	+/0[b]	+/0[c]
German unitholders UCITS			
Austrian-resident UCITS	0	0	+/0[f]
Netherlands-resident (EII) UCITS	0	0	+/0[f]
Netherlands-resident (FII) UCITS	0	+	+/0[f]

Table 8.1 (cont'd)

	Tax Liability of the UCITS	*Relief for the Withholding Tax Charged by the Source State*	*The Withholding Tax Charged by the UCITS Country at the Time of Distribution*
Netherlands-resident (TII) UCITS	0	0	+/0[f]
UK-resident UCITS	–/0[a]	+/0[b]	+/0[f]
Netherlands unitholders* UCITS			
Austrian-resident UCITS	0	–	+/0[h]
German-resident UCITS	0	–	–[h]/+[i]/0
UK-resident UCITS	–/0[a]	–[b]/+[g]/0	+/0[h]
UK unitholders UCITS			
Austrian-resident UCITS	+[j]/0	–/0[b]	+[k]/0
German-resident UCITS	+[j]/0	–/0[b]	–/+[k]/0[l]
Netherlands-resident (EII) UCITS	+[j]/0	–/0[b]	+[k]/0
Netherlands-resident (FII) UCITS	+[i]/0	[g]/ | [b]/0	–/+[k]/0[h]
Netherlands-resident (TII) UCITS	+[j]/0	–/0[b]	+[k]/0

+, Cross-border trading is facilitated as a result of a tax advantage.

0, Cross-border trading is not affected in the absence of a tax advantage or tax disadvantage.

–, Tax disadvantage that hinders the cross-border trading.

[a] Where the UCITS solely derives UK-source dividends or satisfied the qualifying investment test at all times during the financial year.

[b] If the UCITS satisfied the qualifying investment test at all times during the financial year.

[c] In the case individual and corporate unitholders hold units in a UCITS, which invests in the equity of companies residing in Austria.

Table 8.1 (cont'd)

[d] If the UCITS invests in the equity of companies residing in Austria.

[e] If the units in the UCITS are held by exempt corporate unitholders and the UCITS invests in bonds and other debt securities.

[f] If the units in the UCITS are held by exempt corporate unitholders and the UCITS invests in bonds and debt securities other than profit-sharing and convertible ones.

[g] Where the foreign tax credit granted to UK-resident UCITS exceeds the partial relief granted to Netherlands-resident (FII) UCITS.

[h] In the case exempt corporate unitholders held units in the UCITS.

[i] If individual and corporate unitholders held units in a UCITS, which invests in bonds and debt securities other than profit-sharing and convertible ones.

[j] If the units in the UCITS are held by exempt corporate unitholders and a comparable UK-resident UCITS would not only derive exempt UK dividends or would not satisfy the qualifying investment test at all times during the financial year.

[k] In the case a comparable UK-resident UCITS would derive only UK dividends or satisfy the qualifying investment test and its units are held by individuals.

[l] If the UCITS invests in bonds and other debt securities.

* In comparison with a Netherlands-resident (FII) UCITS. After all, most Netherlands-resident UCITS have opted for the status of fiscal investment institution (FII) for tax purposes.

A more detailed explanation of the distortions shown in the table above is provided in the Sections 8.2–8.4.

8.2. MEASURES TAKEN TO AVOID ECONOMIC DOUBLE TAXATION

8.2.1. Introduction

The avoidance of economic double taxation at the level of UCITS and that of the unitholders differs in Austria, Germany, the Netherlands, and the United Kingdom. The following sections show that these differences distort the trade in units of UCITS in the countries studied. A comparison of the avoidance of taxation at the level of Austrian, German, Netherlands, and UK-resident UCITS shows the distortions.

8.2.2. Cross-Border Trade of Units in Austria

8.2.2.1. Austrian Unitholder and German-Resident or Netherlands-Resident UCITS

Trading in units of German and Netherlands-resident UCITS in Austria is not affected by the measures taken by Germany and the Netherlands, the UCITS

Figure 8.1. A Comparison of the Avoidance of Taxation at the Level of the UCITS

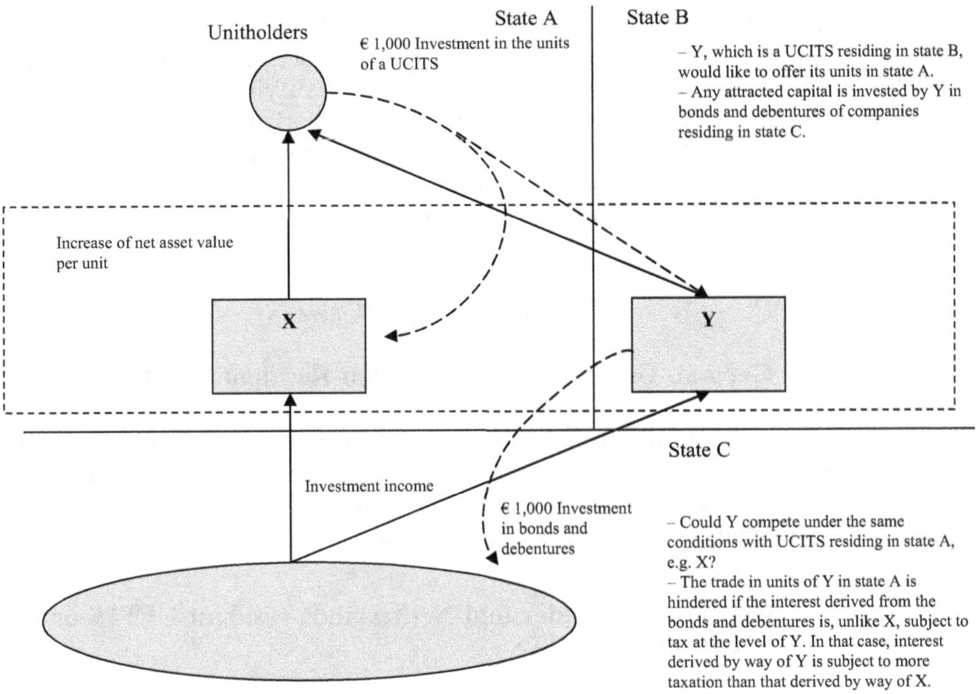

countries, to avoid double taxation at the level of the UCITS. Like Austria, Germany and the Netherlands avoid double taxation at the level of the UCITS. Taxation of income from the underlying investments at the level of German and Netherlands-resident UCITS therefore does not differ for Austrian investors from that at the level of Austrian-resident UCITS.

8.2.2.2. Austrian Unitholder and UK-Resident UCITS

The measures taken by the United Kingdom, in its capacity as the UCITS country, to avoid double taxation hinder UK-resident UCITS by attracting capital in Austria. The United Kingdom, unlike Austria, avoids double taxation at the level of the unitholders. The income from the underlying investments of UK-resident UCITS is therefore subject to corporate income tax at the level of UK-resident UCITS at a rate of 20%. The domestic laws of the UK or the UK tax treaty with Austria, however, do not provide compensation for taxation at the level of the UCITS for Austrian unitholders.[1] Taxation at the level of UK-resident UCITS therefore

1. The UK tax treaty provides initially for compensation for the taxation at the level of the UCITS in the form of a repayment of the part of the tax credit that exceeds a tax at 15% on the dividend and

exceeds that at the level of Austrian-resident UCITS, which results in a tax disadvantage.

Trading in units of UK-resident UCITS in Austria, however, is not affected by the measures taken by the United Kingdom, the UCITS country, to avoid double taxation, if the UCITS solely derives UK dividends or satisfied the qualifying investment test at all times during the year. The qualifying investment test is generally satisfied only by bond funds and money market funds. In that case, the United Kingdom, like Austria, avoids double taxation at the level of the UCITS. The effect of these measures on taxation at the level of a UK-resident UCITS does not differ from Austrian-resident UCITS.

8.2.3. Cross-Border Trade of Units in Germany

8.2.3.1. German Unitholder and Austrian-Resident UCITS

Trading in units of Austrian-resident UCITS in Germany is not hindered by the measures taken by Austria, the UCITS country, to avoid double taxation. The measures taken in Austria avoid economic double taxation at the level of the UCITS. This does not differ from German-resident UCITS.

8.2.3.2. German Unitholder and Netherlands-resident UCITS or UK-Resident UCITS

The conditions under which trading in units of Netherlands and UK-resident UCITS in Germany is affected by the measures taken by the United Kingdom, the UCITS country, to avoid economic double taxation do not differ from those discussed in Section 8.2.2 for Austria.[2]

8.2.4. Cross-Border Trade of Units in the Netherlands

8.2.4.1. Dutch Unitholder and Austrian or German-Resident UCITS

For the same reasons as discussed in Sections 8.2.2 and 8.2.3, the measures taken by the UCITS countries to avoid double taxation do not hinder Austrian and German-resident UCITS by attracting capital in the Netherlands.

---

the tax credit together. As the tax credit is one-ninth of the dividend paid to the unitholders, the amount of the tax credit never exceeds the tax charged at 15% so that Austrian individual and corporate unitholders are never granted any compensation for the taxation at the level of a UK-resident UCITS.

2. The UK tax treaty with Germany does not provide for any compensation for taxation at the level of UK-resident UCITS.

8.2.4.2. Dutch Unitholder and UK-Resident UCITS

Trading in units of UK-resident UCITS in the Netherlands is affected by the measures taken by the United Kingdom, the UCITS country, under the same conditions and for the same reasons as discussed in Section 8.2.2 for Austria.[3]

8.2.5. Cross-Border Trade of Units in the United Kingdom

8.2.5.1. UK Unitholder and Austrian-Resident UCITS

Trading in the units of Austrian-resident UCITS to individual and corporate investors in the United Kingdom is facilitated by the measures taken by Austria, the UCITS country, to avoid double taxation. In Austria, double taxation is fully avoided at the level of the UCITS, whereas the United Kingdom does not fully remove double taxation at the level of the unitholder. An investment in the units of an Austrian-resident UCITS is therefore more attractive to UK individual and corporate unitholders than an investment in the units of UK-resident UCITS.

The absence of taxation at the level of Austrian-resident UCITS in Austria, the UCITS country, also facilitates these UCITS to attract capital from UK exempt corporate investors. Any of the measures taken by Austria at the level of the UCITS also avoid double taxation for UK exempt corporate unitholders, whereas these Unitholders are not compensated in the United Kingdom for taxation at the level of UK-resident UCITS. An investment in the units of an Austrian-resident UCITS therefore results in a tax advantage for UK exempt corporate investors compared to an investment in the units of UK-resident UCITS.

Trading in units of Austrian-resident UCITS in the United Kingdom is not affected by the measures taken by Austria, the UCITS country, to avoid double taxation if it solely derives UK dividends or satisfied the qualifying investment test at all times during the year. The qualifying investment test is generally fulfilled only by bond funds and money market funds. In that case, taxation at the level of Austrian-resident UCITS does not differ from that of UK-resident UCITS, because the measures taken by Austria and the United Kingdom both avoid double taxation at the level of the UCITS.

8.2.5.2. UK Unitholder and German-Resident UCITS or Netherlands-Resident UCITS

Taxation in the Germany and Netherlands, the UCITS countries, affects trading in units of German and Netherlands-resident UCITS in the United Kingdom under the same conditions as discussed above for Austrian-resident UCITS.

---

3. The UK tax treaty with the Netherlands does not differ from the UK tax treaty with Austria in respect to compensation for taxation at the level of UK-resident UCITS.

8.3. THE MEASURES TO PROVIDE RELIEF FOR THE WITHHOLDING TAX CHARGED BY THE SOURCE STATES

8.3.1. Introduction

The availability and the amount of relief for withholding tax charged by the source states varies among Austria, Germany, the Netherlands and the United Kingdom. The cross-border trade in units of UCITS in the countries studied is distorted by the differences in the availability and the amount of the relief. The source of the distortions is examined in the following sections by means of a comparison of the availability and the amount of relief for foreign withholding tax at the level of Austrian-, German-, Netherlands-, and UK-resident UCITS.

8.3.2. Cross-Border Trade of Units in Austria

8.3.2.1. Austrian Unitholder and German-Resident UCITS

Trading in units of German-resident UCITS in Austria is not affected by the absence of relief granted by Germany, the UCITS country, for foreign withholding

Figure 8.2 A Comparison of the Availability and the Amount of Relief for Foreign Withholding Tax at the Level of the UCITS

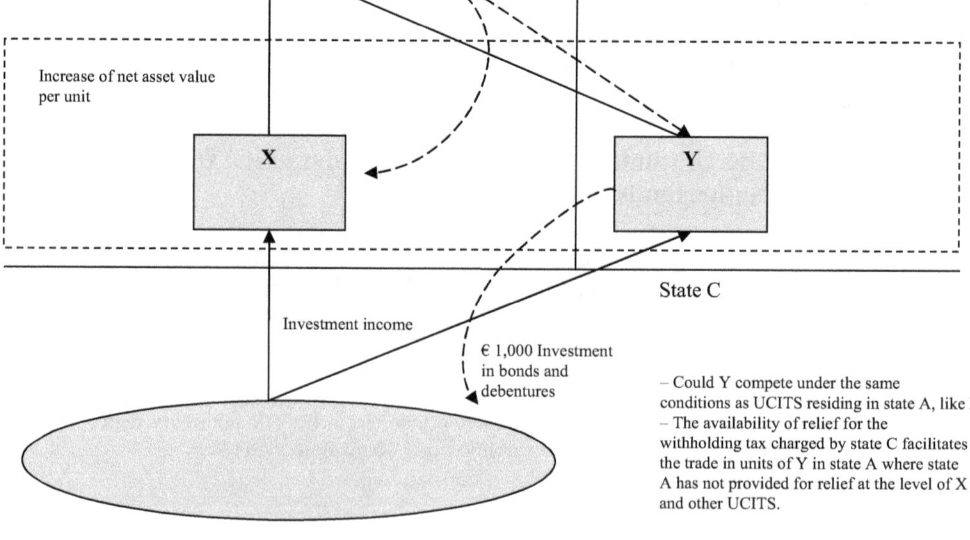

tax charged at source on income. After all, Austrian-resident UCITS are not granted relief for foreign withholding tax either. The attractiveness of units in German-resident UCITS therefore does not differ from that of the units of Austrian-resident UCITS.

8.3.2.2. Austrian Unitholder and Netherlands-Resident (EII/TII) UCITS

The absence of relief granted by the Netherlands, the UCITS country, for foreign withholding tax charged at source, for the same reasons as mentioned earlier for German-resident UCITS, does not affect trading in units of Netherlands-resident (EII/TII) UCITS in Austria.

8.3.2.3. Austrian Unitholder and Netherlands-Resident (FII) UCITS

Trading in units of Netherlands-resident (FII) UCITS is facilitated by the relief granted by the Netherlands, the UCITS country, for foreign withholding tax charged at source on income. No relief is available for Austrian-resident UCITS. The units of Netherlands-resident (FII) UCITS are therefore more attractive for Austrian investors than those of Austrian-resident UCITS. Furthermore, the more non-resident Unitholders are entitled to a reduction or exemption from withholding tax under a tax treaty, the less relief is granted to Netherlands-resident (FII) UCITS; see Section 6.3.3.2 for more details.

8.3.2.4. Austrian Unitholder and UK-Resident UCITS

The relief granted by the United Kingdom, the UCITS country, for foreign withholding tax charged at source of income facilitates UK-resident UCITS by attracting capital in Austria for the same reasons as discussed previously for Netherlands-resident (FII) UCITS.

Trading in units of UK-resident UCITS in Austria is not affected by the absence of relief granted by the United Kingdom, the UCITS country, if the UCITS satisfies the qualifying investment test at all times during a financial year. In that case the attractiveness of UK-resident UCITS does not differ from that of Austrian-resident UCITS.

8.3.3. Cross-Border Trade of Units in Germany

8.3.3.1. German Unitholder and Austrian-Resident UCITS

Trading in units of Austrian-resident UCITS in Germany is not affected by the absence of relief granted by Austria, the UCITS country, for foreign withholding tax. German-resident UCITS are not granted relief for foreign withholding tax, either. The attractiveness of units in Austrian-resident UCITS thus does not differ from the units of German-resident UCITS.

8.3.3.2. German Unitholder and Netherlands-Resident (EII/TII) UCITS

The absence of relief granted by the Netherlands, the UCITS country, for foreign withholding tax does not affect trading in units of Netherlands-resident (EII/TII) UCITS in Germany for the same reasons as discussed earlier for Austrian-resident UCITS.

8.3.3.3. German Unitholder and Netherlands-Resident (FII) UCITS

Trading in units of Netherlands-resident (FII) UCITS in Germany is facilitated by the relief granted by the Netherlands, the UCITS country, for foreign withholding tax. No relief is available for German-resident UCITS. An investment in the units of a Netherlands-resident (FII) UCITS therefore results in a tax advantage for German-resident investors. As follows from Section 6.3.3.2, Netherlands-resident (FII) UCITS are not entitled to full relief for foreign withholding tax if some of the unitholders are entitled to a reduction or an exemption from withholding tax under a tax treaty.

8.3.3.4. German Unitholder and UK-Resident UCITS

The relief granted by the United Kingdom, the UCITS country, for foreign withholding tax affects trading in UK-resident UCITS in Germany under the same conditions as mentioned for Austria in Section 8.3.2.

8.3.4. Cross-Border Trade of Units in the Netherlands

8.3.4.1. Dutch Unitholder and Austrian-Resident UCITS

Trading in units of Austrian-resident UCITS in the Netherlands is hindered by the absence of relief granted by Austria, the UCITS country, for foreign withholding tax. Relief is available for Netherlands-resident (FII) UCITS. Austrian-resident UCITS are therefore less attractive than Netherlands-resident (FII) UCITS.

8.3.4.2. Dutch Unitholder and German-Resident UCITS

The absence of relief granted by Germany, the UCITS country, for foreign withholding tax hinders trading in units of German-resident UCITS in the Netherlands for the same reason as discussed earlier for Austrian-resident UCITS. German-resident UCITS are therefore less attractive than Netherlands-resident (FII) UCITS.

8.3.4.3. Dutch Unitholder and UK-Resident UCITS

Trading in units of UK-resident UCITS in the Netherlands is hindered by the amount of relief granted by the United Kingdom, the UCITS country, for foreign withholding tax in case the Netherlands grants more relief to Netherlands-resident (FII) UCITS. The Netherlands grants conditional relief in the form of a payment reduction for the amount of withholding tax on dividends and interest while the relief granted by the United Kingdom on the basis of the ordinary tax credit is limited to at most the reduced tax rate of 20% but is generally less due to the deduction of expenses. The units in an UK-resident UCITS are in that case less attractive than those of a Netherlands-resident (FII) UCITS.

The availability and amount of relief granted by the United Kingdom, the UCITS country, facilitates trading in the units of UK-resident UCITS in the Netherlands if it exceeds the relief granted by the Netherlands to Netherlands-resident (FII) UCITS. This is the case if a source state charges a withholding tax on other portfolio income.

Trading in units of UK-resident UCITS in the Netherlands is hindered by the absence of relief granted by the United Kingdom, the UCITS country, in case the UCITS satisfied the qualifying investment test. The reasons for this do not differ from those discussed above for Austrian-resident UCITS.

8.3.5. Cross-Border Trade of Units in the United Kingdom

8.3.5.1. UK Unitholder and Austrian-Resident UCITS

Trading in units of Austrian-resident UCITS in the United Kingdom is hindered by the absence of relief granted by Austria, the UCITS country, for foreign withholding tax. Austrian-resident UCITS are, in contrast to UK-resident UCITS, not granted relief by the UCITS country. The units in Austrian-resident UCITS are, therefore, less attractive than those of UK-resident UCITS.

The absence of relief granted by the UCITS country does not affect trading in the units of Austrian-resident UCITS in the United Kingdom if it satisfied the qualifying investment test at all times during a distribution period. In that case, Austrian-resident UCITS as well as UK-resident UCITS are not granted any relief for foreign withholding.

8.3.5.2. UK Unitholder and German-Resident UCITS or Netherlands-Resident (EII/TII) UCITS

The absence of relief granted by Germany and the Netherlands, the UCITS country, affects trading in units of German-resident UCITS and Netherlands-resident (EII/TII) UCITS in the United Kingdom under the same conditions as discussed above for Austrian-resident UCITS.

8.3.5.3. UK Unitholder and Netherlands-Resident (FII) UCITS

The conditions under which the units in Netherlands-resident (FII) UCITS in the United Kingdom are affected by the amount of relief granted by the Netherlands, the UCITS country, do not differ from those discussed in Section 8.3.3 for trading in units of UK-resident UCITS in the Netherlands.

8.4. TAXATION ON DISTRIBUTIONS BY UCITS TO THE UNITHOLDERS

8.4.1. INTRODUCTION

The amount of withholding tax, if any, charged by the UCITS country at the time of distribution varies among Austria, Germany, the Netherlands, and the United Kingdom. The following sections demonstrate that these differences distort the cross-border trade in units of UCITS in the countries studied. The distortions to trading in units of UCITS are identified by means of a comparison of the

Figure 8.3. A Comparison of the Withholding Tax Charged by the UCITS Country at the Time of Distribution at the Level of the UCITS

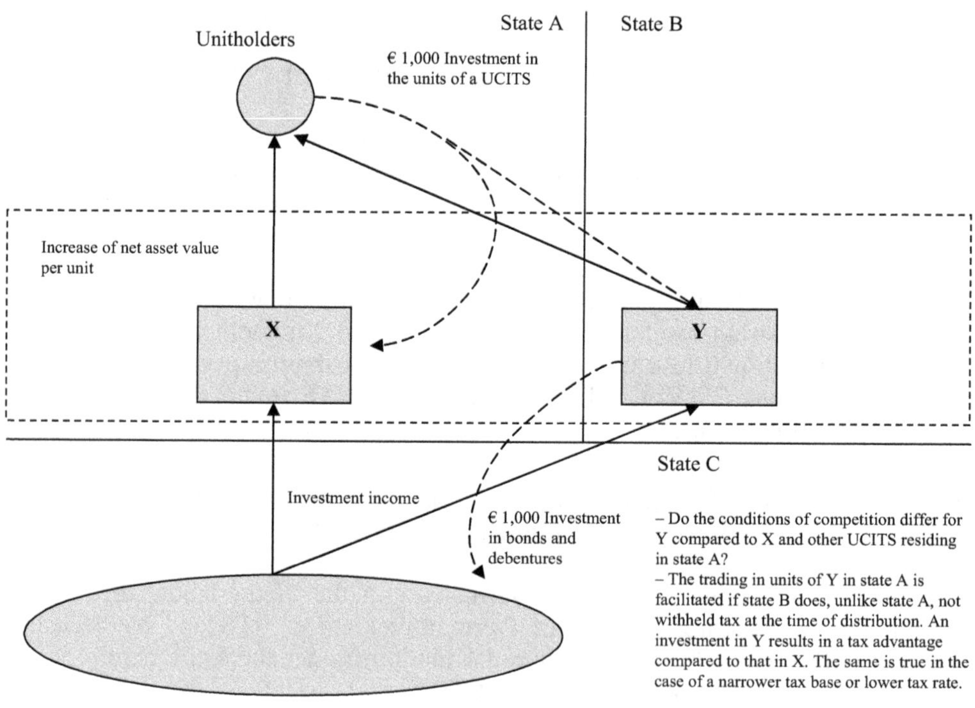

withholding tax charged by Germany, the Netherlands, and the United Kingdom at the time of distributions.

8.4.2. CROSS-BORDER TRADE OF UNITS IN AUSTRIA

8.4.2.1. Austrian Unitholder and German-Resident UCITS

Trading in units of German-resident UCITS to individual and corporate investors in Austria is facilitated by the withholding tax charged by Germany, the UCITS country, at the time of distribution. Under the tax treaty with Austria, Germany charges a withholding tax of 15% at the time of distribution, which is less than the 25% withholding tax charged by Austria.

The withholding tax charged by Germany, the UCITS country, at the time of distribution hinders trading in the units of German-resident UCITS to exempt corporate unitholders in Austria if the UCITS. The part of a distribution that is related to dividends is subject to withholding tax in Germany at a rate of 26.375%, which is higher than the Austrian withholding tax of 25%. The units of German-resident UCITS are therefore less attractive to Austrian exempt corporate investors than those of Austrian-resident UCITS.

The withholding tax charged by Germany, the UCITS country, also hinders trading in the units of German-resident UCITS that invest in the equity of Austrian-resident companies in Austria. Austria, unlike Germany, provides for an exemption from withholding tax for the part of a distribution that is related to Austrian-source dividends. Austrian investors will, therefore, favour Austrian-resident UCITS over German-resident UCITS for investments in Austrian equity.

Trading in units of German-resident UCITS, however, is facilitated by the absence of a withholding tax charged by Germany, the UCITS country, if the UCITS invests in bonds and other debt securities. Germany, in contrast to Austria, does not charge a withholding tax on the part of the distribution to non-resident unitholders that is related to interest. The units of German bond funds and money market funds are therefore more attractive than those of their Austrian counterparts.

8.4.2.2. Austrian Unitholder and Netherlands-Resident (EII/TII) UCITS

Trading in units of Netherlands-resident (EII/TII) UCITS in Austria is facilitated by the absence of a withholding tax charged by the Netherlands, the UCITS country, at the time of distribution. Austria, on the other hand, charges a withholding tax of 25% from Austrian-resident UCITS at the time of distribution. An investment in the units of Netherlands-resident UCITS, therefore, results in a tax advantage compared to Austrian-resident UCITS.

The absence of a withholding tax charged by the Netherlands, the UCITS country, at the time of distribution does not affect trading in units in Netherlands-resident (EII/TII) UCITS if they invest in the equity of Austrian-resident companies. Austria does not charge a withholding tax on the part of the distribution by Austrian-resident UCITS that is related to dividends paid by an Austrian-resident company.

8.4.2.3. Austrian Unitholder and Netherlands-Resident (FII) UCITS

Trading in units of Netherlands-resident (FII) UCITS to individual and corporate investors in Austria is facilitated by the withholding tax charged by the Netherlands, the UCITS country, at the time of distribution. The 15% withholding tax charged by the Netherlands at the time of distribution is less than the 25% withholding tax charged from Austrian-resident UCITS at the time of distribution. The units in Netherlands-resident (FII) UCITS are therefore more attractive than those of Austrian-resident UCITS.

If a Netherlands-resident (FII) UCITS invests in the equity of Austrian-resident companies, the 15% withholding tax charged by the Netherlands, the UCITS country, at the time of distribution hinders trading in the units of the UCITS to individual and (exempt) corporate unitholders in Austria. Contrary to the Netherlands, Austria does not charge withholding tax on the part of a distribution that is related to Austrian-source dividends. Austrian individual and corporate unitholders will therefore find taxation from Austrian-resident UCITS at the time of distribution more attractive for Austrian equity than that from Netherlands-resident (FII) UCITS at the time of distribution.

Trading in units of Netherlands-resident (FII) UCITS to Austrian pension funds is not facilitated by the refund of the withholding tax charged by the Netherlands, the UCITS country, at the time of distribution. Austria exempts distributions to pension funds from withholding tax at the time of distribution. The attractiveness of Netherlands-resident (FII) UCITS therefore does not differ for Austrian pension funds from that of Austrian-resident UCITS. A refund of Netherlands withholding tax, however, is not available under all circumstances; see Section 6.5.3.2 for the conditions.

The availability of a refund of the withholding tax charged at the time of distribution facilitates the trade in units of Netherlands-resident (FII) UCITS to Austrian exempt corporate unitholders other than pension funds. Unlike the Netherlands, Austria does not provide for a refund of the tax withheld at the time of distribution. An investment in the units of Netherlands-resident (FII) UCITS may therefore be more attractive to these investors than in units of an Austrian-resident UCITS.

Trade in units of Netherlands-resident (FII) UCITS to Austrian exempt corporate unitholders for investments in the equity of Austrian companies is not affected by the availability of a refund of the tax withheld at the time of distribution. As a result of an exemption from withholding tax in Austria, taxation of distributed Austrian-source dividends in the Netherlands equals that in Austria.

8.4.2.4. Austrian Unitholder and UK-Resident UCITS

Under the same conditions as discussed earlier for Netherlands-resident (EII/TII) UCITS, the absence of a withholding tax charged by the United Kingdom, the UCITS country, at the time of distribution affects trading in units of UK-resident UCITS in Austria.

8.4.3. Cross-Border Trade of Units in Germany

8.4.3.1. German Unitholder and Austrian-Resident UCITS

Trading in units of Austrian-resident UCITS in Germany is facilitated by the absence of a withholding tax charged by Austria, the UCITS country, at the time of distribution. The distributions of German-resident UCITS are, however, subject to withholding tax at a rate of 26.375%. For that reason, German unitholders will find the units of Austrian-resident UCITS more attractive than those of German-resident UCITS.

The absence of a withholding tax charged by Germany, the UCITS country, at the time of distribution does not affect trading in units of Austrian-resident UCITS that invest in bonds and other debt securities to exempt corporate unitholders in Germany. Germany likewise does not charge withholding tax on the part of a distribution of a German-resident UCITS to exempt corporate unitholders that is related to interest. The attractiveness of Austrian and German-resident UCITS therefore does not differ for German investors.

8.4.3.2. German Unitholder and Netherlands-Resident (EII/TII) UCITS

Trading in units of Netherlands-resident (EII/TII) UCITS in Germany is facilitated by the absence of a withholding tax in the Netherlands, the UCITS country, at the time of distribution under the same conditions as discussed earlier for Austrian-resident UCITS.

8.4.3.3. German Unitholder and Netherlands-Resident (FII) UCITS

The withholding tax charged from Netherlands-resident (FII) UCITS at the time of distribution facilitates trading in units of these UCITS to individual and corporate investors in Germany. The 15% withholding tax charged from Netherlands-resident (FII) UCITS at the time of distribution is less than the 26.375% withholding tax charged from German-resident UCITS at the time of distribution. The units in Netherlands-resident (FII) UCITS are therefore more attractive to German individual and corporate investors than those of a German-resident UCITS.

The refund of the withholding tax charged by the Netherlands, the UCITS country, at the time of distribution facilitates trading in units of

Netherlands-resident (FII) UCITS to exempt corporate unitholders in Germany. Contrary to the Netherlands, Germany does not provide for a refund of the withholding tax charged from German-resident UCITS at the time of distribution. German exempt corporate unitholders may, for that reason, favour an investment in units of Netherlands-resident (FII) UCITS over an investment in those of German-resident UCITS. See Section 6.5.3.2 for the conditions under which the withholding tax charged at the time of distribution is refunded by the Netherlands.

Because of the application of different withholding tax rates, trade in units of Netherlands-resident (FII) UCITS to German exempt corporate unitholders is also facilitated if a refund of withholding tax is not available. Taxation in the Netherlands is in that case still less than that in Germany.

This is, however, not true for the part of a distribution that is related to interest from bonds and debentures, because the latter are exempt from withholding tax in Germany. In that case, taxation in the Netherlands exceeds that in Germany. In the absence of a full refund, the trade in units of Netherlands-resident (FII) UCITS that keep investments in bonds and debentures to German exempt corporate unitholders is hindered by the absence of a refund of the withholding tax charged at the time of distribution.

8.4.3.4. German Unitholder and UK-Resident UCITS

The conditions under which trading in units of UK-resident UCITS in Germany is affected by the absence of a withholding tax charged by the United Kingdom, the UCITS country, at the time of distribution do not differ from those discussed previously for Austrian-resident UCITS.

8.4.4. Cross-Border Trade of Units in the Netherlands

8.4.4.1. Dutch Unitholder and Austrian-Resident UCITS

Trading in units of Austrian-resident UCITS to individual and corporate investors in the Netherlands is, compared to Netherlands-resident (FII) UCITS, facilitated by the absence of a withholding tax charged by Austria, the UCITS country, at the time of distribution. Instead, the Netherlands charges a withholding tax of 15% on distributions by Netherlands-resident (FII) UCITS. Netherlands individual and corporate investors will therefore find the units of Austrian-resident UCITS more attractive than those of Netherlands-resident (FII) UCITS.

The absence of a withholding tax charged at the time of distribution facilitates the trade in units of Austrian-resident UCITS to Netherlands exempt corporate unitholders where the distributed income has been subject to foreign withholding tax for which a Netherlands-resident (FII) UCITS may claim payment reduction. In that case the tax withheld on the distribution of a Netherlands-resident (FII) UCITS would not be fully refundable for exempt corporate unitholders. Austrian-resident UCITS are in that case more attractive those that of Netherlands-resident (FII) UCITS.

Trade in units of Austrian-resident UCITS to Netherlands exempt corporate unitholders is not affected by the absence of a withholding tax at the time of distribution in the case that the distributed income has not been subject to foreign withholding tax for which a Netherlands-resident (FII) UCITS may claim payment reduction. Taxation in Austria does then not differ from that in the Netherlands, because these unitholders are in that case entitled to a refund of the tax withheld by Netherlands-resident (FII) UCITS at the time of distribution.

8.4.4.2. Dutch Unitholder and German-Resident UCITS

Where German-resident UCITS hold investments in equity, trading in units of the UCITS to individual and corporate investors in the Netherlands is not affected by the withholding tax charged by Germany, the UCITS country, at the time of distribution. The distribution is, in accordance with the German tax treaty with the Netherlands, subject to a withholding tax at a rate of 15%, which is equal to the withholding tax charged by the Netherlands from Netherlands-resident (FII) UCITS.

Trading in units of German-resident UCITS that invest in bonds and other debt securities to individual and corporate investors in the Netherlands is facilitated by the absence of a withholding tax charged by Germany, the UCITS country. Contrary to Germany, the Netherlands charges a 15% withholding tax on distributions of Netherlands-resident (FII) UCITS. The units of German bonds funds are therefore more attractive than those of Netherlands-resident (FII) UCITS.

The 26.375% withholding tax charged by the UCITS country at the time of distribution hinders trading in units of German-resident UCITS that invest in equity to exempt corporate unitholders in the Netherlands. The Netherlands, contrary to Germany, provides for a refund of the 15% withholding tax charged from Netherlands-resident (FII) UCITS at the time of distribution.

For the same reasons as discussed earlier for Austrian-resident UCITS, trading in units of German-resident UCITS that invest in bonds and other debt securities to exempt corporate unitholders in the Netherlands is not affected by the absence of a withholding tax by Germany, the UCITS country, at the time of distribution.

8.4.4.3. Dutch Unitholder and UK-Resident UCITS

The absence of a withholding tax at the time of distribution facilitates trading in units of UK-resident UCITS in the Netherlands under the same conditions as discussed previously for Austrian-resident UCITS.

8.4.5. Cross-Border Trade of Units in the United Kingdom

8.4.5.1. UK Unitholder and Austrian-Resident UCITS

Trading in units of Austrian-resident UCITS in the United Kingdom is not affected by the absence of a withholding tax at the time of distribution. The United

Kingdom, the UCITS country, does not charge a withholding tax on distributions, either. The attractiveness of Austrian-resident UCITS thus does not differ from UK-resident UCITS.

The absence of a withholding tax at the time of distribution, however, facilitates trading in units of Austrian-resident UCITS to individual investors in the United Kingdom, where its UK counterparts would satisfy the qualifying investments test. The distributions of UK-resident UCITS to individual unitholders are in that case subject to a 20% withholding tax. UK individual investors will find taxation from Austrian-resident UCITS at the time of distribution more attractive than that from UK-resident UCITS at the time of distribution.

8.4.5.2. UK Unitholder and German-Resident UCITS

The withholding tax charged by Germany, the UCITS country, at the time of distribution hinders trading in units of German-resident UCITS in the United Kingdom where these UCITS invest in equity. Under the German tax treaty with the United Kingdom, Germany charges a withholding tax of 15% on distributions to UK individual and corporate unitholders. The distributions to exempt corporate unitholders are, however, subject to withholding tax at a rate of 26.375%. In either case, a withholding tax is not charged on distributions from UK-resident UCITS.

Trading in units of German-resident UCITS to (exempt) corporate investors in the United Kingdom, however, is not affected by the absence of a withholding tax charged by Germany, the UCITS country, if the UCITS keeps bonds and other debt securities. In that case, Germany, like the United Kingdom, does not charge a withholding tax on the part of the distribution to non-resident unitholders that is related to interest.

The absence of a withholding tax charged by Germany, the UCITS country, facilitates trading in units of a German-resident UCITS to individual investors in the United Kingdom where the UCITS keeps bonds and other debt securities. Germany in that case does not charge a withholding tax on the part of the distribution to non-resident unitholders that is related to interest, whereas the United Kingdom charges a withholding tax of 20% from UK-resident UCITS. The units of German bonds funds and money market funds are therefore more attractive for UK individual investors than those of UK-resident UCITS.

8.4.5.3. UK Unitholder and Netherlands-Resident (EII/TII) UCITS

Trading in units of Netherlands-resident (EII/TII) UCITS in the United Kingdom is affected by the absence of a withholding tax at the time of distribution under the same conditions as those for Austrian-resident UCITS.

8.4.5.4. UK Unitholder and Netherlands-Resident (FII) UCITS

The withholding tax charged by the Netherlands, the UCITS country, at the time of distribution hinders trading in units of Netherlands-resident (FII) UCITS to individual and corporate unitholders in the United Kingdom. In the United

Kingdom, a withholding tax is, unlike in the Netherlands, not charged at the time of distribution. Netherlands-resident (FII) UCITS are therefore less attractive than UK-resident UCITS.

Trading in units of Netherlands-resident (FII) UCITS to UK individual investors for investments that satisfy the qualifying investment test, however, is facilitated by the 15% withholding charged by the Netherlands, the UCITS country, at the time of distribution. The United Kingdom in that case charges a withholding tax of 20% from UK-resident UCITS on distributions to individual unitholders.

The refund of the withholding tax charged at the time of distribution from Netherlands-resident (FII) UCITS does not affect the trade in units of these UCITS. Taxation in the Netherlands does in that case not differ from that in the United Kingdom because the latter does not charge a withholding tax on distributions by UK-resident UCITS to exempt corporate unitholders.

The trade in units of Netherlands-resident (FII) UCITS to UK exempt corporate unitholders is hindered by the absence of a refund of the withholding tax charged by the Netherlands, the UCITS country, at the time of distribution in the case that the distributed income has been subject to foreign withholding tax for which the UCITS has claimed a payment reduction. Taxation in the Netherlands then exceeds that in the United Kingdom for the same reason as discussed earlier.

8.5. CONCLUSION

The units in UCITS cannot freely circulate between the countries studied as a result of differences in taxation at the level of the UCITS. The competition among UCITS therefore does not take place under the same conditions. The UCITS Directive does not remove any of the differences in taxation of income from the investments of UCITS at the level of the UCITS. The scope of the measures taken by the UCITS Directive to remove the restrictions on the free circulation of units in UCITS is too narrow.

On the basis of the previous two chapters, it could be concluded that taxation at the level of UCITS and taxation on distributions are not uniform in the countries studied. The cross-border trade in units of UCITS among the countries studied may be distorted by the differences in the UCITS country. This chapter identifies the distortions in the countries studied.

Part IV
Tax Liability of the Unitholders

The income from the investments should be taxable in the hands of the unitholders at the same time and for the same amount as for a direct investment. However, it may be desirable to provide for the deduction of the costs made at the level of the undertakings for collective investment in transferable securities (UCITS). Furthermore, the nature and source of the income should not be transformed, so that the tax base, exemptions, and special tax rates are applied as if the unitholders had invested directly. Finally, the tax treaties and unilateral rules of the unitholder country should be applied in a similar way to a direct investment so that the same amount of relief is available for the tax withheld at source of income.

Chapters 9–14 demonstrate that the taxation at the level of the unitholders in the countries studied differs considerably for resident and non-resident UCITS and between non-resident UCITS. The tax liability of the unitholders in the unitholder country depends on the country in which the UCITS resides. Among other things, the most significant differences occur in respect of the following:

(1) The tax liability of the unitholder for investments through resident and non-resident UCITS.
(2) The availability of relief for the withholding tax charged by the source states at the level of the unitholders.
(3) The crediting of the withholding tax charged by the UCITS country.

The differences distort the cross-border trade in the units of UCITS for unitholders residing in Austria, Germany, the Netherlands, and the United Kingdom. These distortions limit the cross-border trade in units of UCITS between the countries studied and, therefore, affect the conditions of competition for UCITS in these countries.

The differences facilitate the cross-border trade among the countries studied in some cases, which frustrates the higher aim of the UCITS Directive.

Part IV examines the taxation of dividend, interest, capital gains, and other portfolio income derived by way of UCITS in the unitholder country.

Figure IV.1 Taxation in the Unitholder Country

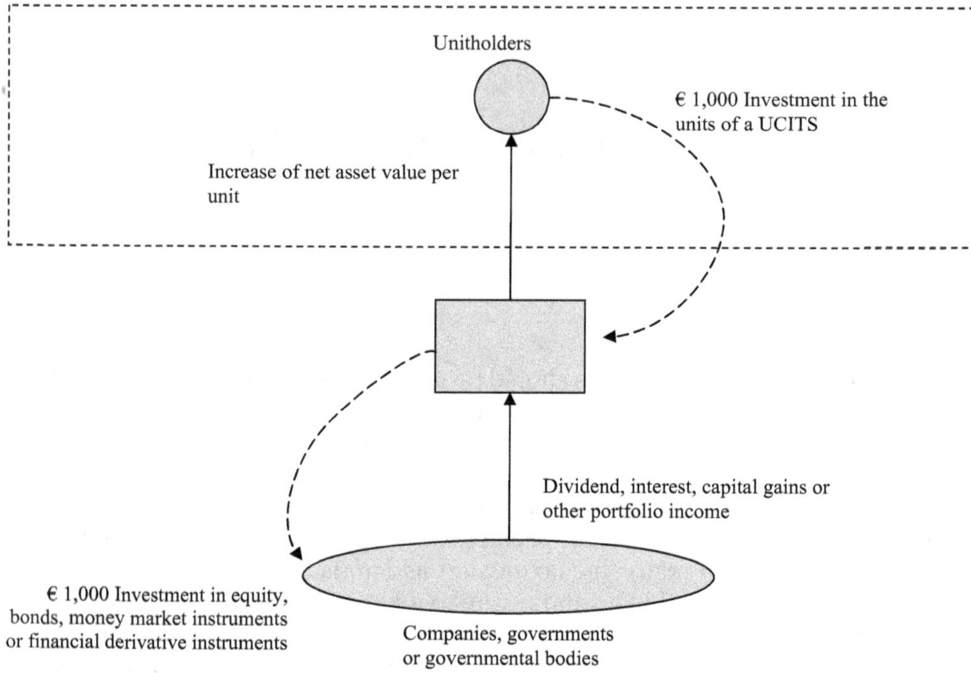

Preface to Chapters 9–12

From Section 3.2 it follows that income from securities and other financial instruments is frequently subject to withholding tax at source. The withholding tax generally concerns a final taxation for non-resident taxpayers, unless they carry on a business by way of a permanent establishment in the source state. For resident taxpayers, the withholding tax is either a prepayment tax or a final taxation. In the case of the latter, the personal and family circumstances are not taken into account. In some states, this is different if the taxation against the general rules results in a lesser taxation.

As mentioned before, the Member States of the European Union (EU) and the European Economic Area (EEA) are sovereign in designing personal and corporate income tax laws. Any rules on the taxation of (portfolio) income from securities and other financial instruments will not be found in the European Community (EC) Treaty, secondary EC legislation or the EEA Treaty; nor is it coordinated by the European Union or the Organization for Economic Cooperation and Development. The countries studied are free to define who is liable to tax, adjust their tax base, set the applicable tax rates, and impose special tax regimes for certain persons or activities, such as UCITS. In the absence of any harmonization or coordination, the taxation of income from securities and other financial instruments in the countries studied may differ from that in other Member States.

Articles 56 and 58 of the EC Treaty and Article 40 of the EEA Treaty, however, forbid a different treatment of domestic and foreign income. Dividends, interest, capital gains, and other portfolio income from foreign securities and other financial instruments may not be taxed more heavily than that from domestic securities and other financial instruments. The countries studied thus may not impose a higher tax rate on foreign income. Nor may an exemption or other relief be restricted to domestic income. Neither should the time that foreign income is considered to be taxable in the hands of resident taxpayer be brought forward compared to domestic income. Taxpayers or the European Commission may bring such discriminatory rules before the European Court of Justice. A number of infringement procedures are pending before the European Court of Justice. The European Commission has started a few procedures to remove discriminatory taxation on foreign dividends paid to individuals.[1]

Chapters 9–12 discuss the level, operation, and transparency of taxation on income from securities and other financial instruments at the level of resident taxpayers in Austria, Germany, the Netherlands, and the United Kingdom. In addition, these chapters examine whether investments in non-resident UCITS are taxed more heavily than those in resident UCITS.[2]

1. See also the press releases by the European Commission of 6 May 2008 (IP/08/712), 28 Feb. 2008 (IP/08/339), 5 Jul. 2007 (IP/071019) and 22 Jan. 2007 (IP/07/67).
2. See also the press release by the European Commission of 26 Jun. 2008 (IP/08/1021).

Chapter 9

Austria: Taxation of Income from Investments in the Country of the Unitholders

Income derived by way of resident UCITS is considered to be that of the unitholders under the domestic laws of Austria. In contrast to a direct investment, the income is not considered to be received upon receipt. Instead, it is considered to be received by the unitholders at distribution, the disposal of units in the undertakings for collective investment in transferable securities (UCITS) and 4 months after the end of the year, whichever is earlier. The exception to the rule is income from speculative transactions and accumulated capital gains.

Unlike a direct investment, income from speculative transactions does not include the capital gains from the disposal of investments within that are disposed within 1 year after the purchase. Instead, it is considered to be one-fifth of the part of the capital gains from the disposal of investments that are not related to bonds or debt securities.

Furthermore, capital gains from the disposal of the underlying investments are not considered to be received by corporate unitholders if they are accumulated. As a result, these gains are not taxed in the hands of these unitholders until the disposal of the units in the UCITS.

Income derived by way of non-resident UCITS is not subject to more taxation than income derived by way of resident UCITS, unless the Austrian tax authorities and unitholders are not properly informed about the amount, nature, and source of the income. The one exception to the rule is the taxation of accumulated capital gains. Unlike an investment in a resident UCITS, these gains are considered to be distributed to corporate unitholders for whom the units in the non-resident UCITS are considered to be business income. This seems to be an infringement of the freedom of capital as laid down in Articles 56 and 58 of the EC Treaty and Article 40 of the EEA Treaty.

The amount of the income derived by way of non-resident UCITS is, however, estimated in the case the non-resident UCITS has not properly informed the Austrian tax authorities or unitholders about the amount, nature, and source of the income. This generally results in more severe taxation. The unitholder however, may prove that the amount of the actual income is less than that of the estimated income.

Any of the foreign tax withheld at source is considered to be that of the unitholders under the domestic laws of Austria. For that reason, the Austrian tax treaties and unilateral rules apply as if the income was derived directly by the unitholders from the underlying investments. This might be the reason why Austria in the case of a non-resident UCITS does not take into account whether any relief for foreign withholding taxes was available at the level of the UCITS.

The tax withheld by the UCITS country at the time of distribution may only be set off against the tax liability of the unitholders if the applicable tax treaty provides for such.

9.1. INTRODUCTION

Under the domestic laws of Austria the income from the underlying investments of UCITS is considered to be that of the unitholders, although it is not considered to be received by them until it is distributed or is considered to be distributed. The income from the underlying investments of German, Netherlands, or UK-resident UCITS, however, is estimated if the Austrian tax authorities and unitholders are not properly informed about the amount, nature, and source of income from the investments or the amount of withholding tax that per-source and per-item charged is at source on the income.

9.2. TAX LIABILITY OF AUSTRIAN-RESIDENT UNITHOLDERS

9.2.1. Income Tax Liability of Austrian-Resident Individual Unitholders

9.2.1.1. Investing Directly in Securities and Other Financial Instruments

Individuals resident in Austria are subject to income tax on their worldwide taxable income. The taxable income of residents includes income from the following sources:

(1) Business income:
   (a) income from agriculture and forestry;
   (b) income from independent (professional) services;
   (c) income from other trade or business.

(2) Other income:
   (a) income from employment;
   (b) income from investments of capital;
   (c) income from rentals, leasing and royalties;
   (d) income from other specific sources as mentioned in section 29 of the Income Tax Act.[3]

Any income that does not qualify as one of these income types is not charged with income tax.

Tax Burden

The taxable income of a calendar year is subject to income tax at a progressive rate of at the most 50% (2009).[4] The income tax liability of some types of income from investment of capital is, however, subject to a 25% withholding tax when that income is paid out domestically.[5] No withholding tax is levied when those income types are paid out abroad.[6] In that case, the gross amount of that income is subject to a special income tax rate of 25% to achieve a tax treatment similar to that for domestically paid out income.[7]

If the income tax liability of income from the investment of capital under the general tax rules would be less than 25%, these tax rules are applied on request of the unitholder. In such a case, the part of the withholding tax that exceeds the income tax liability is refunded.[8] The income tax liability may be lower because of the deduction of costs or the crediting of losses from the same year or other years.

Income from Investment of Capital

Income from investment of capital involves the compensation for the provision of capital.[9] The Income Tax Act contains an exhaustive catalogue of income from investment of capital. It includes the following:

(1) Distributions (dividends), interest and other earnings on shares and equity participations of any kind.
(2) Interest and other income on loans, bonds, deposits, credit balances with banks.[10]

---

3. Section 2(3) Income Tax Act (Einkommensteuergesetz 1988), BGBl. Nr. 400/1988, 7 Jul. 1988.
4. Section 33(1) Income Tax Act.
5. Section 97(1) Income Tax Act.
6. After all, Austria cannot enforce a withholding tax outside its jurisdiction.
7. Section 37(8)(2) and (3) Income Tax Act.
8. Section 97(4) Income Tax Act.
9. H. Kofler & S. Kristen in Bertl, u.a. (Hrsg.), *Handbuch der österreichischen Steuerlehre*, Bd I (London: LexisNexis ARD Orac, 2004), 153.
10. Section 27(1)(1)–(4), and (1)(7) Income Tax Act.

Dividends are considered to be received at the time of payment.[11] If dividend coupons are disposed of before that decision, the proceeds from the disposal are also considered to be dividends at the time of disposal.[12] Bonus shares, however, are explicitly exempt from income tax.[13]

Interest is considered to be received at the time that the debtor and creditor have agreed on or, in the absence of such, at the time of the interest payment. If a bond is disposed of before a pay date, the part of the capital gain from the disposal that is related to the interest accrued since the latest pay date is considered interest, too.[14] The proceeds from the disposal of interest coupons before the pay date are also considered interest at the time of disposal.[15] Interest also includes the compensation given to an individual at the time of purchase in the form of a discount on the par value of a bond[16] or the compensation paid by an individual at the time of purchase in the form of a premium above the par value of a bond.[17,18] A discount or premium, however, is not received by an individual until the repayment date, or if the bonds are disposed of before that date, at the time of disposal. The difference between the par value and the cost price, or issue price, of non-interest-generating bonds is also interest. It is received by an individual at the time of repayment, or if the bonds are disposed of before that date, at the time of disposal.

Exemptions

Moreover, it should be noted that up to an amount of EUR 25,000 dividend and interest from small business finance corporations is exempt in order to stimulate the supply of risk capital and loans for small businesses.[19]

Losses

A loss from investment of capital may be set off against other income. If a loss from investment of capital cannot, or cannot entirely, be credited against other income, the non-creditable part of the loss cannot be carried over to other years.

11. See W. Doralt, *Einkommensteuergesetz Kommentar* (Vienna: WUV-Universitätsverlag, loose leaf), EStG, § 19, 30.
12. Section 27(2)(3) Income Tax Act.
13. Sections 27(1)(1)(a) and 3(29) Income Tax Act.
14. Section 27(3)(3) Income Tax Act.
15. Section 27(2)(3) Income Tax Act.
16. A discount on the par value of a bond is given where the interest rate of the bond is less than the interest rate of the capital market.
17. A premium above the par value of a bond is paid where the interest rate of the bond is more than the interest rate of the capital market.
18. H. Kofler, G. Kofler & S. Kristen in Bertl, u.a. (Hrsg.), *Handbuch der österreichischen Steuerlehre*, Bd I (London: LexisNexis ARD Orac, 2004), at 165.
19. Section 27(3)(3) Income Tax Act.

Other Income

In accordance with section 29 of the Income Tax Act, income from specific sources is taxable as other income. Income from speculative transactions, however, is the only one that is of importance to income from portfolio investments. It includes capital gains realized by the disposal of securities, debt claims, and other economic properties that are disposed of within a year after their purchase.[20] Any capital gains from the disposal of other investments remain exempt from tax.

The capital gain from the disposal of options and futures that are disposed of within a year after their purchase also fall within the capital gain from the disposal of other intangible property. So do other advantages gained with options or futures that are settled within one year after their purchase.[21]

Exemptions

An exemption applies if the income from speculative transactions in a calendar year does not exceed EUR 440.[22]

Losses

A loss from speculative transactions cannot be set off against other income. Nor can it be carried forward to other years.

9.2.1.2. Investment in the Units of Austrian-Resident UCITS

Any income from the underlying investments of a resident UCITS is that of the unitholders, because resident UCITS are considered transparent.[23] In contrast to other structures of joint ownership, the income from the underlying investments is not considered to be received by Austrian individual unitholders at the time it arises.[24] Instead, it is considered received by these unitholders at distribution, the disposal of the units in the UCITS, and 4 months after the end of the financial year of the UCITS,[25] whichever is earlier.

20. Section 30(1)(1)(b) Income Tax Act.
21. See W. Doralt & O. Kempf, *Einkommensteuergesetz Kommentar* (Vienna: WUV-Universitäts-verlag, loose leaf), EStG, § 30, 69–72.
22. Section 30(4) Income Tax Act.
23. W. Doralt & S. Kirchmayr, *Einkommensteuergesetz Kommentar* (Vienna: WUV-Universitäts-verlag, loose leaf), EStG, § 93, 11.
24. See *Ibid.*, 12, P. Reisenhofer, *Investmentfondsgesetz* (Vienna: Manzsche Verlags-und Universitätsbuchhandlung, 2002), 62; and M. Sedlaczek, 'Kapitalertragsteuer und Investmentfonds', in *Kapitalertragsteuer*, ed. E. Lechner, C. Staringer & M. Tumpel (Vienna: Linde Verlag, 2003), 191.
25. Section 40(1) Law on Investment Funds.

Example 9.1

An Austrian-resident UCITS derives from its investments a dividend of EUR 2,500,000 and realizes through the disposal of investments a gain of EUR 10,000,000. In accordance with its fund rules, it accumulates the dividends and the proceeds from the disposal of investments. An Austrian individual unitholder is considered to receive a share in the dividend and the capital gain from the disposal.

Any income from the underlying investments is taxable in the hands of an Austrian individual unitholder if it qualifies as income from the investment of capital or income from speculative transactions. The income from speculative transactions, however, does not include the capital gain realized by the disposal of investments disposed of within 1 year after purchase. Instead, the income is considered to be one-fifth of the part of the capital gain from the disposal of investments that is not related to bonds or debt securities. Any other part of the capital gain remains exempt from income tax.[26]

Example 9.2

An Austrian-resident UCITS derives from its investments a dividend of EUR 2,500,000 and realizes through the disposal of investments in equity a gain of EUR 10,000,000. In accordance with its fund rules, it accumulates the dividend and the capital gain from the disposal of the investments. An Austrian individual unitholder is considered to receive a share in the dividends and the proceeds from the disposal. The share in the dividends is taxable as income from investment of capital, whereas one-fifth of the capital gain from the disposal of an investment in equity is considered to be income from speculative transactions.

Disposal of the Units in an Austrian-Resident UCITS

The part of the capital gain from the disposal that is not related to income from the underlying investments of a resident UCITS is taxable as income from speculative transactions if the units are disposed of within 1 year after their purchase.

Example 9.3

An Austrian-resident UCITS derives from its investments a dividend of EUR 2,500,000 and realizes through the disposal of investments in equity a gain of

26. Section 40(1) Law on Investment Funds.

EUR 10,000,000. The dividends and the capital gain from the disposal of investments are not yet distributed when an Austrian individual unitholder disposes of the units in the UCITS. The dividends and the capital gain from the disposal of the investments are considered to be distributed to the unitholder at the time of disposal. The unitholder's share in the dividend is taxable as income from investment of capital, whereas one-fifth of the share in the capital gain from the disposal of an investment in equity is considered to be income from speculative transactions. The other part of the capital gain from the disposal of the units in the UCITS is taxable as income from speculative transactions if the units are disposed of within 1 year after their purchase.

9.2.1.3. Investment in the Units of UCITS Residing in Germany, the Netherlands, or the United Kingdom

Any income from the underlying investments of a non-resident UCITS is considered to be that of the unitholders. A non-resident UCITS is considered transparent under the domestic laws of Austria, unless it does not qualify as a non-resident undertaking for (collective) investment under the Law on Investment Funds.[27] In that case, it is considered to be a tax opaque entity and as a result of which is considered to be a taxable entity.

Classification of Non-resident UCITS

A UCITS, notwithstanding its legal form, qualifies as a non-resident undertaking for (collective) investment if it is capital that is subject to the laws of another state and it invests the obtained capital in accordance with the principle of the spreading of risk. The latter has to be required by the law of its residence state, its articles of incorporation, or fund rules, or has to be determined on the basis of actual practice. This is a broad definition that does not take into account the characteristics of a non-resident UCITS under the civil law of its residence state. It may comprise UCITS of the corporate type, the contractual type, or the trust type. Indications for a non-resident undertaking for (collective) investment may be that a non-resident UCITS is subject to regulations similar to those of resident UCITS[28] and that the principle of spreading risk is given form in these regulations in the form of qualitative and quantitative restrictions.[29] It does not, however, matter that these restrictions are less strict than those for resident UCITS. Furthermore, (passive) investment activities have to be involved. A UCITS, however, is not allowed to

27. Section 42(1) Law on Investment Funds. See Rz 252 InvFR 2008, P. Quantschnigg, 'Die neue Besteuerung bei ausländischen Investmentfonds', *ÖStZ 1995/1-2*, 7; and C. Reschny-Birox & R. Klaunzer, 'Das Ende der "schwarzen" ausländischen Fonds?', *SWK 2004/23-24*, 1004.
28. Rz 257 InvFR 2008.
29. M. Biegler, 'Zweifelfragen bei der Behandlung von Investmentfonds im außerbetrieblichen Bereich', *SWK 1994*, 18, 405.

have a strong hold on the actual activities of companies in which it keeps shares or holds another kind of equity participation.[30] German-, Netherlands-, and UK-resident UCITS will not have any difficulty in fulfilling all of these conditions.

The income from the underlying investments of these non-resident UCITS is therefore considered to be received by Austrian individual unitholders at the same time, and for the same amount, as income from the underlying investments of resident UCITS is considered to be paid.[31]

Example 9.4

A UK-resident UCITS derives from its investments a dividend of EUR 2,500,000 and realizes through the disposal of investments in equity a gain of EUR 10,000,000. Whether the income from the underlying investments is distributed or accumulated, an Austrian individual unitholder is considered to receive a share in the dividend and the capital gain from the disposal of the investments. The share in the dividend is taxable as income from the investment of capital, whereas one-fifth of the capital gain from the disposal of an investment in equity is considered to be income from speculative transactions.

The income from the underlying investments is taxable in the hands of the unitholders under the same conditions as for resident UCITS.

Estimation of Income

If the amount, nature, and source of the income from the underlying investments of non-resident UCITS are not communicated properly to the tax authorities and the unitholders, it will be estimated. This generally results in more severe taxation. The Law on Investment Funds estimates the income from the underlying investments of the non-resident UCITS in that case because the sum of the amount of the actual distributions and 90% of the amount of an increase in value of the units in the non-resident UCITS (amount of the accumulated income). Under no circumstances is the amount of the accumulated income considered to be less than 10% of the intrinsic value of the units at the end of the year.[32] The amount of the increase in value of the units is the difference between the amount of the intrinsic value of the units at the end of the year and that at the beginning of the year. The amount of the accumulated income is considered to be 10% of the intrinsic value at the end of the year if the increase in value of the units in the non-resident UCITS is less

30. P. Reisenhofer, *Investmentfondsgesetz* (Vienna: Manzsche Verlags-und Universitätsbuchhandlung, 2002), 72.
31. Sections 40(1) and 42 Law on Investment Funds.
32. Section 42(2) Law on Investment Funds.

than that amount. However, a unitholder may provide proof that the amount of the accumulated income is less than the amount of the estimated income. For most non-professional investors, however, this will be a difficult task.

If units of a unitholder are disposed of during the year or within 4 months after the end of the year, the amount of income from the underlying investments that is not yet distributed is considered to be distributed at the time of disposal. The amount, nature, and source of the income from the underlying investments that is considered to be distributed at the time of disposal therefore has to be communicated to the Austrian tax authorities at each issue date.[33] Otherwise, under the Law on Investment Funds the amount of the accumulated income is estimated 100% of the amount of an increase in value of the units in the non-resident UCITS but no less than 0.8% of the intrinsic value of the units at the time of disposal for each month that has begun in the year of disposal.[34] The amount of the increase in value of the units is the difference between the amount of the intrinsic value of the units at the time of disposal and that at the beginning of the year. The amount of the accumulated income is considered to be 0.8% of the intrinsic value at the disposal for each month that has begun where the increase in value of the units in the non-resident UCITS is less than that amount. However, a unitholder may provide proof that the actual amount of the accumulated income is less than the amount of the estimation. For most non-professional investors this will be an even harder task than to provide proof of the amount of the distribution account at the end of the year because UCITS do generally not provide daily reports.

Disposal of the Units in a Non-resident UCITS

The income tax liability for the part of the capital gain realized by the disposal of units in non-resident UCITS does not differ from that for the capital gain from the disposal of units in a resident UCITS.

Example 9.5

A UK-resident UCITS derives from its investments a dividend of EUR 2,500,000 and realizes through the disposal of investments in equity a gain of EUR 10,000,000. The dividend and the capital gain from the disposal of investments are not yet distributed when an Austrian individual unitholder disposes of the units in the UCITS. The dividend and the capital from the disposal of the investments are considered to be distributed to the unitholder at the time of disposal. The unitholder's share in the dividend is taxable as income from investment of capital, whereas one-fifth of the share in the capital gain from the disposal of an investment in equity is considered income from

33. *Ibid.*
34. *Ibid.*

speculative transactions. The other part of the capital gain from the disposal of units in the UCITS is taxable as income from speculative transactions if the units are disposed of within 1 year after their purchase.

9.2.2. Corporate Income Tax Liability of Corporate Unitholders

9.2.2.1. Investing Directly in Securities and Other Financial Instruments

Corporate entities[35] resident in Austria are subject to corporate income tax on their worldwide taxable income. The taxable income of residents includes income from the following sources:

(1) Business income:
   (a) income from agriculture and forestry;
   (b) income from independent (professional) services;
   (c) income from other trade or business.
(2) Other income:
   (a) income from employment;
   (b) income from investments of capital;
   (c) income from rentals, leasing, and royalties;
   (d) income from other specific sources as mentioned in section 29 of the Income Tax Act.[36]

Any income that does not qualify as one of these income types is not charged with corporate income tax.

Partly Exempt Corporate Entities

Among other corporate entities, the corporate income tax liability of Austrian-resident pension funds[37] and charities[38] is limited to income from capital that has been subject to domestic withholding tax or any comparable foreign income that would have been subject to that tax as well if not for its foreign source.[39] In spite of this, the tax base of these entities is reduced substantially for portfolio investments

35. Under the Corporate Tax Act (Körperschafsteuergesetz), BGBl. Nr. 401/1988, 7 Jul. 1988, the following are considered a corporate body: legal persons incorporated under civil law, such as public corporations, private corporations with limited liability and mutual insurance companies, commercial enterprises operated by public bodies, and associations, institutions, foundations without legal personality, and other pools of assets set up for a specific purpose.
36. Section 7(2) Corporate Tax Act in conjunction with s. 2(3) Income Tax Act.
37. Sections 5 and 6(1) Corporate Tax Act. See also the Corporate Tax Guidelines (Körperschaftsteuerrichtlinien 2001).
38. Section 5(6) Corporate Tax Act.
39. H. Kofler, G. Kofler & S. Kristen in Bertl, u.a. (Hrsg.), *Handbuch der österreichischen Steuerlehre*, Bd I (London: LexisNexis ARD Orac, 2004), 595.

by way of an exemption for dividends or a share in the profits other than by liquidation that is paid out on shares or other equity participations held in a resident corporate body and interest from deposits or other debts with domestic credit institutions or a domestic branch of a foreign credit institution, bonds, and other debt securities.[40]

Tax Burden

The taxable income of a financial year is subject to corporate income tax at a flat rate of 25% (2009). A 25% withholding tax discharges the corporate income tax liability of interest from deposits or debts with domestic credit institutions and interest from bonds or other income that is paid out domestically.[41]

If the corporate income tax liability on these types of interest would be less than 25% under the general tax rules, these tax rules are applied on request of the unitholder. The part of the withholding tax that exceeds the corporate income tax liability is refundable.[42] The corporate income tax liability for these types of interest may be less than the withholding tax charged because of the deduction of costs or the crediting of losses from the same year or other years.

Business Income

Income is considered to be business income if it is derived from the business assets of a corporate entity. The portfolio investments of corporate entities that, under commercial law,[43] are obliged to keep books are always considered to be business assets. The portfolio investments of trading or agricultural cooperatives and foundations that operate a business are also considered to be business assets, although such corporate entities are not required to keep books.[44] The foregoing also applies to the portfolio investments of comparable corporate entities that are incorporated under foreign law.[45]

The portfolio investments of other corporate entities are generally not considered to be business assets, unless these investments are purchased with a temporary surplus of liquid assets. This is different only for banks and stockbrokers because they use the portfolio investments for business activities.[46]

40. Section 21(2) and (3) Corporate Tax Act.
41. Section 97(1) Income Tax Act.
42. Section 97(4) Income Tax Act.
43. Section 189 of the Commercial Law contains an obligation to keep books for public corporations, private corporations with limited liability, savings banks, foundations that act as an insurance company on a mutual basis, and some commercial enterprises that are operated by public bodies.
44. Section 7(3) Corporate Tax Act.
45. *Ibid.*
46. W. Doralt, *Einkommensteuergesetz Kommentar* (Vienna: WUV-Universitätsverlag, loose leaf), EStG, § 4, 45, 52, and 53.

Tax Accounting Principles

The business income of a corporate body is determined by a comparison of its business assets.[47] It is the result of the difference between the value of the business assets at the end of the year and that of the business assets at the beginning. Furthermore, this amount has to be corrected with any payments or withdrawals of capital to arrive at the true amount of business income for the applicable year.[48] For the preparation of the fiscal balance sheet, such corporate bodies that are obliged to keep books under commercial law make use of the principles of commercial law to the extent the Income Tax Act does not contain different rules.[49] Other corporate bodies have to base their fiscal balance sheet on double-entry book keeping and the provisions of the Income Tax Act.

Exemptions

An exemption applies to (portfolio) dividends or a share in the profits other than by liquidation that is paid out on shares or other equity participations held in a resident corporate body.[50] Whether the restriction of this exemption to domestic (portfolio) dividends infringes on the free movement of capital under Articles 56 and 58 of the EC Treaty and Article 40 of the EEA Treaty falls outside the scope of this study. The Austrian Supreme Administrative Court recently decided that the restriction to domestic (portfolio) dividends concerns an infringement of Articles 56 and 58 of the EC Treaty.[51] In its view, however, the latter can be removed by way of granting a foreign tax credit.[52,53]

Losses

A loss from business income may be credited against other income. If a loss from business income cannot, or cannot entirely, be credited against other income, the

47. Sections 4(1) and 5(1) Income Tax Act.
48. H. Kofler & S. Kristen in Bertl, u.a. (Hrsg.), *Handbuch der österreichischen Steuerlehre*, Bd I (London: LexisNexis ARD Orac, 2004), 190.
49. Rz 433 Income Tax Guidelines (Einkommensteuerrichtlinien 2000), AÖF 2000/232.
50. Section 10(1) Corporate Tax Act.
51. Austrian Supreme Administrative Court, 17 Apr. 2008, 2008/15/0064.
52. See for a critical discussion of this part of the decision T. Bieber, W. Haslehner, G. Kofler & C.P. Schindler, 'Taxation of Cross-Border Portfolio Dividends in Austria: The Austrian Supreme Administrative Court Interprets EC Law', *European Taxation 2008/583*. See also P. Haunold, M. Tumpel, & C. Widhalm, News aus der EU, *SWI 2007/8*, 377; and R. Beiser, Österreichs Steuern in den Schranken des Gemeinschaftsrechtes, *SWK 2003/30*, 736.
53. The Austrian Department of Finance has recently issued a draft law of s. 10 of the Corporate Tax Act, which provides for an exemption for portfolio dividends paid out on shares or other equity participations held in corporate bodies residing in the European Union. The new draft law therefore seems to remove only a part of the infringement of the freedom of capital as laid down in Arts 56 and 58 of the EC Treaty.

non-creditable part of a loss from business income may be carried forward to other years[54] for up to 75%.

Income from Investment of Capital and Other Income

Income from portfolio investments that do not qualify as business assets is taxable only when it is considered to be income from investment of capital or other income as mentioned in section 29 of the Income Tax Act. These income types are determined as discussed for individuals in Section 9.2.1.1.

Exemptions

The exemption for dividends or a share in the profits other than by liquidation that is paid out on shares or other equity participations held in a resident corporate body is not limited to business income. It thus also applies to any income from investment of capital and other income.

Losses

A loss from investment of capital may be set off against other income. If a loss from investment of capital cannot, or cannot entirely, be credited against other income, the non-creditable part of the loss cannot be carried over to other years.

9.2.2.2. Investment in the Units of Austrian-Resident UCITS

Any income from the underlying investments of a resident UCITS is that of the unitholders, because resident UCITS are considered to be transparent.[55] The income from the underlying investments is, as for individuals, considered to be received by these unitholders on distribution, the disposal of the units in the UCITS and 4 months after the end of the financial year of the UCITS,[56] whichever is earlier. However, if accumulated, the capital gain from the disposal of underlying investments is not realized by corporate unitholders until the disposal of the units in the UCITS.

Example 9.6

An Austrian-resident UCITS derives from its investments a dividend of EUR 2,500,000 and realizes through the disposal of investments a gain of EUR 10,000,000. In accordance with its fund rules, it accumulates the dividend and

54. Section 2(2b) Income Tax Act.
55. W. Doralt & S. Kirchmayr, *Einkommensteuergesetz Kommentar* (Vienna: WUV-Universitätsverlag, loose leaf), EStG, § 93, 11.
56. Section 40(1) Law on Investment Funds.

the capital gain from the disposal of investments. An Austrian corporate unitholder is considered to receive only his share in the dividend.

Any income from the underlying investments is taxable in the hands of an Austrian corporate unitholder if it qualifies as business income, income from the investment of capital or income from speculative transactions. Business income includes any income from the underlying investments of the non-resident UCITS. Income from investment of capital and income from speculative transactions is determined as discussed for individuals in Section 9.2.1.2.

Example 9.7

An Austrian-resident UCITS derives from its investments a dividend of EUR 2,500,000 and realizes through the disposal of investments in equity a gain of EUR 10,000,000. In accordance with its fund rules, it distributes the dividend and the capital gain from the disposal of the investments. If the units in the UCITS qualify as business assets, the distribution is fully taxable as business income.

Exemptions

The exemption for dividends or a share in the profits other than by liquidation that is paid out on shares or other equity participations held in a resident corporate body also applies if this type of income is derived by way of an Austrian-resident UCITS.[57]

Disposal of the Units in an Austrian-Resident UCITS

The part of the capital gain from the disposal that is not related to income from the underlying investments of a resident UCITS is taxable as business income if the units qualify as business assets. Otherwise, they are taxable as income from speculative transactions only where the units are disposed of within 1 year after their purchase.

Example 9.8

An Austrian-resident UCITS derives from its investments a dividend of EUR 2,500,000 and realizes through the disposal of investments in equity a gain of EUR 10,000,000. The dividend and the capital gain from the disposal of investments are not yet distributed when an Austrian individual unitholder

57. Section 10(1) Corporate Tax Act.

disposes of the units in the UCITS. The dividend and capital gain from the disposal of the investments are considered to be distributed to the unitholder at the time of disposal. The unitholder's share in the dividend is taxable as income from investment of capital whereas one-fifth of his share in the capital gain from the disposal of an investment in equity is considered to be income from speculative transactions. The other part of the capital gain from the disposal of the units in the UCITS is taxable as business income where the units qualify as business income.

9.2.2.3. Investment in the Units of UCITS Residing in Germany, the Netherlands, and the United Kingdom by Austrian Corporate Unitholders

Any income from the underlying investments of UCITS residing in Germany, the Netherlands, and the United Kingdom is considered to be that of the unitholders. As discussed for individuals in Section 9.2.1.3, a UCITS residing in Germany, the Netherlands, and the United Kingdom is considered transparent under the Austrian tax legislation.

The income from the underlying investments of these non-resident UCITS is considered to be received by Austrian corporate unitholders at the same time and for the same amount as income from the underlying investments of resident UCITS is considered to be paid out.[58] Any income from the underlying investments is, like that of resident UCITS, taxable if it qualifies as business income, income from investment of capital, or income from speculative transactions. These income types are determined as discussed for individuals in Section 9.2.1.3.

Example 9.9

A UK-resident UCITS derives from its investments a dividend of EUR 2,500,000 and realizes through the disposal of investments a gain of EUR 10,000,000. If the dividend and the proceeds from the disposal of the investments are accumulated, an Austrian corporate unitholder is considered to receive only its share in the dividend.

An exception applies to capital gains realized by the disposal of investments in the case but only if the units in the UCITS are considered to be business assets. In that case, the capital gains are considered to be received by the corporate body as other income. Unlike an investment in resident UCITS, this is also true if these gains are accumulated.[59] By accumulation, capital gains derived by way of non-resident UCITS may be subject to a less favourable tax treatment in the hands of corporate

58. Sections 40(1) and 42 Law on Investment Funds.
59. Sections 42(3) Law on Investment Funds.

bodies compared to capital gains derived by way of resident UCITS. This seems to infringe the freedom of capital as laid down in Articles 56 and 58 of the EC Treaty and Article 40 of the EEA Treaty.

Example 9.10

A UK-resident UCITS derives from its investments a dividend of EUR 2,500,000 and realizes through the disposal of investments a gain of EUR 10,000,000. If the dividend and proceeds from the disposal of the investments are accumulated, an Austrian corporate unitholder is not only considered to receive its share in the dividend but also its share in the capital gain realized by the disposal of the investments.

Exemptions

The same exemptions are available for income derived by way of non-resident UCITS as discussed above for resident UCITS.

Estimation of Income

The Austrian tax authorities and unitholders have to be provided with the information relevant for the corporate income tax liability of the unitholders. The consequences of not communicating the required information, or not communicating that information properly, do not differ from what has been discussed for individuals in Section 9.2.1.3.

Disposal of the Units in a Non-resident UCITS

The corporate income tax liability for the part of the capital gain from the disposal that is not related to income from the underlying investments of UCITS residing in Germany, the Netherlands and the United Kingdom is equal to the corporate income tax liability for that part of the capital gain from the disposal of units in resident UCITS.

Example 9.11

An UK-resident UCITS derives from its investments a dividend of EUR 2,500,000 and realizes through the disposal of investments in equity a gain of EUR 10,000,000. The dividend and the capital gain from the disposal of investments are not yet distributed when an Austrian individual unitholder disposes of the units in the UCITS. For that reason, the dividend and capital gain from the disposal of the investments are considered to be distributed to the unitholder at the time of disposal. The unitholder's share in the dividend is taxable as income from investment of capital while the capital gain from the disposal of an investment in equity is considered to be other income in the case that the units qualify as business income. The other part of the capital gain from the disposal of the units in the UCITS is taxable as business income where the units qualify as business income.

9.2.3. Crediting of the Withholding Tax Charged by the Source State

9.2.3.1. Investing Directly in Securities and Other Financial Instruments

Cross-border investments in securities and other financial instruments have the potential for international double taxation. Like most industrialized states, Austria does not restrict its taxation to domestic assets and activities. It also imposes tax on investments and operations carried out in other states to the degree that they benefit resident taxpayers. This may result in international double taxation because income from foreign securities and financial instruments is often subject to tax in the source state too.

Austria has various regulations to prevent international double taxation in this situation.

Tax Treaties

The most important regulation to prevent international double taxation is the tax treaty. Tax treaties aim to match the taxation under the domestic laws of the Contracting States so that international double taxation as well as double *non*-taxation is prevented. For that reason, tax treaties allocate the right to tax a specific asset, item of income, activity, or person to one of the Contracting States.

The right to tax dividend and interest is generally allocated to both states. Dividends and interest may be taxed in the state in whose jurisdiction the beneficiary resides (residence state). Nevertheless, dividends and interest may also be taxed in the state in whose jurisdiction the paying company or the debtor resides (the source state), but the taxation may not exceed the percentage agreed on in the tax treaty. An overview of the percentages agreed on in the Austrian tax treaties can be found in Tables 3.1 and 3.2 of Chapter 3.

To avoid double taxation, the tax withheld by the source state on dividend or interest may be credited against the beneficiary's tax liability in the residence state (foreign tax credit). The foreign tax credit, however, is limited to the amount of tax that could have been levied by the source state in accordance with the applicable tax treaty.

Instead of the foreign withholding tax that is actually charged on dividend or interest, almost one-fifth of the Austrian tax treaties with developing countries and countries, like Brazil or Turkey, that are not as developed as Austria[60] provide for a foreign tax credit that is higher than the amount of the foreign withholding tax that is actually charged. Austrian-resident investors are, under these tax treaties, allowed either to credit the amount of foreign withholding tax that would have been charged by the source state if the income was taxed in accordance with the general tax rules instead of a special tax incentive (tax sparing credit), or to credit a fictitious percentage of the gross amount of the income (matching credit). The aim of a tax sparing credit or a matching credit is to ensure that the benefits of a special tax incentive of the source state are not, or are not entirely, undone by the taxation of the investor by his state of residence.[61]

Double taxation of capital gains and other portfolio income is in most tax treaties quite easily avoided by allocating the right to tax these items of income exclusively to the residence state of the alienator and the recipient, respectively. Hence, the source state has no right to impose tax.

Nevertheless, a number of tax treaties, which can be found in the Tables 3.3 and 3.4 of Chapter 3, allocate the right to tax capital gains and other portfolio income to both states. To avoid double taxation the tax withheld by the source state may be credited against the alienator or beneficiary's tax liability in the residence state (foreign tax credit).

Unilateral Rules

Regulations on the prevention of international double taxation, however, are not found only in tax treaties. In the absence of a tax treaty, or in the presence of a tax treaty that does not cover certain taxes, does not apply to certain taxpayers, or does not cover certain taxable items; the taxation in the source state and the residence state often show overlap. Most Western states, therefore, have issued unilateral rules that take into account that foreign income may have been subject to tax in the state of residence.

The Austrian unilateral rules for cross-border investments in securities and other financial instruments are found in the Decree on the avoidance of double taxation (hereafter, Dadt).[62] On the basis of the Dadt, the foreign withholding tax may be credited against the beneficiary's tax liability in Austria (foreign tax credit).

60. Brazil, China, Cyprus, Indonesia, Israel, Korea, Malaysia, Malta, Nepal, the Philippines, Portugal, Thailand, Tunisia, and Turkey.
61. H. Kofler & S. Kristen in Bertl, et al., *Handbuch der österreichischen Steuerlehre*, Bd I (London: LexisNexis ARD Orac, 2004), 449 and C. van Raad, *Cursus Belastingrecht (Internationaal belastingrecht)* (Deventer: Kluwer, loose leaf), 3.3.2.D.b.
62. Section 48 Federal Taxation Law (Bundesabgabenordnung), BGBl. 1961/194, 28 Jun. 1961, in combination with s. 1(2) Decree on the Avoidance of Double Taxation (Verordnung des Bundesminister fur Finanzen betreffend die Vermeidung von Doppelbesteuerung), BGBl. Nr. 474/2002.

Ordinary Tax Credit

In spite of the issues discussed in the preceding section, under no circumstances does Austria grant a foreign tax credit that is more than the part of the Austrian (corporate) income tax due on the beneficiary's worldwide income that is related to the foreign income (ordinary tax credit). The aim of the ordinary tax credit is to prevent the foreign tax credit granted by the state of residence from exceeding the (corporate) income tax that the state of residence charges on the foreign income. The ordinary tax credit is determined per country. This means that the Austrian (corporate) income tax that is related to the foreign income has to be calculated separately for each source state. A resident taxpayer, however, may opt for the per-item method in which case the (corporate) income tax that is related to the foreign income is determined per item.

The foreign tax credit cannot exceed 25% of the gross amount of the income from foreign investments of capital if the deduction of domestic withholding tax settles the (corporate) income tax liability of a resident taxpayer.[63] Nevertheless, the crediting of the tax withheld on foreign dividends and other income from shares is even restricted to 15% of the gross amount.[64] Any relief for the amount of the foreign withholding tax that has not been taken into account by the deduction of domestic withholding tax[65] may be requested from the Austrian tax authorities. Although the majority of Austrian tax treaties limit the source state's right to tax dividend and other income from shares to at the most 15% of the gross amount, a resident taxpayer may be entitled to a foreign tax credit of more than 15% of the dividend due to a tax sparing credit or a matching credit. Hence, the crediting of foreign withholding tax is generally settled by deduction of the domestic withholding tax.

Push Through Rule

Any foreign tax credit that cannot be set off against the tax liability of a resident taxpayer may not be carried back to the preceding year or carried forward to the following year;[66] nor is it refunded.

63. Section 48 Federal Taxation Law in combination with s. 1(1) of the Decree on the Relief of Austrian Withholding Tax on Foreign Interest Income and Dividend (Verordnung des Bundesminister für Finanzen zur durchführung der KEST-Entlastung in Bezug auf Auslandszinsen sowie zur Anrechnung ausländischer Quellensteuer bei Kapitalertragsteuerabzug bie Auslandsdividenden), BGBl. Nr. 393/2003.
64. Section 1(2) Decree on the Relief of Austrian Withholding Tax for Foreign Interest Income and Dividend.
65. E. Lechner, 'Kapitalertragsteuer und Doppelbesteuerung', in *Kapitalertragsteuer*, ed. E. Lechner, C. Staringer & M. Tumpel (Vienna: Linde Verlag, 2003), 264 and 265.
66. VwGH 20 Apr. 1999, 99/14/0012, ÖStZB 1999, 696. See also H. Kofler & S. Kristen in Bertl, u.a. (Hrsg.), *Handbuch der österreichischen Steuerlehre*, Bd I (London: LexisNexis ARD Orac, 2004), 451.

9.2.3.2. Investment in the Units of Austrian-Resident UCITS by Austrian Unitholders

Any foreign tax withheld at source on the income derived by way of Austrian-resident UCITS is considered to be charged for the account of the Austrian unitholders of the UCITS under the domestic laws of Austria. The Austrian tax treaties and unilateral rules therefore apply as if the income from underlying investments is derived directly by Austrian unitholders. The crediting of the foreign tax withheld at source on the income takes place as discussed in Section 9.2.3.1.

Relevant Information

The Austrian tax authorities and unitholders have to be provided with an overview of the amount of withholding tax that has been levied per source state and per item. This information is necessary for the Austrian unitholders to file a tax return or a request for the refund of the part of withholding tax that is not levied in accordance with a tax treaty.

9.2.3.3. Investment in the Units of UCITS Residing in Germany, the Netherlands, and the United Kingdom by Austrian Unitholders

Crediting of foreign tax withheld at source on income from underlying investments of non-resident UCITS does not differ from that for Austrian-resident UCITS. German-, Netherlands-, and UK-resident UCITS are likewise considered to be transparent.

Relevant Information

The Austrian tax authorities and unitholders have to be provided with the same information about the foreign withholding tax as for Austrian-resident UCITS.

Withholding Tax Charged by the UCITS Country at Time of Distribution

Non-resident UCITS Considered to be a Resident for the Purposes of a Tax Treaty

Non-resident UCITS are considered to be transparent under the domestic laws of Austria. That might be the reason why it does not take into account that the UCITS country may have withheld tax for the account of the unitholders at the time of distribution. Any regulations regarding the crediting of the tax withheld by the UCITS country at the time of distribution are missing. According to Austrian tax treaties the tax withheld at the time of distribution may be credited by the beneficiary, the unitholder, but only if the distribution is paid by a resident of the UCITS country and is considered to be a dividend.[67]

Non-resident UCITS Not Considered a Resident for the Purposes of a Tax Treaty

If a distribution is not paid by a UCITS that is considered a resident for the purposes of a tax treaty, Austria, as the residence state of the beneficiary, is not obliged to avoid double taxation by way of an exemption or a tax credit. On the basis of the clause on other income, the right to tax is generally allocated exclusively to the residence state of the unitholder. As discussed in Section 2.4.2, states have different views on the meaning of a resident for the purposes of a tax treaty.

A classification conflict arises in cases in which the UCITS country considers the UCITS a resident for the purposes of the applicable tax treaty and withholds tax at the time of distribution whereas Austria does not consider the UCITS to be such resident and does not avoid double taxation by way of a tax credit. In practice, a classification conflict may especially arise with respect to UCITS of the contractual and trust types. According to the Austrian tax authorities, these UCITS are not treaty eligible.[68] Any tax withheld at the time of distribution therefore should be refundable by the UCITS country under the applicable tax treaty.

9.3. CONCLUSION

In Austria, the (corporate) income tax liability of an investment in the units of a UCITS residing in Germany, the Netherlands, or the United Kingdom does not differ from that of an investment in the units of an Austrian-resident UCITS where the non-resident UCITS has properly informed the Austrian tax authorities about the amount, nature, and source of income from the underlying investments. This is different only by the accumulation of capital gains from the disposal of investments. Unlike an investment in a resident UCITS, these capital gains are

67. Whether or not a distribution is considered to be a dividend for the purposes of a tax treaty is determined by the domestic laws of the UCITS country, as the term dividend is generally defined in the Austrian tax treaties as income from shares, jouissance shares or jouissance rights, mining shares, founders' shares, or other rights, not being debt claims, participating in profits, as well as income from other corporate rights that is subjected to the same taxation treatment as income from shares by the laws of the State of which the company making the distribution is a resident. See also BMF 22 Jan. 1996, *SWI* 1996, 99.
68. BMF 4 Mar. 1993, *SWI* 1993, 105. See also D. Aigner & P. Bitzyk, 'Die steuerliche Behandlung von Erträgen aus Anteilen an ausländischen Investmentfonds', *SWI* 1997, 11; and S. Kirchmayr, *National Report of Austria for the IFA Congress of 1997 on the Taxation of Investment Funds* (Brussels: International Fiscal Association, 1997), 266.

considered to be distributed, but only to corporate unitholders for whom the units in the non-resident UCITS are part of the business assets.

The amount of the income derived by way of a non-resident UCITS is estimated in the case in which Austrian tax authorities have not been properly informed about the amount, nature, and source of the income. This may result in more severe taxation.

The withholding tax levied at source on income may also be set off against the (corporate) income tax liability. The Austrian national tax legislation does not take into account whether the foreign withholding tax levied at source is creditable by the UCITS or any relief for that tax is granted to the UCITS by the UCITS country. However, the withholding tax cannot be set off if the UCITS has not informed the Austrian tax authorities per source about the amount that has been levied.

The information that needs to be communicated basically does not differ from that of Austrian UCITS. Nevertheless, it may hinder Austrian unitholders to invest freely in the units of non-resident UCITS. They run the risk for more severe taxation if a non-resident UCITS does not communicate the information, for example, if because of its listing it is not aware of any Austrian unitholders or it is simply too costly to communicate such information to a few Austrian unitholders. Although the unitholders of non-resident UCITS may provide proof that the amount of the accumulated income is less than the amount of the estimated income, for most non-professional investors this will be a difficult task, especially in the case of the amount of the distribution account at an issue date, because UCITS generally do not provide daily reports. Hence, the units in the majority of non-resident UCITS are not available for most Austrian unitholders without the risk for a more burdensome taxation.

Chapter 10

Germany: Taxation of Income from Investments in the Country of the Unitholders

The income from the investments of German-resident undertakings for collective investment in transferable securities (UCITS) is considered to be that of the unitholders under the domestic laws of Germany but only insofar as the Investment Tax Act provides for such transparency. The income is not considered to be received by the unitholders until it is distributed or considered to be distributed at the end of the year.

This is different only for capital gains from the disposal of securities, derivative instruments, or other financial instruments. By accumulation, these gains are not considered to be distributed to the unitholders at the end of the year. As a result, they are not considered to be received by the unitholders until the disposal of the units in the UCITS.

The taxation of income derived by way of non-resident UCITS does not differ from that of income derived by way of resident UCITS if the amount, nature, and source of the income are communicated to the unitholders. Otherwise, the amount of the income is estimated, which usually results in more severe taxation. However, it is not possible for a unitholder to submit evidence that the amount of the actual income is less than the amount of the estimated income.

The German tax treaties and unilateral rules apply as if the unitholders had invested directly in the underlying investments. Like Austria, Germany does not take into account the availability and the amount of relief for these taxes granted at the level of non-resident UCITS, if any.

Under the domestic laws of Germany, the tax withheld by the UCITS country at the time of distribution may be credited against the tax liability of the unitholders, too.

10.1. INTRODUCTION

German tax legislation considers the income from the investments of German-resident UCITS to be that of the unitholders as far as the Investment Tax Act provides for such transparency. The income is not considered to be received by the unitholders until it is distributed or considered to be distributed. This does not differ in the case of an investment in the units of Austrian-, Netherlands-, or UK-resident UCITS, unless the German tax authorities and unitholders are not properly informed about the amount, nature, and source of income from the investments or the amount of withholding that is charged per source and per-item on the income at source.

10.2. TAX LIABILITY OF GERMAN-RESIDENT UNITHOLDERS

10.2.1. INCOME TAX LIABILITY OF GERMAN-RESIDENT INDIVIDUAL UNITHOLDERS

10.2.1.1. Investing Directly in Securities and Other Financial Instruments

Individuals resident in Germany are subject to income tax on their worldwide taxable income. The taxable income of residents includes income from the following sources:

(1) Business income:
   (a) income from agriculture and forestry;
   (b) income from trade and business;
   (c) income from independent (professional) services.
(2) Non-business income:
   (a) income from employment;
   (b) income from investment of capital;
   (c) income from rentals and leasing;
   (d) income from other specific sources as mentioned in section 22 of the Income Tax Act.[1]

Any income that does not qualify as one of these income types is not charged with income tax.

Tax Burden

Progressive Tax Rate

The taxable income of a calendar year is subject to income tax at a progressive rate of at most 47.475% (2009).[2] This percentage includes a solidarity surcharge of

1. Section 2(1) Income Tax Act (Einkommensteuergesetz), BGBl. I 2002/4210, 19 Oct. 2002.
2. Section 32a(1) Income Tax Act.

5.5%, which was introduced to finance the unification of the Federal Republic of Germany and the German Democratic Republic.

Flat Tax Rate

Some items of income from investment of capital are subject to a final withholding tax, but only if they are paid out domestically; see Section 3.2.2.1 for an overview. The paying company or paying agent is obliged to withhold tax at a rate of 26.375% from the gross amount.[3] No tax is withheld where these items of income are paid out outside Germany.[4] In that case, these items of foreign income are subject to income tax in the hands of the taxpayer at a special tax rate of 26.375% from the gross amount. As a result, domestic and foreign income are treated similarly.[5]

Any of the items of income from investment of capital, which have been subject to a final withholding tax, may be taxed on request of the taxpayer against the general tax rules, but only if this would result in a lower income tax liability.[6] In that case the part of the withholding tax that exceeds the income tax liability is refunded.[7]

Income from Investment of Capital

Income from investment of capital includes all benefits that are derived as compensation for providing capital.[8] As from 1 January 2009, it also includes capital gains from the disposal of investments, even while these gains are not a compensation for the provision of capital. The Income Tax Act contains a comprehensive catalogue of income from investment of capital. It includes the following:

(1) Distributions of profit (dividends), and other earnings on shares and other equity participations of any kind.[9]
(2) Interest on debts.[10]
(3) Capital gains from shares and other financial instruments.[11]

Dividends

Dividends are considered to be received at the time that the corporation that pays the dividend has made the decision to do so. If dividend coupons are disposed of

3. Sections 43(1)(2) and 43(1)(7) in conjunction with s. 43a(1)(2) or s. 43a(1)(3) Income Tax Act.
4. After all, Germany cannot enforce a withholding tax outside its jurisdiction.
5. Section 32d(1) Income Tax Act.
6. Section 32d(6) Income Tax Act.
7. Section 36(4) Income Tax Act.
8. E. Littmann, H. Bitz & H. Pust, *Das Einkommensteuerrecht* (Stuttgart: Schäffer Poeschel, loose leaf), EStG, § 20, 5–7.
9. Including a usufruct that includes the right to profits and proceeds from the winding-up of a stock company.
10. Section 20 Income Tax Act.
11. Section 20(2)(1), (2)(3), and (2)(4) Income Tax Act.

before that decision, the proceeds from that disposal are also considered to be dividends. They are considered to be received at the time of the disposal.[12]

Interest

Interest is received by an individual investor when it is payable or it matures.[13] Interest paid by a bank on the bank account of an individual is received at the time that it is credited to the bank account. Nevertheless, regular recurring interest payments that are paid within 10 days before or within 10 days after the end of a calendar year are considered to be received within that calendar year.[14] If interest coupons are disposed of prior to the pay date, the proceeds from that disposal are also considered to be interest. It is considered to be received at the time of disposal.[15] Interest also includes the compensation given to an individual at the time of purchase in the form of a discount on the par value of a bond[16] or the compensation paid by an individual at the time of purchase in the form of a premium above the par value of a bond.[17] A discount or premium, however, is not received by an individual until the repayment date or, if the bonds are disposed of before that date, the time of disposal.[18] The difference between the par value and the cost price, or issue price, of non-interest-generating bonds is also interest. It is received by an individual at the time of repayment or, if these bonds are disposed of before that date, the time of disposal.[19]

Capital Gains from Shares and Other Financial Instruments

As from 1 January 2009, not only capital gains realized by the disposal of shares in a corporation and other financial instruments within a year after the purchase[20] are subject to income tax but also capital gains realized beyond a year. A grandfathering provision, however, applies for those shares and other financial instruments that were already held by a taxpayer before that date. The capital gains accrued before 1 January 2009 is not taxable, unless it is realized within a year after the purchase of the security or other financial instrument.

A capital gain is defined as the difference between the proceeds from the disposal, after deduction of any connecting costs, and the cost price.[21] It also includes a change in the foreign exchange rate where shares or other financial

12. Section 20(2)(1)(2) Income Tax Act.
13. F.E. Harenberg, c.s., *Die Besteuerung privater Kapitaleinkünfte* (Herne: Verlag Neue Wirtschafts-Briefe, 2007), 77.
14. Section 11 Income Tax Act.
15. Section 20(2)(1)(2) Income Tax Act.
16. A discount on the par value of a bond is given where the interest rate of the bond is less than the interest rate of the capital market.
17. A premium above the par value of a bond is paid where the interest rate of the bond is more than the interest rate of the capital market.
18. BFH BStBl. II 1988/252, BMF 24 Jul. 1986, BStBl. I 1986/539, and BFH BStBl. II 2000/259.
19. Section 20(2)(1)(4) Income Tax Act.
20. Before 1 Jan. 2009, these capital gains were taxed as other income instead of income from investment of capital.
21. Section 20(4) Income Tax Act.

instruments are listed in a foreign currency. A gain from a derivative instrument, like an option or future, concerns the cash settlement, transfer, or other advantage connected with the derivative instrument.[22]

Exemptions

The amount of income from investment of capital is exempt up to an amount of EUR 801 to stimulate savings (savings exemption). The amount of the exemption is doubled for spouses. Any expenses connected with the income are explicitly not deductible.[23]

Losses

A loss from investment of capital cannot be set off against other income. It may be, however, carried forward to the following year, although a capital loss from the disposal of shares in a corporation can be credited against capital gains only from the same source; the disposal of the shares in a corporation.[24]

10.2.1.2. Investment in the Units of German-Resident UCITS

Any income from the underlying investments of a resident UCITS is that of the UCITS.[25] The income from the underlying investments is considered to be received by German-resident unitholders on distribution or at the end of the financial year of the UCITS.[26] The part of the income from the underlying investments that is related to capital gains from the disposal of the underlying investments or gains from derivative instruments is not considered to be received if these gains are accumulated. If accumulated, they are not realized by individual unitholders until after disposal of the units in the UCITS.

Example 10.1

A German-resident UCITS derives from its investments a dividend of EUR 2,500,000 and realizes through the disposal of investments a gain of EUR 10,000,000. In accordance with its fund rules, it accumulates the dividend and the proceeds from the disposal of investments. A German individual unitholder is considered to receive only its share in the dividend.

Any income from the underlying investments is taxable in the hands of German individual unitholders as dividends or other distributions on shares. It therefore

22. Section 20(2)(3) Income Tax Act.
23. Section 20(9) Income Tax Act.
24. Section 20(3) Income Tax Act in combination with s. 10d Income Tax Act.
25. A. Ramackers, in *Das Einkommensteuerrecht*, ed. E. Littmann, H. Bitz & H. Pust (Stuttgart: Schäffer Poeschel, loose leaf), InvStG, § 1, 50.
26. Section 2(1) Investment Tax Act (Investmentsteuergesetz), BGBl. I 2003/2724, 15 Dec. 2003.

qualifies as income from investment of capital. Any distributed capital gains from the disposal of the underlying investments or gains from derivative instruments are also fully taxable. This is different only for distributed capital gains acquired before 1 January 2009 that remain exempt from tax.

Example 10.2

A German-resident UCITS derives from its investments a dividend of EUR 2,500,000 and realizes through the disposal of investments a gain of EUR 10,000,000. In accordance with its fund rules, it distributes the dividend and the proceeds from the disposal of investments. The distribution is fully taxable as dividend or other distribution in the hands of a German individual unitholder.

Exemptions

The savings exemption of EUR 801 also applies if income from investment of capital is derived by way of a resident UCITS.

Estimation of Income

The unitholders do not invest directly in the underlying investments, so they must be provided with information relevant for the income tax liability of the unitholders. UCITS therefore have to provide the German tax authorities and the unitholders with detailed information about the amount, nature, and source of the income from the underlying investments. This is the information that is relevant for determination of (corporate) income tax liability, such as the determination of the taxable income, the application of exemptions, and the crediting of foreign withholding tax.

If the amount, nature, and source of the income are not communicated, or are not communicated properly, to the German tax authorities and the unitholders, the amount of the income is estimated while, with the exception of the annual savings exemption, the exemptions do not apply. This generally results in more severe taxation. The Investment Taxation Act estimates the income from the underlying investments in that case as the sum of the amount of the actual distributions, and 70% of the amount of an increase in value of the units in the UCITS (amount of the accumulated income). Under no circumstances is the amount of the accumulated income considered to be less than 6% of the intrinsic value of the units at the end of the year.[27] The amount of the increase in value of the units is the difference between the amount of the intrinsic value of the units at the end of the year and the intrinsic value at the beginning of the year. The amount of accumulated income is considered to be 6% of the intrinsic value at the end of the year if the increase in value of the units in the

27. Section 6 Investment Taxation Act.

UCITS is less than that amount. A unitholder may not provide proof that the amount of the accumulated income is less than the amount of the estimated income.

Disposal of Units in a German-Resident UCITS

The part of the proceeds from the disposal of units in a resident UCITS that is related to interest from investments in bonds or other debt securities, the part of the capital gains from the disposal of bonds or other debt securities that is related to accrued interest, or capital gains from the disposal of interest coupons, is taxable as income from investment of capital.[28]

The difference between the other part of the proceeds from the disposal, after deduction of any connecting costs, and the cost price (capital gain from the disposal) also is taxable in the hands of the unitholders as income from investment of capital.[29] To calculate the amount of the capital gain from the disposal, the proceeds from the disposal must be reduced with the amount of income that is deemed to be distributed in previous years.[30] Otherwise, that part of the proceeds would be subject to tax twice.

Exemptions

The savings exemption is also applicable for capital gains from the disposal of units in a resident UCITS.[31]

Losses

A capital loss from the disposal of units in a resident UCITS may be set off against other income from investment of capital. Any excess may be carried forward to the following year.

10.2.1.3. Investment in the Units of UCITS Residing in Austria, the Netherlands, and the United Kingdom

A non-resident UCITS is considered to be semi-transparent under German tax law if it qualifies as a non-resident investment fund under the Investment Tax Act.[32] The extent of transparency is subject to the provisions of the Investment Taxation Act.[33] If a non-resident UCITS does not qualify as a non-resident investment fund, it is considered to be a corporation, partnership, or other association, whatever comes next.

---

28. Sections 1(4) and 2(1) Investment Taxation Act.
29. *Ibid.*
30. Section 8(5) Investment Taxation Act.
31. Section 20(6) Income Tax Act.
32. Section 1(3) Investment Taxation Act in conjunction with s. 2(8) Investment Act.
33. BFH 11 Oct. 2000, BStBl. II, 2001/22.

Classification of Non-resident UCITS

A UCITS, notwithstanding its legal form,[34] qualifies as a non-resident investment fund if it is capital that is subject to the laws of another state and that invests the obtained capital in accordance with the principle of the spreading of risk in securities, money market instruments, financial derivative instruments, and other listed investments. This is a broad definition that does not take into account the characteristics of a non-resident UCITS under the civil law of its residence state. It may comprise UCITS of the corporate type, the contractual type, or the trust type. Indications for a non-resident investment fund may be that a non-resident UCITS is subject to regulations similar to those of German UCITS and that the principle of spreading risk has been given form in these regulations in the form of qualitative and quantitative restrictions. Furthermore, there have to be (passive) investment activities. A UCITS may not have a strong hold on the actual activities of companies in which it keeps shares or holds another equity participation.[35] Austrian-, Netherlands-, or UK-resident UCITS fulfil generally all of these conditions.

Any income from the underlying investments of UCITS residing in Austria, the Netherlands, or the United Kingdom is considered to be received by German individual unitholders at the same time, and for the same amount, as income from the underlying investments of resident UCITS is considered to be allocated to the investor.[36]

Example 10.3

An Austrian-resident UCITS derives a dividend of EUR 2,500,000 from its investments and realizes through the disposal of investments a gain of EUR 10,000,000. If the dividend and proceeds from the disposal of investments are accumulated, a German individual unitholder is considered to receive only its share in the dividend. If, on the other hand, they are distributed, a German individual unitholder is fully taxed on its share in the dividend as well as in the capital gain from the disposal of the investments.

Any income from the underlying investments is, as is the case for resident UCITS, taxable as dividends or other distributions on shares. It likewise qualifies as income from investment of capital.

Exemptions

The exemptions available for the income derived by way of a non-resident UCITS do not differ from those discussed earlier for income derived by way of resident UCITS.

34. A. Ramackers, in *Das Einkommensteuerrecht*, ed. E. Littmann, H. Bitz & H. Pust (Stuttgart: Schäffer Poeschel, loose leaf), InvStG, § 1, 33.
35. M. Pfüller & R. Schmitt, in J. Brinkhaus & P. Scherer, *KAGG and AuslInvestment-Gesetz – Kommentar* (Munich: C.H. Beck Verlag, 2003), AuslInvestmG, § 1, 55–57.
36. Section 2(1) Investment Taxation Act.

Estimation of Income

German tax authorities and German unitholders of non-resident UCITS must be provided with the same information about the amount, nature, and source of income from the underlying investments that is relevant for determination of (corporate) income tax liability, as is the case for resident UCITS. Germany cannot, however, enforce that obligation in the case of non-resident UCITS.

The amount of income is estimated in the same way as for resident UCITS in case the amount, nature, and source of income is not communicated, or is not communicated properly, to the German tax authorities and the unitholders. With the exception of the annual savings exemption, the exemptions, likewise, do not apply.

Disposal of the Units in a Non-resident UCITS

The income tax liability for the proceeds from disposal of units in a non-resident UCITS does not differ from that for capital gains from disposal of units in resident UCITS.

Exemptions

Capital gains from disposal of units in non-resident UCITS remain exempt under the same conditions as for resident UCITS.

Losses

The treatment of a capital loss from the disposal of units in non-resident UCITS does not differ from that of resident UCITS.

10.2.2. CORPORATE INCOME TAX LIABILITY OF GERMAN-RESIDENT CORPORATE UNITHOLDERS

10.2.2.1. Investing Directly in Securities and Other Financial Instruments

Corporate entities[37] resident in Germany are subject to corporate income tax on their worldwide taxable income. The taxable income of residents includes income from the following sources:

(1) Business income:
   (a) income from agriculture and forestry;

37. The Corporate Tax Act (Körperschafsteuergesetz), BGBl. I 1976/2597 and 2599, 31 Aug. 1976, considers as corporate entities public corporations, private corporations with limited liability, trading or agricultural cooperatives, mutual insurance or pension companies, other legal persons incorporated under civil law, commercial enterprises operated by public bodies, and associations, institutions, foundations without legal personality, and other pools of assets set up for a specific purpose.

    (b) income from trade and business;
    (c) income from independent (professional) services.
(2) Non-business income:
    (a) income from employment;
    (b) income from investment of capital;
    (c) income from rentals and leasing;
    (d) income from specific other sources as mentioned in section 22 of the Income Tax Act.[38]

Any income that does not qualify as one of these income types is not charged with income tax.

Exempt Corporate Entities

Along with some other corporate entities, German-resident pension funds[39] and charities[40] are exempt from corporate income tax. The exemption does not, however, extend to items of income from investment of capital that are subject to German withholding tax.[41] The deduction of withholding tax settles the corporate income tax liability of exempt corporate entities.[42]

Tax Burden

The taxable income of a corporate entity in a financial year is subject to corporate income tax at a flat rate of 15.825% together with the applicable trade tax rate (2009). This percentage includes a solidarity surcharge of 5.5%.[43] The trade tax rate, which is set by the municipality in question, ranges between 14% and 18%. The corporate income tax liability may be credited with the 26.375% withholding tax that is deducted from the gross amount of some items of income from investment of capital paid out domestically. The part of the withholding tax that exceeds the corporate income tax liability is refunded.[44]

Business Income

Income is considered to be business income if it is derived from the business assets of the corporate entity. The portfolio investments of corporate entities[45] that under

38. Section 8(1) Corporate Tax Act in conjunction with s. 2(1) Income Tax Act.
39. Sections 5(3) and 6 Corporate Tax Act.
40. Section 5(9) Corporate Tax Act in conjunction with the ss 51–68 of the Federal Taxation Act.
41. Section 7(2) Corporate Tax Act.
42. Section 32(1) Corporate Tax Act.
43. Sections 2(1) and 4 Solidarity Surcharge Act.
44. Section 31(1) Corporate Tax Act in conjunction with s. 36(4) Income Tax Act.
45. An obligation to keep books applies under the Commercial Law for public corporations, private corporations with limited liability, limited partnerships with stocks, and registered trading or agricultural cooperatives.

commercial law are obliged to keep books are always considered business assets.[46] The portfolio investments of other corporate entities are generally not considered to be business assets, unless they are purchased with a temporary surplus of liquid assets, are investments that can be sold easily, and are more or less free of risk.[47] Despite this, an investment does not qualify as a business asset when it is clear from the beginning that it will incur loss.[48] The portfolio investments of corporate entities are considered to be business assets only for those entities that have a business of dealing in securities,[49] such as banks or stockbrokers, in which case the portfolio investments have an objective or actual connection with the business of the corporate entity.

Tax Accounting Principles

The business income of a corporate entity is determined by a comparison of its business assets. Any change in value of the assets other than a payment or withdrawal of capital is taxed as business income. Those corporate entities that are, under commercial law, obliged to keep books have to prepare their fiscal balance on the basis of their commercial balance.[50] The principles of commercial law also apply to other corporate entities that have a business income of more than EUR 30,000[51] or those that have an income of EUR 30,000 or less but have opted[52] to determine their business income on the basis of a comparison of assets instead of a profit-or-loss account. The principles of commercial law do not apply, however, when a provision of the Income Tax Act or the Corporate Tax Act determines otherwise. The latter Acts may, for tax purposes, contain other regulations regarding the characterization of economic property as business assets and the valuation of business assets than the principles of commercial law.

Exemptions

An exemption applies to 95% of domestic and foreign dividends or other distributions from shares or other equity participations in a company. The Corporate Tax Act also provides for an exemption of 95% of capital gains realized by the

46. Section 8(2) Corporate Tax Act.
47. BFH 18 Dec. 1996 (XI R 52/95), BStBl. 1997/351 and BFH 12 Feb. 1997 (XI R 1/96), BStBl. II 1997/399.
48. BFH 19 Feb. 1997 (XI R 1/96), BStBl. II 1997/399.
49. D. Lübbehüsen, in J. Brinkhaus & P. Scherer, *KAGG and AuslInvestment-Gesetz – Kommentar* (Munich: C.H. Beck Verlag, 2003), KAGG, § 39, 15.
50. Section 5 Income Tax Act.
51. Section 141 Federal Taxation Act. The obligation to keep books for corporate entities that, under commercial law, are not obliged to keep books starts after notice of the German tax authorities. It also stops after such notice and thus does not automatically stop in a year in which a corporate body has a business income of EUR 30,000 or less.
52. See BFH 13 Oct. 1989 (III R 30-31/85), BStBl. II 1990/287.

disposal of shares or other equity participations in resident and non-resident companies.[53]

Losses

A loss from business income may be credited against other income. If a loss from business income cannot, or cannot entirely, be credited against other income, the non-creditable part of the loss may, up to an amount of EUR 511,500, be carried back to the previous year. Any remaining amount may be carried forward to the following years. This is subject to restrictions because only 60% of that part of a remaining loss that exceeds an amount of EUR 1,000,000 may be carried forward.[54]

Income from Investment of Capital

Income from portfolio investments that does not qualify as business assets is taxable only when it is considered to be income from investment of capital. These items of income are determined in the same way as for individuals; see Section 10.2.1.1.

Exemptions

The exemption for 95% of the dividends or other distributions from shares or other equity participations in a German-resident corporation or the capital gain from the disposal of shares or other equity participations in such a corporation is not limited to business income. It also applies to any income from investment of capital.

Losses

A loss from investment of capital may be credited against other income in the year of arising, carried back to the previous year or carried forward to the following years under the same conditions as for individuals; see Section 10.2.1.1.

10.2.2.2. Investment in the Units of German-Resident UCITS

Any income from the underlying investments of a resident UCITS is that of the UCITS.[55] Just as is the case as for individuals, it is considered to be received by German corporate unitholders on distribution or the end of the financial year of the UCITS, whichever is earlier. The part of the income from the underlying investments that is related to capital gains realized by the disposal of the underlying investments, advantages gained with forward contracts, and rights, however, are not considered received if these capital gains are accumulated. If accumulated,

53. Section 8b(1), (2), and (5) Corporate Tax Act.
54. Section 8(1) Corporate Tax Act in conjunction with s. 10d Income Tax Act.
55. A. Ramackers, in *Das Einkommensteuerrecht*, ed. E. Littmann, H. Bitz & H. Pust (Stuttgart: Schäffer Poeschel, loose leaf), InvStG § 1, 50.

these gains are not realized by corporate unitholders until after disposal of the units in the UCITS.

Example 10.4

A German-resident UCITS derives from its investments a dividend of EUR 2,500,000 and realizes through the disposal of investments a gain of EUR 10,000,000. In accordance with its fund rules, it accumulates the dividend and the proceeds from the disposal of investments. A German corporate unitholder is considered to receive only its share in the dividend.

Any other income from the underlying investments is taxable in the hands of German corporate unitholders if it qualifies as business income or income from investment of capital. Business income includes any of the income from the underlying investments that is considered to be received by the unitholders.

Example 10.5

A German-resident UCITS derives from its investments a dividend of EUR 2,500,000 and realizes through the disposal of investments a gain of EUR 10,000,000. In accordance with its fund rules, it distributes the dividend and proceeds from the disposal of investments. Where the units in the UCITS qualify as business assets, the distribution is fully taxable as business income.

If the income does not qualify as business income, it is taxable as income from investment of capital because it is considered a dividend or other distribution. Income from investment of capital is determined in the same way as for individuals; see Section 10.2.1.2.

Exemptions

The exemption for 95% of the dividends or other distributions from shares or other equity participations in a German-resident corporation or the proceeds from the disposal of shares or other equity participations in such a corporation also applies if income is derived by way of a non-resident resident UCITS. It applies to the part of the income from the underlying investments that is related to dividends or other distributions from shares or other equity participations in a German-resident corporation or the proceeds from the disposal of shares or other equity participations in such a corporation.

Estimation of Income

The German tax authorities and unitholders have to be provided with the information relevant for the corporate income tax liability of the unitholders. The consequences of not communicating the required information, or of not communicating that information properly, do not differ from what has been discussed for individuals in Section 10.2.1.2.

Disposal of Units in a German-Resident UCITS

The capital gain realized by the disposal of units in a resident UCITS is fully taxable as business income, unless the units did not qualify as business assets. In that case, the part of the capital gain from the disposal of units in a resident UCITS that is related to interest from investments in bonds or other debt securities, the part of the capital gain from the disposal of bonds or other debt securities that is related to accrued interest, or proceeds from the disposal of interest coupons, is taxable as income from investment of capital.[56] The same applies for the difference between the other part of the capital gain from the disposal, after deduction of any connecting costs, and the cost price (capital gain from the disposal). Any accumulated income that is deemed to be distributed in previous years, however, has to be reduced from the other part of the capital gain from the disposal.[57]

Exemptions

If the capital gain from the disposal is considered to be business income, the part of the gain related to share-related profit remains exempt. The share-related profit includes three income types that would have been exempt in the case of a direct investment. This includes the part of the income from the underlying investments at the time of disposal that is related to dividends from shares in a corporation or the proceeds from the sale of dividend coupons.[58] Furthermore, it includes the part that is related to foreign income that in the case of a direct investment would have been exempt under one of the German tax treaties. In addition, the same applies to the proceeds from the disposal of investments in shares of a corporation that have been accumulated during the period the units were kept by the corporate unitholder and any unrealized changes in value of investments in the shares of a corporation for that period.[59] The amount of the share-related profit is calculated as the difference between the amount of the share-related profit that is included in the redemption price at the time of the disposal and the amount of that profit at the time of the purchase.[60] Resident UCITS are therefore obliged to calculate the share-related profit as a percentage of the redemption price on a daily basis to make the calculation of the share-related profit possible.[61]

---

56. Sections 1(4) and 2(1) Investment Taxation Act.
57. *Ibid.*
58. Section 8 Investment Taxation Act.
59. Section 8 Investment Taxation Act in conjunction with s. 8b Corporate Tax Act.
60. Section 8(3) Investment Taxation Act.
61. The share-related profit has been calculated as a percentage of the redemption price since its introduction in 2004. Therefore, the share-related profit does not include any capital gains and losses that have been realized before 2004. Nor does it include any unrealized capital gains and losses that can be attributed to the period before 2004.

Losses

If the disposal of the units in a non-resident UCITS results in a loss from business income or investment of capital or income from private transactions, the crediting of that loss does not differ from that discussed earlier for a direct investment.

10.2.2.3. Investment in the Units of UCITS Residing in Austria, the Netherlands, or the United Kingdom

As discussed with respect to individuals in Section 10.2.1.3, a non-resident UCITS is considered to be semi-transparent under the domestic laws of Germany.

The income from the underlying investments of non-resident UCITS is considered to be received by German corporate unitholders at the same time, and for the same amount, as the income from the underlying investments of resident UCITS is considered to be paid out.[62] Any income from the underlying investments is, like that of resident UCITS, taxable if it qualifies as business income or income from investment of capital. Business income includes any of the income from the underlying investments that is considered to be received by the unitholders.

Example 10.6

An Austrian-resident UCITS derives from its investments a dividend of EUR 2,500,000 and realizes through the disposal of investments a gain of EUR 10,000,000. If the dividend and the proceeds from the disposal of investments are accumulated, a German corporate unitholder is considered to receive only its share in the dividend. If, on the other hand, they are distributed, the distribution is fully taxable as business income where the units in the UCITS qualify as business assets.

If the income does not qualify as business income, it is, like that of resident UCITS, taxable as income from investment of capital because it is considered to be a dividend or other distribution on shares. Income from investment of capital is determined in the same way as for individuals; see Section 10.2.1.3.

Exemptions

The exemptions for 95% of the dividend or other distributions from shares or other equity participations in a German-resident corporation or the capital gains realized by the disposal of shares or other equity participations in such a corporation also applies if this type of income is derived by way of a non-resident UCITS. The same applies for annual savings exemption for income from investment of capital.

62. Section 2(1) Investment Taxation Act.

Estimation of Income

German tax authorities and corporate unitholders must be provided with the information discussed for resident UCITS in Section 10.2.2.2. Nor do the consequences of not communicating the required information, or not communicating that information properly, differ from what has been discussed with respect to resident UCITS.

Disposal of Units in a Non-resident UCITS

The corporate income tax liability for the capital gain realized by the disposal of units in a non-resident UCITS is determined in the same way as that for the capital gain from the disposal of units in a resident UCITS.

Exemptions

The conditions for the application of the exemption available for the part of the capital gain from the disposal of units in a non-resident UCITS that is related to share-related profit do not differ from those for resident UCITS.

Losses

The same applies to the crediting of a loss from business income or income from investment of capital if that loss results from the disposal of the units in a non-resident UCITS.

10.2.3. Crediting of Withholding Tax

10.2.3.1. Investing Directly in Securities and Other Financial Instruments

Investments in foreign securities and other financial instruments may result in international double taxation for the same reasons as discussed in Section 9.2.3.1 for Austria. Germany has, however, issued several regulations to prevent international double taxation.

Tax Treaties

The majority of German tax treaties, which as mentioned earlier are the most important regulations to prevent international double taxation, allocate the right to tax dividends and interest to both states. Dividends and interest may be taxed not only in the state in whose jurisdiction the beneficiary resides (residence state) but also in the state in whose jurisdiction the paying company or the debtor resides (the source state). The taxation in the source state may not exceed the percentage agreed on in the applicable tax treaty. Tables 3.5 and 3.6 in Chapter 3 provide an overview of the percentages agreed on in the German tax treaties.

The tax withheld by the source state on the dividend or interest may be credited against the beneficiary's tax liability in the residence state (foreign tax credit) to avoid double taxation. The foreign tax credit cannot be more than the amount of tax that could have been withheld by the source state in accordance with the applicable tax treaty.

Several German tax treaties provide for a foreign tax credit that is higher than the withholding tax actually levied. Mostly, these are tax treaties with developing countries or countries such as China or Mexico that are not as developed as Germany.[63] A resident taxpayer may, under these tax treaties, credit either the amount of tax that would have been levied by the source state if the income was taxed in accordance with the general tax rules (tax sparing credit) or a fixed percentage of the gross amount of the income (matching credit). It should be noted, however, that the application of a tax sparing or matching credit is not always open to taxpayers who keep in portfolio investments.

The majority of the German tax treaties prevent double taxation of capital gains and other portfolio income by allocating the right to tax these items of income exclusively to the residence state of the alienator and the recipient, respectively. As a result, these items of income are not subject to tax in the source state.

The opposite is true in some tax treaties for capital gains from the alienation of shares in a company residing in the source state. These tax treaties, as shown in Table 3.7 in Chapter 3, allocate the right to tax these capital gains exclusively to the source state. The tax withheld by the source state cannot be credited by the alienator because these items of income remain exempt from tax in the residence state.

In spite of the considerations discussed earlier, the right to tax capital gains and other portfolio income is allocated to both states in several tax treaties. In these cases, the tax withheld by the source state may be set off against the alienator or beneficiary's tax liability in the residence state to avoid double taxation (foreign tax credit); see the Tables 3.7 and 3.8 in Chapter 3.

Unilateral Rules

In the absence of a tax treaty, or in the presence of a tax treaty that does not cover certain taxes, does not apply to certain taxpayers, or does not cover certain taxable items, the foreign withholding tax may be credited against the beneficiary's tax liability (foreign tax credit).[64] Germany provides for unilateral rules in the Income Tax Act for the same reasons as discussed in Section 9.2.3 for Austria.

---

63. Argentina, Bangladesh, Bolivia, China, Cyprus, Ecuador, Egypt, Greece, India, Indonesia, Iran, Ireland, Israel, Ivory Coast, Jamaica, Kenya, Korea, Liberia, Malaysia, Malta, Mauritius, Mexico, Morocco, Mongolia, the Philippines, Portugal, Singapore, Spain, Sri Lanka, Trinidad and Tobago, Tunisia, Turkey, Uruguay, Venezuela, Vietnam, and Zimbabwe.
64. Section 34c Income Tax Act.

Ordinary Tax Credit

Under no circumstances does Germany grant a foreign tax credit that is more than the part of the German (corporate) income tax due on the beneficiary's worldwide income that is related to the foreign income (ordinary tax credit). The ordinary tax credit is, as is the case for Austrian-resident taxpayers, determined on a per-country basis.

Pass Through Rule

If a foreign tax credit cannot, or cannot entirely, be credited against the (corporate) income tax liability of a resident taxpayer, the excess may not be carried back or forward to other years; nor is it refunded. In this case, a deduction of foreign withholding tax may be more favourable than crediting. However, a resident taxpayer may opt for deduction for foreign withholding tax that is levied in the absence of a tax treaty or a provision concerning that type of income in a tax treaty.[65]

10.2.3.2. Investment in the Units of German-Resident UCITS by German Unitholders

The foreign withholding tax is initially considered to be deducted for the account of resident UCITS under the domestic laws of Germany. However, it cannot be credited by a resident UCITS because it is subjectively exempt from corporate income tax. Under the Investment Taxation Act, a resident UCITS may elect to show foreign withholding tax as either deductible from the taxable income of the unitholders or creditable against the tax liability of the unitholders.

The Investment Tax Act allows German unitholders to apply the German tax treaties and unilateral rules as if they had invested directly in the underlying investments of the UCITS.[66] In that case, crediting of the tax withheld at source on the income from the underlying investments by the German unitholders takes place as discussed in Section 10.2.3.1. The part of the withholding tax not charged in accordance with the applicable tax treaty may also be credited if a refund is refused by the source state.[67] Hence, Germany picks up the check in the case of the unwillingness of the source state to apply the applicable tax treaty to German UCITS or unitholders.

Under no circumstances does Germany grant a foreign tax credit to the German unitholders that is more than the ordinary tax credit. The ordinary tax credit, unlike a direct investment, is determined on an overall basis.[68] This means

65. Section 34c(2) Income Tax Act.
66. Section 4(1) and (2) Investment Tax Act.
67. Section 34c(6)(4) Income Tax Act. See also D. Lübbehüsen, in *KAGG and AuslInvestment-Gesetz – Kommentar*, ed. J. Brinkhaus & P. Scherer (Munich: C.H. Beck Verlag, 2003), KAGG, § 40, 102.
68. Section 4(2) Investment Tax Act.

that the part of the German (corporate) income tax that is related to the foreign income has to be calculated for the combined foreign income from the investments of the resident UCITS.

Relevant Information

The German tax authorities and unitholders have to be provided with an overview of the amount of withholding tax that has been levied per source state and per item. This information is necessary for the German unitholders to file a tax return or a request for the refund of the part of withholding tax that is not levied in accordance with a tax treaty.

10.2.3.3. Investment in the Units of UCITS Residing in Austria, the Netherlands, and the United Kingdom by German Unitholders

The Investment Tax Act allows German unitholders of non-resident UCITS to apply the German tax treaties and unilateral rules as if they had invested directly in the underlying investments of these UCITS.[69] The crediting of foreign withholding tax by German unitholders does thus not differ from what has been discussed for resident UCITS in Section 10.2.3.1. Any German withholding tax is also treated as foreign withholding tax.[70]

Relevant Information

The German tax authorities and unitholders have to be provided with the same information about the foreign withholding tax as for resident UCITS.

Withholding Tax Levied by the UCITS Country at the Time of Distribution

Non-resident UCITS are considered to be transparent for German personal income tax and corporate income tax purposes. Nevertheless, the Investment Tax Act takes into account that the UCITS country may have withheld tax at the time of distribution. The tax withheld by the UCITS country at the time of distribution may be credited against the German tax liability of the unitholder.[71]

69. Section 4(1) and (2) Investment Tax Act.
70. Section 4(2) Investment Tax Act.
71. *Ibid.*

10.3. CONCLUSION

In Germany, the (corporate) income tax liability of an investment in the units of a UCITS residing in Austria, the Netherlands, or the United Kingdom does not differ from that of an investment in the units of a resident UCITS where the non-resident UCITS has properly provided the German tax authorities with information about the amount, nature, and source of income from the underlying investments that is relevant for the (corporate) income tax liability of the unitholders. If the non-resident UCITS has not, or has not properly, informed the German tax authorities, the amount of income will be estimated. Generally, the estimation of income results in more severe taxation.

The withholding tax levied at source of income from the underlying investments of non-resident UCITS may, as is the case for resident UCITS, be set off against the (corporate) income tax liability of the unitholders. The domestic laws of Germany, however, do not take into account whether or not the foreign withholding tax levied at source is, unlike the case for resident UCITS, creditable by the UCITS or whether any relief for that tax is granted to the UCITS by the UCITS country. The withholding tax may not, however, be set off if the UCITS has not informed the German tax authorities per source about the amount that has been levied.

The information that needs to be communicated basically does not differ from that of resident UCITS. Nevertheless, it may hinder German unitholders from investing freely in the units of non-resident UCITS. They run the risk for more severe taxation if a non-resident UCITS does not communicate the information; for example, if because of its listing, it is not aware of any German unitholders or the cost is simply too high to communicate such for a few German unitholders. Although the unitholders of non-resident UCITS may provide proof that the amount of the accumulated income is less than the amount of the estimated income, for most non-professional investors this will be a difficult task, especially with respect to the amount of the distribution account at an issue date because UCITS generally do not provide daily reports. Hence, the units in the majority of non-resident UCITS are not available for most German unitholders without the risk for a more burdensome taxation.

Chapter 11

The Netherlands: Taxation of Income from Investments in the Country of the Unitholders

The legal status of resident undertakings for collective investment in transferable securities (UCITS) determines whether the income from securities and other financial instruments derived by way of UCITS is considered to be that of the unitholders (tax transparent entity) or that of the UCITS (tax opaque entity). Income from the underlying investments of transparent UCITS is considered to be received by the unitholders upon receipt. In the case of tax opaque UCITS, the income is not received by the unitholders until it is distributed or realized by the disposal of units in the UCITS.

Nevertheless, the distinction between transparent and tax opaque UCITS is not of importance for the purposes of personal income tax. Individual taxpayers are not taxed on the actual income from securities and other financial instruments. Instead, the net assets of the taxpayer, that is, the units of the UCITS, are considered to generate a fixed income of 4% of the average of the fair market value at the beginning and the end of the calendar year. The fixed income is taxable as income from savings and investments.

The personal income tax liability for an investment in the units of non-resident UCITS does not differ from that in the units of resident UCITS. The exception on the rule is the application of the exemptions for environmental, social-ethical and cultural investments, which do not apply to non-resident UCITS that do not offer units in the Netherlands. This seems to infringe on the freedom of capital as laid down in Articles 56 and 58 of the EC Treaty or Article 40 of the EEA Treaty. The Income Tax Act does not offer these UCITS or their unitholders the possibility to submit evidence that any of the other conditions for these exemptions are fulfilled.

The different treatment of transparent and tax opaque UCITS is of importance for the purposes of corporate income tax because corporate taxpayers are taxed on the basis of the actual income from securities and other financial instruments.

The taxation of income derived by way of UCITS should not, however, be less than that of income from a direct investment. The units of resident (EII) UCITS therefore need to be valued by corporate unitholders at market value. Any income from the underlying investments is therefore taxable in the hands of these unitholders at the time of arising, although as a capital gain.

The unitholders of resident (FII) UCITS are not required to value the units of these UCITS at market value. Instead, these UCITS have to distribute the annual income within 8 months after the end of the financial year. Nevertheless, capital gains realized by the disposal of the underlying investments do not have to be distributed to the unitholders, if these UCITS have opted for a reinvestment account. In that case, these gains are not subject to tax in the hands of corporate unitholders until disposal of the units in the UCITS.

The corporate income tax liability for an investment in the units of non-resident UCITS is not necessarily the same as that for an investment in the units of resident UCITS. Any income derived by way of non-resident UCITS is considered to be received by corporate unitholders at the time of arising if the UCITS is not subject to corporate income tax and the exemption from corporate income tax does not depend on the distribution of the income from the underlying investments on an annual basis.

Income derived by way of other non-resident UCITS is not taxable in the hands of the unitholder until it is distributed or realized by the disposal of units in the UCITS.

The requirement to value the units of some non-resident UCITS, such as Austrian and German-resident UCITS, at market value seems to infringe on the freedom of capital as laid down in Articles 56 and 58 of the EC Treaty or Article 40 of the EEA Treaty. An investment in units of these non-resident UCITS results in a less favourable treatment than investment in units of resident (FII) UCITS. Any change in the value of the underlying investments of these non-resident UCITS is taxable in the hands of the unitholders at the time of arising, whereas any change in the value of the underlying investments of resident (FII) UCITS that have opted for a reinvestment account is not taxable until disposal of the units in these UCITS.

The Netherlands tax treaties and unilateral rules apply to the unitholders of transparent UCITS as if they had invested directly. This is not the case for unitholders of tax opaque UCITS. In that case, the tax withheld at source is considered to be that of the UCITS and not that of the unitholders.

The unitholders may credit the withholding tax charged by the UCITS country at the time of distribution but only if the applicable tax treaty provides for such.

11.1. INTRODUCTION

The income from the investments of UCITS is, under the domestic laws of the Netherlands, considered to be that of the UCITS. The income from the investments of Netherlands-resident UCITS is, with the exception of individuals, taxable in the hands of the unitholders either at the time it arises or at the time of distribution. This dual approach also applies to the income from the investments of Austrian, German, and UK-resident UCITS. As a result, the time that income from the underlying investments is subject to tax in the hand of the unitholders other than individuals may differ for Austrian-, Netherlands, German, and UK-resident UCITS.

11.2. TAX LIABILITY OF NETHERLANDS-RESIDENT UNITHOLDERS

11.2.1. INCOME TAX LIABILITY OF NETHERLANDS-RESIDENT INDIVIDUAL UNITHOLDERS

11.2.1.1. Investing Directly in Securities and Other Financial Instruments

Individuals resident in the Netherlands are subject to income tax on their worldwide taxable income. The taxable income includes income from the following sources:

(1) income from work and dwellings;
(2) income from substantial interest;
(3) income from savings and investments.

Any income that does not qualify as one of these income types is not charged with income tax.

Tax Burden

Income from savings and investments has its own tax rate. It is taxable at a flat rate of 30% (2009). Dividends that are paid by a resident corporation are subject to a 15% withholding tax. The withholding tax can be credited against the income tax liability of the individual. The part of the withholding tax that exceeds the income tax liability is refunded.

Income from Savings and Investments

Income from savings and investments is the income that is generated by the net assets of an individual taxpayer. The net assets of an individual are considered to generate a fixed income of 4%.[1] The actual income from savings and investments,

1. Article 5.2 Income Tax Act (Wet Inkomstenbelasting, 2001), *Stb.* 2000, 215, 11 May 2000.

if any, is not taken into account; nor are expenses. Among other things, the net assets of an individual include the following:

(1) Personal property except for property that is used for a person's private ends.
(2) Personal property that is used for a person's private ends but mainly serves as investment.
(3) Rights on personal property.
(4) Rights not concerning property, such as money.
(5) Other property rights with an economic value.[2]

The net assets have to be valued at the average of the fair market value at the beginning of the year and their fair market value at the year's end.[3] Investments in securities that are listed on the Euronext exchange in Amsterdam are estimated at the value published in the Official List of the Euronext Amsterdam N.V., although their economic value may be more because of a surplus value or less because of a short value.[4] In the case of securities listed on an exchange other than the Euronext exchange in Amsterdam, the value published in the official list of such an exchange may indicate the economic value of the securities. Nevertheless, the economic value of foreign securities may be less for a resident of the Netherlands because of restrictions regarding the exchange of capital. In that case the economic value may be less, because economic value means the economic value in the Netherlands.[5] On the other hand, the economic value may also be more or less than the value published in a foreign official list. In contrast to securities listed at the Euronext exchange in Amsterdam, the individual is not obliged to use the value published in the official list of the relevant foreign exchange; thus the higher or lesser economic value must be applied. The valuation of securities that are not listed on an exchange is more complicated, because there may not be a daily demand and supply. Tools are available to estimate the value of those securities.

Exemptions

Some investments are entirely or partially exempt because of socioeconomic or environmental reasons. Social investments and investments in start-up capital are exempt up to an amount of EUR 55,145 (2009) each. This amount will be doubled for income tax purposes on the joint request of the individual taxpayer and the taxpayer's partner.[6] Environmentally friendly investments, social-ethical investments, and cultural investments are entirely exempt.[7]

---

2. Article 5.3(2) Income Tax Act.
3. Article 5.2 Income Tax Act.
4. Article 5.21 Income Tax Act in combination with Art. 33b of the Implementing Regulation of the Income Tax Act, *Stb.* 2000, 250, 19 Dec. 2000.
5. L.W. Sillevis, et al., *Cursus Belastingrecht (Inkomstenbelasting)* (Deventer: Kluwer, loose leaf), 5.4.1.C.
6. Articles 5.13, 5.16, and 5.17 Income Tax Act.
7. Articles 5.14, 5.15, and 5.18a Income Tax Act.

The net assets of an individual are exempt up to an amount of EUR 20,661 (2009) to stimulate savings and investments. The amount of the exemption is doubled on the joint request of the individual taxpayer and the taxpayer's partner. Moreover, seniors, individuals who are 65 years or older, are entitled to an additional exemption, which depends on the income from work and dwellings and is at the most EUR 27,350 (2009).

Losses

An actual loss from savings and investments may not be set off against other income, because the net assets of an individual are considered to generate a fixed income of 4%.

11.2.1.2. Investment in the Units of Netherlands-Resident UCITS

The units in a resident UCITS qualify as net assets. They are therefore considered to generate a fixed income of 4% of the average of their fair market value at the beginning of the calendar year and their fair market value at year's end. The fixed income is taxable as income from savings and investments.

Exemptions

The exemptions for environmental, social-ethical and cultural investments also apply to investments made through a resident UCITS. For investments made through a resident UCITS the Income Tax Act requires that at least 70% of the operations of the UCITS consist, according to its statutory goal and actual activities, directly or indirectly of investments in either environmental, social-ethical, or cultural investments.[8]

The annual exemption for the net assets of an individual also applies to an investment in the units of a resident UCITS.

Losses

An actual loss from an investment in the units of a resident UCITS, for the same reason as a direct investment, may not be set off against other income.

11.2.1.3. Investment in the Units of UCITS Residing in Austria, Germany, and the United Kingdom

The units of a UCITS residing in Austria, Germany, or the United Kingdom qualify as net assets. These units are, like those of a resident UCITS, considered to generate a fixed income of 4% of the average of the fair market value of the units at the

8. Articles 5.14(2)(b), 5.15(2)(b), and 5.18a(2)(b) Income Tax Act.

beginning of the calendar year and the fair market value at year's end. The fixed income is, likewise, taxable as income from savings and investments.

Exemptions

The exemptions for environmental, social-ethical, and cultural investments also apply to investments made through a UCITS residing in Austria, Germany, or the United Kingdom. The Income Tax Act sets the same conditions for these exemptions in respect to the operations of non-resident UCITS as for resident UCITS. The exemptions are, however, limited to those non-resident UCITS that have met the requirements to offer their units to the Dutch public.[9] The exemption thus does not apply to an investment in the units of a non-resident UCITS that is purchased in another Member State in the absence of the offering of these units in the Netherlands. It is doubtful whether this restriction is consistent with Articles 56 and 58 of the EC Treaty and Article 40 of the EEA Treaty. Because of the restricted application of the exemption, resident taxpayers may not be inclined to invest in the units of non-resident UCITS that make environmental, social-ethical, or cultural investments but do not offer their units in the Netherlands. Furthermore, it does not seem to be a proportional measure to avoid abuse of these exemptions. The Income Tax Act, namely, does not provide for the possibility for non-resident UCITS that do not offer their units in the Netherlands or their unitholders to prove that an investment in their units fulfils any of the other conditions for the exemptions for environmental, social-ethical, and cultural investments made by the use of a UCITS.

The annual exemption for the net assets of an individual also applies to an investment in the units of a non-resident UCITS.

Losses

An actual loss from an investment in the units of a non-resident UCITS, like that in the units of a Netherlands-resident UCITS, may not be set off against other income.

11.2.2. Corporate Income Tax Liability of Netherlands-Resident Corporate Unitholders

11.2.2.1. Investing Directly in Securities and Other Financial Instruments

Corporate entities[10] resident in the Netherlands are subject to corporate income tax on their worldwide taxable income. The taxable income of residents is business

9. Articles 5.14(2)(b), 5.15(2)(b), and 5.18a(2)(b) Income Tax Act in combination with Arts 28(2), 29(2), and 33a(2) Implementing Order by the Income Tax Act, *Stb.* 2000/250, 19 Dec. 2000.
10. The Corporate Tax Act (Wet op de Vennootschapsbelasting 1969), Stb. 1969, 445, 8 Oct. 1969, considers corporate entities to be public corporations, private corporations with limited liability,

income. Any income that does not qualify as business income is not charged with corporate income tax.

Exempt Corporate Entities

Netherlands-resident pension funds[11] and charities,[12] subject to certain conditions, are exempt from corporate income tax. In the absence of a corporate income tax liability, resident pension funds, charities, and other exempt corporate bodies are, on request, entitled to a refund of the tax withheld at source of dividends paid out by a resident corporation. No refund, however, is available for the part of the withholding tax for which a Netherlands-resident (FII) UCITS has claimed payment reduction.

Tax Burden

A corporate entity's taxable income in the financial year is subject to corporate income tax at a rate of at the most 25.5% (2009). The corporate income tax liability may be credited with the 15% withholding tax that is levied from resident corporations that pay out dividends. The part of the withholding tax that exceeds the corporate income tax liability is refunded.[13]

Business Income

Income is considered to be business income if it is derived from the business assets of the corporate entity. The portfolio investments of public corporations, private corporations with limited liability, cooperatives, foundations on a cooperative basis or those that act as an insurance company or a credit institution on a mutual basis, and mutual insurance companies are always considered to be business income because such entities are considered to carry on their business with their entire capital.[14]

The portfolio investments of funds for joint account[15] and those businesses of public corporate entities[16] that are listed in Article 2(3) of the Corporate Tax Act are also considered business assets.

---

open limited partnerships, other corporations with a capital that is divided in shares, cooperatives, foundations on a cooperative bases or those that act as an insurance company or credit institution, mutual insurance companies, foundations authorized under the Housing Act as an organization that operates in the interest of public housing, other foundations that are not public corporate entities and carry on a business, open funds for joint account, and those businesses of public legal entities that are listed in Art. 2(3) of the Act.

11. Article 5(1)(b) Corporate Tax Act.
12. Article 6 Corporate Tax Act.
13. Article 25(1) Corporate Tax Act.
14. Article 2(5) Corporate Tax Act.
15. Article 2(2) Corporate Tax Act.
16. Article 2(1)(f) Corporate Tax Act.

The portfolio investments of other corporate entities are generally not considered to be business assets, unless they are purchased with a temporary surplus of liquid assets.[17] In this case the corporate entity tries to make these assets profitable only for the short term in which they are unused, so that they are still considered to be business assets.[18] The above situation is different only for banks and brokers for whom the keeping of investments contributes to the carrying on of a business.

Tax Accounting Principles

The taxable income of a corporate entity is determined in accordance with the sound business principle.[19] The principle of sound business practice has been developed in the case law because it is not further defined in the Corporate Tax Act or the Income Tax Act. The aim of this principle is to include just those benefits and expenses in the profits of a financial year that are related to that year only. In principle, a corporate entity may make use of the principles of business economics in the determination of its annual profits, unless these principles are not in accordance with the Corporate Tax Act or the Income Tax Act or the aim or a principle of one of these acts.[20] The sound business principle is based on realism, simplicity, and prudence. The principle of realism requires that payments of benefits and expenses be taken into account in the year, or years, to which they relate. The principle of simplicity says that the determination of the profits must be practical and depends on the size of one's company. The principle of prudence means that losses may be deducted before they are realized, whereas profits do not have to be taken into account if they are not yet realized. It should be noted that each of these elements limits the others.[21]

Exemptions

No exemptions are available for income derived from portfolio investments.

Losses

A loss from investments that are part of the business assets of a corporate entity may be set off against any other business income. If the amount of the loss exceeds the amount of the other business income, the excess can be carried back to the

17. HR 25 May 1977, no. 18 294, BNB 1977/251.
18. J.N. Bouwman, *Wegwijs in de Vennootschapsbelasting* (Amsterdam: Sdu, 2007), 53. See also L.W. Sillevis, et al., *Cursus Belastingrecht (Inkomstenbelasting)* (Deventer: Kluwer, loose leaf), 3.2.7.A.c and 3.2.18.G.a.
19. Article 8(1) Corporate Tax Act in combination with Art. 3.25 Income Tax Act.
20. Supreme Court of the Netherlands, 8 May 1957, *BNB* 1957/208.
21. D. Brüll, J.W. Zwemmer & R.P.C. Cornelisse, *Goedkoopmansgebruik* (Deventer: FED, 1999), 32.

previous year or carried forward to one of the nine following years from 1 January 2007.[22] Before that date the carry forward of losses was not limited in time.

11.2.2.2. Investment in the Units of Netherlands-Resident UCITS

The income from the underlying investments of resident (EII/FII) UCITS is that of the UCITS (tax opaque entity), whereas the unitholders are considered to be the beneficiaries of income from the underlying investments of resident (TII) UCITS (tax transparent entity).

Investment in the Units of Netherlands-Resident (EII) UCITS

Resident (EII) UCITS are not required to distribute the income from the investments to the unitholders. Instead, corporate unitholders are required to value the units in these UCITS at market value.[23]

Example 11.1

The market value of the units of a Netherlands-resident (EII) UCITS is EUR 1,000 in the beginning of the year. The units of the UCITS are listed at EUR 1,500 at the end of the year. The change in value of the units in the UCITS of EUR 500 is taxable in the hands of corporate unitholders because the units are valued at market value.

The market value of the units in resident (EII) UCITS, as discussed in Section 6.4.2.1, does not differ substantially from the net asset value. Any yields from the underlying investments and any change in value of these investments are therefore taxable in the hands of corporate unitholders in the year that they arise.

Investment in the Units of Netherlands-Resident (FII) UCITS

The income from the underlying investments, unlike resident (EII) UCITS, has to be distributed by resident (FII) UCITS within 8 months after the end of the financial year of the UCITS.[24] The part of the income that is related to capital gains from the disposal of investments does not have to be distributed if the UCITS has opted for a reinvestment account.[25] If accumulated, unlike the case for resident (EII) UCITS, these proceeds are, not realized by corporate unitholders until disposal of the units in the UCITS.

---

22. Article 20(2) Corporate Tax Act.
23. Article 3.29a Income Tax Act.
24. Article 28(2)(b) Corporate Tax Act.
25. Articles 1a and 4(2) Decree on Investment Schemes (Besluit Beleggingsinstellingen 1970), *Stb.* 1970, 120, 29 Apr. 1970.

Example 11.2

The income from the underlying investments of a resident UCITS that needs to be distributed is received by corporate unitholders within 8 months of the financial year in which it was originally received by the UCITS. The distributed income is taxable if it qualifies as business income.

Investment in the Units of Netherlands-Resident (TII) UCITS

The income from the underlying investments of transparent resident UCITS is considered to be that of the unitholders. It is considered to be received by the unitholders at the time that it arises. Its nature and source remains intact.

Example 11.3

A Netherlands-resident (TII) UCITS is paid a dividend of EUR 2,500,000. The UCITS also realizes a gain of EUR 10,000,000 by the disposal of one of its investments. The dividend and capital gain are considered to be received by the unitholders of the UCITS at the time of declaration and the time of disposal, respectively.

Estimation of Income

The amount of the income from the underlying investments of resident (TII) UCITS is estimated if it is not communicated to the unitholders. This could be avoided by valuing the units of the UCITS on market value. In that case, any increase in the value of the underlying investments is already taxable at the time of arising.

Exemptions

As in the case of a direct investment, no exemptions are available for the income from portfolio investments derived through a resident UCITS.

Disposal of the Units in a Netherlands-Resident (EII/FII) UCITS

The capital gain realized by the disposal of units in a resident (EII/TII) UCITS is taxable as business income if the units in the UCITS qualify as business assets.

Exemptions

No exemptions are available when the proceeds are considered to be business income.

Losses

The crediting of a loss from the disposal of units in a resident (EII/FII) UCITS does not differ from that discussed above for a direct investment.

Disposal of the Units in a Netherlands-Resident (TII) UCITS

A resident (TII) UCITS is considered to be transparent; thus any capital gains from the underlying investments are considered to be received at the time that these investments are disposed. The taxation at the time of disposal of the units in the UCITS is therefore limited to the part of the capital gain from the disposal of the units in the UCITS that is related to any changes in the value of the underlying investments that are not considered to be realized yet (unrealized capital gains and losses).

11.2.2.3. Investment in the Units of UCITS Residing in Austria, Germany, and the United Kingdom

The characteristics of a non-resident UCITS under the civil law of the UCITS country whether or not in combination with the fund rules determine if the income from the underlying investments is considered to be that of the UCITS (tax opaque entity) or the Netherlands unitholders (tax transparent entity).

Classification of Non-resident UCITS

The income from the underlying investments of a non-resident UCITS is considered to be that of the UCITS if, had the latter been Netherlands-resident, it would have been subject to corporate income tax in the Netherlands. Otherwise, the income is considered to be that of the unitholders. A non-resident UCITS would have been subject to corporate income tax in the Netherlands if it qualified as a corporate entity with a capital that is divided in shares, an open fund for joint account, or another taxable person under the Corporate Tax Act.[26] The characteristics of the UCITS under the civil law of its residence state are taken into account in the examination whether it is a tax opaque or a tax transparent entity.[27] A UCITS qualifies as a corporate entity with a capital that is divided in shares if (1) its unitholders are liable for their share in the capital of the UCITS only, (2) the investments and other assets are owned by the UCITS, and (3) the investments and other assets are for the rest not actually invested for the account and at the risk of the unitholders.[28] A unitholder thus may not be held responsible without

26. See M.L.M. van Kempen, 'Kwalificatie van Buitenlandse Rechtsvormen', *WFR 2005/573*, with regard to joint ventures.
27. See the Opinion of the Advocate General by Supreme Court of the Netherlands, 2 Jun. 2006, no. 40 919, *BNB* 2006/288, 4.2.
28. Supreme Court of the Netherlands, 2 Jun. 2006, no. 40 919, *BNB* 2006/288, 3.2.

limitation for the debts of a UCITS; nor may the ownership of the investments and other assets of the UCITS be in their hands instead of the UCITS. Neither may any income from these investments and assets actually belong to them. These conditions are fulfilled by UK-resident UCITS of the corporate type only.

Austrian, German, and UK-resident UCITS of the trust type, however, may qualify as an open fund for joint account, but only if their units are freely transferable by the unitholders. An open fund for joint account is defined as a fund that is established with the purpose of obtaining income for its participants by way of collective investment or, otherwise, of obtaining capital for as far as its certificates of participation are freely transferable.[29] It is a separate special purpose vehicle, or pool of assets, without legal personality.[30] The income obtained must result from the collective investment or, otherwise, from the capital obtained. In addition, the income has to be intended for the benefit of the unitholders only. The entitlement of the unitholders to a share of the income of the UCITS has to appear from the units of the UCITS. Austrian-, German-, and UK-resident UCITS of the trust type fulfil all of these conditions if their units are freely transferable. Otherwise, they are considered to be a closed fund for joint account, which is a tax transparent entity.

As discussed in Section 6.2.3, the units of UCITS are considered to be freely transferable in the case that a transfer does not depend on the permission of the other unitholders or is not limited to close relatives and in-laws only. It therefore depends on the fund rules of Austrian- and German-resident UCITS or the trust deed of UK-resident UCITS of the trust type whether or not they qualify as a tax opaque entity (open fund for joint account) or a transparent entity (closed fund for joint account).

Tax Opaque Non-resident UCITS

The income from the underlying investments of tax opaque non-resident UCITS is considered to be received by corporate unitholders on distribution and disposal of the units of the UCITS, whichever is earlier. If a non-resident UCITS accumulates the income from the underlying investments, the corporate income tax liability of that income is deferred until it is realized as capital gain by disposal of the units in the UCITS.

Example 11.4

A UK-resident UCITS of the corporate type derives from its investments a dividend of EUR 2,500,000 and realizes through the disposal of investments a gain of EUR 10,000,000. In accordance with the articles of association,

---

29. Article 2(2) Corporate Tax Act.
30. N.H. de Vries, et al., *Cursus Belastingrecht (Vennootschapsbelasting)* (Deventer: Kluwer, loose leaf), 1.0.3.P, b1.

it accumulates the dividend and the proceeds from the disposal of investments. Hence, none of this is received by the Netherlands corporate unitholder until they are realized as a capital gain by the disposal of the units in the UCITS.

The distributed income, like that of a resident (EII/FII) UCITS, is taxable if it qualifies as business income.

Valuation of Units of Non-resident UCITS at Market Value

To prevent the accumulation of income by non-resident UCITS from deferring the corporate income tax liability for the income from the underlying investments, the units in a non-resident UCITS must be valued at market value if the UCITS is not subject to corporate income tax in the UCITS country and the exemption from corporate income tax does not depend on an actual distribution of the income from the investments of the UCITS on an annual basis.[31] The phrase 'not subject to corporate income tax' also seems to include UCITS that are considered to be transparent under the national tax legislation of the UCITS country. An investment in the units of Austrian- and German-resident UCITS therefore needs to be valued by corporate unitholders at market value.

Example 11.5

The market value of the units of a German-resident UCITS is EUR 1,000 at the beginning of the year. The units of the UCITS are listed at EUR 1,500 at the end of the year. The change in value of the units in the UCITS of EUR 500 is taxable in the hands of corporate unitholders, as the units need to be valued at market value.

In the case of an investment in the units of Austrian and German-resident UCITS, the yields from the underlying investments of these UCITS and any change in value of these investments are, as is the case for resident (EII) UCITS, taxable in the hands of corporate unitholders at the time of arising.

The requirement for corporate entities to value the units of certain tax opaque non-resident UCITS at market value seems to infringe the free movement of capital as laid down in Articles 56 and 58 of the EC Treaty and Article 40 of the EEA Treaty. An investment in the units of these non-resident UCITS is treated less favourably than an investment in the units of resident (FII) UCITS. Any change in the value of the underlying investments of these non-resident UCITS is taxable at the time it arises, whereas these changes in the case of an investment in the units of a resident (FII) UCITS that has opted for a reinvestment account are not taxable

31. Article 3.29a Income Tax Act.

until the disposal of the units in the UCITS. The measure therefore does not seem to be proportional.

Transparent Non-resident UCITS

The income from the underlying investments of transparent non-resident UCITS is considered to be received by the unitholders at the same time as discussed in Section 11.2.2.2 for Netherlands-resident (TII) UCITS. Likewise, the nature and source of the income remains intact.

> *Example 11.6*
>
> An Austrian-resident UCITS whose units can be disposed of only to the UCITS itself derives a dividend of EUR 1,000,000, whereas it realizes a capital gain of EUR 1,000,000 when it disposes one of its investments. The Netherlands unitholders of the UCITS are considered to receive their share in the dividend and capital gain at the time of arising.

Like the units of tax opaque non-resident UCITS, the units in transparent non-resident UCITS sometimes need to be valued at fair market value. Likewise, it concerns the units of transparent non-resident UCITS that are not subject to corporate income tax and the exemption from corporate income tax does not depend on the distribution of the income from the underlying investments on an annual basis, that is, the units of Austrian and German-resident UCITS. For the same reasons as discussed earlier for tax opaque non-resident UCITS, the requirement for corporate entities to value the units of certain transparent non-resident UCITS at market value seems to infringe on the free movement of capital as laid down in Articles 56 and 58 of the EC Treaty and Article 40 of the EEA Treaty.

Disposal of the Units in a Tax Opaque Non-resident UCITS

The capital gain realized by the disposal of units in a UCITS residing in Austria, Germany, or the United Kingdom, just as is the case for an investment in the units of a resident UCITS, is taxable as business income if the units in the UCITS qualify as business assets.

Exemptions

No exemptions are available when the capital gain is considered to be business income.

Losses

If the disposal of units in a resident UCITS results in a loss, the loss may be credited under the same conditions as discussed previously for a direct investment.

Disposal of the Units in a Transparent Non-resident UCITS

The corporate income tax liability for the capital gain realized by disposal of the units in the UCITS does not differ from that of the resident (TII) UCITS. It is limited to the part of the proceeds from the disposal that is related to unrealized capital gains.

11.2.3. Crediting of Foreign Withholding Tax

11.2.3.1. Investing Directly in Securities and Other Financial Instruments

Cross-border investments in securities and other financial instruments have the potential for international double taxation for the reasons mentioned in Section 9.2.3.1 for Austria.

Regulations have been issued by the Netherlands to prevent international double taxation.

Tax Treaties

The most important regulations to prevent international double taxation are the tax treaty and the Tax Charter for the Kingdom of the Netherlands, which match the taxation under the domestic laws of the Contracting States by way of allocating the right to tax to one of the Contracting States.

The right to tax dividend and interest, however, is generally allocated to both states. Dividends and interest may be taxed in the state in whose jurisdiction the beneficiary resides (residence state). Nevertheless, dividends and interest also may be taxed in the state in whose jurisdiction the paying company or the debtor resides (the source state) but the taxation may not exceed the percentage agreed on in the tax treaty. An overview of the percentages agreed on in the Netherlands tax treaties can be found in the Tables 3.9 and 3.10 of Chapter 3.

To avoid double taxation, the tax withheld by the source state on the dividend or interest may be credited against the beneficiary's tax liability in the residence state (foreign tax credit). The foreign tax credit is, however, limited to the amount of tax that could have been levied by the source state in accordance with the tax treaty.

Some of the Netherlands tax treaties provide for a foreign tax credit that is higher than the foreign withholding tax actually levied on dividends and interest. As is the case in the treaties of Austria and Germany, this mostly involves tax treaties with developing countries or countries such as Brazil or Mexico that are not as developed as the Netherlands.[32] A Netherlands-resident investor may, under

32. Brazil, China, Mexico, Mongolia, Pakistan, the Philippines, Sri Lanka, Surinam, Tunisia, and Venezuela.

these tax treaties, credit a fixed percentage of the gross amount of dividends or interest (*matching credit*). As discussed in Section 9.2.3.1, a matching credit relates to situations in which the taxation of income in the source state has, in accordance with a tax incentive, been omitted or reduced. Under some tax treaties, whether an individual can actually benefit from a matching credit depends on the source state's domestic law because tax incentives are often limited to business income or certain kinds of (business) activities.

Double taxation of capital gains and other portfolio income is in most tax treaties quite easily avoided by allocating the right to tax these items of income exclusively to the residence state. Hence, the source state has no right to impose tax. As discussed in Section 3.3.4 some tax treaties allocate the right to tax capital gains and other portfolio income to both states. To avoid double taxation, the tax withheld by the source state may be set off against the alienator's or beneficiary's tax liability in the residence state (foreign tax credit).

Unilateral Rules

Regulations on the prevention of international double taxation are not found only in tax treaties. In the absence of a tax treaty, or in the presence of a tax treaty that does not cover certain taxes, does not apply to certain taxpayers, or does not cover certain taxable items, taxation in the source state and the residence state often show overlap. Most Western states therefore have issued unilateral rules that take into account that foreign income may have been subject to tax in the state of residence.

The Dutch unilateral rules for cross-border investments in securities and other financial instruments are found in the Decree on the avoidance of double taxation (hereafter Dadt).[33] The Dadt, however, does not contain relief from international double taxation for all items of income from foreign securities and other financial instruments. It is restricted to dividend and interest paid by a company or debtor that resides within the jurisdiction of some developing countries and more developed countries.[34] In that case only, the beneficiary may credit the tax withheld by the source state against the tax liability in the Netherlands (foreign tax credit).

33. Decree on the avoidance of double taxation (Besluit ter voorkoming van dubbele belasting, 2001), *Stb.* 2000, 642, 21 Dec. 2000.

34. Afghanistan, Albania, Algeria, Armenia, Belize, Benin, Bhutan, Bolivia, Botswana, Burkina Faso, Burundi, Cambodia, Cameron, Cape Verde, Central African Republic, Chad, Colombia, Comoros, Costa Rica, Côte d'Ivoire, Cuba, Democratic Republic of Congo, Djibouti, Dominica, Dominican Republic, Ecuador, El Salvador, Equatorial Guinea, Eritrea, Ethiopia, Fiji, Gambia, Georgia, Ghana, Grenada, Guatemala, Guinea, Guinea-Bissau, Guyana, Haiti, Honduras, Iran, Iraq, Jamaica, Kenya, Kiribati, Laos, Lebanon, Lesotho, Liberia, Madagascar, Maldives, Mali, Marshal Islands, Mauritania, Micronesia, Mozambique, Myanmar, Namibia, Nepal, Nicaragua Niger, North Korea, Palau Islands, the Territories governed by the Palestinian Authorities, Panama, Papua New Guinea, Paraguay, Peru, Republic of Congo, Rwanda, St. Vincent in the Grenadines, Salomon Islands, Samoa, São Tomé and Principe, Senegal, Sierra Leon, Somalia, Sudan, Swaziland, Syria, Tanzania, Togo, Tonga, Tuvalu, Vanuatu, and Yemen.

The amount of the foreign tax credit, however, is maximized at 15% of the gross amount of the dividend or interest. For the purposes of corporate income tax, the maximization applies only to dividends.

Ordinary Tax Credit

Notwithstanding the earlier discussion, the Netherlands under no circumstances grants a foreign tax credit that is more than the part of the Netherlands (corporate) income tax due on the beneficiary's or alienator's worldwide income that is related to the foreign income (ordinary tax credit). The ordinary tax credit may be determined either on a per-country basis or on an overall basis.

The ordinary tax credit, however, does not apply to the tax withheld by a source state on dividend or interest from securities or other financial instruments that are part of an individuals net assets.[35] Instead, the foreign tax credit, as discussed earlier, is maximized to 25% of the gross amount of dividend and interest.

Push Through Rule

If the foreign tax credit cannot, or cannot entirely, be credited against the income tax liability for income from savings of investments[36] or the corporate income tax liability of the unitholder, the excess is not refundable. Instead, it may be carried forward to the following year, even though the Netherlands tax treaties do not provide for that.[37] If a resident taxpayer derives substantial income from foreign investments annually, this may result in a permanent surplus of non-creditable foreign tax credits.

11.2.3.2. Investments in the Units of Netherlands-Resident UCITS

The tax status of the UCITS determines whether or not the foreign withholding tax may be credited by the unitholders.

Netherlands-Resident (EII/FII) UCITS

The income from the investments of resident (EII/FII) UCITS is considered to be that of the UCITS. Any of the withholding taxes levied at source on the income is

35. A relation between the income tax liability of a resident taxpayer and the amount of the foreign income is missing because the income tax liability for (foreign) income from savings and investments is determined on the basis of a fixed amount of the average value of the net assets.
36. In 2001, the amount of the foreign tax credit that exceeded the income tax liability for income from savings and investments could, initially, be set off against the income tax liability for income from work and dwellings or income from substantial interest. This widening, however, was revoked before the end of 2001 (Explanatory Notes of the Decree of 28 Dec. 2001, *Stb.* 2001, 700, at 10).
37. Decree of 21 Jun. 1996, no. IFZ96/619M, *BNB* 1996/292.

thus considered to be charged for the account of the UCITS. The foreign withholding tax therefore may not be credited by the unitholders.

Netherlands-Resident (TII) UCITS

Resident (TII) UCITS are considered to be transparent; thus the Charter for the Kingdom of the Netherlands, the tax treaties, and the unilateral rules are applied as if the unitholders had invested directly in the underlying investments. Any foreign withholding tax may be credited by the unitholders under the same conditions as discussed in Section 11.2.3.1.

Relevant Information

The unitholders need to be provided with an overview of the amount of withholding tax that has been levied per source state and per item. Otherwise, they cannot file a tax return or make a request for the refund of the part of withholding tax that is not levied in accordance with a tax treaty.

11.2.3.3. Investments in Units of UCITS Residing in Austria, Germany, and the United Kingdom

Whether foreign withholding tax may be credited by unitholders depends on the characteristics of the UCITS under civil law of the UCITS country, together with the fund rules.

Tax Opaque Non-resident UCITS

The crediting of the tax withheld at source on the income from the investments of non-resident UCITS does not differ from that of resident (EII/FII) UCITS.

Transparent Non-resident UCITS

Any foreign withholding tax is creditable under the same conditions as discussed earlier for resident (TII) UCITS.

Relevant Information

The unitholders must be provided with the same information about the foreign withholding tax as for resident (TII) UCITS.

Withholding Tax Levied by the UCITS Country at the Time of Distribution

From Section 6.5.4 it follows that the UCITS country often withholds tax at the time of distribution. Whether the tax withheld by the UCITS country at the time of distribution may be credited by the unitholder depends on the UCITS being a person for the purposes of a tax treaty.

Non-resident UCITS Considered a Resident for the Purposes of a Tax Treaty

Unilateral rules on the crediting of the foreign withholding tax charged by the UCITS country are lacking. According to the Netherlands tax treaties the tax withheld at the time of distribution may be credited by the beneficiary, the unitholder, but only if the distribution is paid by a resident of the UCITS country and is considered to be a dividend.

Non-resident UCITS Not Considered a Resident for the Purposes of a Tax Treaty

If a distribution is not paid by a UCITS considered a resident for the purposes of a tax treaty, the Netherlands as the residence state of the beneficiary is not obliged to avoid double taxation by way of an exemption or tax credit. On the basis of the clause on other income, the right to tax is generally allocated exclusively to the residence state of the unitholder. As discussed in Section 2.4.2, states have different views on the meaning of a resident for the purposes of a tax treaty.

A classification conflict arises in the case that the UCITS country considers the UCITS to be a resident for the purposes of the applicable tax treaty and withholds tax at the time of distribution, whereas the Netherlands does not consider the UCITS to be such a resident and does not avoid double taxation by way of a tax credit. In practice, a classification conflict usually does not result in international double taxation because non-resident UCITS are considered by the Netherlands tax authorities to be opaque. Any decree from the state secretary for Finance or other publication from the tax authorities on this practice could not be traced.

11.3. CONCLUSION

11.3.1. Income Tax Liability

In the Netherlands, the income tax liability of an investment in the units of a UCITS residing in Austria, Germany, or the United Kingdom does not differ from that in the units of a Netherlands-resident UCITS. This is different only for the application of the exemption for environmental, social-ethical, and cultural investments, which does not apply to an investment in the units of non-resident UCITS that do not offer their units to the Dutch public. An investment in the units of these non-resident UCITS results in a tax disadvantage compared to Netherlands-resident UCITS.

11.3.2. Corporate Income Tax Liability

The corporate income tax liability of an investment in the units of a non-resident UCITS may differ from a Netherlands-resident UCITS. The corporate income tax liability may be affected by the time that the income from the underlying investments is received by Netherlands corporate unitholders.

The income from the underlying investment of Netherlands-resident (FII) UCITS is received by Netherlands corporate unitholders by way of distribution within 8 months after the end of the financial year in which the income was originally received by the UCITS. Where a Netherlands-resident (FII) UCITS has opted for a reinvestment account, any change in value of the investments is received by Netherlands individual unitholders at the time of disposal of the units in the UCITS. The income of UCITS residing in the United Kingdom is considered received by Netherlands corporate unitholders upon distribution or disposal of the units in the UCITS, whichever is earlier. Any changes in value of the investments cannot be distributed by UK-resident UCITS. By accumulation, the other income from the investments of UK-resident UCITS is not received by Netherlands corporate unitholders until the disposal of the units in the UCITS. The corporate income tax liability for the income is likewise deferred.

Netherlands corporate unitholders of Austrian-resident UCITS, German-resident UCITS and Netherlands-resident (EII) UCITS need to value the units in these UCITS at market value. The yields from the underlying investments and any change in the value of these investments are therefore taxable in the hands of corporate unitholders at the time that they arise. The latter differs from Netherlands-resident (FII) UCITS that have opted for a reinvestment account.

Any income from Netherlands-resident (TII) UCITS is considered to be that of the unitholders. It is considered to be taxable in the hands of corporate unitholders at the time of arising. The same is true for a transparent non-resident UCITS, unless it is not subject to corporate income tax and the exemption from corporate income tax does not depend on the distribution of the income from the underlying investments on an annual basis, like Austrian- and German-resident UCITS. In that case, the units in the UCITS need to be valued at fair market value, as discussed earlier.

11.3.3. Crediting of Foreign Withholding Tax Levied by a Source State

Netherlands-resident unitholders may set off the withholding tax deducted at the source of income from the underlying investments of UCITS against their (corporate) income tax liability but only if the non-resident UCITS is considered to be transparent for Netherlands tax purposes. In that case, the Netherlands tax treaties and unilateral rules are applied as if the unitholders had invested directly. Otherwise, the withholding tax is considered to be levied for the account of the UCITS and, thus, cannot be credited by the unitholders. The Netherlands national tax legislation does not take into account whether the foreign withholding tax levied at source is creditable by non-resident UCITS or any relief for that tax is, as is the case for Netherlands-resident UCITS, granted to the non-resident UCITS by the UCITS country.

11.3.4. Crediting of Foreign Withholding Tax Levied by UCITS Country

The tax withheld by the UCITS country at the time of distribution can be set off against the investor's (corporate) income tax liability where the non-resident UCITS is considered to be a person for tax treaty purposes. If the tax withheld exceeds the investor's (corporate) income tax liability, the excess is, in contrast to the withholding tax levied by the Netherlands at the time of distribution by Netherlands-resident (FII) UCITS, not refunded.

Chapter 12

The United Kingdom: Taxation of Income from Investments in the Country of the Unitholders

Income from securities and other financial instruments derived by way of undertakings for collective investment in transferable securities (UCITS) is not considered to be that of the unitholders. Instead, it is considered that of the UCITS. As a result, it is not taxable in the hands of the unitholders until it is distributed or realized by the disposal of the units in the UCITS.

The tax liability of income derived by way of UCITS should not be less (or more, as the case may be) than that of a direct investment. For that reason, UK-resident UCITS are required to distribute the income from the underlying investments at the end of each distribution period. An exception to the rule applies to capital gains realized by the disposal of the underlying investments. UK-resident UCITS are not allowed to distribute capital gains even to the unitholders. Hence, these gains are not taxable in the hands of the unitholders until they are realized by disposal of the units in the UCITS.

The taxation of income derived by way of a non-resident UCITS is not the same as that of income derived by way of resident UCITS. The characteristics under the civil law of the UCITS country determine whether income derived by way of non-resident UCITS is considered to be that of the unitholders (tax transparent entity) or that of the UCITS (tax opaque entity). The unitholders of transparent non-resident UCITS are considered to receive the income from the underlying investments on receipt, whereas income derived by way of tax opaque non-resident UCITS is not considered to be received by the unitholders until it is distributed or realized by the disposal of units in UCITS.

The different treatment of resident and non-resident UCITS seems to result in some cases in an infringement of the freedom of capital as laid down in Articles 56 and 58 of the EC Treaty or Article 40 of the EEA Treaty.

Domestic and foreign dividends derived by way of non-resident UCITS, for example, are subject to more taxation in the hands of the unitholders as those derived by way of UK-resident UCITS. The available tax credit or exemption for these dividends is, compared to UK-resident UCITS, restricted to domestic dividends only if they are derived by way of transparent non-resident UCITS, whereas they are entirely denied in the case of a tax opaque non-resident UCITS.

Furthermore, the taxation of capital gains realized by the disposal of the underlying investments of transparent non-resident UCITS are subject to tax at the time of disposal, whereas that from the underlying investments of UK-resident UCITS are not taxed until disposal of the units in the UCITS.

Not only the taxation of capital gains realized by the disposal of underlying investments of non-resident transparent UCITS differs from that of UK-resident UCITS but also that of capital gains realized by the disposal of the units in tax opaque non-resident UCITS. These gains, however, are not charged with capital gains tax as a chargeable gain if the non-resident UCITS was not certified as a distribution fund (or a reporting fund for periods commencing on or after October 2009) during the entire period of ownership (i.e. it was a non-qualifying or non-reporting fund). Instead, the profit in that case is charged with income tax as an offshore income gain, which is subject to a less favourable taxation than chargeable gains.

Any of the foreign tax withheld at source of the income derived by way of resident UCITS is considered to be that of the UCITS. The UK tax treaties and unilateral rules are therefore not applied to these taxes as if the unitholders had invested directly. The same applies for tax opaque non-resident UCITS.

The income of transparent non-resident UCITS is, however, that of the unitholders under the domestic laws of the United Kingdom. The UK tax treaties and unilateral rules, therefore, apply as if the income was derived directly by the unitholders from the underlying investments.

The tax withheld by the UCITS country at the time of distribution may be set off against the tax liability of the unitholders where the applicable tax treaty provides for such.

12.1. INTRODUCTION

The income from the investments of UK-resident UCITS is considered under UK tax legislation to be that of the UCITS. The income from the investments is therefore not taxable until it is distributed, or considered to be distributed, to the unitholders. In the case of an investment in the units of Austrian-, German-, or Netherlands-resident UCITS, however, the income is taxable either at the time it arises, is distributed or is realized by disposal of the units in the UCITS. The United Kingdom thus does not impose a uniform tax liability for income derived by way of Austrian-, German-, Netherlands-, and UK-resident UCITS.

12.2. TAX LIABILITY OF UK-RESIDENT UNITHOLDERS

12.2.1. Income Tax and Capital Gain Tax Liability of UK-Resident Individual Unitholders

12.2.1.1. Investing Directly in Securities and Other Financial Instruments

Individuals resident in the United Kingdom are subject to income tax on their worldwide taxable income and chargeable gains. The taxable income includes income from the following sources:

(1) Business income:
  (a) trading income.
(2) Non-business income:
  (a) employment income;
  (b) pension income;
  (c) social security income;
  (d) property income;
  (e) savings and investment income;
  (f) miscellaneous income;
  (g) other amounts which are charged to income tax under the Income Tax Acts.[1]

The chargeable gains include gains from the disposal of assets.[2] Any 'income' that does not qualify as taxable income or chargeable gains is not charged with income tax or capital gain tax.

Tax Burden

Income Tax

The United Kingdom applies different progressive tax rates for non-savings income, savings income, and dividends. Non-savings income is taxable at 10%,[3] 22%,[4] or 40%[5] (2009-2010). Income from savings and investments is subject to income tax at 10%,[6] 20%,[7] or 40%[8] (2009-2010). Dividends are taxed either at 10%[9] or

1. Section 3(1) and (2) Income Tax Act 2007, c.3.
2. Section 1(1) Taxation of Chargeable Gains Act 1992, c.12.
3. The first GBP 2,440 of the taxable income (2009–2010).
4. The part of the taxable income between GBP 2,440 and GBP 37,400 (2009–2010).
5. The part of the taxable income that exceeds GBP 37,400 (2009-2010).
6. The first GBP 2,440 of the taxable income (2009–2010).
7. The part of the taxable income between GBP 2,440 and GBP 37,400 (2009–2010).
8. The part of the taxable income that exceeds GBP 37,400 (2009–10).
9. The first GBP 37,400 of the taxable income (2009–2010).

32.5%[10] (2009–2010). Because the United Kingdom applies different progressive tax rates, the Income and Corporation Taxes Act contains specific rules for the allocation of taxable income of an individual across the different tax rates for non-savings income, savings income, and dividends. The savings income is considered to be the higher part of the taxable income, and dividends the highest part of that part.[11]

Example 12.1

A UK-resident individual has the following taxable income:

(1) income from employment GBP 20,000;
(2) interest GBP 20,000;
(3) UK dividend GBP 5,000.

The first GBP 2,440 of non-savings income is subject to income tax at a rate of 10%. The next non-savings income GBP 17,560 (20,000 –/– 2,440) is taxed at a rate of 22%. The next savings income of GBP 17,400 (37,400 –/– 20,000) is taxed at a rate of 20%. The next savings income of GBP 2,600 (40,000-37,400) is taxed at 40%. Finally, the next dividend GBP 5,000 (45,000 –/– 40,000) is taxed at 32.5%.

The United Kingdom applies a partial imputation system. An individual who receives a domestic qualifying distribution,[12] such as dividends on shares paid by a UK-resident company, is partially compensated for the corporate income tax charged at the level of the company in the form of a credit (dividend tax credit). The amount of the credit is one-ninth of the dividend payment.[13] The dividend tax credit can be set off against the income tax liability of the individual.[14] If the dividend tax credit exceeds the income tax liability of the individual, the excess is generally not refunded.[15] No dividend tax credit is available for foreign dividends. Whether the restriction of the dividend tax credit to domestic dividends infringes on free movement of capital under Articles 56 and 58 of the EC Treaty and Article 40 of the EEA Treaty falls outside the scope of this book.

Interest that is paid out domestically by a deposit taker, certain payments of yearly interest, and payments of UK public revenue dividends are subject to withholding tax of a 20% (2009–2010).[16] The withholding tax may be credited against the income tax liability of the individual. The part of the withholding tax that exceeds the income tax liability, however, is refundable.[17]

---

10. The part of the taxable income that exceeds GBP 37,400 (2009–2010).
11. Section 16(3), (4) and (5) Income Tax Act 2007.
12. Section 209(2) Income and Corporate Taxes Act 1988.
13. Section 397(1) Income Tax (Trading and Other Income) Act 2005, c.5.
14. Section 397(2) Income Tax (Trading and Other Income) Act 2005.
15. J. Tiley, Revenue Law (Hart Publishing, 2008), 879.
16. Section 847 Income Tax Act 2007.
17. D. Smailes & A. Flint, *Tolley's Income Tax 2006–07* (LexisNexis Tolley, 2006), at 23.1.

Capital Gains Tax

Gains from the disposal of assets are subject to capital gains tax at a flat rate of 18%.[18]

Example 12.2

The taxable income of an individual is GBP 40,000. In the same year, the chargeable gains add up to GBP 10,000. The chargeable gains are taxed with capital gains tax at a rate of 18%.

Income from Savings and Investments

A definition of income from savings and investments is missing. The Income Tax (Trading and Other Income) Act, however, contains an exhaustive catalogue of income from savings and investments. Among other things, it includes dividends and other distributions and interest.[19]

Dividend and other distributions are considered to be received by an individual at the time when they become due and payable. Qualifying distributions, like dividends paid by UK-resident companies, must be grossed up with one-ninth of their amount.[20] The aim of the gross-up is so that the corporate income tax levied on the distributed income at the level of the distributing company is partially replaced to tax the distributed income in the hands of the recipient as if it had been earned directly (partial imputation system). Non-qualifying distributions, such as dividends paid by non-UK-resident companies do not have to be grossed up, because a dividend tax credit is granted only for qualifying distributions.

Interest is a payment for the use of money.[21] It is considered to arise at the time that it is received or is made available for a person's benefit. The part of the proceeds from the disposal of bonds or other debt instruments that is related to interest accrued since the latest pay date or interest that has become payable but is not yet cashed, however, is also considered to be interest.[22] Interest, further, includes any discount[23] given to an individual at the time of purchase on the par value of a bond or the premium[24] paid by an individual at the time of purchase above the par value of a bond. A discount or premium is not usually received by an individual until the

18. Section 4 Taxation of Chargeable Gains Act.
19. Section 365(1) Income Tax (Trading and Other Income) Act.
20. Section 398(1) Income Tax (Trading and Other Income) Act.
21. *Schulze v. Bensted*, 1915 2 S.L.T. 382.
22. Section 369(4) Income Tax (Trading and Other Income) Act in conjunction with ss 714 and 716 of the Income and Corporation Taxes Act.
23. A discount on the par value of a bond is given where the interest rate of the bond is less than the interest rate of the capital market.
24. A premium above the par value of a bond is paid where the interest rate of the bond is more than the interest rate of the capital market.

repayment date. The difference between the par value and the cost price, or issue price, of a non-interest-generating bond is also interest if it qualifies as a deeply discounted security. A deeply discounted security is a security whose redemption price exceeds its issue price by more than 15% or, if less, 0.5% per year for the remaining period until the redemption date. It includes, for example, zero-bonds. The profit or loss on a deeply discounted security is considered to be realized at the earlier of the redemption date and disposal of the deeply discounted securities.

Exemptions

The part of the capital gain realized by the disposal of bonds or other debt instruments that is related to interest accrued since the latest pay date or interest that has become payable but is not yet cashed remains exempt from income tax when the nominal value of the securities held by the individual who sold the bond or other debt did not exceed an amount of GBP 5,000 on any day in the calendar year in which the interest period ends or in the previous year.[25] In that case it is subject to capital gain tax as chargeable gain.

Losses

A loss from savings and investments can be credited against other income. If the loss from savings and investments exceeds the other income of an individual, the excess cannot be carried back or forward.

Chargeable Gains

The chargeable gains include the gains from the disposal of assets.[26] Assets include all forms of property.[27] The Taxation of Chargeable Gains Act explicitly provides that assets include options, debts, and incorporeal property generally, as well as currency.[28] Most government securities are excluded from capital gains tax.[29]

The disposal of portfolio investments, such as shares, bonds, and other debt securities, financial options, or financial futures may trigger a taxable event for capital gains tax. The Taxation of Chargeable Gains Act makes sure that the disposal of assets also includes a cash settlement of financial options, among other options.[30] Portfolio investments are considered to be disposed of on a last-in-first-out basis.[31] An individual investor is thus not free to consider those

25. Section 715(1)(b) Income and Corporation Taxes Act 1988.
26. The exception to the rule applies to proceeds from the disposal of assets that are derived by traders for whom these proceeds are considered business income. A discussion of the taxation of individuals who carry on a business as a trader, however, falls outside the scope of the study.
27. Section 21(1) Taxation of Chargeable Gains Act.
28. Section 21(1)(a) and (b) Taxation of Chargeable Gains Act.
29. Section 115 Taxation of Chargeable Gains Act in combination with Sch. 9 of that Act.
30. Section 144A Taxation of Chargeable Gains Act.
31. Section 106A(6) Taxation of Chargeable Gains Act.

investments to be disposed of that he has kept the longest. If he has acquired the same kind of investments on the date of the disposal, those newly acquired investments are considered to be sold first.[32] This rule applies as well to the same kind of investments that are acquired within 30 days after the disposal.[33]

The gain from the disposal of investments is the difference between the market price of the investments at the time of disposal and that at the time of acquisition.[34,35] If the disposal involves bonds or other debt securities, the part of the proceeds from the disposal that is related to interest accrued after the last pay date or interest that became payable but is not yet cashed in is deducted from the gain because that part is subject to income tax. The deduction prevents the accrued interest from being taxed twice.

Exemptions

In addition, the amount of chargeable gains remains up to an amount of GBP 10,100 (2009-2010) exempt (annual exemption).

Losses

A loss from the disposal of non-business assets can be credited against the gain of the disposal of other assets. If a loss cannot, or cannot entirely, be credited against any gains from the disposal of assets, the excess may be carried forward to the following years.[36] It is credited against the gain that remains after the application of the annual exemption in a following year.[37]

12.2.1.2. Investment in the Units of UK-Resident UCITS

Any income from the underlying investments of a resident UCITS is that of the UCITS. The income from the underlying investments, however, must be distributed by a resident UCITS before the end of each distribution period.[38] Any capital gains from the disposal of investments, as mentioned in Section 6.4.4, have to be accumulated. These capital gains are therefore not realized by individual unitholders until the units in the UCITS are disposed.

32. Section 106A(5) Taxation of Chargeable Gains Act.
33. Section 106A(4) Taxation of Chargeable Gains Act.
34. Section 17(1) Taxation of Chargeable Gains Act.
35. For the calculation of the gain from the disposal, the market price of financial options and financial futures does not have to be reduced by the part of the market price that is related to the 'lifetime' of these contracts that has already passed, because they are not considered to be wasting assets (ss 144A and 143(7) and (8) Taxable Chargeable Gains Act).
36. Section 2(2)(b) Taxation of Chargeable Gains Act.
37. Section 3(5)(b) Taxation of Chargeable Gains Act.
38. Sections 18(2) and 22(2) The Authorised Investment Funds (Tax) Regulations 2006, S.I. 2006/964, 29 Mar. 2006.

Example 12.3

A UK-resident UCITS derives from its investments a dividend of EUR 2,500,000 and realizes through the disposal of investments a gain of EUR 10,000,000. It needs to distribute an amount of EUR 2,500,000 to the unitholders.

The income from the underlying investments of a resident UCITS is thus received by individual unitholders in the same distribution period in which it was originally received by the UCITS. The distributed income is taxable as dividends paid by a resident company. It needs to be grossed up with one-ninth, because it involves a qualified distribution. An individual unitholder is granted a dividend tax credit of one-ninth of the amount of the distributed income. It can be set off against the income tax liability of the individual unitholder.

Example 12.4

A UK individual unitholder derives a dividend of EUR 1,000 from units in a UK-resident UCITS. The dividend needs to be grossed up with one-ninth. The unitholder is thus considered to have received a dividend of EUR 1,111 while he is granted a dividend tax credit of EUR 111.

If a resident UCITS satisfies the qualifying investment test, the distributed income is considered to constitute yearly interest. Yearly interest is subject to deduction of tax. A 20% withholding tax is therefore levied at the time of distribution. The withholding tax may be credited against the income tax liability of the individual. Individual unitholders are not granted dividend tax credits.

Example 12.5

A UK individual derives a dividend of EUR 1,000 from units in a UK-resident UCITS. The UK-resident UCITS has satisfied the qualifying investment test. The distributed income is therefore considered yearly interest. The payment of EUR 1,000 is subject to a withholding tax of EUR 200 so that the unitholder actually receives an amount of EUR 800. The gross amount of the yearly interest is taxable in the hands of the unitholder. The withholding tax may be credited against the income tax liability of the individual.

Exemptions

As in the case of a direct investment, no exemptions are available for income derived from the underlying investments of a resident UCITS.

Disposal of the Units in UK-Resident UCITS

The units in a resident UCITS are considered property. The capital gain realized by the disposal of units in resident UCITS is therefore subject to capital gains tax.

Exemptions

The annual exemption also applies to a gain from the disposal of the units in a resident UCITS.

Example 12.6

A UK individual unitholder disposes of its units in a UK-resident UCITS of the corporate type for an amount of EUR 12,500. The annual exemption is not used yet by the unitholder. Hence, only EUR 2,400 of the gain is taxable.

Losses

Where an individual unitholder realizes a loss through the disposal of the units in a resident UCITS, the loss may, like a direct investment, be set off against any gains from the disposal of other assets. If the loss cannot, or cannot entirely, be set off against gains, the excess can likewise be carried forward to the following years.

12.2.1.3. Investment in the Units of UCITS Residing in Austria, Germany, or the Netherlands

The characteristics of the UCITS under the civil law of the UCITS country together with its instruments of incorporation, trust deed, or fund rules determine whether the income from the underlying investments is that of a non-resident UCITS (tax opaque entity) or the UK unitholders (tax transparent entity).[39] The same applies for capital gains realized by the disposal of the underlying investment.

Classification of Non-resident UCITS

Income and the capital gains from the underlying investment are considered to be those of the non-resident UCITS if the UCITS is considered a tax opaque entity. Otherwise, in the case of tax transparent entities, the income is that of the unitholders. Broadly, a non-resident UCITS is considered to be a tax opaque entity if it is a separate entity, which, instead of the unitholders, has the benefit of any proprietary right in the investments or the income from these investments.[40] Furthermore, it needs to have 'separate liability from the ownership of

---

39. *Rae v. Lazard Investment Company Limited* (1963) 41 T.C. 1.
40. *Memec plc v. I.R.C.*, [1996] S.T.C. 1336 at 1353.

the property or liability by or of the person composing the aggregation'.[41] Finally, it must have issued share capital or something else that serves the same function as share capital.[42] These requirements are also found in a statement of the UK tax authorities regarding the criteria it considers in classifying foreign entities.[43,44] Netherlands-resident UCITS of the corporate type fulfil all of these conditions.

These conditions are not fulfilled by Austrian-resident UCITS, German-resident UCITS, and Netherlands-resident UCITS of the contractual type because they lack legal personality. These UCITS are therefore considered to be transparent, although it is assumed that a Luxembourg-resident UCITS of the contractual type, which has similar characteristics, may proceed by default as if it is an entity of a corporate nature[45] or it may, for capital gains tax purposes, be considered as such when its custodian has entered into a declaration of trust governed by English law to the effect that the custodian holds the portfolio of the fund on trust for the unitholders and is thereby bound by the fund rules.[46]

Tax Opaque Non-resident UCITS

The income from the underlying investments of tax opaque non-resident UCITS, like that of Netherlands-resident UCITS of the corporate type, is considered to be that of the UCITS. It is considered received by UK individual unitholders on distribution or disposal of the units in the UCITS, whichever is earlier. The same applies to capital gains realized by the disposal of the underlying investments. When the income from the underlying investments or the capital gains from their disposal are accumulated, the income tax liability is deferred to the disposal of the units in the UCITS.

---

41. *Von Hellfeld v. E Rechnitzer and Mayer Frères & Co.* [1914] 1 Ch 748.
42. *Ryall v. Du Bois* (1933) TC 431.
43. *Tax Bulletin*, Issue 83, June 2006, 1295: (i) Does the foreign entity have a legal existence separate from that of the persons who have an interest in it? (ii) Does the entity issue share capital or something else, which serves the same function as share capital? (iii) Is the business carried on by the entity itself or jointly by the persons who have an interest in it that is separate and distinct from the entity? (iv) Are the persons who have an interest in the entity entitled to share in its profits as they arise; or does the amount of profits to which they are entitled depend on a decision of the entity or its members, after the period in which the profits have arisen, to make a distribution of its profits. (v) Who is responsible for debts incurred as a result of the carrying on of the business: the entity or the persons who have an interest in it? (vi) Do the assets used for carrying on the business belong beneficially to the entity or to the persons who have an interest in it?
44. This statement was, according to the Revenue, drafted in accordance with approach of the Court of Appeal in the case of *Memec plc v. CIR* and the case law preceding that case.
45. M. Smith & S. Davies, 'Offshore Funds', in *Tolley's Taxation of Collective Investment*, ed. S. Newcombe et al. (London: LexisNexis Tolley, 2003), 89.
46. R.O.A. Fraser & J.R. Wood, *Taxation of Offshore Trusts and Funds* (London: LexisNexis Tolley, 2002), 117.

Example 12.7

A Netherlands-resident (EII) UCITS of the corporate type derives from its investments a dividend of EUR 2,500,000 and realizes through the disposal of investments a gain of EUR 10,000,000. In accordance with its articles of association, it accumulates the dividend and the capital gain from the disposal of investments. None of them are thus received by UK individual unitholders until they are realized as capital gains by the disposal of the units in the UCITS.

If the income from the underlying investments of a tax opaque non-resident UCITS is distributed, it is taxable as a dividend paid by a non-resident company. Unlike distribution of a resident UCITS, it does not need to be grossed up with one-ninth, because it involves a non-qualified distribution. An individual unitholder is likewise not granted a dividend tax credit of one-ninth of the amount of the distributed income. The different treatment does not, however, necessarily infringe on the free movement of capital as laid down in Articles 56 and 58 of the EC Treaty and Article 40 of the EEA Treaty. The distributed income of resident UCITS has been subject to corporate income tax while any corporate income tax liability for the income of Netherlands UCITS of the contractual type has been avoided by way of a nil percent tax rate or a subjective exemption. The distributed income of other tax opaque non-resident UCITS, however, may have been subject to (corporate) income tax. Nevertheless, at the time of writing, the UK tax legislation does not take this into account. In some cases, a view might be taken that the UK method for conferring tax credits is non-proportional.

Exemptions

Just as for a resident UCITS, no exemptions are available for income derived from the underlying investments of a tax opaque non-resident UCITS.

Transparent Non-resident UCITS

The income from the underlying investments of Austrian-resident UCITS, German-resident UCITS, and Netherlands-resident UCITS of the contractual type may be considered to be that of the UK unitholders if the relevant tax authorities agree that these vehicles are tax transparent. Income derived from a tax transparent UCITS will be considered to be received by a UK individual unitholder at the time it arises as if the individual had invested directly in the underlying investments. The same applies to the capital gain realized by the disposal of the underlying investments.

Example 12.8

A Netherlands-resident UCITS of the contractual type derives a dividend of EUR 2,500,000 from its investments and realizes through the disposal of investments a gain of EUR 10,000,000. A UK individual unitholder is considered to receive its share in the dividend and the capital gain from the disposal at the time that they arise.

Any income other than dividends paid by a UK company, unlike any distributed income from the underlying investments of a resident UCITS, does not need to be grossed up with one-ninth, because it does not concern a qualified distribution. An individual unitholder is, likewise, not granted a dividend tax credit of one-ninth of the amount of the distributed income. This seems to infringe on the free movement of capital as laid down in Articles 56 and 58 of the EC Treaty and Article 40 of the EEA Treaty. Any distribution of income from the underlying investments of resident UCITS is subject to a more favourable treatment than any income other than a dividend paid by a UK company from the underlying investments of a transparent non-resident UCITS. The performance of an investment in the units of transparent non-resident UCITS is therefore less than that in the units of a resident UCITS.

Exemptions

The annual exemption is also fully applicable to gains from the disposal of the underlying investments of a transparent non-resident UCITS.

Losses

A loss from the disposal of an investment may be set off by individual unitholders against any gains from the disposal of other assets. If the loss cannot, or cannot entirely, be set off against gains, the excess likewise may be carried forward to the following years.

Estimation of Income

If the amount, nature, and source of the income from the underlying investments of transparent non-resident UCITS are not communicated, or are not communicated properly, to the unitholders, it is estimated. An estimation of income may result in more severe taxation.

Disposal of the Units in Tax Opaque Non-resident UCITS

The units in a tax opaque non-resident UCITS are considered to be property. The profit realized by the disposal of the units in tax opaque non-resident UCITS, however, is not charged with capital gains tax as a chargeable gain if the non-resident UCITS was not certified as a distributing fund (or a 'reporting fund' for periods commencing on or after October 2009)[47] during the entire period of ownership (i.e., it was a non-qualifying or non-reporting fund). Instead, any profits fall to be charged within the income tax regime as offshore income gains, which are subject to a less favourable taxation than chargeable gains.[48]

Offshore Funds Tax Regulations

The special tax regulations for non-distributing (or non-reporting funds) are intended to level the playing field between resident and offshore funds. This is the case because the offshore fund tax regulations prevent offshore funds, such as tax opaque non-resident UCITS,[49] from converting income into capital gains, which are subject to a more favourable tax treatment than income. As we have seen previously, this is done by taxing profits realized by the disposal of units in non-qualifying funds (or non-reporting funds) as an offshore income gain.

Without the tax regulations for offshore funds, non-distributing tax opaque non-resident UCITS would not only enable individuals to defer the income tax liability for the income from the underlying investments but also realize the

47. Offshore funds will be able to apply for Reporting fund status for accounting periods beginning on or after 1 Oct. 2009. Because the UK tax authorities have accepted that it could take some time to comply with the new rules, funds may continue to operate the distributor status regime for the first period of the new reporting regime. Reporting status will replace distributor status for all distributor status funds for accounting periods beginning on or after 1 Oct. 2010.
48. A capital gains tax liability is avoided by way of a deduction for offshore income gains from the profit realized by the disposal of units in a non-reporting fund.
49. Tax opaque non-resident UCITS are usually considered to be subject to the tax regulations for offshore funds because they qualify as a collective investment scheme and they are structured as (i) a company resident outside the UK; (ii) a unit trust scheme, the trustees of which are not resident in the UK; or (iii) any arrangements under foreign law that create rights in the nature of co-ownership (s. 3 of The Offshore Funds (Tax) Regulations 2009, S.I. 2009, in combination with s. 756A(1) Income and Corporation Taxes Act). A collective investment scheme is 'any arrangement with respect to property of any description, including money, the purpose or effect of which is to enable persons taking part in the arrangements (whether by becoming owners of the property or any part of it or otherwise) to participate in or receive profits or income arising from the acquisition, holding, management or disposal of the property or sums paid out of such profits or income' (s. 235(1) Financial Services and Markets Act 2000). Furthermore, at least one of the following conditions must be fulfilled: the contributions of the participants and the profits or income out of which payments are to be made to them must be pooled, or the property must be managed as a whole by or on behalf of the operator of the scheme (s. 235(3) Financial Services and Markets Act 2000). Finally, the unitholders may not be involved in the day-to-day management of the UCITS, although they may have a right to be consulted or to give directions (s. 235(2) Financial Services and Markets Act 2000). Netherlands-resident UCITS of the corporate type meet all of these conditions and are thus subject to the special tax regulations for offshore funds. It should be noted that the definition of what should constitute a Collective Investment Scheme is the subject of an ongoing consultation in the United Kingdom and it is possible that the FSA definition may shortly be replaced with a new principle based on the tax definition.

accumulated income as a chargeable gain that is subject to a more favourable tax treatment than income. The tax regulations for offshore funds take away the advantages of accumulated income that is realized as a chargeable gain. These tax regulations, however, do not take away the deferral of the income tax liability for the accumulated income. The old distributor status regime is not considered further below.

Reporting Fund

A non-resident UCITS is on request certified as a reporting fund. Any accumulated reportable income from the underlying investments of a reporting fund is, like that of a resident UCITS, considered to be distributed to the unitholders at the end of the distribution period (distribution date)[50,51] (see earlier discussion for the taxation of a distribution in the hands of the unitholders).

Example 12.9

A Netherlands-resident (EII) UCITS of the corporate type is approved as a reporting fund. During the year, it derives from its investments a dividend of EUR 2,500,000 and realizes a capital gain of EUR 10,000,000 by the disposal of investments. In accordance with its articles of association, it accumulates the dividend and the capital gain from the disposal of investments. The dividend is considered to be received by UK unitholders at the end of the reporting date.

A reporting fund needs to provide the UK tax authorities and unitholders with a calculation of its reportable income for each period of account.[52] The reportable income is broadly the same as the income shown in the distribution account as available for distribution for resident UCITS. It concerns the total return after adjustments for the Statement of Recommended Practice relating to Authorised Funds; see Section 6.4.4.

The reportable income needs to be determined in accordance with international accounting standards or the generally accepted accounting practice.[53] The latter concerns either UK generally accepted accounting practice or an alternative. The UK tax authorities will remain a list of alternative generally accepted accounting practices. It is expected, however, that a non-resident UCITS makes use of the generally accepted accounting practice of the UCITS

50. The distribution date is in a case that the reporting fund issues its report to the participants within a period of 6 months beginning with the day immediately following the last date of the reporting period, the date on which the report is issued. Otherwise, it concerns the last day of the reporting period.
51. Section 71 of The Offshore Funds (Tax) Regulations 2009.
52. Section 57 of The Offshore Funds (Tax) Regulations 2009.
53. Section 53 of The Offshore Funds (Tax) Regulations 2009.

country rather than another alternative. The exception to the rule is where a developed, generally accepted accounting practice is missing in the UCITS country.[54] Either way, it is up to the non-resident UCITS to demonstrate that the proposed generally accepted accounting practice is a true alternative to the international accounting standards.[55]

Certification

The manager of a non-resident UCITS or other offshore fund may make an application to be certified as a reporting fund. The certification remains valid until the fund gives notice for voluntary withdrawal;[56] for example, it ceased to have any UK unitholders or breaches the reporting fund requirements.[57] Among other things, a reporting fund is required to provide the UK tax authorities for each period of account its computation of the reported income of each UK unitholder (with the name and address of the unitholder) together with its computation of its reported income based on its audited financial statement and a copy of the latter statement.

Exemptions

The annual exemption applies only to a gain from the disposal of the units in a tax opaque non-resident UCITS if the latter was certified as a distributing offshore fund during the entire period of ownership. The same applies for the flat tax rate of 18%.

Example 12.10

A UK individual unitholder disposes of its units in a Netherlands-resident UCITS of the corporate type for an amount of EUR 13,500. The units were acquired for an amount of EUR 1,000 ten years ago. The Netherlands-resident UCITS was certified as distributing offshore funds during the entire period of ownership. The gain of EUR 12,500 is therefore reduced by the annual exemption. Hence, only EUR 2,400 of the gain is taxable.

If a tax opaque non-resident UCITS was not certified during the entire period of ownership, the capital from the disposal of the units in that UCITS is considered to be income. The annual exemption is therefore not applicable. Nor does the flat tax rate of 18%.

---

54. See Draft Statutory Instrument for consultation. The Offshore Funds (Tax) Regulations 2008 (HMRC, May 2008), 22.
55. Offshore funds: a discussion paper (HMRC, October 2007), at 3.18.
56. Section 89 of The Offshore Fund (Tax) Regulations 2009.
57. Section 80 of The Offshore Fund (Tax) Regulations 2009.

Example 12.11

A UK individual unitholder disposes of his units in a Netherlands-resident UCITS of the corporate type for an amount of EUR 13,500. The units were acquired for an amount of EUR 1,000 ten years ago. The Netherlands-resident UCITS was not certified as distributing offshore fund during the entire period of ownership. The gain of EUR 12,500 therefore is not reduced by the annual exemption. Hence, the gain is fully taxable as offshore income gain.

Losses

A loss from the disposal of the units in a tax opaque non-resident UCITS may be set off by an individual unitholders against any gains from the disposal of other assets, regardless of whether the UCITS was certified as a reporting fund during the entire period of ownership. An offshore income loss does not exist. It is thus subject to the general provisions for capital gains tax.[58] If the loss cannot, or cannot entirely, be set off against gains, the excess may likewise be carried forward to the following years.

Disposal of the Units in Transparent Non-resident UCITS

The capital gain from the disposal of the units in a transparent non-resident UCITS does not result in a chargeable gain for capital gains tax because the UCITS is transparent.[59] This is different only for any increase in the value of the underlying investments, which is not yet realized. Such increase is considered to be realized at the time of disposal of the units in the UCITS.

12.2.2. Corporate Income Tax Liability of UK-Resident Corporate Unitholders

12.2.2.1. Investing Directly in Securities and Other Financial Instruments

Companies[60] resident in the United Kingdom are subject to corporate income tax on their worldwide taxable profits. The taxable profits of residents

---

58. M. Smith & S. Davies, 'Offshore Funds', in *Tolley's Taxation of Collective Investment*, ed. S. Newcombe et al. (London: LexisNexis Tolley, 2003), 332 and 333.
59. *Ibid.*, 334.
60. A company means any body corporate or unincorporated associations other than a partnership, local authority, or local authority association.

include income from the following sources, which are known as Schedules or Cases:[61]

(1) Business income:
   (a) annual profits or gains from rents and similar payments from land in the United Kingdom (Schedule A);
   (b) profits or gains from any trading (Schedule D, case I);
   (c) profits or gains from a profession or vocation (Schedule D, case II).
(2) Non-business income:
   (a) interest, annuities and other annual payments and discounts (Schedule D, case III);
   (b) profits or gains from foreign possessions (Schedule D, case V);
   (c) other annual profits or gains not falling in the other Schedules and Cases (Schedule D, case VI).

The taxable profits also include chargeable gains, that is, gains from the disposal of business or other assets.

Any 'income' that does not qualify as one of these income types, that is, domestic dividends that do not qualify as business income or as a gain from the disposal of assets, is not charged with corporate income tax.

Exempt Companies

UK-resident pension funds[62] and charities,[63] among other companies, are exempt from corporate income tax but not on trading income. Generally, any dividend tax credits cannot be set off by exempt companies. These credits, however, are not refundable.[64] No withholding tax applies to interest paid domestically by deposit-takers to exempt companies.[65]

Tax Burden

The taxable profits of the financial year of a company are subject to corporate income tax at a progressive rate of at the most 28% (2009). No withholding tax applies to interest paid domestically by deposit-takers to companies.[66]

Business Income

Income is considered to be business income if it is derived from business assets. The portfolio investments of companies are generally not considered business

61. Section 6(4)(a) Income and Corporation Taxes Act.
62. Sections 186 and 187(4) FA 2004 and s. 271 Taxation of Chargeable Gains Act.
63. Section 505 Income and Corporation Taxes Act.
64. J. Tiley, *Revenue Law* (Oxford: Hart Publishing, 2008), 830 and 878.
65. Section 481(4) and (4A) Income and Corporation Taxes Act.
66. *Ibid.*

assets; for most companies the sale of portfolio investments is not undertaken in the ordinary course of carrying on a business or profession. This is different only for companies that carry on a business of buying and selling portfolio investments with a view to profit, such as share dealers and banks.[67]

Tax Accounting Principles

The taxable income of a company is determined in accordance with generally accepted accounting practice.[68] Generally accepted accounting practice is defined in relation to the affairs of a company or other entity that prepares accounts in accordance with international financial reporting standards, generally accepted accounting practice with respect to such accounts and, in any other case, UK generally accepted accounting practice with respect to accounts.[69] Companies are free to choose one of those accounting principles.[70] The generally accepted accounting practice, however, applies to the extent the (corporate) income tax laws or principles do not determine otherwise.[71]

Exemptions

An exemption applies to qualified distributions, such as a dividend, paid by a UK-resident company, unless it is received by a dealer.[72] In that case, it is part of the dealer's profits from a trade or the carrying on of a business. A dealer, for this purpose, not only means share dealers but also banks and certain other financial institutions.[73] As mentioned earlier, whether the restriction of the exemption to domestic dividends and other distributions infringes on the free movement of capital as laid down in Articles 56 and 58 of the EC Treaty[74] and Article 40 of the EEA Treaty falls outside the scope of this study.

Losses

A loss from business income may be set off against other profits, income, or chargeable gains of the same financial year.[75] If the loss cannot, or cannot entirely, be set off, the excess may be carried back to the preceding period of 12 months.[76]

67. K. Walton, *Simon's Calculating Taxable Trading Profits* (London: LexisNexis Tolley, 2002), 3.7.
68. Section 42 FA 1998.
69. Section 50 FA 2004.
70. J. Tiley, *Revenue Law* (Oxford: Hart Publishing, 2008), 405.
71. See D. Smailes & A. Flint, *Tolley's Income Tax 2006–07* (London: LexisNexis Tolley, 2006), 82.20.
72. Sections 95(1) and 208 Income and Corporation Taxes Act.
73. *Simon's Direct Tax Service* (London: Butterworths, loose leaf), D1.404.
74. See also J. Tiley, *Revenue Law* (London: Hart Publishing, 2008), 881.
75. Section 393A(1)(a) Income and Corporation Taxes Act.
76. Section 393A(2) Income and Corporation Taxes Act.

However, it is carried forward to the following years if it cannot entirely be set off against the profits, gains, or chargeable gains in the preceding period of 12 months.[77] The crediting in the following years is limited to business income of the same trade or business.[78]

Where the amount of the business income of the trade in the following years is not sufficient to credit the loss, it may also be set off against interest or dividends on investments.[79] It involves interest or dividends on investments that would have been taxable as business income if it were not because of specific other provisions in the Income and Corporation Taxes Act, just as for loan relationships, that determine otherwise. Whether interest or dividends on investments would qualify as business income depends on the nature of business carried on by a company. As discussed earlier, the investments of only a few companies qualify as business assets.

Interest, Annuities, and Other Annual Payments and Discounts

The Income and Corporation Taxes Act contains an exhaustive catalogue of interest, annuities, and other annual payments and discounts that are not considered to be business income. It involves the following:[80]

(1) Any interest of money, whether yearly or otherwise, or annuity or other annual payment, whether such payment is payable within or without the United Kingdom, either as a charge on property of the person paying the same by virtue of any deed or will or otherwise, or as reservation out of it, or as a personal debt or obligation by virtue of any contract or whether the same is received and payable half-yearly or at any shorter or more distant periods, but not including any payment chargeable under Schedule A.
(2) Discounts.
(3) Income from securities that is payable out of the public revenue of the United Kingdom or Northern Ireland.

It also includes any profits, gains, and losses from bonds and other debt securities as well as financial options and financial futures. It involves changes in value of bonds and other debt securities and interest generated by them. The time that any change in value or interest is included as interest, annuities and other annual payments, and discounts does not differ from business income.

Exemptions

There are no exemptions available for profits, gains, and losses from bonds and other debt securities, nor for financial options and financial futures.

---

77. Section 393(1) in combination with s. 393A(1)(b) Income and Corporation Taxes Act.
78. Section 393(1) Income and Corporation Taxes Act.
79. Section 393(8) Income and Corporation Taxes Act.
80. Section 18(3) Income and Corporation Taxes Act.

Losses

Any loss from bonds or other debt securities may be set off against any profits of a company in the same year.[81] The part that cannot be set off may be carried back to interest, annuities and other annual payments, and discounts of previous years or carried forward to non-trading profits of the following year.[82]

Profits or Gains from Foreign Possessions

The Income and Corporations Taxes Act does not define the profits or gains from foreign possessions that are not considered to be business income. Among other things this includes dividends from shares in non-resident companies.

Any foreign dividend is considered to be received by a company at the time that it becomes due and payable.

Exemptions

The exemption for qualifying distributions is limited to dividends and other distributions paid by UK-resident companies. Whether the restriction of the exemption to domestic dividends and other distributions infringes on the free movement of capital as laid down in Articles 56 and 58 of the EC Treaty[83] and Article 40 of the EEA Treaty falls outside the scope of this book.[84]

Losses

Any loss from foreign possessions may be set off only against income from such possessions. If the loss exceeds the other income from foreign possessions, the excess may be carried forward to income from foreign possessions in a following year.[85]

Chargeable Gains

Gains from the disposal of assets that do not qualify as business assets are taxable as chargeable gain. In the case of portfolio investments of companies, however, it is limited to the proceeds from the disposal of shares, because any profits, gains or losses from bonds and other debt securities, as well as that from financial options and futures is taxable as interest, annuities and other annual payments, and discounts. A chargeable gain is determined in the same manner as discussed for individuals in Section 12.2.1.1.

---

81. Section 83(2) FA 1996.
82. Section 83(2) and (3) FA 1996.
83. See also J. Tiley, *Revenue Law* (Oxford: Hart Publishing, 2008), 881.
84. It should be noted that at the time of writing, the UK tax authorities are in the consultation process for issuing new draft tax legislation for the taxation of foreign profits.
85. Section 396 Income and Corporation Taxes Act.

Exemptions

The annual exemption and the flat tax rate of 18% described earlier, do not apply to companies. Instead, a company is entitled to indexation relief to provide allowance for inflation. The indexation relief reduces the capital gains. It runs from the month that an asset is obtained until the month in which disposal of the asset occurs.[86]

Losses

A loss from the disposal of assets, in the same manner as discussed for individuals in Section 12.2.1.1, may be credited against the gain of the disposal of other assets only. If a loss cannot, or cannot entirely, be credited against any gains from the disposal of other assets, the excess may, as for individuals, be carried forward to the following years.[87] It is credited against the gain that remains after the application of the annual exemption in a following year.[88]

12.2.2.2. Investments in the Units of UK-Resident UCITS

Any income from the underlying investments of resident UCITS is that of the UCITS. The income from the underlying investments, however, has to be distributed by a resident UCITS before the end of a distribution period. Any capital gains from the disposal of the underlying investments, as mentioned earlier for individuals, may not be distributed to the unitholders. The capital gains therefore are not realized by corporate unitholders until disposal of the units in the UCITS.

The income from the underlying investments is received by UK corporate unitholders in the same year. It is taxable in the hands of UK corporate unitholders if it qualifies as business income or annual payments. The part of the income that is not related to qualifying distributions needs to be grossed up with one-ninth of the amount. It is considered to be an annual payment that has been received by a corporate unitholder after deduction of income tax at a rate of 10% (2009).[89] The deemed deduction of income tax may be credited against the corporate income tax liability of the company. The part that cannot be credited is refunded.[90]

If a resident UCITS satisfies the qualifying investment test, the distributed income is considered to be yearly interest. In that case, none of the income needs to be grossed up. No tax is deducted at the time of distribution where yearly interest is paid to a company, including exempt companies such as pension funds and charities.[91]

---

86. Section 53 Taxation of Chargeable Gains Act.
87. Section 2(2)(b) Taxation of Chargeable Gains Act.
88. Section 3(5)(b) Taxation of Chargeable Gains Act.
89. Section 48(2) The Authorised Investment Funds (Tax) Regulations 2006.
90. L. Shirley, 'Authorised Unit Trusts and OEICs', in *Tolley's Taxation of Collective Investment*, ed. S. Newcombe et al. (London: LexisNexis Tolley, 2003), 38.
91. Sections 26(4)(a) and 47(2) The Authorised Investment Funds (Tax) Regulations 2006.

Exemptions

The exemption for qualifying distributions applies only to the part of the distributed income that is related to qualifying distributions, because the other part is considered to be an annual payment instead of a dividend paid by a UK-resident company.[92] The part of the distributed income that is considered to be an annual payment is determined by way of the following formula:[93]

U = (A * C)/D

where *U* is the part of the distribution that is considered to be an annual payment.
A is the amount of the dividend distribution.
C stands for such amount of the income available for distribution that does not derive from franked investment income, as reduced by an amount equal to the corporate income tax liability in respect to the income available for distribution. It concerns the corporate income tax liability that remains after crediting of any foreign tax credits.
D is the amount of the gross income, as reduced by an amount equal to the corporate income tax liability in respect to the income available for distribution. It concerns the corporate income tax liability that remains after crediting of any foreign tax credits.

Example 12.12

A UK-resident UCITS derives the following from its investments:

(1) UK dividends of EUR 2,500,000
(2) Overseas dividends of EUR 2,500,000
(3) UK interest of EUR 2,500,000
(4) Overseas interest of EUR 2,500,000

The overseas income has been subject to withholding tax of EUR 250,000. The corporate income tax liability of the UCITS that remains after the crediting of foreign tax credit is EUR 500,000. The UK-resident UCITS distributes an amount of EUR 6,750,000 to the unitholders. A UK corporate unitholder derives from the units in that UK-resident UCITS a dividend of EUR 675. The part of the dividend that is taxable as an annual payment and needs to be grossed up with one-ninth is as follows: U = (A * C)/D = (EUR 6,750,000* [EUR 10,000,000 –/– EUR 2,500,000 –/– EUR 500,000])/(EUR 10,000,000 –/– EUR 500,000) = EUR 4,973,684, or 73.7% of the distribution. The other part of the distribution remains exempt because it is considered to be a qualifying distribution.

---

92. Section 48(2) The Authorised Investment Funds (Tax) Regulations 2006.
93. Section 49 The Authorised Investment Funds (Tax) Regulations 2006.

The exemption for qualifying distributions does not apply if a resident UCITS satisfies the qualifying investment test. In that case the distributed income is considered to be yearly interest.

Disposal of Units in UK-Resident UCITS

A capital gain from the disposal of units in a resident UCITS is taxable either as business income or a chargeable gain.

Exemptions

No exemptions are available where the capital gain is considered to be business income. The indexation allowance applies if a capital gain from the disposal of the units in resident UCITS qualifies as a chargeable gain.

Losses

A loss from the disposal of units in resident UCITS, like a direct investment, may be set off against other profits, income, or chargeable gains of the same financial year if the units qualified as business assets. If the loss cannot, or cannot entirely, be set off, the excess may be carried back or forward under the same conditions as for a direct investment.

Where the units in a resident UCITS do not qualify as business assets, the loss, like a direct investment, may be set off against any gains from the disposal of assets. If the loss cannot, or cannot entirely, be set off against gains, the excess may likewise be carried forward to the following years.

12.2.2.3. Investments in the Units of UCITS Residing in Austria, Germany, or the Netherlands

As discussed for individuals in Section 12.2.1.3, the characteristics of non-resident UCITS under the civil law of the UCITS country determines whether the income of the underlying investments is that of the UCITS or the UK unitholders.

Tax Opaque Non-resident UCITS

As discussed for individuals in Section 12.2.1.3, the income from the underlying investments of tax opaque non-resident UCITS, like Netherlands-resident UCITS of the corporate type, is considered to be that of the UCITS.

The income from the underlying investments of tax opaque non-resident UCITS is considered to be received by UK corporate unitholders at distribution or disposal of the units in the UCITS, whichever is earlier. If the income from the underlying investments of a resident UCITS is distributed, it is taxable as business income or a profit or gain from foreign possessions.

The capital gains from the disposal of the underlying investments are also received by UK corporate unitholders at distribution or disposal of the units in the UCITS, whichever is earlier. When the income from the underlying investments or the capital gains from their disposal are accumulated, the income tax liability is deferred until the disposal of the units in the UCITS.

Exemptions

The exemption for qualifying distributions, unlike for an investment in the units of resident UCITS, does not apply to the part of the distribution that is related to qualifying distributions. The distributed income is fully considered to be a non-qualifying distribution because it is paid by a non-resident company. This seems to infringe on the free movement of capital as laid down in Articles 56 and 58 of the EC Treaty and Article 40 of the EEA Treaty. Domestic dividends are subject to a more favourable tax treatment than foreign dividends. The performance of an investment in the shares of non-resident companies is, as for individuals, less than that in the shares of a resident UCITS because any dividends on these shares are not exempt from UK corporate income tax.[94]

Transparent Non-resident UCITS

As discussed in Section 12.2.1.3, the income from the underlying investments of Austrian-resident UCITS, German-resident UCITS, and Netherlands-resident UCITS of the contractual type is considered to be that of the UK unitholders.

The income from the underlying investments of transparent non-resident UCITS is, unlike that of resident UCITS, considered to be received by UK corporate unitholders at the time of its arising. The same applies to the capital gains from the disposal of investments. The income and capital gains are taxable if they qualify as business income, interest, annuities and other annual payments and discounts, profit or gain from foreign possessions, or chargeable gain.

Exemptions

The exemption for qualifying distributions is fully applicable, as for any qualified distributions that are derived by way of a transparent non-resident UCITS, are considered to be paid out directly to a UK corporate unitholder.

94. It should be noted that at the time of writing, the UK tax authorities are in the consultation process for issuing new draft tax legislation for the taxation of foreign profits. The current draft legislation suggests that an overseas dividend will be exempt from tax if it falls within any of one of five 'exempt clauses'. These are dividend received in respect to companies controlled (a defined term), dividends received in respect to less than 10% holdings (i.e., portfolio holdings), dividends not designed to reduce tax, dividends paid in respect of non-redeemable ordinary shares, and dividends accounted for as loan relationships.

Furthermore, the indexation allowance applies where the gains are considered to be a chargeable gain.

Losses

A loss from the disposal of one of the underlying investments of a transparent non-resident UCITS, like a direct investment, may be set off against other profits, income, or chargeable gains of the same financial year if the investment qualified as business assets. If the loss cannot, or cannot entirely, be set off, the excess may be carried back or forward under the same conditions as for a direct investment.

Where the investment did not qualify as business assets, the loss may, like a direct investment, be set off against any gains from the disposal of assets. If the loss cannot, or cannot entirely, be set off against gains, the excess may likewise be carried forward to the following years.

Estimation of Income

If the amount, nature, and source of the income from the underlying investments of transparent non-resident UCITS are not communicated, or are not communicated properly, to the unitholders, it is estimated. This generally results in more severe taxation.

Disposal of Units in Tax Opaque Non-resident UCITS

The capital gains from the disposal of units in a tax opaque non-resident UCITS are taxable either as business income or a chargeable gain. The tax regulations for offshore funds affect corporate unitholders for the indexation allowance that is available under the Taxation of Chargeable Gains Act.[95]

Exemptions

The indexation allowance applies to a gain from the disposal of units in tax opaque non-resident UCITS if the latter was certified as a reporting fund during the entire period of ownership and the units of the UCITS were not part of the business assets of the corporate unitholder. In that case the capital gain is reduced with the indexation allowance.

Losses

A loss from the disposal of units in resident UCITS may, like a direct investment, be set off against other profits, income or chargeable gains of the same financial year if the units qualified as business assets. If the loss cannot, or cannot entirely, be

95. Section 37(1) Taxation of Chargeable Gains Act.

set off, the excess may be carried back or forward under the same conditions as for a direct investment.

Where the units in a resident UCITS did not qualify as business assets, the loss may, like a direct investment, be set off against any gains from the disposal of assets. If the loss cannot, or cannot entirely, be set off against gains, the excess may likewise be carried forward to the following years.

Disposal of the Units in Transparent Non-resident UCITS

As discussed for individuals in Section 12.2.1.3, the capital gains from the disposal of the units in a transparent non-resident UCITS do not result in a chargeable gain for capital gains tax. The UCITS is, after all, transparent.

12.2.3. Crediting of Foreign Withholding Tax

12.2.3.1. Investing Directly in Securities and Other Financial Instruments

Cross-border investments in securities and other financial instruments may result in international double taxation for the same reasons as discussed in Section 9.2.3.1 for Austria.

The United Kingdom, however, has regulations to prevent international double taxation.

Tax Treaties

Most UK tax treaties prevent double taxation of dividends and interest by allocating the right to tax to both Contracting States. Not only the state in whose jurisdiction the beneficiary of the dividend and interest resides (residence state) but also the state in whose jurisdiction the paying company or the debtor resides (the source state) may tax these items of income. The taxation in the source state, however, is restricted to the percentage agreed on in the applicable tax treaty. The percentages agreed on in the UK tax treaties can be found in the Tables 3.13 and 3.14 of Chapter 3.

The tax withheld by the source state on the dividend or interest may be credited against the beneficiary's tax liability in the residence state (foreign tax credit). The foreign tax credit cannot, however, exceed the amount of tax that could have been withheld by the source state in accordance with the applicable tax treaty.

Some UK tax treaties provide for a foreign tax credit that is higher than the foreign withholding tax actually levied. These are mostly tax treaties concluded with developing countries or countries such as Argentina or Mexico that are not as developed as the United Kingdom.[96] Under these treaties a resident taxpayer may

96. Argentina, Bulgaria, Croatia, Cyprus, Egypt, Ghana, India, Ivory Coast, Kenya, Macedonia, Malaysia, Malta, Mauritius, Mexico, Mongolia, Morocco, Nigeria, Pakistan, Sri Lanka, Thailand, Tunisia, Turkey, Vietnam, and Zambia.

credit the amount of withholding tax that would have been levied by the source state if the income or capital gain had been taxed in accordance with the general tax rules (tax sparing credit). A tax sparing credit relates to situations in which the taxation of income in the source state, in accordance with a tax incentive, has been omitted or reduced. However, whether a resident taxpayer can actually benefit from a tax sparing credit for portfolio income depends on the source state's domestic law because tax incentives are often limited to business income or certain kinds of (business) activities. Furthermore, even where a resident taxpayer may benefit from a tax sparing credit, it is sometimes limited in time. The tax sparing credit provided for in the tax treaty with India is, for example, available only for a period of 10 years after the exemption or reduction of Indian tax was first granted.[97]

To avoid double taxation, the right to tax capital gains and other portfolio income is allocated exclusively by most of the UK tax treaties to the residence state of the alienator and the recipient, respectively. These items of income thus remain exempt from tax in the source state.

A number of tax treaties, however, allocate the right to tax capital gains and other portfolio income to both states. To avoid double taxation, the tax withheld by the source state may be credited against the tax liability of the alienator or beneficiary in the residence state (foreign tax credit).

Unilateral Rules

Any foreign withholding tax that has been levied on dividends, interest, capital gains, or other portfolio income in the absence of a tax treaty, or although a tax treaty is present it does not cover certain taxes, does not apply to certain taxpayers or does not cover the taxation of certain items of income may, under certain circumstances, be credited against a UK-resident investor's (corporate) income tax or capital gain tax liability (unilateral relief). Unilateral relief is not granted when the foreign tax levied does not correspond to UK (corporate) income tax or capital gain tax. The latter is not the case for taxes on income levied by a province, state, or other part of a country.[98]

Ordinary Tax Credit

Notwithstanding the earlier discussion, the United Kingdom under no circumstances grants a foreign tax credit for more than the UK (corporate) income tax or capital gain tax on the foreign income or the foreign capital gain. This is calculated as the difference between the amounts of income tax that would be borne by the individual for the year (1) if the individual were charged to tax on total income or chargeable gains (before foreign tax relief) for the year and (2) if the individual were charged to tax on the same income or chargeable gains excluding

97. Article 24(5) Tax Treaty between India and the United Kingdom.
98. Section 790(12) Income and Corporation Taxes Act and s. 277(1) Taxation on Chargeable Gains Act.

the foreign income or foreign capital gain (ordinary tax credit).[99] The ordinary tax credit is determined on a per-item basis.[100] Where an individual has more than one item of foreign income, the ordinary tax credit for the first item of foreign income is calculated as mentioned above. For the calculation of the ordinary tax credit for the second item, the amount of the total income mentioned under (1) has to be reduced by the amount of the first item that has already been taken into account. And so on for any third or subsequent item of foreign income. To obtain the highest ordinary tax credit, an individual should generally start with the item that has borne the highest rate of foreign tax.[101]

12.2.3.2. Investment in the Units of UK-Resident UCITS

The income from the investments of a UK-resident UCITS is considered to be that of the UCITS. Any of the withholding taxes levied at source of income is thus considered to be deducted for the account of the UCITS as well. The foreign withholding tax may therefore not be credited by the UK unitholders.

12.2.3.3. Investments in the Units of UCITS Residing in Austria, Germany, and the Netherlands

As discussed in Section 12.2.1.3, the characteristics of non-resident UCITS under the civil law of the UCITS country determine whether the income of the underlying investments is that of the UCITS or the UK unitholders, and thus for whose account the foreign withholding tax has been deducted at source.

Tax Opaque Non-resident UCITS

The income from the underlying investments of opaque non-resident UCITS, such as Netherlands-resident UCITS of the corporate type, is, like that of a UK-resident UCITS, considered to be that of the UCITS. Any of the withholding tax levied at source of income is likewise considered to be levied for the account of these non-resident UCITS. The foreign withholding tax therefore cannot be credited by UK unitholders.

Transparent Non-resident UCITS

The crediting of foreign withholding taxes takes place differently for transparent non-resident UCITS. UK tax treaties and unilateral rules are considered to apply as if the income from the underlying investments of Austrian-resident UCITS, German-resident UCITS, and Netherlands-resident UCITS of the contractual type is derived

99. Section 796(1) Income and Corporation Taxes Act and s. 277(1) Taxation on Chargeable Gains Act.
100. Section 796(2) Income and Corporation Taxes Act and s. 277(1) Taxation on Chargeable Gains Act.
101. M. Finney, *UK Taxation for Students: a Simplified Approach* (London: Spiramus, 2005), 130.

directly by UK unitholders. The tax withheld at source on the taxable income is, under the same conditions as discussed for a direct investment in Section 12.2.3.1, creditable on the basis of the UK tax treaties and unilateral rules (foreign tax credit).

Example 12.13

An Austrian-resident UCITS receives an interest payment of GBP 100,000, which is paid by a Brazilian resident corporation. The income is considered by Brazil to be that of the unitholders. The United Kingdom has not concluded a tax treaty with Brazil, which levies, for example, a withholding tax of 25% on the interest. The withholding tax per unit is assumed to be GBP 25. The foreign tax credit is the lower of the foreign withholding tax levied and the ordinary tax credit. The latter depends on the tax liability of the unitholder. In the absence of any deductible expenses or creditable losses, the ordinary tax credit is limited for individual unitholders to GBP 10, GBP 20, or GBP 25, whereas in the case of corporate unitholders it varies from GBP 20 to a maximum of GBP 25.

The amount of the foreign tax credit available for unitholders of transparent non-resident UCITS may exceed the amount of the foreign tax credit that is available for UK-resident UCITS because the latter is subject to corporate income tax at a reduced tax rate.

Relevant Information

The unitholders have to be informed about the amount of withholding tax that has been levied per source state and per item. They need this information to file a tax return or a request for the refund of the part of withholding tax that is not levied in accordance with a tax treaty.

Withholding Tax Charged by the UCITS Country at the Time of Distribution

Non-resident UCITS Considered a Resident for the Purposes of a Tax Treaty

The UK has not adopted any unilateral rules on the crediting of the foreign withholding tax charged by the UCITS country. According to the UK tax treaties the tax withheld at the time of distribution may be credited by the beneficiary, the unitholder, but only if the distribution is paid by a resident of the UCITS country and is considered to be a dividend.

Non-resident UCITS Not Considered a Resident for the Purposes of a Tax Treaty

If a distribution is not paid by a UCITS that is considered a resident for the purposes of a tax treaty, the United Kingdom, as the residence state of the beneficiary, is not obliged to avoid double taxation by way of an exemption or a tax credit. On the basis of the clause on other income, the right to tax is generally allocated exclusively to the residence state of the unitholder. As discussed in Section 2.4.2, states have different views on the meaning of a resident for the purposes of a tax treaty.

A classification conflict arises in the case that the UCITS country considers the UCITS to be a resident for thc purposes of the applicable tax treaty and withholds tax at the time of distribution, whereas the United Kingdom does not consider the UCITS to be such resident and does not avoid double taxation by way of a tax credit.

12.3. CONCLUSION

12.3.1. Income Tax Liability and Capital Gains Tax Liability

In the United Kingdom, the income tax liability and capital gains tax liability of an investment in the units of a UCITS residing in Austria, Germany, or the Netherlands differs from that in the units of a UK-resident UCITS. The income tax liability is affected by differences in respect to the time that any of the income and the proceeds from disposal are received by UK individual unitholders and the nature and source of the income.

12.3.2. Time of Receipt of Income

The income from the underlying investment of UK-resident UCITS is received by UK individual unitholders by way of distribution in the same distribution period that the income was originally received by the UCITS. The income of Austrian-resident UCITS, German-resident UCITS, Netherlands-resident UCITS of the contractual type and is considered to be received by UK individual unitholders at the time it arises. The time of receipt of the income of these UCITS thus does not differ much from that of UK-resident UCITS. The income of Netherlands-resident (FII) UCITS of the corporate type, however, is received at the earlier of a distribution and the disposal of the units in the UCITS. In accumulation, the income of Netherlands-resident (EII) UCITS of the corporate type is not received by UK individual unitholders until the disposal of the units in the UCITS. The income tax liability for the income is likewise deferred.

The capital gain realized by the disposal of investments of UK-resident UCITS is received by UK individual unitholders at the earlier of a distribution and the disposal of the units in the UCITS. The same applies to the proceeds of Netherlands UCITS of the corporate type. The proceeds from the disposal of investments of Austrian-resident UCITS, German-resident UCITS, and Netherlands-resident UCITS of the contractual type, however, are considered to be received by UK individual unitholders at the time they arise. The income tax liability for the capital gain from the disposal of the underlying investments, unlike an investment in the units of a UK-resident UCITS, cannot be deferred until the disposal of the units in the UCITS. The UK national tax legislation does not provide the same treatment.

12.3.3. Nature and Source of Income

Any distributed income from the underlying investments of UK-resident UCITS is considered to be a qualifying distribution. Therefore, it needs to be grossed up with one-ninth of the amount of the distribution, whereas UK individual unitholders are granted a dividend tax credit of one-ninth of the amount of the distribution. Only the part of the income from the underlying investments of Austrian-resident UCITS, German-resident UCITS, and Netherlands-resident UCITS of the contractual type that is related to qualifying distributions is considered to be such a distribution. None of the distributed income of Netherlands-resident UCITS of the corporate type is considered to be a qualifying distribution.

The capital gain from the disposal of units in UK-resident UCITS is subject to a special tax rate for capital gains. The special tax rate is also available for capital gains realized by the disposal of investments of tax transparent non-resident UCITS. In the case of tax opaque non-resident UCITS, the application of the special tax rate is limited to units in tax opaque non-resident UCITS that were certified as reporting offshore fund during the entire period of ownership. Otherwise, they are not available because the capital gain from the disposal of units in a tax opaque UCITS is in that case taxable with income tax as offshore income gain.

12.3.4. Corporate Income Tax Liability

The corporate income tax liability of an investment in the units of a UCITS residing in Austria, Germany, or the Netherlands differs from that in the units of a UK-resident UCITS. It is affected by differences with respect to the time that any of the income and capital gains from the disposal of the underlying investments are received by UK individual unitholders and the nature and source of the income.

12.3.5. Time of Receipt of Income

The differences regarding the time that the income from the underlying investments of UK-resident UCITS, tax opaque non-resident UCITS, and transparent non-resident UCITS is considered to be received by corporate unitholders does not differ from individuals. The same applies for the proceeds from the disposal of investments.

12.3.6. Nature and Source of Income

Any distributed income from the underlying investments of UK-resident UCITS is considered to be a qualifying distribution. It therefore needs to be grossed up with one-ninth of the amount of the distribution; UK individual unitholders are granted a dividend tax credit of one-ninth of the amount of the distribution. Only the part of the income from the underlying investments of Austrian-resident UCITS, German-resident UCITS, and Netherlands-resident UCITS of the contractual type that is related to qualifying distributions is considered to be such a distribution. None of the distributed income of Netherlands-resident UCITS of the corporate type is considered to be a qualifying distribution.

12.3.7. Crediting of Foreign Withholding Tax Levied by a Source State

The withholding tax levied at source on income from the underlying investments of UK-resident UCITS may not be credited by UK unitholders against their (corporate) income tax liability or capital gain tax liability because it is considered to be levied for the account of the UCITS. The same applies for tax opaque non-resident UCITS. The withholding levied at source on income from the underlying investments of transparent non-resident UCITS, however, may be credited by UK unitholders because it is considered to be levied for the account of the unitholders. The UK tax legislation does not take into account whether the foreign withholding tax levied at source is creditable by non-resident UCITS or whether any relief for that tax is, as is the case for UK-resident UCITS, granted to the non-resident UCITS by the UCITS country.

12.3.8. Crediting of Foreign Withholding Tax Levied by UCITS Country

The withholding tax levied by the UCITS country at the time of distribution results in a tax disadvantage if it cannot be credited against the investor's tax liability under the applicable tax treaty. A tax disadvantage may also arise in the case in which the withholding tax cannot entirely be credited by the UK unitholder. The excess is, in contrast to the withholding tax levied by the United Kingdom at the time of an interest distribution, not refunded. Nor is the withholding tax levied by the UCITS country, as is the case for the UK withholding tax, refunded to UK exempt companies.

12.3.9. Relevant Information

Transparent non-resident UCITS, unlike UK-resident UCITS, have to provide UK unitholders with information about the amount, nature, and source of the income from the underlying investments that is relevant for the (corporate) income tax liability and capital gains tax liability of these unitholders. This may hinder UK unitholders to invest freely in the units of non-resident UCITS. They run the risk for more severe taxation if a non-resident UCITS does not communicate the information; for example, if because of its listing it is not aware of any UK unitholders or it is simply too costly to communicate this for a few UK unitholders. Although the unitholders of non-resident UCITS may provide proof that the amount of the accumulated income is less than the amount of the estimated income, this will be a difficult task for most non-professional investors. Hence, for most UK unitholders the units in the majority of non-resident UCITS are not available without the risk for more severe taxation.

Chapter 13

Comparison of Taxation in the Unitholder Country of Income Derived by Way of Austrian-, German-, Netherlands-, and UK-Resident UCITS

Transparency is not favoured by the countries studied to make sure that the tax liability of income derived by way of undertakings for collective investment in transferable securities (UCITS) in the unitholder country does not differ from that of a direct investment. It is used by a limited number of countries, Austria, and the Netherlands. Nonetheless, transparency is a quite efficient instrument. It does not only establish that income derived by way of UCITS, like a direct investment, is that of the unitholders but also establishes that income is likewise considered to be received at the time of arising.

An inconvenience of transparency is that the underlying investments are not only considered to be disposed of by their sale or redemption, but also each time that these UCITS issue units. After the issuing of units, the underlying investments are shared by more unitholders than before. A part of the share in the underlying investments is thus disposed by the existing unitholders to the new unitholders. Hence, a UCITS needs to inform the unitholders about the part of the underlying investments that is disposed for each issue date.

This inconvenience may be the reason why Austria does not use transparency for capital gains realized by the disposal of the underlying investments. By accumulation, these capital gains are not considered to be received by the unitholders until they are actually distributed or realized by the disposal of the units in the UCITS.

Semi-transparency is favoured by most of the countries studied as an alternative to transparency. In these countries, the income from the investments is that of the UCITS and not of the unitholders. For that reason, a fiction establishes that the income is considered to be distributed to the unitholders at a certain time, for example, the end of the financial year. Without that fiction, the income is not taxable in the hands of the unitholder until it is distributed or realized by the disposal of the units in the UCITS.

Unlike transparency, it does not establish that the nature and source of the income remains the same. This requires additional measures. The necessity of additional measures depends on the domestic laws of the countries studied. The more special tax rates or exemptions there are for certain items of income, the more additional measures are needed. Otherwise, income derived by way of UCITS may be subject to more taxation (or less taxation, as the case may be) than a direct investment.

One of the countries studied, the Netherlands, requires some resident UCITS to distribute the income from the underlying investments within eight months after the end of the financial year. The distribution makes sure that the income is taxable in the hands of corporate unitholders, although as dividend from a resident company. The Netherlands has failed to make sure that the source and nature of the income remains the same, but then the Corporate Tax Act does not distinguish between dividends, interest, capital gains, and other portfolio income.

The taxation of income derived by way of resident and non-resident UCITS is not always the same in the countries studied. Some of the countries studied, the Netherlands and the United Kingdom, have failed to introduce measures that would have established such. As a result, the taxation of income derived by way of non-resident UCITS depends on the legal characteristics of UCITS under the civil law of the UCITS country.

In the Netherlands, the legal characteristics of the UCITS are not taken into account in the case of non-resident UCITS that are not subject to corporate income tax and the exemption from corporate income tax does not depend on the distribution of income from the underlying investments on an annual basis. Corporate unitholders are required to value the units of these UCITS at fair market value so that any income is considered to be derived by the unitholders at the time of arising, although as a capital gain.

Transparency is also used in some cases to establish that the tax treaties and unilateral rules of the countries studied apply as if the unitholders had invested directly. In other cases the countries studied have failed to do so. In these cases the foreign tax withheld at source may not be credited by the unitholders.

Only one of the countries studied, Germany, has ensured that tax withheld by the UCITS country at the time of distribution can be set off against the tax liability of unitholders. The other countries have not introduced measures so that the crediting of the tax withheld by the UCITS country depends on the applicable tax treaty, which may give different results.

13.1. INTRODUCTION

In this chapter follows a review and assessment of the instruments used by the countries studied to ensure that the income derived by way of UCITS is taxed in the hands of the unitholders as if they had invested directly. In Section 13.2, the tax liability of income derived by way of resident and non-resident UCITS is examined. Section 13.3 evaluates the crediting of the tax withheld at source, and that of the tax withheld at the time of distribution is examined in Section 13.4.

13.2. COMPARISON OF THE TAX LIABILITY OF INCOME DERIVED BY WAY OF UCITS

As shown in Table 13.1 the instruments used by Austria, Germany, the Netherlands, and the United Kingdom to establish that the tax liability of taxpayers for income derived by way of UCITS does not differ from a direct investment do not generate the same results for resident and non-resident UCITS. The taxation of unitholders residing in the countries studied for income derived by way of UCITS therefore differs for Austrian-, German-, Netherlands-, and UK-resident UCITS. Moreover, it is affected by the accumulation of income.

Table 13.1 A Comparison of the Tax Liability of Income Derived by Way of UCITS

UCITS Country	*Resident UCITS*	*Non-resident UCITS*	*Consequences of the Taxation in Unitholder Country*
Austria	Transparency although the income is not considered to be derived until it is distributed, the units in the UCITS are disposed or 4 months after the end of the year, whichever is earlier. Accumulated capital gains are not considered to be realized by corporate	Transparency although the income is not considered to be derived until it is distributed, the units in the UCITS are disposed or 4 months after the end of the year, whichever is earlier. Accumulated capital gains are not considered to be realized by corporate	No uniform taxation in the unitholder country for income derived by way of resident and non-resident UCITS in case a non-resident UCITS has not informed the Austrian tax authorities and unitholders about the amount, nature, and source of the income.

Table 13.1 (cont'd)

UCITS Country	*Resident UCITS*	*Non-resident UCITS*	*Consequences of the Taxation in Unitholder Country*
	unitholders until disposal of units in UCITS.	unitholders until disposal of units in UCITS. The amount of the income is estimated where the UCITS has not informed or not properly informed the Austrian tax authorities and unitholders about the amount, nature, and source of the income.	By the selection of UCITS the promise that a UCITS informs the tax authorities and the unitholders about the amount, nature, and source of the income derived by way of that UCITS is of importance.
Germany	Semi-transparency although the income is not considered to be derived until it is distributed or the units in the UCITS are disposed or the end of the year, whichever is earlier. An exception applies to accumulated capital gains. The amount of the income is estimated where the UCITS has not informed or not properly informed the	Semi-transparency although the income is not considered to be derived until it is distributed or the units in the UCITS are disposed or the end of the year, whichever is earlier. An exception applies to accumulated capital gains. The amount of the income is estimated where the UCITS has not informed or not properly informed the German tax	By the selection of UCITS the promise that a UCITS informs the tax authorities and the unitholders about the amount, nature, and source of the income derived by way of that UCITS is of importance.

Table 13.1 (cont'd)

UCITS Country	*Resident UCITS*	*Non-resident UCITS*	*Consequences of the Taxation in Unitholder Country*
	German tax authorities and unitholders about the amount, nature, and source of the income.	authorities and unitholders about the amount, nature, and source of the income.	
Netherlands	Transparency, semi-transparency, or by way of an annual distribution, although capital gains may be accumulated.	Semi-transparency or time of distribution or time of disposal of units in UCITS, whichever is earlier. The amount of income derived by way of transparent non-resident UCITS is estimated where the UCITS has not informed the unitholders about thc amount of the income.	No uniform taxation in the unitholder country for income derived by way of resident and non-resident UCITS and between non-resident UCITS. By the selection of UCITS the taxation in the residence state of the UCITS is of importance.
United Kingdom	Semi-transparency although capital gains are accumulated.	Transparency; semi-transparency; or time of distribution or time of disposal of units in UCITS, whichever is earlier. The amount of income derived by way of transparent	No uniform taxation in the unitholder country for income derived by way of resident and non-resident UCITS and between non-resident UCITS By the selection of UCITS the characteristics of

Table 13.1 (cont'd)

UCITS Country	*Resident UCITS*	*Non-resident UCITS*	*Consequences of the Taxation in Unitholder Country*
		non-resident UCITS is estimated where the UCITS has not informed the unitholders about the amount of the income.	an UCITS under the civil law of the UCITS is of importance.

13.2.1. Availability of Instruments to Establish that Income Derived by Way of UCITS Is Taxed at the Same Time and for the Same Amount as a Direct Investment

Transparency

Austria, and, for Netherlands-resident (TII) UCITS, the Netherlands consider income derived by way of UCITS to be that of the unitholders. Nevertheless, they apply different rules in respect of the time that the income is considered to be received by the unitholders. Like in the case of a direct investment, the income is considered to be received by Dutch unitholders at the time of arising, whereas Austrian unitholders, unlike in the case of a direct investment, are considered to have received the income at the time of distribution, the disposal of the units in the UCITS, or 4 months after the end of the financial year, whichever is earlier. In either case the tax liability of the unitholders is not deferred compared to a direct investment by the accumulation of the income. An exception to the rule is the accumulation of capital gains, but only for Austrian corporate unitholders for whom the units in the UCITS are part of their business assets.

Example 13.1

W, a corporate unitholder residing in Austria, holds units in X, an Austrian-resident UCITS. The units in X are part of W's business assets. X is paid a dividend of EUR 100,000 by Y, a company resident in Z. Shortly after the dividend payment, the shares of Y are disposed by X. By the disposal of the shares, X realizes a capital gain of EUR 500,000. The dividend and capital gain are in accordance with the fund rules accumulated by X. The dividend is, nevertheless, considered to be derived by W 4 months after the end of the financial year of the UCITS.

As dividend, interest, capital gains, and other portfolio income derived by way of UCITS is considered to be that of the unitholders, the nature, and source of these income types remain intact. This is different in Austria for income from speculative transactions that is derived by way of UCITS. Instead of the part of the capital gains that is related to disposals of investments within a year after the purchase, it is simply determined as one-fifth of the capital gains from investments other than bonds and debentures. For any other income, the nature and source remain intact so that any exemptions and special tax rates are applied as if the unitholders had invested directly.

Example 13.2

X in Example 13.1 is considered to have derived a dividend paid by a company residing in Z.

To tax dividend, interest, capital gains, and other portfolio income derived by way of UCITS as if they had invested directly, the Austrian tax authorities and unitholders have to be informed by UCITS about the amount, nature, and source of the income from the underlying investments. Austrian-resident UCITS are required to do so.

Semi-Transparency

Dividend, interest, capital gains, and other portfolio income that are derived through UCITS is in Germany, the Netherlands except for Netherlands-resident (TII) UCITS, and the United Kingdom considered to be that of the UCITS. The income is not considered to be received by the unitholders until it is distributed or realized by the disposal of the units of the UCITS. All three countries therefore provide for fictions to establish that the tax liability for portfolio income derived by way of UCITS is not deferred by way of accumulation by UCITS. They do, however, apply different rules in respect to the time that the income is considered to be distributed to the unitholders. Germany applies a fiction that the income is considered to be distributed to the unitholders at the time that it is distributed, it is realized by the disposal of units in the UCITS, or the end of the financial year, whichever is earlier. In the Netherlands and the United Kingdom, the income is considered to be distributed to the unitholders at the time of arising and the end of the distribution period, respectively. The income that is in the Netherlands considered to be distributed to the unitholders also includes unrealized capital gains. The application of the Netherlands fiction, however, is restricted to Netherlands-resident (EII) UCITS, although it also applies to individual unitholders of Netherlands-resident (FII) UCITS.

The accumulation of income by UCITS thus does not defer the tax liability of the unitholders. Both Germany and the United Kingdom apply an exception for capital gains. By accumulation of capital gains, the tax liability of the unitholders is deferred until the units in the UCITS are disposed of. In Germany, the deferral of the tax liability is limited to corporate unitholders for whom the units in the UCITS are part of their business assets.[1]

Example 13.3

Some of the units in W, a UCITS residing in Germany, are held by X, a German-resident corporate unitholder for whom the units in W qualify as business assets. W derives a dividend of EUR 100,000 from Y, a Z-resident company. X disposes the shares of Y not long after the dividend payment. X realizes a capital gain of EUR 500,000 by the disposal of the shares. X accumulates the dividend and capital gain in accordance with its fund rules. The dividend is, nonetheless, considered to be derived by X at the end of the financial year of the UCITS.

Any dividend, interest, capital gains, and other portfolio income derived through UCITS is, as mentioned above, considered by Germany, the Netherlands, and the United Kingdom to be that of the UCITS. As a result, the nature and source of dividend, interest, capital gains, and other portfolio income that is derived by UCITS is affected. By distribution to the unitholders, it is considered to be a dividend paid by a company. Germany, however, applies a fiction that the nature and source of the income remains intact if it is related to interest, capital gains, or foreign income for which an exemption applies under a tax treaty. As a result, the unitholders are entitled to the same exemptions and special tax rates as for a direct investment. Furthermore, the exemption for inter-corporate dividends is, like a direct investment, limited to the part of the income derived through UCITS that is related to dividends.

Example 13.4

The dividend that is considered to be derived by W in example 13.4 is considered to be a dividend derived from a Z-resident company.

Contrary to Germany, the Netherlands and the United Kingdom do not provide for any measures to establish that the nature and source of income that is derived by way of UCITS remains intact. As transparency is realized in the Netherlands by way of the requirement that the units in the UCITS are valued at fair market value, the income is considered to be a capital gain. The lost of the nature and source of income derived by way of UCITS, however, does not affect the tax liability of Dutch unitholders compared to a direct investment. Neither the Netherlands Income Tax Act nor the Netherlands Corporate Tax Act provides for any special tax treatment of dividend, interest, capital gains, and other portfolio income. Furthermore, the exemptions for environmental, social-ethical, or cultural

1. The tax liability of other unitholders is not affected as an exemption applies to capital gains.

investments do under conditions also apply to investments that are held by way of resident UCITS.

Example 13.5

W, a corporate unitholder residing in the Netherlands, derives by way of X, a Netherlands-resident (EII) UCITS, a dividend of EUR 100,000. The dividend is paid by Y, a company residing in Z. The shares in Y are not long after the payment of dividend disposed by X. A capital gain of EUR 500,000 is realized by the disposal of the shares. In accordance with the fund rules, the dividend and capital gain are accumulated by X. The dividend, however, is taxable in the hands of W because the units in X have to be valued at fair market value, which includes the dividend paid by Y. Instead of a dividend, W is considered to have derived an unrealized capital gain from a change in value of shares in X.

In the United Kingdom, any distributions by UCITS are considered to be a dividend paid by a company or, in the case of an UK-resident UCITS that satisfies the qualifying investment test at all times during the year, yearly interest. As a result, the tax liability may differ from a direct investment because any exemptions or special tax rates are not applied for dividend, interest, capital gains, and other portfolio income, as if the unitholders had invested directly. An exception on the rule is the exemption for UK inter-corporate dividends, which applies only to the part of the distribution of UK-resident UCITS that is related to UK-source dividends.

Example 13.6

W, a UCITS residing in the United Kingdom, is paid a dividend of EUR 100,000 by X, a company residing in Y. The units in X are disposed after the dividend payment. The disposal of the units results in a capital gain of EUR 500,000. The dividend is distributed by W while the capital gain is accumulated. Nevertheless, the dividend is considered to be paid by W to Z, a UK-resident company, and other unitholders. The dividend derived by Z is considered to be a dividend paid by a UK company.

An Annual Distribution

Dividend, interest, capital gains, and other portfolio income derived by way of UCITS are, as mentioned above, considered to be that of the UCITS. As a result, the income is not considered to be received by the unitholders until it is distributed or realized by the disposal of the units of the UCITS. As mentioned earlier, corporate unitholders of Netherlands-resident (FII) UCITS are not required to value the units of these UCITS at fair market value. Instead, dividend, interest, capital gains, and other portfolio income derived by way of Netherlands-resident (FII) UCITS need to be distributed to the unitholders within 8 months after the end of each financial year. A Netherlands-resident (FII) UCITS may opt to accumulate capital gains. The tax liability for dividend, interest, and other portfolio income cannot be deferred by way of accumulation.

Example 13.7

W, a Netherlands-resident corporation, keeps some of the units in X, a Netherlands-resident (FII) UCITS. A dividend of EUR 100,000 is derived by X from Y, a company residing in Z. Shortly after the dividend payment, X realizes a capital gain of EUR 500,000 by the disposal of the shares in W. X distributes the dividend to the unitholders while the capital gain is accumulated. The distributed dividend is taxable in the hands of Z.

Any income that is distributed by Netherlands-resident (FII) UCITS is considered to be a dividend paid by a Netherlands-resident company. This does not affect the tax liability for dividend, interest, capital gains, and other portfolio income derived by way of these UCITS because these income types are not taxed differently in the Netherlands.

Example 13.8

In Example 13.7, Z is considered to have derived a dividend from a company residing in the Netherlands.

13.2.2. Application Of Instruments to Establish Taxation as If Invested Directly in the Case of Investments in Non-resident UCITS

The taxation of the unitholder for income derived by way of UCITS does not differ for resident and non-resident UCITS in Austria, but only where a non-resident UCITS has properly communicated the amount, nature, and source of the portfolio income that is derived from the underlying investments. Otherwise, the amount of income derived by way of the non-resident UCITS is estimated, whereas none of the exemptions are available to the unitholders. This generally results in more severe taxation. The unitholders may provide proof that the amount of income is less than the estimated amount. Although non-professional unitholders may already have difficulty in obtaining information about the amount of income that is not distributed at the end of the UCITS's financial year, information about the amount of income that is derived by the disposal of the units in a non-resident UCITS is almost impractical to obtain because the majority of German-, Netherlands-, and UK-resident UCITS do not provide for financial reports on a daily basis. Nor is that required under the UCITS Directive. This reduces the number of

German-, Netherlands-, and UK-resident UCITS for non-professional investors to choose from without risking or experiencing more severe taxation.

Example 13.9

W, an individual unitholder residing in Austria, holds units in X, a UK-resident UCITS. The intrinsic value of a unit in X is EUR 1,000 at the beginning of the financial year in January. In May, X is paid a dividend of EUR 100,000, or EUR 10 per unit, by Y, a company resident in Z. The dividend is in accordance with the articles of incorporation accumulated by X. At the end of May, the value of the shares in Y has increased with EUR 200,000 or EUR 20 per unit. The dividend and capital gain is realized by W at the end of May when he disposes the shares in X on the stock exchange. Instead of a dividend of EUR 10 and a capital gain of EUR 20, W is considered to have derived an amount of EUR 40 at the time of disposal because X has not informed the Austrian tax authorities and X about the amount, nature, and source of income that was derived at the time of disposal. W fails to prove that the amount of the dividend and capital gains derived by way of UCITS is less than the estimated amount as X does not provide for a financial report on a monthly basis.

The taxation of unitholders in Germany is equal to that in Austria with the exception that the income derived by way of both resident and non-resident UCITS is estimated in case the amount, nature, and source of income is not communicated, or not communicated properly, to the German tax authorities and unitholders. Nevertheless, it is still an ambivalent measure because Germany does not make it possible for the unitholders to provide proof that the amount of income derived by way of UCITS is less than the estimated amount.

The taxation of the unitholders in the Netherlands and the United Kingdom is, on the other hand, affected by the use of different instruments to establish that the taxation of dividend, interest, capital gains, and other portfolio income derived by way of resident and non-resident UCITS does not differ from a direct investment and the absence of such instruments, respectively. As a result, the time that income derived by way of UCITS is considered to be taxable in the hands of the unitholders differs for resident and non-resident UCITS and between non-resident UCITS. In the United Kingdom, the differences in the taxation of unitholders are increased by a different application of the exemption for inter-corporate dividends for UK-source dividends derived by resident and non-resident UCITS and between non-resident UCITS.

Example 13.10

V, a UK-resident company, keeps units in W, a UCITS residing in the United Kingdom, and X, a UCITS residing in Germany. V and X, both keep shares issued by Y, a company residing in Z. During the year, W and X dispose the units in Y. By accident, they both realize a capital gain of EUR 500,000 by the disposal of the units in Y. The capital gain is accumulated by W and X. Nevertheless, the capital gain that is derived by way of X is considered to be received by V at the time that it arose. The capital gain derived by way of X, however, is not taxable in the hands of V until disposal of the units in W.

13.2.3. Conclusion

The instruments used by Austria, Germany, the Netherlands, and the United Kingdom establish that the tax liability of taxpayers for income derived by way of UCITS is not deferred compared to that of a direct investment. In the Netherlands, the tax liability of taxpayers for capital gains derived by way of UCITS differs from a direct investment. Any change in value of the underlying investments as from the purchase of the units is already taxable in the hands of the unitholders at the time of arising. An exception applies for Netherlands-resident (FII) UCITS. The Netherlands does not provide measures for capital gains derived by way of these UCITS.

By accumulation, the tax liability of capital gains derived by way of UCITS in Austria, Germany, and the United Kingdom, unlike a direct investment, is deferred until the disposal of the units in the UCITS. The deferral of the tax liability, however, provides that the unitholders are taxed only on the part of the capital gains that arose during the period of ownership of the units in the UCITS, whether realized or not. In Austria and Germany, the deferral of the tax liability for capital gains is limited to corporate unitholders for whom the units of UCITS are part of the business assets. It is not necessary for Austria and Germany to provide a similar rule for individual unitholders and corporate unitholders for whom the units in the UCITS do not qualify as business assets as capital gains are for these unitholders exempt from tax.

The taxation of taxpayers in Austria, Germany, the Netherlands, and the United Kingdom varies for income derived by way of resident and non-resident UCITS and between non-resident UCITS. It is affected in Austria and Germany in the case in which a non-resident UCITS has not informed the tax authorities or unitholders about the amount, nature, and source of the income while the taxpayer did not provide proof that the income derived by way of the UCITS in question is less than the estimated amount. In the Netherlands and the United Kingdom, the taxation of the unitholders is affected by the application of different measures to resident and non-resident UCITS and even between non-resident UCITS.

13.3. THE CREDITING OF THE WITHHOLDING TAX CHARGED BY SOURCE STATES ON INCOME DERIVED BY WAY OF UCITS

Austria and Germany have taken measures to establish that the crediting of the withholding tax charged by source states on income derived by way of UCITS does not differ from a direct investment. The measures taken by the United Kingdom, however, generate different results for resident and non-resident UCITS. The Netherlands has not taken measures at the level of the unitholders of resident (EII/FII) UCITS (Table 13.2).

Table 13.2 A Comparison of the Crediting of Withholding Tax Charged by Source States on Income Derived by Way of UCITS

UCITS Country	*Resident UCITS*	*Non-resident UCITS*	*Consequences of the Taxation in Unitholder Country*
Austria	Transparency	Transparency	No notice is taken of the relief provided in the UCITS country.
Germany	Semi-transparency	Semi-transparency	No notice is taken of the relief provided in the UCITS country.
Netherlands	Transparency but not for resident (EII/FII) UCITS	Transparency but not for tax opaque non-resident UCITS.	No notice is taken of the relief provided in the UCITS country.
United Kingdom	None	Transparency but not for tax opaque non-resident UCITS.	No uniform taxation in the unitholder country for income derived by way of resident and non-resident UCITS and between non-resident UCITS.

13.3.1. Availability of Instruments for the Crediting of the Tax Withheld at Source as If Invested Directly

13.3.1.1. Transparency

Dividend, interest, capital gains, and other portfolio income derived by way of UCITS are in Austria and, for Netherlands-resident (TII) UCITS, the Netherlands considered to be that of the unitholders. Any tax withheld at source of income derived by way of these UCITS is therefore considered to be charged for the account of the unitholders too. The application of tax treaties and unilateral rules for the crediting of foreign withholding tax does, thus, not differ from a direct investment. The foreign withholding tax, however, can be set off by unitholders only if they are per source and per item informed about the amount of foreign withholding tax that is charged.

Example 13.11

W, an Austrian-resident individual, derives by way of X, a UK-resident UCITS, a dividend of EUR 100,000. The dividend is paid by Y, a company residing in Z. The latter charges a withholding tax of EUR 10,000 on the dividend. The withholding tax may be credited by W.

Semi-Transparency

As mentioned in Section 13.2, Germany considers dividend, interest, capital gains, and other portfolio income derived by way of UCITS as that of the UCITS. For that reason, the withholding tax charged by source states is considered to be charged for the account of the UCITS too. It can, thus, not be credited by the unitholders. Germany therefore applies a fiction to make it possible for unitholders to apply the German tax treaties and unilateral rules for the crediting of foreign withholding tax as if they had invested directly. For the same reason as mentioned earlier for Austria, it is necessary that unitholders are informed by a UCITS about the amount of foreign withholding tax per source and per item.

Example 13.12

Some of the units in W, a UK-resident UCITS, are held by X. A dividend of EUR 100,000 is paid by Y, a Z-resident company to W. The dividend is subject to a withholding tax of EUR 10,000 in Z. The withholding tax charged by Z, however, can be credited by X under the same conditions as a direct investment.

Absence of Measures to Establish Transparency

Similar to Germany, dividend, interest, capital gains, and other portfolio income derived by way of UCITS is for Netherlands-resident (EII/FII) UCITS in the Netherlands and for UK-resident UCITS in the United Kingdom considered to be that of the UCITS. Contrary to Germany, the Netherlands and the United Kingdom have not provided measures to establish that the crediting of foreign withholding tax charged on income derived by way of UCITS does not differ from a direct investment. Instead, these two countries provide relief for foreign withholding tax at the level of the UCITS (see for a comparison Section 7.3).

Example 13.13

W, a UK-resident company, keeps units in X, a resident UCITS. X is paid a dividend of EUR 100,000 by Y, a Z-resident company. Z has deducted a withholding tax of EUR 10,000 from the dividend. The withholding tax charged by Z cannot be set off against the income tax liability of W.

13.3.2. Application of Instruments to Establish Taxation as If Invested Directly in the Case of Investments in Non-resident UCITS

In addition to the availability of measures to establish that the crediting of the tax withheld does not differ from a direct investment, the taxation of unitholders in the United Kingdom is affected by the application of these measures for income derived by way of resident and non-resident UCITS. The crediting of foreign withholding tax by the unitholders is determined on the basis of the characteristics of a non-resident UCITS under the civil law of the country where the UCITS resides because the crediting is restricted to transparent non-resident UCITS. As a result, the taxation in the unitholder country for income derived by way of UCITS differs for resident and non-resident UCITS and between non-resident UCITS. The same is true in the Netherlands.

Example 13.14

V, a UK-resident company, keeps units in W, a UCITS residing in the United Kingdom, and X, a UCITS residing in Germany. W and X both keep bonds issued by Y, a company residing in Z. Y pays W and X interest of EUR 100,000. Z is required to withhold a tax of EUR 5,000 on the interest paid to W and X. V may credit the withholding tax charged by Z on income derived by way of X only.

13.3.3. Conclusion

The instruments used by Austria, Germany, and for Netherlands-resident (TII) UCITS the Netherlands provide that the crediting of withholding tax charged on income derived by way of UCITS takes place as if the unitholders had invested directly. The Netherlands, except for Netherlands-resident (TII) UCITS, and the

United Kingdom have not provided measures to establish transparency in respect to the crediting of foreign withholding tax.

In the United Kingdom, the crediting of withholding tax charged by source states on dividend, interest, capital gains, and other portfolio income derived by way of UCITS gives different results for resident and non-resident UCITS and between non-resident UCITS. It is affected by the restriction of the crediting of withholding tax charged on income derived by way of UCITS to unitholders of transparent non-resident UCITS.

13.4. THE CREDITING OF THE WITHHOLDING TAX CHARGED BY THE UCITS COUNTRY

Table 13.3 demonstrates that the instruments used by Austria, Germany, the Netherlands, and the United Kingdom to provide relief for withholding tax charged by the UCITS country at the time that income is considered to be derived by the unitholders does not provide the same results for resident and non-resident UCITS. As a result, the taxation of unitholders in the countries studied differs for income derived by way of resident and non-resident UCITS.

Table 13.3 Relief Available at the Level of the Unitholders for Withholding Tax Charged by UCITS Country

UCITS Country	*Resident UCITS*	*Non-resident UCITS*	*Tax Consequences of the Taxation in the Unitholder Country*
Austria	Refundable	Creditable but only for tax opaque non-resident UCITS.	No uniform taxation in the unitholder country for income derived by way of resident and non-resident UCITS.
Germany	Refundable	Creditable	No uniform taxation in the unitholder country for income derived by way of resident and non-resident UCITS.
Netherlands	Refundable	Creditable but only for tax opaque non-resident UCITS.	No uniform taxation in the unitholder country for income derived by way of resident and non-resident UCITS.

Table 13.3 (cont'd)

UCITS Country	*Resident UCITS*	*Non-resident UCITS*	*Tax Consequences of the Taxation in the Unitholder Country*
United Kingdom	Refundable	Creditable but only for tax opaque non-resident UCITS	No uniform taxation in the unitholder country for income derived by way of resident and non-resident UCITS.

13.4.1. Availability of Instruments for Crediting Tax Withheld at Time of Distribution

13.4.1.1. Refund

Each of the countries studied should, in accordance with the tax treaties between the countries studied, provide relief for the withholding tax charged by a UCITS country at the time that dividend, interest, capital gains, and other portfolio income derived by way of UCITS is considered to be distributed to the unitholders. The withholding tax charged on income distributed by resident UCITS is considered to be surtax for the (corporate) income tax liability of the unitholders. The withholding tax can therefore be set off against that tax liability. The non-creditable part of the withholding tax is refunded to the unitholders because it was meant as surtax only.

Example 13.15

Some of the units in W, an Austrian-resident UCITS, are held by X, an individual unitholder residing in Austria. W derives interest of EUR 100,000 on bonds issued by Y, a Z-resident company. The interest payment is in accordance with the fund rules accumulated by W. Nevertheless, the interest is considered to be distributed by W 4 months after the end of its financial year. Austria charges a withholding tax at the time of distribution. Because of costs, W is able to credit only half of the withholding tax. W is paid a refund of the other half.

13.4.2. Application of Instruments for Crediting of Tax Withheld at the Time of Distribution in the Case of Investments in Non-resident UCITS

The taxation in the unitholder country is affected by the application of different methods to provide relief for the tax withheld by itself at the time of distribution or another UCITS country. The application of a refund of the non-creditable part of the withholding tax is determined on the basis of the residence state of the UCITS because the application of the refund is limited to resident UCITS. As a consequence, the taxation of the unitholders in Austria, Germany, the Netherlands, and the United Kingdom varies for income derived by way of resident and non-resident UCITS.

Example 13.16

W, an individual residing in Austria, keeps units in X, a German-resident UCITS. Y, a Z-resident company, derives interest of EUR 100,000 on bonds issued by Y, a company residing in Z. In accordance with the fund rules, the interest is accumulated by W. Nevertheless, the interest is considered to be distributed by W 4 months after the end of its financial year. Germany charges a withholding tax at that time. Because of costs, only half of the German withholding tax can be set off against the income tax liability of W. No refund is available in Austria for the other half.

13.4.3. Conclusion

The taxation in the unitholder country for income derived by way of resident and non-resident UCITS in Austria, Germany, the Netherlands, and the United Kingdom is not uniform. The taxation in the unitholder country is affected by restriction of a refund of the non-creditable part of the withholding tax that is charged by a UCITS country at the time of distribution to resident UCITS.

Chapter 14 discusses the consequences of the differences in the taxation at the level of the unitholders for the cross-border trading in units of UCITS in Austria, Germany, the Netherlands and the United Kingdom.

Chapter 14

Distortions to the Cross-Border Trade in Units of UCITS Caused by Differences in the Taxation in the Unitholder Country

The countries studied have failed to provide a level playing field for trade in units of undertakings for collective investment in transferable securities (UCITS). Investments in non-resident UCITS are subject to more taxation than those in resident UCITS. Investors residing in the countries studied are therefore discouraged from making use of non-resident UCITS. This is different in Austria and Germany only if the UCITS has informed the tax authorities or unitholders about the amount, nature, and source of the income together with the amount of tax withheld at source. Because the UCITS Directive does not require the communication of this information, the number of non-resident UCITS to choose from without experiencing or risking a higher tax burden is likely to be narrowed.

14.1. INTRODUCTION

As shown in Chapters 9–13, taxation in unitholder countries for investments in UCITS residing in Austria, Germany, the Netherlands, and the United Kingdom varies significantly in the countries studied. The cross-border trade in units of UCITS in the countries studied is distorted by these differences in taxation because income derived by way of non-resident UCITS is, compared to income derived by way of resident UCITS, sometimes subject to more severe taxation (tax disadvantage), whereas other times a lesser taxation occurs (tax advantage). The competition among UCITS in the countries studied therefore does not take place under the same conditions.

14.1.1. Tabular Overview

An overview of the distortions is illustrated in the Table 14.1. For Austrian, Dutch, German, and UK unitholders Table 14.1 indicates which tax advantages or disadvantages arise from the differences in taxation in the UCITS country for income derived by way of non-resident UCITS compared to income derived by way of resident UCITS. The table demonstrates that the distortions are connected with the resident state of UCITS.

Table 14.1 Taxation of Income from Underlying Investments of Non-resident UCITS at the Level of the Unitholder

	Tax Liability of the Unitholders	*Relief for the Withholding Tax Charged by Source State*	*Relief for the Withholding Tax Charged by the UCITS Country*
Austrian unitholders UCITS			
German-resident UCITS	0/–[a,b]	0/–[c]	0/–[d,e]
Netherlands-resident (EII) UCITS	0/–[a,b]	0/–[c]	0
Netherlands-resident (FII) UCITS	0/–[a,b]	0/–[c]	0/–[d]
Netherlands-resident (TII) UCITS	0/–[a,b]	0/–[c]	0
UK-resident UCITS	0/–[a,b]	0/–[c]	0
German unitholders UCITS			
Austrian-resident UCITS	0/–[a]	0/–[c]	0
Netherlands-resident (EII) UCITS	0/–[a]	0/–[c]	0
Netherlands-resident (FII) UCITS	0/–[a]	0/–[c]	0/–[d]
Netherlands-resident (TII) UCITS	0/–[a]	0/–[c]	0
UK UCITS	0/–[a]	0/–[c]	0

Table 14.1 (cont'd)

	Tax Liability of the Unitholders	*Relief for the Withholding Tax Charged by Source State*	*Relief for the Withholding Tax Charged by the UCITS Country*
*Netherlands unitholders**			
UCITS			
Austrian-resident UCITS	0[f]/–[g,h]	–	0
German-resident UCITS	0[f]/–[g,h]	–	0/–[d,e]
UK-resident UCITS	0[f]/–[g]/+[i]	0/–[j]	0
UK unitholders			
UCITS			
Austrian-resident UCITS	0/–[a]	+/–[c]	0
German-resident UCITS	0/–[a]	+/–[c]	0/–[d,e]
Netherlands-resident (EII) UCITS	0/–[k,l,m]	0/+[n]/–[o]	0
Netherlands-resident (FII) UCITS	0/–[k,l,m]	0/+[n]/–[o]	0/–[d]
Netherlands-resident (TII) UCITS	0/–[a]	+/–[c]	0

+, Cross-border trading is facilitated as a result of a tax advantage.

0, Cross-border trading is not affected in the absence of a tax advantage or tax disadvantage.

–, Tax disadvantage that hinders cross-border trading.

[a] In case the tax authorities or the unitholders are not informed about the amount, nature, and source of the income.

[b] Where capital gains from the disposal of investments are accumulated but only for corporate unitholders.

[c] If the tax authorities or the unitholder are not informed per source and per item about the amount of tax withheld at source of the taxable income.

[d] Where the withholding tax charged by the UCITS country cannot, or cannot completely, be set off against the tax liability of the unitholder.

Table 14.1 (cont'd)

[e] If the unitholder country does not consider German-resident UCITS to be a person for tax treaty purposes.

[f] Individual unitholders.

[g] For individual unitholders if the UCITS keeps environmental, social-ethical, and cultural investments and does not offer its units in the unitholder country.

[h] Corporate unitholders.

[i] By accumulation of the yields from the underlying investments of the UCITS.

[j] In case the UCITS has satisfied the qualifying investment test at all times during the financial year.

[k] If a UCITS of the corporate type is not certified as a reporting offshore fund.

[l] If a UCITS of the corporate type distributes dividends received from UK-resident companies.

[m] Where a UCITS of the contractual type has not communicated, or has not properly communicated, the amount, nature and source of the income to the unitholders.

[n] In the case of an investment in the units of a UCITS of the contractual type.

[o] If a UCITS of the contractual type has not, per source and per item, informed the unitholders about the amount of tax withheld at source of the taxable income.

* In comparison with a Netherlands-resident (FII) UCITS, as most Netherlands-resident UCITS have opted to be treated as a fiscal investment institution (FII) for tax purposes.

A more detailed discussion about the source of the distortions shown in Table 14.1 above is given in Sections 14.2–14.4.

14.2. MEASURES TO TAX INCOME AT THE SAME TIME AND FOR THE SAME AMOUNT AS A DIRECT INVESTMENT

14.2.1. Introduction

The taxation of income derived by way of resident and non-resident UCITS in the countries studied differs. In some cases, it is affected by differences in the time that income is considered to be derived by the unitholders. In other cases, it is caused by the restriction of certain exemptions to resident UCITS only. Sometimes, it depends on whether or not information on the amount, nature, and source of income is provided to the tax authorities or the unitholders in accordance with the domestic laws of the unitholder state. The taxation of the unitholders in the countries studied does not only distort the conditions of competition for resident and non-resident UCITS but also between resident UCITS.

Investors may be discouraged by the differences in taxation to invest in units of non-resident UCITS. This hinders marketing of units in non-resident UCITS in the countries studied.

Figure 14.1 Investors May Be Discouraged to Make Use of Non-resident UCITS if the Taxation of Income Derived by Way of Non-resident UCITS Is Brought Forward

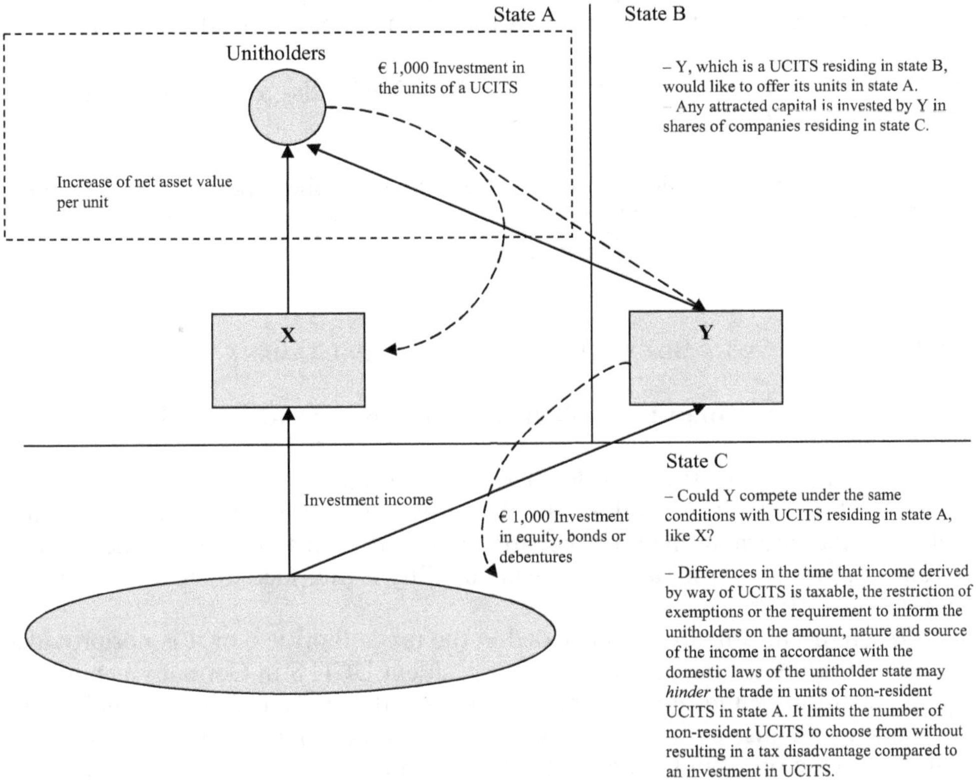

14.2.2. Cross-Border Trading of Units in Austria

14.2.2.1. Austrian Unitholder and German-Resident UCITS

Trading in the units of German-resident UCITS in Austria is hindered by the taxation of the unitholders if the tax authorities and unitholders are not provided, or not provided properly, with information about the amount, nature, and source of the income that is relevant for the (corporate) income tax liability. In that case, the amount of the income is estimated. This generally results in more burdensome taxation. Although the unitholders of non-resident UCITS may provide proof that the amount of the income is less than the amount of the estimated income, this will be a difficult task for most non-professional investors.

Where the tax authorities and the unitholders are probably provided with information about the amount, nature, and source of the income, taxation of the unitholders does not hinder German-resident UCITS by attracting capital in Austria. In that case the (corporate) income tax liability on the income available for distribution is determined like that for the income of a resident UCITS.

14.2.2.2. Austrian Unitholder and Netherlands- and UK-Resident UCITS

The conditions under which trading in the units of Netherlands- and UK-resident UCITS in Austria is affected by taxation of the unitholders do not differ from those of German-resident UCITS; nor do the reasons.

14.2.3. Cross-Border Trading of Units in Germany

14.2.3.1. German Unitholder and Austrian-Resident UCITS

Trading in units of Austrian-resident UCITS in Germany is, for the same reasons as discussed for Austria in Section 14.2.2, not hindered by the taxation of the unitholders if the information about the amount, nature, and source of the income that is relevant for the (corporate) income tax liability is provided to the tax authorities and the unitholders.

Where no information is provided to the tax authorities, or it is not provided properly, trading in the units of Austrian-resident UCITS in Germany is hindered by the taxation of the unitholders. In that case the income from the underlying investments is, just as in Austria, estimated. Unlike in Austria, the unitholders cannot provide proof in Germany that the amount of income from the underlying investments is less than the estimated amount.

14.2.3.2. German Unitholder and Netherlands-Resident UCITS or UK-Resident UCITS

Trading in units of Netherlands and UK-resident UCITS in Germany is affected by taxation of the unitholders under the same conditions as discussed earlier for Austrian-resident UCITS.

14.2.4. Cross-Border Trading of Units in the Netherlands

14.2.4.1. Dutch Unitholder and Austrian-Resident UCITS

Trading in units of Austrian-resident UCITS in the Netherlands is not hindered by taxation of individual unitholders, unless it concerns UCITS that mainly hold environmental, social-ethical, and cultural investments and that do not offer their units to the Dutch public. The exemptions for environmental, social-ethical, and cultural investments in that case do not apply.

The taxation of corporate unitholders hinders the trading of units in Austrian-resident UCITS in the Netherlands. The units of these UCITS have to be valued at market value so that the yields from the underlying investments and any change in value of these UCITS are taxable in the hands of Dutch corporate unitholders at the time they arise. This results in a tax disadvantage compared to resident (FII) UCITS. A change in value of the underlying investments of resident (FII) UCITS is not received by corporate unitholders until the disposal of the units in the UCITS if the latter has opted for a reinvestment account.

Trade in units of Austrian-resident UCITS, whose units are not freely transferable, is hindered by the taxation of corporate unitholders in the Netherlands. Any capital gains realized by the disposal of the underlying investments are considered to be derived in the hands of these unitholders at the time of arising. This results in a tax disadvantage compared to resident (FII) UCITS for the reasons mentioned previously.

14.2.4.2. Dutch Unitholder and German-Resident UCITS

The conditions under which trading in units of German-resident UCITS in the Netherlands is affected by taxation of the unitholders do not differ from those of Austrian-resident UCITS; nor do the reasons.

14.2.4.3. Dutch Unitholder and UK-Resident UCITS

Taxation of individual unitholders affects trading in units of UK-resident UCITS under the same conditions as discussed earlier for Austrian-resident UCITS.

Trading in units of UK-resident UCITS in the Netherlands, however, is facilitated by taxation of corporate unitholders if the income from the underlying investments is accumulated by these UCITS. By accumulation, the yields from the investments, unlike that of resident (FII) UCITS, are not taxable in the hands of corporate unitholders until they are realized on disposal of the units in the UCITS.

14.2.5. Cross-Border Trading of Units in the United Kingdom

14.2.5.1. UK Unitholder and Austrian-Resident UCITS

Trading in units of Austrian-resident UCITS in the United Kingdom is hindered by the taxation of the unitholders. These UCITS are considered by the United Kingdom to be transparent. The income from the underlying investments and capital gains from the disposal of investments are therefore considered to be received by the unitholders at the time they arise. This causes a tax disadvantage because capital gains from the disposal of investments, in the case of a UK-resident UCITS, are not considered to be received by the unitholders until the disposal of the units in the UCITS.

14.2.5.2. UK Unitholder and German-Resident UCITS or Netherlands-Resident UCITS of the Contractual Type

Taxation of unitholders affects trading in units of German-resident UCITS and Netherlands-resident UCITS of the contractual type in the United Kingdom, similar to that of Austrian-resident UCITS.

14.2.5.3. UK Unitholder and Netherlands-Resident UCITS of the Corporate Type

Trading in units of Netherlands-resident UCITS of the corporate type is not hindered by taxation of individual unitholders if they are certified as a reporting offshore fund. In that case the income tax liability for the income available for distribution is determined just as that for the income of a UK-resident UCITS.

The taxation of individual unitholders hinders trading of units in Netherlands-resident UCITS of the corporate type where they are not certified as a reporting offshore fund. In that case the exemptions under the Taxation of Chargeable Gains Act do not apply to capital gain from disposal of units in the UCITS because they are considered income. This results in a higher tax liability. The deferral of the tax liability for accumulated income, however, is not removed by the United Kingdom.

Trading in units of Netherlands-resident (EII) UCITS of the corporate type to corporate investors in the United Kingdom is facilitated by the taxation of corporate unitholders if the income from the underlying investments is accumulated by the UCITS. In that case the corporate income tax liability for the yields from the investments, unlike for UK-resident UCITS, is deferred until the disposal of the units in these UCITS. This results in a tax advantage compared to UK-resident UCITS.

The taxation of corporate unitholders does not affect the trading in units of Netherlands-resident UCITS (FII) of the corporate type. The income available for distribution, like that of UK-resident UCITS, has to be distributed by these UCITS to the unitholders.

Trading in the units of Netherlands-resident UCITS to corporate investors in the United Kingdom, however, is hindered if the UCITS invests in the equity of UK companies. Unlike UK-resident UCITS, the part of the distribution of Netherlands-resident UCITS that is related to dividends paid by UK-resident companies is not exempt from corporate income tax. Netherlands-resident UCITS are therefore less attractive to corporate investors for investments in UK equity than UK-resident UCITS.

14.3. MEASURES TO PROVIDE RELIEF FOR WITHHOLDING TAX CHARGED BY THE SOURCE STATE

14.3.1. INTRODUCTION

The countries studied do not apply the same rules for the crediting of foreign withholding tax for investments in resident and non-resident UCITS (foreign tax credit). In some cases, the availability of a foreign tax credit, unlike resident UCITS, depends on the characteristics of non-resident UCITS under the civil law of the UCITS country. In other cases, the availability of a foreign tax credit is determined by the conditions under which the units in the non-resident UCITS can be transferred. Sometimes, submission of information per source and per item about the amount of tax withheld at source affects the crediting of this tax. Resident and non-resident UCITS therefore do not compete under the same conditions; see also Section 8.3.

As a result, the trade in units of non-resident UCITS in the countries studied may be hindered (or supported as the case may be) because resident individual and (exempt) corporate investors may be discouraged (or encouraged) to invest by way of non-resident UCITS.

Figure 14.2 Investors May Be Encouraged to Make Use of Non-resident UCITS if They May, Unlike Investments in Resident UCITS, Credit Foreign Withholding Tax

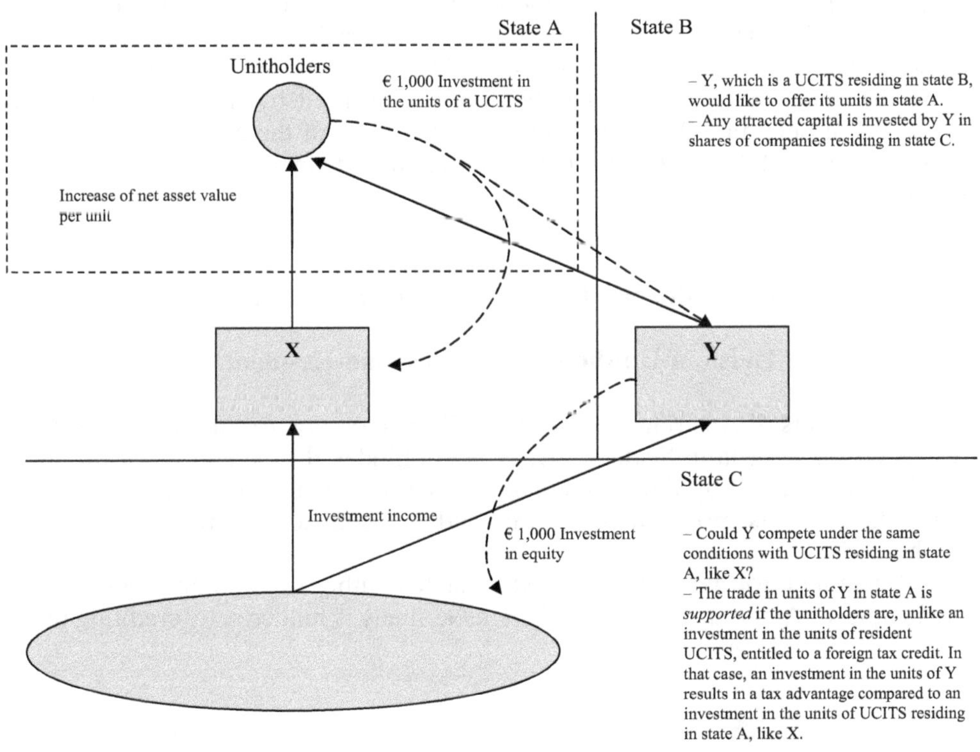

14.3.2. Cross-Border Trading of Units in Austria

14.3.2.1. Austrian Unitholder and German-Resident UCITS

Trading in units of German-resident UCITS is not affected by crediting of the withholding tax charged by source states if Austrian tax authorities and unitholders are informed per source and per item about the amount of tax withheld at source of taxable income. Austria provides relief for the withholding tax charged by the source state at the level of the unitholders in the form of a credit for foreign withholding tax.

If the information about the tax withheld at source is not communicated, or is not properly communicated, crediting of the withholding tax charged by the source states hinders the trading in the units of German-resident UCITS in Austria. The unitholders are in that case not granted relief for the withholding tax charged by the source state.

14.3.2.2. Austrian Unitholder and Netherlands-resident UCITS or UK-resident UCITS

The conditions under which crediting of the withholding tax charged by the source states affects trading of the units in Netherlands and UK-resident UCITS in Austria do not differ from those for German-resident UCITS. Austria, however, does not take note of the relief provided at the level of Netherlands-resident (FII) UCITS and UK-resident UCITS in the form of payment relief or a foreign tax credit, respectively. The unitholders of these UCITS are therefore indirectly provided more than once relief for the withholding tax charged by the source state. As discussed in Section 8.2.2, relief granted at the level of the Netherlands-resident (FII) UCITS and UK-resident UCITS facilitates trading in the units of these UCITS in Austria.

14.3.3. Cross-Border Trading of Units in Germany

14.3.3.1. German Unitholder and Austrian-Resident UCITS

Trading in units of Austrian-resident UCITS in Germany, for the same reasons as discussed for Austria in Section 14.2.2, is not hindered by crediting of the withholding tax charged by the source states if the information about the amount of withholding tax is provided per source and per item to the tax authorities and unitholders.

Where no information is provided to the tax authorities and unitholders, trading in units of Austrian-resident UCITS in Germany is hindered by crediting of the withholding tax charged by the source states for the same reasons as given for Austria in Section 14.2.2.

14.3.3.2. German Unitholder and Netherlands- and UK-resident UCITS

Crediting of the withholding tax charged by the source states affects trading in units of Netherlands and UK-resident UCITS in Germany under the same conditions as mentioned earlier for Austrian-resident UCITS. Like Austria, Germany does not take notice of relief granted for foreign withholding tax at the level of the UCITS. Trading in units of Netherlands-resident (FII) UCITS and UK-resident UCITS in Germany is facilitated for the same reasons as discussed earlier for trading of the units of these UCITS in Austria.

14.3.4. Cross-Border Trading of Units in the Netherlands

14.3.4.1. Dutch Unitholder and Austrian-Resident UCITS

Trading in units of Austrian-resident UCITS in the Netherlands is hindered by crediting of the withholding tax charged by the source states. The Netherlands provides relief for the withholding tax charged by the source state at the level of the UCITS in the form of a payment. No relief is available at the level of the unitholders. It does not take into account that no relief is provided at the level of Austrian-resident UCITS. As discussed in Section 8.3, this results in a tax disadvantage compared to an investment in the units of resident (FII) UCITS. It does not differ from resident (EII) UCITS.

Crediting of the withholding tax charged by the source states, however, supports trade in units of Austrian-resident UCITS to individual and corporate Unitholders in the Netherlands if the units are not freely transferable and the unitholders are informed about the amount of withholding tax per source and per item. In that case, the Netherlands grants the unitholders of these UCITS relief for the withholding tax charged by the source states in the form of a foreign tax credit. The amount of the foreign tax credit may exceed that of the payment relief granted to Netherlands-resident (FII) UCITS, because the latter is restricted to at most 15% of the gross amount of the dividend or interest. It does not, however, differ from that for resident (TII) UCITS.

14.3.4.2. Dutch Unitholder and German-Resident UCITS

Crediting of the withholding tax charged by the source states hinders trading in units of German-resident UCITS in the Netherlands. An investment in the units of German-resident UCITS, for the same reason as for that in the units of Austrian-resident UCITS, results in a tax disadvantage.

14.3.4.3. Dutch Unitholder and UK-Resident UCITS

Trading in units of UK-resident UCITS in the Netherlands is not affected by crediting of the withholding tax charged by the source states. The United Kingdom, like the Netherlands, provides for relief at the level of the UCITS. Trading in units of UK-resident UCITS in the Netherlands in respect to that relief is discussed in Section 8.3.

Crediting of the withholding tax charged by the source state supports trade in units of UK-resident UCITS of the trust type to individual and corporate unitholders, but only if the units are not freely transferable for the same reasons as discussed for Austrian-resident UCITS. The Netherlands does not seem to take into account that UK-resident UCITS are granted a foreign tax credit.

Trading in units of UK-resident UCITS is hindered by crediting of the withholding tax charged by the source states in the case that the UCITS satisfied the qualifying investment test at all times during a distribution period. In that case, it is not granted relief for the withholding tax charged by the source states. This results in a tax disadvantage compared to resident (FII/TII) UCITS for the same reasons as mentioned earlier for Austrian-resident UCITS. It does not differ from resident (EII) UCITS.

14.3.5. Cross-Border Trading of Units in the United Kingdom

14.3.5.1. UK Unitholder and Austrian-Resident UCITS

Trading in units of Austrian-resident UCITS in the United Kingdom is facilitated by crediting of the withholding tax charged by the source states if the information about the amount of withholding tax is provided per source and per item to the unitholders. The United Kingdom grants unitholders of these UCITS relief for the withholding tax charged by the source states in the form of a foreign tax credit. The amount of the foreign tax credit, however, may exceed that of the foreign tax credit granted to UK-resident UCITS, because the latter is subject to a reduced tax rate.

Where no information is provided to unitholders, crediting of the withholding tax charged by the source states hinders trading in units of Austrian-resident UCITS in the United Kingdom for the same reasons as discussed for Austria in Section 14.2.2.

14.3.5.2. UK Unitholder and German-Resident UCITS or Netherlands-Resident (EII/FII/TII) UCITS of the Contractual Type

The conditions under which trading in units of German-resident UCITS and Netherlands-resident (EII/FII/TII) UCITS of the contractual type in the United Kingdom is either facilitated or hindered by crediting of the withholding tax

charged by the source states do not differ from those for Austrian-resident UCITS. The United Kingdom, like Austria and Germany, does not take into account relief provided at the level of Netherlands-resident (FII) UCITS of the contractual type. This facilitates trading in units of these UCITS in the United Kingdom, as discussed in Section 8.2.2.

14.3.5.3. UK Unitholder and Netherlands-Resident (EII) UCITS of the Corporate Type

Trading in units of Netherlands-resident (EII) UCITS of the corporate type in the United Kingdom is hindered by crediting of the withholding tax charged by the source states. The United Kingdom does not grant relief to the unitholders because it assumes that the UCITS country has granted relief at the level of the UCITS. The Netherlands does not, however, provide relief for Netherlands-resident (EII) UCITS. This results in a tax disadvantage compared to UK-resident UCITS.

14.3.5.4. UK Unitholder and Netherlands-Resident (FII) UCITS of the Corporate Type

Crediting of the withholding tax charged by the source states does not affect trading in the units of Netherlands-resident (FII) UCITS of the corporate type in the United Kingdom. The Netherlands, like the United Kingdom, provides for relief at the level of these UCITS. The absence of relief at the level of the unitholders therefore does not result in a tax disadvantage compared to UK-resident UCITS. From Section 7.3 it follows that the amount of relief granted at the level of Netherlands-resident (FII) UCITS may differ from that at the level of UK-resident UCITS.

14.4. MEASURES TO PROVIDE RELIEF FOR THE WITHHOLDING TAX CHARGED BY THE UCITS COUNTRY

14.4.1. Introduction

In the countries studied the availability of a refund for the tax withheld at the time of distribution is not the same for investments in resident and non-resident UCITS. The refund of the non-creditable part of the tax withheld at the time of distribution is restricted to investments in resident UCITS. No refund is available for the tax withheld at the time of distribution by non-resident UCITS. The conditions of competition between resident and non-resident UCITS are thus not the same.

The trade in units of non-resident UCITS in the countries studied may therefore be hindered. Resident individual and (exempt) corporate investors may be discouraged to invest by way of non-resident UCITS.

Figure 14.3 A Comparison of the Availability of Relief for the Withholding Tax Charged by the UCITS Country at the Time of Distribution

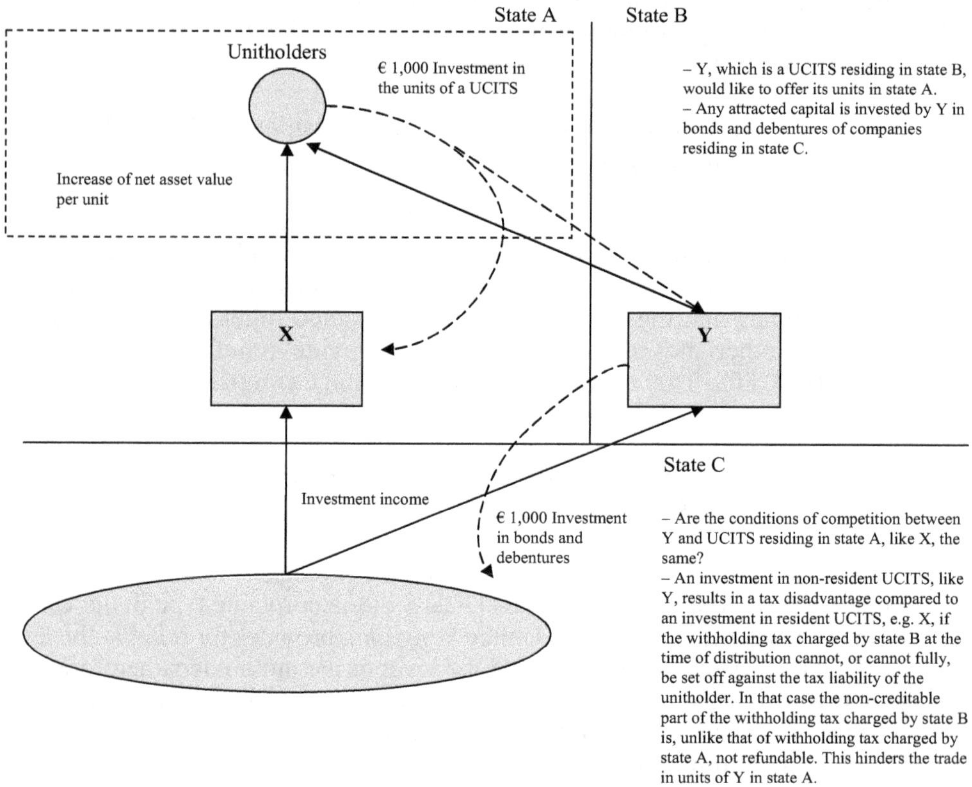

14.4.2. Cross-Border Trading of Units in Austria

14.4.2.1. Austrian Unitholder and German-Resident UCITS

Trading in the units of German-resident UCITS in Austria is hindered by crediting of the withholding tax charged at the time of distribution by Germany, the UCITS country. The tax withheld at the time of distribution may be credited against the tax liability of Austrian unitholders under the Austrian tax treaty with Germany, but only if the German-resident UCITS is considered to be a person for the purposes of that tax treaty. From Section 3.3.2 it follows that Austria does not consistently consider German-resident UCITS to be a person for tax treaty purposes. An investment in the units of German-resident UCITS is therefore less attractive than that in the units of resident UCITS.

14.4.2.2. Austrian Unitholder and Netherlands-Resident (EII/TII) UCITS

Crediting of the withholding tax charged at the time of distribution does not affect the trade in units of Netherlands-resident (EII/TII) UCITS. The distributions of these UCITS are, in contrast to those of resident UCITS, exempt from withholding tax at the time of distribution. The withholding tax charged from resident UCITS, however, is fully creditable or refundable so that the tax disadvantage from the withholding tax is completely removed by the taxation of the unitholders.

14.4.2.3. Austrian Unitholder and Netherlands-Resident (FII) UCITS

Crediting of the withholding tax charged by the Netherlands, the UCITS country, at the time of distribution does not hinder trading in units of Netherlands-resident (FII) UCITS in Austria if the tax withheld can be completely set off against the tax liability of the unitholders. The result from crediting in that case does not differ from the crediting or refunding of the withholding tax charged from resident UCITS.

If the withholding tax cannot be, or cannot be completely, set off against the tax liability of the unitholder, trading in units of Netherlands-resident UCITS in Austria is hindered by crediting of the withholding tax charged by the UCITS country at the time of distribution. The part of the withholding tax that cannot be set off, unlike the withholding tax charged from resident UCITS at the time of distribution, is not refundable.

14.4.2.4. Austrian Unitholder and UK-Resident UCITS

Trading in units of UK-resident UCITS in Austria, for the same reasons as given for Netherlands-resident (EII/TII) UCITS, is not affected by crediting of withholding tax charged at the time of distribution.

14.4.3. Cross-Border Trading of Units in Germany

14.4.3.1. German Unitholder and Austrian-resident UCITS

In the absence of any withholding tax charged at the time of distribution, crediting of the withholding tax charged at the time of distribution does not affect trading in units of Austrian-resident UCITS in Germany. The distributions of these UCITS, in contrast to those of resident UCITS, are exempt from withholding tax at the time of distribution. The withholding tax charged from resident UCITS, however, is fully creditable or refundable. The tax disadvantage from the withholding tax charged at time of distribution by resident UCITS is completely removed by the taxation of the unitholders.

14.4.3.2. German Unitholder and Netherlands-Resident (FII) UCITS

Trading in units of Netherlands-resident (FII) UCITS is under the same conditions affected by crediting of the withholding tax charged by the Netherlands, the UCITS country, at the time of distribution, as discussed in Section 14.4.2 for Austria.

14.4.3.3. German Unitholder and Netherlands-Resident (EII/TII) UCITS or UK-resident UCITS

For the same reasons as for Austrian-resident UCITS, trading in units of Netherlands-resident (EII/TII) UCITS and UK-resident UCITS is not affected by crediting of the withholding tax charged by the UCITS country.

14.4.4. Cross-Border Trading of Units in the Netherlands

14.4.4.1. Dutch Unitholder and Austrian-Resident UCITS

Crediting of the withholding tax charged at the time of distribution does not affect the trading in units of Austrian-resident UCITS in the Netherlands for the same reasons as discussed in Section 14.4.3 for trading in units of these UCITS in Germany.

14.4.4.2. Dutch Unitholder and German-Resident UCITS

Trading in the units of German-resident UCITS in the Netherlands is hindered by crediting of withholding tax charged at the time of distribution by Germany, the UCITS country. According to the tax treaty with Germany, tax withheld at the time of distribution may be set off by the unitholders against the tax liability, but only if the German-resident UCITS is considered to be a person for the purposes of that tax treaty. The Netherlands does not consistently consider German-resident UCITS to be a person for tax treaty purposes; see Section 3.3.2. Netherlands investors therefore may not be inclined to make use of German-resident UCITS.

14.4.4.3. Dutch Unitholder and UK-Resident UCITS

Crediting of the withholding tax charged at the time of distribution does not affect trading in units of UK-resident UCITS in the Netherlands. The reasons for this do not differ from those for Austrian-resident UCITS.

14.4.5. Cross-Border Trading of Units in the United Kingdom

14.4.5.1. UK Unitholder and Austrian-Resident UCITS

Trading in the units of Austrian-resident UCITS in the United Kingdom, for the same reasons as discussed for Germany in Section 14.4.3, is not hindered by crediting of the withholding tax charged at the time of distribution.

14.4.5.2. UK Unitholder and German-Resident UCITS

Trading in units of German-resident UCITS in the United Kingdom is hindered by crediting of the withholding tax charged at the time of distribution by Germany, the UCITS country. In accordance with the UK tax treaty with Germany, tax withheld at the time of distribution may be set off against the unitholder's tax liability but only if the German-resident UCITS is considered to be a person for the purposes of that tax treaty. It is not clear whether the United Kingdom considers German-resident UCITS to be a person for tax treaty purposes. An investment in the units of German-resident UCITS is therefore less attractive than that in the units of resident UCITS.

14.4.5.3. UK Unitholder and Netherlands-Resident (EII/TII) UCITS

Crediting of the withholding tax charged at the time of distribution, for the same reasons as for Austrian-resident UCITS, does not affect the trading in the units of Netherlands-resident (EII/TII) UCITS in the United Kingdom.

14.4.5.4. UK Unitholders and Netherlands-Resident (FII) UCITS

The conditions under which trading in units of Netherlands-resident (FII) UCITS in the United Kingdom is affected by crediting of the withholding tax charged by the Netherlands, the UCITS country, at the time of distribution do not differ from those discussed in Section 14.4.2 for the trading of these units in Austria.

14.5. CONCLUSION

Trade in units of UCITS between the countries studied is distorted by the differences in the taxation at the level of the unitholders. The conditions of competition in the countries studied diverge for resident and non-resident UCITS and between non-resident UCITS. The UCITS Directive has not removed the differences in the taxation of income from the investments in UCITS at the level of the unitholders.

We have learned from the previous five chapters that investments in resident and non-resident UCITS are not necessarily subject to the same taxation in the unitholder country. This may hinder non-resident UCITS to attract capital from investors residing in other Member States. This chapter gives an overview of the distortions to the trade in units of UCITS in the countries studied.

Part V

Removal of Tax Advantages and Tax Disadvantages

Investors residing in the countries studied cannot, or cannot always, freely invest in the units of non-resident undertakings for collective investment in transferable securities (UCITS) without experiencing or risking a higher tax burden than for investments in units of resident UCITS. As Chapters 3–14 demonstrate, some of these tax disadvantages are caused by discrimination resulting from the fact that a country treats non-resident taxpayers or foreign income differently from resident taxpayers or domestic income. The majority of the tax disadvantages, however, are the result of differences between the tax laws of the countries studied instead of differences between the taxpayers or income.

The very same differences facilitate trading in units of other non-resident UCITS. Although this results in a tax advantage for the unitholders, it undermines the higher aim of the UCITS Directive.

Taxation also hinders some of the UCITS residing in the countries studied from investing in other Member States or third countries.

Chapter 15 provides a comprehensive overview of the tax advantages and disadvantages that occur in cross-border trading. This is done in the form of schedules. Finally, some solutions for these distortions of the internal market are offered. Moreover, a recommendation for amendment of the Organization for Economic Cooperation and Development (OECD) Model Tax Convention and its Commentary is provided.

Chapter 15
Analysis and Recommendations

In the absence of harmonization or coordination, each of the Member States has introduced its own rules for taxation of investments in and by undertakings for collective investment in transferable securities (UCITS). The tax liability, tax base, tax rate and available relief from taxation for investments in and by UCITS therefore differs for each of the Member States.

Taxation of investments in and by UCITS in the Member States shows some substantial differences. These differences in taxation of investments in and by UCITS will harm the competition between UCITS if investments in non-resident UCITS result in a tax disadvantage (or a tax advantage, as the case may be) compared to investments in resident UCITS. In that case, UCITS do not compete under the same conditions.

For that reason, this study has examined taxation of investments in and by UCITS in Austria, Germany, the Netherlands and the United Kingdom. From this study follows that the taxation in the countries studied is not the same, not only at the level of the underlying investments, but also at the level of the UCITS and that of the unitholders. Because of the differences in taxation, investors residing in the countries studied cannot, or cannot always, freely invest in non-resident UCITS without experiencing or risking more severe taxation than for investments in resident UCITS (tax disadvantage). Sometimes these differences result in a lesser taxation (tax advantage). Either way, the differences frustrate the higher aim of the UCITS Directive – to bring about a European capital market and improve conditions of competition between UCITS in the European Union.

Tax disadvantages that hamper UCITS in attracting capital from investors residing outside the UCITS country probably could be removed by negative harmonization. These tax disadvantages seem to be caused by a different treatment of non-resident taxpayers or foreign income compared with resident taxpayers and domestic income in one state. This infringes on the freedom of capital as laid down in Articles 56 and 58 of the European Community (EC) Treaty and Article 40 of the European Economic Area (EEA) Treaty.

The tax advantages and most of the tax disadvantages cannot be removed by means of negative harmonization. They are the result of differences between tax laws of the countries studied. An appeal to the principle of the freedom of capital does not give comfort. The differences can be removed only by way of positive harmonization. It is recommended to harmonize the taxation of investments in and by UCITS because taxation has been identified and ranked as one of the most important obstacles to cross-border investments in UCITS.

In an amendment of the UCITS Directive or the draft of a new Directive, it should be laid down that income from the investments of UCITS is considered to be that of the unitholders under the domestic laws of the unitholders and for tax treaty purposes. Transparency is the most efficient instrument to establish that the investments in and by UCITS are not taxed more heavily (or less heavily, as the case may be) than a direct investment.

From a political point of view, however, it may be more desirable to have a dual approach to gain the support of the industry. Under a dual approach, the management company of the UCITS at the time of incorporation chooses for the income to be either that of the unitholders (transparency) or that of the UCITS (intransparency). Transparency may be attractive for professional funds, whereas intransparency may be more practical and convenient for retail funds.

If Member States cannot agree on the harmonization of the taxation of investments in and by UCITS, tax advantages and disadvantages also could be removed by way of tax coordination or spontaneous amendments of the domestic laws of the Member States.

Application of the UCITS Directive is not limited to the EU. It also applies in the other Member States of the EEA. It is therefore desirable that these states also participate in discussions on harmonization or coordination of taxation of investments in and by UCITS.

Some Member States may be more willing to cooperate to remove tax advantages and disadvantages that hinder cross-border investments in and by UCITS if such is done by way of the OECD. After all, the OECD Model Tax Convention and its Commentary are not binding on them.

15.1. INTRODUCTION

The first part of this chapter gives an overview of the most considerable tax advantages and disadvantages (and how they originated) that hamper attracting capital from unitholders residing in other Member States, that is, Austria, Germany, the Netherlands and the United Kingdom (Section 15.2).

In the second part of this chapter (Sections 15.3–15.7), it is recommended to remove the Member States' diverging tax laws and tax treaties in respect to taxation of investments in and by UCITS and replace them by unified or harmonized rules. From a political view, it may not be feasible to unify or harmonize taxation of income from investments in and by UCITS. Therefore, some alternatives are provided.

15.2. ANALYSIS OF TAXATION OF INCOME FROM INVESTMENTS BY AND IN UCITS

The cross-border trade in units of non-resident UCITS is hindered (or facilitated, as the case may be) by the taxation at the following levels:

(1) The underlying investments (at source).
(2) The UCITS.
(3) The unitholders.

15.2.1. Taxation in the Source Country

The tax treatment at source on income from the investments by a UCITS residing in one of the countries studied may hamper or facilitate investments in these UCITS by non-resident unitholders because of differences in the following:

(1) The withholding tax rate, available exemptions from withholding tax and available refunds of the tax withheld at source (disparity/discrimination).
(2) The number of tax treaties concluded by the UCITS country or the country of the unitholders (disparity).
(3) The provisions of the tax treaties concluded between a source state and the UCITS country or the country of the unitholders (disparity).
(4) The application of the tax treaties concluded between a source state and the UCITS country or the country of the unitholders (disparity).

15.2.1.1. Differences in the Withholding Tax Rate, Available Exemptions from Withholding Tax and Available Refunds of the Tax Withheld at Source

Reasons for Differences in Tax Treatment

A part of the differences in the source taxation on income from investments in the countries studied is caused by the absence of uniform tax rates for resident and non-resident UCITS. In some cases, income paid to non-resident UCITS is subject to less taxation than that paid to resident UCITS (tax advantage) as a result of the application of a reduced tax rate under a tax treaty. Taxation differs not only between resident and non-resident UCITS, but also between non-resident UCITS. After all, the application of tax treaties to UCITS is not the same, as will be discussed more in depth in the next subsection.

Example 15.1

X, a company residing in Austria, pays a dividend of EUR 100,000 to Y, an Austrian-resident UCITS, and to Z, a Netherlands-resident (FII) UCITS. X needs to withhold a tax of EUR 25,000 on the dividend paid to Y, whereas the withholding tax on the dividend paid to Y, in accordance with the Austrian tax treaty with the Netherlands, only EUR 15,000.

Most differences in source taxation in the countries studied are the result of restriction of an exemption from withholding tax or a refund of the tax withheld to resident UCITS. As a result, income paid to non-resident UCITS is frequently taxed more heavily than income paid to resident UCITS (tax disadvantage). This seems to infringe on the freedom of capital as laid down in Articles 56 and 58 of the EC Treaty and Article 40 of the EEA Treaty.

Example 15.2

X, a UCITS residing in Germany, and Y, a UCITS residing in the United Kingdom, both keep shares issued by Z, a German-resident company. Z pays to X and Y a dividend of EUR 100,000. Z is required to withhold EUR 26,375 and EUR 15,000 tax on the dividends paid to X, respectively Y. The tax of EUR 26,375 withheld on the dividend paid to X is refunded to X, whereas that withheld on the dividend paid to Y is not.

As a result of differences in the source taxation in the countries studied, resident and non-resident UCITS do not compete under the same conditions for domestic investments. A non-resident UCITS therefore may have difficulty in attracting capital from individual and institutional investors residing in one of the countries studied.

15.2.1.2. Differences in the Number, Provisions and Application of Tax Treaties

Reasons for Differences in Tax Treatment

Differences in source taxation on income from foreign investments can be partly traced to the number and provisions of the tax treaties concluded by the countries studied. A source state's right to tax is in most cases limited in the presence of a tax treaty if the beneficiary of the income is a person for tax treaty purposes. The size of the tax treaty network of the countries studied, however, is not the same. For portfolio investments, it varies from 77 tax treaties concluded by Austria to 107 tax treaties in the case of the United Kingdom. Nevertheless, the tax treaty network of the countries studied does not fully overlap and shows some significant gaps; for an overview of the tax treaty network of these countries, see Tables 3.1–3.16.

Example 15.3

W, a corporate body residing in the Netherlands, holds units in X, a Netherlands-resident (FII) UCITS, and in Y, a UK-resident UCITS. X and Y derive interest of EUR 100,000 from bonds issued by Z, a company residing in Chile. Z is, in the absence of a tax treaty with the Netherlands, required to withhold EUR 21,690 as tax on the interest payment to X, whereas the withholding tax charged on the interest payment to Y is in accordance with the Chilean tax treaty with the United Kingdom reduced to EUR 15,000.

A source state's right to tax may be limited if a tax treaty provides for a reduction of withholding tax or an exemption from withholding tax. The majority of the tax treaties of the countries studied limits a source state's right to tax dividend or interest to a percentage agreed on in the tax treaty. The countries studied, however, have not agreed on the same percentages. Moreover, tax treaties may provide for special tax rates for interest paid by the Government or a governmental body of the Contracting State, or interest paid to banks, financial institutions, or pension funds.

Example 15.4

W, an individual residing in Austria, invests in units of X, an Austrian-resident UCITS, and that of Y, a Netherlands-resident (FII) UCITS. X and Y are paid EUR 100,000 interest on bonds issued by Z, a Venezuelan-resident company. In accordance with the Venezuelan tax treaty with Austria and the Netherlands, respectively, Z withholds EUR 10,000 as tax on the dividend paid to X and EUR 5,000 on that paid to Y.

Even though the right to tax capital gains realized on the disposal of portfolio investments or other portfolio income generally is allocated exclusively to the state of residence of the alienator or the beneficiary of the income, the countries studied have agreed on different allocation rules in a substantial number of tax treaties.

Example 15.5

A part of the shares in X, an Argentinean-resident company, is held by Y and Z. Y is a Netherlands-resident (FII) UCITS, and Z is a UK-resident UCITS. During the year, Y and Z dispose of the shares in X. Y is paid the full amount of the proceeds from the disposal, whereas the credit institution or financial service provider, which is charged by Z to execute the disposal, is obliged to deduct a 15% withholding tax from the proceeds from the disposal.

For the most part, differences in source taxation are caused by the application of tax treaties. A tax treaty may limit a source state's right to tax, but only if the beneficiary of the income is considered to be a person for tax treaty purposes. The beneficiary of the income is considered to be a person for the purposes of a tax treaty if the beneficiary is liable to tax in a state that is a party to the tax treaty by reason of domicile, residence, place of management, or any other criterion of a similar nature under the domestic laws of that Contracting State. The objective and subjective tax liability of UCITS, however, is not the same in the countries studied.

Thus, the application of tax treaties is not the same either. In some cases, tax treaties are applied to unitholders, whereas in other cases they apply to the UCITS. In the third case, the application of tax treaties is denied to both UCITS and the unitholders. The application of tax treaties to UCITS is not only convenient and practical for the unitholders, it also enables non-resident unitholders to take advantage of the tax treaty network of the UCITS country (tax treaty shopping) if that country has concluded more tax treaties with countries in a certain region or with a specific country that has not concluded a tax treaty with the unitholder's residence state. The same applies in the case of a provision in one of the tax treaties of the UCITS country that is more attractive than that of the tax treaty of the unitholder's residence state.

Example 15.6

W, a pension fund residing in Germany, holds units in X, a German-resident UCITS, and in Y, a Netherlands-resident (FII) UCITS. X and Y both derive interest of EUR 100,000 from bonds issued by Z, a US-resident company. Because of the denial of the US tax treaty with Germany, Z may be required to withhold EUR 30,000 tax from the interest paid to X, whereas the interest paid to Y remains exempt from tax in accordance with the US tax treaty with the Netherlands.

Because of the differences in the number, provisions and application of tax treaties, income from investments by non-resident UCITS is in a substantial number of cases subject to more taxation (tax disadvantage) or less taxation (tax advantage) than is the case for investments by resident UCITS. The competition between UCITS for foreign investments therefore does not take place under the same conditions.

Overview

The materials discussed earlier are shown in more detail in the schedule in Table 15.1. For Austrian-, German-, Netherlands- and UK-resident unitholders the table indicates which tax advantages and disadvantages compared to resident UCITS were found in the examination of the cross-border trade in units of UCITS.

Table 15.1 Overview of Tax Advantages and Disadvantages Caused by Taxation of Investments by UCITS in the Source State

	Advantage	*Disadvantage*
Austrian unitholders Investments in and by:		
Resident UCITS	(1) Individual/corporate/exempt corporate unitholders: Exemption from withholding tax for interest paid by an Austrian debtor to the UCITS	(3) Exempt corporate unitholders: Austrian tax treaties not applicable.
	(2) Individual/corporate unitholders: Austrian tax treaties applicable.	
German-resident UCITS	(1) Individual/corporate/exempt corporate unitholders: Refund for the tax withheld at source on dividends paid by a German-resident company or interest paid in Germany on profit sharing or convertible bonds or debt securities.	(3) Individual/corporate/exempt corporate unitholders: The absence of an exemption from withholding tax for interest paid by an Austrian debtor to the UCITS.
	(2) Individual/corporate unitholders: In a number of cases the Austrian tax treaties are applicable.	(4) Individual/corporate/exempt corporate unitholders: Austrian or German tax treaties often not applicable.
Netherlands-resident (EII) UCITS		(1) Individual/corporate/exempt corporate unitholders: The absence of an exemption from withholding tax for interest paid by an Austrian debtor to the UCITS.

(continued)

Table 15.1 (cont'd)

	Advantage	*Disadvantage*
		(2) Individual/corporate/exempt corporate unitholders: Austrian or Netherlands tax treaties not applicable.
Netherlands-resident (FII) UCITS	(1) Individual/corporate/exempt corporate unitholders: The application of a reduced tax rate for dividends paid by an Austrian-resident company (under the applicable tax treaty). (2) Individual/corporate/exempt corporate unitholders: Exemption from withholding tax for interest paid by an Austrian debtor to the UCITS (under the applicable tax treaty). (3) Individual/corporate/exempt corporate unitholders: Refund for the tax withheld at source on dividends paid by a Netherlands-resident company. (4) Individual/corporate/exempt corporate unitholders: Netherlands tax treaties applicable. This enables the unitholders to do some tax treaty shopping.	
Netherlands-resident (TII) UCITS	(1) Exempt corporate unitholders: Exemption from withholding tax for interest paid by an Austrian debtor to the UCITS. (2) Individual/corporate unitholders: Austrian tax treaties applicable.	(3) Individual/corporate unitholders: Absence of an exemption from withholding tax for interest paid by an Austrian debtor to the UCITS. (4) Exempt corporate unitholders: Austrian tax treaties not applicable.

UK-resident UCITS	(1) Individual/corporate/exempt corporate unitholders: The application of a reduced tax rate for dividends paid by an Austrian-resident company (under the applicable tax treaty). (2) Individual/corporate/exempt corporate unitholders: Exemption from withholding tax for interest paid by an Austrian debtor to the UCITS (under the applicable tax treaty). (3) Individual/corporate/exempt corporate unitholders: UK tax treaties generally applicable, although in a few cases the Austrian ones are applied as if the unitholders had invested directly. This enables the unitholders to do some tax treaty shopping.	(4) Exempt corporate unitholders: In a few cases the UK tax treaties are not applicable.
German unitholders		
Investments in and by: Resident UCITS	(1) Individual/corporate/exempt corporate unitholders: Refund of the tax withheld at source on dividends paid by a German-resident company or interest on profit sharing or convertible bonds or debt securities paid by a German debtor. (2) Individual/corporate/exempt corporate unitholders: Exemption from withholding tax for interest (other than from profit sharing or convertible bonds or debt securities) paid by a German debtor to the UCITS. (3) Individual/corporate unitholders: In a number of cases the German tax treaties applicable.	(4) Individual/corporate/exempt corporate unitholders: German tax treaties generally not applicable.

(continued)

Table 15.1 (cont'd)

	Advantage	*Disadvantage*
Austrian-resident UCITS	(1) Exempt corporate unitholders: exemption from withholding tax for interest (other than from profit sharing or convertible bonds or debt securities) paid by a German debtor to the UCITS. (2) Individual/corporate unitholders: German tax treaties applicable.	(3) Individual/corporate/exempt corporate unitholders: No refund of the tax withheld at source on dividends paid by a German-resident company or interest paid in Germany on profit sharing or convertible bonds or debt securities. (4) Individual/corporate unitholders: The absence of an exemption from withholding tax for interest (other than from profit sharing or convertible bonds or debt securities) paid by a German debtor to the UCITS. (5) Exempt corporate unitholders: German tax treaties not applicable.
Netherlands-resident (EII) UCITS		(1) Individual/corporate/exempt corporate unitholders: No refund of the tax withheld at source on dividends paid by a German-resident company or interest paid in Germany on profit sharing or convertible bonds or debt securities. (2) Individual/corporate/exempt corporate unitholders: The absence of an exemption from withholding tax for interest (other than from profit sharing or convertible bonds or debt securities) paid by a German debtor to the UCITS.

		(3) Individual/corporate/exempt corporate unitholders: Netherlands or German tax treaties not applicable.
Netherlands-resident (FII) UCITS	(1) Individual/corporate/exempt corporate unitholders: Refund for the tax withheld at source on dividends paid by a Netherlands-resident company.	(4) Individual/corporate/exempt corporate unitholders: No refund of the tax withheld at source on dividends paid by a German-resident company or interest paid in Germany on profit sharing or convertible bonds or debt securities.
	(2) Individual/corporate/exempt corporate unitholders: Exemption from withholding tax for interest (other than from profit sharing or convertible bonds or debt securities) paid by a German debtor to the UCITS (under the applicable tax treaty).	
	(3) Individual/corporate/exempt corporate unitholders: Netherlands tax treaties applicable. This enables the unitholders to do some tax treaty shopping.	
Netherlands-resident (TII) UCITS	(1) Exempt corporate unitholders: Exemption from withholding tax for interest (other than from profit sharing or convertible bonds or debt securities) paid by a German debtor to the UCITS.	(3) Individual/corporate/exempt corporate unitholders: No refund of the tax withheld at source on dividends paid by a German-resident company or interest paid in Germany on profit sharing or convertible bonds or debt securities.
	(2) Individual/corporate unitholders: German tax treaties applicable.	(4) Individual/corporate unitholders: The absence of an exemption from withholding tax for interest (other than from profit

(continued)

Table 15.1 (cont'd)

	Advantage	*Disadvantage*
		sharing or convertible bonds or debt securities) paid by a German debtor to the UCITS.
		(5) Exempt corporate unitholders: German tax treaties not applicable.
UK-resident UCITS	(1) Individual/corporate/exempt corporate unitholders: Exemption from withholding tax for interest paid by a German debtor to the UCITS (under the applicable tax treaty).	(3) Individual/corporate/exempt corporate unitholders: No refund of the tax withheld at source on dividends paid by a German-resident company or interest paid in Germany on profit sharing or convertible bonds or debt securities.
	(2) Individual/corporate/exempt corporate unitholders: UK tax treaties are generally applicable although in a few cases the German ones are applied as if the unitholders had invested directly. This enables the unitholders to do some tax treaty shopping.	(4) Exempt corporate unitholders: in a few cases the UK tax treaties are not applicable.
Netherlands unitholders		
Investments in and by: Resident (FII) UCITS*	(1) Individual/corporate/exempt corporate unitholders: Refund of the tax withheld at source on dividends paid by a Netherlands-resident company.	

	(2) Individual/corporate/exempt corporate unitholders: Netherlands tax treaties applicable.	
Austrian-resident UCITS	(1) Individual/corporate/exempt corporate unitholders: Netherlands tax treaties applicable.	(2) Individual/corporate/exempt corporate unitholders: No refund of the tax withheld at source on dividends paid by a Netherlands-resident company. (3) Exempt corporate unitholders: Netherlands tax treaties not applicable.
German-resident UCITS	(1) Individual/corporate/exempt corporate unitholders: Refund of the tax withheld at source on dividends paid by a German-resident company or interest paid in Germany on profit sharing or convertible bonds or debt securities.	(3) Individual/corporate/exempt corporate unitholders: No refund of the tax withheld at source on dividends paid by a Netherlands-resident company.
	(2) Individual/corporate unitholders: In a number of cases the Netherlands tax treaties applicable.	(4) Individual/corporate/exempt corporate unitholders: Netherlands or German tax treaties generally not applicable.
UK-resident UCITS	(1) Individual/corporate/exempt corporate unitholders: UK tax treaties generally applicable, although in a few cases the Netherlands treaties are applied as if the unitholders had invested directly. This enables the unitholders to do some tax treaty shopping.	(2) Individual/corporate/exempt corporate unitholders: No refund of the tax withheld at source on dividends paid by a Netherlands-resident company. (3) Exempt corporate unitholders: In a few cases the UK tax treaties are not applicable.

(continued)

Table 15.1 (cont'd)

	Advantage	Disadvantage
UK unitholders		
Investments in and by: Resident UCITS	(1) Individual/corporate/exempt corporate unitholders: Exemption from withholding tax for interest paid by a UK deposit-taker to the UCITS. (2) Individual/corporate/exempt corporate unitholders: UK tax treaties generally applicable.	(3) Exempt corporate unitholders: In a few cases the UK tax treaties are not applicable.
Austrian-resident UCITS	(1) Corporate/exempt corporate unitholders: Exemption from withholding tax for interest paid by a UK deposit-taker to the UCITS. (2) Individual/corporate unitholders: UK tax treaties applicable.	(3) Individual unitholders: The absence of an exemption from withholding tax for interest paid by a UK deposit-taker to the UCITS. (4) Exempt corporate unitholders: UK tax treaties not applicable.
German-resident UCITS	(1) Corporate/exempt corporate unitholders: Exemption from withholding tax for interest paid by a UK deposit-taker to the UCITS. (2) Individual/corporate/exempt corporate unitholders: Refund of the tax withheld at source on dividends paid by a German-resident company or interest paid in Germany on profit sharing or convertible bonds or debt securities. (3) Individual/corporate unitholders: In a number of cases the UK tax treaties applicable.	(4) Individual unitholders: The absence of an exemption from withholding tax for interest paid by a UK deposit-taker to the UCITS. (5) Individual/corporate/exempt corporate unitholders: German or UK tax treaties generally not applicable.

Netherlands-resident (EII) UCITS of the contractual type	(1) Corporate/exempt corporate unitholders: Exemption from withholding tax for interest paid by a UK deposit-taker to the UCITS.	(2) Individual unitholders: The absence of an exemption from withholding tax for interest paid by a UK deposit-taker to the UCITS. (3) Individual/corporate/exempt corporate unitholders: Netherlands or UK tax treaties not applicable.
Netherlands-resident (EII) UCITS of the corporate type	(1) Individual/corporate/exempt corporate unitholders: Exemption from withholding tax for interest paid by a UK deposit-taker to the UCITS.	(2) Individual/corporate/exempt corporate unitholders: Netherlands or UK tax treaties not applicable.
Netherlands-resident (FII) UCITS	(1) Individual/corporate/exempt corporate unitholders: Exemption from withholding tax for interest paid by a UK deposit-taker to the UCITS. (2) Individual/corporate/exempt corporate unitholders: Refund of the tax withheld at source on dividends paid by a Netherlands-resident company. (3) Individual/corporate/exempt corporate unitholders: Netherlands tax treaties applicable. This enables the unitholders to do some tax treaty shopping.	
Netherlands-resident (TII) UCITS	(1) Corporate/exempt corporate unitholders: Exemption from withholding tax for interest paid by a UK deposit-taker to the UCITS. (2) Individual/corporate unitholders: UK tax treaties applicable.	(3) Individual unitholders: The absence of an exemption from withholding tax for interest paid by a UK deposit-taker to the UCITS. (4) Exempt corporate unitholders: UK tax treaties not applicable.

* After all, the majority of Netherlands-resident UCITS have chosen for the status of fiscal investment fund.

In summary, the main disadvantages are due to the denial of a reduction of withholding tax available under the domestic laws of the source state or a tax treaty to both the UCITS and unitholders. The main advantages are the result of the application of tax treaties to the UCITS instead of the unitholders.

15.2.2. Taxation in the UCITS Country

The tax treatment of investments by and in UCITS in the countries studied may hamper or facilitate investments in these UCITS by non-resident unitholders as a result of differences in the following:

(1) The objective and subjective tax liability of UCITS (disparity/discrimination).
(2) The availability and the amount of relief for the withholding tax levied by the source state (disparity/discrimination).
(3) The withholding tax imposed by the UCITS country at the time of distribution (disparity).

15.2.2.1. Differences in the Objective and Subjective Tax Liability of UCITS

Reasons for Differences in Tax Treatment

Differences in taxation of investments by UCITS in the UCITS country are partly the result of the fact that the objective and subjective tax liability of UCITS has not been harmonized or unified. The objective and subjective tax liability of UCITS has to avoid entirely or partly that income from the investment is taxed twice – at the level of the UCITS and the level of the unitholders (double taxation).

Most of the countries studied favour avoiding double taxation at the level of the UCITS. In the countries studied, different instruments are used to achieve this result – transparency, a reduced tax base, a reduced tax rate, or a subjective exemption. Each of these instruments prevents income derived by way of UCITS being subject to more taxation than a direct investment. This is true not only for resident unitholders, but also for non-resident unitholders (tax advantage).

Example 15.7

W, an individual residing in Austria, keeps units in X, an Austrian-resident UCITS, and in Y, a UK-resident UCITS. Z, a Chinese company, pays a dividend of EUR 100,000 to both X and Y. The dividend derived by Y is, in contrast to that of X, subject to UK corporate income tax. The UK corporate income tax liability of Y is EUR 20,000. The dividend is distributed by X and Y to the unitholders. W is paid by X and Y an amount of EUR 1,000 and EUR 800, respectively.

The exception to the rule is the United Kingdom, which for some kinds of income reduces double taxation at the level of the unitholders. The unitholders of UK-resident UCITS are partly compensated for taxation at the level of the UCITS, but only if they are liable to personal or corporate income tax in the United Kingdom. Exempt corporate unitholders, like pension funds and charities, are not liable to tax in the United Kingdom. The same is generally true for non-resident unitholders. These unitholders are thus not compensated for taxation at the level of UK-resident UCITS (disadvantage).

Example 15.8

W, an individual residing in Austria, keeps units in X, an Austrian-resident UCITS, and in Y, a UK-resident UCITS. Z, a Chinese company, pays a dividend of EUR 100,000 to both X and Y. The dividend derived by Y is, in contrast to that of X, subject to UK corporate income tax. The UK corporate income tax liability of Y is EUR 20,000. The dividend is distributed by X and Y to the unitholders. W is paid by X and Y an amount of EUR 1,000 and EUR 800, respectively.

Besides different tax treatment in respect to the objective and subjective tax liability of UCITS, a different tax treatment of domestic and foreign dividends in one of the countries studied, the United Kingdom, explains another part of the differences in the taxation of investments by UCITS in the UCITS country. For domestic dividends, the United Kingdom avoids taxation at the level of the UCITS by way of an exemption. The exemption is not available for foreign dividends. As a result, foreign dividends are subject to more taxation than domestic dividends (tax disadvantage). This seems to be an infringement of the freedom of capital as laid down in Articles 56 and 58 of the EC Treaty and Article 40 of the EEA Treaty.

Example 15.9

X, a UK-resident UCITS, is paid a dividend of EUR 100,000 by Y, a Netherlands-resident company, and another dividend of EUR 100,000 by Z, a UK-resident company. The Netherlands dividend is subject to corporate income tax in the hands of X at a rate of 20%, whereas the UK dividend is not.

The differences in the taxation of some investments by UK-resident UCITS may hamper the trade in units of these UCITS in other Member States. Foreign dividends derived by way of UK-resident UCITS are subject to more taxation than foreign dividends derived by way of non-resident UCITS. UK-resident UCITS therefore do not compete under the same conditions as Austrian-, German-, and Netherlands-resident UCITS. In addition, the more severe taxation of foreign dividends may also discourage UK-resident UCITS to invest in equity outside the United Kingdom.

15.2.2.2. Differences in the Availability and the Amount of Relief for the Withholding Tax Levied by the Source State

Reasons for Differences in Tax Treatment

The differences in the taxation of investments by UCITS in the UCITS country are partly caused by the absence of uniform rules as to the level at which relief for the tax withheld by the source state should be available. Some of the countries studied provide relief at the level of the unitholders. The other countries do so at the level of the UCITS.

Example 15.10

W, an individual residing in Germany, keeps units in X, a German-resident UCITS, and in Y, a Netherlands-resident (FII) UCITS. Z, a Chinese company, pays a dividend of EUR 100,000 to both X and Y. Z has to withhold EUR 10,000 as tax on the dividend. X is, unlike Y, not provided by the UCITS country with relief for the Chinese withholding tax of EUR 10,000.

The relief for foreign withholding tax is granted in the form of a payment reduction for the tax withheld at the time of distribution or a foreign tax credit. Any foreign withholding tax on dividend and interest may be set off by a Netherlands-resident (FII) UCITS against the 15% tax that needs to be withheld for the account of the unitholders at the time of distribution. A Netherlands-resident (FII) UCITS thus does not have to pay the full amount of the withholding tax to the tax authorities, whereas the tax withheld is fully creditable by the unitholders.[1] The relief for foreign withholding tax is limited to 15% of the gross amount of each dividend or interest.

Example 15.11

The unitholders of X, a Netherlands-resident (FII) UCITS, are paid a distribution of EUR 100,000. X needs to withhold EUR 15,000 tax from the gross amount of the distribution. No withholding tax is paid by X to the Netherlands tax authorities, because of EUR 15,000 of Austrian withholding tax, which may be set off against the tax withheld at the time of distribution.

The relief available to Netherlands-resident (FII) UCITS, however, is reduced if some of the unitholders (other than EU pension funds, charities, and some other exempt corporate bodies) are entitled to a reduction of withholding tax or an exemption from withholding tax under a tax treaty (tax disadvantage). The

1. The difference between the tax withheld on the distribution and the tax paid to the tax authorities increases the intrinsic value of the units in the UCITS.

reduction of the relief may discourage Netherlands-resident (FII) UCITS to attract capital from unitholders who reside in another Member State or a third state whose tax treaty with the Netherlands provides a reduction of or an exemption from withholding tax. It therefore seems to infringe on the freedom of capital as laid down in Articles 56 and 58 of the EC Treaty and Article 40 of the EEA Treaty.

Example 15.12

X, a Netherlands-resident (FII) UCITS, is paid a dividend of EUR 100,000 by Y, a German-resident corporation. Y needs to withhold a tax of EUR 15,000 from the gross amount of the dividend. The tax withheld on the dividend qualifies for relief. Half of unitholders are resident in the Netherlands. The other half of the unitholders consists of Czech, Portuguese, and Slovakian individuals. At the time of distribution these unitholders are entitled to a reduction of EUR 2,500. The UCITS is granted a partial relief of EUR 12,500 (EUR 15,000 –/– EUR 2,500).

The withholding tax charged by the source state on dividend, interest, and other portfolio income is creditable against the tax liability of UK-resident UCITS in accordance with the UK tax treaties and unilateral rules. Under no circumstances does the United Kingdom grants a foreign tax credit for more than the part of the corporate income tax liability of the beneficiary that is related to the foreign income (ordinary tax credit).

Example 15.13

Y, a UK-resident UCITS, is paid a dividend of EUR 100,000 by Z, a company residing in China. Z needs to withhold a tax of EUR 10,000 on the dividend. The Chinese withholding tax of EUR 10,000 can be set off against the corporate income tax liability of Y.

None of the withholding tax is creditable, if the UCITS satisfies the qualifying investment test at all times during the financial year. In that case, the corporate income tax liability is nullified because of the deduction of the distributed income or income that is considered to be distributed.

Example 15.14

X, a UK-resident UCITS, is paid interest of EUR 100,000 by Y, an Ecuadorian company. Y is required to withhold EUR 25,000 as tax on the interest payment. However, X is not entitled to relief by the UCITS country for the Ecuadorian withholding tax of EUR 25,000 if it satisfied the qualifying investment test at all times during the distribution period.

Trade in units of Netherlands-resident (FII) UCITS and UK-resident UCITS may be facilitated by the available relief for the tax withheld by a source state. The relief granted to these UCITS may be more than that granted to other UCITS, if any. A level playing field for UCITS is, therefore, missing in the countries studied and probably in other Member States as well.

15.2.2.3. Differences in the Tax Imposed by the UCITS Country at the Time of Distribution

Reasons for the Differences in Tax Treatment

Differences in the taxation of investments in UCITS in the UCITS country can be partly traced to the differences in the tax base, tax rates, and available exemptions from withholding tax at the time of distribution.

Example 15.15

X, a French company, pays interest for an amount of EUR 100,000 to Y, an Austrian-resident UCITS, and Z, a Netherlands-resident (FII) UCITS. The interest payment of EUR 100,000 is fully distributed by the UCITS to the unitholders. Y is obliged to deduct EUR 25,000 withholding tax from the gross amount of the distribution, whereas Z needs to withhold EUR 15,000 tax.

For another part, the differences in the taxation of investments in UCITS can be explained by differences in the taxation at source of income from domestic investments (investments situated within the UCITS country). Some items of income are subject to withholding tax at source. Other items are exempt from withholding tax, or the tax withheld at source is refundable. Instead, these items are subject to withholding tax at the time of distribution.

Example 15.16

X, a Netherlands-resident (EII) UCITS is paid a dividend of EUR 100,000 by Y, a Dutch-resident company. Y is obliged to deduct EUR 15,000 tax from the gross amount of the dividend. Later on, the dividend is distributed by X to the unitholders. X does not have to withhold tax from the gross amount of the distribution. The distribution is exempt from withholding tax.

Trade in units of UCITS in the countries studied may be hampered or facilitated by differences in the tax imposed by the UCITS country at the time of distribution. Taxation at the time of distribution by a non-resident UCITS may be less than that at the time of distribution by a resident UCITS. The opposite also may be true.

The conditions of competitions for Austrian, German, Netherlands, and UK-resident UCITS are thus not the same.

Overview

In more detail, the schedule in Table 15.2 illustrates the information provided above. With respect to Austrian, German, Netherlands, and UK-resident unitholders, tax advantages and disadvantages compared to resident UCITS were found by the studying of the cross-border trade in units of UCITS.
Table 15.2 shows that the most important disadvantages are caused by the taxation of some items of income at the level of UK-resident UCITS and the main advantages are the result of the availability of relief for the tax withheld at source or the absence of a withholding tax at the time of distribution.

15.2.3. Taxation in the Country of the Unitholders

The tax treatment of investments in non-resident UCITS in the countries studied may hamper or facilitate investments in these UCITS by resident unitholders due to differences in:

(1) The personal and corporate income tax liability of unitholders (disparity/discrimination).
(2) The availability of relief for the withholding tax levied by the source state (disparity).
(3) The availability of relief for the tax imposed by the UCITS country at the time of distribution (disparity/discrimination).
(4) The provision of information relevant for the (corporate) income tax liability of the unitholders (disparity/discrimination).

15.2.3.1. Differences in Personal and Corporate Income Tax Liability of Unitholders

Reasons for Differences in Tax Treatment

For the most part, differences in taxation of investments in resident and non-resident UCITS in the countries studied can be explained by timing issues. Income derived by way of non-resident UCITS is considered to be received by the unitholders at other times than that derived by way of resident UCITS.

In two of the countries studied, Austria and Germany, the taxation of investments in non-resident UCITS does not differ from that of investments in resident UCITS. This is different only if the UCITS has not informed the tax authorities or the unitholders of the amount, nature, and source of income. In that case the amount of the income is estimated, which usually results in more severe taxation.

Table 15.2 Overview of Tax Advantages and Tax Disadvantages Caused by Taxation of Investments in and by UCITS in the UCITS Country

	Advantage	*Disadvantage*
Austrian unitholders Investments in and by:		
Resident UCITS	(1) Individual/corporate/exempt corporate unitholders: The avoidance of double taxation at the level of the UCITS. (2) Individual/corporate/exempt corporate unitholders: The absence of withholding tax on Austrian-source dividends at the time of distribution. (3) Pension funds: The absence of withholding tax on interest at the time of distribution.	(4) Individual/corporate/exempt corporate unitholders: A withholding tax of 25% at the time of distribution.
German-resident UCITS	(1) Individual/corporate/ exempt corporate unitholders: The avoidance of double taxation at the level of the UCITS. (2) Individual/corporate/ exempt corporate unitholders: The absence of withholding tax on interest at the time of distribution.	(4) Individual/corporate/exempt unitholders: Withholding tax on Austrian-source dividends at the time of distribution. (5) Exempt corporate unitholders: A withholding tax of 26.375% on dividends.

	(3) Individual/corporate unitholders: A withholding tax of 15% on dividends at the time of distribution.	
Netherlands-resident (EII) UCITS	(1) Individual/corporate/exempt corporate unitholders: The avoidance of double taxation at the level of the UCITS. (2) Individual/corporate/exempt corporate unitholders: The absence of withholding tax at the time of distribution.	
Netherlands-resident (FII) UCITS	(1) Individual/corporate/exempt corporate unitholders: The avoidance of double taxation at the level of the UCITS. (2) Individual/corporate/exempt corporate unitholders: Relief for the tax withheld at source on dividends and interest and not all of the unitholders (other than EU pension funds and charities) are entitled to a reduction or exemption from withholding tax under a tax treaty. (3) Individual/corporate/exempt corporate unitholders: Withholding tax of 15% at the time of distribution. (4) Exempt corporate unitholders: A refund of the tax withheld at the time of distribution. The refund is restricted to the part of the tax withheld for which the UCITS has not claimed payment reduction.	(5) Individual/corporate/exempt unitholders: a withholding tax of 15% on Austrian-source dividends at the time of distribution.

(continued)

Table 15.2 (cont'd)

	Advantage	*Disadvantage*
Netherlands-resident (TII) UCITS	(1) Individual/corporate/exempt corporate unitholders: The avoidance of double taxation at the level of the UCITS. (2) Individual/corporate/exempt corporate unitholders: The absence of withholding tax at the time of distribution.	
UK-resident UCITS	(1) Individual/corporate/exempt corporate unitholders: The avoidance of double taxation at the level of the UCITS, but only for UK dividends or in the case that the qualifying investment test is satisfied. (2) Individual/corporate/exempt corporate unitholders: A foreign tax credit for the tax withheld at source, unless the qualifying investment test is satisfied. (3) Individual/corporate/exempt corporate unitholders: The absence of withholding tax at the time of distribution.	(4) Individual/corporate/exempt corporate unitholders: Some kind of income is subject to taxation at the level of the UCITS.
German unitholders Investments in and by:		
Resident UCITS	(1) Individual/corporate/exempt corporate unitholders: The avoidance of double taxation at the level of the UCITS.	(3) Individual/corporate/exempt corporate unitholders: A withholding tax of 26.375% at the time of distribution.

	(2) Exempt corporate unitholders: The absence of withholding tax on interest at the time of distribution.	
Austrian-resident UCITS	(1) Individual/corporate/exempt corporate unitholders: The avoidance of double taxation at the level of the UCITS. (2) Individual/corporate/exempt corporate unitholders: The absence of withholding tax at the time of distribution.	
Netherlands-resident (EII) UCITS	(1) Individual/corporate/exempt corporate unitholders: The avoidance of double taxation at the level of the UCITS. (2) Individual/corporate/exempt corporate unitholders: The absence of withholding tax at the time of distribution.	
Netherlands-resident (FII) UCITS	(1) Individual/corporate/exempt corporate unitholders: The avoidance of double taxation at the level of the UCITS. (2) Individual/corporate/exempt corporate unitholders: Relief for the tax withheld at source on dividends and interest, unless all of the unitholders (other than EU pension funds and charities) are entitled to a reduction or exemption from withholding tax under a tax treaty. (3) Individual/corporate/exempt corporate unitholders: Withholding tax of 15% at the time of distribution.	(5) Exempt corporate unitholders: Withholding tax of 15% on interest at the time of distribution.

(continued)

Table 15.2 (cont'd)

	Advantage	*Disadvantage*
	(4) Exempt corporate unitholders: A refund of the tax withheld at the time of distribution. The refund is restricted to the part of the tax withheld for which the UCITS has not claimed payment reduction.	
Netherlands-resident (TII) UCITS	(1) Individual/corporate/exempt corporate unitholders: The avoidance of double taxation at the level of the UCITS. (2) Individual/corporate/exempt corporate unitholders: The absence of withholding tax at the time of distribution.	
UK-resident UCITS	(1) Individual/corporate/exempt corporate unitholders: The avoidance of double taxation at the level of the UCITS but only for UK dividends or in the case that the qualifying investment test is satisfied. (2) Individual/corporate/exempt corporate unitholders: A foreign tax credit for the tax withheld at source, unless the qualifying investment test is satisfied. (3) Individual/corporate/exempt corporate unitholders: The absence of withholding tax at the time of distribution.	(4) Individual/corporate/exempt corporate unitholders: Some kind of income is subject to taxation at the level of the UCITS.

Netherlands unitholders Investments in and by:		
Resident (FII) UCITS*	(1) Individual/corporate/exempt corporate unitholders: The avoidance of double taxation at the level of the UCITS. (2) Individual/corporate/exempt corporate unitholders: Relief for the tax withheld at source on dividends and interest. (3) Exempt corporate unitholders: A refund of the tax withheld at the time of distribution. The refund is restricted to the part of the tax withheld for which the UCITS has not claimed payment reduction.	(4) Individual/corporate/exempt corporate unitholders: A withholding tax of 15% at the time of distribution.
Austrian-resident UCITS	(1) Individual/corporate/exempt corporate unitholders: The avoidance of double taxation at the level of the UCITS. (2) Individual/corporate/exempt corporate unitholders: The absence of withholding tax at the time of distribution.	(3) Individual/corporate/exempt corporate unitholders: The absence of relief for the tax withheld at source on dividends and interest.
German-resident UCITS	(1) Individual/corporate/exempt corporate unitholders: The avoidance of double taxation at the level of the UCITS. (2) Individual/corporate/exempt corporate unitholders: The absence of withholding tax on interest at the time of distribution.	(3) Individual/corporate/exempt corporate unitholders: The absence of relief for the tax withheld at source on dividends and interest. (4) Individual/corporate/exempt corporate unitholders: A withholding tax of 15% on dividends at the time of distribution.

(continued)

Table 15.2 (cont'd)

	Advantage	*Disadvantage*
UK-resident UCITS	(1) Individual/corporate/exempt corporate unitholders: The avoidance of double taxation at the level of the UCITS but only for UK dividends or in the case that the qualifying investment test is satisfied. (2) Individual/corporate/exempt corporate unitholders: A foreign tax credit for the tax withheld at source on dividends, interest, and other portfolio income, unless the qualifying investment test is satisfied. (3) Individual/corporate/exempt corporate unitholders: The absence of withholding tax at the time of distribution.	(4) Individual/corporate/exempt corporate unitholders: Some kinds of income are subject to taxation at the level of the UCITS. (5) Individual/corporate/ exempt corporate unitholders: The absence of a foreign tax credit for the tax withheld at source in the case that the qualifying investment test is satisfied.
UK unitholders Investments in and by:		
Resident UCITS	(1) Individual/corporate/exempt corporate unitholders: The avoidance of double taxation at the level of the UCITS, but only for UK dividends or in the case that the qualifying investment test is satisfied. (2) Individual/corporate unitholders: The avoidance of double taxation for some income at the level of the unitholders.	(5) Exempt corporate unitholders: Some kinds of income are subject to taxation at the level of the UCITS. (6) Individual/corporate/exempt corporate unitholders: The absence of a foreign tax credit for the tax withheld at source in the case that the qualifying investment test is satisfied.

	(3) Individual/corporate/exempt corporate unitholders: A foreign tax credit for the tax withheld at source on dividends, interest and other portfolio income, unless the qualifying investment test is satisfied. (4) Individual/corporate/exempt corporate unitholders: The absence of withholding tax at the time of distribution.	(7) Individual unitholders: A withholding tax of 20% at the time of distribution in the case that the UCITS satisfies the qualifying investment test.
Austrian-resident UCITS	(1) Individual/corporate/exempt corporate unitholders: The avoidance of double taxation at the level of the UCITS. (2) Individual/corporate/exempt corporate unitholders: The absence of withholding tax at the time of distribution	(3) Individual/corporate/exempt corporate unitholders: The absence of a foreign tax credit for the tax withheld at source on dividends, interest, and other portfolio income.
German-resident UCITS	(1) Individual/corporate/exempt corporate unitholders: The avoidance of double taxation at the level of the UCITS. (2) Individual unitholders: The absence of withholding tax on interest at the time of distribution.	(3) Individual/corporate/exempt corporate unitholders: The absence of a foreign tax credit for the tax withheld at source on dividends, interest, and other portfolio income. (4) Individual/corporate unitholders: A withholding tax on dividends of 15% at the time of distribution. (5) Exempt corporate unitholders: A withholding tax on dividends of 26.375% at the time of distribution.
Netherlands-resident (EII) UCITS	(1) Individual/corporate/exempt corporate unitholders: The avoidance of double taxation at the level of the UCITS. (2) Individual unitholders: The absence of withholding tax at the time of distribution.	(3) Individual/corporate/exempt corporate unitholders: The absence of a foreign tax credit for the tax withheld at source on dividends, interest, and other portfolio income.

(continued)

Table 15.2 (cont'd)

	Advantage	*Disadvantage*
Netherlands-resident (FII) UCITS	(1) Individual/corporate/exempt corporate unitholders: The avoidance of double taxation at the level of the UCITS. (2) Individual/corporate/exempt corporate unitholders: Relief for the tax withheld at source on dividends and interest, unless all of the unitholders (other than EU pension funds and charities) are entitled to a reduction or exemption from withholding tax under a tax treaty. (3) Individual unitholders: A withholding tax of 15% in the case that a resident UCITS would satisfy the qualifying investment test. (4) Exempt corporate unitholders: A refund of the tax withheld at the time of distribution. The refund is restricted to the part of the tax withheld for which the UCITS has not claimed payment reduction.	(5) Individual/corporate/exempt corporate unitholders: The absence of relief for the tax withheld at source on other portfolio income. (6) Individual/corporate/exempt corporate unitholders: A withholding tax of 15% at the time of distribution.
Netherlands-resident (TII) UCITS	(1) Individual/corporate/exempt corporate unitholders: The avoidance of double taxation at the level of the UCITS. (2) Individual/corporate/exempt corporate unitholders: The absence of withholding tax at the time of distribution	(3) Individual/corporate/exempt corporate unitholders: The absence of a foreign tax credit for the tax withheld at source on dividends, interest and other portfolio income.

* After all, the majority of Netherlands-resident UCITS have chosen for the status of fiscal investment fund.

Example 15.17

Some German individual and corporate investors have invested in units of X, a German-resident UCITS, and in those of Y, a Netherlands-resident UCITS. Both UCITS are paid a dividend of EUR 100,000 by Z, an Austrian-resident company. The dividend is accumulated in accordance with the fund rules of both UCITS. Nevertheless, the German unitholders are considered to have received their share in the divided at the end of the financial year.

The one exception to the rule in Austria is taxation of accumulated capital gains. Unlike an investment in a resident UCITS, these gains are considered to be distributed to corporate unitholders for whom the units in the non-resident UCITS are considered to be business income. This seems to be an infringement of the freedom of capital as laid down in Articles 56 and 58 of the EC Treaty and Article 40 of the EEA Treaty.

Example 15.18

W, an Austrian-resident corporate body, keeps some of the units in X, an Austrian-resident UCITS, and in Y, a Netherlands-resident (FII) UCITS. The units in both UCITS are considered part of W's business assets. During the year, both UCITS realize a capital gain of EUR 500,000 by the disposal of shares issued by Z, a German-resident company. The capital gain is accumulated in accordance with the fund rules of both. The capital gain derived by way of X is not considered to be received by W until it is realized by the disposal of the units in X, whereas that derived by way of Y is considered to be received, and thus taxable, in the hands of W four months after the end of the year.

The other countries studied, the Netherlands and the United Kingdom, have not established that taxation of investments in non-resident UCITS does not differ from that of investments in resident UCITS. In the Netherlands, taxation of investments in non-resident UCITS depends on the legal characteristics of the UCITS under the civil law of the UCITS country. These characteristics determine whether the income from the investments is that of the unitholders (transparent) or that of the UCITS (intransparent). Income from the investments of transparent non-resident UCITS is considered to be received by the unitholders on receipt, whereas the unitholders of tax opaque non-resident UCITS are not considered to receive any of the income from the investments until distribution or disposal of the units of the UCITS.

The legal characteristics of the UCITS, however, are not taken into account in the case of non-resident UCITS that are not subject to corporate income tax, and the exemption from corporate income tax does not depend on distribution of income from the underlying investments on an annual basis. The Dutch Corporate Tax Act requires corporate unitholders to value units in these UCITS at fair market value. As a result, any income derived by way of non-resident UCITS is considered to be received by corporate unitholders at the time of arising of the UCITS.

The requirement to value the units of some non-resident UCITS, such as Austrian and German-resident UCITS, at market value seems to infringe on the freedom of capital as laid down in Articles 56 and 58 of the EC Treaty or Article 40 of the EEA Treaty. An investment in units of these non-resident UCITS results in a less favourable treatment than that in the units of resident (FII) UCITS. Any realized and unrealized capital gains from the underlying investments of these non-resident UCITS are taxable in the hands of corporate unitholders at the time of arising, whereas those from the underlying investments of Netherlands-resident (FII) UCITS that have opted for a reinvestment account are not taxable until the disposal of the units in these UCITS.

Example 15.19

Some of the units in W, an Austrian-resident UCITS, and in X, a Netherlands-resident (FII) UCITS, are held by Y, a corporate body residing in the Netherlands. During the year, both UCITS realize a capital gain of EUR 500,000 by the disposal of shares issued by Z, a Canadian-resident company. The capital gain is accumulated in accordance with the fund rules of both. Nonetheless, the capital gain that is derived by way of W is considered to be received, and thus taxable, by Y at the time that it arose, whereas Y is not taxed on the capital gain derived by way of X until disposal of the units in X.

The legal characteristic of the UCITS under the civil law of the UCITS country also determines the taxation of investments in non-resident UCITS in the United Kingdom. Like in the Netherlands, income from investments of transparent non-resident UCITS is considered to be received by the unitholders on receipt, whereas unitholders of tax opaque non-resident UCITS are not considered to receive any of the income from the investments until distribution or disposal of the units of the UCITS.

Because of the different treatment of resident and transparent non-resident UCITS, capital gains from disposal of the underlying investments of transparent non-resident UCITS are subject to tax at the time of disposal, whereas those from disposal of the underlying investment of UK-resident UCITS are not taxed until disposal of the units in the UCITS. This seems to be an infringement of the freedom of capital as laid down in Articles 56 and 58 of the EC Treaty and Article 40 of the EEA Treaty for the same reasons as discussed earlier for the Netherlands.

Not only does taxation of capital gains realized by disposal of underlying investments of non-resident transparent UCITS differ from that of UK-resident UCITS but also that of capital gains realized by disposal of units in tax opaque non-resident UCITS. These gains, however, are not charged with capital gains tax as a chargeable gain if the non-resident UCITS was not certified as a reporting fund during the entire period of ownership (non-reporting funds). Instead, the profit in that case is charged with income tax as an offshore income gain, which is subject to a less favourable taxation than chargeable gains.

Separate from the time that income is considered to be received by the unitholders, the differences in the taxation of investments in resident and non-resident UCITS in the Netherlands and the United Kingdom also can be explained by the denial of some exemptions. The exemptions for environmental, social-ethical, and cultural investments in the Netherlands for example do not apply to investments in non-resident UCITS that do not offer units in the Netherlands. This seems to infringe the freedom of capital as laid down in Articles 56 and 58 of the EC Treaty and Article 40 of the EEA Treaty. The Income Tax Act does not offer these UCITS or their unitholders the possibility to submit evidence that any of the other conditions for these exemptions are fulfilled.

Example 15.20

W, an individual residing in the Netherlands, invests in units of X, an Austrian-resident UCITS, and Y, a Netherlands-resident UCITS. In accordance with their fund rules, both UCITS solely hold environmental, social-ethical, and cultural investments. Assuming that the units in X are, contrary to those of Y, not offered in the Netherlands, W is, for that reason, not entitled to the exemption for environmental, social-ethical, and cultural investments.

In the United Kingdom, the exemption for domestic dividends is restricted to domestic dividends only if they are derived by way of transparent non-resident UCITS, whereas they are entirely denied in the case of a tax opaque non-resident UCITS. As a result, domestic dividends derived by way of non-resident UCITS are subject to more taxation in the hands of the unitholders than those derived by way of UK-resident UCITS. This seems to be an infringement of the freedom of capital as laid down in Articles 56 and 58 of the EC Treaty or Article 40 of the EEA Treaty.

Example 15.21

W, a corporate body residing in the United Kingdom, keeps units in X, a Netherlands-resident (FII) UCITS of the corporate type, and that of Y, a UK-resident UCITS. Y, a UK-resident company, pays both UCITS a dividend of EUR 100,000. Both UCITS are required to distribute the UK dividend to the unitholders. The UK dividend derived by way of X, however, is fully taxable in the hands of W, whereas an exemption applies to the UK dividend derived by way of Y.

Investments in resident and non-resident UCITS are taxed in the same way but only if the tax authorities or unitholders are informed about the amount, nature and source of the income from the underlying investments. This requirement limits the number of non-resident UCITS in which Austrian and German may invest without experiencing or risking a higher tax burden than an investment in a resident UCITS. After all, most non-resident UCITS do not provide the unitholders with information about the amount, nature, and source of the income in accordance with the Austrian and German tax laws. Nor are they required to do so under the UCITS Directive. This may especially be true for German investors because the German Income Tax Act does not allow the unitholders to submit proof that the amount of the actual income derived by way of non-resident UCITS is less than the amount of the estimated income.

The differences in the taxation of investments of resident and non-resident UCITS in the Netherlands and the United Kingdom may hamper non-resident UCITS in attracting capital from unitholders residing these countries. Taxation of income derived by way of non-resident UCITS is often more heavy than that of income derived by way of resident UCITS. Non-resident UCITS thus do not compete under the same conditions in the Netherlands and the United Kingdom as resident UCITS.

Furthermore, the restriction of the exemption for environmental, social-ethical, and cultural investments discourages Netherlands individual investors to make use of non-resident UCITS for such investments. The same is true in the United Kingdom for investments in UK equity.

15.2.3.2. Differences in the Availability of Relief for the Withholding Tax Levied by the Source State

Reasons for the Differences in Tax Treatment

The differences in taxation of investments in resident and non-resident UCITS in the countries studied are the result of absence of uniform rules as to the level at which relief for tax withheld by the source state should be available.

In Austria and Germany, available relief for the withholding tax levied by the source state does not differ for resident and non-resident UCITS. This is different only in the case in which a non-resident UCITS has not informed the tax authorities or the unitholders about the amount of the foreign withholding tax per source and per item.

The Netherlands and the United Kingdom have failed to make sure that the availability of relief for the withholding tax levied by the source state does not differ for investments in resident and non-resident UCITS.

The differences in availability of relief for tax withheld at source of income for investments in non-resident UCITS may hamper or facilitate trade in units of UCITS in the Netherlands and the United Kingdom. After all, it may be more or less than the relief available for investments in resident UCITS. Because of the differences in the availability of relief, the Netherlands and the United Kingdom have failed to establish that resident and non-resident UCITS compete under the same conditions.

15.2.3.3. Differences in the Availability of Relief for the Tax Imposed by the UCITS Country at the Time of Distribution

Reasons for the Differences in Tax Treatment

The differences can be explained by the diverse treatment of the withholding tax charged from resident and non-resident UCITS at the time of distribution. In each of the countries studied, the part of the withholding tax charged from resident UCITS at the time of distribution that is not creditable against the tax liability of the unitholder is refunded to the unitholders. The refund, however, is restricted to the withholding tax charged from resident UCITS. An investment in a non-resident UCITS therefore causes a tax disadvantage compared to an investment in units of a resident UCITS, where the withholding tax charged at the time of distribution cannot, or cannot fully, be credited against the corporate income tax liability of the unitholder.

Example 15.22

W, an Austrian-resident corporate body, invests in the units of X, an Austrian-resident UCITS, and in Y, a Netherlands-resident (FII) UCITS. X had to withhold EUR 25,000 on a distribution to W, whereas X was required to deduct a withholding tax of EUR 15,000 on a distribution to W. Different from the withholding tax charged from X at the time of the distribution, no refund is available for the part of the withholding tax charged from Y at the time of distribution that cannot be set off against the corporate income tax liability of W.

After all, the tax imposed by the UCITS country at the time of distribution may be set off against the tax liability of the unitholders only if the applicable tax treaty provides for such. This is different only in one of the countries studied. Either way, no refund is available for the part of the tax withheld that cannot, or cannot fully, be credited against the corporate income tax liability of the unitholder.

The trading in units of UCITS between Austria, Germany, the Netherlands, and the United Kingdom is distorted by differences in the availability of a refund for the non-creditable part of the withholding tax charged by the UCITS country at the time of distribution. The competition between UCITS in the countries studied therefore does not take place under the same conditions.

Overview

The information discussed earlier is illustrated in Table 15.3, which shows tax advantages and disadvantages compared to investing in resident UCITS found in examining the cross-border trade in units of UCITS for Austrian, German, Netherlands, and UK-resident unitholders.

Table 15.3 Overview of Tax Disadvantages and Tax Advantages of Taxation of Investments in UCITS in the Unitholder Country

	Advantage	*Disadvantage*
Austrian unitholders Investments in and by:		
Resident UCITS	(1) Corporate unitholders: Any accumulated capital gains are not considered to be received by the unitholders until disposal of the units in the UCITS. (2) Individual/corporate unitholders: A foreign tax credit for the tax withheld at source on dividends, interest, and other portfolio income. (3) Individual/corporate unitholders: The part of the tax withheld at the time of distribution that cannot be set off against the unitholder's tax liability is refundable.	(4) Individual/corporate unitholders: Any income or realized capital gains from the underlying investments are considered to be received at the time of distribution or disposal or 4 months after the end of the year, whichever is earlier.
German-resident UCITS	(1) Individual/corporate unitholders: A foreign tax credit for the tax withheld at source on dividends, interest, and other portfolio income.	(2) Individual/corporate unitholders: Any income or realized capital gains from the underlying investments are considered to be received at the time of distribution or disposal or 4 months after the end of the year, whichever is earlier. This is also true for accumulated capital gains, unless the units in the UCITS are not considered to be business assets.

		(3) Individual/corporate unitholders: It is not clear whether the tax withheld at the time of distribution by Germany may be set off against the unitholder's tax liability.
Netherlands-resident (EII) UCITS	(1) Individual/corporate unitholders: A foreign tax credit for the tax withheld at source on dividends, interest, and other portfolio income.	(2) Individual/corporate unitholders: Any income or realized capital gains from the underlying investments are considered to be received at the time of distribution or disposal or 4 months after the end of the year, whichever is earlier. This is also true for accumulated capital gains, unless the units in the UCITS are not considered to be business assets.
Netherlands-resident (FII) UCITS	(1) Individual/corporate unitholders: A foreign tax credit for the tax withheld at source on dividends, interest, and other portfolio income.	(2) Individual/corporate unitholders: Any income or realized capital gains from the underlying investments are considered to be received at the time of distribution or disposal or 4 months after the end of the year, whichever is earlier. This is also true for accumulated capital gains, unless the units in the UCITS are not considered to be business assets. (3) Individual/corporate unitholders: The part of the tax withheld at the time of distribution by the Netherlands that cannot be set off against the unitholder's tax liability is not refundable.
Netherlands-resident (TII) UCITS	(1) Individual/corporate unitholders: A foreign tax credit for the tax withheld at source on	(2) Individual/corporate unitholders: Any income or realized capital gains from the

(continued)

Table 15.3 (cont'd)

	Advantage	*Disadvantage*
	dividends, interest, and other portfolio income.	underlying investments are considered to be received at the time of distribution or disposal or 4 months after the end of the year, whichever is earlier. This is also true for accumulated capital gains, unless the units in the UCITS are not considered to be business assets.
UK-resident UCITS	(1) Individual/corporate unitholders: A foreign tax credit for the tax withheld at source on dividends, interest, and other portfolio income.	(2) Individual/corporate unitholders: Any income or realized capital gains from the underlying investments are considered to be received at the time of distribution or disposal or 4 months after the end of the year, whichever is earlier. This is also true for accumulated capital gains, unless the units in the UCITS are not considered to be business assets.
German unitholders Investments in and by:		
Resident UCITS	(1) Individual/corporate unitholders: Any accumulated capital gains are not considered to be received until disposal of the units in the UCITS. (2) Individual/corporate unitholders: a foreign tax credit for the tax withheld at source on dividends, interest and other portfolio income.	(4) Individual/corporate unitholders: Any income or realized capital gains from the underlying investments are considered to be received at the time of distribution or disposal or 4 months after the end of the year, whichever is earlier.

	(3) Individual/corporate unitholders: The part of the tax withheld at the time of distribution that cannot be set off against the unitholder's tax liability is refundable.	
Austrian-resident UCITS	(1) Individual/corporate unitholders: Any accumulated capital gains are not considered to be received by the unitholders until the units in the UCITS are disposed of. (2) Individual/corporate unitholders: A foreign tax credit for the tax withheld at source on dividends, interest, and other portfolio income.	(3) Individual/corporate unitholders: Any income or realized capital gains from the underlying investments are considered to be received at the time of distribution or disposal or 4 months after the end of the year, whichever is earlier.
Netherlands-resident (EII) UCITS	(1) Individual/corporate unitholders: Any accumulated capital gains are not considered to be received by the unitholders until disposal of the units in the UCITS. (2) Individual/corporate unitholders: A foreign tax credit for the tax withheld at source on dividends, interest. and other portfolio income.	(3) Individual/corporate unitholders: Any income or realized capital gains from the underlying investments are considered to be received at the time of distribution or disposal or 4 months after the end of the year, whichever is earlier.
Netherlands-resident (FII) UCITS	(1) Individual/corporate unitholders: Any accumulated capital gains are not considered to be received by the unitholders until disposal of the units in the UCITS. (2) Individual/corporate unitholders: A foreign tax credit for the tax withheld at source on dividends, interest, and other portfolio income.	(3) Individual/corporate unitholders: Any income or realized capital gains from the underlying investments are considered to be received at the time of distribution or disposal or 4 months after the end of the year, whichever is earlier. (4) Individual/corporate unitholders: The part of the tax withheld at the time of

(continued)

Table 15.3 (cont'd)

	Advantage	*Disadvantage*
		distribution by the Netherlands that cannot be set off against the unitholder's tax liability is not refundable.
Netherlands-resident (TII) UCITS	(1) Individual/corporate unitholders: Any accumulated capital gains are not considered to be received by the unitholders until disposal of the units in the UCITS. (2) Individual/corporate unitholders: A foreign tax credit for the tax withheld at source on dividends, interest, and other portfolio income.	(3) Individual/corporate unitholders: Any income or realized capital gains from the underlying investments are considered to be received at the time of distribution or disposal or 4 months after the end of the year, whichever is earlier.
UK-resident UCITS	(1) Individual/corporate unitholders: Any accumulated capital gains are not considered to be received by the unitholders until disposal of the units in the UCITS. (2) Individual/corporate unitholders: A foreign tax credit for the tax withheld at source on dividends, interest, and other portfolio income.	(3) Individual/corporate unitholders: Any income or realized capital gains from the underlying investments are considered to be received at the time of distribution or disposal or 4 months after the end of the year, whichever is earlier.
Netherlands unitholders Investments in and by:		
Resident (FII) UCITS*	(1) Corporate unitholders: Realized and unrealized capital gains from the underlying investments are not considered to be received until disposal of the units in	(4) Corporate unitholders: Any income from the underlying investments is received within 8 months after the end of the financial year (distribution requirement).

	the UCITS, but only if the UCITS has not opted for a reinvestment account. (2) Individual unitholders: The application of the exemptions for environmental, social-ethical and cultural investments. (3) Individual/corporate unitholders: The part of the tax withheld at the time of distribution that cannot be set off against the unitholder's tax liability is refundable.	(5) Individual/corporate unitholders: The absence of a foreign tax credit for the tax withheld at source on dividends, interest, and other portfolio income.
Austrian-resident UCITS	(1) Individual/corporate unitholders: A foreign tax credit for the tax withheld at source on dividends, interest, and other portfolio income, but only if the units of the UCITS are not freely transferable.	(2) Corporate unitholders: Any income from the underlying investments is considered to be received at the time of arising. (3) Individual/corporate unitholders: Have to make individual request for refund or payment of withholding tax levied by the UCITS country at the time of distribution. (4) Individual unitholders: The denial of the exemptions for environmental, social-ethical, and cultural investments, but only in the case of UCITS that do not offer units in the Netherlands.
German-resident UCITS	(1) Individual/corporate unitholders: A foreign tax credit for the tax withheld at source on dividends, interest, and other portfolio income, but only if the units of the UCITS are not freely transferable.	(2) Corporate unitholders: Any income from the underlying investments is considered to be received at the time of arising. (3) Individual unitholders: The denial of the exemptions for environmental, social-ethical, and cultural investments, but only in the case of UCITS that do not offer units in the Netherlands.

(continued)

Table 15.3 (cont'd)

	Advantage	*Disadvantage*
		(4) Individual/corporate unitholders: It is not clear whether the tax withheld at the time of distribution by Germany may be set off against the unitholder's tax liability.
UK-resident UCITS	(1) Corporate unitholders: Any accumulated income from the underlying investments is not considered to be received until disposal of the units in the UCITS.	(2) Corporate unitholders: Any distributed income is considered to be received upon distribution. (3) Individual unitholders: The denial of the exemptions for environmental, social-ethical, and cultural investments, but only in the case of UCITS that do not offer units in the Netherlands. (4) Individual/corporate unitholders: The absence of a foreign tax credit for the tax withheld at source on dividends, interest, and other portfolio income.
UK unitholders Investments in and by:		
Austrian-resident UCITS	(1) Corporate unitholders: The application of the exemption for UK dividends derived by way of the UCITS. (2) Individual/corporate unitholders: A foreign tax credit for the tax withheld at source on dividends, interest, and other portfolio income.	(3) Individual/corporate unitholders: Any income or realized capital gains from the underlying investments are considered to be received at the time of arising.
German-resident UCITS	(1) Corporate unitholders: The application of	(3) Individual/corporate unitholders: Any

	(2) Individual/corporate unitholders: A foreign tax credit for the tax withheld at source on dividends, interest, and other portfolio income.	received at the time of arising. (4) Individual/corporate unitholders: It is not clear whether the tax withheld at the time of distribution by Germany may be set off against the unitholder's tax liability.
Netherlands-resident (EII) UCITS of the contractual type	(1) Corporate unitholders: The application of the exemption for UK dividends derived by way of the UCITS. (2) Individual/corporate unitholders: A foreign tax credit for the tax withheld at source on dividends, interest, and other portfolio income.	(3) Individual/corporate unitholders: Any income or realized capital gains from the underlying investments are considered to be received at the time of arising.
Netherlands-resident (EII) UCITS of the corporate type	(1) Corporate unitholders: Realized and unrealized capital gains from the underlying investments are not considered to be received until disposal of the units in the UCITS.	(2) Corporate unitholders: Any income from the underlying investments is received within 8 months after the end of the financial year (distribution requirement). (3) Corporate unitholders: The denial of the exemption for any UK dividends derived by way of the UCITS. (4) Individual/corporate unitholders: The absence of a foreign tax credit for the withholding tax levied by a source state.
Netherlands-resident (FII) UCITS of the contractual type	(1) Corporate unitholders: The application of the exemption for UK dividends derived by way of the UCITS. (2) Individual/corporate unitholders: A foreign tax credit for the tax withheld at source on dividends, interest, and other portfolio income.	(3) Individual/corporate unitholders: Any income or realized capital gains from the underlying investments are considered to be received at the time of arising. (4) Individual/corporate unitholders: The part of the tax withheld at the time of distribution by the Netherlands that cannot be set off

(continued)

Table 15.3 (cont'd)

	Advantage	*Disadvantage*
		against the unitholder's tax liability is not refundable.
Netherlands-resident (FII) UCITS of the corporate type	(1) Corporate unitholders: Realized and unrealized capital gains from the underlying investments are not considered to be received until disposal of the units in the UCITS, but only if the UCITS has opted for a reinvestment account.	(2) Corporate unitholders: Any income from the underlying investments is received within 8 months after the end of the financial year (distribution requirement). (3) Corporate unitholders: The denial of exemption for any UK dividends derived by way of the UCITS. (4) Individual/corporate unitholders: The absence of a foreign tax credit for the withholding tax levied by a source state. (5) Individual/corporate unitholders: The part of the tax withheld at the time of distribution by the Netherlands that cannot be set off against the unitholder's tax liability is not refundable.
Netherlands-resident (TII) UCITS	(1) Corporate unitholders: The application of the exemption for UK dividends derived by way of the UCITS. (2) Individual/corporate unitholders: A foreign tax credit for the tax withheld at source on dividends, interest, and other portfolio income.	(3) Individual/corporate unitholders: Any income or realized capital gains from the underlying investments are considered to be received at the time of arising.

* After all, the majority of Netherlands-resident UCITS have chosen for the status of fiscal investment fund.

Table 15.3 shows that the largest tax advantages and disadvantages are the result of timing issues and the denial of exemptions.

15.3. TOWARDS HARMONIZATION OF THE TAXATION OF UCITS

15.3.1. Introduction

The analysis shows that investing through a non-resident UCITS may be advantageous or disadvantageous depending on the circumstances. It is considered desirable to harmonize taxation of investments in and by UCITS to establish a level playing field for these undertakings.

15.3.2. Negative Harmonization

Some tax disadvantages that hinder the cross-border trade in units of UCITS can be removed by means of negative harmonization. These tax disadvantages are caused by different treatment of resident and non-resident taxpayers or domestic and foreign income in one state and thus are considered discriminatory.

15.3.3. Positive Harmonization

The tax advantages and the majority of the tax disadvantages that hinder the cross-border trade in units of UCITS cannot be removed by means of negative harmonization. They are caused by differences between the tax laws of the countries studied. An appeal to the principle of non-discrimination therefore does not give comfort. The differences between the tax laws of the countries studied can be removed only through positive harmonization.[2]

15.3.4. Desirability of Harmonization

Investments in UCITS are currently fragmentized by the national borders of the Member States, as discussed in the Introduction. As a result of the fragmentation, the average UCITS is currently five times smaller than its counterparts in the United States. Because of the scale effect, unitholders pay an estimated EUR 2 to EUR 6 billion per year more in fees than what they would have if the fund market were unified. It is therefore considered necessary to achieve the aim of the UCITS Directive – 'the removal of the restrictions on the free circulation of the units of

2. Court of Justice of the European Communities, *Gilly* case (C – 336/96).

collective investment undertakings in the Community, and [. . .] to bring about a European capital market'.

Taxation has been identified and ranked as one of the most important obstacles to cross-border investments in UCITS. It is therefore recommended to do the following:

(1) Remove any discriminatory tax rules that hinder cross-border investments in and by UCITS through negative harmonization.
(2) Improve the conditions of competition between UCITS even more by removing the Member States' diverging tax laws by harmonized rules on the taxation of investments in and by UCITS (positive harmonization).

This brings us to the question whether such amendments are feasible.

15.3.5. Feasibility of Harmonization

The EC treaty and the EEA Treaty provide the European Commission with the necessary tools to bring a less favourable treatment of investments in and by non-resident UCITS in the EU Member States before the European Court of Justice (infringement procedure). The European Free Trade Association (EFTA) Surveillance Authority has at its disposal similar tools in the case of less favourable treatment in Iceland, Liechtenstein, and Norway, although these obstacles are brought before the EFTA Court of Justice instead.[3]

The European Commission does not have the power to unify or harmonize the taxation of investments in and by UCITS. Nor does the EFTA Surveillance Authority. The European Commission, however, may make a proposal for the harmonization or coordination of the Member States' laws, regulations, and administrative procedures to fully establish an internal market or fix operative problems. Such a proposal is presented to the Member States in the European Council after consulting the European Parliament and the Economic and Social Committee. A discussion on whether the unification or harmonization of the taxation of investments in and by UCITS requires the support of a qualified majority[4] of the Member States, or the support of all Member States[5] falls outside the scope of the study. The same applies for a discussion on the competence of the EEA Joint Committee to adopt any EC secondary law on the taxation of investments in and by UCITS.[6]

Obstacles to Positive Harmonization

It does not seem likely that the differences between tax laws of the Member States create an obstacle to the harmonization of the taxation of investments in and by

3. Article 31 of the EFTA Court Agreement.
4. In accordance with the Arts 47(2) and 48 of the EC Treaty.
5. In accordance with Art. 94 or 308 of the EC Treaty.
6. Article 98 of the EEA Treaty.

UCITS. From the tax laws of the countries studied follows that the use of fictions for the beneficiary of income from the investments of UCITS is widespread. The same is true for the use of fictions with respect to the time that the income is considered to be received by the unitholders and for what amount.

In Sections 15.4 and 15.5 a proposal for the form and contents of EC legislation on the taxation of investments in and by UCITS is formulated.

15.4. FORM OF THE PROPOSED EUROPEAN COMMUNITY LEGISLATION

15.4.1. European Union Tax

Harmonization of taxation of the income from investments of UCITS could be combined with the plans of the European Commission for a common consolidated tax base. A common consolidated tax base system provides for common rules in respect to determination of the tax base of companies or certain companies. The amount of the common consolidated tax base is allocated to the Member States on the basis of a formula. The common consolidated tax base of companies would be administrated by the EU or in a modified form by the Member States.

Alternatives for the common consolidated tax base are an EU company income tax or a harmonized tax base. An EU company income tax involves a single corporate tax code for the EU with a single tax rate. In a modified form, the Member States may apply their own tax rates to that part of the tax base that is allocated to them. In the case of a harmonized tax base, the corporate income tax legislation of the Member States is replaced by a harmonized tax base. The Member States thus apply the same (corporate) income tax regulation, although they can set their own tax rates. The harmonized tax base could also be shared between the EU and the Member States. In that case, the corporate income tax legislation of the Member States could also refer to the EU harmonized tax base. Any changes immediately affect the harmonized tax base of the Member States. The harmonized tax base would be administered by the Member States.

Whether the Member States opt for an EU company income tax, a harmonized tax base, or a common consolidated tax base, special tax regulations for UCITS are required to avoid double taxation of the income from the investments and to establish that that income is not taxed higher or lower than a direct investment.

15.4.2. Amendment of UCITS Directive

Some Member States,[7] have indicated that they will not agree to a common consolidated tax base. It is likely that these Member States will also raise objections to

7. Among others, the Baltic States, Ireland, and the United Kingdom.

an EU corporate income tax, harmonized corporate income tax, or a combination of both. From a political point of view, it is therefore more feasible to amend the UCITS Directive or to draft a new Directive for the harmonization of taxation of income from investments of UCITS. It might be less difficult to arrive at harmonization on a subfield.

15.5. CONTENTS OF THE PROPOSED EUROPEAN COMMUNITY LEGISLATION

It is essential for the removal of the obstacles to cross-border trade in units of UCITS that the harmonized tax rules apply to all UCITS, regardless of whether they have non-resident unitholders or they invest abroad.

15.5.1. Taxpayer

In an amendment of the UCITS Directive or the draft of a new Directive it should be laid down that the income from the investments of UCITS is for tax purposes considered to be that of the unitholders (tax transparent entity) or that of the UCITS (tax opaque entity). It is submitted that transparency is more favourable than intransparency. It is the most efficient instrument to establish that the taxation of investments in and by UCITS is not more (or less as the case may be) than a direct investment.

Alternative – Dual Approach

From a political point of view it might be more desirable to have a dual approach to gain the support of the industry. A dual approach should comprehend both tax transparent UCITS and tax opaque UCITS. The management company 'checks the box' by the incorporation of an UCITS for either a tax transparent entity or a tax opaque entity. Tax transparent UCITS may be favourable for UCITS with a limited number of institutional unitholders (professional funds) whereas tax opaque UCITS are more convenient and practical for UCITS that are listed or otherwise available to a broad public (retail funds).

For that reason, the Sections 15.5.1.1 and 15.5.1.2 do not discuss only the contents that should be included in an amendment of the UCITS Directive or a new Directive on the taxation of investments in and by transparent UCITS but also for tax opaque UCITS.

15.5.1.1. Transparent UCITS

The income from the investments of transparent UCITS should be considered to be that of the unitholders under the domestic laws of the Member States and for tax treaty purposes. The taxation of investments by and in UCITS would, therefore, take place as if the unitholders had invested directly. On the other hand, the UCITS needs to inform the unitholders about any circumstances relevant to their tax liability, such as the amount, nature, and source of the items of income from the underlying investments and any tax withheld at source.

Taxation at the Level of the Investments

An advantage of transparent UCITS is that the application of reduced tax rates or exemptions from withholding tax under the domestic laws of the source state or a tax treaty does not differ from a direct investment. The applicable tax treaty is that between the source state and the unitholder's resident state, which reduces tax treaty shopping. The tax treaty network of the UCITS country is not of importance for taxation in the source state; nor are the objective and subjective tax liability of the UCITS. Like a direct investment, the application of a tax treaty depends on the tax liability of the unitholders.

The Member States, or the EU on their behalf, should, within a reasonable period, negotiate a Memorandum of Understanding with the tax treaty partners outside the EU about the beneficial ownership of income from investments by transparent UCITS. The Memorandum of Understanding should ensure that the unitholders are considered to be the beneficiaries of the income not only from investments within the EU but also from investments outside the EU.

Issues Arising from This Approach

A disadvantage of transparency is that the unitholders have to file separate requests to each source state for a reduction of withholding tax or an exemption from tax under the domestic laws of that state or the applicable tax treaty. This is inconvenient, is impractical, and creates an administrative burden for the UCITS and the unitholders.

An amendment of the UCITS Directive or a draft of a new Directive should therefore provide for the possibility of a collective request by the UCITS on behalf of the unitholders for a reduction of withholding tax or an exemption from withholding tax under the domestic laws of a Member State or the applicable tax treaty.[8] A collective request should be available on behalf of those unitholders that are residing in the EU and are entitled to a refund under the domestic laws of the Member State or the applicable tax treaty. It would be preferable that the amount of the difference between the domestic tax rate and the reduced tax rate is, like a direct investment, paid directly to unitholders who are entitled to such

8. Of course, the administrative burden for the unitholders could also simply be avoided by abolishing the levy of a withholding tax at source on the income from the investments within the European Union. The abolishing of withholding taxes, however, does not do justice to the source principle. The source state has also provided the unitholders with possibilities to generate the income from those portfolio investments that are located within its jurisdiction. The right to tax is therefore, in my view, rightly shared between the source state and the residence state of the unitholder.

reduction or exemption. Otherwise, the unitholders who are entitled to the refund have to share the amount of the refund with the other unitholders. Further research is necessary to formulate adequate administrative procedures.

In addition, the Member States, or the EU on their behalf, should, within a reasonable period, renegotiate the existing tax treaties with countries outside the EU in respect to a collective request by UCITS on behalf of those unitholders residing in the EU that are entitled to a refund under the tax treaty with the source state and their resident state, whereas the Member States have to be bound to take down such a collective request in any new tax treaties.

Taxation at the Level of the UCITS

Transparency simply avoids taxation at the level of the UCITS. The income from the investments of transparent UCITS is for tax purposes directly considered to be that of the unitholders. This is not different for non-resident unitholders.

Taxation at the Level of the Unitholders

An amendment of the UCITS Directive or the draft of a new Directive does not have to restrict the Member States' sovereignty in the field of the taxation of portfolio investments. Transparency establishes that the income from the investments of resident and non-resident UCITS is taxable in the hands of the unitholders at the same time and for the same amount as for a direct investment. From a political point of view, this might lower the threshold for the Member States to agree on the harmonization of the taxation of investments in and by UCITS.

Issues Arising from this Approach – I

It might be desirable to make an exception to the previously discussed rule for accumulated capital gains. An inconvenience of transparency is that the underlying investments are considered to be disposed of not only by their sale or redemption, but also each time a UCITS issues units; see the abstract of Chapter 13. This inconvenience could be removed by stipulating that capital gains realized by the disposal of the underlying investments are not considered to be received by the unitholders until they are actually distributed or realized by the disposal of the units in the UCITS.

An exception to accumulated capital gains should not have to be impossible for the Member States to overcome. After all, the countries studied do not, or do not always, consider accumulated capital gains to be received at the time of arising. Instead, they are often not considered to be received until disposal of the units in the UCITS.

Issues Arising from this Approach – II

Transparency brings an administrative burden for the UCITS and the unitholders. Because the unitholders are taxed as if they had invested directly, the UCITS has to administer and communicate the amount, nature, and source of the income that is considered to be received by each unitholder and the amount of tax withheld at source (per item and per source). Otherwise, the unitholders cannot file their tax return.

For the convenience of comparison, it is recommended that an amendment of the UCITS Directive or the draft of a new Directive provides for a standard form. Instead of a paper version of the standard form, it might also be possible to provide for a pan-European online database, which could be consulted by the tax authorities and unitholders. In that case, the UCITS could enter relevant information in the database. Nonetheless, the unitholders should, on request, be provided with a paper version of the form. The information should be available within a reasonable period after the end of the distribution period so that fund of funds are also able to determine their income within a reasonable period.

15.5.1.2. Tax Opaque UCITS

In the case of a dual approach, the income from the investments of some UCITS would initially be considered to be that of the UCITS under the domestic laws of the Member States and for tax treaty purposes (tax opaque UCITS). In addition, unitholders are taxed as if they had invested in a company. This is different only where an amendment of the UCITS Directive or the draft of a new Directive provides for such.

Taxation at the Level of the Investments

The application of reduced tax rates or exemptions from withholding tax under the domestic laws of the Member States or a tax treaty depends on the legal characteristics under the civil law of the UCITS country or the objective and subjective tax liability of the UCITS. Unlike a direct investment, the tax liability of the unitholders is not taken into account. This may result in a tax disadvantage for pension funds and charities, which are in the case of a direct investment often entitled to an exemption from withholding tax for certain items of income.

To establish a level playing field, the amendment of the UCITS Directive or the draft for a new Directive should stipulate that the domestic laws of the Member States apply as if all UCITS were companies. Otherwise, the source taxation in the Member States still may not be the same. Some of the exemptions available in the Member States depend on the legal characteristics of the recipient. After all, UCITS are either incorporated or established by contract or under a trust deed.

A level playing field could also be established by way of an exemption from withholding tax or a refund of the tax withheld at source. Instead, the income would be subject to tax by the UCITS country at the time of distribution. Such approach, in my view, does not do justice to the fact that the source state in the case of portfolio income contributes more to generation of the income than the UCITS country. In addition, it would require harmonization of the tax base, tax rate, and available exemptions at the time of distribution, which currently differ quite substantially among the Member States. Harmonization of taxation on distributions would restrict Member States' sovereignty more than necessary to establish that the source taxation does not differ between UCITS.

Application of Tax Treaties

The applicable tax treaty would be the one between the source state and the UCITS country. Contrary to a direct investment, application of the applicable tax treaty depends on the objective and subjective tax liability of the UCITS. As a corporation, a UCITS would initially be liable to tax in the UCITS country by reason of domicile, residence, place of management, or any other criterion of a similar nature under the domestic laws of that Contracting State. It should thus be considered to be a person for tax treaty purposes.

Issues Arising from this Approach – I

This is practical and convenient for individual and corporate unitholders. They do not have to file individual requests to each source state for the application of a reduction of withholding tax or an exemption from withholding tax in accordance with the applicable tax treaty. It is also practical and convenient for the source state because it does not have to make a refund to numerous unitholders, but merely to the UCITS.

On the other hand, application of the tax treaty to the UCITS usually results in a tax advantage for exempt corporate unitholders. These unitholders, with a few exceptions, would not be entitled to a reduction of withholding tax or an exemption from withholding tax in the case of a direct investment. The tax advantage, however, comes for the account of the Member State, which acts as the source state.

Issues Arising from this Approach – II

Tax treaties across Member States are not the same for each. It differs in size and contents. The application of tax treaties to the UCITS will therefore still result in substantial differences in the source taxation. The differences in the tax treaty network of the Member States for portfolio income could be removed by the introduction of an EU tax treaty network for portfolio income. From a political point of view, however, this might be a bridge too far (or more likely several bridges too far) for the Member States.

In the meantime, differences in the number and provisions of the tax treaties concluded by the Member States enable individual and corporate unitholders to take advantage of the tax treaty network of the UCITS countries (tax treaty shopping). Again, tax treaty shopping takes place at the expenses of the Member State that acts as a source state.

Application of Tax Treaties for Investments Outside the EU

Third countries may have a different view on the term 'liable to tax (. . .) by reason of his domicile, residence, place of management or any other criterion of a similar nature under the domestic laws of that Contracting State'. They do not necessarily apply tax treaties to UCITS. It is therefore necessary that the Member States, or the EU on their behalf, make sure that their tax treaty partners also consider UCITS as a corporation to be a person for tax treaty purposes by their tax treaty partners.

The tax treaty partners of Member States may be reluctant to agree on the application of tax treaties to UCITS. Acting as a source state, these countries pay the bill for application of tax treaties not only to exempt corporate unitholders, but also for individual and corporate unitholders taking advantage of the tax treaty network of the UCITS country (tax treaty shopping).

Taxation at the Level of the UCITS

As a corporation, tax opaque UCITS are initially subject to corporate income tax. As a result, the income from the investments may be subject to tax twice (economic double taxation). Investors therefore may be declined to make use of tax opaque UCITS.

For that reason, the amendment of the UCITS Directive or the draft for a new Directive should specify which method needs to be used by the Member State to avoid (economic) double taxation either at the level of the UCITS or that of the unitholders. The following methods avoid taxation at the level of the UCITS:

(1) Subjective exemption.
(2) Reduced tax base.
(3) Reduced tax rate.

These methods avoid double taxation for both resident and non-resident unitholders. In the absence of a tax liability, a tax credit for the tax withheld at source is, however, missing.

(Economic) double taxation also can be avoided at the level of the unitholders. This could be done by tax credit or exemption. The methods of tax credit or exemption compensate unitholders for taxation at the level of the UCITS. In the presence of a tax credit, the tax treaties and unilateral rules of the UCITS country may provide for a tax credit at the level of the UCITS for the tax withheld at source.

It is submitted that avoidance of double taxation takes place at the level of the UCITS. The avoidance of taxation at the level of the unitholders in the form of a (refundable) tax credit seems to be unnecessary burdensome, whereas the personal and family circumstances of unitholders are not taken into account in the case of an exemption at the level of unitholders.

Issues Arising from this Approach – I

An inconvenience of tax opaque UCITS is that the tax withheld at source cannot be set off by the UCITS or the unitholders. Instead, the UCITS country could provide for a payment reduction of the tax withheld at the time of distribution. Like in the Netherlands, any of the tax withheld at source could be set off by UCITS against the tax that needs to be withheld for the account of the unitholders at the time of distribution. A UCITS thus does not pay the full amount of the withholding tax to the tax authorities, whereas the tax withheld is fully creditable by the unitholders. The difference between the tax withheld on the distribution and the tax paid to the tax authorities increases the intrinsic value of units in the UCITS.

Issues Arising from this Approach – II

Without further measures, any distributions of income by tax opaque UCITS are considered to be a dividend paid by a company, which is often subject to withholding tax. The levying of a withholding tax at the time of distribution, however, results in a more severe tax burden than in the case of a direct investment. It is therefore desirable that an amendment of the UCITS Directive or the draft of a new Directive provides for an exemption from withholding tax on distributions of tax opaque UCITS. If the Member States decide otherwise, it is necessary to harmonize the amount of withholding tax that is charged by the UCITS country at the time of distribution. After all, the tax base, tax rates, and available exemptions from withholding tax as demonstrated by this study and discussed earlier differ substantially among the Member States.

Taxation at the Level of the Unitholders

The income from the underlying investments is considered to be that of the UCITS. It is not received by the unitholders until it is distributed or realized by the disposal of the units in the UCITS.

The amendment of the UCITS Directive or the draft for a new Directive should determine that any income from the underlying investments that is available for distribution is considered to be distributed at the end of each distribution period (distribution fiction). Like in the United Kingdom, a distribution period should be at the most a year, but it would not cause problems if the articles of incorporation, fund rules, or trust deed provide for a shorter distribution period, for example, a month or a quarter or half of a year.

Issues Arising from this Approach

A disadvantage of a distribution fiction is that some of the unitholders may be taxed on (deemed) distributed income for which they have paid compensation at the issue date. The issue price of units in an UCITS contains compensation for the balance of the unrealized capital gains from the underlying investments at the issue date. The compensation prevents the watering down of these capital gains per unit.[9] An amendment of the UCITS Directive or the draft of a new Directive should provide that the compensation paid at the issue date for unrealized capital gains could be set

9. Otherwise, these capital gains would, after the issuing of units, be divided among more units than before, as a result of which the gains per unit would become less. The compensation provides that the amount of the annual income per unit remains unaffected by the issuing of units.

off against the part of the (deemed) distribution or deemed distribution that is related to capital gains from the underlying investments.[10]

Nature and Source of the Income

The distributions or deemed distributions of tax opaque UCITS are taxable in the hands of the unitholders as a dividend paid by a company. Without further measures, the nature and source of the income thus does not remain the same.

Issues Arising from this Approach

Taxation of distributions and deemed distributions by UCITS is simple and does not necessarily result in an administrative burden for the UCITS and unitholders. The simplicity comes at the expense of transparency. Any special tax rates and exemptions do not apply as if the unitholders had invested directly. The same is true for the application of tax treaties and unilateral rules. After all, the nature and source of the income from the underlying investments do not remain the same. This could be restored by additional measures, but then transparency would be far more efficient.

15.5.2. Timing Issues and Tax Accounting Principles

Irrespective of an agreement by the Member States for transparency or a dual approach, it is advisable that the amendment of the UCITS Directive or the draft for a new Directive sets out at what time and for what amount the income is considered to be arisen from the investments (harmonized tax base and tax accounting principles). In the case of transparent UCITS, it is also necessary to harmonize the nature and source of the income. Otherwise, the amount of the income has to be determined in accordance with the non-harmonized tax laws of twenty-seven Member States. For that purpose, the UCITS should keep twenty-seven administrations. From the examination of the taxation of an investment in resident and non-resident UCITS in the countries studied it follows that this is precisely one of the problems at this time.

It is therefore preferable to apply a harmonized tax base and tax accounting principles for income from investments of UCITS. In that case, one administration will do for all Member States. From the examination of the taxation of UCITS in the countries studied it follows that the differences among these countries should not be impossible to overcome. The most considerable differences arise with regard to the time that a capital gain or loss from an investment is taken into

10. Alternatively, the amendment or the draft could simply determine that UCITS cannot distribute capital gains to the unitholder and neither are they considered to be distributed. In that case, the capital gains are not realized by unitholders until the disposal of the units in the UCITS. This, however, results in a tax advantage compared to a direct investment.

account and whether a loss may be set off against other income or carried over to a following year. Further research is necessary with regard to other portfolio investments because this study was limited to the mainstream income from investments in equity, bonds and other debt securities, and financial options and futures.

The tax authorities of the UCITS country should be in charge of the supervision about the UCITS. These authorities, thus, have to check whether the UCITS has determined the tax base and has drafted the standard forms correctly. In which way any mistakes or errors should be corrected is subject for further research.

15.6. WHAT IF EUROPEAN UNION HARMONIZATION IS NOT FEASIBLE?

In the EU, it is difficult to arrive at harmonization in the field of direct taxation. So far, the Member States have agreed on only four directives on direct taxation – the Parent-Subsidiary Directive, the Merger Directive, the Interest and Royalty Directive, and the Savings Taxation Directive. It is therefore likely that Member States will not be able to agree on harmonization of taxation of the income from investments of UCITS.

Tax advantages and disadvantages that hinder the cross-border trade in units of UCITS, however, also could be removed through tax coordination or spontaneous amendments of national legislation.

15.6.1. Tax Coordination

In the absence of harmonization, tax coordination could also provide for the use of one method by the Member States, or certain Member States, to avoid double taxation and for the application of the same on other measures necessary to ensure that an investment in units of a UCITS is not taxed higher or lower than a direct investment. In addition, it could standardize communication of the amount, nature, and source of income to the tax authorities of the unitholders' residence state and the unitholders so that it is sufficient for UCITS to provide one standard form with information.

Such tax coordination could be established by bilateral agreements between the EU and Member States or by a multilateral agreement between the Member States or certain Member States.

15.6.1.1. Canadian Provincial and Territorial Legislation as Example

An example of successful coordination of the taxation of collective investment funds can be found in Canada. In Canada, a federation of ten provinces[11] and three

11. Alberta, British Columbia, Manitoba, New Brunswick, New Foundland and Labrador, Nova Scotia, Ontario, Prince Edward Island, Québec and Saskatchewan.

territories,[12] the authority to impose income tax legislation is, as in the EU, divided over several jurisdictions. The Constitution Act, 1867[13] granted the authority to enact income tax legislation to the federal and provincial legislators. The income tax of most provinces[14] and all territories is, on the basis of the Tax Collection Agreements with the federal government, collected by the federal government on behalf of the provinces. To facilitate the collection and assessment of taxes by the federal government,[15] the provinces and all territories have, under the Tax Collection Agreements, agreed to refer to the federal income tax legislation for the tax base of taxpayers, including collective investment funds (mutual funds). By way of reference to the federal income tax legislation, most provinces and all territories apply the same method to avoid double taxation and other measures necessary to ensure that an investment in the unit of a mutual fund is not taxed higher or lower than a direct investment. Tax coordination is established by bilateral agreements between the federation and the provinces. A model of the (corporate) income tax legislation of the provinces is attached to the bilateral agreement.

The provinces that have not agreed to refer to the federal income tax legislation, nevertheless, define the tax base under the provincial (corporate) income tax legislation in an almost identical way as that of the federal income tax legislation. In addition, these provinces apply the same method, or a method that gives the same result, to avoid double taxation and other measures to ensure that an investment in the units of a mutual fund is not taxed higher or lower than a direct investment.

The cross-border trading in units of undertakings for collective investment in the provinces and territories does not seem to result in any tax advantages or disadvantages,[16] because they make use of the same method to avoid double taxation and other measures to ensure that an investment in the units of a mutual fund is not taxed higher or lower than a direct investment. The taxation of an investment in the units of a mutual fund residing in another province or territory than the unitholder therefore does not differ from that of an investment in the units of a mutual fund that resides in the same province or territory as the unitholder. Therefore investors are free to invest in the units of mutual funds. Such a form of coordination might also be feasible for the EU.

15.6.1.2. EU Model Provisions for Tax Treaties

Alternatively, the EU could also provide for model provisions for tax treaties with regard to the taxation of income from investments of UCITS at source.

12. Northwest Territories, Nunavut and Yukon.
13. Constitution Act, 1867, 30 & 31 Vict., c. 3 (Imp.) (formerly the British North America Act) as amended.
14. Québec has not entered into a Tax Collection Agreement with the federal government for the collection of corporate and personal income taxes, and Alberta and Ontario have agreed only on the collection of personal income tax.
15. V. Krishna, *The Fundamentals of Canadian Income Tax* (Toronto: Thomson Carswell, 2006), 12.
16. From the discussion of the federal income tax legislation in the Canadian literature, one can conclude that the provincial and territorial income taxes do not cause any major problems.

These provisions could provide that, notwithstanding the legal form of a UCITS, for tax treaty purposes, it is considered transparent. To lower the administrative burden for unitholders, a tax treaty should, as discussed in Section 15.5.1.1, provide for a collective request by the UCITS for a refund of the part of withholding tax that is not levied in accordance with the applicable tax treaty. A collective request should be made possible for all unitholders residing in the EU who would have been entitled to a refund in the case of a direct investment. The refund should, for the reasons mentioned in Section 15.5.1.1, be paid directly to the unitholders entitled to it. The scope of any model provisions for tax treaties is, however, limited to taxation of the income at source. They cannot remove the existing differences at the level of taxation of the UCITS and that of the unitholder.

15.6.2. Spontaneous Amendments of National Legislation

The cross-border trade in units of UCITS may be improved through spontaneous harmonization. Member States may spontaneously apply the same tax legislation at one or more of the levels involved in taxation of the income from the investments of UCITS. An example of spontaneous harmonization is the subjective exemption for UCITS as laid down in section 6a of the Dutch Corporate Tax Act for Exempt Investment Institutions (EII), which is based on the Luxembourg tax legislation for UCITS of the corporate type. Care should be taken that spontaneous harmonization does not result in a worsening of the overall tax burden for unitholders. Under section 6a of the Dutch Corporate Tax Act, individual and corporate unitholders residing in the Netherlands cannot credit the withholding taxes levied at source on income. Neither can a UCITS that opts for these tax regulations apply for any relief for these taxes. This causes a worsening of taxation of the income from investments of UCITS compared to the at that time already existing tax regulations for Fiscal Investment Institutions (FII). UCITS that have opted for the latter tax regulations are provided with relief for these taxes.[17]

15.7. THIRD COUNTRIES

The harmonization, coordination, or spontaneous amendments of national legislation of taxation of income from the investments of UCITS solves only the problems of cross-border investments in and by UCITS within the European Union.

15.7.1. EEA

The UCITS Directive does not apply only in the EU, but also applies in the other Member States of the EEA. Therefore it is desirable that these other states also will

17. R.P.C. Adema, Nieuw op de (Wijn)kaart: een VBI-regime, *Onderneming & Financiering* 67 (2005): 106.

be involved in discussions on the harmonization or coordination of taxation of the income from investments of UCITS and its design.

15.7.2. OECD

The Organization for Economic Cooperation and Development (hereafter, OECD) currently studies the part of the problems discussed in this book related to the application of tax treaties.[18] If the OECD comes to the conclusion that it is desirable and feasible to include specific regulations in bilateral tax treaties for income from portfolio investments of UCITS and similar collective investment funds, it could consider the following:

(1) Notwithstanding the legal form of the UCITS, the income from its portfolio investments is considered to be derived by the unitholders. In that case, only those unitholders that are liable to tax may file a request for a refund of that part of the withholding tax that has not been levied in accordance with the applicable tax treaty. Notwithstanding the state of residence of the UCITS, the applicable tax treaty is the one concluded between the source state and the residence state of the unitholder. Any tax treaty shopping by the unitholders is thus obstructed.

(2) Transparency of the UCITS causes an administrative burden for the unitholders. They have to file individual requests for refund of withholding tax. As discussed in Section 15.5.1.1, the administrative burden of unitholders could be relieved through a collective request by the UCITS on their behalf. Just as for the EU, further research is necessary to formulate adequate administrative procedures.

It should be noted that because it is already difficult to arrive at tax harmonization and coordination within the EU, it may be even more difficult to achieve harmonization or coordination within the OECD. Nevertheless, Member States may be more willing to cooperate, because the OECD Model Tax Convention and its Commentary are not binding on them.

This chapter analyses the consequences of taxation on the trade in units of UCITS between Austria, Germany, the Netherlands, and the United Kingdom. It further formulates recommendations for the taxation of investments in and by UCITS in the EU.

---

18. See the report of the informal consultative group on the taxation of collective investment vehicles and procedures for tax relief for cross-border investors on the granting of treaty benefits with respect to the income of collective investment vehicles. The views expressed in this report, however, are not that of the OECD or its Member States. It is therefore unclear whether it will eventually result in an amendment of the OECD Model Tax Convention. For that reason, this report is not discussed in this study.

Summary

This book provides a study of the taxation of UCITS in Austria, Germany, the Netherlands, and the United Kingdom. It analyses the tax consequences of the cross-border trade in units of UCITS for unitholders residing in the countries studied. The study ends with recommendations to remove the tax advantages and tax disadvantages that occur in cross-border trading.

The Concept and the Taxation of UCITS

An introduction of the concept of UCITS is provided in Chapter 1. In 1985, the agreement of the European Council on the UCITS Directive had to remove the restrictions on free circulation of units of UCITS and to establish a European capital market. The UCITS Directive therefore coordinated the laws, regulations and administrative provisions in respect to the obligations and control of UCITS by standardized rules so that cross-border trade in the units of UCITS within the EU is guaranteed. In 1994, the scope of the UCITS Directive was expanded to the EEA.

In spite of the aim of the UCITS Directive, trading in units of UCITS is for the most part still fragmentized by the national borders of Member States. In a study by the Centre for European Economic Research in Mannheim, taxation is ranked as one of the most important obstacles to cross-border trading in units of UCITS and other collective investment funds. Academic and industry studies have identified tax regulations of Member States that discriminate or restrict investments in non-resident UCITS. These studies, however, have not examined whether differences between the tax laws of the Member States are so substantial that investments in the units of non-resident UCITS, or certain non-resident UCITS, may at all times result in a higher tax burden for investors.

Taxation of UCITS is not covered by the UCITS Directive; nor is it elsewhere in secondary EC law. In the absence of any coordination or harmonization, Member States have referred to the existing tax regulations for collective investment funds. To prevent an investment in units of a UCITS resulting in a higher tax burden than as for a direct investment, most Member States have adopted the concept of transparency for taxation of income derived through UCITS and other collective investment funds. According to this concept, investors who invest by way of a UCITS or other collective investment fund should not be taxed more or less than if they had invested directly. From Chapter 2 follows that measures used by Member States to establish that income derived from investments of UCITS is not subject to more or less tax than in the case of a direct investment differ substantially because they are based on the diverging tax laws of the Member States.

The cross-border trade in units of UCITS may be affected by differences in the tax laws of Member States, because these differences may result for an investment in units of non-resident UCITS, or certain non-resident UCITS, in a tax advantage or disadvantage. Investors therefore may be less or more attracted to non-resident UCITS. In either case, the dissimilarities may affect the conditions of competition among UCITS. Parts II to IV examined whether the cross-border trade in the units of UCITS between Austria, Germany, the Netherlands and the United Kingdom actually results in any tax advantages or disadvantages.

Taxation at Source

Income derived from the investments of UCITS is usually subject to withholding tax in the source state. To ensure that income derived by way of UCITS is not subject to more or less withholding tax than a direct investment, the tax status of unitholders should be taken into account instead of that of the UCITS. This applies both when invested domestically as well when invested abroad. In the latter case the application of tax treaties should not differ from that in a direct investment.

Chapters 3–5 demonstrate that the taxation at source of income from the investments of UCITS differs substantially for UCITS residing in Austria, Germany, the Netherlands and the United Kingdom. To prevent tax disadvantages, it is recommended that investors take notice of the state of residence of the UCITS and the investment policy of the UCITS.

The countries studied do not take into account the tax status of the unitholders. Instead, they avoid taxation at source of income from investments situated within their jurisdiction or refund the tax withheld to the UCITS. In Germany and, for Netherlands-resident (FII) UCITS, the Netherlands, the refund of withholding tax is restricted to UCITS residing in these countries so that the amount of tax withheld at source of German and Netherlands source income differs among Austrian, German, Netherlands and UK-resident UCITS.

The same is true for the application of tax treaties for income from investments situated outside the jurisdiction of the UCITS country. A uniform application of tax treaties to UCITS of the countries studied is lacking. The application of tax treaties is affected by the measures taken to avoid taxation at the level of the UCITS. As a result of these measures the income from the investments of Austrian-resident UCITS and Netherlands-resident (TII) UCITS is considered to be that of the unitholders, whereas that of German, Netherlands and UK-resident UCITS is that of the UCITS. The tax liability of unitholders is therefore taken into account only for investments through Austrian-resident UCITS.

Netherlands-resident (FII) UCITS and UK-resident UCITS enable non-resident investors to do some tax treaty shopping.

Instead of the tax liability of unitholders, the application of tax treaties to German-resident UCITS, Netherlands-resident (EII/FII) UCITS and UK-resident UCITS depends on the tax liability of the UCITS. Netherlands-resident (FII) UCITS and UK-resident UCITS are generally considered to be liable to tax while German-resident UCITS and Netherlands-resident (EII) UCITS are not considered to be liable to tax because they are subjectively exempt from corporate income tax. The application of tax treaties to Netherlands-resident (FII) UCITS and UK-resident UCITS results for exempt corporate unitholders in a tax advantage compared to a direct investment, whereas the denial of tax treaties to German-resident UCITS and Netherlands-resident (EII) UCITS causes a tax disadvantage for individual and corporate unitholders.

The application of tax treaties to Netherlands-resident (FII) UCITS and UK-resident UCITS, further, enables non-resident investors to make use of the tax treaties network of the Netherlands or the United Kingdom. This results in a benefit in the case in which the tax treaty network of these countries is in a specific region wider than that of the resident state of the unitholder or in the case of a Netherlands or UK tax treaty with a particular state that has not concluded a tax treaty with the resident state of the investor. The same applies if the source state's right to tax is in one or more of the Netherlands or UK tax treaties more restricted than in the tax treaties of the state of residence of the investor. In either case, the non-resident investor benefits from the investment by way of Netherlands-resident (FII) UCITS or UK-resident UCITS; a benefit that the would not have had in case of a direct investment.

In some cases, German-resident UCITS are assumed wrongfully to be transparent, so that the tax treaties are, like Austrian-resident UCITS and Netherlands-resident (TII) UCITS, applied as if the unitholders had invested directly. The same applies in a few cases for UK-resident UCITS of the trust type. An overview of the states that wrongfully assume that German-resident UCITS or UK-resident UCITS of the trust type are transparent, however, could not be found.

From the overview of taxation at source provided in Chapter 5 follows that the cross-border trade in units of UCITS results in a considerable number of tax advantages and disadvantages for unitholders residing in Austria, Germany, the Netherlands and the United Kingdom compared to an investment in the units of a resident UCITS.

Taxation at the Level of the UCITS

To ensure that the income from investments of UCITS is not subject to more tax than in case of a direct investment, any taxation at the level of the UCITS should be avoided. Neither should any withholding tax be charged from the UCITS at the time of distribution. Furthermore, the UCITS should not be provided with relief for the withholding tax charged at source of the income. Otherwise, the relief is indirectly available for unitholders that would, in the case of a direct investment, not be entitled to such relief.

Chapters 6–8 show that the taxation at the level of UCITS residing in Austria, Germany, the Netherlands and the United Kingdom differs considerable. It is therefore advisable for investors to take notice of the state of residence of the UCITS and its investment policy to avoid tax disadvantages.

The countries studied prevent taxation at the level of the UCITS by way of transparency, a subjective exemption, a reduced tax base, or a reduced tax rate, although any taxation at the level of UK-resident UCITS is not prevented in case it does not satisfy the qualifying investment test at all times during the financial year. The unitholders are partly compensated for the tax liability of the UCITS if they are liable to tax in the United Kingdom. UK exempt corporate entities and non-resident investors, however, are generally not liable to tax in the United Kingdom. As a result, income derived by UK exempt corporate entities and non-resident investors through UK-resident UCITS is subject to more tax than income that is derived by way of Austrian, German and Netherlands-resident UCITS.

Except for Netherlands-resident (EII/TII) UCITS, the countries studied charge withholding tax from UCITS at the time of distribution because they provided an exemption at source of income or a refund for tax withheld at source of income. However, they apply different tax bases, tax rates and exemptions so that the amount of tax withheld by the UCITS country at the time of distribution differs for Austrian, German, Netherlands and UK-resident UCITS.

Furthermore, the countries studied do not provide for uniform rules regarding the availability of relief for withholding tax charged by source states. Austria and Germany do not provide relief to UCITS for withholding tax that is charged by source states, whereas in the Netherlands and the United Kingdom, UCITS are granted relief for such withholding tax. The relief granted by the Netherlands, however, is limited to Netherlands-resident (FII) UCITS. Finally, the amount of relief granted to Netherlands-resident (FII) UCITS is determined differently from the amount of relief that is granted to UK-resident UCITS. The availability and amount of relief to UCITS in the countries vary substantially.

Chapter 8 demonstrates that the differences between taxation at the level of UCITS result in numerous tax advantages and tax disadvantages by cross-border trading in units of UCITS. The differences between taxation at the level of UCITS affect the conditions of competition between UCITS because investors will be declined to invest in units of an UCITS if it results in a tax disadvantage. The opposite is true if a tax advantage occurs.

Taxation at the Level of the Unitholders

The time that the income from the investments of UCITS is considered to be received by the unitholders should not differ from a direct investment. Nor should the amount, nature and source of the income be considered to be different from those of a direct investment so that the same tax base, exemptions and special tax rates are applied as for a direct investment. Furthermore, the unitholders should, in accordance with the tax treaties and unilateral rules of the unitholder country, be entitled to credit any of the withholding tax charged by the source state applied as if they had invested directly in the underlying investments.

From the Chapters 9 to 14 follows that taxation at the level of the unitholders for resident and non-resident UCITS and between non-resident UCITS varies substantially in the countries studied. It is therefore unwise for investors not to take notice of these differences by the selection of UCITS, to prevent tax disadvantages.

Austria and Germany apply a uniform rule in respect to the time that the income derived from the investments of resident and non-resident UCITS is considered to be received by unitholders. The income from investments of UCITS is considered to be received by Austrian unitholders at the earlier of a distribution or disposal or four months after the end of the financial year, whereas German unitholders are considered to have received the income at the earlier of a distribution or the end of the financial year.

The Netherlands, on the other hand, does not apply a uniform rule for the time that income from investments of UCITS is considered to be received. The income from investments of Netherlands-resident (FII) UCITS is actually distributed to the unitholders within eight months after the end of the financial year, whereas the income from investments of Netherlands-resident (EII/TII) UCITS is taxable in the hands of corporate unitholders at the time of arising. The latter rule also applies to Austrian- and German-resident UCITS. The income from investments of UK-resident UCITS, however, is subject to corporate income tax at the time that it is distributed or realized by the disposal of the units in the UCITS. By accumulation, the corporate income tax liability for the income from the investments in UK-resident UCITS is deferred until disposal of the units in these UCITS.

Uniform rules regarding the time that the income from the investments of UCITS is considered to be received by the unitholders are also lacking in the United Kingdom. The income from UK-resident UCITS is considered to be distributed to unitholders at each distribution date. In the case of Austrian resident-UCITS, German-resident UCITS and Netherlands-resident UCITS of the contractual type, the income is considered to be received by unitholders at the time of arising. The income from Netherlands-resident UCITS of the corporate type, on the other hand, is taxable in the hands of unitholders at the earlier of a distribution or the disposal of the units in the UCITS. If the income is accumulated in accordance with the instrument of incorporation of a Netherlands-resident (EII) UCITS of the corporate type, it is thus not taxable in the hands of the unitholders until disposal of the units in the UCITS.

Furthermore, the tax treaties and unilateral rules may, for the crediting of the withholding tax charged by the source states, be applied by Austrian, German and, in the case of transparent non-resident UCITS, UK unitholders of UCITS as if they had invested directly. The tax laws of these countries do not take notice of the part of the withholding tax for which relief was available at the level of Netherlands-resident (FII) UCITS or UK-resident UCITS. As a result, Austrian, German, or UK unitholders of these UCITS may be provided relief more than once for the withholding tax charged by the source state.

On the other hand, it is not possible for unitholders of UCITS residing in the Netherlands or, in the case of tax opaque non-resident UCITS, the United Kingdom to credit any of the withholding tax charged by the source states. The withholding tax is, under the Netherlands and UK tax legislation, considered to be charged for the account of the UCITS even in the case in which no relief is provided at the level of the UCITS.

As shown in the overview of taxation at the level of the unitholders provided in Chapter 14, the cross-border trade in units of UCITS results in a considerable number of tax advantages and disadvantages for unitholders residing in Austria, Germany, the Netherlands and the United Kingdom compared to an investment in the units of a resident UCITS. In the countries studied, UCITS do not compete under the same conditions.

Removal of the Tax Disadvantages and Tax Advantages

Parts II to IV demonstrate that the cross-border trade in units of UCITS results in a substantial number of tax advantages and disadvantages for unitholders residing in Austria, Germany, the Netherlands and the United Kingdom. Some of these tax disadvantages can be removed by negative harmonization. It concerns those distortions caused by a different treatment of a taxable subject or a taxable object in one state.

The majority of tax advantages and disadvantages, however, are the result of a different treatment in two or more states. As a result of the differences in the tax laws of the countries studied, the cross-border trade in units of UCITS at all times results in tax advantages or disadvantages, which undermines the conditions of competition between UCITS. The differences in the tax laws can be removed only by way of positive harmonization.

Cross-border trading in the units of UCITS would no longer be distorted by differences in the tax laws of Member States in case the taxation at source of income from the investments of UCITS, at the level of the UCITS and at the level of the unitholders would be harmonized. It is therefore advisable to amend the UCITS Directive or to draft a new Directive. It is recommended to lay down in the amendment of the UCITS Directive or the draft of a new Directive that UCITS are considered to be transparent so that the income from investments of UCITS is that of unitholders at the time of arising. Furthermore, income from investments of UCITS should be subject to the same amount of withholding tax as if the unitholders had invested directly. The same applies for the application of tax treaties. To avoid unitholders having to file individual requests to each source state for a refund of the part of the withholding tax that is not charged in accordance with the applicable tax treaty, tax laws of Member States should provide for a collective request by UCITS on behalf of those unitholders that are entitled to a refund, whereas the existing tax treaties with countries outside the EU should be renegotiated by Member States or on their behalf by the EU.

An amendment of the UCITS Directive or a draft of a new Directive should further provide for uniform rules regarding the time that income is considered to be arisen and the amount, nature and source of the income. Moreover, the information that needs to be communicated by UCITS to the tax authorities and unitholders should be harmonized so that it is sufficient for UCITS to provide one standard form for the tax authorities and unitholders of all Member States. The same applies for the amount of withholding tax charged by the source states.

If Member States cannot agree on an amendment of the UCITS Directive or the draft of a new Directive regarding taxation of UCITS, tax coordination may be an alternative method to standardize methods used to establish that income derived from investment of UCITS is not subject to more or less tax than as for a direct investment. Otherwise, any standardization of the taxation of income derived by way of UCITS depends on spontaneous amendments of the national tax legislation of the Member States.

Bibliography

Adema, R.P.C. 'Nieuw op de (Wijn)kaart: een VBI-regime'. *Onderneming & Financiering* 67 (2005): 106.

Adema, R.P.C. 'Collective Investment Vehicles and the Savings Taxation Directive from a Dutch Perspective'. In *The Taxation of Interest Savings Income in the European Capital Market.* Edited by D. Aigner, L. Glaser & M. Trumpel. Vienna: Linde Verlag, 2006.

Beckmann, K. In *Investment*: *Handbuch für das gesamte Investmentwesen.* Edited by K. Beckmann, R. Scholtz & L. Vollmer. Berlin: Erich Schmidt Verlag, loose leaf. 44.

Beiser, R. 'Österreichs Steuern in den Schranken des Gemeinschaftsrechtes'. *SWK* 30 (2003): 736.

Biegler, M. 'Zweifelfragen bei der Behandlung von Investmentfonds im auβerbetrieblichen Bereich'. *SWK* 18 (1994): 405.

Bongaarts, P.J.M. & L.J. Ed. *General Report of the IFA Congress of 1997 on the Taxation of Investment Funds.* Brussels: International Fiscal Association, 1997.

Bouwman, J.N. *Wegwijs in de Vennootschapsbelasting.* The Hague: Sdu, 2007.

Brüll, D., J.W. Zwemmer & R.P.C. Cornelisse. *Goedkoopmansgebruik.* FED, 1999.

Burns, L. & R. Krever. 'Taxation of Income from Business and Investment'. In *Tax Law Design and Drafting.* Edited by V. Thuronyi. Washington, D.C.: International Monetary Fund, 1998.

Davies, G.T. *European Union – Internal Market Law.* London: Cavendish, 2003.

Doralt, W. *Einkommensteuergesetz Kommentar.* Vienna: WUV-Universitätsverlag, loose leaf, 2005.

Doralt, W. & O. Kempf. *Einkommensteuergesetz Kommentar.* Vienna: WUV-Universitätsverlag, loose leaf.

Doralt, W. & S. Kirchmayr. *Einkommensteuergesetz Kommentar.* WUV-Universitätsverlag, loose leaf.

Dungworth, E. & O. Farnworth. 'Authorised Unit Trusts and OEICs'. In *Tolley's Taxation of Collective Investment.* Edited by S. Newcombe et al. London: LexisNexis Tolley, 2003.

Easson, A.J. & V. Thuronyi. 'Fiscal Transparency'. In *Tax Law Design and Drafting*. Edited by V. Thuronyi. Washington, D.C.: International Monetary Fund, 1998.

Elser, T. In *Investment – Handbuch für das gesamte Investmentwesen.* Edited by Beckmann, R. Scholtz & L. Vollmer. Berlin: Erich Schmidt Verlag, loose leaf.

Finney, M. *UK Taxation for Students – A Simplified Approach.* London: Spiramus, 2005.

Fraser, R.O.A. & J.R. Wood. *Taxation of Offshore Trusts and Funds.* London: LexisNexis Tolley, 2002.

Grundmann-Van der Krol, C.M. *Koersen door de Wet op het financieel toezicht.* Deventer: Kluwer, 2007.

Hallas, W. *Die Prüfung von Investmentfonds.* Vienna: Verlag Orac, 1997.

Haunold, P., M. Tumpel & C. Widhalm. 'News aus der EU'. *SWI* 8 (2007): 377.

Hayton, D.J. *The Law of Trusts.* London: Sweet & Maxwell, 2003.

Hurley, C. *National Report on the United Kingdom of the IFA Congress of 1997 on the Taxation of Investment Funds.* Washington, D.C.: International Fiscal Association, 1997.

Invesco. *Building of an Integrated European Fund Management – Cross Border Mergers of Funds, a Quick Win?* Toronto: Invesco, 2005.

Jacobs, O.H. & J. Haun. 'Financial Derivatives in International Tax Law – A Treatment of Certain Key Considerations', *Intertax* (1995): 407

Kapteijn, P.J.G. & P. Verloren van Themaat. *Inleiding tot het recht van de Europese Gemeenschappen.* Deventer: Kluwer, 1995.

Kempen, M.L.M. van, Kwalificatie van. Buitenlandse Rechtsvormen. *WFR* 573 (2005).

Kirchmayr, S. *National Report of Austria for the IFA Congress of 1997 on the Taxation of Investment Funds.* Washington, D.C.: International Fiscal Association, 1997.

Kofler, H., G. Kofler & S. Kristen. In *Handbuch der österreichischen Steuerlehre*, Bd I, Edited by R. Bertl, et al. (Hrsg.). Vienna: LexisNexis ARD Orac, 2004.

Kofler, H. & S. Kristen. In *Handbuch der österreichischen Steuerlehre*, Bd I. Edited by Bertl, et al. (Hrsg.). Vienna: LexisNexis ARD Orac, 2004.

Kosters, L.F. & H. Mooij. *National Report on the Netherlands of the IFA Congress of 1997 on the Taxation of Investment Funds.* Washington, D.C.: International Fiscal Association, 1997.

Krishna, V. *The Fundamentals of Canadian Income Tax.* Toronto: Thomson Carswell, 2006.

Lang, M. *The Application of the OECD Model Tax Convention to Partnerships.* Vienna: Linde Verlag/Kluwer Law International, 2000.

Lechner, E. 'Kapitalertragsteuer und Doppelbesteuerung'. in *Kapitalertragsteuer.* Vienna: Linde Verlag, 2003.

Lübbehüsen, D. In *KAGG and AuslInvestment-Gesetz – Kommentar*. Edited by J. Brinkhaus & P. Scherer. Munich: Verlag C.H. Beck, 2003.

Luja, R.H.C. 'Investment Funds, Tax Planning and State Aid'. *European Taxation* 12 (2006): 565–569.

Macfarlanes. *Collective Investment Schemes: the Law and Practice.* London: Sweet and Maxwell, loose leaf,.

Organization for Economic Cooperation and Development. *Taxation of Collective Investment Institutions.* Paris: OECD, 1977.

Organization for Economic Cooperation and Development. *Taxation of New Financial Instruments.* Paris: OECD, 1994.

Organization for Economic Cooperation and Development. *Taxation of Cross Border Portfolio Investment: Mutual Funds and Possible Tax Distortions.* Paris: OECD, 1999.

Plambeck, C.T., H.D. Rosenbloom & D.M. Ring. *General Report of the IFA Congress of 1995 on the Tax Aspects of Derivative Financial Instruments.* Brussels: International Fiscal Association, 1995.

Ponsen, N.V. & P. Klemann. 'Beleggingsinstellingen nader belicht'. In *Preadviezen voor de Vereniging voor Effectenrecht 2000.* Deventer: Kluwer, 2000.

PricewaterhouseCoopers. *Discriminatory Tax Barriers in the Single European Investment Funds Market – A Discussion Paper.* Report commissioned by the Fédération Européenes des Fonds en Sociétés d'Investissement, 2001.

PricewaterhouseCoopers. *Discriminatory tax barriers in the Single European Investment Funds market: A Progress Report.* Report commissioned by the Fédération Européenes des Fonds en Sociétés d'Investissement, 2003.

PricewaterhouseCoopers. *Tax discrimination against foreign funds: Light at the end of the tunnel.* Report commissioned by the European Fund and Asset Management Association, 2005.

Quantschnigg, P. 'Die neue Besteuerung bei ausländischen Investmentfonds'. *ÖStZ* 1-2 (1995): 7.

Raad C. van. *Cursus Belastingrecht (Internationaal Belastingrecht).* Deventer: Kluwer, loose leaf.

Ramackers, A. In *Das Einkommensteuerrecht.* Edited by E. Littmann, H. Bitz & H. Pust. Stuttgart: Schäffer Poeschel, loose leaf.

Reisenhofer, P. *Investmentfondsgesetz.* Vienna: MANZ'sche Verlags-und Universitätsbuchhandlung, 2002.

Renk, E.G. Fiscal Problems Arising in Connection with Investment Trusts of International Character – General Report. The Hague: Cahiers de Droit Fiscal International, 1962.

Reschny-Birox, C. & R. Klaunzer. 'Das Ende der "schwarzen" ausländischen Fonds?' *SWK* 23-24 (2004): 1004.

Schödermeier, M. & C. Baltzer. In *KAGG and AuslInvestment-Gesetz – Kommentar.* Edited by J. Brinkhaus & P. Scherer. Munich: Verlag C.H. Beck, 2003.

Sedlaczek, M. 'Kapitalertragsteuer und Investmentfonds'. In *Kapitalertragsteuer.* Vienna: Linde Verlag, 2003.

Shirley, L. 'Authorised Unit Trusts and OEICs'. In *Tolley's Taxation of Collective Investment.* Edited by S. Newcombe et al. London: NexisLexis Tolley, 2003.

Sillevis, L.W., et al. *Cursus Belastingrecht (Inkomstenbelasting).* Deventer: Kluwer, loose leaf.

Simon's Direct Tax Service. London: Butterworths, loose leaf.

Smailes, D. & A. Flint. *Tolley's Income Tax 2006–07.* London: LexisNexis Tolley, 2006.

Smith, M. & S. Davies. 'Offshore Funds'. in *Tolley's Taxation of Collective Investment.* London: LexisNexis Tolley, 2003.

Sorgenfrei, U. 'Steuerlichter Transparenzgrundsatz und DBA-Berechtigung deutscher offener Investmentfonds'. *IStR* 10 (1994): 468 and 469.

Täske, J. *National Report on Germany of the IFA Congress of 1997 on the Taxation of Investment Funds.* Washington, D.C.: International Fiscal Association, 1997.

Tiley, J. *Revenue Law.* Oxford: Hart Publishing, 2005.

Verhagen, P.M. *Financiële derivaten in de fiscale winst.* Lelystad: Vermande, 1997.

Viitala, T. *Taxation of Investment Funds in the European Union.* Amsterdam: IBFD, 2005.

Vogel, K. *Klaus Vogel on Double Taxation Conventions: a Commentary to the OECD, UN and US Model Conventions for the Avoidance of Double Taxation of Income and Capital – With Particular Reference to German Treaty Practice.* Amsterdam: Kluwer Law International, 1997.

Vries, N.H. de, et al. *Cursus Belastingrecht (Vennootschapsbelasting).* Deventer: Kluwer, loose leaf.

Walton, K. *Simon's Calculating Taxable Trading Profits.* London: LexisNexis Tolley, 2002.

Index

T

U

EUCOTAX Series on European Taxation

(1) Peter HJ Essers, Guido JME de Bont & Eric CCM Kemmeren (eds), *The Compatibility of Anti-Abuse Provisions in Tax Treaties with EC Law*, 1998 (ISBN 90-411-9678-1).
(2) Gerard TK Meussen (ed.), *The Principle of Equality in European Taxation*, 1999 (ISBN 90-411-9693-5).
(3) Michael Lang (ed.), *Tax Treaty Interpretation*, 2001 (ISBN 90-411-9857-1).
(4) Pasquale Pistone, *The Impact of Community Law on Tax Treaties: Issues and Solutions*, 2002 (ISBN 90-411-9860-1).
(5) René Offermanns, *The Entrepreneurship Concept in a European Comparative Tax Law Perspective*, 2002 (ISBN 90-411-9887-3).
(6) Michael Lang & Mario Züger, *Settlement of Disputes in Tax Treaty Law*, 2002 (ISBN 90-411-9904-7).
(7) Carlo Pinto, *Tax Competition and EU Law*, 2003 (ISBN 90-411-9913-6).
(8) Michael Lang, Hans-Jörgen Aigner, Ulrich Scheuerle & Markus Stefaner, *CFC Legislation, Tax Treaties and EC Law*, 2004 (ISBN 90-411-2284-2).
(9) Mattias Dahlberg, *Direct Taxation in Relation to the Freedom of Establishment and the Free Movement of Capital*, 2005 (ISBN 90-411-2363-6).
(10) Michael Lang, Judith Herdin & Ines Hofbauer, *WTO and Direct Taxation*, 2005 (ISBN 90-411-2371-7).
(11) Dennis Weber, *Tax Avoidance and the EC Tray Freedoms: A Study of the Limitations under European Law for the Prevention of Tax Avoidance*, 2005 (ISBN 90-411-2402-0).
(12) Félix Alberto Vega Borrego, *Limitations on Benefits Clauses on Double Taxation Conventions*, 2005 (ISBN 90-411-2370-9).
(13) Michael Lang, Josef Schuch & Claus Staringer, *ECJ-Recent Developments in Direct Taxation*, 2006 (ISBN 90-411-2509-4).
(14) Reuven S. Avi-Yonah, James R. Hines Jr. & Michael Lang, *Comparative Fiscal Federalism. Comparing the European Court of Justice and the US Supreme Court's Tax Jurisprudence*, 2007 (ISBN 978-90-411-2552-1).
(15) Christiana HJI Panayi, *Double Taxation, Tax Treaties, Treaty-Shopping and the European Community*, 2007 (ISBN 978-90-411-2658-0).
(16) Dennis Weber, *The Influence of European Law on Direct Taxation: Recent and Future Developments*, 2007 (ISBN 978-90-411-2667-2).
(17) Michael Lang & Pasquale Pistone, *The EU and Third Countries: Direct Taxation*, 2007 (ISBN 978-90-411-2665-8).
(18) Oskar Henkow, *Financial Activities in European VAT: A Theoretical and Legal Research of the European VAT System and Preferred Treatment of Financial Activities*, 2007 (ISBN 978-90-411-2703-7).
(19) Michael Lang (ed.), *Tax Compliance Costs for Companies in an Enlarged European Community*, 2008 (ISBN 978-90-411-2666-5).

(20) Michael Lang (ed.), *Source versus Residence. Problems Arising from the Allocation of Taxing Rights in Tax Treaty Law and Possible Alternatives*, 2008 (ISBN 978-90-411-2763-1).
(21) Ioanna Mitroyanni, *Integration Approaches to Group Taxation in the European Internal Market*, 2008 (ISBN 978-90-411-2779-2).
(22) Rolf Eicke, *Tax Planning with Holding Companies. Repatriation of US Profits from Europe: Concepts, Strategies, Structures*, 2008 (ISBN 978-90-411-2794-5).
(23) Peter Essers et al. (ed.), *The Influence of IAS/IFRS on the CCCTB, Tax Accounting, Disclosure and Corporate Law Accounting Concepts: 'A Clash of Cultures'*, 2008 (ISBN 978-90-411-2819-5).
(24) Tonny Schenk-Geers, *International Exchange of Information and the Protection of Taxpayers*, 2009 (ISBN 978-90-411-3142-3).
(25) Raymond Adema, *UCITS and Taxation: Towards Harmonization of the Taxation of UCITS*, 2009 (ISBN 978-90-411-2839-3).

www.ingramcontent.com/pod-product-compliance
Lightning Source LLC
LaVergne TN
LVHW020647300926
849161LV00004B/860